# Time Out

# Los Angeles Guide

**Penguin Books**

PENGUIN BOOKS

Published by the Penguin Group
Penguin Books Ltd., 27 Wrights Lane, London, W8 5TZ, England
Penguin Books USA Inc., 375 Hudson Street, New York, New York 10014, USA
Penguin Books Australia Ltd., Ringwood, Victoria, Australia
Penguin Books Canada Ltd., 10 Alcorn Avenue, Toronto, Ontario, Canada M4V 3B2
Penguin Books (NZ) Ltd., 183-190 Wairau Road, Auckland 10, New Zealand

Penguin Books Ltd., Registered offices: Harmondsworth, Middlesex, England

First published 1997
10 9 8 7 6 5 4 3 2 1

Colour reprographics by Precise Litho, 34-35 Great Sutton Street, London EC1
Mono reprographics, printed and bound by William Clowes Ltd, Beccles, Suffolk NR34 9QE

## Edited and designed by

Time Out Magazine Limited
Universal House
251 Tottenham Court Road
London W1P OAB
Tel: 0171 813 3000
Fax: 0171 813 6001
E-mail: net@timeout.co.uk
http://www.timeout.co.uk

## Editorial

**Managing Editor** Peter Fiennes
**Editor** Ruth Jarvis
**Consultant Editor** Frances Anderton
**Deputy Editor** Cathy Phillips
**Listings Editor/Staff Writer** Matthew Duersten
**Indexer** Jacqueline Brind

## Design

**Art Director** Warren Beeby
**Art Editor** John Oakey
**Designers** Paul Tansley, Mandy Martin
**Design Assistants** Carrie Lambe, Marcus Ludewig
**Picture Editor** Catherine Hardcastle
**Picture Researcher** Michaela Freeman

## Advertising

**Group Advertisement Director** Lesley Gill
**Sales Director** Mark Phillips
**Advertisement Sales (LA)** JCI New York

## Administration

**Publisher** Tony Elliott
**Managing Director** Mike Hardwick
**Financial Director** Kevin Ellis
**Marketing Director** Gillian Auld
**Production Manager** Mark Lamond

## Features in this guide were written and researched by:

**Introduction** Frances Anderton. **Essential Information** Matt Duersten. **Getting Around** David Eimer (*It's better by bus* Matt Duersten/Cathy Phillips). **Accommodation** Erika Lenkert. **Sightseeing** Victoria Tilney. **By Season** Katie Klapper. **Geography** Mick Farren (*Earthquake survival* Ruth Jarvis/Lesley O'Toole). **History** William Fulton (*Noir* David Eimer). **LA Today** Mick Farren (*LA by numbers* Matt Duersten, *Gangs* Kathryn Harris). **Latino LA** Martin Hernàndez. **Architecture** Michael Webb. **Car City** Frances Anderton. **Celebrity LA** Lesley O'Toole. **Los Angeles by Neigbourhood** Frances Anderton (Orientation, Westside: Beach Towns); Laura Connolly (Westside: Inland); Dan Epstein (Midtown & Hollywood, East of Hollywood); David Eimer (Downtown); William Fulton (The Valleys); Martìn Hernàndez (East LA); Rochelle Mills (South-Central); Cary Darling (Long Beach & the South Bay, Orange County); Katie Klapper (*A river runs rhrough it*). **Restaurants** Kathryn Harris. **Coffeehouses** Victoria Tilney (*Coffeespeak* Victoria Tilney, Matt Duersten). **Bars** Dan Epstein. **Shopping & Services** Kathryn Harris. **Media** Dan Epstein (*LA talk radio* Matt Duersten). **Active LA** Nick Karno, David Eimer, Kathryn Harris, Katie Klapper. **Comedy** Dan O'Connor. **Dance Clubs** Peter Relic. **Film** David Eimer (*And the winner is* Ruth Jarvis). **Museums & Galleries** Lisa Auerbach (*Picture this* Matt Duersten). **Music** Martin Fleischmann. **Theatre** Victoria Tilney. **Dance** Joanne Parkes. **Business** Laura Connolly. **Children** Dian Phillips. **Gay** John D'Amico. **Lesbian** Kimberly Wallace. **Students** Rebecca Epstein. **Trips Out of Town** Frances Anderton, Gus Funnell (*Wine country* Richard Neill). **Survival** Lesley O'Toole (*Site seeing – LA on line* and *Hot lines* Matt Duersten).

### The Editors would like to thank the following:

Carl Hall, David Gyepes, Scott Grusky, Gus Funnell, Mark and his Cadillac, Brad Brillowski, Chris Feldmeier, John Chase, Lisa Sichi, the Metropolitan Transit Authority, Sarah Guy, Ian Smith, Katy O'Dowd, Tom Charity, California Tourism, Frank Broughton and the staff of *Time Out New York*.

**Maps** pages 278-184 by Streetwise; pages 288-290 by John Oakey.

**Photography** by Danny Hole except for pages 3, 184 LACVB/Michele and Tom Grimm; 47, 242, 247, 250, 251, 252 LACVB/Robert Holmes; 54, 55, 69 Telegraph Colour Library; 57, 58 Seaver Center, The Natural History Museum of Los Angeles County; 59, 64, 120 Corbis; 71 AP; 225, 240, 245, 248 Cathy Phillips; 240, 244, 246, 256 Ruth Jarvis; 276-7 Science Photo Library. Pictures on pages 11, 17(t), 50, 136, 156, 193, 194, 213, 215, 222, 241 were supplied by the featured establishments/organisations. With thanks to Danny Chau Photolabs for black and white printing.

# Contents

**About the Guide** vi
**Introduction** 1
**Essential Information** 3
**Getting Around** 9
**Accommodation** 15
**Sightseeing** 33
**By Season** 47

## In Context

Geography 52
History 56
LA Today 66
Latino LA 72
Architecture 75
Car City 79
Celebrity LA 82

## By Neighbourhood

Orientation 88
Westside: Beach Towns 89
Westside: Inland 94
Midtown & Hollywood 99
Downtown 104

East of Hollywood 109
The Valleys 111
Long Beach & the South Bay 113
East LA 115
South-Central 117
Orange County 119

## Eating & Drinking

Restaurants 122
Coffeehouses 145
Bars 149

## Shopping & Services

Shopping & Services 154

## Arts & Entertainment

Media 180
Active LA 184
Comedy 193
Dance Clubs 195
Film 199
Museums & Galleries 205
Music 212
Theatre & Dance 221

## In Focus

Business 226
Children 228
Gay & Lesbian 231
Students 236

## Trips Out of Town

Trips Out of Town 240

## Survival

Survival 258

**Further Reading** 266
**Index** 267
**Advertisers Index** 273
**Maps** 275

MICKEY MOUSE

# Essential Information

**Back to basics – all the facts and figures you'll need to plan and enjoy your stay in the Big Orange.**

For more practical information, *see chapter* **Survival**. For information on the abbreviations used in this guide, *see page vi* **About the Guide**.

## Attitude

The people you will come across in LA will be perfectly polite, chatty even (unless they're in their cars, of course, where they suffer from the usual pumped-up motormania). Be polite back and communication is unlikely to be a problem. Note that on the freeway, locals often don't signal to change lanes, but will simply extend their hand out of the window and point to the space they want.

## Banks

Most banks are open 10am-4.30pm Monday to Thursday, 9am or 10am to 6pm Friday and 9-10am to 2-3pm on Saturday. Some of the more prominent are the Bank of America, Home Savings of America, Great Western, Wells Fargo and the First Federal Bank of California, all of which have numerous locations all over the city and most of which offer competitive currency exchange rates, along with international banking services, including cable transfers, foreign drafts on overseas banks and import/export financing. They can also raise cash on a credit card.

### ATMs

ATMs (Automated Teller Machine) are as numerous as cars in LA, found in and outside banks, in some of the bigger shopping malls and in stores such as 7-Eleven. ATMs sometimes incur a $1-$2 surcharge for withdrawal; the maximum withdrawal varies between $200 and $300 per day. There are many different card networks, including Star and Interlink, but the main ones are **Cirrus** (1-800 424 7787 for locations) and **Plus** (1-800 843 7587). Banks worldwide link into these two systems; if you have the appropriate symbol on your cash card you will be able to get money out using your usual PIN. Most ATMs will also dispense cash advances from MasterCard and Visa and some will also take American Express. There is a small interest charge for cash advances.

Try to get to an ATM before the sun goes down, and in somebody else's company, as robbing ATM customers is a popular sport in LA. Panhandlers will hang out by them as well, presumably for maximum guilt factor ('Hey, man, it's right there in your hand!').

### Bureaux de change

The majority of currency exchange can be taken care of at Los Angeles International Airport, where Lenlyn Limited (7am-11pm daily; 1-310 417 0366) and Traveler's Exchange (6am-11pm daily; 1-310 649 1656) both have offices in

*Pershing Square, in the financial district.*

Terminals 2 and 5 and in the Tom Bradley International Terminal. The *Wall Street Journal* and the *LA Times'* Business section publish exchange rates daily. Some of the more prominent bureaux de change include:

**American Express Travel Services**
*327 North Beverly Drive, between Brighton & Dayton Ways, Beverly Hills (1-310 274 8277/lost or stolen cards 1-800 528 4800/lost or stolen travellers cheques 1-800 221 7282). Bus 4, 20, 27, DASH Beverly Hills/I-10, exit Robertson Boulevard north.* **Open** 10am-6pm Mon-Fri.
**Branches**: Third Street, at La Cienega Boulevard, West Hollywood; 937 Westwood Boulevard, between La Conte & Weyburn Avenues, Westwood (1-208 6191).

**Associated Foreign Exchange**
*433 North Beverly Drive, between Brighton Way & Little Santa Monica Boulevard, Beverly Hills (1-310 274 7610). Bus 4, 20, 21, 22, 320/I-10, exit Robertson Boulevard north.* **Open** 9am-4.30pm Mon-Fri.

**Thomas Cook Foreign Exchange Service**
*452 North Bedford Drive, between Brighton Way & Little Santa Monica Boulevard, Beverly Hills (1-800 287 7362 for any location).* **Open** 9am-5pm Mon-Fri.
**Branches**: 735 South Figueroa Street, between Seventh & Eighth Streets, Downtown; 8901 Santa Monica Boulevard, at San Vincente Boulevard, West Hollywood.

## Climate

'There are no seasons here' is the common grouse of both tried-and-true Angelenos and passers-through; to which many more would reply: 'exactly!'. With an annual average of 300 clear days, Los Angeles offers sun, blue skies, white clouds, palm trees and near-perfect 70-75° weather for those weary of less predictable and user-friendly

We travel the world
for you

to bring the most exciting fashions
for you, your family and your home under one roof. Stop by the
visitors center with this guide and a bloomingdale's same-day
receipt to receive a bloomingdale's gift.*

CENTURY CITY · SHERMAN OAKS · NEWPORT BEACH · STANFORD
BEVERLY CENTER (MARCH 1997)
*LIMIT ONE PER CUSTOMER.

# bloomingdale's
It's Like No Other Store In The World

environments. Unfortunately, it's the smog (which refracts the desert sun) combined with the heat (especially in the San Fernando Valley), usually around 102° in midsummer, that can be nightmarish. The best times to visit are between September and November or March and May, since these 'seasons' offer mid-range temperatures and consistently beautiful days. For those wishing to avoid LA's environmental foibles, January's cooler temperatures and frequent rainfall take the edge off the smog and heat – and the Santa Ana winds in July-August and October/November bring it back with a vengeance. In June/July the coastal cities are swathed for most of the day in sea mist, referred to as June gloom.

To check the weather, call **Los Angeles Weather Information** on 1-213 554 1212, or **Los Angeles Surf & Weather** on 1-310 578 0478. For daily smog and air-quality checks, call **Southcoast Air Quality Management District** on 1-800 242 4022 (8am-6pm Mon-Fri).

## Credit cards

The two major credit cards accepted just about everywhere in the United States are **MasterCard** (1-800 826 2181) and **Visa** (1-800 336 8472). **American Express** (1-800 528 4800) is also a prominent card, although some establishments will not accept them because of the high processing costs. Other, less ubiquitous ones are Discover (1-800 347 2683), Carte Blanche, JCB and Diner's Club (1-800 234 6377), more likely to be accepted at higher-end places. Don't even think of coming to LA without at least one major credit card, unless you have a fistful of dollar travellers cheques.

## Currency

As they say in LA: 'Cash talks; bullshit walks'. The United States' monetary system is decimal based: the US dollar ($) is divisible into 100 cents (¢). Coin denominations run from

# Yo! LA speaks!

**Ass-out** (*n; Gen-X*): When someone does something foolish.

**Crib** (*n; hip-hop*): House; apartment.

**Cushion weed** (*n; limo drivers*): Inebriated, usually unconscious, limousine passenger.

**Da bomb** (*n; hip-hop*): Terrific; okay. ('Baby, you're da bomb in that dress!')

**Deconono** (*n; architectural*): Post-WW II architecture remodelled to the point to where the original no longer exists.

**Dis** (*n, v; hip-hop*): To disrespect, ignore or blow off. South of the I-10, the penalty for this is death.

**Dope** (*n; hip-hop*): Awesome; cool; fantastic.

**Frigidaires** (*n; Hollywood*): Badly capped front teeth.

**Gangsta** (*n; hip-hop*): Way of dress, speak and life in LA gang culture that spawned a multi-million dollar rap industry and popular culture movement. Also *OG* (Original Gangsta), the highest title bestowed upon any gang member.

**Glomming** (*v; surfer/Valley/Gen-X*): Freeloading, borrowing beyond the pale of acceptable manners; also known as *mooching* or *bungeing*. (*See also* **Kato, pulling a**.)

**Goofing** (*v; surfer; stoner; hip-hop*): Bothering someone; derived from a 1960s term meaning to take drugs and hang out among straight people.

**Green room** (*v; surfer*): To get inside the tube of water created by a wave. ('Did you see the way Zig green-roomed that?')

**Hey** (*Gen-X*): How young Angelenos greet each other.

**Homie** (*n; hip-hop*): Term of respect and affection; more casual than *dude* or *man*.

**Indier-than-thou** (*adj*): Pompous band which refuses to be signed to a major label.

**Iowa** (*n; Hollywood*): Hopelessly amateurish screenplay.

**Kato, pulling a** (*v*): Freeloading.

**Kewl** (*Valley*): A twist on the word cool.

**Kook** (*n; surfer*): Anybody who shows up at a beach and is not a local person.

**Leslie** (*n*): A frizzy, slightly out-of-control hairstyle. Named after the Menendez brothers' defence attorney Leslie Abramson.

**Like** (*Valley/Gen-X*): Used as a punctuation mark, like a comma or caesura. ('Like, I was, like, way upset that he like, totally, like dumped me.')

**Lincoln drop** (*n*): Dish of pennies next to cash register of any store.

**Looky loos** (*n; LAPD*): Intrusive bystanders at a crime or celebrity scene, known elsewhere as rubberneckers.

**Monet** (*n*): Someone who looks attractive from, and only from, afar.

**The Mouse** (*n; Hollywood*): Disney Studios.

**Nonpro** (*n; Hollywood*): Someone not in the entertainment business.

**Odelay!** (*exclam; East LA*): Term used by Latinos in Los Angeles; usually a celebratory exclamation, like alright! or hey!

**OJ, doing an** (*v*): Buying justice.

**Over the Hill, to go** (*v; Valley/Westside*): going either to the Valley from the Westside or vice versa.

**Pasadena** (*v; Hollywood*): To pass on a screenplay.

**Tenpercentary** (*n; Hollywood*): A talent agency.

**Willie from Philly** (*n; LAPD*): LAPD's nickname for LAPD Police Chief Willie L Williams.

**Willis** (*n*): Studiospeak for any blockbuster action-adventure film.

**What's up?**: Basically – 'Speak quickly; I don't have time'.

**What's up with that?**: 'What's going on?' or 'Explain what's behind that.'

the copper penny (1¢; Abraham Lincoln); the silver nickel (5¢; Thomas Jefferson); dime (10¢; Franklin Delano Roosevelt); quarter (25¢; George Washington); and the less common half-dollar (50¢; John F Kennedy). Notes ('greenbacks'), all the same size, come in $1 (George Washington); $5 (Abraham Lincoln); $10 (Alexander Hamilton); $20 (Andrew Jackson); $50 (Ulysses S Grant); and $100 (Benjamin Franklin) denominations. Should you find yourself with the Susan B Anthony silver $1 coin, or the Thomas Jefferson $2 bill, *don't spend them*; they are collectors' items reflecting the US's resistance to change.

Obtain travellers cheques – in US dollars and from a well-known company – before your trip. Almost all stores, restaurants, and the like will accept them with a valid passport or other identification, save for the occasional establishment that requires a minimum purchase. If you need to buy travellers cheques in LA, many commercial banks sell them for 1-3% of the face value.

If you need money wired to you, then **American Express MoneyGram** (1-800 926 9400 for locations) or **Western Union** (1-800 325 6000) can receive funds from anywhere in the world, although their high commission (usually around 10%) underscores their 'emergency only' status.

## Disabled

Since 1982, California's strict state building codes have ensured easy and equal disabled access to all city facilities, businesses, parking lots, restaurants, hotels and other public places; consequently, the newer facilities will be more accommodating than the older ones, which, in many cases, have been retrofitted to comply with the barest requirements of the codes. The MTA has special reduced fares and specific 'lift' buses with fixed times and schedules. To locate areas with handicapped facilities or access, just look for the blue and white handicapped symbol of a wheelchair.

There are a number of organisations which can assist you in planning your trip and supply information and referrals, among them the **Junior League of Los Angeles** (1-213 937 5566), which publishes a booklet entitled 'Around Town With Ease' ($2); and the **Society for the Advancement of Travel for the Handicapped** (1-212 447 7284/fax 1-212 725 8253).

## Electricity

Rather than the standard 220-240V, 50-cycle AC used in Europe, LA and the United States use a 110-120V, 60-cycle AC voltage. Except for dual-voltage, flat-pin plug shavers, you will need to run any appliances you bring with you via an adaptor, available at airport shops.

## Immigration & customs

A necessary evil of international travel (even more so now that idiots like the Unabomber can shut down LAX with just one phone call). It begins even before you hit the ground, when your flight attendant gives you two forms to fill out (one for immigration and one for customs). When you land, expect the customs/immigration process to take about an hour. Customs officials are a no-nonsense bunch, so smiling a lot and looking cutely foreign will not get you through any faster. Just accept your entry permit and move on.

The current US customs regulations allow foreign visitors to import the following, duty-free: 200 cigarettes or 50 cigars (not Cuban; over-18s only), or 2kg of smoking tobacco; one litre (1.05 US quart) of wine or spirits (over-21s only); and up to $100 in gifts ($400 for returning Americans). You can take up to $10,000 in cash, travellers cheques or endorsed bank drafts in or out of the country tax-free, and goods worth up

to $1000 (you pay a flat tax rate of 10% on any excess). For more customs information contact the **US Customs Service** at LAX (1-310 215 2414).

## Insurance

Baggage, trip-cancellation, and medical insurance should be taken care of before you even get on the plane from your starting point. The US is renowned for its superb healthcare facilities; the catch is that the cost will most likely put you back in the hospital. The majority of medical centres require that you give details of your insurance company and your policy number if you require treatment. For further information, *see chapter* **Survival**.

## Liquor laws

Bars, dance clubs, restaurants, liquor stores and supermarkets that sell liquor can do so between 6am and 2am. Strip or burlesque clubs are not allowed to serve alcohol at all. Twenty-one is the legal age for purchase and consumption

*LA benchmarks: they want your money.*

of alcoholic beverages. Picture ID, whether state or foreign driver's licence or passport, is strictly required for all patrons who wish to imbibe.

## Opening times

Although many establishments – such as city, state or government agencies, museums and coffeeshops – open at 8am or 9am, in LA, the magic hour is 10am. Most places you will travel to will open their doors at this time, and close them at 5pm. Many shops, boutiques and museums will have one or two days during the week when they are open until 8pm or 9pm; and many stay open on Sunday from noon-5pm or later.

## Post offices

Post offices are generally open 9am-5pm, but often have last collections at 6pm. Many are open on Saturdays from 9am to 1pm or 2pm. There are often stamp vending machines and scales in the lobby, open out of hours. For general postal information and locations, check the front of any Pacific Bell LA Metropolitan phone book, or dial **1-800 725 2161**.

US mailboxes are red, white and blue with the US Mail bald eagle logo printed clearly on the front and side. Pull the handle down and put your post (no packages) in the slot.

## Safety

Unlikely though it may sound, the place that invented the terms 'car-jacking' and 'drive-by shooting' is actually a safer place for visitors than, say, Florida. Common sense should be the rule of the day: keep your car doors locked while driving; don't fumble with your wallet on streets or street corners; avoid parking in questionable areas (when in doubt, use valet parking); avoid walking alone at night; always plan where you're going; and always lock your car. As a pedestrian, walk with a brisk confidence; this should help discourage panhandlers, and people will most likely stay out of your way. As a motorist, avoid coming off the freeway in unfamiliar areas, never cut anyone off in traffic or yell epithets at other drivers, never drive too slowly or too quickly (65mph is a good, median speed), and take a map with you wherever you go. Another precaution, if you can afford it, is to rent a cellular phone (*see chapter* **Business**). If you have car trouble, there are over 4,000 free emergency phone boxes (yellow in colour) located on the side of LA's freeways.

A few areas that you should be careful about travelling to or through after dark include parts of Silver Lake, Hollywood (especially Hollywood Boulevard), Koreatown, Compton, Echo Park, Downtown and Venice. Relatively safe areas include Santa Monica, West Hollywood, Beverly Hills, Westwood/UCLA, Marina del Rey, Sherman Oaks, Studio City, Encino and Burbank.

## Telephones

There are three area codes in LA: **310** (West LA, Long Beach, Santa Monica), **213** (Downtown, Hollywood) and **818** (San Fernando Valley). Others you might be dialling frequently are 619 (San Diego), 415 (San Francisco), 702 (Las Vegas), 714 (Orange County) and 805 (Santa Barbara).

For local calls *within* your area code, pick up the phone and dial the number. For local calls *outside* your area code or national long-distance calls, dial 1 + [area code] + [the number]. For any local long-distance enquiries (ie within the 310,

213 and 818 areas), call 411; for national long-distance enquiries, dial 1 + [area code] + 555 1212 (if you don't know the area code, dial 0 for the operator).

For international calls, dial 011 followed by the country code (UK 44; New Zealand 64; Australia 61, Germany 49; Japan 81 – see the phone book for others). For enquiries on toll-free numbers (prefaced by 1-800), dial 1-800 555 1212. If you're just plain befuddled, dial 0 for operator assistance and collect (reverse charge) calls. **For police, fire, or medical emergencies, dial 911**.

In hotels, you may have to dial an 0 or 9 before all these numbers to get a line. You will also pay a surcharge – ask how much at your hotel, as quite often using a phonecard, credit card or pay phone (*see below*) will work out cheaper, especially on long-distance/international calls.

Public telephones are plentiful in LA. To use a public phone, pick up the receiver, listen for a dialling tone and feed it change. Operator and directory calls are free. Local calls cost 25¢ (some are 20¢), with the cost increasing with the distance (a recorded voice will tell you to feed in more quarters). Make sure you have plenty of change as pay phones only take nickels, dimes and quarters. It's nigh on impossible to make international calls this way, but you can use your MasterCard with AT&T (1-800 225 5288) or MCI (1-800 950 5555) or buy phonecards ($4-$50) from large stores like Thrifty and Payless Drug, which give you a fixed amount of time anywhere in the US – or less time internationally.

Voicemail is inescapable in LA; note that the 'pound' key is marked # and the 'star' key *. The local Pacific Bell Yellow Pages' Customer Guide is a valuable resource section that gives essential emergency numbers, instructions on how to use public phones and information on call rates.

## Time

California operates on **Pacific Standard Time**, which is eight hours behind Greenwich Mean Time (London), three hours behind Eastern Standard Time (New York), one hour behind Mountain Time (Denver), and two hours behind Central Time (Chicago). Clocks go forward by an hour on the last Sunday in April, and back again on the last Sunday in October. Many outdoor establishments, such as beaches, gardens, driving tours and even some museums, change their hours accordingly.

## Tourist information

### Visitor Information Centres

*685 South Figueroa Street, between Seventh Street & Wilshire Boulevard, Downtown (1-213 689 8822). Metro 7th Street/Metro Center/bus 26, 60, 427, 434, 460, Commuter Express 437, 448, Foothill Transit 495, DASH A/1-110, exit Ninth Street east.* **Open** 8am-5pm Mon-Fri; 8.30am-5pm Sat.

*The Janes House, 6541 Hollywood Boulevard, at Hudson Avenue, Hollywood (1-213 689 8822). Bus 1, 180, 210, 212/US101, exit Hollywood Boulevard west.* **Open** 9am-5pm Mon-Sat.

## Smoking

Los Angeles has some of the most stringent anti-smoking laws on record. Smoking is strictly prohibited in cinemas, stage-production or musical-recital theatres (save for designated areas of lobbies), libraries, museums, art galleries, train, cruise ship, airport and bus depot waiting areas and ticket lines, city buses, elevators, public bathrooms and bathhouses and allowed only in the bar and outdoor areas of restaurants, at the proprietors' discretion. Most hotels prohibit smoking altogether, except in designated rooms. By January 1997, even tighter laws may be introduced.

# Getting Around

**Sacrilegious but true: you don't actually need a car to get around LA – though it helps.**

Given the sheer size and sprawl of LA, it's hardly surprising that Angelenos have a special relationship with the car: they spend a lot of time sitting in them. And it's always been that way: as far back as 1916, there were over 50,000 cars chugging around LA. Driving is simply the quickest and easiest way to get around the city and, once you get the hang of the freeways, it can actually be fun. But, if you don't have access to a car, it doesn't mean that you're condemned to staying within walking distance of your hotel. Los Angeles has a very efficient bus system that goes just about everywhere, as well as a number of infant Metro (subway train) lines that are slowly gaining in popularity as they start to extend across the city. Because of the distances to be covered, if you're planning to use public transport to get around, be prepared to plan ahead and always allow plenty of time for your journey.

For more on Los Angeles' unique automobile culture, *see chapter* **Car City**. For a map of LA's freeway system, *see* **Maps** at the back of the guide.

## To & from the airports

## Los Angeles International Airport (LAX)

*Information 1-310 646 5252.*

### By shuttle

LAX is situated on the Westside, practically on the sea, and has eight terminals; flights from Europe usually arrive at the Tom Bradley International Terminal. A fleet of shuttles flits between the airport and every neighbourhood in LA, 24 hours a day. Most will drop you at your hotel; fares start at $15. You pick them up immediately outside the arrival terminals: dispatchers will advise you on which one to take. If you're flying out of LAX, **SuperShuttle** (1-213 775 6600/ 1-310 782 6600), **Californian Dream Airport Shuttle** (1-800 503 7326) and **Shuttle 2000** (1-800 977 7872) will pick you up from wherever you are to take you to the airport. It's a good idea to order these 24 hours in advance.

### By taxi

Taxis can be found immediately outside the arrival terminals. If you're staying on the Westside, a taxi ride from LAX will cost around $20 plus tip. If you're heading to Hollywood or beyond, it'll be at least $40 and a tip. There's a flat-rate of $24 between LAX and Downtown.

### By bus

There's a free shuttle from LAX to the nearby MTA bus terminal at Vicksburg Avenue and 96th Street. From there,

buses go all over the city. If you're arriving at night, it's probably better to hop on a shuttle rather than the bus.

## Burbank-Glendale-Pasadena Airport

*Information 1-818 840 8847.*

If you're flying from a US airport, you may fly into Burbank rather than LAX, but it's still served by shuttles and taxis, and a free shuttle will connect you to the MTA bus stop at Hollywood Way and Thornton Avenue, Burbank.

## Major international airlines

For more airlines, consult the *Yellow Pages.*

**Air New Zealand** 1-800 262 1234
**American Airlines** *domestic* 1-800 433 7300/ *international* 1-800 624 6262
**British Airways** 1-800 247 9297
**Continental Airlines** *domestic* 1-800 525 0280/ *international* 1-800 231 0856
**Delta Air Lines** *domestic* 1-800 325 8224/*international* 1-800 221 1212
**Northwest Airlines** *domestic* 1-800 225 2525/ *international* 1-800 447 4747
**TWA** *domestic* 1-800 221 2000/*international* 1-800 892 4141
**USAir** 1-800 428 4322
**United Airlines** 1-800 241 6522
**Virgin Atlantic Airways** 1-800 862 8621

## Public transport

## Information

LA's public transport system is run by the **Metropolitan Transportation Authority (MTA)**. For information on bus and Metro train timetables, fares and passes, phone **1-213 626 4455** or **1-800 266 6883** (and expect to wait on hold for a while). The operators can plan your journey for you, including connections, if you tell them where you are and where you want to go. Alternatively, during the week, you can visit the MTA centres at 515 South Flower Street (at Fifth Street, Downtown LA; 7.30am-3.30pm Mon-Fri) and 6249 Hollywood Boulevard (at Vine Street, Hollywood; 10am-6pm Mon-Fri). For a copy of the MTA's *Self-Guided Tours,* write to Metro, 425 Main Street, LA, CA 90013-1393.

## Buses

The main mode of public transport in Los Angeles are the **MTA** buses, their white with orange and red trim paintwork often covered in garish advertising, covering over 200 routes throughout the LA area. The **DASH** (Downtown Area Short Hop) A, B, C, D and E are five express shuttles (running every 15-45 minutes) that service Downtown LA and most of its important sites and landmarks, including the Garment District, Convention Center, MOCA, City Hall, USC, Union Station, Little Tokyo, Exposition Park and the Music Center. DASH also provides express shuttle services to other areas,

We travel the world
for you

to bring the most exciting fashions
for you, your family and your home under one roof. Stop by the
visitors center with this guide and a bloomingdale's same-day
receipt to receive a bloomingdale's gift.*

CENTURY CITY · SHERMAN OAKS · NEWPORT BEACH · STANFORD
BEVERLY CENTER (MARCH 1997)
*LIMIT ONE PER CUSTOMER.

# bloomingdale's
It's Like No Other Store In The World

*LAX's* **Theme Building**: *welcome to LA, the aliens have landed...*

including Beverly Hills, Venice, Hollywood, West Hollywood, Pacific Palisades, Crenshaw and Van Nuys/ Studio City. For more information, call 1-213 580 5444.

Municipal bus services include **Santa Monica City Bus Lines**, aka'The Big Blue Bus' (1-310451 5444), which serves Santa Monica, Malibu and Venice; **West Hollywood Cityline** (1-7800 447 2189), a shuttle service covering 18 locations in West Hollywood; **Commuter Express** (1-800 266 6883), essentially a commuter bus service from Downtown LA to, among other destinations, Glendale, Encino, Westwood, Brentwood, Culver City and the San Fernando Valley; **Foothill Transit** (1-818 967 3147), primarily serving the San Gabriel and Pomona Valleys; and **Culver CityBus** (1-310 253 6500), covering Culver City, Venice, Mar Vista, LAX and Westwood/UCLA. The MTA can also advise on these services.

On busy lines, buses run every 5-10 minutes during peak hours; at night, it's every half hour or so. On the main crosstown routes the service is 24-hour, but there's only one bus an hour after 11pm. The buses stick to their schedules, more or less, and they also provide an insight into a different side of LA – people only take the bus if they haven't got a car; consequently, they're mainly used by the poor, the old and recent immigrants. They are safe, however. Given the distances you may have to cover, taking the bus is by necessity slow, so allow plenty of time.

### Fares & bus stops

One trip on an MTA bus costs $1.35; children under five travel free. You'll need the exact fare; the machines on the buses take notes. If you plan to change buses, ask the driver for a transfer (25¢), which you can use on a subsequent journey that day. On Santa Monica buses, the basic fare is 50¢; transfers cost 25¢. DASH buses cost 25¢. Fares on other bus lines fall into a similar price range. The MTA bus stop sign is a big orange 'M' on a white rectangle. In Santa Monica, it's a blue triangle on a light pole marked 'Big Blue Bus'.

### Tokens & travel passes

If you're going to use the buses a lot, you can buy tokens from supermarkets and local stores. A bag of 10 costs $9 and

it's one token per journey. Alternatively, you can get a monthly pass for $49. You can also use tokens on the Metro train system (*see below*).

### Outside LA

For long-distance buses, the main **Greyhound Terminal** (1-213 629 8400/1-800 231 2222; open 24 hours daily) is at 1716 East Seventh Street, between South Alameda & Decatur Streets, Downtown. This is a distinctly dodgy area, but the terminal itself is safe. You can get to or from the terminal on MTA bus routes 60, 470 and 471.

## Trains

The concept of a **Metro** subway line is a new one for LA and public awareness of the three lines – Red, Blue and Green – is still fairly low. As a result, the trains are rarely crowded, but then they only cover certain areas of the city. The MTA is opening new stations as fast as they can be built, so by the time you read this there will probably have been a couple of additions to the network. One trip costs $1.35 and transfers (between lines and between buses and trains) are available. Trains run 4.45am-11.30pm daily.

**Metro Red Line**
A genuine underground subway, this is the newest line: it opened in 1993 and starts at Union Station in Downtown and runs through to Wilshire Boulevard and Western Avenue. By 2001, the line is scheduled to go as far as Hollywood.

**Metro Blue Line**
Starting at the Red Line station at Seventh Street and Figueroa Street in Downtown, the Blue Line heads south, above ground, through South-Central, before ending up in Long Beach. The view along the way offers a glimpse of a part of LA not normally seen by visitors.

**Metro Green Line**
This overground route links the area around LAX (no station at the airport) with South-Central and then Norwalk to the east. It's unlikely you'll need to use this particular route.

# It's better by bus

With over 2,700 buses lumbering around the 465-square mile Greater Los Angeles area, MTA provides more than enough bus lines of note to help the car-less visitor reach their destination. Here are a few of the most useful:

**1** From Downtown along Hollywood Boulevard.
**2** From Downtown along Sunset Boulevard to the Pacific Coast Highway. The **302** is a limited-stop service along the same route.
**3** From Downtown along Sunset Boulevard and Beverly Drive to Beverly Hills.
**4** From Downtown along Santa Monica Boulevard to Santa Monica Beach. (Limited-stop service **304**.)
**10 & 11** From Downtown along Melrose Avenue.
**20** From Downtown all the way down Wilshire Boulevard to Santa Monica.
**21** From MacArthur Park along Wilshire Boulevard to Westwood/UCLA.
**22** From MacArthur Park along Wilshire Boulevard to Century City and Brentwood. (Limited-stop **322**.)
**33** From Downtown along Venice Boulevard to Venice Beach. (Limited-stop **333**.)
**60** From Downtown to Long Beach.
**96** From Downtown to Griffith Park (via Los Angeles Zoo), Burbank, Studio City and Sherman Oaks.

**180 & 181** From Hollywood to Pasadena via Glendale.
**212** From Hollywood down La Brea Avenue (crossing Melrose Avenue, Beverly Boulevard and Wilshire Boulevard) all the way to Inglewood.
**401** Express route from Downtown to downtown Pasadena.
**420** Express route from Downtown to Universal City Studios, the Hollywood Bowl and the Lankershim/Cahuenga spine.
**434** Express route from Downtown via the I-10 to Santa Monica and along the Pacific Coast Highway to Malibu.
**460** From Downtown to Disneyland and Knott's Berry Farm (via a 2-hour, circuitous route through Norwalk, Pico Rivera and Downey).

## Santa Monica City Bus Lines

**1** From Venice along Santa Monica Boulevard through Santa Monica to UCLA.
**2** From Venice along the seafront to Santa Monica and along Wilshire Boulevard to UCLA.
**3** From LAX along Lincoln Boulevard through Venice and Santa Monica, then along Montana Avenue to UCLA.
**9** From West LA along Olympic Boulevard through Santa Monica to Pacific Palisades.

## Outside LA

**Union Station** (800 North Alameda Street, Downtown; 1-213 683 6987) is the place to go for any train heading out of LA. The **Metrolink** (1-213 808 5465) suburban lines cover Orange County, Riverside County and San Bernadino County. All **Amtrak** trains (1-800 872 7245), to destinations in California and all over the US, depart from here.

## Taxis & limousines

Because of LA's size, taxis are not a cheap way of getting around, but they do take credit cards. The basic fee is $1.90 and then $1.60 per additional mile. You can't hail them, although there are taxi ranks in certain areas. Supermarkets and restaurants will often call cabs for you. Companies include **Yellow Cab Co** (1-213/310/818 808 1000); **Independent Cab Co** (1-800 521 8249) and **Checker Cab Co** (1-800 300 5007), all 24-hour.

The limo is the quintessential LA form of transport; you'll see more limos here than just about anywhere else in the world. The cost of hiring a limo starts at around $40 an hour and the driver will expect a decent tip. Companies include **Mirage Transportation Corporation** (1-310 419 0911); **The Ultimate Limousine** (1-800 710 1498) and **A1-West Coast Limousine Service** (1-310 671 8720).

## Driving

Driving in LA presents its own unique challenges. At first sight, the five-lane freeways seem like racetracks with cars jockeying for position by overtaking on both sides and weaving in and out of lanes. But intimidating as it may initially seem, you'll quickly get used to it and, when it's late at night and the freeways are less crowded, driving can be a positive pleasure. You can also console yourself with the thought that if you can drive in LA, you can drive anywhere.

## Freeway etiquette

Freeways are referred to by their numbers – the 10, 110, 405 and so on – and often by names as well. The I-10 (I stands for Interstate) west of Downtown, for example, is known as the Santa Monica Freeway. On the freeways there is a speed limit of 65mph, but you'll see many cars going much faster. Don't expect people to indicate when they change lanes. The outside lanes are the fast lanes (though it's perfectly normal to overtake on the inside): it's best to stay in the middle ones until you need to exit. Any road apart from a freeway is known as a surface street. When you merge onto a freeway from a surface street, it's important to accelerate to freeway speed; similarly, be prepared to brake sharply when exiting. Exits are marked by the name of the surface street you join; remember that you may be exiting off either side of the freeway.

Always plan your route before you leave: the freeway system does not take you directly from A to B and it moves swiftly, so you must know your freeway entrance and exit and the direction you are going (north, south, east or west) before you start. Otherwise, you can easily find yourself being sucked off at the wrong exit and getting lost in an unknown area. Often there will be a car-pool lane, which only cars carrying two or three people (depending on the signs) can use. This is not a members-only scheme; if you fit the criterion, you can use the lane (but make sure you get out of it well before your exit).

On the surface streets, driving is much the same as in any US city. You can turn right on a red light if your way is clear and the speed limit is 35mph, though, again, it's often flouted. At four-way crossings, 'courtesy driving' is expected: cars cross in the order that they arrive at the junction.

## Parking

Because LA is a car-dependent city, parking isn't usually a problem. Remember that you must park in the same direction that the traffic is going. Don't block driveways or fire hydrants and pay particular attention to kerb markings: if they're red, don't park there or you could get towed. Then go and look at all the signs on your side of the block – they will tell you the local parking laws. Parking enforcement officers are everywhere and illegal parking of any sort, even for a short time, usually results in a ticket. Use car parks (known as parking lots) whenever you can; for recommended car parks and more information on driving, *see chapter* **Survival**.

Note that California law requires all occupants to wear a seatbelt. Always keep ID and papers with you in the car in case you're stopped by the Highway Patrol.

## Car rental

To rent a car in the States – almost always an automatic – you'll need a credit card and a driver's licence. Most companies won't rent to anyone under 25 (or, if they do, will add on a hefty surcharge). There are dozens of car rental companies in LA and it obviously pays to shop around. The national companies, which tend to offer the best deals and the most reliable vehicles, all have free 1-800 numbers; many companies require you to book on these rather than at the local office. Rates seesaw wildly, depending on demand; it can be a good idea to make a reservation weeks in advance (possible now that 1-800 numbers are accessible from the UK). You can put a hold on a car without committing yourself (and if they run out of a car in that class, they will upgrade you – a frequent and pleasurable occurrence). As a rule, you will not be allowed to take a rental car into Mexico.

Remember that the price quoted will not include state sales tax or any form of insurance, but also that you may qualify for a discount: AA members do, and you can sometimes wangle a corporate deal if you show your business card. Insurance will almost double your bill, but it is essential – and you are unlikely to be covered by your domestic policy. You will be offered both liability insurance (for damage you cause to other cars and their occupants) and a collision damage waiver (CDW), both around the $9-a-day mark. We recommend that you take out both – even though it will make the insurance as costly as the rental itself. Unlike other states, the baseline fee gives you no cover at all in California.

Bearing all this in mind, it is probably worth considering fly-drive deals, renting via your home travel agent or getting quotes from a local branch of an international company.

### Car rental companies

**Alamo** 1-800 327 9633; **Avis** 1-800 831 2847; **Budget** 1-800 527 0700; **Dollar** 1-800 800 4000; **Enterprise** 1-800 325 8007; **Hertz** 1-800 654 3131; **National Car Rental** 1-800 227 7368; **Thrifty Car Rental** 1-800 367 2277; **Rent-A-Wreck** 1-800 535 1391

## Motorbike rental

If you want to cruise the streets on a Harley, then try **Eagle Rider Motorcycle Rental** on 1-310 320 3456 (20917 Western Avenue, at Torrance Boulevard, South Bay. You need to be over 21 and have a credit card and motorbike licence.

## Cycling

You can cycle the bike paths that head down the coast from Santa Monica and mountain bike in Griffith Park and Topanga Canyon, but otherwise the volume of traffic and distances involved make cycling difficult in LA. For other bike paths and rentals, *see chapter* **Active LA**.

## On foot

Perversely, certain sections of LA are best covered on foot. In particular, Downtown, central Hollywood and the Santa Monica and Venice beachfronts are best explored by walking. Jaywalking – crossing the street anywhere except at a designated pedestrian crossing – can get you a $100 ticket. Seriously.

# Accommodation

*If you want posh, palatial and posey, you're in the right town – but if eccentric, exotic or just plain budget is more your scene, LA can accommodate you, too.*

Like everything else in Los Angeles, hotels here are all about image. Many have been around since Hollywood's golden years and each has its own history, local legends and style; and whatever identity each hotel chooses, most take it over the top in an only-in-California way. What this means for you is that you get not only a place to crash, but also a scene, an attitude and an unforgettable experience that comes free with the price of the room.

If you haven't figured it out already, LA is absolutely huge – so huge, in fact, that where you choose to stay will dictate what kind of holiday you have. A room in Santa Monica guarantees you quick shoreline access, a cooler climate and a beachy California vibe; Beverly Hills offers a decadent dose of Hollywood glamour, star-sightings, upscale shopping and Sunset Boulevard's nightlife; while Downtown digs generally cater to conventioneers.

## PRICES & SERVICES

Expect to pay (for a double room, per night) from $40-$110 in a budget hotel; $90-$200 in a mid-range hotel; and from about $200 (to the sky's the limit)

in a first-class hotel. Prices can very enormously, depending on location and exactly which establishment you've picked: there are some very, very luxurious and very, very expensive hotels in Los Angeles. The cheapest form of accommodation (bar camping) is to get a shared room in a hostel; these start from around $17 per person per night. The budget chain motels can be quite cheap (*see page 21* **Hotel chains**), especially if there are four of you; double rooms usually have two large double beds. The rates will be lower the further out you go, but it can be worth the commute, especially since motels are never far from the freeway.

Remember that the quoted rates are 'rack rates' ('official' published rates) and that the actual cost can be half as much, depending on day of the week, season, availability, any promotions that might be running and whether you are eligible for a discount – ask about corporate, AAA, weekend, promotional and any other kind of discount you can think of. However, rates do not include hotel taxes, which range from 12-15 per cent (depending on which city the hotel is in).

*Bed down in a set of dentures at the art deco* **Argyle***. See page 20.*

You will always get a TV in your room – they're as much part of the furniture as a bed – and parking facilities (this is LA, after all). Parking is usually free at budget and mid-range hotels but the hefty rates at the larger and more costly places can increase your bill substantially (rates quoted are per night). Expect to pay a service charge (from 25¢ for a local call) for using the phone. All hotels offer no-smoking rooms.

## Booking & rental services

### Los Angeles Convention & Visitors Bureau
*685 South Figueroa Street, LA, CA 90017 (1-213 689 8822/fax 1-213 236 2395).* **Open** 8am-5pm Mon-Friday; 8.30am-3pm Sat.

### Preferred Hotels & Resorts Worldwide
*10877 Wilshire Boulevard, Suite 403, LA, CA 90024 (1-800 323 7500/1-310 208 2884/fax 1-310 208 2994).*

### Central Reservation Service
*505 Maitland Avenue, Suite 100, Altamonte Springs, FL 32701 (1-800 548 3311/1-407 339 4116/fax 1-407 339 4736).*

### Hotel Reservations Network
*8140 Walnut Hill Lane, Suite 203, Dallas, TX 75231 (1-800 964 6835/1-214 361 7311/fax 1-214 361 7299).*

## Westside: beach towns
### First-class

### Hotel Oceana
*849 Ocean Avenue, between Montana Avenue & Idaho Street, Santa Monica, CA 90403 (reservations 1-800 777 0758/front desk 1-310 393 0486/fax 1-310 458 1182/ e-mail: beachsuite@aol.com/website: http://www.smweb. com/oceana).* Bus 22, 322/I-10, exit Fourth-Fifth Street north. **Rates** one-bedroom suite $190-$265; two-bedroom suite $275-$325. **Credit** AmEx, DC, Disc, JCB, MC, V.
Across the street from Santa Monica beach (with unobstructed views) and two blocks away from Third Street Promenade is the brand-new Hotel Oceana. Each of the 63 luxurious but informal suites aim to recall the art deco era of the Cote d'Azur, with primary colours, vibrant patterns, wrought-iron and wicker. Bonuses include granite and marble bathrooms, a CD stereo and fully equipped kitchens (larger suites only), free continental breakfast and daily

*Pool life at the **Hotel Figueroa**. See p27.*

*Home on the range at the **Bel-Air**. See p22.*

newspapers. Many rooms have large balconies facing onto Ocean Avenue, while others face the swimming pool that dominates the courtyard. No on-site restaurant but in-suite gourmet dining is provided by Wolfgang Puck's Café. One of the best hotels in Santa Monica.
**Hotel services** *Limited air-conditioning. Babysitting. Bar. Car park ($10; $15 valet). Disabled: access; rooms. Fax. Fitness facilities (spa). Laundry. Lifts. Multi-lingual staff.*
**Room services** *Fax/modem hookups. Hair dryer. Mini-bar. Radio. Refrigerator. Room service. Stereo with CD player. Telephone. VCR on request.*

### Loews Santa Monica Beach Hotel
*1700 Ocean Avenue, between Colorado Avenue & Pico Boulevard, Santa Monica, CA 90401 (reservations 1-800 235 6397/front desk 1-310 458 6700/fax 1-310 458 6761).* Bus 20, 22, 33, 320, 322, 333, 434, Santa Monica 1, 7, 8, 10/I-10, exit Fourth-Fifth Street north. **Rates** single $225-$345; double $245-$365. **Credit** AmEx, DC, Disc, JCB, MC, V.
The 319-room Loews is what you'd expect from Southern California: it's light and airy, warm and beachy, casual but elegant – and even the guests are attractive. The four-storey atrium lobby takes full advantage of its scenic surroundings offering views of the beach and beyond. Location is key; the beach is just across the street and the oceanfront park, pier, restaurants and Third Street Promenade a painless stroll away. Good stuff-your-face Sunday brunch.
**Hotel services** *Air-conditioning. Babysitting. Bar. Beauty salon. Car park ($15). Conference facilities. Disabled: access; rooms. Fax. Fitness facilities (cardio room, free weights, Jacuzzi, sauna, steam). Laundry. Lifts. Multi-lingual staff. Pool. Two restaurants. Safe.*
**Room services** *Fax. Hair dryer. Mini-bar. Radio. Refrigerator. 24-hour room service. Telephone. VCR.*

# WESTLAKE
### PLAZA INN

## A RAMADA INN HOTEL

The Westlake Plaza Inn Hotel, welcomes each guest into an Oasis of tranquil beauty with unequalled personal attention.

Located downtown in the city's fashionable west end, just minutes from the city hall. The Westlake Plaza Inn Hotel provides every service and facility to ensure the perfect stay.

The elegantly furnished accommodation will satisfy even the most discerning of tastes.

Luxurious Suites ✦ Jacuzzi Suites ✦ Guest Rooms

**611 SOUTH WESTLAKE AVENUE, LOS ANGELES, CA 90057
TEL: (213) 483-6363 ✦ FAX: (213) 483-0088**

*Reservation: 1-800-688-8389*

## Shutters on the Beach

*1 Pico Boulevard, at Ocean Avenue, Santa Monica, CA 90405 (reservations 1-800 334 9000/hotel operator 1-310 458 0030/fax 1-310 458 4589). Bus 20, 33, 320, 434, Santa Monica 1, 7, 10/I-10, exit Fourth Street south.* **Rates** *single/double $280-$450; suite from $675.* **Credit** AmEx, DC, Disc, MC, V.

Named after the sliding doors in all guest rooms, Shutters opened in 1993 and is the only hotel in Santa Monica that's actually on the beach. Its location, along with its New England beach home-styling and luxury amenities, make it one of the most popular destinations in the area – just ask Oasis. Its lobby has two wood-burning fireplaces and original artworks by David Hockney and Roy Lichtenstein. There are 186 rooms and 12 suites, custom-furnished in upscale beach décor, with upholstered headboards, lounge chairs and walnut desks. The marble bathrooms with whirlpool tubs are above par.

**Hotel services** *Air-conditioning. Babysitting. Bar. Bike rental. Car park ($17; valet $17 overnight; $3 first 3 hours, $2 each additional hour daytime). Conference facilities. Currency exchange. Disabled: access; rooms. Fax. Laundry. Lifts. Multi-lingual staff. Fitness facilities (cardio, free weights, Nautilus, spa). Pool. Two restaurants.*

**Room services** *Hair dryer. Mini-bar. Radio. 24-hour room service. Safe. Telephone. VCR.*

## Mid-range

### Casa Malibu

*22752 Pacific Coast Highway, between Malibu Pier & Los Flores Canyon, Malibu, CA 90265 (reservations 1-800 831 0858/front desk 1-310 456 2219/fax 1-310 456 5418). Bus 434/I-10, exit PCH north.* **Rates** *single/double $99-$199.* **Credit** AmEx, MC, V.

Owners Joan and Richard Page are slowly renovating this small, two-storey motel –and what they've done so far makes it the best affordable choice along the northern shore. Each room has classy furnishings, fax/modem hookups, a coffee maker and refrigerator; some have fireplaces, kitchens and/or private decks. Upgraded rooms include Italian tiling and the kind of seriously stunning bathrooms you'd expect from a luxury hotel. The buildings are covered with flowing vines and surround a garden courtyard and a brick patio that looks directly onto the hotel's private beach.

**Hotel services.** *Limited air-conditioning. Babysitting on request. Free covered car park. Fax. Laundry. Private beach. Safe.*

**Room services** *Fax/modem hookups. Hair dryer. Radio. Refrigerator. Telephone. VCR.*

### Shangri-La

*1301 Ocean Avenue, at Arizona Avenue, Santa Monica, CA 90401 (reservations 1-800 345 7829/front desk 1-310 394 2791/fax 1-310 451 3351). Bus 4, 20, 22, 33, Santa Monica 1, 7, 8, 10/I-10, exit Fourth-Fifth Street north.* **Rates** *single/double $115; one-bedroom suite $155-$235; two-bedroom suite $265-$450.* **Credit** AmEx, DC, Disc, JCB, MC, V.

Across from oceanfront Palisades Park, the 1939 art deco Shangri-La prides itself on its spacious rooms and great ocean views. The 55 rooms and suites are nothing too fancy, but they are large and adorned with beautiful – though sometimes scuffed – deco furniture (beware: there are some tacky elements). There are full kitchens in almost every room and the bathrooms are clean and roomy. The only down side is that there's no pool, room service, restaurant or bar. Continental breakfast is included.

**Hotel services** *Air-conditioning. Free car park. Fax. Fitness facilities (cardio, free weights). Laundry. Lifts. Multi-lingual staff. Safe.*

**Room services** *Hair dryer. Refrigerator. Telephone.*

## Budget

### Bayside Hotel

*2001 Ocean Avenue, at Bay Street, Santa Monica, CA 90405 (front desk 1-310 396 6000/fax 1-310 451 1111). Bus 20, 22, 320, 322, 434/I-10, exit Fourth Street south.* **Rates** *single/double $49-$99.* **Credit** AmEx, Disc, MC, V.

A few blocks south of Santa Monica's shopping and dining action, the Bayside is casual but surprisingly well-appointed considering it's an elderly motel. Rooms range from a box to a suite, are decorated in beiges and pastels and have huge windows, somewhat spongy mattresses, a TV and an ancient coffee maker; none have phones. Bathrooms, though clean, are small and unmemorable. Tables and chairs along the balcony walkway are a perfect perch for afternoon sun-catching. A few extra bucks will get you a kitchen or an unobstructed ocean view. Weekly rates.

**Hotel services** *Air-conditioning. Fax. Free car park. Telephones.*

**Room services** *Refrigerator.*

### Belle Blue Inn by the Sea

*1670 Ocean Avenue, between Pico Boulevard & Colorado Avenue, Santa Monica, CA 90401 (front desk 1-310 393 2363/fax 1-310 393 1063). Bus 20, 22, 320, 322, 434, Santa Monica 1, 7, 10/I-10, exit Fourth Street south.* **Rates** *single $60-$90; double $65-$110.* **Credit** AmEx, MC, V.

The Belle Blue captures the casual and colourful essence of Santa Monica – and considering it's sandwiched between the Loews hotel and a string of commercial properties, is a short walk from the beach and reasonably priced, it's also exceptionally charming and exclusive. Each room is entered via a private entrance on a quaint, gated cul-de-sac lined with homes and greenery. Rooms are on the small side, but have brightly painted walls with individual and cosy furnishings and an all-round homey feel. A courtyard terrace offers umbrella-covered tables and chairs – and is the only place you can smoke. Continental breakfast included.

**Hotel services** *Free car park. Fax.*

**Room services** *Refrigerator. Telephone.*

### The Cadillac

*8 Dudley Avenue, at Speedway, Venice, CA 90291 (front desk 1-310 399 8876/fax 1-310 399 4536). Bus 33, 436, Santa Monica 1, 2/I-10, exit Lincoln Boulevard south.* **Rates** *hostel bed $20; single/double $79-$90; suite $110-$125.* **Credit** AmEx, JCB, MC, V.

Vibrant as its beachfront surroundings, this four-storey hotel's front yard is the heart of infamous Venice Beach, complete with restaurants, rollerbladers, bikers and sunbathers; the revamped deco interior is a mixture of artistic and vibrant, tasteful and cheesy. The hotel has private rooms (on the tackier side of deco, with black lacquer furnishings and industrial carpeting) and hostel rooms with two bunk beds and a shared bath. Common areas include an upstairs sun deck and a lounge with pool table. Built in 1905, the Cadillac was once the summer residence of Charlie Chaplin.

**Hotel services** *Babysitting. Free car park. Disabled: access; rooms. Fitness facilities (gym, sauna). Self-service laundry. Vending machine with snacks and stamps.*

**Room services** *Safe. Telephone.*

### Hotel Carmel by the Sea

*201 Broadway, at Second Street, Santa Monica, CA 90401 (reservations 1-800 445 8695/front desk 1-310 451 2469/fax 1-310 393 4180). Bus 4, 33, 434, Santa Monica 7, 8, 10/I-10, exit Fourth-Fifth street north.* **Rates** *shared bath $55; single $75; double $85; suite $115.* **Credit** AmEx, DC, Disc, JCB, MC, V.

Before its recent renovation, Hotel Carmel's 74-year-old walls were showing their age, but that didn't stop young tourists

**The Cadillac:** *right in the whirling epicentre of Venice Beach. See page 19.*

from packing the place – the rates and location are one of the best combos in the area (it's one block from the beach and around the corner from Third Street Promenade). The 110 rooms (including 13 with shared bathrooms) have wooden furnishings and colourful bedspreads; bathrooms are basic with aged towels and no frilly toiletries. Expect the quirks that come with every old building, don't expect a great view – and you'll be perfectly happy here.
**Hotel services** *Car park ($6.60 overnight; $2.20 two hours daytime). Currency exchange. Fax. Hair dryer. Laundry. Lifts. Multi-lingual staff. Safe.*
**Room services** *Hair dryer (suites only). Radio. Refrigerator (suites only). Telephone.*

## Westside: inland

### First-class

#### The Argyle
*8358 Sunset Boulevard, at La Cienega Boulevard, West Hollywood, CA 90069 (reservations 1-800 225 2637/ front desk 1-213 654 7100/fax 1-213 654 9287). Bus 2, 3, 429/I-10, exit La Cienega Boulevard north.* **Rates** single/double $170-$325. **Credit** AmEx, DC, MC, V.
Enter this magnificent 1931 art deco building (previously the Saint James Club) in the heart of the wild side of Sunset Boulevard and you are immediately transported into the past by elaborate ceiling mouldings, light fixtures and period furnishings. The rooms capture the essence of deco luxury with stunning, custom-made Italian furniture, including an oval scalloped bed, a postcard desk and even a cute-enough-to-steal deco ice-bucket. Add a stereo system, VCR and a TV that electronically sinks into its own custom-made credenza, and you've got one of the swankiest rooms in town. The bathrooms are equally stylish, and some have steam showers with Jacuzzi tubs. If you really want to live the high life, rent one of the spacious penthouses (where John Wayne once lived), complete with rooftop balcony.

**Hotel services** *Air-conditioning. Babysitting. Bar. Car park ($17). 24-hour concierge. Conference facilities. Currency exchange. Disabled: access; rooms. Fax. Fitness facilities (cardio). Laundry. Lifts. Multi-lingual staff. Pool. Restaurant.*
**Room services** *Fax. Hair dryer. Mini-bar. Radio. 24-hour room service. Safe. Telephone.*

#### Beverly Hills Hotel & Bungalows
*9641 Sunset Boulevard, at Rodeo Drive, Beverly Hills, CA 90210 (reservations 1-800 283 8885/front desk 1-310 276 2251/fax 1-310 887 2887). Bus 2, 429/I-405, exit Sunset Boulevard east.* **Rates** single/double $300-$400; suite $600-$3,000; bungalow $300-$3,000. **Credit** AmEx, DC, MC, V.
Whoever said money can't buy love hasn't stayed at the Beverly Hills Hotel. A celebrity favourite since its 1912 opening, it has hosted such regulars as Elizabeth Taylor (who bungalowed here with six of her seven husbands), and after its $100 million renovation (by new owner the Sultan of Brunei), has recently become a parading ground for the nouveaux riche. Its biggest draw is its true Hollywood feel – grandiose, glamorous and expensive. The decor is pink'n' palatial with banana-leaf wallpapered hallways and luxurious but homey guest rooms. Each is tastefully appointed and giddy with trinkets, gilded mirrors, a great stereo system, two phones with voicemail and a fax. Bathrooms are extravagantly oversized, with a glorious marble bath and separate shower. Lounge in the lobby at tea-time, walk in the 12-acre grounds, sunbathe at the fabulous pool (with cabanas for $100 per day) or hang out at the happening Polo Lounge bar – you can't help but feel that Beverly Hills vibe.
**Hotel services** *Air-conditioning. On-call babysitting. Bar. Beauty salon. Car park ($15). Conference facilities. Currency exchange. Disabled: access; rooms. Fitness facilities. Laundry. Lifts. Multi-lingual staff. Pool. Jogging trails. Four restaurants.*
**Room services** *Hair dryer. Mini-bar. Modem hookup. Radio. Room service. Telephones (3). VCR/stereo.*

## Beverly Prescott Hotel

*1224 South Beverwil Drive, at Pico Boulevard, LA, CA 90035 (reservations 1-800 421 3212/front desk 1-310 277 2800/fax 1-310 203 9537). Bus 3, Santa Monica 7, 13/I-10, exit National Boulevard/Overland Avenue north.* **Rates** single/double $190-$275; suite $350-$700. **Credit** AmEx, DC, Disc, MC, V.

The 1970s-style, high-rise exterior gives no hint of the Prescott's whimsical, colourful and artistic interior, but once in the door, there's no mistaking it. Beyond the lobby, the lounge is pure creative fantasy, and the rooms boldly follow suit in a whirlwind of colour and design detail. Each is playfully tasteful, with good original art, a comfortable bed with an enormous black-and-tan checkered headboard, wrought-iron lamps, and an overstuffed, striped lounge chair. All rooms have a balcony, some looking onto the nearby hills to the north (sadly via the parking lot); others to the flatlands to the south. Bathrooms have plenty of elbow room and granite detail. It's not a walkable neighborhood, but then again, it's peaceful because of it.

**Hotel services** *Air-conditioning. Babysitting. Bar. Car park ($15.40). Conference facilities. Currency exchange. Disabled: access; rooms. Fax. Laundry. Lifts. Multi-lingual staff. Fitness facilities (cardio, free weights). Restaurant.*
**Room services** *Fax. Hair dryer. Mini-bar. Radio. 24-hour room service.Telephone. VCR on request.*

## Century Plaza Hotel and Tower

*2025 Avenue of the Stars, at Constellation Boulevard, Century City, CA 90067 (reservations 1-800 228 3000/front desk 1-310 277 2000/fax 1-310 551 3355). Bus 22, 27, 28, 316, 328, Santa Monica 5, Antelope Valley 786/I-405, exit Santa Monica Boulevard east.* **Rates** single $215-$265; double $265-$290. **Credit** AmEx, DC, MC, V.

The Century Plaza's 20-storey high, block-long main building is so enormous that it screams 'convention hotel'. However, the business pill is sweetened by good service, class and respectable style. Rooms (over 1,000 of them) are adorned with stately furnishings; all come with a secretary desk, coffee maker, a small balcony with table and chairs plus views partly obstructed by surrounding high-rises. Bathrooms can be small and not all have baths. Public spaces attempt to scale down the vast environment with quiet sitting nooks and artworks, but the best common areas are by the pool, where swimming is accompanied by fitness facilities and patio lunching. Its location, near the ABC Entertainment Center, Schubert Theater and the Century City Shopping Center, makes entertainment and retail cravings easy to satisfy.

**Hotel services** *Air-conditioning. Babysitting. Two bars. Beauty salon. Car park ($19.50). Conference facilities. Currency exchange. Disabled: access; rooms. Fax. Fitness facilities. Laundry. Lifts. Multi-lingual staff. Pool. Two restaurants.*
**Room services** *Hair dryer. Mini-bar. Radio. Room service. Safe. Telephone. VCR on request.*

## Château Marmont

*8221 Sunset Boulevard, between Sweetzer Avenue & Havenhurst Drive, Hollywood, CA 90046 (reservations 1-800 242 8328/front desk 1-213 656 1010/fax 1-213 655 5311). Bus 2, 3, 429/I-10, exit La Cienega Boulevard north.* **Rates** single/double $190-$1,400. **Credit** AmEx, DC, MC, V.

Since 1933, stars like Greta Garbo, Clark Gable, Roman Polanski, Jim Morrison and the unfortunate John Belushi (who overdosed in his bungalow here) have called the Marmont home. Standing just above Sunset Strip, it's a seven-storey structure modelled after the Loire Valley's Château Amboise. Over the years, the steady stream of partying rock stars took its toll on the place, but in 1990 the new owners returned it to its original funky-but-chic aes-

thetic. Rooms are large and unpretentious (ask for a bungalow for the ultimate homey-apartment feel); furnishings are straight out of a Barbara Stanwyck movie, and the service is casual and discreet. Add a hip and famous clientele and a serious dose of old Hollywood exclusivity, and you've got one of the most popular hotels in LA. An added bonus is Bar Marmont, the hip and popular next-door lounge and restaurant.

**Hotel services** *Air-conditioning. Babysitting. Bar. Car park ($12.50). Disabled: access. Fax. Fitness facilities (cardio, free weights). Laundry. Lifts. Multi-lingual staff. Pool. Restaurant.*
**Room services** *CD library. Hair dryer. Mini-bar. Radio. Refrigerator. 24-hour room service. Safe. Telephone (2, with voicemail). Stereo with CD player. VCR.*

## Four Seasons at Beverly Hills

*300 South Doheny Drive, at Burton Way, Beverly Hills, CA 90048 (reservations 1-800 332 3442/front desk 1-310 273 2222/fax 1-310 859 9048). Bus 27, 316, 576/ I-10, exit Robertson Boulevard north.* **Rates** single $295-$365; double $325-$395; suite $460-$3,500. **Credit** AmEx, DC, JCB, MC, V.

Look through any doorway in the first-floor common areas, filled with original art and bountiful flower arrangments, and you'll see beautifully landscaped gardens. At weekends, when press junkets are in full force, you'll probably sight a famous face, too. The rooms are being renovated floor by floor during 1997; the textiles will be replaced but the walk-out balcony, secretary desk, three phones, an armoire and impeccable bathrooms will remain. The luxury and premiere suites bring in folks important (and wealthy) enough to rent out entire floors. The clincher, however, is the chi-chi, fourth-floor pool, which has cabanas, an awning-covered outdoor gym and a luncheon patio – all sprinkled with the Beautiful People. Renowned and utterly refined.

**Hotel services** *Air-conditioning. Babysitting. Bar. Car park (free self-park; $18 valet). Continental breakfast. Conference facilities. Currency exchange. Disabled: access;*

# Hotel chains

There are hundreds of chain hotels, ranging from budget to luxury, throughout Los Angeles. Contact any of the following and they're likely to have a property in the area of your choice.

### First-class

**The Ritz-Carlton** 1-800 241 3333
**Hilton Hotels** 1-800 445 8667
**Hyatt** 1-800 233 1234
**Sheraton Hotels & Inns** 1-800 325 3535

### Mid-range

**Holiday Inn** 1-800 465 4329
**Howard Johnson** 1-800 654 2000
**Marriott** 1-800 228 9290
**Radisson** 1-800 333 3333

### Budget

**Best Western** 1-800 528 1234
**Comfort Inns** 1-800 228 5150
**Days Inn** 1-800 325 2525
**Motel 6** 1-800 466 8356
**Super 8** 1-800 800 8000
**Travelodge** 1-800 578-7878

*rooms. Fax. Laundry. Lifts. Multi-lingual staff. Safe.*
*Fitness facilities (cardio, free weights). Pool. Restaurants.*
**Room services** *Hair dryer. Mini-bar. Radio.*
*Refrigerator. Room service. Safe (suites only). Telephone.*

## Hotel Bel-Air

*701 Stone Canyon Road, at Bellagio Road, Bel Air, CA*
*90077 (reservations 1-800 648 4097/front desk 1-310*
*472 1211/fax 1-310 476 5890). I-405, exit Sunset*
*Boulevard east.* **Rates** single/double $315-$435; junior
suite $495; suite $550-$2,500. **Credit** AmEx, Disc, JCB,
MC, V.

The 12-acre, 92-room Bel-Air is sophisticated, luxurious,
romantic and surprisingly pastoral – and stars and bigwigs
have been retreating here since long before Marilyn booked
her room by the pool. Picture this: a bridged entryway surrounded by Swan Lake (yes, real swans); lavish wild-yet-
sculptured gardens, cocktails in the traditional,
wood-panelled bar; a pool surrounded by palms and
bougainvillaea. The rooms themselves, in the two-storey,
pink stucco, 1920s Mission-style buildings, are impeccably
stylish; each has a private entrance from the gardens, an
elaborate bathroom and comes with a welcoming Asian tea
basket. It's not unusual to see celebs (Nancy Reagan still
lunches here), but don't ask for any commemorative pics –
exclusivity means that no cameras are allowed.

**Hotel services** *Air-conditioning. On-call babysitting.*
*Bar. Beauty salon. Free car park. Conference facilities.*
*Currency exchange. Disabled: access; rooms. Fax. Fitness*
*facilities. Laundry. Multi-lingual staff. Restaurant. Safe.*
**Room services** *Hair dryer. Mini-bar. Radio.*
*Refrigerator (suites with kitchens only). 24-hour room*
*service. Telephone. VCR.*

## Hotel Nikko at Beverly Hills

*465 South La Cienega Boulevard, at Clifton Way, LA,*
*CA 90048 (reservations 1-800 645 5624/hotel operator*
*1-310 247 0400/fax 1-310 247 0315). Bus 27, 105,*
*576/I-10, exit La Cienega Boulevard north.* **Rates** single
$270-$295; double $295-$320. **Credit** AmEx, DC, Disc,
JCB, MC, V.

Worldly business travellers know the Nikko is one of the
finest contemporary hotels in LA. The marble lobby is dominated by a Japanese-style rock garden with fountains and a
towering atrium; behind the Hana Lounge is the pool area
(which you might recall from the film *Indecent Proposal*); and
upstairs, the 300 rooms range from deluxe to the $18,000-per
night Presidential Suite. Each room is adorned with contemporary Japanese-style furnishings, tastefully subdued
lighting and luxuriously soft, canopied beds. Bathrooms are
huge and some have sunken Japanese tubs. Most impressive
are the new suites, which combine full-blown luxury with
New York apartment appeal, and offer all the facilities a busi-
nessperson could want.

**Hotel services** *Air-conditioning. Babysitting. Bar. Car*
*park (free self-park, $16.50 valet). Conference facilities.*
*Currency exchange. Disabled: access; rooms. Fax. Fitness*
*facilities (cardio, free weights, sauna). Laundry. Lift.*
*Multi-lingual staff. Pool. Restaurant.*
**Room services** *CD player. Hair dryer. Mini-bar. Radio.*
*Refrigerator. Room service. Safe. Telephone. VCR.*

## Mondrian Hotel

*8440 Sunset Boulevard, at La Cienega Boulevard, West*
*Hollywood CA 90069 (reservations 1-800 525 8029/*
*front desk 1-213 650 8999/fax 1-213 650 5215). Bus 2,*
*3, 429/I-10, exit La Cienega Boulevard north.* **Rates**
single/double $185; suite $210-$750. **Credit** AmEx, DC,
Disc, JCB, MC, V.

Ian Schrager Hotels, renowned for its Paramount and
Royalton hotels in New York and the Delano in Miami, recently acquired this giant 12-storey property, and renovations
have been in the works for the past year. You, the visitor, are
part of the landscape: a walking piece of art in an environment

where everything plays on scale and illusion. Expect huge
terracotta pots cradling short trees; indoor furniture outside
and vice-versa; free-form light sculptures in the lobby; plenty of play on Hollywood glamour; and, of course, wonderfully chic rooms, most with kitchens, large windows and an
upscale down-home feel. Common areas include an outdoor
New England-style pool and a Caribbean whisky bar.
**Hotel services** *Air-conditioning. Babysitting. Bar.*
*Beauty salon. Car park ($17.50). Children's play area.*
*Conference facilities. Currency exchange. Disabled: access;*
*rooms. Fax. Fitness facilities (sauna, steam, 24-hour*
*gym, Jacuzzi). Laundry. Lifts. Multi-lingual staff. Pool.*
*Restaurants.*
**Room services** *Hair dryer. Mini-bar. Radio. Room*
*service. Safe. VCR on request.*

## The Peninsula Beverly Hills

*9882 Little Santa Monica Boulevard, at Wilshire Boulevard,*
*Beverly Hills, CA 90212 (reservations 1-800 462 7899/front*
*desk 1-310 551 2888/fax 1-310 788 2319). Bus 4, 304/*
*I-405, exit Wilshire Boulevard east.* **Rates** single $315-$500;
double $345-$500; suite $600-$3,000. **Credit** AmEx, DC,
Disc, JCB, MC, V.

Bellhops in starched white uniforms and gold-crested caps
greet the famous, the wealthy and the corporate elite at the
Peninsula's discreet location, eight blocks off Rodeo Drive.
The mahogany lobby bar packs in the cigar-smokers, gold-
diggers and men on the prowl. The enormous Living Room
is an out-and-out luxury lounge, where guests sip tea or
champagne and look out onto the sculpted garden. Rooms
are conservative and refined, with Tiffany amenities and
Rodeo's finest linens. The pool is a fabulous spot, with patio
dining and a Jacuzzi overlooking the city and the hills. Dining
is five-star, of course, as is every inch of this ultra-exclusive
hotel, opened in 1991.
**Hotel services** *Air-conditioning. Babysitting. Bar.*
*Car park ($17). Conference facilities. Disabled: access;*
*rooms. Fax. Laundry. Lifts. Multi-lingual staff. Fitness*
*facilities (cardio, free weights, spa). Outdoor heated*
*pool. Restaurant.*
**Room services** *Hair dryer. Mini-bar. Radio.*
*Refrigerator. 24-hour room service. Safe. Telephone. VCR.*

## The Regent Beverly Wilshire

*9500 Wilshire Boulevard, between Rodeo & El Camino*
*Drives, Beverly Hills, CA 90212 (reservations 1-800 421*
*4354/front desk 1-310 275 5200/fax 1-310 274 2851).*
*Bus 20, 21, 22, 320, 322/I-10, exit Wilshire Boulevard*
*east.* **Rates** single $255-$380; double $275-$400. **Credit**
AmEx, Disc, MC, V.

This 275-room, Italian Renaissance-style hotel (as featured
in *Pretty Woman*) is one of LA's favourite luxury hotels. Built
in 1928, it is renowned for its old-world opulence and high-
brow and famous clientele. Rooms are in two wings: the original Wilshire wing and the more recently constructed
Beverly wing. The latter is currently being renovated, but
the cognoscenti prefer the Wilshire wing anyway (Warren
Beatty, at the height of his playboy career, shacked up here
for 12 years). The establishment is organised like a fine
European four-star hotel with everything radiating out from
the central lobby, including the cosy bar frequented by cigar-
smoking businessmen, tourists and expensively dressed
women. The rooms are largish, the beds wondrously comfy,
the décor antiquely luxurious and the bathrooms elegant and
lavish in black Carrera marble. Topping it off are the vibe –
this is *the* place to be – and the welcoming tray of fresh straw-
berries, brown sugar and sour cream.
**Hotel services** *Air-conditioning. Babysitting. Ballroom.*
*Bar. Beauty salon. Car park ($18). Conference facilities.*
*Currency exchange. Disabled: access; rooms. Fax. Fitness*
*facilities (health spa, hot tubs). Laundry. Lifts. Multi-*
*lingual staff. Pool. Three restaurants.*
**Room services** *Hair dryer. Mini-bar. Radio.*
*Refrigerator. 24-hour room service. Safe. VCR.*

## Sunset Marquis Hotel & Villas

*1200 North Alta Loma Road, at Sunset Boulevard, West Hollywood, CA 90069 (reservations 1-800 858 9758/ front desk 1-310 657 1333/fax 1-310 652 5300). Bus 2, 3, 20, 27, 429/I-10, exit La Cienega Boulevard north.* **Rates** single/double from $235.20. **Credit** AmEx, DC, MC, V.

Bang in the middle of West Hollywood, this 114-room, three-storey building was once part of Lionel Barrymore's estate. Now it's divided into one- and two-bedroom suites with private patios and balconies, many overlooking the pool. Suites in the main building are tastefully furnished, whistle-clean and luxurious. The 12 private villas clustered around a smaller, more exclusive pool have boarded stars such as Julio Iglesias and Aerosmith's Steven Tyler and come with their own private butler. While the Sunset Marquis doesn't have a sit-down restaurant, it does have the Whiskey Bar, one of the hottest watering holes in Los Angeles, where you might look up at the TV monitors and see artists such as Jimmy Page recording his latest in The Studio, the Sunset Marquis' on-site, state-of-the-art recording room.

**Hotel services** *Air-conditioning. Babysitting. Bar. Car park ($10). Conference facilities. Disabled: access. Fax. Laundry. Lifts. Multi-lingual staff. Fitness facilities (cardio, free weights). Pool. Two restaurants.*
**Room services** *Hair dryer. Radio. Room service. Rooms for disabled. Safe. Stereo with CD player. Telephone. VCR.*
**Branch: Westwood Marquis** 930 Hilgard Avenue, at Le Conte Avenue, Westwood, CA 90024 (reservations 1-800 421 2317 (US)/0800 897 529 (UK)/front desk 1-310 208 8765/fax 1-310 824 0355).

## Wyndham Bel Age Hotel

*1020 North San Vicente Boulevard, at Sunset Boulevard, West Hollywood, CA 90069 (reservations 1-800 996 3426/front desk 1-310 854 1111/fax 1-310 854 0926). Bus 2, 3, 105, 302, 429/I-10, exit La Cienega Boulevard north.* **Rates** $169-$199 corporate, single/double $350-$385. **Credit** AmEx, DC, Disc, JCB, MC, V.

Located just below Sunset Strip and around the corner from the infamous Viper Room nightclub, this nine-storey, brown stucco structure contains 200 one- and two-bedroom suites. The cosy cocktail lounge is where Jack Nicholas romanced Kathleen Turner in *Prizzi's Honor*. Other attractions include the top-class Diaghilev Restaurant and the La Brasserie nightclub, which has sweeping views over LA and an impressive roster of performers. A kitschy collection of sculptures and artworks in the common areas add a dash of flavour, and the rooftop pool allows for fun in the sun. The suites are large and comfortable, but showing some wear.

**Hotel services** *Air-conditioning. Babysitting. Two bars. Beauty salon. Car park ($16; valet $16 overnight; $6 2 hours, $2 additional hours daytime). Conference facilities. Disabled: access; rooms. Fax. Fitness facilities (cardio, Jacuzzi, Universal weights). Laundry. Lifts. Multi-lingual staff. Pool. Two restaurants. Safe.*
**Room services** *Hair dryer. Mini-bar. Radio. Refrigerator. 24-hour room service. Telephone. VCR (some rooms).*

# Mid-range

## Beverly Plaza

*8384 West Third Street, at Orlando Avenue, LA, CA 90048 (reservations 1-800 624 6835/front desk 1-213 658 6600/fax 1-213 653 3464). Bus 16/I-10, exit La Cienega Boulevard north.* **Rates** single/double $129-$184. **Credit** AmEx, DC, JCB, MC, V.

The trendy Beverly Plaza is an artsy 98-room hotel with fanciful décor and a popular restaurant. Nearby are Miracle Mile's shopping and La Cienega Boulevard's Restaurant Row. The oversized rooms were renovated in 1996 with custom furnishings, hand-painted headboards and plenty of taupe. Bathrooms are on the small side, but the perks –

including bath robes, natural shampoos and soaps, gourmet chocolates from San Francisco's Joseph Schmidt, free newspapers, $10 taxi coupons per day – and an eager-to-please staff make up for such shortcomings. There's also a small but respectable fitness centre and a petite outdoor pool.
**Hotel services** *Air-conditioning. Babysitting. Bar. Car park ($10). Conference facilities. Disabled: access; rooms. Fax. Fitness facilities (sauna, spa, massage, manicure, pedicure). Laundry. Lifts. Multi-lingual staff. Pool. Safe.*
**Room services** *Hair dryer. Mini-bar. Radio. 24-hour room service. Telephone. VCR to hire.*

## Hilgard House Westwood Village

*927 Hilgard Avenue, at Le Conte Avenue, Westwood, CA 90024 (reservations 1-800 826 3934/front desk 1-310 208 3945/fax 1-310 208 1972). Bus 2, 21, 429, 576, Santa Monica 1, 2, Culver City 6/I-405, exit Wilshire Boulevard north.* **Rates** single $99; double $109. **Credit** AmEx, DC, Disc, MC, V.

Across from the Westwood Marquis is the understated but elegant 47-room Hilgard House. The lobby looks like an English library while the rooms are cosy European in style. It lacks extra hotel perks, such as a pool, gym, bar or restaurant, but with the free continental breakfast, free parking and its location (surrounded by UCLA and Westwood shopping) you've got yourself a darn good deal.
**Hotel services** *Air-conditioning. Babysitting. Free car park. Fax. Laundry. Lifts. Multi-lingual staff. Safe.*
**Room services** *Hair dryer. Radio. Refrigerator. Telephone.*

## Le Montrose Suite Hotel

*900 Hammond Street, at San Vincente Boulevard & Doheny Drive, West Hollywood, CA 90069 (reservations 1-800 776 0666/front desk 1-310 855 1115/fax 1-310 657 9192). Bus 2, 3, 105, 429/I-405, exit Santa Monica Boulevard east.* **Rates** single/double $200 junior; $300 executive; $375 one-bedroom suite. **Credit** AmEx, DC, JCB, MC, V.

What Le Montrose lacks in service and amenities, it makes up for with affordable comfortable rooms and central location (just two blocks south of Sunset Boulevard). Each suite is spotless and tastefully furnished in contemporary style and the beds are wonderfully spacious. The rooftop pool has a commanding view of LA and looks out over the nearby Beverly Center. Perfectly suited to families and couples wanting a comfortable weekend hideaway.
**Hotel services** *Air-conditioning. Babysitting. Bicycles. Car park ($14). Conference facilities. Currency exchange. Disabled: access; rooms. Fax. Gym. Laundry. Lifts. Multi-lingual staff. Pool. Restaurant.*
**Room services** *Hair dryer. Mini-bar. Radio. Refrigerator. Room service. Safe. Telephone.*

## Summit Hotel Rodeo Drive

*360 North Rodeo Drive, at Brighton Way, Beverly Hills, CA 90210 (reservations 1-800 468 3541/front desk 1-310 273 0300/fax 1-310 859 8730). Bus 20, 21, 22/I-405, exit Wilshire Boulevard east.* **Rates** single/double $150-$390; suite $350-$425. **Credit** AmEx, DC, Disc, JCB, MC, V.

The 86-room Summit Hotel Rodeo is squeezed into the middle of Rodeo's exorbitant retail action – the optimum spot for folks in need of a little shopping therapy. Built in 1962, the hotel recently changed hands, and though there's talk of redecorating, it's still on the drawing board. There's not much public space, only a second-floor sun deck and an adjoining restaurant (which happens to be the only eaterie on Rodeo and is an excellent spot for star-spotting). There is, however, a free shuttle to Summit's Bel Air property, which has a pool and sports facilities. The rooms are not as impressive its ultra-chi-chi address, but are comfortable. Expect to find French provincial furnishings, a coffee maker, small sitting area and a disappointingly small and plain bathroom.

**Hotel services** *Air-conditioning. Babysitting. Bar. Car park ($12). Disabled: access. Fax. Off-site fitness facilities (pool, spa, tennis). Laundry. Lifts. Multi-lingual staff. Restaurant. Safe.*
**Room services** *Hair dryer. Mini-bar. Radio. Refrigerator (suites only). Room service. Telephone.*

## Budget

### Beverly House Hotel

*140 South Lasky Drive, at Little Santa Monica Boulevard, Beverly Hills, CA 90212 (reservations 1-800 432 5444/ front desk 1-310 271 2145/fax 1-310 276 8431). Bus 4, 20, 21, 22, 27/I-405, exit Santa Monica Boulevard east.* **Rates** single $83-$99; double $93-$99. **Credit** AmEx, DC, JCB, MC, V.

The name Beverly Hills might evoke glamour, but the place Beverly Hills has some less than glitzy corners, and this is one of them. It's an old, plain hotel that's not remotely spectacular, but it is affordable, very clean and close to Rodeo Drive. The rooms (some of which need a paint job) have modest antique wooden furnishings, dark maroon carpeting and small, simple bathrooms. Perks include a free continental breakfast.

**Hotel services** *Air-conditioning. Free car park. Fax. Laundry. Lifts. Multi-lingual staff. Safe.*
**Room services** *Radio. Refrigerator (some rooms). Telephone. VCR (some rooms).*

### Westwood Inn Motel

*10820 Wilshire Boulevard, at Glendon Avenue, Westwood, CA 90024 (1-310 474 3118/fax 1-310 474 3213). Bus 21, 22, Commuter Express 431, 534, 573/ I-405, exit Wilshire Boulevard east.* **Rates** single $48; double $54-$58. **Credit** AmEx, DC, JCB, MC, V.

New management took over the Westwood six years ago and has been slowly and lovingly sprucing up these old digs. It's still an old motel, but the nicely painted rooms (20 in all, with showers only) are large enough to do a jig in, have new carpets, picnic-style table and chairs and an interesting collection of bedside lamps. Some even have two bedrooms. Best of all, the price. For under 60 bucks, you get easy access to Westwood's shopping and UCLA and free local calls (well, the first 10 minutes of each call). Weekly rates.

**Hotel services** *Air-conditioning. Free car park. Fax. Laundry. Room services Hair dryer. Refrigerator. Safe. Telephone. VCR.*

## Hollywood & Midtown

### First-class

#### Hotel Sofitel Los Angeles

*8555 Beverly Boulevard, at La Cienega Boulevard, West Hollywood, CA 90048 (reservations 1-800 521 7772/ front desk 1-310 278 5444/fax 1-310 657 2816). Bus 14, 16, 105, DASH Fairfax, Hollywood/I-10, exit La Cienega Boulevard north.* **Rates** single/double $230-$250; suite $265-$500. **Credit** AmEx, DC, MC, V.

The mature and tasteful, French-owned, 311-room Sofitel attracts its guests with its calming and well-appointed lobby, its location – directly across the street from the Beverly Center and near Restaurant Row – and rooms decorated with flowery wallpaper, adobe-coloured paint and above-par fabrics. There's no wacky Hollywood vibe here, just peaceful surroundings and upscale classic décor, which attract plenty of older business clientele. Guests get a freshly baked baguette upon check-out.

**Hotel services** *Air-conditioning. Babysitting. Bar. Car park ($16.50). Conference room. Currency exchange. Disabled: access; rooms. Fax. 24-hour fitness facilities*

*(free weights, dry sauna, Stairmaster, treadmills). Laundry. Lifts. Multi-lingual staff. Pool. Restaurant. Safe.*
**Room services** *Fax/modem hook-ups. Hair dryer. Mini-bar. Radio. 24-hour room service. Telephone (2, with voicemail). VCR to hire.*

## Mid-range

### Clarion Hollywood Roosevelt Hotel

*7000 Hollywood Boulevard, between Highland & La Brea Avenues, Hollywood, CA 90028 (reservations 1-800 252 7466/front desk 1-213 466 7000/fax 1-213 466 9376). Bus 1, 180, 181, 212/US101, exit Highland Avenue south.* **Rates** single $109-$119; double $129-$139. **Credit** AmEx, DC, Disc, JCB, MC, V.

In the middle of gritty Hollywood Boulevard stands the surprisingly pleasant 320-room Hollywood Roosevelt, a 1927 landmark building that was once the hub of Hollywood hullabaloo. The first Academy Awards were held here, Marilyn Monroe lived here for eight years and legend has it that Bill 'Bojangles' Robinson taught Shirley Temple how to tap dance up the lobby staircase. Staff members say the place is haunted by Montgomery Clift and Marilyn (her room is still intact, her wardrobe mirror hangs in the lower lobby and some claim they've seen her face in it), and you can't help but feel the old Hollywood magic in the air. The two-story Spanish Colonial lobby, with hand-stencilled ceilings and arched doorways, is impressive and well-kept. Rooms are less glamorous, but are individually decorated and clean, with smallish bathrooms. There's a David Hockney painting on the bottom of the pool.

**Hotel services** *Air-conditioning. On-call babysitting. Two bars. Car park ($9.50). Conference facilities. Currency exchange. Disabled: access; rooms. Fitness facilities (treadmill, stationary bike, dumbells, bench presses). Fax. Valet laundry. Lifts. Pool. Restaurant.*
**Room services** *Mini-bar. Radio. Room service. Safe. Telephone.*

## Budget

### Beverly Laurel Motor Hotel

*8018 Beverly Boulevard, at Laurel Avenue, LA, CA 90048 (1-213 651 2441/fax 1-213 651 5225). Bus 14, 217, DASH Fairfax/I-10, exit La Cienega Boulevard north.* **Rates** single $55-$65; double $60-$70. **Credit** AmEx, DC, MC, V.

It looks like a dive, it's priced like a dive, but someone with an artistic hand has turned the Beverly Laurel into one of the most tasteful and stylish motels around, with gold-and-black checkered bedspreads, wooden headboards inlaid with black-and-white photos, black vinyl chairs and groovy deco tables. In most rooms, one wall is painted brilliant blue. Be sure to request a newer room,

unless you'd prefer the old-style wooden décor. The adjoining restaurant, Swingers, is a popular breakfast and late-night spot for West LA hipsters. Staff can sometimes be unaccommodating.

**Hotel services** *Air-conditioning. Free car park. Fax. Lifts. Pool. Restaurant.*
**Room services** *Microwave. Refrigerator. Telephone.*

### Bevonshire Lodge Motel

*7575 Beverly Boulevard, at Curson Avenue, LA, CA 90036 (1-213 936 6154/fax 1-213 936 6640). Bus 14, DASH Fairfax/I-10, exit La Brea Avenue north.* **Rates** single $39.50; double $42.50. **Credit** AmEx, MC, V.

The enormous rubber tree growing from a hole in the lobby carpet and extending along the two-storey windows is an indication of how long this motel has been around. Though a splash of paint is needed in some areas, overall, it's in fine shape. The rooms are sizeable, have tiled bathrooms and many come with complete kitchens ($6 extra); all circle the courtyard pool. There's no restaurant, but the ever-popular Authentic Café is across the street and many of Beverly's trendy boutiques and eateries are in close range.

**Hotel services** *Air-conditioning. Free car park. Fax. Safe.*
**Room services** *Hair dryer on request. Refrigerator. Telephone.*

### Highland Gardens Hotel

*7047 Franklin Avenue, at La Brea Avenue, Hollywood Hills, CA 90028 (reservations 1-800 404 5472/front desk 1-213 850 0536/fax 1-213 850 1712). Bus 1, 2, 3, 4, 212, 420/US101, exit Highland Avenue south.* **Rates** single $55-$80; double $60-$80; suite $80-$110. **Credit** AmEx, MC, V.

Rooms here may be reminiscent of a *Brady Bunch* set, but they're huge, dirt cheap and a few blocks from star-paved Hollywood Boulevard. Common areas consist of a breakfast room (where guests grab free cups of coffee and pastries), a simple lobby and a heated courtyard pool. Rooms surround the pool and offer the basic necessities in 1970s colours and décor, enormous bedrooms, kitchens and/or living rooms. Per square foot, no hotel in town can touch this for value.

**Hotel services** *Air-conditioning. Free car park. Fax. Laundry. Multi-lingual staff. Pool.*
**Room services** *Hair dryer. Radio. Refrigerator. Safe. Telephone. VCR to hire.*

### Magic Hotel

*7025 Franklin Avenue, between La Brea & Orange Avenues, Hollywood, CA 90028 (1-800 741 4915 reservations;1-213 851 0800 front desk/1-213 851 4926 fax). Bus 1, 180, 181, 212, 217, 429/US101, exit Highland Avenue north.* **Rates** single $55; deluxe single

# The best hotels for...

### ...pooling it

**Four Seasons'** rooftop pool offers panoramic views, but you're more likely to focus on the Bronzed and the Beautiful who lounge cabana-side or work out in the adjoining open-air gym. Runners-up are the **Beverly Hills Hotel** (*pictured*), where handsome young pool-hands cater to your every whim, and **The Peninsula Beverly Hills**, whose Jacuzzi is surrounded by a rooftop lawn and is perhaps the perfect place in the metropolis to catch a romantic sunset.

### ...playing hip

Only the perpetually stylish book a room at the retro-cool **Château Marmont**. Here, it's almost impossible not to see a famous face passing in the lobby or sipping a martini at the now overly trendy adjoining bar.

### ...blowing your wad

Whether it's parking your car, sponsoring pool guests or dining, nothing comes cheaply at the **Beverly Hills Hotel**. But then, of course, that's the point.

### ...ogling sexy rollerbladers

From an oceanfront room at the funky **Cadillac** on Venice Beach, you can watch California's young blades flaunt it as they cruise up and down the boardwalk.

### ...ghost-spotting

The **Clarion Hollywood Roosevelt** has housed some of Hollywood's greatest bygone entertainers, and apparently, even post-mortem, some still haven't checked out.

### ...star-spotting

With its exclusive top-floor rooms and weekend press junkets, you're almost guaranteed to get a glimpse of someone famous during a stay at the classy **Four Seasons**. **Château Marmont** and **The Regent Beverly Wilshire** are also favourite hideouts for Hollywood's elite.

### ...entertaining business clients

Hold your business meeting in one of the new high-tech and ultra-smooth **Nikko** suites; the swanky but serious décor is bound to seal that deal.

### ...picking up poseurs

The **Peninsula**'s refined digs may be 100 per cent kosher, but some of the bar's clientele are definitely telling tall tales as they puff cigars and attempt to impress the ladies.

### ...escaping Los Angeles' chaos

Spend even an afternoon at the pastoral **Hotel Bel-Air** and you'll feel pampered and rejuvenated. The **Ritz-Carltons Huntington** and **Laguna Niegel** also do the trick, combining grand surroundings with impeccable service and an air of exclusivity.

### ...budget bargains

The **Belle Blue Inn** offers beach access along with a dose of funky Santa Monica living and a free continental breakfast. Inland, the **Beverly Laurel Motor Hotel**'s strategic location and hip décor combined with rock-bottom prices makes it a best bet. Downtown, even the luxury hotels don't have the atmosphere that comes free at the **Hotel Figueroa**.

The cathedral-like lobby at the **Regal Biltmore**. *See page 27.*

$85; double $95; executive suites $70. **Credit** AmEx, DC, JCB, MC, V.

Across the street from the Highland is the motel-like Magic Hotel. Here, too, rooms are large and tidy, with newer furnishings and carpeting and stiff mattresses. Old magic show posters adorn the walls in reference to the neighbouring Magic Castle, a private magicians' club. All rooms surround the courtyard, which has a pool and lounge furniture, and all (bar singles) have a kitchen.

**Hotel services** *Air-conditioning. Free car park. Fax. Laundry. Multi-lingual staf. Pool. Safe.*
**Room services** *Hair dryer on request. Radio. Refrigerator. Telephone.*

## Downtown

## First-class

### Hotel Inter-Continental

*251 South Olive Street, at Second Street, LA, CA 90012 (reservations 1-800 442 5251/front desk 1-213 617 3300/fax 1-213 617-3399). Metro Civic Center/Tom Bradley/Bus 14, 24, 420, Commuter Express 418, 425/I-110, exit Fourth Street east.* **Rates** single $190-$210 (club level $240); double $210-$230 (club level $250).
**Credit** AmEx, Disc, MC, V.

A welcome departure from generic business hotels, the new high-rise Inter-Continental blends the traditional with the boldly creative – and the result is impressive. An enormous light lobby, with grand floral arrangements, a huge, bright yellow sculpture and calming orchestral music give way to soothing taupe and olive rooms. Each has a an en-suite bath and shower, a chaise longue, a comfy love seat and an oversized desk, all a step above corporate. Perks include speaker phones with modem capability and oversized terrycloth robes. 'Club level' guests are housed on floors 16 or 17, with access to the hotel's business centre. The Museum of Contemporary Art is next door.

**Hotel services** *Air-conditioning. Babysitting. Bar. Car park ($18; valet $20 overnight; $2.20 per 20 mins daytime). Conference facilities. Currency exchange. Disabled: access; rooms. Fax. Fitness facilities (sauna, steam). Valet laundry. Lifts. Multi-lingual staff. Pool. Two restaurants. Safe.*
**Room services** *Hair dryer. Mini-bar. Modem hookup. Radio. Refrigerator. 24-hour room service. Telephone (with voicemail).*

### Regal Biltmore, Los Angeles

*506 South Grand Street, at Fifth Street, LA, CA 90071 (reservations 1-800 245 8673/front desk 1-213 624 1011/fax 1-213 612 1545). Metro 7th Street/Metro Center/Bus 16, 18, 78, 96, Foothill Transit 492/I-110, exit Sixth Street east.* **Rates** single $195-$235; double $225-$235.
**Credit** AmEx, Disc, JCB, MC, V.

Built in 1923, the 11-storey Biltmore is the oldest hotel in Downtown LA, and still maintains the Italian-Spanish Renaissance elegance that enticed such VIPs as Princess Margaret, the Duke of Kent and presidents Truman, Kennedy, Ford, Carter and Reagan to pay a visit. The cathedral-like lobby and common areas are absolute masterpieces, with hand-painted frescos (by Italian artist Giovanni Smeraldi, who also contributed to the White House and the Vatican), bas-relief décor, a fountain, wooden floors, beautifully ornate ceilings with glass inlay and hand-painted detail and stupendous floral arrangements. Some rooms look a little worn, but have original art, peach walls and floral prints. You'd be better off on the executive floor, which has newly decorated rooms with twice-daily maid service, beautiful furnishings, designer soaps and dataports. The health club has a Pompeii-style pool, steam room, Jacuzzi and sauna.

**Hotel services** *Air-conditioning. Babysitting on request. Three bars. Beauty salon. Car park ($17.90). Conference*

facilities. Currency exchange. Disabled: access; rooms. Fax. Fitness facilities. Laundry. Lifts. Multi-lingual staff. Pool. Three restaurants. Safe.
**Room services** *Hair dryer (9-11th floors only). Mini-bar (most rooms). Radio. Refrigerator (most rooms). 24-hour room service. Telephone (with voicemail).*

### Wyndham Checkers Hotel

*535 South Grand Avenue, between Fifth & Sixth Streets, LA, CA 90071 (reservations 1-800 996 3426/front desk 1-213 624 0000/fax 1-213 626 9906). Metro 7th Street/Metro/Bus 37, 78, 79/I-110, exit Sixth street east.* **Rates** single $159-$259; double $179-$279.
**Credit** AmEx, DC, Disc, JCB, MC, V.

Combine first-class service and a boutique environment and you've got Checkers, a downtown favourite. The recently renovated, Asian-influenced lobby is full of worldly visitors chatting over cappuccino while the award-winning Checkers Restaurant serves lofty fare to an upscale clientele. Light and airy rooms are individually decorated in understated luxury, with original art and marble sidetables and bathrooms.

**Hotel services** *Air-conditioning. On-call babysitting. Bar. Car park ($18). Conference facilities. Disabled: access; rooms. Fax. Fitness facilities (sauna, whirlpool). Laundry. Lifts. Multi-lingual staff. Pool. Restaurant. Safe.*
**Room services** *Fax/modem hookups. Hair dryer. Mini-bar. Radio. 24-hour room service. Telephone (3, with voicemail).*

## Mid-range

### Hotel Figueroa

*939 South Figueroa Street, at Olympic Boulevard, LA, CA 90015 (reservations 1-800 421 9092/front desk 1-213 627 8971/fax 1-213 689 0305). Metro 7th Street/Metro Center or Westlake/Macarthur Park/Bus 27, 28, 81, 328, 427, Commuter Express 419/I-110, exit Ninth Street east.* **Rates** single $74-$84; double $84-$94. **Credit** DC, JCB, MC, V.

An exotic oasis near the Convention Center, the 285-room Figueroa is funky-chic and wildly decorated in Southwestern colour, collected artefacts and wrought iron. It's a whirlwind of hand-painted everything, including elevators, doors and ceilings, with Mexican tables and chairs and huge pots filled with exotic plants. Some rooms are large, some small, and each is uniquely decorated; the older TVs and furnishings could be ugly on their own, but in combination they make the place work. Especially cool are the Clay Pit Indian restaurant and the crowded Verandah Bar, which overlooks the pool and garden.

**Hotel services** *Air-conditioning. Two bars. Free car park. Fax. Laundry. Lifts. Multi-lingual staff. Three restaurants. Safe.*
**Room services** *Hair dryer on request. Radio. Refrigerator (most rooms). Telephone.*

### Westin Bonaventure Hotel and Suites

*404 South Figueroa Street, at Fourth Street, LA, CA 90071 (reservations 1-800 228 3000/front desk 1-213 624 1000/fax 1-213 612 4800/website: http://www.westin. com). Metro 7th Street/Metro Center/Bus 53, 60, 471, Montebello 40/I-110 north, exit Third Street east.* **Rates** single $139-$177; double $139-$195. **Credit** AmEx, DC, Disc, JCB, MC, V.

Five gargantuan mirrored cylindrical towers fused together, the Bonaventure is a major contributor to Downtown LA's skyline. From the outside, it's a visual wonder; from the inside, a mini city. Occupying an entire city block, the hotel has 12 glass elevators that shoot you to your (rather small) room. Each room has floor-to-ceiling windows, wall safes, voicemail and modem access and are decorated in dark wood. Tower suites are twice the size. There's an 85,000sq ft health, tennis, and fitness centre, a revolving rooftop

lounge and a shopping gallery with over 40 shops and restaurants. There's also one all-suite tower with a Japanese guest floor (24-hour translation, Japanese newspapers, TV and breakfast), and sky bridges to World Trade Center.
**Hotel services** *Air-conditioning. Two bars. Beauty salon. Car park ($18.50). Conference facilities. Currency exchange. Disabled: access; rooms. Fax. Fitness facilities (cardio, free weights, pool, spa). Laundry. Lifts. Multilingual staff. Two restaurants.*
**Room services** *Fax/modem hookups. Hair dryer. Radio. Refrigerator on request. 24-hour room service. Safe. Telephone (voicemail).*

## Budget

### Kawada Hotel

*200 South Hill Street, at Second Street, LA, CA 90012 (reservations 1-800 752 9232/front desk 1-213 621 4455/ fax 1-213 687 4455). Metro Civic Center/Tom Bradley/Bus 420, 425/I-110, exit Ninth Street east.* **Rates** single $79-$109; double $89-$119; corporate single/double $75. **Credit** AmEx, MC, V.
What the four-storey Kawada lacks in décor, it more than makes up for with cleanliness and value. Take the slow lift to spotless rooms, complete with kitchenette, coffee maker, desk and radio. Though watercolour paintings, pot-pourri, pretty soaps and a bathroom phone attempt to make the place feel upscale, rooms here are hardly luxurious. Some can be small (request a larger one), there's no closet (only a clothing nook) and most offer a view that will inspire you to keep the blinds drawn. But the only real bummer is that parking is uncovered and half a block away.
**Hotel services** *Air-conditioning. Bar. Car park ($6.60). Conference facilities. Disabled: access; rooms. Fax. Laundry. Lifts. Multi-lingual staff. Restaurant. Safe. Free shuttle to Downtown.*
**Room services** *Radio. Refrigerator. Kitchenette. Room service. Telephone. VCR.*

### Stillwell Hotel

*838 South Grand Avenue, between Eighth & Ninth Streets, LA, CA 90017 (front desk 1-800 553 4774/1-213 627 1151/fax 1-213 622 8940). Metro 7th Street/Metro Center/Bus 78, 79, 96, 404, 484, Foothill Transit 486/I-110, exit Ninth street east.* **Rates** single $39-$49; double $49-$59. **Credit** AmEx, DC, MC, V.
Aged and ultra-budget, the 232-room Stillwell ain't much to look at, but it's certainly cheap and located a few blocks from the LA Convention Center and the California Mart, which makes it perfect for convention-goers. The staff can be unfriendly, but they do offer an all-you-can-eat Indian buffet lunch for $7.95, as well as an old bar with authentic barflies and a budget restaurant.
**Hotel services** *Air-conditioning. Bar. Car park ($3). Conference facilities. Disabled: access; rooms. Fax. Laundry. Lifts. Multi-lingual staff. Three restaurants.*
**Room services** *Radio. Refrigerator. Telephone.*

## The Valleys

### First-class

### Ritz-Carlton Huntington

*1401 South Oak Knoll Avenue, at Wentworth Avenue, Pasadena, CA 91106 (reservations 1-800 241 3333/ front desk 1-818 568 3900/fax 1-818 568 3900). Bus 485/I-110, exit Glenarm Street east.* **Rates** single $185-$295; double $200-$1,310; suite $400-$2,000. **Credit** AmEx, DC, Disc, JCB, MC, V.
On 23 pristine acres in Pasedena, the Ritz's 1907 palace stands amid Japanese gardens and vast grassy expanses. It's a perfect escape from the traffic and crowds of LA; the kind

of place where Jim Carrey rents the Presidential Suite when he's in the neighbourhood. Rooms and the more-private cottages are elegant, and the service divine. Splash in the pool, stroll through the gardens, snack on sushi, swing dance on Friday night or indulge in Sunday's champagne brunch; whatever you do, you'll be hard-pressed to find a reason to leave this peaceful (albeit pricey) retreat.
**Hotel services** *Air-conditioning. Babysitting. Bar. Beauty salon. Bicycles. Car park ($15). Conference facilities. Currency exchange. Disabled: access; rooms. Fax. Fitness facilities (cardio, free weights, karate, tennis, swimming lessons, yoga). Laundry. Lifts. Multi-lingual staff. Two restaurants.*
**Room services** *Hair dryer. Mini-bar. Radio. Refrigerator. Room service. Safe. Telephones (3). VCR.*

## Mid-range

### Sheraton Universal

*333 Universal Terrace Parkway, at Lankershim Boulevard, Universal City, CA 91608 (reservations 1-800 325 3535/front desk 1-818 980 1212/fax 1-818 985 4980). Bus 420, 425, 522/US101, exit Lankershim Boulevard north.* **Rates** single $205; double $225. **Credit** AmEx, DC, Disc, MC, V.
Renovated in 1994, the 444-room Sheraton Universal is an upscale corporate-style hotel situated in Universal City, near burgeoning Universal CityWalk, Universal Studios and all the major freeways. There's a respectable gym, complimentary shuttle to Universal Studios, and special holiday packages that include admission to the Universal Studios Tour. Club-level rooms offer plenty of extra perks.
**Hotel services** *Air-conditioning. Babysitting. Bar. Car park ($14). Conference facilities. Disabled: access; rooms. Fax. Fitness (cardio, free weights, whirlpool). Laundry. Lifts. Multi-lingual staff. Pool. Restaurant.*
**Room services** *Fax/modem hookups. Hair dryer. Mini-bar. Radio. Room service. Safe. Telephone (with voicemail, call-waiting). VCR on request.*

## Orange County & Anaheim

### First-class

### Ritz-Carlton Laguna Niegel

*33533 Ritz-Carlton Drive, at Pacific Coast Highway, Dana Point, CA 92629 (reservations 1-800 241 3333/front desk 1-714 240 2000/fax 1-714 240 0829). Bus Orange County Transit 1/I-5, exit Crown Valley Parkway west.* **Rates** single/double $215-$415; club floor $275-$475; suite $500-$2,750. **Credit** AmEx, DC, Disc, MC, V.
California's only five-star and five-diamond resort is perched upon a 150ft bluff in Dana Point, overlooking the adjoining golf course and the shimmering Pacific Ocean. The four-storey Mediterranean-style hotel is about as good as it gets, with a substantial collection of art, an art gallery, three renowned restaurants, and every type of resort recreation your could wish for (including two miles of hotel-front beach). The kids' programme will keep young folk busy all day while you relax, and you can always blast over to Disneyland, which is 35 miles away. The rooms have private balconies (many looking onto the ocean) and Italian marble bathrooms with a great selection of toiletries.
**Hotel services** *Air-conditioning. Babysitting. Two bars. Beauty salon. Business centre. Car park ($17). Car & limo rental. Conference facilities. Croquet. Currency exchange. Disabled: access; rooms. Fax. Fitness facilities (cardio,*

*You should be able to get a room at the* **Westin Bonaventure Hotel**. *See page 27.*

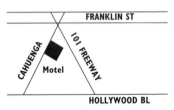

*free weights, aerobics, yoga, golf, massage, sauna, tennis, whirlpool). Laundry. Lifts. Multi-lingual staff. Two pools. Three restaurants.*
**Room services** *Hair dryer. Mini-bar. Radio. Refrigerator. 24-hour room service. Safe. Telephones (3).*

### The Disneyland Hotel

*1150 West Cerritos Avenue, between West & Walnut Streets, Anaheim, CA 92802 (reservations 1-800 821 8976/front desk 1-714 778 6600/fax 1-714 956 6597). Bus 460/I-5, exit Ball Avenue west.* **Rates** single/double $175-$210. **Credit** AmEx, DC, MC, V.
**Hotel services** *Air conditioning. Babysitting. Bar. Car park ($10). Conference facilities. Currency exchange. Disabled: access; rooms. Fax. Fitness facilities. Laundry. Lifts. Multi-lingual staff. Restaurants (12). Safe.*
**Room services** *Hair dryer. Mini-bar. Radio. Refrigerator on request. Room service. Telephone.*

### The Disneyland Pacific Hotel

*1717 South West Street, at Katella Avenue, Anaheim, CA 92802 (reservations 1-800 821 8976/front desk 1-714 999 0990/fax 1-714 776 5763). Bus 460/I-5, exit Ball Road west.* **Rates** single/double $170-$210. **Credit** AmEx, DC, MC, V.
**Hotel services** *Air conditioning. Babysitting. Two bars. Car park ($10). Conference facilities. Currency exchange. Disabled: access; rooms. Fax. Fitness facilities. Laundry. Lifts. Multi-lingual staff. Two restaurants. Safe.*
**Room services** *Hair dryer. Radio. Refrigerator on request. Room service. Telephone. VCR (concierge level only).*
Both of Disney's properties are adjacent to the park and surrounded by restaurants, a pond (used as an ice-rink in winter), paddle boats, outdoor pool with sandy shore and volleyball court, shops, and the monorail, which picks passengers up and shuttles them to Disneyland. The rooms themselves are rather disappointing, not in quality, but because they're not fantastical or Disney-oriented like the rest of the area. You can expect Mickey toiletries and some themed artwork, but the rest is basic California décor. However, the common areas of both hotels were renovated in 1996, with the intent of Disneyfication. The Disneyland Hotel (1,000-plus rooms), features traditional Disney (Mickey, Donald et al) while the Pacific (500 rooms) honours modern Disney (*Beauty and the Beast, The Lion King*). Kids are especially fond of the Disneyland's Goofy's Kitchen, where they can breakfast with their favourite Disney characters, and 'Practically Perfect Tea', a Pacific Hotel treat that's reminiscent of Mary Poppins. The Pacific, the more upscale of the two, is currently less cheerful, but when Disney's enormous new addition is completed (in 2001), the hotel will look directly onto the new park. Big bonus: with the purchase of a basic Disney passport (one-day $34 adults, $26 children; two-day $59 adults, $44 children) guests can enter the park an hour and a half before the general public.

## Mid-range

### Candy Cane Inn

*1747 South Harbor Boulevard, at Katella Avenue, Anaheim, CA 92802 (1-800 345 7057/front desk 1-714 774 5284/fax 1-714 772 5462). Bus 460/I-5, exit Harbor Boulevard south.* **Rates** single/double $74-$95. **Credit** AmEx, DC, Disc, MC, V.
Ask locals where to stay and they're likely to direct you to the Candy Cane Inn. No, it's not pink and stripy. The name dates back to the Inn's beginnings, when Disneyland first opened, but the motel's come a long way since then. Today, it's one of the best mid-range options in the area. There's plenty of greenery (considering it's on a busy street), a pool and children's wading area, free continental breakfast – and it'll look even better after the $1 million renovation, which is slated for completion as we go to press. The management really cares about its guests and does everything possible to make their stay above par.

**Hotel services** *Air-conditioning. Free car park. Disabled: access; rooms. Fax. Laundry. Safe. Free shuttle to Disneyland.*
**Room services** *Radio. Refrigerator (deluxe rooms only). Telephone.*

## Budget

### Penny Sleeper Inn

*1441 South Manchester Avenue, at Harbor Boulevard, Anaheim, CA 92802 (reservations 1-800 854 6118/front desk 1-714 991 8100/fax 1-714 533 6430). Bus 460, Orange County Transit 43, 46/I-5, exit Harbor Boulevard south.* **Rates** single $36-$39; double $40-$46. **Credit** AmEx, Disc, MC, V.
You're likely to hear cars passing on the neighbouring freeway and the beds and furniture may not have been updated since the 1970s (think bright orange), but if you're looking for a clean crash pad with a pool for next to nothing, this 100-room hotel is the spot. Free continental breakfast.
**Hotel services** *Air-conditioning. Babysitting. Free car park. Disabled: access; rooms. Fax. Laundry. Pool. Free shuttle to Disneyland.*
**Room services** *Hair dryer. Radio. Safe. Telephone. VCR to hire.*

## Hostels & B&Bs

### Banana Bungalow Hollywood

*2775 West Cahuenga Boulevard, between Mulholland Drive & Franklin Avenue, Hollywood, CA 90068 (reservations 1-800 446 7835/front desk 1-213 851 1129/fax 1-213 851 1569). Bus 163, 420/US101, exit Hollywood Bowl/Highland Avenue north.* **Rates** shared room $18; single/double $45; triple $60. **Credit** MC, V.
This small international village just above the Bowl is the perfect place from which to explore Hollywood. Eleven well-kept bungalows (sleeping 4 to 10) make up the dormitory accommodation and there are 12 private rooms, each with a TV, lockers and bathroom. Guests have access to a pool, kitchen, pool table, video games, a simple restaurant serving sandwiches and burgers for under five bucks, and three dance parties a week. Its location is a bit removed from the action, but the hostel provides almost every service a visitor needs, including free transport from air, train and bus terminals and daily shuttles to attractions and nightlife.
**Hotel services** *Free car park. Disabled: access. Fax. Free weights. Laundry. Market. Restaurant.*
**Room services** *Lockers.*

### Hollywood Wilshire YMCA

*1553 North Schrader Boulevard, between Sunset Boulevard & Selma Avenue, CA 90028 (1-213 467 4161). Bus 1, 26, 213/I-10, exit Highland Avenue.*
**Registration** 7am-10pm. **Rates** dorm with sheets $15. The maximum stay here is seven nights, and you have to be out of your dorm between 10am and 4pm, but the location is good and the sports centre excellent – with two pools, state-of-the-art fitness equipment, courts for racquetball, handball and volleyball, saunas, steam rooms and an aerobics studio. The only other YMCA with residential facilities is at 140 North Louise Street, at Wilson Avenue, Glendale, CA 91206 (1-818 240 4130). It offers longer-term accommodation along with the usual fitness facilities.
**Hotel services** *Childcare centre. Fitness facilities (sports centre/gym). Lounge. Launderette. Microwave oven. Parking. Payphone. Storage facilities. Vending machine.*

### Hostelling International Los Angeles

*1436 Second Street, at Santa Monica Boulevard, Santa Monica, CA 90401 (reservations 1-800 909 4776/front desk 1-310 393 9913/fax 1-310 393 1769). Bus 4, 20,*

**The Venice Beach House Historic Inn**. *You might as well be in Bournemouth.*

*33, 434, Santa Monica 1, 2, 3, 10/I-10, exit Fourth-Fifth Street south.* **Rates** dorm without sheets $16.80 members, $19.80 non-members; dorms with sheets $18-$20 members, $21-$22 non-members; private room with sheets $49 members, $52 non-members. **Credit** MC, V.

If a beach vacation is your thing, book in advance at this enormous Santa Monica hostel located two blocks from the shore and a few strides from Third Street Promenade. Guests are buzzed through the secured entrance of this four-storey building, where rooms are either dorm-style (sleeping four, six, eight or ten) or private. The latter are small and basic – nothing more than a bed, side table, lamp, mirror and dresser (no wardrobe). But they're spotless, and provide all you'll need for a comfortable stay. Bring flip-flops to wear in the shower. All baths are shared.

**Hotel services** *Conference facilities. Disabled: access. Fax. Games room. Kitchen. Laundry. Lifts. Lockers. Multi-lingual staff. Pool table. Restaurant.*

### Venice Beach House Historic Inn

*15 30th Avenue, at Washington Boulevard & Pacific Avenue, Venice, CA 90291 (1-310 823 1966/fax 1-310 823 1842). Bus 108, Culver City 1, Commuter Express 437/I-10, exit Fourth-Fifth Street south.* **Rates** single/double $85-$165. **Credit** AmEx, MC, V.

Unlike the larger, less personal hostels, the nine-room Venice Beach House offers luxurious yet homey B&B accommodation on a quaint and quiet Venice street. It's a historic wooden house, built in 1911 and impeccably fashioned with dark wood, rich fabrics and antique everything – right down to the beautiful and well-appointed shared baths. You get a full breakfast, gourmet coffee and tea and a peaceful romantic environment just 80 steps from the beach. There's not much of a view other than the garden, but the trees and bushes ensure privacy and add to the serene atmosphere. For a jolt back to reality, step outside and walk along the beachfront promenade, where freaks, tourists and bikini-clad California girls are in full force. No smoking inside the hostel.

**Hotel services** *Free car park. Fax. Room services. Radio. Telephone.*

## Camping

It's worth considering camping in LA: obviously it's cheap, but it's also pleasant – state campgrounds tend to be located in beautiful surroundings and each site has a picnic table and fire ring. Yes, it involves a drive – but what doesn't in LA?

### Leo Carrillo State Beach

*3500 Pacific Coast Highway, Malibu, CA 90265 (1-818 880 0350/1-800 444 7275 reservations).* **Price** $17-$18 per site per night.

Tent camping is allowed in the park, except on the north side of the beach, which is blacktop, and so only open to camper vans. There are 127 sites, bathrooms, pay showers, a small shop and access to the beach and hiking/biking trails.

### Malibu Beach RV Park

*25801 Pacific Coast Highway, Malibu, CA 90265 (1-310 456 6052/1-800 622 6052 reservations).* **Price** from $16.80 tents, from $26 RVs.

A commercial (and so less lovely) site largely aimed at RV (recreational vehicle) campers, but with 50 tent sites and vast amounts of facilities, including a Jacuzzi.

## Rented accommodation

Rent is relatively cheap in Los Angeles but most rental agreements are for one year. If you're staying for at least two weeks, you could try **Oakwood Corporate Housing**, a nationwide organisation specialising in short-term lets. Most rents are for a minimum of one month, though its Marina del Rey location will rent apartments for two weeks. Call 1-800 888 0808 for its central booking office and price details (website at http://www.oakwood.com).

# Sightseeing

**Life's a beach in LA, where pleasure seekers can gratify their every whim. Bask, gawp, shop or cruise, but whatever you do, enjoy.**

'If this is hell, why is it so popular?', wrote the *New York Times*'s Bryce Nelson of LA, a city where people think a building erected in the 1950s is a historic monument, where youth and beauty are embraced with myopic madness, where stars are made and dreams really can come true. It's a city of attitude, with no centre and possibly no heart: experiencing it is as much about eaves-dropping, people-watching and gradual osmosis as checking sights off a list. That said, this is the nation's second largest city and is not a place in which you can get bored. The man-made – amusement parks, movie studios, museums, shops and restaurants – vies with the natural – a gorgeous coastline, great weather and in-city mountains – for your attention. Kick off your shoes and jump in. LA is not called the City of Angels for nothing.

Many of the attractions listed here also feature in other chapters; check the index for details.

## Beaches

On a clear day, with mountain ranges, sea, and sky overlapping with postcard perfection, the beaches from the South Bay up through Venice and Santa Monica north to Malibu epitomise the West Coast's powers of seduction. But don't let the sun and palm trees (imported, incidentally) kid you – the Pacific here is almost as cold as the Atlantic. By summer's end, however, the water temperature reaches a warm and refreshing 70°F. Smog and pollution are bigger considerations. The rule of thumb is that the farther you are from Santa Monica Bay (where waste is pumped into the ocean), the cleaner the water and sky. Late summer and early autumn is the smog season, though almost any time of year can surprise with a heaven-sent blue sky.

Beaches usually open at sunrise and close at sunset, but stay late one day to enjoy one of Southern California's breathtaking sunsets

# Best beaches for...

### ... surfing
Tied for first: **Malibu Surfrider Beach**, where the ocean is freckled with surfers riding the pompadour waves, and **Huntington Beach**, which remains one of the hardcore surf capitals with its varietal breaks and multi-directional swells. The Beach Boys didn't include them in the lyrics of *Surfin' Safari* for nothing.

### ... children
**Santa Monica Beach**, with its busy, bright pier complete with food stalls and game arcades, as well as beachfront rentals of almost anything you can think of, plus sea, sand, and plenty of open space.

### ... quintessential Californian sand and surf
**Zuma Beach**, where the soft silty carpet stretches wide and long; where the waves roll in big and deliciously refreshing.

### ... watching sunset
**El Matador Beach**, because being in its rugged embrace – and maybe somebody else's – as the sun bleeds down is about as good as it gets.

### ... clean water
**Zuma Beach**, far enough north to escape the squalor of the Santa Monica Bay.

### ... catching a game of volleyball
**Manhattan Beach**, where the young and the beautiful play as if they were born with a volleyball in their hands.

### ... rollerblading
The stretch between **Will Rogers State Beach** in Santa Monica and **Venice Beach**, where the paved boardwalk, marked for two-way traffic, meanders through the sand; ocean on one side, Venice streetlife on the other. You can even get a group lesson at one of the rental booths.

### ... people-watching
**Venice Beach**: the land of the eccentric and the beautiful.

### ... rollerhockey
**Will Rogers State Beach**, where asphalt parking lots are in abundance and empty out early and late in the day, perfect for pick-up games.

### ... sailboarding & sailing
The beach at **Marina del Rey**, the main port of call for all things nautical.

### ... oceanfront dining
**Venice**, **Santa Monica**, **Malibu** and beyond: drive north on the Pacific Coast Highway and countless restaurants lure you in with fresh fish, outdoor dining and views to make you weep.

(ironically much of the intense colour is caused by smog in the air). Most welcome children, but not dogs, and have space and rental gear for rollerblading, rollerhockey, bicycling, surfing and volleyball, as well as serviceable showers and toilets, refreshment on hand, and parking. For more information on the beach of your choice, call the Department of Beaches & Harbors on 1-310 305 9503. *See also chapter* **Active LA**.

### Santa Monica

Accessible and close to LA proper, this big beach is usually crowded and has a fun, festive, summer-holiday feel to it. However, because the water is dirty and few brave the waves, Santa Monica Pier is one of the highlights. Restored to its original dimensions and about to embark on its second century, the Pier is about three city blocks in length and offers typical and endearingly low-tech distractions: pier fishing, video arcades, free twilight dance concerts in summer, fortune tellers, shops, fairground games, snack foods, rides and an 11-storey Ferris wheel – from the top of which, on a clear day or night, you can see forever. The carousel is a national historic monument. Touristy, but fun.

### Venice

Venice Beach is a country all of its own, with the least homogeneous set of residents and visitors you could imagine. People-watching is the raison d'être here, and you'll soon tick off every last category in your *I Spy* book, California wackos included. Amid the pedestrian streetlife, Ocean Front Walk offers shops, restaurants and food stands. Seawards from the Walk, jump into the flow of the winding boardwalk – rollerblade, bike or indulge in any other wheeled sport you can come up with; watch or play volleyball or basketball; check out the Incredible Hulk-sized muscle men and women who work out endlessly at Muscle Beach, the almost legendary outdoor gym; or just enjoy the sun-warmed sand. Swimming is an unwise choice; the water is dirty. Venice Pier, to the south, with its food and entertainment stalls, is amusing, but second fiddle to Ocean Front Walk. There are several beachside parking lots – try the end of Rose Avenue or Windward Avenue, off Pacific Avenue, where you'll pay $5-$7. Street parking is usually jammed solid, and can be dodgy in any case.

### Malibu

Unfortunately, the best beaches in Malibu are the private property of the rich and famous. The majority of the public beaches, spotted with commercial restaurants and certainly nothing out of the ordinary, make tourists wonder where the real Malibu could be. Nonetheless, swimming, sunning and playing here is popular, especially among those who enjoy watching the do-or-die surfers riding the waves. As for the supposedly glamorous side of Malibu, with its stars, wealthy eccentrics and bikini-clad beauties, well, you'll have to search. Drive out near Point Doom and beyond and you will see incredible houses – some of which are built precariously on the edge of rocky bluffs – with lush gardens and ocean views. Ironically, the bigger and more expensive the mansion, the more dangerously it is situated. Paradise has its price – mudslides, rains, brush fires and other natural counterbalances.

### Zuma

Quintessentially Southern California, Zuma Beach is about as good as it gets. Four miles north of Malibu, enduring the sometimes long and traffic-clogged drive on the PCH, you come upon the long sprawl of sand and surf. The water is clean and the waves strong enough to endanger your bikini top. Zuma can get crowded, but dish out the $5 to park (a must, because the parking enforcement people are ruthless) and you're set for the day. Lifeguards man the beach and there are toilets, showers and a few hot dog and soda carts. The best bet is to bring your own picnic and plenty to drink.

Although there are often volleyball games and surfing, Zuma is best for long beach walks, swimming, sunbathing and beach fun with friends and family.

### El Matador

Small, beautiful and dominated by monuments of rocky outcrop, El Matador looks more like a European beach. It's six miles north of Malibu and just past Zuma Beach, then a walk down a steep gravelly path. Wear shoes and don't bring too much heavy gear or picnic paraphernalia. You should be able to find some privacy here; visitors can spread their towels in the cupped hands of the rocks. Arriving early or staying late should reward you with a memorable dawn or sunset.

### South Bay beaches

**Manhattan**, **Huntington** and **Hermosa** Beaches are the best of the South Bay beaches. Right out of a postcard of Southern California, they offer clean water, sand that stretches out of sight, small piers and all the accoutrements – volleyball, sailing and beachfront paths for walking, running, biking and rollerblading. The charm of these beaches is the local flavour. Visitors can swim, picnic and bask in the sun alongside residents and local fishermen as well as other tourists. The surf's not bad either. Huntington Beach picks up swells from a variety of directions, which makes for good waves, and the waters are often less crowded than, say, Malibu Beach. For those who prefer dry land, Manhattan Beach hosts an annual Volleyball Open, which is televised and attended by throngs of enthusiasts.

# Attractions

### Farmers' Market

*6333 West Third Street, at Fairfax Avenue, Park La Brea (1-213 549 2140). Bus 16, 217/I-10, exit Fairfax Avenue north.* **Open** 9am-7pm daily. **Admission** free.
As much a destination for locals as for tourists, the Farmers' Market was originally established as a co-op where the townspeople could buy produce from local farmers. Today, there are more than 165 stalls selling foods from gumbo to falafel, fruits, vegetables, pastries, exotic spices, dried fruits and home-made sweets as well as shops selling candles, jewellery, clothes and tourist stuff. Although the market can get a bit crowded, and finding a table under the shade of an umbrella can be a challenge, the effort is worth it, especially on Thursday, Friday and Saturday evenings from 7-9pm, when bands play.
*Designated smoking areas.*

### Hollywood Bowl

*2301 North Highland Avenue, at Odin Street, Hollywood (1-213 850 2000). Bus Hollywood Bowl/US101, exit Highland Avenue/Hollywood Bowl.* **Open** June-Sept; *box office* 10am-9pm Mon-Sat; noon-8pm Sun; *rehearsals* 9.30am-12.30pm day of performance. **Tickets** prices vary; call to check. **Credit** AmEx, Disc, MC, V.
The Hollywood Bowl has long been an icon in Los Angeles. Celebrating its 75th anniversary in 1995, it draws crowds of every age and type to its summer concerts. People come with picnic baskets to enjoy in the grounds beforehand or to dip into during the show itself. The off-season home of the LA Philharmonic (morning rehearsals are open to the public), this outdoor bandshell nestled in the hills has hosted countless notable conductors and classical musicians and been featured in more than 50 films. The Hollywood Museum is an extra bonus with its exhibitions on the history of the Bowl.
*Parking Hollywood Bowl $10-$24.20; park and ride $5 round trip; shuttle $2.50 round trip.*

*The Waterworld spectacular at **Universal Studios**. See page 40.*

# Water covers 2/3 of the world.

## We cover the rest.

| | |
|---|---|
| 150 countries. | |
| 5,400 locations. | |
| 2,000 at airports. | |
| 500,000 cars. | |
| 18,000 staff. | |

**W**herever you are going in the world, whether it's for business or pleasure, you can rely on an unbeatable combination of price and service from Hertz.

**T**o find out more, or to make a reservation, simply visit your local Travel Agency or call Hertz direct on:

## 0990 90 60 90

The World's #1 Car Rental Company

## The Henry E Huntington Library, Art Collections & Botanical Gardens

*1151 Oxford Road, second entrance at corner of Orlando Road & Allen Avenue, San Marino (1-818 405 2100/ recorded information 1-818 405 2141). Bus 79/I-110, exit Arroyo Parkway north.* **Open** *winter* noon-4.30pm Tue-Fri; 10.30am-4.30pm Sat, Sun; *summer* 10.30am-4.30pm Tue-Sun. **Admission** $7.50 adults; $6 senior citizens; $4 students; free under-12s; free first Thur of the month. **Credit** MC, V.

This cultural institution was founded in 1919 by Henry E Huntington, a savvy businessman whose passions, besides business, were books, art and gardens. Dedicated to research, education and the pursuit of beauty, it includes a library, containing an impressive collection of rare books and manuscripts on British and American history and literature; an art collection, one of the most comprehensive assemblies of British and French art from the 18th and 19th centuries; and botanical gardens, containing over 14,000 different kinds of plants, including some lovely cacti. Highlights include the Ellesmere manuscript of Chaucer's *Canterbury Tales*, a few early editions of Shakespeare and high tea in the Rose Garden Room on afternoons from Tuesday to Friday.

## Hollywood Wax Museum

*6767 Hollywood Boulevard, at Highland Avenue, Hollywood (1-213 462 5991/recorded information 1-213 462 8860). Bus 1, 163, 180, 181, 210/I-10, exit La Brea Avenue north.* **Open** 10am-midnight Thur, Sun; 10am-2am Fri, Sat. **Admission** $8.95 adults; $7.50 senior citizens; $6.95 6-12s. **Credit** AmEx, MC, V.

Rather ragged around the edges, the Hollywood Wax Museum is still amusing even if the sets do seem to have been locked in a time capsule for a decade. Many of the celebrities, presidents, athletes and historical figures immortalised in wax look more like relatives of the people they're supposed to portray, some close, others long-lost and some by marriage. Its redeeming feature is the Chamber of Horrors, which despite its campness can be a bit spooky. Why visitors are driven to throw coins at the wax 'Last Supper' continues to be a mystery. Combo discount admission available for the Hollywood Wax Museum and the Guinness Book of World Records Museum across the street.

## La Brea Tar Pits

*5801 Wilshire Boulevard, between La Brea & Fairfax Avenues, Park La Brea (1-213 857 6311/George C Page Museum 1-213 936 2230). Bus 20, 21, 22/I-10, exit La Brea Avenue north.* **Open** 10am-5pm Tue-Sun.

**Admission** $6 adults; $3.50 students, senior citizens; $2 5-10s; free first Tue of the month. **Credit** AmEx, Disc, V.

As you peer into these vast pits oozing with tar (*brea* in Spanish) in Hancock Park, you may wonder what's the big deal. The big deal is the history: early settlers and natives used the tar to seal boats and roofs, and before that, mastodons used it as a graveyard. In 1906 geologists discovered fossils of over 200 varieties of mammals, plants, reptiles, birds and insects from the Pleistocene Era encrusted in these mucky pits. The George C Page Museum of Tar Pit Discoveries near the pits will enlighten you through holograms, films, demonstrations, exhibitions and dinosaur replicas.

*Parking $7.50.*

## Mann's Chinese Theater

*6925 Hollywood Boulevard, between Highland & La Brea Avenues, Hollywood (1-213 461 3331/recorded information 1-213 464 8111/reservations 1-310 289 6266). Bus 1, 26, 213/I-10, exit Highland Avenue.* **Open** first show 12.15pm. **Admission** $7.50 adults; $5.25 students; $4.50 under-12s, senior citizens; $4.50 first two performances Mon-Fri; $5 Sat, Sun. **Credit** MC, V.

Mann's is where you will find the famous courtyard where movie greats have made imprints of their hands and feet. Master showman Sid Grauman, in true Hollywood style,

*Mexican cacti at the* **Huntington***.*

commissioned architects Meyer and Holler to create a Chinese temple as a new stage on which to perform his prologues. Legend insists that Norma Talmadge accidentally stepped into the wet cement outside the new building and, in spirited response, Sid fetched Mary Pickford and Douglas Fairbanks to repeat the 'mistake' with their feet and hands. And so it began. The theatre was the spot where the first gala premieres took place... limousines, fur-wrapped starlets, the works. The courtyard can choke with camera-snapping tourists measuring their own hands and feet against the likes of John Wayne, Jimmy Stewart and Judy Garland, but the cinema itself is well preserved, clean and still a great place to catch a movie.

## Olvera Street

*Bounded by North Spring, North Alameda & Arcadia Streets and West Cesar Chavez Boulevard, Downtown (visitor centre 1-213 628 1274). Metro Union Station/ Bus DASH B.*

As part of an urban renewal programme in the 1930s, Olvera Street, home to some of LA's earliest buildings, was pedestrianised, and is now a buzzing walkway of museums, restaurants and food and craft stalls that attracts tourists in droves but still has a genuine Mexican feel. It is part of the El Pueblo de Los Angeles Historical Monument, the site of the original settlement, and contains a park and 27 historic or architecturally significant buildings, including the Avila Adobe, LA's oldest house, and Sepulveda House, both open to the public (Sepulveda House doubles as a visitors' centre). These few blocks are constantly busy and alive, especially at weekends, when there's often live music, and on special Mexican festival days such as the Blessing of the Animals in the spring, Cinco de Mayo in May and Los Posadas before Christmas (*see chapter* **Los Angeles by Season***). Free guided tours are available.

*Parking on Main Street $1.25 first 20 mins; $7.50 all day Mon-Fri; $5 all day Sat, Sun.*

# CENTRAL PARK SummerStage

## New York City's favorite FREE music, dance, and spoken word festival. Every summer.

**Pick up a copy of TIME OUT NEW YORK when you arrive this summer for a complete schedule of Central Park SummerStage events. Call the CPSS hotline at 212-360-2777 for calendar details.**

## Queen Mary

*1126 Queens Highway, Pier J, Long Beach (1-310 435 3511/hotel booking 1-800 437 2934). Metro Transit Mall/ I-405, exit I-710 south.* **Open** *winter* 10am-6pm daily; *summer* 10am-6pm Mon-Fri; 10am-9pm Sat, Sun. **Admission** $10 adults; $8 senior citizens; $6 3-11s. **Credit** AmEx, DC, MC, V.

Having retired from active duty in 1967, the Queen Mary now resides in Long Beach. A popular tourist target, though only mildly diverting unless you have a thing for cruise ships, the majestic liner offers some fun tours such as the Ghost Tour and the Engine Room Tour. In fact, pick an area of the liner in which you are especially interested, and staff will tailor a tour to match. The Queen Mary was used for interior shots for the film *The Poseidon Adventure* and guides are happy to share shooting anecdotes. There are shops and restaurants both in the boat and in the adjacent Marketplace, designed as a quaint English shopping village. For those who like heart-stopping adventure, jumping from MegaBungee, the tallest freestanding bungee tower on the continent, will be something to brag about. *Parking $5-$7.*

## Ripley's Believe It or Not

*6780 Hollywood Boulevard, at Highland Avenue, Hollywood (1-213 466 6335). Bus 1, 210, 212, 217/ US101, exit Highland Avenue.* **Open** 10am-10pm daily. **Admission** $8.95 adults; $5.95 5-11s. **Credit** MC, V.

Based on Robert Ripley's book, *Believe It or Not*, this attraction stretches the definition for a museum. The wacky, fact-filled book works very nicely, but the concept hasn't made a particularly successful leap from the page. However, if the mood strikes you, go and see 'exhibits of facts' including: 'Three-ball Charlie', a man who could put three balls in his mouth and whistle simultaneously; weapons and torture devices of tribal cannibals; the man who walked across the

continent backwards; and the world's strangest gravestones. Just one question: why is it so hard to believe that someone created a sculpture of Marilyn Monroe out of a quarter of a million dollars or a life-size portrait of John Wayne from laundry lint? People do these things – the real question is why.

## Spadena House (Witch's House)

*Carmelita Ave & Walden Drive, Beverly Hills.*

If you stare long enough at this bizarre fairytale house, you might think you can see a wart-faced witch summoning Hansel and Gretel inside with her gnarled finger. The Witch's House was originally the administration building of Irving V Willat Productions in Culver City. Designed with peaked roofs, tilted windows and a fabulous witch-and-broomstick spirit, the house was often used as a set in Willat's pictures. It is now a private residence, so be careful not to incite the wrath of the residing witch, warlock, or law-abiding citizen.

## Watts Towers

*1765 East 107th Street, between Alameda Street & Central Avenue, Watts (1-213 485 2433/arts centre 1-213 847 1646). Bus 56, 251/Metro 103rd Street/I-10, exit Century Boulevard north.* **Open** 10am-4pm Tue-Sat; noon-4pm Sun. **Admission** free.

Working in construction by day, plasterer Sam Rodia kept his sleeves rolled up into the night and spent 33 years (1921-1954) building his Eiffel Tower in Watts. An unlettered Italian, Rodia created the 99½ft high towers with only his artistic vision to keep him company. 'How could I have been helped?' he asked. 'I couldn't tell anyone what to do; most of the time, I didn't know myself.' Structuring his towers from salvaged steel rods and cast-off pipe structures, bed frames and cement, Rodia incorporated pieces of broken bottles, ceramic tiles, organic materials and china cups and plates into his folk-art masterpieces. He scaled the towers on a window-washer's belt and bucket and decorated them with over 25,000 seashells, so encrusted became the surface that the towers look as if they were made of nothing more than calcified coral and shell. Rodia deeded Watts Towers to the neighbourhood, and they have since become a source of Black civic pride. They are currently being restored and are closed to the public until 1998, but it's still worth coming to look at the exterior. The adjacent community centre hosts exhibitions of Third World and African-American art, workshops and a couple of festivals a year. Watts is a high-crime area, so it's best not to hang around after dark.

# Theme parks

## Disneyland

*1313 Harbor Boulevard, Anaheim, Orange County (1-714 999 4565/1-714 781 4560). Bus 460/I-5, exit Harbor Boulevard.* **Open** *winter* 10am-6pm Mon-Fri; 9am-10pm Sat, Sun; *summer* 8am-midnight Mon-Thur, Sun; 8am-1am Fri, Sat; hours can vary, so call in advance. **Admission** $34 adults; $30 senior citizens; $26 3-11s. **Credit** AmEx, MC, V.

Called 'the happiest place on earth', Disneyland is all it's cracked up to be, if you like that kind of thing. If you don't, on the other hand, you may need sectioning after your visit. This immaculate world (deliveries and rubbish removal are all done underground) will take you to Tomorrowland, Fantasyland, Frontierland and Adventureland; through the middle of it all runs Main Street, always busy but positively throbbing on parade days. Although new rides come on line with movie-studio productivity, some of the old favourites still draw enormous crowds: Space Mountain, which takes you, in utter darkness, on a fast and scream-inducing ride through time, space and black holes; the Matterhorn, where you take a bobsled rollercoaster ride around the bald summit of a Swiss Alp; the Haunted Mansion, where in true Disney style the ghosts trill and smile; and Pirates of the Caribbean, where singing pirates

**Watts Towers**, *made from found materials.*

*Famous imprints at* **Mann's Chinese Theater**. *See page 37.*

capture your heart during their drunken spree. A word of advice: if you hate having a song stick in your head, skip It's a Small World, which is sadly outdated and no more than an incitement to strangle the person who wrote the inane tune. Disneyland is good fun, but get there early to beat the crowds, be prepared to queue, and pace yourself – it's big. *Parking $6.*

### Knott's Berry Farm

*8039 Beach Boulevard, at La Palma Avenue, Buena Park, Orange County (1-714 220 5200/1-714 220 5220). Bus 420/I-5, exit Beach Boulevard south.* **Open** *winter* hours vary, so call ahead; *summer* 9am-midnight daily. **Admission** $29.95 adults; $19.95 senior citizens, 3-11s; *after 4pm* $14.95 adults, senior citizens. **Credit** AmEx, DC, Disc, MC, V.

Knott's Berry Farm started as a farm stand selling the delicious home-made jams, jellies, and preserves of one Mrs Cordelia Knott. Although Mrs Knott and family have long since left the farm, her jams are still for sale, as are tasty homestyle fried chicken dinners at the restaurant outside the gates. Inside the park, which portrays an idealised, kinder America, there are water rides, the 20-storey Sky Jump parachute ride, and Montezooma's Revenge, a seemingly tame rollercoaster that still gives you that stomach-flying-out-of-your-mouth sensation. Many of the buildings in the park were transplanted from old mining towns, which fits in with the feeling of nostalgia that hovers in the air. Children are bound to like Ghost Town: good, clean, nostalgic fun complete with smiling can-can girls and gun-slinging cowboys. *Parking $5.*

### Six Flags California

*Magic Mountain Parkway, off the I-5, Valencia (1-805 255 4100/recorded information 1-805 255 4111). I-5, exit Magic Mountain Parkway.* **Open** *both* from 10am daily; closing hours vary, so call ahead; *Hurricane Harbor* closed in winter. **Admission** *Magic Mountain* $33 adults; $19 over-55s; $15 children under 48in;

*Hurricane Harbor* $15 adults; $10 children, senior citizens. **Credit** *both* AmEx, MC, V.

Six Flags California comprises Six Flags Magic Mountain and its new watery cousin, Six Flags Hurricane Harbor Water Park. Both give you rides, rides, and more rides, and spectacular rides at that: rollercoasters and water rides for every level of screamer, the most famous of them the Colossus, the largest wooden-framed roller coaster ever built. Those whose idea of fun is to feel their kidneys and livers shifting around inside shouldn't miss the Viper, a loop-de-loop rollercoaster, but make sure you don't consume too much of the ubiquitous hot dogs or soda before embarking on this corkscrew journey. The upside-down, track-above-your head Backlot is also out there. Raging Waters, albeit undeniably wet, is a ball, as is the new Superman, the Escape: bragging some technological whizzkiddery, it catapults you straight up a 41-storey tower at 100 mph – in seven seconds. Freefalling down at the same speed, you wish you were wearing the superhero's cape. Set scenically on the hip of the San Fernando Mountains and created for kids and adults, Six Flags is fun with a screamingly huge capital F. *Parking $6.*

### Universal Studios Hollywood & CityWalk

*100 Universal City Plaza, Universal City (1-818 508 9600). Bus 420/US101, exit Universal Center Drive.* **Open** *winter* 8am-10pm daily; last tram tour 4.15; *summer* 7am-11pm daily; last tram tour 6.15pm. **Admission** $34 adults; $29 senior citizens; $26 3-11s. **Credit** AmEx, DC, Disc, MC, V.

Although four million visitors a year can't all be wrong, unless you like pre-packaged cheese, doing Universal can seem like a rite of passage that you're glad you experienced, but only once it's over. Although you can opt to attend animal acts, stroll round the Lucille Ball museum, experience the *Back to the Future* flight simulator, go on rides such as Jurassic Park or watch scripted shows inspired by recent TV programmes or movies such as *ET, Waterworld* and *The Flintstones*, the best way to see Universal is to take the tram. The ride takes you through the backlot of the working studio, where you will see the likes of King Kong, all 13,000lbs of him, moving rather arthritically, the shark from *Jaws* leaping out of the water and snapping its mechanical mouth at you, the parting of the Red Sea, the 'Big One' earthquake (really nothing like the real thing), and the *Psycho* house. The best part of the tram is that you glimpse slices of studio life: casts and crews rushing about, dilapidated old props stashed here and there. And of course, while on the tram, you get to sit down – and you'll need it. The tram ride alone lasts five to seven hours. Allow a full day for Universal and start early. The complex also houses one of LA's big concert venues, Universal Amphitheater, the 18-screen Universal City Cinemas and Universal CityWalk, an LA-themed shopping (and eating) 'street'. Although mobbed most of the time, the CityWalk is at its glitzy best at night when the two blocks of collaged LA architecture come alive. *Parking $6.*

## Areas

*See also chapter* **By Neighbourhood**.

### Beverly Hills, Bel Air & Rodeo Drive

Whether you're a hard-core shopper or a sociologist, don't miss a walk or drive down **Rodeo Drive**. In the very heart of **Beverly Hills**, these few blocks, on which some of the superswank shops require appointments for entrance, embody conspicuous consumption at its best or worse. Trinkets sell for thousands and men, women and children don furs, silks, and giant gemstones for a regular afternoon outing. The epitome of the American dream, with its tree-lined streets, perfectly manicured gardens, low crime rate, and beautiful people, Beverly Hills became a city in 1880, before which it was known chiefly for its crops of robust lima beans. The houses are big, as expected, and built in every style imaginable. Don't be afraid to drive off the main drag and explore some side streets to get the full effect.

**Bel Air**, also home to the rich and famous, is a posh hillside community west of Beverly Hills. Known for their privacy and pretty views, the houses in this gated neighbourhood are undoubtedly visual feasts, but unfortunately, visitors driving the meandering roads won't see much save the names of these mansions lettered on the mailboxes, since the best houses are hidden from sight.

## Downtown

Downtown LA is an odd stew of old and new, vibrant and stagnant, beautiful and ugly, made up of the skyscraper-studded financial downtown, El Pueblo de Los Angeles – the site of the original settlement, *see above* **Olvera Street** – City Hall, Chinatown and Little Tokyo. Much of it can be explored on foot during the day, but be careful at night as some parts can be dangerous. Some of LA's most stunning architecture is found downtown, such as the romantic **Union Station**, where you expect to see Bogie and Bergman kissing a star-crossed good-bye. Other landmarks include the **Bradbury Building** (304 South Broadway), as featured in *Blade Runner*, and the space-age **Westin Bonaventure Hotel** (404 South Figueroa Street). Also of note are the **Music Center**, whose Dorothy Chandler Pavilion hosts the Oscar ceremony, the **Museum of Contemporary Art** (MOCA), the **Angels Flight** funicular railway (Hill Street, between Third & Fourth Streets) and **Broadway**, a thriving Mexican shopping street. In the 1940s, LA's Community Redevelopment Agency developed **Little Tokyo**, **Chinatown** and **Koreatown** to the east, which have blossomed into thriving communities, great spots for food, shops and religious shrines.

## Hollywood Boulevard

Gone are the dream-come-true days of fur-wrapped starlets and tuxedoed leading men. Now Hollywood Boulevard, with its X-rated cinemas, tacky tourist shops and vagrants, is where dreams become dirty, lost and forgotten. To say Hollywood Boulevard is anticlimactic would be an understatement, but there are nevertheless a few places on this long street worth a look: the historic **Mann's Chinese** and **El Capitan** Theaters, the old **Roosevelt Hotel** and the beautifully designed **Pantages Theater** among them. Don't expect much and you will enjoy what used to be the heart of Hollywoodland. The **Walk of Fame**, with bronze stars embedded in the pavement paying tribute to over 2,500 Hollywood greats (and not-so-greats, so long as they had a good publicist and some spare cash), extends in all directions from the junction of Hollywood Boulevard and Vine Street, with the longest stretch running westwards to La Brea Avenue.

## Melrose Avenue

Melrose Avenue is a mecca of LA trendiness. Locals and tourists throng to it like ants on an anthill, especially the stretch between La Brea and Fairfax Avenues. Lined with funky restaurants, art galleries, theatres, comedy clubs and shops selling everything from vintage clothes and used Levi's to designer sunglasses and art, it attracts the young and the old, the business-suited and the punk-grunge hippies with its adrenaline pulse. A few highlights: **Aardvark** for vintage clothing, **Caffe Luna** for espresso and mouthwatering tiramisu, **Wacko** for bizarro gifts, **The Wound & Wound Toy Company** for wind-up toys and music boxes and the **Groundlings Improv Theatre** where many of the *Saturday Night Live* greats served their apprenticeship. Melrose Avenue suffers from a lack of parking: some space can be found on the neighbouring cross streets, but read signs carefully for restrictions.

## Old Town Pasadena

Named 'the crown of the valley' by the Chippewa Indians, Pasadena, at the foot of the San Gabriel Mountains, was one of the first areas in Los Angeles to be settled. A holiday refuge for rich East Coasters, it was – and remains – the toney antithesis of the coastal hustle, exuding class in its educational and cultural institutions, museums and old-money mansions (some of which have such TV alter-egos as the Carrington mansion in *Dynasty* and Bruce 'Batman' Wayne's bat-base). The 12 square blocks of artsy **Old Town**

# The Hollywood sign

Built in 1923, the gargantuan Hollywood sign was originally an advertisement for a real estate development called Hollywoodland. In 1949, the city tore down the last four letters and kept the other nine as a landmark. Hovering over Hollywood like the ultimate aspirational icon, it has now become such a potent symbol of stardom that it's a surprise to hear that it's been the jumping-off point for only one suicide.

Urban legend has it that a young starlet, Lillian Millicent Entwistle, known as Peg, threw herself off the sign one breezy September night in 1932. She had had her 15 minutes of fame as one of the youngest actresses ever to star in a Broadway show. In the wake of her success, she transplanted herself and her hopes to the land of celluloid stardom. Soon after arriving in LA, she signed a contract with RKO Studios, but they declined to pick up her option

when they saw her first film. Young Peg, only 24, was devastated. She dragged herself up through the scratchy brush of Mount Lee to the sign, climbed the 50-foot ladder, stood on top of the 'H' and leaped.

Today, to protect against vandals and hopeless hearts like Peg's, the Hollywood sign, repainted five times a year, is defended by a million-dollar security system. However, even the sophisticated alarms and infrared lights cannot keep out all wilful trespassers who want to get their messages out to the world. For brief moments, this legendary sign and its 5,000 lights have become 'Ollywood' (after Iran-Contra messenger Colonel Oliver North), 'Holly-weed' in appreciation of the powers of marijuana, and a support message to the US troops fighting in the Gulf War, when a massive yellow ribbon was tied around the letters.

*Be the complete tourist – buy a map locating the addresses of the stars.*

**Pasadena** are best explored on foot. Walk among Beaux Arts-style buildings and Craftsman-style homes such as the **Gamble House** (4 Westmoreland Place; 1-818 793 3334) or browse in the **Norton Simon Museum of Art** or the **Henry E Huntington** library, art collections and botanical gardens (*see above* **Attractions**). Also worth checking out, for its art and architecture, is the **Pasadena Playhouse**. There's plenty of parking on the outskirts.

## Sunset Strip

The famous **Sunset Strip** is the section of Sunset Boulevard that runs from Doheny Drive to Laurel Canyon in West Hollywood. Studded with billboards and bright lights, it has been the centre of LA nightlife since the 1920s. Along its length are such landmarks as the **Whisky A-Go-Go** music club, the **Comedy Store**, the **House of Blues** and the **Viper Room**. Lots of restaurants and shops, too.

## Third Street Promenade, Santa Monica

Created in the late '80s for pedestrians only, this four-block promenade is at its best on weekend nights, when the street performers are out, cafés, bars, restaurants and some shops open late and vendors fill the street with carts selling silver jewellery, organic cotton clothes and Bonsai trees. Almost anything you could ask for is at hand: good food, shops both practical and whimsical, several multi-screen cinemas, an indoor mall and sidewalk tables to sit at, sip coffee and watch the world go by. Some find it all rather contrived and antiseptic, but it's not only tourists who come here – though any visitor daunted by the magnitude of the city will be reassured by the very blandness that puts others off. Handy for the beach, and with ample parking in lots on Second and Fourth Streets.

## Venice

At the turn of the century, builders, government and, most notably, tobacco magnate Abbot Kinney transformed this area into the 'Venice of America', complete with canals, bridges, imported gondolas, meandering streets and a bohemian spirit. The canals were condemned in 1940, but since then have been restored, reopened and partly regentrified: art and architecture studios as well as private homes thrive. Only those with relatively robust pocketbooks can live along the quaint waterways, but anyone can wander among them. Enter the network by turning south off Venice Boulevard onto Dell Avenue, about a quarter of a mile back from the beach.

Venice as a whole is a mixed and magnetic community of post-'60s hippies, the elderly, artistic, and free-spirited, with a bit of gang territory thrown in (watch yourself and your car in inland areas, especially after dark). **Abbot Kinney Boulevard** is a good place to window shop or enjoy a coffee or meal at a local café or restaurant. And then, of course, there's **Venice Beach** (*see above* **Beaches**).

## Drives

Yes, you can get around LA by bus, but everyone should see it through a windscreen at least once – it's what it was designed for.

## Sunset Boulevard

In its 20-mile plus length from its coastal beginnings (it joins Pacific Coast Highway) to its metamorphosis into Cesar Chavez Boulevard just north of downtown, Sunset changes from the LA version of a country road into an urban drag, and from the most desirable address to a rather seedier one. From the ocean it winds its way up through wealthy **Pacific Palisades** and **Brentwood**, then passes between the **UCLA** campus and **Bel Air** before becoming one of the main arteries of **Beverly Hills**. Turnings to the north access state parks and canyon roads (such as Beverly Glen Boulevard and Coldwater Canyon Road, which lead to the dramatic Mulholland Drive and Valley views). To fully appreciate the opulence of Beverly Hills, it's best to leave Sunset and explore, but you will see evidence of supertax bracketeers in the large properties that line the road and the famous 1920s-built pink **Beverly Hills Hotel**. After Beverly Hills, you hit **West Hollywood** and **Sunset Strip** (*see above* **Areas**). The Boulevard then ceases to meander and becomes a straight east-west conduit, a couple of blocks south of Hollywood Boulevard, with which it merges as it turns south east to become a main drag for the mixed communities of **Silver Lake** and **Echo Park**. In these eastern stretches it becomes increasingly scruffier and more urban, but no less interesting. It ends just past the **Hollywood Bowl**; fittingly, for its last couple of miles, it becomes Route 66.

## Pacific Coast Highway

The Pacific Coast Highway (SR1 or Highway 1), more commonly known as the PCH, hugs the LA coastline for most of its length, north to **Malibu** and beyond and south to the end of **Orange County**. We don't recommend that you drive the whole thing, but the northern stretch up from Venice to Malibu and beyond is particularly scenic.

## Wilshire Boulevard

Running from just west of downtown to the coast, Wilshire crosses some of the most diverse areas of LA. It can take a good 90 minutes to do its 16-mile length in bad traffic, but there are exit points onto the I-10 if it all gets too much. Out of downtown, you'll pass **MacArthur Park**, lined with what were, before its recent degeneration into a poor, crime-ridden neighbourhood, desirable apartment buildings. This is followed by the splendid but sadly closed art deco **Bullocks** department store and, a mile or so on, **Koreatown**, extending north and south at the intersection of Wilshire and Western, where the art deco **Wiltern Theater** stands. A couple of miles later, you reach **Miracle Mile**, where some of LA's best museums are clustered, along with **Hancock Park**, home of the **La Brea Tar Pits** (*see above* **Attractions**). Also of interest in this area are the **El Rey Theater**, built in 1936 in Streamline Moderne style, the beautiful 1940 **May Co** department store, now closed and a reminder of the area's decline, and **Park La Brea** to the north, an ugly 1950s gated community. From here, Wilshire progresses through upmarket **Beverly Hills** and **Westwood**, via the impressively gracious **Veterans Administration** (whose streets are named after famous US generals) into **Santa Monica**, where it passes **Third Street Promenade** (*see above* **Areas**) on its way to join Ocean Avenue at the seafront.

## Museums

*See also chapter* **Museums & Galleries**.

### The J Paul Getty Museum at the Getty Villa

*17985 Pacific Coast Highway, Malibu (1-310 458 2003). Bus 434/I-10 west, exit PCH north.* **Open** 10am-5pm Tue-Sun. **Admission** free; book parking 7-10 days in advance. **Credit** AmEx, MC, V.

### The J Paul Getty Center for the Fine Arts

*1200 Getty Center Drive, at the I-405, Brentwood. Bus 561/I-405, exit Getty Center Drive.* **Open** Tue-Sun (hours to be decided). **Admission** free; book parking 2 weeks in advance. **Credit** AmEx, MC, V.

Perched like royalty on the canyon hills of the PCH, the impressive Getty Museum is a modelled after a Roman villa buried by Mount Vesuvius's efflux. Endowed with a trust by the extremely wealthy J Paul, the Getty contains some outstanding collections including Roman and Greek antiquities, French furniture and works by Renaissance masters. It also has great gardens, and although no picnics are allowed, you can eat in an outdoor café and look out over the sweeping

vistas of mountains, sea, sky, and city. In autumn 1997, a new $733 million Getty Center will open its doors in Brentwood. The Malibu Getty will then close for three years and reopen in the year 2000, when it will hold only the antiquities – the rest of the collection will be housed in the new museum.

## Museum of Contemporary Art (MOCA)

*250 South Grand Avenue, at Third Street, Downtown (1-213 626 6222/). Metro Civic Center/Tom Bradley or Pershing Square. Bus 30, 31, 40, 42, 436, 445, 466, DASH A, D/I-110, exit Fourth Street east.* **Open** 11am-5pm Tue, Wed, Fri-Sun; 11am-8pm Thur. **Admission** $6 adults; $4 students, senior citizens; free under-12s; free 5-8pm Thur. **Credit** AmEx, MC, V.

Only ten years old and the first major US building by famous Japanese architect Arata Isozaki, MOCA has large galleries and massive windows that give it an open, free feeling. International in scope, the museum presents the works of such contemporary artists as Louise Nevelson, Mark Rothko and Franz Kline. The courtyard is a great place to have lunch or a drink, and the gift shop is one of the best, though not cheap. MOCA also has an auditorium where films and performing arts are shown.

## Los Angeles County Museum of Art (LACMA)

*5905 Wilshire Boulevard, between Fairfax & La Brea Avenues, Miracle Mile (1-213 857 6000). Bus 20, 21, 22, 320/I-10, exit Fairfax Avenue north.* **Open** 10am-5pm Tue-Thur; 10am-9pm Fri; 11am-6pm Sat, Sun. **Admission** $6 adults; $4 students, senior citizens; $1 6-17s; free second Wed of the month. **No credit cards**.

As well as housing a variety of art from various periods and countries, from a huge collection of Asian and Near Eastern art and textiles to works from the Baroque and Rococo periods, LACMA also offers one of LA's best ongoing film and concert series in its 500-seat Bing Theater. A modern wonder of glass, limestone, glass brick and green terracotta, this architecturally intriguing building sits smack in the middle of Miracle Mile. In the outdoor Plaza courtyard, you can enjoy free jazz on Friday evenings and Sunday afternoons. *Parking $5 Wilshire Boulevard & Spaulding Avenue; free after 5pm Fri.*

## Viewpoints

### Griffith Park & Observatory

*Griffith Park, entrances at Vermont Avenue, Los Feliz Boulevard & Western Avenue, Los Feliz (1-213 665 5188). Bus 96/I-5, Los Feliz Boulevard exit west.* **Open** 5am-10pm daily.

*Griffith Park Observatory & Planetarium, 2800 East Observatory Road, Griffith Park (1-213 664 1181/ recorded information 1-213 664 1191/Laserium 1-818 901 9405). Bus 96/I-5, exit Los Feliz Boulevard west.* **Open** *summer* 12.30-10pm daily; *winter* 2-10pm Tue-Fri; 12.30-10pm Sat, Sun. **Admission** *Planetarium shows* $4 adults; $3 senior citizens; $2 children; *Laserium shows* $7 adults; $6 senior citizens, children; under-5s not admitted. **Credit** MC, V.

Open until ten at night (except on Mondays), when the city sparkles like an open jewel box below, the Observatory is a good perch from which to enjoy the view both up to the skies and down to the city. Complete with its bronze domes, it has been part of the Hollywood Hills landscape since 1935. The inside of the mother dome serves as a screen for the multimedia presentations that change every few months. Summer and weekends offer the most frequent planetarium and laser shows, but weekdays are less crowded. If you prefer the real thing, you can get up close and personal with your favourite constellations with the help of intensely strong rooftop telescopes. Leave time for the Hall of Science and a gander at the Foucault pendulum, the solar telescope, the cosmic ray

cloud chamber, and more. As for the park itself, the sprawling acres offer myriad hiking and walking trails, picnic areas and charity events including road and bike races.

### Yamashiro

*1999 North Sycamore Avenue, at Franklin Avenue, Hollywood (1-213 466 5125). Bus 1/US101, exit Highland Avenue.* **Dinner** 5.30-10pm Mon-Thur, Sun; 5.30-11pm Fri, Sat. **Average** $27. **Credit** AmEx, MC, V

Originally a brothel (or so legend tells us), this regal pagoda in the Hollywood Hills is the oldest building in LA. Now one of Hollywood's best-known Japanese restaurants, the imported oriental structure is more than 600 years old. The food is only so-so – though you can always just have a drink in the bar – but the view is definitely worth the drive or climb up the meandering approach. Book a window seat.

### Top of Mulholland Drive

Winding and precariously narrow, the ridge that Mulholland Drive follows boasts some geometric hairpin turns and a view that would make anyone fall in love with the city below. It's at its most glorious at night, when the City of Angels is alive with winking lights. One of the best stretches is the three or so miles between Coldwater and Laurel Canyon Roads, where there are places to pull over, get out of the car, stand on the edge of the city and look down. Mulholland Drive has inspired many celluloid tributes, notably Roman Polanski's *Chinatown*.

### The Radisson Huntley Hotel

*1111 Second Street, between Wilshire Boulevard & California Avenue, Santa Monica (1-310 394 5454/ 1-800 333 3333/Toppers restaurant 1-310 393 8080). Bus 1, 2, 3, 4/ I-405, exit Wilshire Boulevard west.* **Breakfast** 6am-11am, **lunch** 11am-2pm, **dinner** 3pm-midnight, **bar** until 2am, daily. **Credit** AmEx, DC, Disc, MC, V.

Toppers, the Mexican restaurant and cantina on the top floor of the Radisson Huntley offers one of the most beautiful and sweeping views of the coast. On a clear day, you can see all the way to Catalina Island and the endless roll of the San Bernardino Mountains. Take the outside glass elevator to the top. Starting at 8.30pm each night, free musical entertainment fills the glass-walled restaurant. Since the city has ruled against the erection of buildings over eight storeys, the Huntley is in no danger of losing its exquisite view. All this and cocktails too.

*Parking $7.50 overnight; $2.75 day.*

## Outdoors

### Forest Lawn Memorial Parks

*Forest Lawn Memorial Park Glendale, 1712 South Glendale Avenue, between Los Feliz Boulevard & San Fernando Road, Glendale. I-5, exit Los Feliz Boulevard east.*

*Forest Lawn Memorial Park Hollywood Hills, 6300 Forest Lawn Drive, at SR134 & Barham Boulevard. Bus 163/SR134, exit Forest Lawn Drive.*

**Both** *1-800 204 3131.* **Open** *summer* 8am-6pm daily; *winter* 9am-5pm daily.

Without spending a cent, you can spend the day at the Forest Lawn cemeteries (there are two, one in the Hollywood Hills, just west of Griffith Park, and one in Glendale, on the eastern side of the I-5 from Griffith Park) and feel as if you have had a whirlwind tour of some of the world's greatest works of art and architecture (replicas, but who cares). Founder Hubert Eaton envisioned 'the greenest, most enchanting park you ever saw in your life... vistas of sparkling lawns, with shaded arborways and garden retreats and beautiful, noble statuary'. The imitation art includes Michelangelo's 'David', Leonardo da Vinci's 'The Last Supper', Lorenzo Ghiberti's 'Paradise Doors' and a 14th-century Scottish church. But remember: respect. Forest Lawn is first and foremost a burial ground. *Parking free.*

## Will Rogers Historic State Park

*14253 Sunset Boulevard, at Will Rogers State Park Road, Pacific Palisades (1-310 454 8212). Bus 434/I-405, exit Sunset Boulevard west.* **Open** *summer* 8am-7pm daily; *winter* 8am-6pm daily.

Will Rogers was a busy man. Humorist, writer, performer, cowboy and rope-trickster, he was also the first honorary mayor of Beverly Hills. Since Rogers was the only man in Hollywood who 'never met a man he didn't like', it seems fitting that upon his death, his ranch house and land became a national park welcoming one and all. The 31-room house is maintained as it was when the 1930s box-office star lived there, the living room full of Western-style furniture, Indian rugs and lariats. The grounds give access to some good hikes and also hosts polo matches on Saturdays and Sundays. *Parking $5.*

## Horse riding

*Sunset Ranch, 3400 North Beachwood Drive, at Franklin Avenue, Hollywood (1-213 469 5450). US101, exit Beachwood Drive north.* **Open** 9am-5pm daily. **Horses** $15 per hour.

Sunset Ranch offers riding lessons, moonlight rides and hourly rentals in the Hollywood Hills. Don't miss the evening margarita ride, up and over the hills and into the Valley, where you stop at a Mexican restaurant for burritos and margaritas. At least one person always falls off on the way home.

## Self-Realization Fellowship Lake Shrine

*17190 Sunset Boulevard, off Pacific Coast Highway, Pacific Palisades (1-310 454 4114/1-213 225 2471). Bus 2, 434/I-10, exit PCH north.* **Open** 9am-4.45pm Tue-Sat; 12.30-4.45pm Sun; services 9am, 11am Sun. **Admission** free.

Opened in 1950, this Buddhist retreat is an oasis of peace and beauty. Surrounded by a spring-fed lake, trees, flowers, paths, birds and turtles,you can stroll the grounds, ponder in private garden nooks or meditate in the Windmill Chapel. *Parking free.*

## Hollywood Reservoir & Dog Park

*Lake Hollywood Drive, Hollywood Hills. Bus 420/US101, exit Barham Boulevard north.*

Set in the Hollywood Hills, above the Hollywood Bowl and below the Hollywood Sign and Madonna's enormous estate, Hollywood Reservoir attracts runners, walkers and the occasional cyclist. If you can get out of bed, the reservoir is at its best when the gates open at 6.30am. The aroma of dewmoist pines envelops you as you run or walk on the three-mile pebbly dirt road around the reservoir's circumference. Early evenings and weekends are much more crowded, but rarely do you feel as if people outnumber trees. From one side of the reservoir, you can get a fantastic view of the Hollywood Sign. Tucked behind the Hollywood sign Beachwood Canyon is the Hollywood Dog Park. It's not uncommon to catch a glimpse of a jogging star who thinks they're successfully incognito under their baseball cap. The Dog Park is a great place to enjoy the freedom of sprawling sky and enthusiastic canines.

# Tours

## Starline Tours

*Information & bookings 1-213 463 3333.*

Some of Starline's vast range of tours go out in minibuses, which give you access to the meandering streets of the more star-studded areas. Tour 1 visits the lavish homes of stars including Charlie Chaplin, Barbra Streisand, Steve Martin, Lucille Ball, Jimmy Stewart, Phil Collins, Tori Spelling, and of course, Marilyn Monroe. The longer, narrated Tour 21 swings by movie stars' homes, Universal Studios and city highlights from Sunset Strip to Beverly Hills, with shop stops. Most of the tours run all year round and offer several departure times each day.

**Also recommended**: Gray Line Tours, 6333 West Third Street, Building 1030A, LA (1-213 525 1212) and Oskar J's Sightseeing Tours, 4334 Woodman Avenue, Sherman Oaks (1-818 501 2217).

## Los Angeles Conservancy Walking Tours

*Information & bookings 1-213 623 2489.* **Tours** usually 10am, 11am Sat. **Cost** $5. Booking required.

Yes, it can be done on foot, especially downtown. Try the Marble Masterpieces Tour, which explores the use of marble in historic and new buildings, from the 1931 One Bunker Hill Building to the post-modern Coast Savings Building. A shorter tour would be around the Biltmore, one of LA's most venerable and glamorous hotels. Other Conservancy walking tours, all one to two hours long, include Little Tokyo, LA City Hall, Union Station, Pershing Square and the Higashi Hongwanji Buddhist Temple. Intelligent and sophisticated, these tours are for those interested in the preservation and revitalisation of urban architectural heritage.

## Grave Line Tours

*Information & bookings 1-213 469 4149.* **Tours** 9.30am daily, from the east side of Mann's Chinese Theater, Hollywood Boulevard, at Orchid & Highland Avenues. **Cost** $40. **Credit** MC, V.

Ex-mortician Greg Smith will take you in the comfort of his converted Cadillac hearse for a two-plus hour jaunt to the homes where 80 stars took their last breaths and fill you in on some tasty titbits about their lives. Booking is required for the tour.

## Helinet Tours

*Information & bookings 1-818 902 0229.* **Credit** MC, V. *Van Nuys Airport, Van Nuys: bus 164, 236/I-405, exit Victory Boulevard west.*

Three helicopter tours are on offer: a 25-minute tour, for $85 per person, which leaves from Van Nuys Airport and spins you over Universal Studios, the Hollywood Sign, Griffith Park, Dodger Stadium, downtown and Beverly Hills and back. The long tour (50 minutes, $139 per person) adds on a westward jaunt over Santa Monica, up the Malibu Coast and over, around and through some breathtaking canyons. The Night Tour, often organised for weddings and other special events, costs $279 a pop. The helicopter picks you up in Van Nuys, takes you over the sparkling city on the short tour, then drops you at the four-star Tower Restaurant on top of the TransAmerica Building. After dinner a limo returns you to the airport or any other destination of your choice. The price includes everything except dinner drinks.

## Nursery Nature Walks

*Information 1-310 998 1151/bookings 1-310 364 3591.* **Tickets** free; $5 donation requested. **Credit** MC, V.

These nature walks in the Santa Monica Mountains aim to introduce families to the outdoors while instilling respect for wilderness areas. Most of the walks are pushchair-accessible. They're run by a non-profit organisation, which also offers various nature and animal-related festivals and events – phone for details.

## The Next Stage Tours

*Information & bookings 1-213 939 2688.* **Cost** $30-$60. **Credit** MC, V.

Come to Next Stage if you're fed up of production-line tours: owner Marlene Gordon will pay you individual attention and offers some unusual themes which give a real insight into the city. Try the Famous Insomniacs Tour, which takes you to the Flower and Produce Markets among other stops and ends on top of a skyscraper at sunrise; the Scentimental Journey, which introduces you to the whiff and sniffs of LA or the really quite odd LA Has Its Ups and Downs Tour, which takes you to numerous escalators and elevators from downtown to the sea.

# Los Angeles by Season

*There are celebrations galore in multicultural LA, from Thai New Year to the Mexican Day of the Dead, from Japanese festivals to surfing championships.*

Seasons in Los Angeles are distinguished not so much by weather – yes, it's always good – as by air quality and cloud cover. Expect grey skies (and occasional rain) in winter and again in early summer, when the long cloudy days of coastal 'June gloom' can get on people's nerves. Warm weather and smog arrive in July and climax with some spectacular heatwaves in September and October. But winter visitors, do not despair. The Santa Anas – brisk, hot, desert winds – often return beach weather to the region at unexpected times.

Lacking snow and falling leaves, most Angelenos clock the seasons using traditions imported from their place of origin. With a population that speaks most of the world's languages as well as English in the accent of 50 states (and not a few Commonwealth countries), California dreamin' is celebrated year-round.

### National holidays

New Year's Day (1 Jan); Martin Luther King Jr Day (3rd Mon in Jan); President's Day (3rd Mon in Feb); Memorial Day (last Mon in May); Independence Day (4 July); Labor Day (1st Mon in Sept); Columbus Day (2nd Mon in Oct); Election Day (1st Tue in Nov); Veteran's Day (11 Nov); Thanksgiving Day (4th Thur in Nov); Christmas Day (25 Dec).

## Spring

### The Academy Awards

*Usually at Dorothy Chandler Pavilion, Music Center, 135 North Grand Avenue, at First Street, Downtown.* **Date** mid-late Mar.

You'll have to camp out all night and hang out all day for even the vaguest chance of spotting any celebs – best to watch the whole shebang on TV, like the rest of the world. Alternatively, since the stars are otherwise engaged, this is a choice night to get a good table at any posh restaurant that's not holding its own Oscars party.

**The Rose Parade** *wends its weird way through the streets of Pasadena. See page 50.*

### Santa Clarita Cowboy Poetry & Music Festival

*Information 1-805 255 4910. Melody Ranch, Santa Clarita.* **Date** late Mar/early Apr.
Re-live the old West with a weekend of trail rides, poetry, storytelling, Western swing dance, chuck wagon food and music by top cowboy artists, held at Gene Autry's former ranch, as seen in the movies *High Noon* and *Gunsmoke*.

### City of Los Angeles Marathon

*Information 1-310 444 5544. Citywide; check newspapers for route.* **Date** first Sun in Mar.
It's an all-city traffic-clogging festival, so if you're located within the course, join in the fun. Eleven 'entertainment centres' and more than 100 live bands and performers line the route.

### Blessing of the Animals

*Information 1-213 628 7164. Pueblo de Los Angeles Historical Monument, Olvera Street, Downtown LA.* **Date** Easter Sat.
A bedecked cow leads a procession of farm animals and local pets to be sprinkled with holy water by the Cardinal of Los Angeles in a tradition dating from the fourth century.

### Thai New Year (Songran Festival)

*Information 1-818 785 9552. Wat Thai of Los Angeles, 8225 Coldwater Canyon Avenue, at Roscoe Boulevard, North Hollywood.* **Date** mid Apr.
Visit this Buddhist temple to pay homage to the orange-robed monks, watch Thai boxing, classical dance and the Miss Songkran beauty contest and eat authentic delicacies.

### California Poppy Festival

*Information 1-805 723 6077. Lancaster City Park, 43011 10th Street West, between Avenues L & K-8, Lancaster.* **Date** second weekend in Apr.
Yes, it's just like the Wizard of Oz, especially after a rainy winter. Take advantage of helicopter rides and free shuttles from the park to the California Poppy Preserve. Call the Wildflower Hotline (1-818 768 3533) for details of what's blooming where.

### Fiesta Broadway/Cinco de Mayo

*Information 1-310 914 0015. Broadway, Hill & Spring Streets, Downtown LA.* **Date** last Sun in Apr.
Billed as 'the nation's largest Cinco de Mayo celebration', but it's a bit commercial. Ignore the corporate sponsors and zero in on a feast of Latino music.

### Topanga Banjo Fiddle Contest, Dance & Folk Arts Festival

*Information 1-818 382 4819. Paramount Ranch, entrance on Cornell Road, Agoura.* **Date** mid May.
A bluegrass blowout, with old-time, railroad and hobo music, cowboy poetry and traditional dance demonstrations. Bring your instrument and a blanket.

### Annual Cajun & Zydeco Festival

*Information 1-310 427 3713. Rainbow Lagoon Park, behind Long Beach Convention Center, East Shoreline Drive, Long Beach.* **Tickets** $20 on gate; $15 in advance. **Date** first weekend in June.
Louisiana exports its best for a weekend of music, food and dancing. Work off the calories at this taste of LA in LA.

---

# Events outside Los Angeles

### Riverside County Fair & National Date Festival

*Information 1-619 863 8236. Riverside County Fairgrounds, at US111, Indio, Riverside County.* **Date** Feb.
This 10-day event presents a uniquely Middle Eastern take on the traditional American county fair. In addition to agricultural exhibits, expect daily camel and ostrich races, date milkshakes and weirdly costumed desert denizens.

### Temecula Balloon & Wine Festival

*Information 1-909 676 6713. Lake Skinner, 37701 Warren Road, Temecula, Riverside County.* **Tickets** $12 Sat; $10 Sun. **Date** last weekend in Apr.
Antique cars, wine-tasting and live jazz and rock – but the real reason to visit the rolling hills of this wine district is to witness the mass ascension of more than 60 hot-air balloons. Get up early to catch this breathtaking 7am sight.

### Ramona Pageant

*Information 1-800 645 4465/1-909 658 3111. Ramona Bowl, 27400 Ramona Bowl Road, Hemet, Riverside County.* **Date** late Apr-early May.
With a cast of 350, this hokey/wonderful spectacular is based on an early California inter-racial love story. Set in a stunning mountain amphitheatre, the show features mariachis, dancing, native American rituals and charging horsemen. A then-unknown Raquel Welch once took part.

### Pageant of the Masters & Sawdust Festival

*Information 1-714 494 1145. Irvine Bowl, 650 Laguna Canyon Road, Laguna Beach, Orange County.*

**Tickets** $15-$40. **Date** July-Aug.
Famous works of art are recreated with astonishing accuracy with Laguna locals posing in 'tableaux vivant', presented nightly in the beautiful Irvine Bowl. Spend the day at the Sawdust Festival's hundreds of arts and crafts displays.

### US Open of Surfing & 'Surf City' Beach Exposition

*Information 1-714 443 6187. Huntington Beach Pier, Main Street, at PCH, Huntington Beach, Orange County.* **Date** first week in Aug.
Part of the ASP World Championships tour, this six-day event draws many internationally top-rated surfers, as well as 400 other competitors. Enthusiasts cheer them on at summer's biggest beach party.

### Southern California Indian Center Pow Wow

*Information 1-714 530 0225. Orange County Fairgrounds, 88 Fair Drive, between Fairview & Arlington Roads, Costa Mesa, Orange County.* **Date** early Aug.
The biggest Native American event of the year features a weekend of drumming and dancing, foods and exhibits from American Indians across the States.

### The Glory of Christmas

*Information 1-714 971 4000) Crystal Cathedral, 12141 Lewis Street, at Chapman Avenue, Garden Grove, Orange County.* **Date** late Nov-Dec.
Hollywood values make this spectacular 'living nativity' a must. Set in the famed glass-and-steel church with a cast of hundreds, a breathtaking starlit sky and live camels. At the ministry known for originating drive-in churches.

# Summer

Summer is the season for outdoor concerts, with the LA Philharmonic sharing the Hollywood Bowl, with rock and jazz acts (*see chapter* **Music**) and a series of noon and evening performances of everything from opera to tap dance in California Plaza in Downtown LA (information 1-213 687 2159).

## The Will Geer Theatricum Botanicum

*Information 1-310 455 3723. 1419 North Topanga Canyon Boulevard, at Cheney Drive, Topanga.* **Tickets** $15. **Date** mid June-mid Sept.
Shakespeare and other theatrical classics presented on a wooded hillside in LA's last remaining hippy stronghold.

## The Last Remaining Seats

*Information (1-213 623 2489). Broadway cinemas, Downtown LA.* **Date** four Wednesdays in June.
Festival of old films – both silents and talkies – with live musical accompaniment in grand old movie palaces reopened especially for this event.

## Gay & Lesbian Pride Celebration

*Information 1-213 860 0701. Festival in West Hollywood Park, 647 North San Vicente Boulevard, at Roberston Boulevard, West Hollywood. Parade goes along Santa Monica Boulevard, from Crescent Heights Boulevard to the park.* **Tickets** $10. **Date** late June.
Weekend of free concerts, Sunday parade and two-day festival. Politics and pride, flamboyance and freedom. Fun.

## Independence Day

*LA Fire Department public information 1-213 881 2411.* **Date** 4 July.
Americana, LA-style. Picnic, barbecue, go to the beach, take in a parade and watch some fireworks. Check papers for some 50 fireworks displays, from the Rose Bowl to Dodger Stadium, Marina del Rey to Magic Mountain, as well as oddities such as the Mr & Ms Muscle Beach Venice Physique Contest.

## Santa Monica Pier Twilight Dance Series

*Information 1-310 458 8900. Santa Monica Pier, at Colorado & Ocean Avenues, Santa Monica.* **Date** 7.30-9.30pm Thur; July-Labor Day.
Santa Monica Pier rocks with stellar performers, from blues to regional, world beat to straight-out rock 'n' roll.

## Brazilian Summer Festival

*Information 1-818 566 1111. John Anson Ford Theater, 2580 Cahuenga Boulevard, at Vine Street, Hollywood.* **Tickets** $15. **Date** July.
LA's vibrant Brazilian community makes this a happening like no other, with music, arts, cuisine and capoeira.

## Outfest: The Los Angeles Gay & Lesbian Film Festival

*Information 1-213 951 1247.* **Date** July.
Just like it sounds. Very high quality.

## Lotus Festival

*Information 1-213 485 1310. Echo Park Lake, Glendale Boulevard, at Bellevue Avenue, Echo Park.* **Date** second weekend in July.
With the largest lotus bed in the States, this festival celebrates Asia and the Pacific Islands with dance, music, martial arts, exotic plants and, best of all, dragon boat races.

## Festival of the Chariots

*Information 1-310 836 2676. Venice Beach Pavilion, Venice.* **Date** first Sun in Aug.

The best thing this side of Benares. See Krishna transported from Santa Monica Pier to Venice on three ornate 60ft chariots. Booths promote Indian culture and there's also rock'n'roll, dancing and food.

## LA à la Carte

*Information 1-714 753 1551. North-east corner of Wilshire & Veteran Boulevards, Westwood.* **Tickets** $8 adults; $3 children. **Date** early Aug.
LA's premier food event: a weekend of tastings from restaurants and musical entertainment on three stages, including top acts in the league of James Brown and Los Lobos.

## Nisei Week Japanese Festival

*Information 1-213 687 7193. Little Tokyo, Downtown LA.* **Date** Aug.
Martial arts, the tea ceremony, Taiko drumming, Japanese arts, ondo dancing, a parade and lots more in this eight-day event.

## LA African Marketplace & Cultural Faire

*Information 1-213 734 1164. Rancho Cienega Park, 5001 Rodeo Road, at Martin Luther King Jr Boulevard, Baldwin Hills.* **Date** last three weekends in Aug.
A dusty African village environment where over 350 merchants show their wares and six stages provide non-stop entertainment. African, Afro-influenced Caribbean, roots and contemporary African-American music, dance and food.

# Autumn

## Leimert Park Jazz Festival

*Information 1-213 960 1625. Leimert Park Village, 43rd Place & Crenshaw Boulevard, Crenshaw.* **Date** late Aug-early Sept.
Top jazz artists converge on a neighbourhood that is the creative centre of LA's African-American community.

## Day of the Drum/Simon Rodia Watts Towers Jazz Festival

*Information 1-213 485 1795. 1727 East 107th Street, between Willowbrook Avenue & 103rd Street, Watts.* **Date** late Sept.
These back-to-back events feature international drumming, jazz, gospel and R&B. Good eats, arts and a great excuse to visit one of LA's quirkiest and most beautiful landmarks.

## AFI International Film Festival

*Information (1-213 856 7707). Various cinemas in Santa Monica & Hollywood.* **Date** mid Oct.
Over 90 films are presented in this two-week event.

## Hallowe'en in West Hollywood

*Information 1-213 848 6547. Santa Monica Boulevard, between La Cienega & Robertson Boulevards, West Hollywood.* **Date** 31 Oct.
In a city full of parties, this one is probably LA's most popular spot for costume viewing. Expect food, music and entertainment – the lip-sync competition is a must. Dress up, but be prepared to hike in; parking is a nightmare.

## Day of the Dead (Dia de Los Muertos)

*Information 1-213 881 6444. Self-Help Graphics, 3802 Cesar E Chavez Avenue, at Gage Avenue, East LA.* **Date** 2 Nov; art exhibition until end of month.
This hip organisation of Latino artists brings together art, altars and musical and theatrical groups to celebrate the Mexican tradition of honouring the dead. Skeletons galore.

## Doodah Parade

*Information 1-818 449 3689. Starts at Raymond Avenue & Holly Street, travels west on Colorado Boulevard, ends at Union Street, Old Town Pasadena.* **Date** 2pm, Sun before Thanksgiving.

*Holy Cow! It's the **Blessing of the Animals**. See page 48.*

A spoof version of the Rose Parade with just-plain-folks goofing on whatever is topical. Perennial favourites include the Precision Marching Briefcase Drill Team and the Lounge Lizards, a group of Sinatra-crooning reptiles.

### Hollywood Christmas Parade
*Information 1-213 469 2337. Travels west on Sunset Boulevard, from Van Ness to Highland Avenues, north to Hollywood Boulevard, and east to Bronson Avenue.* **Date** Sun after Thanksgiving.
If Hollywood is a state of mind, its namesake boulevard is a tacky embarrassment. Join one million fans for an evening of over 100 B-level celebrities, bands and equestrian units.

## Winter

### Mariachi Festival
*Information 1-213 485 0709. Intersection of First, Boyle & Pleasant Streets, Boyle Heights.* **Date** mid Nov.
Fun and funky opportunity to experience a wide range of mariachi styles – right beside the doughnut shop that serves these musicians as an employment agency. Great Mexican food.

### Las Posadas
*Information 1-213 628 7164. Olvera Street, Downtown LA.* **Date** 7pm, 16-24 Dec.
A candlelit procession re-enacts Joseph and Mary's search for shelter, finishing with traditional Mexican Christmas music and a piñata party for children.

### Parades of Lights & Marina del Rey Christmas Boat Parade
*Information 1-310 821 7614. Marina del Rey.*
**Date** second Sat in Dec.
While many US citizens decorate their homes for Christmas, Southern California's temperate weather lets locals take this tradition afloat. Check the press for details of ceremonies at marinas from Santa Barbara to San Diego. Probably the best in-town offering is at Marina del Rey.

### Tournament of Roses Rose Parade
*Information 1-818 795 4171. Pasadena; route begins at South Orange Grove Boulevard & Ellis Street, turns east on Colorado Boulevard, turns north on Sierra Madre Boulevard, ends at Paloma Street.* **Date** 8.05am, 1 Jan.
What is supposedly the world's largest parade, started as a marketing ploy to show off California's great climate. It still works.

### Whale watching
*Information American Cetacean Society (1-310 548 6279); Cabrillo Marine Aquarium (1-310 548 7562).* **Date** mid Dec-mid Mar, best in Jan.
Each winter, about 12,000 grey whales migrate from Alaska to Baja California to breed. This amazing spectacle can be observed on boat trips launched from harbours along the coast. Check the press for boat charter ads or call the numbers above.

### Chinese New Year
*Information 1-213 617 039). Chinatown; parade along North Broadway, between Cesar E Chavez Avenue & Bernard Street.* **Date** Sat before President's Day.
A street fair, races and, best of all, the Golden Dragon parade. In true LA style, you will see every ethnic mix participating.

### Bob Marley Day
*Information 1-310 436 3661. Long Beach Convention Center, East Shoreline Drive, Long Beach.* **Date** mid Feb.
Jamaica exports its top acts – from Burning Spear and Judy Mowatt to Sugar Minott – for this three-day festival, and LA's rastas and reggae enthusiasts show up in force.

### National Hot Rod Association Chief Winternationals
*Information 1-818 914 4761. Pomona Raceway, 2780 Fairplex Avenue, at Arrow Highway, Pomona.* **Tickets** $15-$58. **Date** first weekend in Feb.
The sport of drag racing began over 40 years ago along the back roads and dry lake beds of Southern California. Catch its chrome and flash at this four-day event. Bring earplugs.

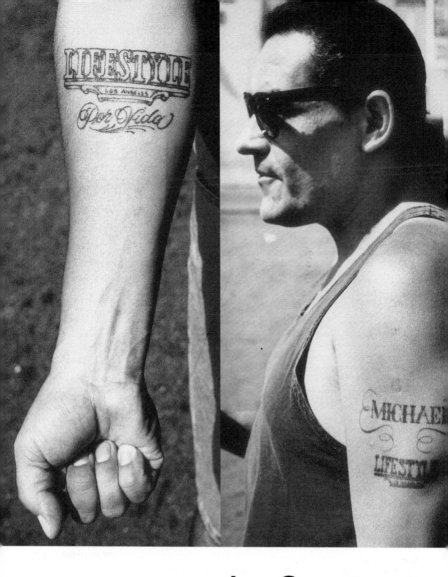

# In Context

| | | | | |
|---|---|---|---|---|
| Geography | **52** | Latino LA | **72** |
| History | **56** | Architecture | **75** |
| LA Today | **66** | Car City | **79** |
| | | Celebrity LA | **82** |

# Geography

**LA's earthquakes are only one ingredient in a geographical molotov cocktail that flares regularly and could combust at any time.**

*What a difference a day makes – the after-effects of an LA mudslide.*

Built on land reclaimed from the desert, blasted by the arid Santa Ana winds and eroded by a cycle of fire and flood, LA's ecology is uniquely precarious, and coping with natural disasters is high on the list of urban survival techniques. In addition to the best-known hazard of earthquakes, the area is also subject to bushfires, floods and mudslides.

An earthquake is a profoundly unsettling experience. In the lower ranges of the Richter scale, a seismic tremor is little more than a intrusive vibration, like a passing underground train where no underground actually exists. At higher magnitudes, the sway is not unlike an express crossing the points at high speed. Objects are jolted off shelves, pictures drop from the wall and furniture 'walks'. A major event, like the 6.7 Northridge quake of 1993, is all but indescribable, an Olympian hammer blow followed by a shaking so violent that you start to doubt that the building you are in is going to survive the stress, and hiding under a table or standing in a doorway seems close to fatuous. The 20 or so seconds of quake duration feels like a lifetime and, unless you're terminally blasé or heavily drugged, the imminent possibility of death swamps the consciousness.

The aftermath is as surreal as the quake is violent. The dust settles to a science fiction chorus as every car alarm in the city goes off simultaneously. Flashes light the sky as downed power lines short out. Then the dogs start barking. Where cats take cover, dogs launch into vocal protest. The next question is whether the fat lady has truly finished her aria or is merely clearing her metaphorical throat. Will an aftershock of equal force drop the last straw on structures already weakened by the initial jolt? To paraphrase Tennessee Ernie Ford's 'Sixteen Tons', if the first one don't get you, the second (or third) one will. It's then that Angelenos anxiously watch the clock, remembering the combination of statistics and folklore that claims that the odds against a bad aftershock diminish by 25% for every hour that passes.

Concern also switches to what might be happening elsewhere. Earthquakes and the damage caused are totally unpredictable. One block may be totalled while the next remains unscathed. One neighbourhood may make it through with nothing more than a high pulse rate and broken knick-knacks, but another can burn like Nero's Rome. If the power is on and the cable still up, radio or TV are supposedly the answer but invariably prove little or no help. Walter Cronkite is not around to aid and comfort. In a hastily heated up newsroom, the number two sports guy and a cub reporter, both more scared than you are, attempt to put out emergency coverage with absolutely no information except what they can see from the studio roof or obtain by phone from viewers. Since all the LA TV stations now boast their own seismograph, the media response is largely reduced to anecdotal chat and action replays of a quivering pen. It takes at least a couple of hours for the reassuring Expert From Cal Tech to start disseminating some hard facts.

Cal Tech is the world's leading seismology study centre, but even its experts are quick to

# Earthquake survival

Earthquakes can happen at any time in Los Angeles and the surrounding areas, though recently the major temblors (as they're called locally) have taken place very early in the morning. Should you experience large jolts or unusual ground movement, it is likely to be an earthquake. In the event of a major earthquake (5 and above on the Richter Scale), the worst activity is generally at the beginning. Movement will get less intense as time goes on but will continue in a stream of aftershocks for several days. In the event of a major earthquake, power lines are invariably ruptured. It is therefore prudent to carry a small torch with you at all times.

● Whether you're inside or out, get away from anything which may collapse or break.

● If you're inside, stand under a solid door frame or sturdy piece of furniture, for example a large table or desk. Hold onto it firmly until all movement has subsided.

● If you're outside, try to stand away from any structure which may collapse (notably trees, bridges and power lines).

● If you're in a car, pull over and stop where it is safe. Avoid flyovers and power lines.

● After the earthquake, think before you act. Do not use lighters or candles or light a cigarette. Do not turn on lights or use any electrical appliance, including the telephone. Major earthquakes often rupture gas, electricity and water lines.

## American Red Cross LA

*2700 Wilshire Boulevard, Los Angeles, CA 90057 (1-213 739 5200).*

The Red Cross helps co-ordinate disaster relief operations and can also send out information packs on earthquake preparedness (write to Disaster Services at the above address, enclosing postage). They recommend that non-nationals caught in a quake phone a friend or relative at home as soon as they can, to avoid the phonelines being clogged up with enquiries (outgoing calls are more likely to get through than incoming ones).

explain that earthquakes are very big and human beings are very small. We still know next to nothing about how quakes really work, and what we do know is constantly being revised. Cal Tech will happily explain the rudiments of plate tectonics and how the continents basically float on the planet's semi liquid core. They will pinpoint the earthquake's epicentre and explain how shockwaves radiate from that point causing diminishing degrees of damage as they move outward. They cite, however, the 8.0+ quake in Chile in the summer of 1995 that has thrown much previous earthquake thinking into serious disarray. A quake of that size would, in theory, total a city like LA, but, in fact, the Chilean quake did no surface damage whatsoever, since its epicentre was buried deep beneath the Andes. At this point the experts' faces take on a 'go figure' expression.

Lately, though, the Cal Tech boffins have actually delivered a couple of pieces of possible good news. Due to the local plate structure, the quakes in Southern California have a side-to-side shaking motion as opposed to the vertical bouncing experienced on the other side of the seismic 'ring of fire' in Japan. In January 1995, a 7.2 jolt all but flattened the historic Japanese city of Kobe, but, because of this difference in motion, in a quake of the same magnitude, Los Angeles might escape similar devastation. For the same reason, LA is also spared the tsunami-like tidal waves that follow many Japanese tremors.

For as long as most Angelenos can remember, the fear has been of the Big One, the unthinkable moment when the San Andreas Fault, which runs up the centre of California, finally shrugs off a century of accumulated stress in a 8.5 or even a 9.0 grand slam that takes out the entire LA Basin in a catastrophe of multi-megaton proportions. But current (although maybe wishful) thinking claims that the Big One may never happen, and the fact that LA stands on a veritable mosaic of smaller branching faults could cushion the worst if the San Andreas decided suddenly to do the cool jerk.

If Los Angeles only had earthquakes it would be bad enough, but, from around the end of June to when the rains come in December or January, the outlying suburbs are also hazardously flammable. In a tinder-dry, semi-desert, lightning-sparked brushfires are nature's highly efficient method of thinning the undergrowth. Conflagration is only to be expected, but no-one ever seems to expect it. Many of the homes in the dry canyons and desert margins are wooden buildings from the *Bonanza* school of architecture. Wood shingle roofs that explode with a spark were only recently outlawed. Many suburban areas, being unwilling to pay the extra taxes, also resist incorporating into the city and lack local fire departments or adequate emergency water. In the Malibu canyon fires of 1994, most of the hydrants didn't work because of lack of maintenance.

Those still fighting the class war can take comfort that brushfire is something that mainly happens to the rich – they're the ones who can afford the vulnerable but desirable locations – and can

relish the TV images of the inferno bearing down on the estates of movie moguls or software tycoons. On the other hand, in LA, tossing cigarettes out of the car window is antisocial, heavily jumped on by the LAPD, and subject to severe penalties. What starts as an unextinguished Marlboro can finish up as ten thousand acres of blackened moonscape – and it doesn't always belong to Demi Moore.

Floods are only a problem for one month in the year. Sometime between Boxing Day and the end of March, the rains come in a grand and biblical manner, pushing the LA storm drain system far beyond its limits, and, as in the winter of '94-'95, causing extensive flooding. The original design of the LA storm drains was OK, one of the things they actually got right, but, with the permanent budget crisis, the system is neither maintained nor improved. Through the summer and fall, the network of drains, culverts, concrete channels and flow-off areas like the Sepulveda Basin – where parkland can be converted into a temporary lake in a crisis – become clogged with trash, old bicycles and even abandoned Toyotas. (And who can forget the 1954 movie *Them*, in which giant radioactive ants made their nests in the storm sewers?)

These spring rains also wash hundreds of tons of assorted toxins straight into the Santa Monica Bay, decimating marine life and causing surfers problems with their immune systems.

And then we have the mudslides. When heavy rain falls on bone-dry, sandy soil, it becomes dirty blancmange, and whole hillsides flow into new hydrolastic contour patterns, taking out any roads or buildings that happen to be in the way. As with fire, the mudslide problem is exacerbated by greed and poor planning. Many of the places worst hit are the skim developments that were used for moving money around during the Reagan-era Savings And Loan rip-offs. It's in those security-gated monuments to voodoo economics, with names like Paradise Hills and Ocean Heights, that luxury homes all too frequently find themselves breaching the sandbags and slithering majestically into the valley below. Often a swimming pool is involved, which adds a few hundred thousand more gallons of water to the general mess.

The obvious question has to be: who was stupid enough to erect a city on the site of Los Angeles anyway? Aren't the man-made menaces bad enough – armed psychotics in freeway gridlock, car-culture air quality and double the national average of kids with asthma? Why does anyone in their right mind live in a place that floods and burns and where the very ground gets up and shimmies like a stripper at the Casbah Room? The answer is, of course, no-one really plans a city. It's an organic thing that simply happens for a multitude of reasons. That LA exists at all in all its fatuous overcrowded glory has to be a testament to the capacity of human beings to live in the moment and avoid all thoughts of the future. Isn't that right, Mr Rotten?

# History

*From its origins as an Indian village to the mega-sprawl of today, LA has been moulded by a sometimes explosive mix of job-hungry immigrants, enterprising industrialists and real-estate speculators.*

## PRE-1888: MISSIONS & COW TOWNS

Perhaps it shouldn't be surprising, given Los Angeles' more recent history, that human settlement here began with a series of Native American single-family suburbs scattered across the landscape in seemingly haphazard fashion. Prior to the arrival of Spanish colonists in the latter part of the eighteenth century, what is now metropolitan LA was populated by some 30,000 Native Americans. But they were not farmers – they relied on hunting and native plants for food – and, unlike the Iroquois and other tribes in North America, had not organised into strong political confederations. Instead, they lived in small settlements surrounding the area's few rivers, each group adopting a separate identity (the names most of them are known by today – Gabrieleno, Juaneno, Luisenos and so on – were given them by the Spanish).

The Spanish arrived in 1769 and established a string of Franciscan missions along the Californian coast (the first at San Diego), backed by military muscle. The San Gabriel Mission was founded in 1771, marking the first Spanish foray into the Los Angeles area. The supposed purpose of the missions was to spread the Christian faith and the early Franciscan missionaries, especially their leader Father Junipéro Serra, have been glorified over the centuries. In fact, mission life was feudal and even brutal, especially for the reluctant Native American converts. They were rounded up from their small settlements and virtually enslaved by the Franciscans, and thousands died – a problem that required the missions to expand deep into the countryside in search of more converts.

The history of Los Angeles as a city dates back to 1781 – the same year that the British surrendered to George Washington in Virginia, ending the American War of Independence – when the Spaniards decided they needed a settlement, or pueblo, in Southern California to serve as a way-station for the military. A site was selected nine miles east of the San Gabriel mission, where the Los Angeles River widened from a narrows. California's military governor, Felipe De Neve, laid out a plaza 275ft by 180ft, with lots around it, each with a 55ft-wide frontage on the plaza. He commissioned his aides to recruit 24 settlers and their families from Sonora, and on 18 August 1781, after a forced march

of 100 days through desert heat, what remained of these settlers arrived at the plaza: 12 men, 11 women and 21 children. They were immediately quarantined because of smallpox. What is left of the plaza can be viewed at El Pueblo de Los Angeles Historical Monument (more commonly known as Olvera Street), a 44-acre historical area in downtown LA, bounded by Alameda, Arcadia, Spring and Macy Streets. As many writers have observed, El Pueblo de Nuestra Senora la Reina de Los Angeles began as it has always grown – not with a hardy band of motivated settlers, but with a real estate agent looking for customers.

The new settlement remained a dusty cow town for decades – in 1800 the population was 315 people and 12,500 cows. But other missions were added in what would become the Los Angeles area, including San Buenaventura, San Fernando and San Juan Capistrano (for more information on the Spanish Missions and how to visit them, *see chapter* **Trips out of Town**).

After Mexico declared itself independent and annexed California in 1822, Spanish-born priests were ordered out of California, the mission system broke down and powerful local families – eager to exploit the possibilities of mission land – received dozens of large land grants from the Mexican government. Most of these 'ranchos', typically several thousand acres in size, were recognised as valid claims of title when California entered the United States in 1850. Many of them remained intact into the twentieth century – one of many factors that allowed large-scale, mass-production land development to occur in Los Angeles.

The Americans had been informally colonising LA throughout the era of Mexican rule, as opportunists arrived in town, married into prominent 'Spanish' families, and called themselves 'Don Otto' or 'Don Bill'. The actual transfer of the cow town into US hands occurred during the forcible annexation of California, triggering the Mexican-American war of June 1846. A couple of months later, on 13 August, Commodore RF Stockton landed at San Pedro with 500 marines and started his march to the pueblo. With political support from the 'Dons', he captured the settlement without firing a shot. The US-Mexican treaty of 1848 confirmed US dominion over California and in 1850 it officially became the 31st State of the Union.

*Graumans (now **Mann's**) Chinese Theater, site of countless glittering, star-studded nights.*

Los Angeles grew steadily but unspectacularly for the next 20 years, gaining a reputation as a wild-west town of Dodge City proportions and typical Western crudity (water, always in shortage, was delivered by open ditch, for example). But with the completion of the transcontinental railroad to San Francisco in 1868, expectations of a boom rose. The 1872 publication of Helen Hunt Jackson's novel *Ramona*, which romanticised rancho life at the expense of historical accuracy, sparked a period of national publicity and interest in Southern California.

In 1886, the transcontinental railroad from St Louis to Los Angeles was completed, bringing with it the long-expected – but short-lived – boom. A price war broke out among the railroads, and the cost of a one-way ticket to LA dropped from $125 to $1. In 1887, Southern Pacific Railroad transported 120,000 people to Los Angeles, then a city of about 10,000 residents. The result was LA's first real-estate boom, with more than 100 communities subdivided in a four-year period.

Paper fortunes were made overnight – and then lost when the boom shrivelled in 1889. 'I had half a million dollars wiped out in the crash,' one fictional character reported in a novel. 'And what's worse, $500 of it was cash.' But the population had grown dramatically, in part because many immigrants could not afford to leave. Despite the crash, the boom of the 1880s had permanently transformed Los Angeles from a cow town into a fast-growing hustlers' paradise.

## 1888-1929: BOOMS AND BUSTS

After the boom of the 1880s, the land barons and real estate operators who came to dominate Los Angeles' growth were determined to build a more solid basis for expansion. Forming the Los Angeles Chamber of Commerce in 1888, they took the unprecedented step of embarking on a nationwide campaign, focused on the Midwest, to attract new immigrants. It was this campaign that led the journalist Morrow Mayo, writing in the 1930s, to conclude that Los Angeles is not a city but 'a commodity; something to be advertised and sold to the people of the United States like automobiles, cigarettes and mouth washes'.

The Chamber of Commerce began sending speakers, advertisements and brochures to the Midwest; 1902 saw the launch of the Rose Bowl (a college football game held on New Year's Day) and the preceding Rose Parade (in which flower-covered floats parade through Pasadena), as a promotion for LA's sunny climate. It was not long before the advertisements had the desired effect and, as commodity prices rose in the first decade

*Long before the freeways, Angelenos loved to cruise up the (muddy) coast.*

of the new century, thousands of Midwestern farmers sold out and a new boom ensued.

Encouraged by the boom, the city's land barons successfully undertook one of the most audacious and duplicitous schemes ever devised to ensure a city's future greatness. In 1904, a former mayor of Los Angeles named Fred Eaton went to the Owens Valley – a high-desert region 230 miles north of Los Angeles – claiming that he was working on a dam project for the federal government, and began buying land along the Owens River. Once the land was purchased, Eaton said the federal project was dead and revealed his true purpose: to divert the Owens River through an aqueduct to Los Angeles.

Whipped into a frenzy by trumped-up fears of a drought, LA voters approved a bond issue in 1905 to build an aqueduct from the Owens Valley to the city. LA had enough water to serve the population at the time, but not enough to grow. As William Mulholland, the city's water engineer, put it at the time: 'If we don't get it, we won't need it'. Mulholland, a self-taught Irish immigrant, then accomplished one of the great engineering feats in US history. Eighty years after its completion, his 230-mile aqueduct still operates, without electrical power, entirely on a gravity system. 'There it is,' Mulholland told the people of Los Angeles when the floodway opened in 1913. 'Take it.'

The aqueduct didn't come to Los Angeles proper, however. Instead, it went only as far as the San Fernando Valley, an adjacent farming region. In the last – and most masterful – part of the aqueduct scam, Los Angeles' land barons had secretly bought the valley cheaply, annexed it to the city, and then splashed Owens Valley water onto it for irrigation, greatly increasing its value. Today, the San Fernando Valley, population 1.3 million, is the prototypical US suburb, and its people regularly chafe under the LA city controls that brought water to their valley in the first place.

With the water in place, Los Angeles boomed in the Teens and Twenties as did no other US city – partly on the strength of real-estate speculation, and partly on the rise of three new industries: petroleum, aircraft and movies.

With little natural wood and almost no coal, isolated Los Angeles had always had a fuel crisis almost as severe as its water crisis. The discovery of oil throughout metropolitan Los Angeles between 1900 and 1925 changed all that. Oil fields were discovered around the La Brea Tar Pits and in Huntington Beach and Santa Fe Springs. The result was a plentiful supply of oil that enriched the region and helped to fuel the city's growing love affair with the car.

More dispersed than any other US city, Los Angeles took to the car more readily than anywhere except Detroit. Soon the city had its own thriving oil, automobile and tyre industries, each with their own monuments. In 1928, Adolph Schleicher, president of Samson Tire & Rubber Co, constructed an $8 million tyre plant modelled after a royal palace once built by the king of Assyria. The plant (at 5675 Telegraph Road, City of Commerce) has recently been reborn as a retailing mecca known as The Citadel.

Movies and aircraft came to LA during the Teens, and for the same reasons: the area's temperate weather, low rainfall and cheap land provided the wide-open spaces that both needed to operate. Donald Douglas founded his aircraft company (a predecessor to McDonnell-Douglas) at Clover Field in Santa Monica – now the Santa Monica Municipal Airport – in 1921, while the Lockheed Brothers started their company in Santa Barbara in 1914 before moving it to LA. Jack Northrop, who had worked with both Douglas and the Lockheeds, started his own company in Burbank in 1928. All three firms later formed the foundation of the US's 'military-industrial' complex.

Filming began in Los Angeles around 1910, and moved to Hollywood when the Blondeau Tavern at Gower Street and Sunset Boulevard was turned into a movie studio overnight in 1911. At the time, Hollywood was being marketed as a pious and sedate suburb of large homes, and the intrusion of the film industry was resented. The movie industry was never really geographically centred on Hollywood, however; Culver City and Burbank, which both have studios, have equally strong claims as the centre of film land. Nevertheless, Hollywood became the financial and social centre of the industry, growing from a population of 4,000 in 1910 to 30,000 in 1920 to 235,000 in 1930, and the wealth of the period is still visible today in the magnificent commercial architecture along Hollywood Boulevard between Cahuenga and Highland Avenues. For more on the history of the film industry, *see chapter* **Film**.

In the 1920s, when LA's population doubled, the city was a kind of 'national suburb' where the middle class sought refuge from the teeming immigrant classes evident in other large cities. During this period, civic leaders worked hard to build the edifices and institutions they thought a big city should have, including the Biltmore Hotel and the adjacent

# O come all ye faithful

Los Angeles is known for its long history of kooks, zealots and unconventional religious leaders, but probably none has ever matched the charisma, the public relations skill or the sheer audacity of Aimee Semple McPherson.

Like so many prominent Angelenos of the 1920s (including her contemporary, the oil-stock swindler CC Julian), Aimee was Canadian. Born in 1890, she married young, worked in China as a missionary and married again when her husband died of typhoid. By 1918, she had devised her own evangelical religion known as the Foursquare Gospel. She divorced her husband and travelled with her two children and her mother to LA, with the slogan 'Jesus Is Coming Soon – Get Ready' emblazoned on the side of her touring car.

Within five years, McPherson had developed such a following that she was able to build the 4,300-seat Angelus Temple in Echo Park. Calling herself Sister Aimee, she prefigured such modern-day media preachers as Jerry Falwell and Pat Robertson by purchasing her own radio station and publishing house, the better to reach her ministry. She made a connection with her audiences by using comic props; for example, she sometimes dressed as a USC football player 'carrying the ball' for Christ.

In 1926, McPherson reached the height of her fame when she disappeared off the beach near Ocean Park. A massive search did not find her and she was presumed drowned. After a memorial service at Angelus Temple some four weeks later, she resurfaced, claiming she had

been kidnapped and had escaped from her captors in Mexico. In all likelihood, she had spent the time shacking up in Carmel with a married man who worked at her radio station. Thereafter, she became the subject of public ridicule, though her faithful followers stuck with her. Like so many others who have migrated to Southern California and found their fortune here, she knew how to sell.

Los Angeles Central Library, Los Angeles City Hall, the University of Southern California and adjacent Exposition Park, and Los Angeles Coliseum.

Los Angeles also became the financial capital of the West Coast during the 1920s with the creation of the Los Angeles (now Pacific) Stock Exchange. The 'Wall Street of the West' was centred on Spring Street, between Third and Eighth Streets, where many of the original buildings remain today. The early movie palaces were built not in Hollywood but downtown on Broadway, adjacent to Spring Street. Most of these theatres are still in operation today, including the Million Dollar Theater (307 South Broadway), which dates from 1918 and now shows Spanish-language films.

However, this same process of making LA the great 'white' city marginalised the minority groups that had always been a part of life here. The Mexican and Mexican-American population, which was growing rapidly to provide labourers for the expanding city, was pushed out of downtown into what is now the East LA barrio. African-Americans, who had previously lived all over the city, became confined to an area south of downtown straddling Central Avenue, which became known as South Central. Both these developments laid the foundation for later social unrest.

Still, Los Angeles in the 1920s had an irrepressible energy that even its critics loved. The boom and the arrival of so many newcomers created a rootlessness that manifested itself in a thousand different ways, many of which provided the seeds for the city's later kooky reputation. Those in need of companionship were drawn to the city's many cafeterias (invented in LA), which served as incubators of random social activity. Those in need of a restored faith had (and still have) their choice of any number of high-profile faith-healers, such as Aimee Semple McPherson (*see box* **O come all ye faithful**). And those with a little cash searching for a quick profit were drawn to the tantalising claims of local oil companies in search of investors.

Indeed, nothing captures a sense of the primal energy of Los Angeles during the 1920s as well as stories from the oil business. With a steady supply of gushers spouting in the suburbs (often in subdivided residential neighbourhoods), oil promoters had a ready-made promotional device with which to attract investors. With a stream of equity-rich farm refugees from the Midwest, they also had a ready-made pool of gullible investors. The promoters took out newspaper ads, held weekend barbecues at the gushers and used other strong-arm tactics to attract investment.

The most skilled oil promoter was a Canadian immigrant named CC Julian, who attracted millions of dollars to his oil company with a string of daily newspaper ads that had the narrative drive of a continuing soap opera. When it became clear that Julian couldn't deliver on his investment promises, he was elbowed out of his own firm by an array of other swindlers who continued the scam and turned it into the longest-running scandal of the 1920s. By the time it was all over, Julian Petroleum had issued millions of bogus shares and the district attorney had been indicted on a bribery charge. The end came in 1931, when a defrauded investor opened fire in a LA courtroom on a banker who had been involved in the scam. The failed investor had 10 cents in his pocket when he was arrested; the crooked banker had $63,000 in his pocket when he died. The murder epitomised the disreputable state that Los Angeles was in by the time the 1920s' boom ended.

## 1929-1965: GROWING UP

The 1930s was a more sober period for LA, as elsewhere in the US. With the boom over and the Depression settling in, the city grew more slowly, and the new arrivals were very different from their predecessors. Instead of wooing wealthy Midwestern farmers, LA now attracted poor white refugees from the so-called 'Dust Bowl' of Oklahoma and Texas — the 'Okies' made famous in John Steinbeck's novel *The Grapes of Wrath*. These unskilled workers wound up as farm labourers and hangers-on in the margins of society.

Dealing with these newcomers proved difficult for Los Angeles, and was intertwined with another problem – how to handle the equally poor and unskilled Mexican and Mexican-American population. Since farm owners chose to hire the Okies over the Mexicans, LA County was overwhelmed with the cost of public relief and resorted to forcibly 'repatriating' even those Mexicans who were born and raised in Los Angeles.

Meanwhile, the continual arrival of Okies and other 'hobos' caused a nasty public backlash. But it also built a liberal political mood among the have-nots, which culminated in the near-election of reformer and novelist Upton Sinclair as governor of California in 1934. Having moved to Pasadena in the Teens, Sinclair wrote a diatribe called *I, Governor of California, and How I Ended Poverty*. As a result, he founded the End Poverty In California (EPIC) movement and won the Democratic gubernatorial nomination. Only a concerted effort by reactionary political forces (aided by movie-house propaganda from the film industry) defeated Sinclair's bid. Afterwards, he wrote another book, this one called *I, Governor of California, and How I Got Licked*.

The region was also set back by other downturns, such as the 1933 Long Beach earthquake, the first major quake to hit the city since it became populous. But by the mid-1930s, optimism had returned, heralded by the 1932 Olympic Games, which were held at the city's Coliseum. To celebrate the games, Tenth Street was expanded, spruced up, renamed Olympic Boulevard and lined with palm trees – thus setting the fashion for palms in LA. In 1939, the first local freeway was built: the Arroyo Seco Parkway, now the Pasadena Freeway (*see box* **Trolleys, trains & automobiles**). A new aqueduct bringing water from the Hoover Dam along the Colorado River opened in 1941. But the coming of World War II caused the biggest upheaval Los Angeles had seen to that point, and set the stage for the modern metropolis.

Already at the forefront of aviation, Los Angeles industrialised rapidly as it became a major military manufacturing centre and staging ground for the US's fight against Japan in the Pacific Ocean. More than 5,000 new manufacturing plants were built in LA during the war, mostly in outlying locations. New dormitory communities sprang up to accommodate the workers. Many were 'model' communities sponsored by industrialists or the military, and they helped to establish the sprawling pattern of city development that came to characterise LA in the post-war period.

Los Angeles' population quickly diversified, further laying the groundwork for the racial unrest that would later characterise the city. During the war, more than 200,000 African-Americans moved to the city, mostly from Texas and Louisiana, to take advantage of job opportunities. But the South Central ghetto wasn't allowed to expand geographically to accommodate them, resulting in the creation of an overcrowded (though lively) district. In need of labourers, Los Angeles again welcomed the return of Mexicans and Mexican-Americans who had been pushed out a decade before. However, a backlash once again ensued.

After a murder at the Sleepy Lagoon swimming hole in East LA in 1942, the authorities arrested more than 300 Latino youths, putting 23 of them on trial for first-degree murder. Most were minors. In a trial thick with racial epithets, 17 of the defendants were convicted. The convictions were later overturned by an appeal court, but several months later, a mob, including many servicemen, attacked Latinos and others in what became known as the 'Zoot Suit' riots. Thereafter, local newspapers, stoking the fires of prejudice, stopped referring to Latinos as Mexicans and, instead, called them 'zoot suits' or *pachucos*, after the baggy suits the men often wore.

Discrimination against LA's growing Japanese community was even more pronounced. Most

# Noir culture

There's an obvious irony that a city famous for its sunshine should also be the birthplace of noir culture, but for every resident who delights in the climate, beaches and mobility of LA society, you will find another who mutters darkly about the racism, poverty and uniformity that also exist under the blue skies of LA. This polarity of opinion is typical of the city and it's always been that way.

It was the great depression of the 1930s that fully crystalised these two divergent perspectives. With little heavy industry in the area, the hardest hit were the aspirant middle classes who had flocked to the region after World War I. Inspired by the pioneer spirit that had brought their families to America in the first place, they were property developers and oil speculators, small businessmen and insurance agents. Their anger and frustration was the first sign that LA might not be the promised land after all. Soon writers like James M Cain, Raymond Chandler, Nathanael West and Chester Himes began to express this rage in novels that portrayed LA as the antithesis of the American dream. At the same time, a group of painters were also set on debunking the prevailing myth of LA. The Group of Independent Artists drew on European and Mexican influences to attack the romanticism of the landscape painters who had dominated Southern Californian art up to that point.

Equally important to the birth of noir culture was the mass exodus of Central Europeans to LA in the 1930s. When Hitler came to power, virtually the entire German film industry packed up and headed for Hollywood. They brought with them European cynicism and expressionism, the dominant style of the German cinema. It was dark and foreboding, full of shadows and suspicion, and when it was combined with the writing of the likes of Chandler, Cain and Dashiell Hammett, it became film noir. The brilliant *Double Indemnity*, a Chandler adaptation of a Cain story that was directed by the Austrian exile Billy Wilder, is the high point of the noir cycle that resulted in countless movies in the early 1940s. Noir remains a potent force in cinema. *Blade Runner* is perhaps the best example of a recent version of it, while *Chinatown* was a 1970s take on 1940s noir.

The noir tradition in writing has also continued. Writers from Joan Didion to Bret Easton Ellis have portrayed LA as a city without remorse, a place which brings out the worst in those foolish enough to live there, and the crazed crime novels of James Ellroy continue where Chandler left off. Mixing fact with fiction in such books as *The Black Dahlia*, Ellroy has brought noir into the 1990s, and so potent is the genre that it is likely to outlast the 20th century.

*Homeless in downtown LA: the cash-starved city seems to have few solutions.*

Japanese-Americans on the West Coast were interned in camps by the federal government during World War II, no matter how patriotic they were (in a supreme irony, some young men were permitted to leave the internment camps to join the US armed forces). Most Japanese lost their property, then concentrated in the Little Tokyo area of LA just east of City Hall. It took decades for Little Tokyo to return to prosperity, but an infusion of Japanese capital in the 1970s and 1980s has created a thriving district characterised by such institutions as the New Otani Hotel (120 South Los Angeles Street).

Many African-Americans, Latinos and Japanese from Los Angeles were fighting for the United States during World War II. When they returned and continued to suffer from housing discrimination, police brutality and the general LA attitude that they were not 'real Americans', their sense of alienation grew further. But, because LA WAS a highly segregated city, most whites could ignore the race problem – especially after the war, when it reaped the benefits of industrialisation and a new suburban boom began.

The post-war era in LA is often recalled by long-time residents as an idyllic period of prosperity and harmony. In fact, it was an unsettled period in which the city struggled to keep up with the demands of massive growth. Taxes rose in order to build new facilities and heavily over-subscribed schools went on double-sessions, teaching two classes in the same classroom at different times of the day. Most of all, the entire Los Angeles region devoted itself to building things.

Freeway construction, which was stymied by the war, exploded in 1947, when California imposed an additional gas tax to pay for it. Virtually the entire freeway system – truly a marvel of modern engineering – was built between 1950 and 1970. Perhaps its most important long-term effect was to open up vast tracts in outlying areas for urban development, especially in the San Fernando Valley and Orange County, which was linked to LA by Interstate 5, the Golden State Freeway. A seminal event in this suburbanisation was the opening, in 1955, of Disneyland. It was the first theme park ever built and helped to legitimise Orange County as an emerging area.

Other leisure attractions also helped to establish LA as a major city during this period. In 1958, the city achieved 'major-league' status by luring New York's Brooklyn Dodgers baseball team. But, as has so often been the case in LA's history, even this event was marred by the tense relationship between the races. To obtain the team, the city gave the Dodgers a spectacular site in Chavez Ravine, overlooking downtown Los Angeles. Located in a low-income Latino neighbourhood, the site had been earmarked for use as a public housing project, which was never built. However, Dodger Stadium (1000 Elysian Park Avenue, LA) remains one of the finest sports facilities in the US.

As suburbanisation continued in the 1950s and 1960s, more and more neglected areas were left behind as LA prospered. On a hot summer night in 1965, the pent-up frustrations of the black ghetto exploded into one of the first and most destructive of the US's urban riots. The Watts riots began when an African-American man was pulled over on a drink-driving charge; by the time they were over, dozens of people had been killed and hundreds of buildings had been destroyed. For many Angelenos living in their comfortable suburbs, the Watts riots were the first indication that all was not well in their metropolis.

## 1965-1996: THE METROPOLIS

After the Watts riots, Los Angeles began to suffer from an image problem for the first time, and the city struggled for the better part of a decade. National publications proclaimed the end of the California Dream. The Los Angeles Police Department, under a series of hard-line chiefs, continued to treat minority

# Trolleys, trains & automobiles

Los Angeles is perceived today as a town created by freeways, but it would be more accurate to say that the freeways were created by the town. The geography of LA – especially the positions of the mountain ranges and the passes – gives the Los Angeles area a logical pattern of about five transportation corridors. These corridors have been followed in turn by foot, stage, rail and the freeways themselves.

In large part, Los Angeles became decentralised through the efforts of Henry Huntington, who built the Pacific Electric system – the most extensive inter-urban trolley system in the country, stretching from San Bernardino to Santa Monica. PE even built a one-mile subway out of downtown LA; the Subway Terminal Building, where it ended, is still in existence (at 417 South Hill Street, Downtown), and, though the subway tunnel is now closed, its mouth can still be seen at the intersection of Beverly and Glendale Boulevards, near Echo Park. The PE trolley system was gradually dismantled between 1930 and 1961.

When cars became commonly available in the 1910s, Angelenos flocked to them to free themselves from Huntington's monopolistic practices. The roads were soon jammed, and in 1937 the Automobile Club of Southern California proposed 'a network of traffic routes for the exclusive use of motor vehicles, over which there shall be no crossing at grade and along which there shall be no interference from land use activities'. The club's accompanying map 'Showing General Location of Proposed Motorways in the Los Angeles Metropolitan Area' outlined almost exactly the Los Angeles freeway system as it was eventually built.

In time, the freeways came to define LA so completely that they became the object of almost perverse affection. 'Actual participation requires a total surrender,' Joan Didion once wrote about freeway driving in LA, 'a concentration so intense as to seem a kind of narcosis, a rapture-of-the-freeway. The mind goes clean. The rhythm takes over'. In the 1960s, one local magazine profiled a family that supposedly lived in the freeways in a motor home, commuting between launderettes, stores and Dad's job at the Lockheed factory in Burbank, stopping only occasionally at parking lots to sleep. The story kicked up such a fuss that the magazine was forced to disclose that the whole thing had been a hoax. 'What was designed as a satire,' its writer said, 'was too close to the truth'.

LA's newly emerging rail transit system is the result of 70 years of public bickering. The first proposal for 'rapid transit' was put forth in 1925, but was quickly swallowed up in a disagreement among the major railroads about where the main downtown train station should be. After some 15 years of delay, the magnificent Union Terminal (800 North Alameda Street) was built – far away from the bustle of downtown, and only a few years before freeways and air travel made it virtually obsolete.

Local officials unsuccessfully attempted to obtain voter support for a new rail transit system throughout the 1960s and 1970s before success came in 1980. Since then, the Red Line subway has opened downtown, along with the Blue Line to Long Beach and the Green Line, which runs from the Blue Line station in Norwalk to Los Angeles international airport (LAX). A commuter rail system to outlying counties operates out of Union Station. Today, one cent of the 8.25 cent-per-dollar sales tax in LA County goes to public transport.

So far, these rail systems have not been a notable popular success – unlike the city's most famous rail system, the one-block Angels Flight funicular railway that runs up Bunker Hill at Third Street between Hill Street and Grand Avenue. Originally opened in 1904 to connect downtown to a seedy flophouse district atop Bunker Hill, it was removed in 1969 to make way for urban renewal. It reopened in 1996 – connecting a now seedy part of downtown to the gleaming office towers that have been built on top of the hill.

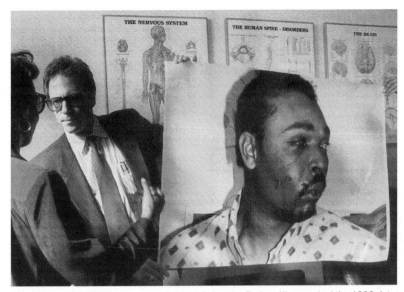

The acquital of LAPD officers accused of brutally beating Rodney King sparked the 1992 riots.

neighbourhoods as if they were occupied territory. As in other US cities, the breakdown of African-American families left black teenagers with few male role models, and they began to form gangs.

In 1966, LA actor Ronald Reagan, with no previous experience in politics, was elected state governor on a law-and-order platform. Three years later, the Charles Manson cult killed actress Sharon Tate and others at a home in Benedict Canyon, disturbing the sense of tranquility even in that high-end Beverly Hills suburb. In 1971, the city suffered its worst earthquake in 38 years, an event that managed not to cause enormous damage only by the fact that it struck at 6am.

Out of this troubled situation, however, emerged a towering political figure capable of healing the city. Tom Bradley was an African-American police captain who had grown up in the segregated world of Central Avenue and later held his own in such white-dominated enclaves as UCLA and the LAPD. In the 1950s, Bradley was assigned to improve relations with beleaguered Jewish shopkeepers in black neighbourhoods, a task he used to create the foundation for a cross-racial political alliance that sustained him for 30 years.

After retiring from the police force, Bradley was elected to the City Council and, with strong support in South Central and the largely Jewish Westside, ran for mayor. He lost in 1969 but ran again in 1973 and won, becoming the first African-American mayor of a predominantly white city (LA is only about 15% black). By moving into the mayor's mansion, he helped desegregate the Hancock Park neighbourhood, which had violently resisted the arrival of Nat King Cole some years before.

A low-key man with a calming personality, Bradley ruled the city for 20 years through the power of persuasion. Especially in the first decade, he was successful. During the 1970s, he sought to heal the racial wounds, while in the early 1980s, he turned his attention to business development, reviving downtown and courting international business; the 1984 Olympics were his greatest triumph. Bradley's efforts also benefited from a huge flow of Japanese capital into Los Angeles real estate in the 1980s.

However, this period proved to be a mere respite from Los Angeles' chronic social and racial tensions. The area became more polarised in the 1970s, as affluent whites grew more conservative and found little in common with the immigrants who were turning LA into the new US melting pot. Long the national suburb, Los Angeles had traditionally drawn its immigrants from the rest of the US. From the 1960s, however, most of its newcomers came from abroad.

The decline of agriculture in Latin America made LA a magnet for immigrants – legal and illegal – from rural Mexico and elsewhere; political strife in Central America also brought in hundreds of thousands. The city's position on the edge of the burgeoning Pacific Rim also attracted people (and capital) from Korea, the Philippines, Taiwan and Hong Kong.

The vast central areas of Los Angeles were re-energised by these newcomers. Tourism, trade and the garment industry boomed, as did the rapidly expanding Koreatown. But, as the neighbourhoods changed, friction grew. Latin American immigrants began crowding into historically black South Central, creating a culture clash with middle- and working-class homeowners. African-Americans, in particular, felt more alienated than ever.

These tensions, fuelled by a declining economy shattered by the Pentagon cutbacks at the end of the Cold War, turned Los Angeles into a social tinderbox at the beginning of the 1990s. The arrest of black motorist Rodney King by four LAPD officers in 1991 (captured on tape by a home-video enthusiast) proved to be the turning point. When a jury acquitted the officers in 1992, it touched off a riot far more widespread and destructive than the Watts riots of 1965. It lasted three days, during which 50 people died and over 1,000 buildings were destroyed by fire and looting. More than 1,000 people were arrested, more of them Latino than black. It was the worst urban riot in US history.

Since then, racial tensions have remained high but the economy has improved and the city regained a sense of optimism. The arrest and trial of football and TV star OJ Simpson in 1995 gripped the city as it did the nation. Simpson, an African-American divorced from a white woman, was accused of killing his ex-wife and another man; his acquittal stunned white residents and reassured black residents, but did not lead to more violence.

Meanwhile, the Latino community has grown dramatically. Latinos are now the dominant racial group in LA County, though they haven't attained strong representation in the political and business leadership. Many older shopping areas have been revived with Latino commerce, including Broadway in downtown LA and Pacific Boulevard in Huntington Park. Asian immigrants are helping with the current economic recovery.

As Los Angeles ponders the twenty-first century, the city faces the challenge of casting aside its history as the national suburb once and for all, and finding ways to harness its multicultural strength in order to remain one of the world's great cities.

# Key events

**1771** Spanish mission established at San Gabriel.
**1781** Pueblo of Los Angeles founded on present site of the Olvera Street Plaza.
**1822** Mexico declares independence from Spain and annexes California, freeing LA from Spanish rule.
**1846** US marines land at San Pedro and take LA pueblo from the Mexican army without a fight.
**1848** US-Mexican treaty confirms US dominion over California.
**1850** California becomes the 31st State of the Union.
**1851** California recognises most large Spanish land grants in the LA area.
**1868** Transcontinental railroad reaches San Francisco, opening up California to the East.
**1886** Transcontinental railroad reaches LA.
**1887** Fare war drops cost of one-way trip from St Louis to LA from $125 to $1.
**1888** City experiences first real estate boom.
**1888** Chamber of Commerce is set up and begins promoting LA in the Midwest.
**1889** City experiences first real estate bust.
**1902** Rose Parade is founded.
**1906** LA announces plans to build aqueduct from Owens Valley.
**1913** Owens Valley aqueduct opens.
**1917** US enters World War I.
**1923** Biltmore Hotel opens in downtown LA.

**1928** District attorney Asa Keyes is indicted on bribery charge after losing case against oil-stock swindlers.
**1929** Stock market crashes; Depression begins.
**1932** LA hosts the Olympics for the first time.
**1933** Long Beach earthquake.
**1934** Upton Sinclair nearly elected Governor of California.
**1937** Auto Club of Southern California proposes freeway system.
**1939** Arroyo Seco Parkway (Pasadena Freeway) opens.
**1941** US enters World War II.
**1943** Zoot Suit riots.
**1955** Disneyland opens in Anaheim.
**1958** Brooklyn Dodgers baseball team moves to LA.
**1965** Watts riots erupt.
**1966** Ronald Reagan elected Governor of California.
**1969** Charles Manson and followers murder Sharon Tate.
**1971** Sylmar earthquake hits.
**1973** Tom Bradley elected mayor of LA.
**1984** LA hosts the Olympics for the second time.
**1990** Defence cutbacks hit LA.
**1991** Rodney King arrested.
**1992** King verdict sparks widespread rioting.
**1994** Northridge earthquake hits.
**1995** OJ Simpson acquitted of murdering wife.

# LA Today

*According to some, the American dream is hurtling towards millennial nightmare – with its epicentre in LA. Paranoia or prophecy, asks Mick Farren.*

The sunsets in Los Angeles come with an irony both fabulous and symbolic. The greater the pollution, the more spectacular the sky. When smog advisories warn those with respiratory problems to stay indoors, the sun can be guaranteed to go down in the kind of purple and magenta glory that prompted Jim Morrison to write the line 'bloody red sun of fantastic LA'.

The brand-new Hollywood home of producer Aaron Spelling, the creator of Dynasty, Beverly Hills 90210 and Melrose Place, looks directly into those crimson sunsets. It sits on the summit of a specially sawn-off mountain, just to the east of Laurel Canyon, a stark modern structure that greatly resembles a grounded concrete UFO. Eventually it will be screened from the public gaze by a grove of trees, but, until poplars and cypress grow to their full height, it stands proudly visible, easily seen by the hookers on Sunset Boulevard, the speedfreak trash on Santa Monica and the homeless around Plummer Park. Apparently Spelling spared no expense in either the construction or furnishing of his eyrie. The joke among those who claim to have visited is that, to find the bathroom, you 'turn left at the second Van Gogh'.

Chez Spelling says it all about modern LA. The gulf between rich and poor may yawn as wide in other cities of the developed world, but few allow it to be so blatantly juxtapositioned. Los Angeles has always been a city of extremes and paradox, but here in the 1990s, they seem flagrantly flaunted. Entertainment mogul Michael Eisner took home a reputed $213 million personal paycheck for the 1995 tax year, while down on Fifth Street (the Nickel), winos stab each other over the five cent deposit on an empty Coke can. As I write this, the lead stories on The Channel 2 News At Eleven are Oscar-nominated Robert Downey Jr being busted in his car with cocaine, heroin and a .357 magnum, and three anonymous Compton crack dealers in a white Monte Carlo engaging in a lethal firefight with the LAPD. The visual for Downey was a clip of him playing a junkie Gen-Xer in the movie *Less Than Zero*. For the Compton shootout, it was the bullet-riddled car being hauled away by a wrecking truck. The message was that bad news can fall on both the humble and the exalted. What is not stressed is that Downey will probably do a hundred hours of community service. One of the Compton gangstas is dead and the others are liable to get ten to life.

Since the start of the '90s, the news in LA has been pretty much all bad. The Cold War ended, and the local defence industry all but closed down. The tax base rapidly eroded and the Southern Californian economy continued to lay flat on its back, not even sharing the sluggish recovery enjoyed by the rest of the country. The unemployment rate hung between 10% and 12%, and, to cap it all, both natural and man-made disasters came so thick and fast that they started to take on an air of almost biblical retribution. Floods were followed by fire and earthquake, and pestilence changed lives and lifestyles. To cap it all, the tragic progression through the Rodney King beating, the riots and the protracted OJ Simpson judicial circus left many of us with the distinct impression that we were living through the end of civilisation as we knew it, and that maybe the Four Horsemen were using the LA basin to warm up before riding onto the actual Apocalypse.

The scary part is that an apparent majority of Angelenos almost seem to accept the currently deplorable state of the city as something they deserve. Okay, so the place is rapidly degenerating into a collection of uneasy enclaves separated along lines of race and purchasing power, sinking into a *Blade Runner* dystopian futurism, cheaply disguised with pink and turquoise paint and sub-tropical vegetation. The air is unbreathable, the water undrinkable, the transit system impenetrable and cabs are an endangered species, but maybe we're the ones responsible. Did we have it idyllic for too long? Maybe it's karmic justice for the folly of the freeways, the endless summer, the flashy irresponsibility and the easy hedonism of decades past. We know the experiment with car culture was a fundamental failure, but we'll still go broke making the payments on that '95 Mustang. Even the religious cults that have always flourished in the Californian sun have turned grimly apocalyptic. Where once new agers muttered their mantras, interfaced with their crystals and channelled ancient Native American shamans, they now anxiously eye the millennium and wonder when the benign aliens are going to arrive and save them from the horror of 2000AD.

Economically, a certain degree of payback is in fact taking place. Through the 1980s, ex-governor and LA homeboy Ronald Reagan made it possible

# LA by numbers

| | |
|---|---|
| Population of Los Angeles (1781) *(First US Census Report)* | **44** |
| Population of LA City (1995) *(Economic Development Corp.)* | **3.7 million** |
| Population of LA County (1995) *(Economic Development Corp.)* | **9.3 million** |
| Area of LA City *(World Almanac)* | **465 miles** |
| Annual per capita income LA County *(LA Economic Development Corp.)* | **$22,376** |
| Average per capita income Beverly Hills | **$84,564** |
| Amount of money made in parking tickets in 1995 | **$60 million** |
| Annual economic impact of the entertainment industry *(LA Economic Development Corp.)* | **$43 billion** |
| Cumulative AIDS cases, 1996 *(APLA)* | **33,107** |
| Clear days in 1995 *(US Weather Bureau)* | **291** |
| Total number of days air declared 'unbreathable' in 1993 *(California Air Resources Board)* | **162** |
| Number of 'vehicles on LA freeways per hour | **15,000** |
| Rush-hour volume of a one-mile stretch of the I-405 (just south of the I-10) *(Dept. of Transportation)* | **25,500 vehicles** |
| Estimated number of people who moved out of LA in 1994 *(California Dept. of Finance)* | **23,500** |
| Number of people who moved to LA in 1994 *(Californian Dept. of Finance)* | **65,000** |
| Estimated black population of LA County (1990) | **934,776** |
| Estimated Latino population (1990) | **3,351,242** |
| Estimated Asian/Pacific population (1990) *(US Census)* | **907,810** |
| Estimated gay and lesbian population of LA County *(Gay & Lesbian Center of Los Angeles)* | **600,000** |
| Number of screenplays submitted to Writers Guild West in 1996 | **40,000** |
| Possibility of the Big One occuring in the next twelve years *(US Geological Survey)* | **60%** |
| Total damages from 1994 earthquakes *(US Facts on File)* | **$30 billion** |
| Annual felony cases prosecuted (1995) *(LA District Attorney)* | **70,000** |
| Street lights in LA | **217,385** |
| Yearly electricity bill for city (1995) | **$15 million** |
| Number of fireworks exploded at Rose Bowl 4th of July Celebration | **1,000** |
| Year fortune cookies were invented in LA | **1916** |
| Number of points scored by LA Laker Kareem Abdul-Jabbar | **44,149 (NBA record)** |
| Number of adult drug arrests (1994) *(California Dept. of Justice)* | **29,593** |

for Southern California to all but rob the rest of the country blind. He ensured that his SoCal military industrial cronies were able to plant their snouts firmly in the Federal Government hog trough. Massive tax breaks were given to the mushrooming computer industry, defence contracts were virtual licenses to print money, and LA was the Western hub of the $300 billion Savings and Loan banking scandal. Now, with a president who is both a Democrat and a southerner, such favoured status is long gone.

This is not to say that corruption has ended. Far from it. Just last year, Orange County, the suburban area south of metropolitan LA, the home of Disneyland and McDonnell Douglas, declared bankruptcy. One of the richest per-capita neighbourhoods on the entire planet had been driven into hopeless debt by a County Supervisor playing the bond market margins with public funds. Currently, the City of Los Angeles is building a subway system, despite all protests that tunnelling a London/New York-style underground rail system through soft alluvial soil in a notorious earthquake zone is not such a smart idea. One projected subway route will follow Wilshire Boulevard and pass within yards of the La Brea tarpits, adding

the possibility of benzine and methane gas leakage to the package of disasters waiting to happen. Already major cave-ins have occurred in the tunnel being built under Hollywood Boulevard, the most recent of which threatened the foundations of landmarks like the Mann's Chinese Theatre and the Roosevelt Hotel and all but halted construction on the subway, but, in the end, with the help of Mayor Richard Riordan, the contractors prevailed. The subway contracts are worth a fortune whether anyone ultimately rides on the system or not.

In the last half dozen national and local elections, crime has been a major issue, but, when candidates wax macho about longer prison terms and the building of bigger and better jails, they're talking crime among the poor and minorities, drugs and street crime. Few express righteous indignation about corporate crime, white collar millionaire crime, or mention the unfolding saga of how Ollie North and the CIA may have engineered the crack epidemic in Compton. Amid the rhetoric stand the twin towers of one of the biggest, best and most modern of prisons, a monument to corruption disguised as law and order. The downtown Men's Jail, just a few blocks from the courthouse where OJ went on trial, is completely empty. Simpson himself was one of the few

---

# Gangland culture

*'The most dangerous black man in America is the ghetto hustler. He is internally restrained by nothing. He has no religion, no concept of morality, no civic responsibility, no fear – nothing.'*
*Malcolm X in The Autobiography of Malcolm X*
Malcolm X's haunting words are particularly resonant in Los Angeles, commonly referred to as the gang capital of the world. But while the portrayal of the 'ghetto hustler' as a man without morality strikes a biting contemporary chord, to characterise LA's gang activity as a black problem, as it is often perceived outside the city, is innacurate. Latino gangs predate the black gangs – who first became prominent after the Watts riots of 1965 – and also outnumber them, and Asian gangs, with connections to their mainland counterparts, are on the rise. There are also other gangs from other ethnic communities, including whites, and a growing number of girl gangs.

The subject of gangs provokes a confused, often cagey set of responses from Angelenos. Some are swept away by paranoia, but many think that their city – and its varous ethnic groups – have been unfairly singled out for sensationalist attention and that the white Establishment, primarily in the form of politicians and the police, are manipulating the situation for its own ends. Media coverage is plentiful, but can lean toward the hysterical and inaccurate, giving rise to a mass of conflicting myth and false assumptions. But gang violence is nevertheless a fact of life: in California firearms have surpassed auto accidents as the leading cause of injury-related death among young people, and nowhere outside military battle has society created so many crippled young men, some of whom, unable to conceive of an alternative lifestyle, are still armed and firing from their wheelchairs.

It's easy to be simplistic about the causes of gang activity, but inevitably poverty and institutionalised racism are major factors. In the most deprived areas the once-stabilising forces of family, church, school and community are disintegrating, and gang fetishism, with its particular graffiti, mannerisms, language and style of clothing, holds out the promise of an alternative structure. Equally inevitably, one way that gangs have found to elevate themselves above the poverty line and thus find some legitimacy, however spurious, is the sale of drugs. The arrival of crack cocaine on the scene in the mid 1980s is blamed for a concurrent escalation in gang activity, as opposing factions fought to control the market. Crack is the number one employer of minority youth.

prisoners ever to be incarcerated there. After its construction, no money remained in the city budget to staff it and bring it on line.

The Men's Prison fiasco notwithstanding, crime will continue to be a big-ticket issue among political hopefuls, and the primary focus will inevitably stay on the gang problem. Like so many other things, however, crime is a matter of perception not actuality. Rather than expanding out of control as the pundits would have us believe, the crime rate – with the single exception of homicide by teenagers – has actually dropped in the '90s.

Even the world fascination with the LA gang culture is more a product of rap records, overemphasised news reporting and movies like *Boyz N the Hood*. The image of the black gangsta has become so all-pervading that now even LA residents, who ought to know better, see every black kid on the Venice promenade in baggy ankle swingers and a turned-round baseball cap as an armed and dangerous Shoreline Crip.The truth is that the black population of Los Angeles is becoming progressively smaller as the traditional neighbourhoods like Watts and Compton are being squeezed by the massive influx of Latino and Asian immigrants. Organised street crime and

particularly drug dealing, both in and out of the prison system, is almost totally controlled by the loosely knit, but ruthlessly efficient Mexican Mafia. Vietnamese gangs and even the newly arrived Russian mob, are rapidly carving out areas of influence. The black gangs may maintain their hold on the romantic image, but their numbers – and the threat that they represent – are in serious decline. The tourist in LA may see gang graffiti sprayed on walls, but, unless he or she makes a determined excursion to gangsta turf, they are highly unlikely to ever encounter a single gangbanger.

A popular saying around town is that the biggest and most dangerous gang is the Los Angeles Police Department, and the visitor, if not actually experiencing a close encounter with them, will see them everywhere. In the post-Rodney King, post-OJ world, the LAPD are a demoralised force, highly aware of their bad reputation, but reacting to it by behaving even more like the bullyboys of an occupying army. The popular conception that they are bunch of trigger happy racists is wrong in so far as it actually doesn't go far enough. My own personal observation is that the average LA police officer is an equal-opportunity misanthrope – much like Tim Robbins character in the film *Short Cuts*

1996's revelations that the CIA may have been implicated in putting crack onto the streets of South Central to raise funds for the Contras would seem to confirm many people's suspicions that the authorities are playing the situation for their own ends. Many believe that the LAPD prefers the gangs at each others' throats, on a path of self-destruction, to that unthinkable nightmare: a unified group of angry, underprivileged youth. Interestingly, the police stayed off the streets during the 1992 riots, ostensibly to 'avoid further provocation' – an alternative interpretation is that it was a conspiracy to stir up more alienation between whites and blacks.

## HOW GANGS WORK

Gang activity is focussed in inner city areas, largely in scattered patches of East LA, South Central and Long Beach, including parts of Compton, Boyle Heights, Watts and Van Nuys. Gangs are often known by the area they control – the Rollin' 60s, the Eight Trey Gang and Five Duce Crips – and defend this territory zealously.

The two best-known – and biggest – gangs in LA are the Crips and the Bloods, which developed in the aftermath of the 1965 Watts riots. The Crips wear blue and the Brims (the original name for the Bloods) don red; the Crips will often pierce their left ear, while the Bloods hole their right. Crips will refer to each other as 'Cuz' and the Bloods as 'Bloods'. Trademark attire is oversized plaid shirts, bandannas, trousers that hang below the waist, exposing undershorts, hair braids on males and the much-reported 'colours' which designate turf.

The easy accessibility of guns means that now most gang violence involves shooting, with the drive-by as the favourite method. It's this relatively uncontained warfare that is most likely to affect non gang-members, hence the increase in the number of 'civilians' caught in the crossfire and the accompanying rise in urban paranoia.

– who divides the world into a simple binary equation of cops and civilians – and believes that civilians are venal, stupid, lying, untrustworthy and possibly dangerous. The best advice, if pulled over by the LAPD, or otherwise forced into interaction with them is relax. Become as robotlike as they are. Give only your name rank and serial number and do nothing to suggest that you might look good inside the County Jail or bleeding on the sidewalk.

If this all sounds dauntingly grim, don't be discouraged. The bottom line is that LA hasn't really changed that much through the 1990s. Everything from AIDS to the alarming availability of firearms has put a crimp in a lot of behaviour, but the sun still shines, the surf still breaks out by Malibu, the palms still sway – even though the water is piped in from north of Las Vegas – and you can still be stuck in traffic with Jack Nicholson in the car behind you. Many of the perceived evils are, once again, much more a matter of perception than reality. The basic problem is that, through the 1950s and '60s, LA was sold as the American Dream made real. It was only natural. Hollywood was the company town of the Dream Machine, and many Angelenos saw themselves as custodians of the Dream. Although the Dream has proved unworkable, too rough on the environment and too heavy on the natural resources, many have difficulty letting it go. With a Hollywood sense of drama, they believe that the only substitute for paradise has to be hell. It's that old LA extremism. One can only replace a consumer utopia – with a pool in every backyard and fins on every Cadillac – with an apocalyptic nightmare of a machine gun in every home and the crouching fear that the gangstas, the illegals and the psychos are on their way. The city of Los Angles only starts to make sense with the realisation that the former was a Doris Day exaggeration and the latter is Quentin Tarantino paranoia.

The sun still sets in its blaze of *Gone With The Wind* glory and, as the light rapidly fades, you can still wind your way up one of the canyons to Mulholland Drive. You look out across the rectilinear jewel field of lights, and, sure, you know that bad things lurk in the darkness, but that doesn't stop the view being absolutely breathtaking.

# Within these walls

Hey, you've got a bit of money, you're probably white, you like all the good things that LA has to offer – so why should you live in fear of crime? Why not buy your way out of the urban jungle by barricading yourself and your family in a nice self-contained residential compound where high walls and sturdy gates mean that the only thing to worry about is what to wear to your neighbour's drinks party?

Despite a reported decline in crime figures in Los Angeles, *fear* of crime is on the increase, in part due to increasingly inflammatory news reporting. The 1992 riots only compounded the pervasive mistrust of 'them' – read blacks and Latinos – which has given rise to 'white-flight' (the exodus of white middle-class families from the inner city to the suburbs) and the creation of these walled residential estates.

Gated communities are not new to the city. But the famously exclusive Bel Air Estates, the equally select Palos Verdes Estates and Devonshire Highlands, an early gated community in San Fernando Valley, were sold, in the '50s, 'more on the basis of snob appeal than survivalism', according to urban commentator Steven Flusty. The gates to these estates were more symbolic than restrictive. In recent years, however, vigilantly patrolled developments have spread like a virus. Complete with guard-houses manned by security patrols or remotely activated gates, hidden cameras and high surrounding walls or fences, gated communities typically are new suburban estates containing hundreds of homes and sometimes built around private golf courses, sports clubs and other facilities.

There are also increasing numbers of newly-gated communities – streets or estates that have chosen to fence themselves in. An example is Park La Brea, a 1950s era compound of ugly, regimented apartment towers and two-storey garden houses (inexplicably the residence of choice for many young architects), covering several acres in the Wilshire district. In 1990, the owners closed off all public entrances with manned guard-houses and fenced in the entire complex. To exit such a place, you have to drive right up to the automated gates, triggering the electric opening mechanism, a fact not obvious to newcomers, who have been known to drive hopelessly around in search of an open exit, believing themselves to be trapped in a residential prison.

The irony of gated communities is that it seems they do not provide the security promised in the developers' hype. Figures suggest no long-term drop in crime, and even hint at an increase. Gated estates appear by definition to have something to steal and, furthermore, the gates and fences serve as a greater obstacle to police cars than to practised burglars.

*From fame to shame:* **Robert Downey Jr** *facing drug charges in Malibu, 1996.*

# Latino LA

**There's no ignoring the fact that LA is a Latino city.**

Latinos are no minority in Los Angeles, except, that is, in the status afforded them by the establishment. According to some estimates, they already outnumber Anglos and, by the next century, have been forecast to overtake all other ethnic groups combined. Much as the paranoid Anglos might like to trade on stereotypes, the plethora of countries, cultures and economic backgrounds represented results in a diverse and ubiquitous culture, from the descendants of the early Mexican migrants in the San Fernando Valley, who now harvest college educations where their forbears harvested crops, to dishwashers in Westside restaurants where Latino attorneys and film executives conduct their power lunches; from the Central American street vendors who plead their case to Chicano city council members to the Mexican and Central American day labourers in the South Side; from the Chicano and Mexican working class of the East Side, historically the entry point for immigrants, to the teeming masses on Downtown's main thoroughfare, Broadway.

## THE MEXICAN WAVE

When Mexico gained its independence from Spain in 1822, large tracts of land were deeded to local families, who were recognised as Mexican citizens. Many of the descendants of the original settlers grew prosperous as ranchers and merchants. Trade with the nascent United States brought more prosperity as well as American settlers, and the two cultures clashed. Animosity between the two groups increased and when the city fell into the hands of the US after the Mexican-American war in 1848 it was the end of the era of Mexican supremacy and the advent of US domination.

Los Angeles claims the distinction of containing the largest population of Mexicans outside Mexico City, and the Mexican influence in Los Angeles is the most distinct one, from the historic adobe houses of Olvera Street in Downtown down to the names of the major thoroughfares, such as La Cienega Boulevard, Figueroa Street, Sepulveda Boulevard, Ventura Boulevard and Santa Monica Boulevard.

Mexican holidays such as Cinco de Mayo (the Fifth of May), celebrating a crucial military victory over the French invaders in 1862, and Diez y Seis de Septiembre (16 September), commemorating Mexico's Independence Day, carry as much weight as such American holidays as the Fourth of July and Labor Day, with their own celebrations and fiestas. The City of Los Angeles even sponsors its own Diez y Seis de Septiembre party on the steps of City Hall, broadcasting the festivities from Mexico City on large TV screens, including the Mexican president's ceremonial speech from the presidential palace. And many local restaurants and bars, Mexican and otherwise, sponsor a Cinco de Mayo party, offering margaritas and cerveza (beer) at reasonable rates to bolster the custom of fiesta as well as their profits.

---

# Lowriders

Until the police cracked down several years ago, Saturday nights made Whittier Boulevard in East LA a virtual parking lot as Mexican-American youth jammed the streets with their souped-up automobiles, looking for romance, excitement and sometimes a fight. 'Cruising the Boulevard' was a teenage rite of passage for decades, a modern interpretation of a Mexican courting ritual in which young men and women strolled through a park looking for their true love. In this newer version, young *vatos* (dudes) drove in their 'lowriders' and tried to pick up on the *rucas* (girls), who more than likely had borrowed Dad's sedan for the night.

Lowriders, usually Chevrolet Impalas or Buick Rivieras, are customised cars sporting elaborate paint jobs, chrome wheels and hydraulic lifts on the front and rear wheels that make them bounce as they prowl the street. Many a duel would ensue between two *vatos* over which car could bounce the highest. While the cruising tradition continues in other parts of LA, it is mourned by many who experienced the Boulevard tradition, though many lowrider clubs still exist and they display their fancy *ranflas* in car shows.

*Opposite: lowriders – a peacock show.*

## THE CENTRAL AMERICANS ARRIVE

Increasingly, the Mexican influence is in competition with a Central American one. The divergent influences of these newly arrived immigrants are creating not a cohesive body of people but a sometimes difficult, sometimes beneficial, nexus of cultures and peoples. Political ideology, class conflict and nationalistic antagonisms have followed the growing waves of Central Americans who have fled here, and each population brings with it its own cultural, political and social contradictions.

Civil wars in El Salvador and Nicaragua during the 1980s saw a huge influx of refugees seeking political and economic asylum from death squads and poverty. The city now boasts large populations of immigrants from El Salvador, Guatemala, Nicaragua and other Central American, South American and Caribbean countries. After years as refugees and resident aliens, many see the futility of returning to their respective countries and are now making diligent efforts to become US citizens.

Organisations founded by displaced Central American revolutionaries to aid refugees and support their comrades back home are turning their attention to local issues. They are now asking for their piece of the pie that has long been denied them by the more established Mexican-American and African-American politicos of the city, as well as the Anglo ruling class.

## THE OPPRESSED MAJORITY

While the number of Latinos is growing in Los Angeles, their political clout is still nascent, due in some part to the dynamics mentioned above, but mostly to forces outside their control. But with increasing numbers of immigrant Latinos becoming citizens and registering to vote, and their American-born children taking up their voting rights, Latinos are seen as a growing political and economic threat to the status quo of the ruling class of the city. Their response has been a chilling example of the lengths those in power will go to stay in control.

In 1994 a state-wide ballot initiative, the nefarious Proposition 187, sought to disqualify 'illegal immigrants' ('undocumented aliens' is the preferred term among the progressive community) from public social services, education and medical care. Insecurities caused by the economic recession of the late 1980s and early 1990s were exploited to full advantage by the racist and right-wing forces pushing Prop 187. Proponents tapped into the fears of the increasingly disenfranchised and newly laid-off white working class and the long economically oppressed African-American population, who didn't blame capital flight or corporate capitalism on their downward mobility but 'those damned immigrants taking our jobs'.

While the initiative did pass in the November elections, an October 1994 pro-immigrant march drew well over 100,000 to streets of downtown Los Angeles, the largest march in the city's history. Many of the progressive multi-ethnic coalitions of college students, labour unions, political activists, politicians and others that mobilised for the march have held together and are a burgeoning political force in the city. Immigrants with a history of political activity in the own countries serve as leaders in many of these coalitions and bring their own unique perspective to the fray.

The moribund and beleaguered labour movement has even had a much-needed shot in the arm. Drawing support from the abundant low-wage Latino immigrant working class – janitors, waiters, busboys, hotel maids, garment workers, factory workers and others – local unions are working to improve the conditions of this increasingly exploited workforce. Efforts to organise the mostly Mexican and Central American workers, many of whom were active politically in their own countries, are forging a strong militant political consciousness with sophisticated strategies and tactics. Along with the local multi-ethnic coalitions, these groupings serve as a focus of hope for true economic and social change as well as a shift in the balance of political power in Los Angeles.

## CULTURAL DOMINATION

While the political influence is wanting, the cultural is not. Latino musical styles have long had a voice in Los Angeles. The Mexican styles of mariachi, banda, romances and ranchera blare on such top-rated radio stations as KLAX-FM 97.5 and KLVE FM-107.5, while the Caribbean Afro-Cuban beats of samba and mambo and Central American salsa and merengue draw dancers to such hot night spots as Club Bahia, La Masia, Zabumba and Leonardo's. The burgeoning Rock en Español movement is represented in LA rock clubs as eclectic bands perform their own brand of new wave, punk and rock 'n' roll, sung exclusively in Spanish. And East LA's own Los Lobos have fulfilled their crossover dream, recording on a major label, touring nationwide and serving as inspiration for many Latinos with aspirations for success.

Local Latino theatre groups perform the works not only of Spanish and Latin American playwrights but of Europeans and Americans as well, at such venues as the Bilingual Foundation of the Arts and Plaza de la Raza in East LA, and Nosotros Theater in Hollywood. Latino performance artists, poets and writers present their work at Highways and Midnight Special Books in Santa Monica, Regeneraciòn and Arroyo Books in Highland Park and Self-Help-Graphics in East LA. And the leading Spanish language newspaper, *La Opinion*, boasts a circulation of 100,000-plus.

The divergent Latino groups are creating a new dynamic in the city. Long the downtrodden, they are becoming a force to be reckoned with, and the future holds great promise.

# Architecture

**It might seem like a random roadside sprawl, but originality has always flourished in LA, where architecture is continually reinventing itself.**

Los Angeles was founded and repeatedly reinvented by adventurers and fortune-seekers, some of whom came laden with cultural baggage, others with 'nothing to declare but their genius' – as Oscar Wilde told a US customs officer. This helps to explain why most of Los Angeles and its 170 contiguous communities is a chaotic mishmash of borrowed styles, executed with little finesse or imagination. But originality has also flourished here, ever since the arrival of the intercontinental railroad in 1887 and the rapid transformation of a dusty cow town into a metropolis.

There are few major public buildings or landmark corporate structures. Like Tokyo, Los Angeles appears bewilderingly vast, featureless and horizontal from the freeways; one needs to explore the neighbourhoods to discover its extraordinary diversity and well-concealed treasures. Topography offers a clue; much of the best work is tucked away in the hills, clinging to 'unbuildable' sites that appeal to clients whose ambitions outrun their budgets.

For tours that feature architecture, art and design, contact Architours (1-213 294 5825). Occasional house tours are offered by the LA chapter of the American Institute of Architects (1-310 785 1809), the Los Angeles Conservancy (1-213 623 2489) and the Society for Architectural Historians (1-800 972 4722). For more information on many of the buildings mentioned here, *see chapters* **Sightseeing, Film** *and* **Theatre & Dance.**

## A CITY IS BORN

Only a few fragments remain of the early settlement with the long-winded name, El Pueblo de Nuestra Senora la Reina de Los Angeles. Misty-eyed preservationists blather on about the city's roots and the adobe tradition, but the evidence is unconvincing: dull provincial buildings, rebuilt or prettified, are best forgotten. There is, however, a rich legacy of buildings from the land boom of the late 1880s, notably the houses built in the Queen Anne and Eastlake styles on the 1300 block of Carroll Avenue in Angelino Heights, just northwest of Downtown. One of the Victorian offices that early residents commuted to by streetcar was the **Bradbury Building**; behind its century-old brick facade is a stunning skylit atrium surrounded by

Step inside the **Bradbury Building**.

tiled galleries, with polished wood balustrades and open-cage lifts. It was inspired by a science fiction novel and was featured in the film *Blade Runner*.

Ten miles north-east, at the foot of the San Gabriel Mountains lies Pasadena, which flourished as a winter resort for rich Easterners around the turn of the century. Remnants of the flamboyant resort hotels survive, as do many handsome Craftsman-style 'bungalows', of which the standout is the **Gamble House**, built by Charles and Henry Greene in 1908, a marvel of polished mahogany and Tiffany glass.

### Bradbury Building

*304 South Broadway, at Third Street, Downtown (1-213 626 1893). Metro Civic Center/Tom Bradley or Pershing Square/bus 1, 2, 3, 4, 10/I-10, exit Fourth Street east.* **Open** (ground floor only) 9am-6pm Mon-Fri; 9am-5pm Sat, Sun. **Admission** free.

The glorious art deco **Wiltern Theater**, movie palace turned rock venue.

### Gamble House

*4 Westmoreland Place, at Walnut Street, Pasadena (1-818 793 3334). Bus 177, 267/I-10, exit Orange Grove Boulevard north.* **Open** noon-3pm Thur-Sat (tours every 20 mins). **Admission** $5 adults; $4 senior citizens; $3 under-12s.

### INTERWAR BOOM

During the growth years of the 1920s, Southern California embraced the Mediterranean tradition, building thousands of pocket haciendas, Churrigueresque car showrooms and abstracted Andalusian farmhouses. The city developed an indiscriminate appetite for all things foreign and exotic: Wallace Neff and George Washington Smith set the pace, but all Beaux Arts-trained architects were masters of period style, and every builder could run up a mosque, a medieval castle or an Egyptian tomb to satisfy a devotee of romantic fiction. Hollywood legitimised this exuberant eclecticism, but the impulse came from newcomers who flocked to LA from around the world, dreaming of fortune or an easy life in the sun.

The greatest personal fantasy to survive is **Watts Towers** (1921-54), which a poor Italian immigrant, Sam Rodia, spent three decades building. Every day he hoisted himself up one of the slender iron cages, implanting scraps of broken china and glass in wet cement. Experts are now struggling with the problems of conservation and the towers are closed to the public until 1998. **Spadena House** (Walden Drive, at Carmelita Avenue, Beverly Hills), also known as the Witch's House, was designed for a 1921 movie (Hansel and Gretel, one assumes) in Culver City and was later moved to its present site.

Mass fantasies found their outlet in exotic movie palaces. Still flourishing is **Mann's Chinese Theater** (6925 Hollywood Boulevard); newly reborn is **El Capitan Theater** (at number 6838). Other palaces are now used for the performing arts: art deco fans should catch a show at the **Pantages Theater** (6233 Hollywood Boulevard) or the **Wiltern Theater** (Wilshire Boulevard, at Western Avenue). There is a cluster of decaying vintage movie palaces on South Broadway.

Recently restored and extended by US firm Hardy Holzman Pfeiffer, Bertram Goodhue's **Central Library** embodies the civic pride and Beaux Arts scholarship of the 1920s in its Egyptian massing, lofty inscriptions and spirited murals. Its commercial counterpart was **Bullocks Wilshire** (3050 Wilshire Boulevard), the grandest of department stores and the first to be designed so that motorists could unload beneath a *porte cochère* – a drive-through canopy attached to the entrance – and park in the rear. It has recently been transformed into a law school, with its art deco facades and ornament preserved.

Frank Lloyd Wright and his Austrian-born protégés, Rudolph Schindler and Richard Neutra, pioneered modern architecture in Southern California from 1920 onwards. Highlights include Wright's **Hollyhock House** and **Ennis-Brown House**, both of which are open to the public. The **Schindler House** in West Hollywood, built as the architect's live-work space, is a dazzling combination of tilt-up concrete walls, redwood partitions, rooftop 'sleeping baskets' and outdoor living rooms. Another major work by Schindler is the concrete-frame **Lovell Beach House** (13th Street, at Beach Walk, Balboa Island, Orange County).

Neutra had a 40-year career in Los Angeles: among his finest International Modern residences are the **Lovell Health House** (416 Dundee Drive, at the southern end of Griffith Park) and the **Strathmore Apartments**, stacked up a hillside in Westwood (11005 Strathmore Drive).

Another influential Los Angeles architect born out of Frank Lloyd Wright's organic modern tradition was John Lautner, designer of structurally dynamic futuristic buildings, such as the 1960 **Chemosphere** (776 Torreyson Drive, north of Mount Olympus), most familiar as the exotic setting of choice in James Bond films. Lautner first came to Los Angeles in 1939 to supervise construction of Frank Lloyd Wright's Sturges house and was sickened by the ugliness of what he saw. But he realised, as Wright had in the 1920s, that he could realise his vision here, in the soft clay of a burgeoning community, as he never could in the tradition-bound East or Midwest. He settled in and built a succession of daring, highly original houses – although he did no more than scrape a living and achieved widespread fame only in the last few years before his death in 1994.

The Los Angeles region fared better than most during the Depression, but the old extravagance was gone, and New World Streamline Moderne replaced European models for many public buildings and a few homes. You can drive by the **Coca-Cola Bottling Plant** (1334 Central Avenue, at 14th Street), which resembles an ocean liner moored amid the warehouses of Downtown, and take a train from **Union Station**, last of the great US passenger terminals.

### Watts Towers
*1765 East 107th Street, between Alameda Street & Central Avenue, Watts (art centre 1-213 847 4646). Metro 103rd Street/bus 56, 251/I-10, exit Century Boulevard north.* **Open** *art centre* 10am-4pm Tue-Sat; noon-4pm Sun. **Admission** free.

### Broadway movie palaces
*Million Dollar, Los Angeles, Orpheum, United Artists, Broadway, between Third Street & Olympic Boulevard, Downtown. Metro Pershing Square or 7th Street/Metro Center/bus 10, 11, 40, 45/I-110 north, exit Sixth Street east.* **Open** Orpheum for films; others for church services, special events and on Los Angeles Conservancy tours. **Information** Orpheum 1-213 239 0949; others 1-213 623 2489.

### Central Library
*630 West Fifth Street, between Flower Street & Grand Avenue, Downtown (1-213 228 7000/public events 1-213 228 7040). Metro Pershing Square or 7th Street/bus DASH E/I-110 north, exit Sixth Street east.* **Open** 10am-5.30pm Mon, Thur-Sat; noon-8pm Tue, Wed; 1-5pm Sun.

### Hollyhock House
*4800 Hollywood Boulevard, between Vermont Avenue & Edgewood Drive, Los Feliz (1-213 913 4157). Bus 1, 180, 181, 204, 217/US101, exit Vermont Avenue north.* **Open** noon-3pm (tours on the hour) Tue-Sun. **Admission** $2 adults; $1 senior citizens; free under-12s.

### Ennis-Brown House
*2655 Glendower Avenue, near intersection of Vermont Avenue & Los Feliz Boulevard, Los Feliz (1-213 660 0607). Bus 180, 181/US101, exit Vermont Avenue north.* **Open** *tours* second Sat of Jan, Mar, May, July, Sept, Nov; at other times by reservation. **Tours** $10 adults; $5 students, senior citizens. **No credit cards**.

### MAK Center/Schindler House
*835 North Kings Road, between Santa Monica Boulevard & Melrose Avenue, West Hollywood (1-213 651 1510). Bus 4, 105, 304/I-10, exit La Cienega Boulevard north.* **Open** 11am-6pm Wed-Sun. **Admission** $5.

## POST-WAR GROWTH

The population of Southern California exploded in the 1950s and new suburbs obliterated fields and citrus orchards, extending, with the freeways, over the mountains and into the desert. Business interests spurred the renewal of Downtown, razing the decaying Victorian mansions atop Bunker Hill and creating, from the early 1960s onwards, a corridor of office towers. But, as freeways clogged and public transportation lagged, Century City and other commercial hubs grew to serve an increasingly fragmented and suburban metropolis.

From 1945-62, the influential magazine *Arts + Architecture* sponsored the Case Study House programme, a visionary project fuelled by post-war optimism whose mission was to create prototypical low-cost houses utilising new prefabricated materials and building methods. Although they never achieved the anticipated mass popularity, the Case Study Houses stand as icons of Southern Californian modern design, characterised by interpenetrating landscape and open-plan glass and steel volumes. One of the best was the steel-framed **Eames House**, a fusion of poetry and technology by Charles and Ray Eames, the US's most talented husband-and-wife design team, built in 1949 from off-the-shelf components.

Just as Frank Lloyd Wright had inspired the first generation of modernists in Southern California, so did Toronto-born Frank Gehry (who has worked in Los Angeles since the early 1960s) serve as mentor to several generations of free-spirited architects. Gehry's many buildings include the **Temporary Contemporary Museum** (152 North Central Avenue, at First Street, Downtown), a subtle warehouse conversion; **Loyola Law School** (1441 West Olympic Boulevard, between Albany and Valencia Streets, Downtown); Gehry's own house in Santa Monica (22nd Street, at Washington Avenue) and the West Coast headquarters for the **Chiat/Day** advertising agency (340 Main Street, at Rose Avenue, Venice), with its eye-catching portico in the form of an upturned pair

# The Googie legacy

In 1949, John Lautner designed an angular, wood and glass coffee shop called Googie's, next door to the legendary Schwab's drugstore on Sunset Strip. Both landmarks have now vanished, replaced by a pastel shopping/movie theatre complex, but the name Googie lives on as short-hand for the post-war generation of coffee shops that epitomise 1950s and 1960s drive-by design.

America had emerged from Depression and war: there was a mood of optimism and of faith in technology. Cars were designed to look like jet fighters, and the coffee shops (like car washes) also strove to look as though they were moving at warp speed. Lloyd Wright (Frank's son) and Lautner led the charge; other architects picked up on the sensuous curves, expansive windows and splayed walls of such buildings as Wright's Guggenheim Museum and Taliesin West.

The coffee shop began to replace the old diner and the greasy spoon café, flourishing on the new commercial strips that served the burgeoning suburbs. They drew on an earlier tradition of the building as sign: the overscaled doughnuts, windmills and hot dogs that had lured passing motorists in the 1930s. In the 1950s, everyone was getting a car and had more to spend: Denny's, Coffee Dan's, Ships and Norms offered families and young couples a clean, well-

lit space from which to observe their neighbours speeding by. Flashing neon signs towered over these single-storey boxes; within, the furnishings were a mix of cosy and gee-whizz – Naugahyde booths and space-age lamps.

Of the survivors, the best may be Pann's (at the intersection of La Tijera, La Cienega and Centinela Boulevards, Inglewood) and Ship's Culver City (Overland Avenue, at Washington Boulevard; *pictured*). The earliest surviving McDonald's (Lakewood Boulevard, at Florence Avenue, Downey) shares the aesthetic. The best reference source is still *Googie* by Alan Hess (Chronicle Books, 1985), which goes in and out of print but can usually be found second-hand.

of binoculars designed by Claes Oldenburg. Alas, Gehry's masterpiece, the Walt Disney Concert Hall in Downtown, is currently stalled for lack of money.

There are several must-see buildings by architects influenced by Gehry's idiosyncratic forms and inventive use of (often low-cost industrial) materials. The UCLA campus in Westwood has one striking example: the **'Towell' (Temporary Powell) Library**, a sizzling temporary structure designed by Hodgetts and Fung. And, in Culver City, Eric Owen Moss has remodelled a succession of drab warehouses, creating cutting-edge workspaces for innovative companies, including **The Box** (8520 National Boulevard) and **Samitaur** (3457 South La Cienega Boulevard).

Outstanding examples of contemporary architecture in downtown Los Angeles include the **Museum of Contemporary Art** (250 South Grand Avenue), a powerful complex of geometric solids and skylit galleries designed by Japanese architect Arata Isozaki, and Pei Cobb Freed's soaring extension to the **LA Convention Center**. For relaxation, there's **Pershing Square**, LA's second-oldest public space. It was dramatically

re-landscaped in 1994 by Laurie Olin, with colourful architectural features by Ricardo Legorreta.

Twelve miles west, in Brentwood, the new **Getty Center** opens in October 1997 on a hilltop campus designed by Richard Meier, while the **J Paul Getty Museum**, a replica Roman villa in Malibu, is being remodelled to house classical antiquities. Meier also designed the crisp **Museum of Radio & Television** in Beverly Hills. In Burbank, Robert Stern brings smiles to motorists crawling home on the I-34 with his cartoon-like **Disney Animation Building**. To the south, in Orange County, Philip Johnson and John Burgee created the aptly named **Crystal Cathedral** for one of California's leading pop preachers.

### Eames House
*203 Chautauqua Boulevard, off PCH, Pacific Palisades. Bus 9, 434/I-10, exit PCH north.* **Open** *office* 10am-5pm Mon-Fri. Exterior tours only; *information* 1-310 396 5991.

### Crystal Cathedral
*12141 Lewis Street, at Chapman Avenue, Garden Grove (1-714 971 4000). I-5 south, exit The Center Drive to Chapman Avenue west.* **Open** 9am-3.30pm Mon-Sat (except during weddings and funerals); tours every 20 mins. **Admission** free.

# Car City

**More than any other city in the world, LA owes its existence, form and character to the automobile, and driving its roads and freeways is the quintessential LA experience.**

'I drive, therefore I am,' should be the motto of Los Angeles, a city whose culture, urban form and image is predicated on ownership of an automobile.

Not that this was always so. The vast agglomeration that is contemporary LA was in its early years a collection of small, distinct cities, such as Pasadena, Santa Monica, Venice and Los Angeles (now Downtown), that were connected first by carriage and horse tracks, then by steam, and subsequently by the Redline electric railroad.

Downtown emerged as the commercial and transit centre, with Union Station as the hub of an efficient network of trams and rail. By the 1940s the area had become highly congested and, in order to avoid it altogether, a burgeoning car-driving populace voted for the development of the boulevard system. The boulevards, traversing LA from west to east and criss-crossing north-to-south avenues, were the first step towards the decentralisation of Los Angeles and the amalgamation of the separate cities into Greater Los Angeles (*see also chapter* **Orientation**).

## BUILDING THE FREEWAYS

In 1939, the Pasadena Freeway (US110), the first of its kind and now considered a classic, was constructed. Designed for cars going at 45 miles an hour, it is a charming byway that weaves its way under bridges and through rolling landscapes from Downtown LA to Pasadena.

In the 1950s, major freeway construction began. The planning of the routes was a highly politicised process. Avoiding the wealthier communities on the Westside, the freeways gouged their way through disenfranchised neighbourhoods, leaving in their wake broken communities and a network of concrete and tarmac viaducts that have become the chief arteries and defining forms of the city.

Freeway construction more or less stopped in the 1970s (though a painful 30-year battle to prevent the extension of the Pasadena Freeway into picturesque South Pasadena still rages). The last freeway to be completed, after a lengthy construction process, was US105 (aka Century or Glenn Anderson Freeway) in 1995. This dramatic feat of engineering (immortalised on film while still under construction when an as yet incomplete stretch of overpass was jumped during the bus chase in the movie *Speed*) supposedly heralds the freeway of

*The pattern of LA life.*

the future. It comes complete with high-tech sensors and a rail system along the centre.

The latter reflects a new stage in the evolution of Los Angeles. To cater to an expanding population, a vast, federally funded public transit project, comprising overground train and subway systems and intended to wean the populace from car dependency, is underway. Administered by the Metropolitan Transit Authority (MTA), this, too, is a highly politicised undertaking, which has not only been riddled with scandal and construction problems from its inception but also ill serves the poorer neighbourhoods that need it most and neglects to improve the existing bus system.

The result is that locals have little faith in the prospect of becoming a public transit based city and, despite the many measures conceived to mitigate the environmental impact of cars (including catalytic converters, emission-free gasoline and incentives to car-pool), car use continues to rise.

## THE DRIVING EXPERIENCE

Driving in LA delivers ecstacy and agony in equal measure. It offers the pleasure of navigating a road system designed for the driver, and the frustration of trying to traverse the city by any other means. The ecstacy of whizzing along the freeway towards infinity, music playing, is countered by the pain of being stuck on that same freeway in rush hour, or worse, breaking down on it, ending up huddled in a locked car on the hard shoulder, praying for the arrival of the Automobile Club of Southern California (at around $50 per year for roadside assistance and four free pick-ups, it's the club for sensible Los Angelenos).

Delight in acquiring the vehicle of one's choice – be it classic, wrecked, customised or hot off the production line – and the availability of ridiculously cheap petrol is tempered by the direct and hidden costs of car use. Quite apart from the obvious expenses of insurance (the highest in the US), maintenance, registration, smog tests, parking tickets and so on, a good half of California tax-revenue goes towards the construction and maintenance of the highways system and the California Highway Patrol that protects it. Driving in LA also presents the conflicting feelings of joy at being on the open road in one of the most spectacular terrains on the planet, and guilt that such liberation is achieved at the expense of that self-same natural environment.

## A CITY BUILT FOR THE CAR

Car dependence has left its mark on the city not only in the network of freeways but in the form of the city itself. Car use encouraged the characteristic suburban LA lifestyle that emphasises private over public. Acres of land are covered by tracts of one- and two-storey, single-family housing, with wide streets and driveways, two-car garages, large front yard and backyard complete with swimming pool and barbecue – the portable barbecue, incidentally, was invented by Henry Ford, who promoted the idea of 'picnicking' as one of the joys of leisure driving.

Car use also spawned a city zoned into residential neighbourhoods, some of which do not even have pavements, and commercial boulevards: 'strips' lined with buildings designed to cater to the driver. If not actually the originator, Los Angeles popularised stores with their entrances on the rear parking lot (the historic Bullocks building on Wilshire Boulevard was the first of this type), corner mini-malls and drive-in motels (take Sunset Boulevard between Fairfax and La Brea Avenues to see some classics).

Drive-through fast-food restaurants and diners flourished on the strips. McDonald's, Jack In The Box, Taco Bell and In n Out Burger (the undisputed best of the burger chains) are ubiquitous and largely anonymous – though must-see fast food-eries include a great new retro-style In n Out in

Westwood Village, a sculptural Kentucky Fried Chicken on Western Avenue and one of the earliest McDonald's in Pomona. Some classic diners, built in the 1950s and 1960s 'Googie' era of LA architecture, such as Bob's Big Boy in Burbank, still exist (for more on Googie diners, *see chapter* **Architecture**). Catch them before they disappear.

Most noticeable of all, however, are the signs. Since business owners found they needed to catch the eye of a motorist skating by at 40 or more miles an hour, commercial art – huge advertising billboards, ads painted on the sides of buildings and buildings as signs in themselves – have emerged as the vernacular artform of Los Angeles. Drive along Sunset Strip between Doheny Drive and La Cienega Boulevard for the most sensational, eye-popping sequence of huge signs. Take in the Cabazon Monster (a lifesize model of a dinosaur) on the I-10 east of LA, and visit the Tail-o'-the-Pup on North San Vicente Boulevard in West Hollywood or the Big Donut on West Manchester Boulevard in Inglewood to experience the few remaining iconic incarnations of buildings-as-signs.

Los Angeles is also the city of car lots, lube shops, 'body shops', car showrooms (visit Heritage Classics on Santa Monica Boulevard at La Peer Drive; 1-310 657 9699), carwashes – try Sunset Carwash on Sunset Boulevard, opposite the Screen Actors Guild (1-213 656 2777) for a classic carwash experience combined with the chance of seeing a star in a car – and, most of all, parking lots, which cover huge amounts of land.

## YOU ARE WHAT YOU DRIVE

Car culture has bred a weird sense of time and space – locals measure the length of a journey by the time it takes rather than the distance covered, because the road system is designed to enable Angelenos to drive vast distances quickly. It has also generated a mindset where other forms of locomotion are confined to leisure activities, such as walking or cycling – you drive to the gym to use the step machine – and a dependence on technology that spawns dependence on more technology; hence the ubiquitous car phone/fax/stereo and the 'intelligent' freeway, with in-built sensors supposed to alert drivers of traffic problems ahead.

Car culture has also bred a snobbery based on the car you drive, with those thousands who do not drive or own a car being the untouchables (or, one might say, 'immobiles') at the bottom of the social ladder; a condition reinforced by the fact that the California driving licence is the most commonly used form of ID in the state. It is used instead of a bank card to authorise a cheque, get access to clubs and to prove you're old enough to buy alcohol.

People go to absurd extremes to keep up automobile appearances. Many cars on the road in LA are not actually owned but leased, for a night or for as long as you can keep up the monthly pay-

*Buildings as billboards – unmissable at any speed.*

ments. Among many urban myths is the belief that certain Beverly Hills divorcees down on their uppers live in their cars, and, in so doing, maintain some semblance of their former glory.

Some people define themselves by their car, as they define their location by the freeway exit to which it is closest, and within the hierarchy of car ownership are numerous automobile subcultures – tribes include Latino lowriders, Valley Boy hot-rodders, media trendies in Jeep Wranglers, executive Lexus owners, proud custodians of classic American cars (still going strong here because the desert dryness means that cars do not rust), wannabe macho dudes on pumped-up pick-up trucks and urban survivalist Westside mothers battling the streets in four-wheel Ford Explorers.

The cult of the car has bred a whole battery of gimmicks and services for car users, from bizarre personalised number plates – BRAK NEK, FAT LADY, BZAZAB (think about it...), SHRINK and ALI CAT are some we've spotted – to valet parking. Legions of besuited valet parkers marking the entrances to restaurants, clubs and, sometimes, car parks are the answer to parking in a city that has run out of space (never forget to tip your valet).

You can probably rent any type of car in LA, but for a *California Dreamin'* experience, try Dreamboats (1-310 828 3014) or the infamous car-wreck supplier to the studios, Rent-A-Wreck, on Pico Boulevard (1-310 478 0676). Depending on your budget, at R-A-W you can hire anything from a beat-up old Ford to a pink convertible Caddy. And, if you want to do the movie star thang, the car rental of choice has to be a stretch limousine. Limos, used to transport people in style to Prom nights, the Oscars and the Grammies, or as mobile party rooms for stag nights, are available for hire any time, in numerous different makes and lengths. Try Mercedes Limousines (9641 Sunset Boulevard, Beverly Hills; 1-310 271 8559), where, for $60 an hour (plus tip) you can hog the road in a stretch Lincoln, for $110 you can command a stretch Mercedes and, for $95, a Roller.

Car culture has also bred some terrific radio. Tune into KCRW-FM 89.9, a favourite on the Westside for eclectic music and great news programming; KPWR-FM 106.3 for hip-hop and rap; KROQ-FM 106.7 for rock; KPFK-FM 90.7 for earnest radicalism; or KXEZ-FM 100 for the easy listening playing in the white BMW on Hugh Grant's fateful night. If you want to experience contemporary American culture at its most shrill, sample the talk radio shows on several AM stations, especially KFI-AM 640. For more on drive-time shows, *see chapter* **Media**.

On the down side, car dependence has given rise to drive-by shootings, car-jacking, impossible building codes (demanding unachievable levels of parking space to accompany a new building), acquisitiveness, smog and traffic school. This last is an only-in-LA institution, dreamed up by insurance companies, whereby you pay to attend a day of traffic school instead of getting an endorsement on your driving licence. It's a total con but has given rise to all sorts of creative variations, such as Comedy Traffic School and Chocoholics and Ice-cream Lovers' School.

But, surprisingly, reliance on automobiles has also bred a generosity of sorts. With a collective sense of 'there but for the grace of God, go I, and my car', Angelenos will drive miles out their way to give acquaintances a ride home, porter friends to and from the airport and often freely lend out cars (insurance permitting), exhibiting a casualness that results from taking the car for granted.

If you want to find out more about the evolution of automobile culture in LA as well as see some fabulous historic cars, visit the Petersen Automotive Museum on Wilshire Boulevard. Founded by the owner of Petersen Publishing Company, a producer of numerous car magazines, it offers a largely uncritical view of the automobile, but is great fun nonetheless (*see chapter* **Museums & Galleries**). For more information on driving in LA, including car rental, *see chapters* **Getting Around** *and* **Essential Information**.

# Celebrity LA

**This is no city to be cool in – so go star-spotting crazy and gawk to your heart's content. Here's where.**

There are more celebrities in Los Angeles than any other city in the world. Though Hollywood is synonymous with film, LA is also the world's television capital and, would like to think, music too. Just turn on the local news on any given night and a celeb scandal will invariably come before the world's latest terrorist atrocity. It's never easy to forget you're in Los Angeles but it's very easy to forget there's a rest of the world.

Economically, the effect of Hollywood on Los Angeles is smaller than you might think. Its impact is more psychological. Though you won't spot a celeb every day, you might. Many Los Angelenos feel a vicarious thrill, simply by virtue of living in the same city as many of the world's most famous people – and many more who want to be famous. Sometimes, in certain parts of town, there's no escaping Mr or Ms Wannabe. That handsome guy waiting on you is probably an actor. The receptionist at your hotel is probably a screenwriter. Ninety nine per cent of these people never make it. There are a lot of sad desperate people in Hollywood who, despite years of rejection, forlornly cling to the dream that their big break could be just around the corner. The thing is, it just could be. The unlikeliest big breaks happen every day; there is still magic in Hollywood and it just might happen to you. That's showbiz.

## Celebrity spotting

Celebs are everywhere. But they're not usually at the addresses given on the star maps sold on Hollywood street corners, which are horribly out of date.

Most celebs live in Hollywood Hills, Beverly Hills, Bel Air, Brentwood, Santa Monica and Malibu. But you have to know where to go. If you devote a day to celeb-hunting, chances are you'll find at least one if you haunt a selection of the places listed below. It may be the bloke who played JR's second cousin on *Dallas*, it may be Arnold Schwarzenegger. That's the beauty of LA.

Some stars love to frequent the places Where Celebs Go. Others have zero interest in the celebrity scene. Your best bet for spotting the reclusive (ie classy) stars is at premieres or promotional parties. Finding out what's happening is tricky if you're only in town for a while. Try calling Hollywood News Calendar (1-213 872 1507), a fax service giving details of events and big names in town.

## Homes

Some people are so famous everyone knows where they live. If you want to spot TV mogul Aaron Spelling or his Beverly Hills 90210 actress daughter Tori, you could go and hang outside their mansion in Bel Air. Take Sunset Boulevard west through Beverly Hills and Bel Air and make a left on Mapleton Drive. Take it all the way to the end. That last huge house on the left is the place. OK, you can't see the private ice-rink or cinemas – and definitely not the present-wrapping room – but it still looks impressive.

A much better bet is the little-discussed Broad Beach, home to the likes of Steven Spielberg, Kurt Russell and Goldie Hawn, Robert Downey Jr, Ali MacGraw, Sylvester Stallone, Mel Gibson and Sting (when he's in town). These people like to say they live in Malibu, which throws people off the (beaten) track slightly, as Broad Beach is actually part of Zuma Beach up the coast. To find Chez Spielberg, take Pacific Coast Highway north, go through Malibu and continue to Broad Beach Road. Make a left and drive a little way along the street. Walk to the beach (there are a number of narrow pathways down to the sea) and look for the dark brown wooden house with the lawn. It's not tricky; Spielberg is the only person there rich enough to have a lawn. Oh, and Stallone's is the pink house.

If you're more of a front-of-camera star, you need to live somewhere safer and less accessible – such as Malibu Colony, essentially a glorified housing estate for the rich and famous. If you're not a resident or on the guest list, you can't get in.

## Supermarkets

Supermarkets are prime celeb-spotting haunts. After all, celebs have to eat. Many don't do their own shopping (darling, they have personal assistants for stuff like that) but a surprising amount do. Here's the pick of the best:

### Brentwood Country Mart

*225 26th Street, at San Vincente Boulevard, Brentwood (1-310 395 6714).*
An odd collection of shops and a supermarket which has attracted the likes of Messrs Spielberg, Stallone and Hanks.

### Gelsons Market

*15424 Sunset Boulevard, at Temescal Canyon Road, Pacific Palisades (1-310 459 4483).*
Gourmet to the nth degree, as appreciated by star shoppers.

### Hughes

*23765 West Malibu Road, at Malibu Colony Plaza, Malibu (1-310 456 2917).*
Just outside Malibu Colony, therefore on the doorstep of more celebs than any other supermarket.

### Mayfair Market

*5877 Franklin Avenue, at Bronson Avenue, Hollywood (1-213 464 7316).*
Situated at the bottom of a popular section of the Hollywood Hills. Celebs who drop by for takeaway sushi include Brad Pitt and Jason Priestley.

### Pavilions

*8969 Santa Monica Boulevard, at Robertson Boulevard, West Hollywood (1-310 273 0977).*

### Wholefoods

*239 North Crescent Drive, at Wilshire Boulevard, Beverly Hills (1-310 274 3360).*

## Shops

Celebs like to shop. In fact, the more shops they can find in one place, the better.

### Barneys of New York

*9570 Wilshire Boulevard, between Camden & Peck Drives, Beverly Hills (1-310 276 4400).*
LA's most expensive, most exclusive department store: just perfect.

### Beverly Center

*8500 Beverly Bouleard, at La Cienega Boulevard, West Hollywood (1-310 854 0070).*
Three floors of shops plus food and a cinema makes this one tough for any celeb to resist.

### Century City Shopping Center and Marketplace

*10250 Little Santa Monica Boulevard, between Avenue of the Stars & Century Park West, Century City (1-310 277 3898).*

### Fred Segal

*8100 Melrose Avenue, at Crescent Heights Boulevard, West Hollywood (1-213 651 4129).*
With the exception of the couture houses on Rodeo Drive, this is possibly the most expensive clothes shop in the city. The café is just as fashionable as the store.

## Restaurants

Weekends are the times when Mr and Mrs Jo Schmuck like to eat out. Mr and Mrs Celeb, as a result, prefer weekdays. Most of these restaurants are very smart so if you show up not looking the part and toting a large camcorder, you're likely to be conspicuous. Although most of these restaurants are far from cheap, many have bars.

### Chianti

*7383 Melrose Avenue, at Martel Avenue, West Hollywood (1-213 653 8833).*
So dark that celebs feel they can take off their sunglasses.

### Drai's

*730 North La Cienega Boulevard, between Melrose & Waring Avenues, West Hollywood (1-310 358 8585).*
Paparazzi heaven any weekday evening.

### Eclipse

*8800 Melrose Ave, at Robertson Boulevard, West Hollywood (1-310 724 5959).*
Celebrity staple.

### El Coyote

*7312 Beverly Boulevard, between Poinsettia Place & Fuller Avenue, Park La Brea (1-213 939 2255).*
Young Hollywood loves the killer margaritas and the classless co-mingling.

### Hugo's

*8401 Santa Monica Boulevard, at Kings Road, West Hollywood (1-310 654 3993).*
Fashionable venue that attracts a big gay crowd at weekends. Celebs do weekday brunch.

### Kate Mantilini

*9101 Wilshire Boulevard, at Doheny Drive, Beverly Hills (1-310 278 3699).*
Huge, perennially trendy celeb hangout.

### Kokomo Café

*6333 West Third Street, at Fairfax Avenue, West Hollywood (1-213 933 0773).*
One of the numerous restaurants in the Farmers' Market. Weekdays are prime spotting time as it's next door to CBS.

### Matsuhisa

*129 North La Cienega Boulevard, between Wilshire Boulevard & Clifton Way, Beverly Hills (1-310 659 9639).*
Almost LA's most expensive sushi, which always attracts celebs anxious to maintain their washboard stomachs.

### Mortons

*8764 Melrose Avenue, at Robertson Boulevard, West Hollywood (1-310 276 5205).*
Monday dinner is unoffical celeb heaven.

### Musso & Frank Grill

*6667 Hollywood Boulevard, at Cherokee Avenue, Hollywood (1-213 467 7788).*
Hollywood's oldest surviving restaurant has served everyone from Ernest Hemingway and F Scott Fitzgerald to Steve McQueen and Brad Pitt.

### Orso

*8706 West Third Street, between Robertson & San Vincente Boulevards, Beverly Hills (1-310 274 7144).*
Very low-key and therefore much loved by celebs trying not to be celebs for at least the duration of dinner.

### Rainbow Bar & Grill

*9015 West Sunset Boulevard, at Doheny Drive, West Hollywood (1-310 278 4232).*
Seconds away from legendary rock venues the Whiskey and the Roxy, the Rainbow always boasts a band that has just played or a celeb who has caught them.

### Spago

*1114 Horn Avenue, at Sunset Boulevard, West Hollywood (1-310 652 4025); from spring 1997 176 North Canon Drive, Beverly Hills (1-310 652 4025).*
Designer pizza and a photographer always on hand.

## Bars & cafés

Hotel bars are invariably good bets as they're more than likely to be frequented by visiting celebs staying there.

### Bar Marmont

*8171 Sunset Boulevard, between Sweetzer Avenue & Crescent Heights Boulevard, West Hollywood (1-213 650 0575).*
At the time of going to press, this was the hottest bar in town, and is likely to endure because it's attached to Los Angeles' coolest hotel for over a century – Chateau Marmont.

# How to be a celeb for a day

*Honestly, some people will do anything to get their picture in the papers.*

**8am**: Greet your stretch limo driver at the entrance to your hotel, the Four Seasons. Your people have booked through Music Express (1-213 849 2244), which handles numerous celebrities plus the Oscars and most big events.

**8.30am**: Breakfast at Barney Greengrass, the rooftop restaurant at the most glamorous department store of them all, Barneys New York.

**10am**: Barneys opens its doors to shoppers.

Peruse all floors to buy anything sporting a Barneys logo. Everyone back home must know you've been to the world's most stylish department store. And, anyway, it gives you an excuse to tell them again and again about being in the fitting room at the same time as Michelle Pfeiffer.

**11am**: Work out at the very famous Golds Gym (1016 North Cole Avenue, at Santa Monica Boulevard, Hollywood; 1-213 462 7012). Join for

## Cat & Fiddle Pub

*6530 Sunset Boulevard, between Highland Avenue &*
*Cahuenga Boulevard, Hollywood (1-213 468 3800).*
Rockers galore drink Guinness under the trees on the patio.

## Formosa Café

*7156 Santa Monica Boulevard, at Formosa Avenue,*
*Hollywood (1-213 850 9050).*
One of LA's oldest and most-loved bars. It never goes out
of fashion so it's always a sure fire bet for the more trend-
conscious celebs.

## Four Seasons at Beverly Hills

*300 South Doheny Drive, at Burton Way, Beverly Hills*
*(front desk 1-310 273 2222).*
Very popular celeb digs. Also, a venue for film companies'
PR efforts, so full of film stars promoting their latest project.

## Jones

*7205 Santa Monica Boulevard, between Poinsettia Place*
*& Formosa Avenue, West Hollywood (1-213 850 1726/7).*
A bar and restaurant, though most are there to pose at the
bar. A favourite of Young Hollywood.

## Kings Road Café

*8361 Beverly Boulevard, at Kings Road, West Hollywood*
*(1-213 655 9044).*
It looks pretty normal, but it's actually a hub for beautiful
people and the entertainment industry. Great coffee.

## Peninsula

*9882 Santa Monica Boulevard, at Wilshire Boulevard,*
*Beverly Hills (1-310 551 2888).*
A classy assortment of A-list stars plus serious Hollywood
powerbrokers power-breakfasting on the roof by day, power-
drinking in the bar by night.

## Sunset Marquis Hotel & Villas

*1200 North Alta Loma Road, at Sunset Boulevard, West*
*Hollywood, CA 90069 (front desk 1-310 657 1333).*
The hotel's Whisky Bar is one of the coolest in town, though
it's no longer as frighteningly trendy as it once was, but the
hotel is still the rock superstar's preferred LA home.

## Village Coffee Shop

*2695 North Beachwood Drive, at Westshire Drive,*
*Hollywood (1-213 467 5398).*

---

anything from a day to a week to a year. Try not
to stare at Jodie Foster on the treadmill next to you.
**12.30pm**: Lunch at the Beverly Hills Hotel's
Polo Lounge (9641 West Sunset Boulevard, at
Rodeo Drive, Beverly Hills; 1-310 276 2251).
Since the famous 'pink palace' reopened after
extensive renovation, it has become even more
popular with the rich and famous. Try to be discreet when using your mobile phone at the table.
Only wannabes show them off.

**2pm**: Your limo whizzes you to an unassuming
grey building in Koreatown. 'Hmm,' you mutter
disconsolately into your Evian. 'We must be
lost.' Not at all. Welcome to Beverly Hot Springs,
the only natural mineral spa in Los Angeles (308
North Oxford Avenue, Koreatown; 1-213 734
7000). Relax in the hot and cold pools, then enjoy
a shiatsu massage or the ultimate luxury treatment, Body Care, which involves being smothered in a mixture of baby oil, cucumber and milk.
Heavenly (honest).

**4pm**: Tongue scrape (the latest beauty fad) at
the office of Dr Douglas Hauck (8920 Wilshire
Boulevard, at La Peer Avenue, Beverly Hills; 1-
310 659 5399).

**4.30pm**: Time to prepare for your big night. Cut
and blow-dry at the hottest hair and beauty
place – Juan Juan in Beverly Hills. After bouff-
ing by Juan Juan himself (Uma Thurman has to
wait while he finishes your hair), amble a few
doors down for your sugar leg wax. (Hair salon
is at 9667 Wilshire Blvd, at Bedford Drive,
Beverly Hills; 1-310 278 5826, the beauty salon
at 9675 Wilshire; 1-310 246 0808.)

**6pm**: Your people have already arranged (via
the hotel concierge) for a personal make-up artist
to prepare you for the long night ahead. If you
would prefer something a little more exclusive,
have them call Cloutier, darling (1-310 394 8813).
This hair, make-up and styling agency primps
and coiffs all the big names.

**7pm**: Drinks at Le Colonial, sitting next to Clint
Eastwood and Susan Sarandon (8783 Beverly
Boulevard, at Robertson Boulevard, West
Hollywood; 1-310 289 0660). There's so much
networking to do, the limo driver has to call you
on the mobile to let you know you'll miss your
dinner reservation if you don't leave now.

**9pm**: Dinner at Geoffrey's, high on a cliff overlooking the sea off Malibu (27400 Pacific Coast
Highway, at Latigo Canyon Road; 1-310 457
1519). Pronounce the name correctly – it sounds
like Joffrey's – or you'll come off as a tourist. Try
not to gawk at Pamela Anderson Lee's breasts.

**11pm**: Drinks (preferably margarita with the
latest fashion tequila) in the pretending-to-be
scruffy splendour of Bar Marmont (*see chapter*
**Bars**). Marvel at Keanu Reeves with facial hair.

**12.30am**: Dancing at the Viper Room (*see*
**Where they died**). Yes, that really is co-owner
Johnny Depp at a booth in the main room. You're
lucky: he normally views the punters from an
upstairs office via a two-way mirror.

**1am**: Coffee in the Four Seasons' bar. Spot celeb
at next table. Ask for a light, not an autograph.
Pretend you have no idea who they are. Wander
upstairs to your room loudly bemoaning the
thought of that 7am power-breakfast tomorrow.

Known by everyone as the Beachwood Café, this is the place to be for weekday brunch, when you might catch a bleary-eyed celeb. In the shadow of the Hollywood sign at the bottom of a celeb-packed area of the Hollywood Hills.

## Celebrity sites

### Where they died

### John Belushi
*Bungalow 2, Chateau Marmont, 8221 West Sunset Boulevard, West Hollywood (1-213 656 1010).*
Belushi overdosed here on a speedball, the same lethal combination of cocaine and heroin that killed River Phoenix.

### Janis Joplin
*Landmark Hotel, 7047 Franklin Avenue, between Ceritos Avenue & North Orange Drive, Hollywood.*
The hotel where Joplin overdosed is now an apartment block.

### Robert F Kennedy
*Ambassador Hotel, 3400 Wilshire Boulevard, between Alexandria & Mariposa Avenues, Mid-Wilshire (1-213 387 7011).*
Kennedy was assassinated in the kitchen by Sirhan Sirhan.

### Marilyn Monroe
*12305 Fifth Helena Drive, Brentwood.*

### River Phoenix
*The Viper Room, 8852 West Sunset Boulevard, West Hollywood (1-310 358 1800).*
Phoenix died right on the pavement of Sunset Boulevard, by the club's back door (the entrance is on Larrabee Street).

### Bugsy Siegel
*810 Linden Drive, between Lomitas Avenue & Whittier Drive, Beverly Hills.*
Mafia bigwig – the Warren Beatty film *Bugsy* is based on his life – was shot a billion times here.

### Where they're buried

### Forest Lawn Cemetary
*1712 South Glendale Avenue, between San Fernando Road & Los Feliz Boulevard, Glendale (1-800 204 3131).*
Humphrey Bogart, Clark Gable, Walt Disney and Spencer Tracy lie at rest here.

### Hollywood Memorial Cemetary
*6000 Santa Monica Boulevard, between Gower Street & Van Ness Avenue, Hollywood (1-213 469 1181).*
Cecil B DeMille, Rudolph Valentino, Peter Lorre, Douglas Fairbanks, Virginia Rappe (actress whom Fatty Arbuckle was accused of murdering).

### Holy Cross Cemetary
*5835 West Slauson Avenue, at Bristol Parkway, Culver City (1-310 670 7697).*
Bing Crosby, Bela Lugosi.

### Westwood Memorial Cemetary
*1218 Glendon Avenue, at Wilshire Boulevard, Westwood (1-310 474 1579).*
Here lie Marilyn Monroe, Natalie Wood, Roy Orbison and Buddy Rich.

### Where they used to live

### Charlie Chaplin
*1085 Summit Drive, at Cove Way, Beverly Hills.*

### Clark Gable & Carole Lombard
*4543 Tara Drive, at Ashley Oaks, Encino.*
The house looks exactly as it did when Hollywood's golden couple were in residence.

### Joan Crawford
*426 North Bristol Avenue, between Evanston & Hanover Streets, Brentwood.*

### James Dean
*Sigma Nu, 601 Gayley Avenue, at Strathmore Drive, Westwood.*
Dean lived at this UCLA fraternity house while at the university. He was expelled for punching a fraternity brother.
*3908 Barham Boulevard, Burbank.*
Dean lived in an apartment here, close to Warner Brothers Studios, where he made most of his films.

### Jayne Mansfield
*10100 Sunset Boulevard, between Baroda Drive & Charing Cross Road, Bel Air.*
One of the original LA mansions, still featuring a heart-shaped pool with 'I love you Jaynie' written on the bottom. Subsequently owned by Engelbert Humperdinck and Sylvester Stallone.

### Elvis & Priscilla Presley
*144 Monovale Drive, at Ladera Drive, Bel Air.*

### Miscellaneous

### Corner of Sunset Boulevard & Courtney Avenue
Just north of here was where Hugh Grant employed Divine Brown for her most fruitful job yet.

### Clarion Hollywood Roosevelt Hotel
*7000 Hollywood Boulevard, between Highland & La Brea Avenues, Hollywood (front desk 1-213 466 7000).*
Back in the 1940s, many of Hollywood's biggest names would congregate here every Monday night in the Blossom Room. Montgomery Clift stayed here while filming *From Here to Eternity*; his ghost supposedly haunts room 928. The manager's office also houses a mirror which once hung in Monroe's room – her image has been seen in it more than once.

### Garden of Allah
*8150 West Sunset Boulevard, between Crescent Heights Boulevard & Havenhurst Drive, West Hollywood.*
Sadly, now a Great Western bank, the Garden of Allah was the first star hotel, providing rooms for everyone from David Niven to Errol Flynn. There is a rather pathetic model of the hotel inside the bank.

### Knickerbocker Hotel
*1817 North Ivar Avenue, at Yucca Street, Hollywood.*
Now a retirement complex, this hotel was once the in place to stay. Frequent guests included Frank Sinatra, Elvis Presley and Bette Davis.

### Peter Lawford's House
*625 Palisades Beach Road, Pacific Palisades.*
Peter Lawford was the Kennedy brothers' friend and confidante. This is the site of Marilyn Monroe and John F Kennedy's alleged trysts.

### Villa Capri
*6735 Yucca Street, between Highland & Las Palmas Avenue, Hollywood.*
Site of a famous restaurant where James Dean had his last dinner. Frequented by members of the original Brat Pack, including Humphrey Bogart, Judy Garland, Frank Sinatra and Lauren Bacall.

# By Neighbourhood

| | | | |
|---|---|---|---|
| Orientation | **88** | East of Hollywood | **109** |
| Westside: Beach Towns | **89** | The Valleys | **111** |
| Westside: Inland | **94** | Long Beach & the South Bay | **113** |
| Midtown & Hollywood | **99** | East LA | **115** |
| Downtown | **104** | South-Central | **117** |
| | | Orange County | **119** |

# Orientation

**Don't be daunted by the sheer size of LA. Some basic information is all you need to point you in the right direction.**

The one sign you will not see when you arrive in Los Angeles is the one directing you to the city centre. Because there isn't one. Greater LA is an amorphous, sprawling, urban agglomeration spread over a huge flood basin, which is subdivided by freeways and bounded by ocean and mountains: on its western edge by 160 miles of Pacific Rim coastline, and then, clockwise, by the Santa Monica, San Gabriel, San Bernadino, San Jacinto and Santa Ana Mountains.

## THE CITY OF LOS ANGELES

As you drive around what you think is Los Angeles, you may be confused by signs pointing to 'Los Angeles'. This is because the City of Los Angeles is a distinct city within the County of Los Angeles. LA County contains 88 incorporated cities, each with their own downtowns, including Malibu, Santa Monica, Beverly Hills, West Hollywood, Culver City, Inglewood, Pasadena and Los Angeles. Together, they add up to the LA of popular imagination. On the other hand, Hollywood, which seems to be a distinct place, is just one of many neighbourhoods in the amorphous City of Los Angeles, which also includes Downtown.

In turn, LA County is one of the counties in the Los Angeles Five County Area. Together with Riverside, Ventura, Orange and San Bernadino Counties, the Five County Area constitutes a colossal area of about 34,000 square miles and 14.5 million people. LA County loosely consists of various recognisable regions: Downtown LA, East LA (largely Latino) and Midtown, the Valleys, the Westside and South Central LA (comprising many black and Latino neighbourhoods). These areas are in turn made up of smaller neighbourhoods.

LA is also subdivided by numerous freeways and by a loose grid of large arteries – the boulevards and avenues. These non-freeway streets are referred to as 'surface streets'. Boulevards typically (but not exclusively) go east to west (with street numbers starting at zero in Downtown and ascending westwards), while avenues run north to south. Sometimes the boulevards and avenues are divided into 'North' and 'South' and 'East' and 'West' and the numbering will restart at a city boundary (North Robertson Boulevard, for example, changes numbers three times as it passes through three cities), so check which stretch of road you want and watch the numbers carefully.

## THE FREEWAYS

In the central portion of LA County, the flood basin where you are likely to spend most of your time, the I-10 (or Santa Monica Freeway) traverses LA from west to east and separates Hollywood and Midtown from South and South Central LA. The I-405 (San Diego Freeway) goes north to south on the west side of the City of Los Angeles, separating the affluent coastal and inland cities from the rest of LA. This region, the Westside, is considered by some to extend beyond the I-405 to the more easterly La Cienega Boulevard, taking in Beverly Hills and West Hollywood. You will also see some guidebooks refer to the Westside as only the inland neighbourhoods, rather than including the beach towns of Malibu, Santa Monica, Venice and Marina del Rey, as we have done. Basically, the Westside is a place and an attitude; it is synonymous with affluence and white culture. Westsiders are mocked for never venturing east of La Cienega Boulevard or south of the I-10. Within the Westside is an area called, confusingly, West LA. This refers to a western portion of Los Angeles that is loosely situated between the distinct cities of Santa Monica, Beverly Hills and Culver City.

The I-110 (Harbor Freeway) also goes north to south, on the east side, separating Downtown and East LA from west and central LA. The US101 (Hollywood Freeway) and the I-5 (Golden State Freeway) head north-west from Downtown into the Valleys. The Valleys – San Fernando to the north-west and San Gabriel to the north-east – are separated, physically, and spiritually, from the rest of LA by the Santa Monica Mountains. The San Fernando Valley is Quentin Tarantino land, flat, hot and post-war, while the San Gabriel Valley contains older cities such as Pasadena.

When planning a journey in LA make sure you find out not only the address but the nearest cross-street – for example, La Cienega and Third. If you're taking the freeway, find out the exit nearest to your destination. Unless you are sure of the district you are heading for, also get the city and the zip code (Highland Avenue, Santa Monica, CA 90405, for example). Remember that the same street name will occur in different cities.

Most importantly, if you are intending to do any driving in LA, get hold of *The Thomas Guide* to Los Angeles County. Although it will set you back 30 bucks or so, this is LA's indispensable street directory.

# Westside: Beach Towns

*Welcome to the archetypal LA of Baywatch, beautiful people and palm-fringed beaches. Bimbo city? Far from it.*

There's more to the Westside beach towns than just sun, sea and sand. Santa Monica, Venice, Marina del Rey, Pacific Palisades and Malibu are all home to feisty communities who have created neighbourhoods with distinct character and plenty to do. Just remember that the beach cities are not at their best in June, during which they are swathed in morning cloud known as June Gloom.

For information on the beaches themselves, *see* chapter **Sightseeing**.

## Santa Monica

With the Santa Monica Mountains to the north, the glistening Pacific Ocean to the west, palm-tree lined cliffs and almost year-round sun tempered by ocean breezes, affluent Santa Monica is indisputably the the jewel of LA's Westside. Known locally as 'the people's republic of Santa Monica', it is also the heartland of bourgeois liberalism, noted for its environmental causes, rent control and tolerance of the homeless.

The Santa Monica area was settled for centuries by the Gabrieleno Indians, then by Spanish settlers who named the city and many of the major streets. It was acquired by Anglo pioneers in the late nineteenth century and snowballed from a small vacation town into today's city of about 87,000. Brits abound in Santa Monica (aka Santa Margate) as do Iranians (since the fall of the Shah), many other immigrant groups, retirees (septuagenarians on wheels are the biggest danger on the city's streets), health fanatics, beach bums and entertainment industry titans – residents include Michelle Pfeiffer, Ted Danson and Arnold Schwarzenegger. The muscled one also owns a chunk of commercial property in Santa Monica and a mediocre restaurant, **Schatzi on Main** (3110 Main Street).

As well as the tourist-oriented beaches, pier and shops, Santa Monica also boasts some of the best restaurants in the LA basin, a burgeoning creative business centre and a thriving art, coffeehouse and literary scene (there's one bookshop every quarter of a square mile). It has some great modern architecture: much of Frank Gehry's work is here,

Joggers on **Fourth Street Steps**.

including his own house, as well as some art deco, such as the **Shangri-La Hotel** (1301 Ocean Avenue, at Arizona Avenue) and good '50s Modern, such as the **Santa Monica Civic Auditorium** (1855 Main Street, at Pico Boulevard).

Santa Monica has three main shopping and entertainment areas: Montana Avenue, Third Street Promenade and Main Street.

## Montana Avenue

Montana Avenue runs parallel to Wilshire Boulevard, the city's main east-west artery, towards the north, affluent end of town bordering on the Santa Monica Canyons. Montana Avenue metamorphosised in the 1970s from a bland commercial strip into the Rodeo Drive of the coast. Locals divide their leisure time between such treats as spiritual and physical sustenance at **Yoga Works** (at 1426) and supper at **Louise's Trattoria** (at 1008). North of Montana, at Fourth Street and Adelaide Drive, are the infamous **Fourth Street Steps**: 189 concrete steps that serve as a cliffside Stairmaster and, reputedly, a pick-up place for fit singles.

## Third Street Promenade

South of Montana Avenue, below Wilshire Boulevard at Third Street, is the wildly popular **Third Street Promenade**. Anchored by three cineplexes, the Frank Gehry-designed **Santa**

**Monica Place** at the southern end (approach from Main Street to the south for a surprising facade) and adjacent parking structures, these four blocks of pedestrianised streets are by day and night a hugely popular shopping, eating and entertainment zone. With regular street performers, farmers' markets on Wednesday and Saturday mornings and seasonal festivals, as well as the trendy **Congo Square** coffee bar (the yogi tea is a must), **Urban Outfitters** clothing store and **Gotham Hall** club and pool house, Third Street Promenade offers a pumped-up version of *paseo*. People do walk in LA.

## Main Street

Even further south is Main Street, an upmarket commercial strip two blocks west of the Santa Monica Boardwalk. A popular breakfast-time haunt for early-morning joggers, Main Street offers an eclectic mix of fashion and knick-knack stores, as well as numerous coffee bars and eateries. Highlights include the **Novel Café**, an extremely laid-back bookstore/coffee bar at Pier Avenue, Wolfgang Puck's **Chinois on Main** (2709 Main Street) and the Frank Gehry-designed **Edgemar Complex** (2437 Main Street), a sculptural mall which houses the **Santa Monica Museum of Art**, the **MOCA Store** (Museum of Contemporary Art; great for presents) and the high-class **Röckenwagner** restaurant.

*Venice: hanging trainers mark gang territory.*

Main Street runs through Ocean Park, a hilly, bohemian neighbourhood at the south end of Santa Monica, whose intense light and tranquillity was celebrated on canvas by late resident Richard Diebenkorn in his famous Ocean Park Paintings.

Worth visiting inland is the new **Bergamot Station**, a complex of art galleries created at a former Red Trolley terminus (accessible from Michigan Avenue, off Cloverfield Boulevard), and **Santa Monica Airport**. Built before much of the rest of Santa Monica, the airport is the hip hangout for airplane enthusiasts. Top gun Tom Cruise keeps his Pitts Special biplane here; mere mortals, with a licence, can rent a plane for a mere $60 an hour or take a simulated flight at the **Museum of Flying**. Large parties are held at the airport, architects and designers have offices in hangars and there are two good restaurants there, **DC3** and **Typhoon**, both serving excellent Californian cuisine in full view of the aeroplanes.

### Santa Monica Visitor Center

*1400 Ocean Avenue, Santa Monica, CA 90401 (1-310 393 7593).* **Open** *winter* 10am-4pm daily; *summer* 10am-5pm daily.
Visitor information and literature.

# Venice

Santa Monica is so perfect that it can, in some areas, seem a bit precious, something that could never be said of its southerly neighbour, Venice. Despite gentrification during the 1980s, Venice remains the bohemian quarter of Los Angeles, populated by ageing hippies, artists, students and young professionals in creative industries who can't yet afford a place in Santa Monica. It is also home to transients and a poor black – and increasingly Latino – community beset by drug dealing and gang fights that make the Oakwood area (circumscribed by Lincoln and Venice Boulevards and Sunset and Electric Avenues) a no-go zone after dark.

Formerly a beach resort, the section of Venice west of Lincoln Boulevard has rows of tumbledown clapboard beach houses, walk-streets (pedestrian-only alleyways leading to the beach) and, in the more affluent southern end, canals. Venice owes its existence to entrepreneur Abbot Kinney, who founded it in 1900, envisaging it as the hub of a cultural renaissance in America. He oversaw the construction of canals, a lagoon and buildings in the Venetian style, even importing two dozen genuine gondoliers to complete the effect (one of whom apparently got so homesick that he tried to sail back to Italy and made it as far as San Pedro). The **Venice Canals**, south of Venice Boulevard, are an idyllic enclave of bridges, waterways and eclectic architecture.

Although Kinney failed to achieve the cultural rebirth – visitors were far more interested in amusing themselves – he did succeed in creating a

Take a stroll round the **Venice Canals** – one place where the car isn't king.

successful resort known in its heyday as the Playland of the Pacific. Venice's main commercial street, Abbot Kinney Boulevard, is named in his honour, and well worth visiting for its collection of art galleries, accessories and bric-à-brac, design stores and good eateries, including **Hal's Bar & Grill** at number 1349, by California Avenue, the eternally hip hangout for local meedja folk (the atmosphere compensates for the overpriced food), **Joe's Restaurant** (No.1023) for excellent food in simple surroundings, **Mobays** (No.1031) for Caribbean cuisine on a delightful patio, and the **Abbot's Habit** (No.1401) for coffee and snacks.

In the 1980s, Venice became a hotbed of architectural activity. You can see several buildings by acclaimed contemporary local architects, such as Frank Gehry's Norton and Spiller houses, the Bergren, Sedlak and 2-4-6-8 houses by Morphosis, Dennis Hopper's residence by Brian Murphy as well as Frank Israel's renovation of the former Charles and Ray Eames studio, now Bright and Associates, and Frank Gehry's **Chiat/Day Building** (near Rose Avenue). You can't miss the latter as its entrance is marked by an enormous pair of Claes Oldenburg-designed binoculars, one of the better examples of public art that can be found in Venice. A more controversial art piece is Jonathan Borofsky's unmissable *Dancing Clown* perched on the corner of Main Street and Rose Avenue. For a tour of the public artworks, many of which are near Ocean Front Walk (aka Venice Boardwalk), contact the Social and Public Art Resource (SPARC) on 1-310 822 9560.

Many renowned Southern Californian artists have maintained studios in Venice for years, among them Laddie John Dill, Guy Dill, Billy Al Bengston, Ed Moses and Chuck Arnoldi. If you are here in May you might catch the yearly Venice Artwalk, a charitable event in aid of the Venice Family Free Clinic, in which you can tour more than 60 artists' studios.

Venice has also been a mecca for kooky California culture – the **Psychic Eye** bookstore, incorporating the New Age Center, at 218 Main Street is a must – and fitness fanaticism. Three of LA's most famous gyms are here, **Gold's** (360 Hampton Drive), the Schwarzenegger-owned **World Gym** (812 Main Street) and **Powerhouse Gym** (245 Main Street). Their buff clientele can be strutting their stuff in many Venice locales; you can't miss them chowing down on protein-packed brunches at the **Firehouse Restaurant**, a vivid red-painted former fire station on the corner of Rose Avenue and Main Street.

Other notable Venice spots include St Marks restaurant/club at the beach end of Windward Avenue – go there for salsa lessons on Sundays. This is one block south of Market Street, where you can take in the prominent **LA Louver** art gallery and trendy restaurant **72 Market St**. The other key strip is Rose Avenue, an east-west commercial street at the north end of Venice. There are a few interesting thrift shops, but the main attraction is the **Rose Café** (no. 220); adorned with large painted roses; it's a self-serve and sit-down restaurant with an attractive garden and crafts store.

**Marina del Rey**: *a 1970s period piece.*

**Venice Chamber of Commerce**
*583¾ Venice Boulevard, Venice, CA 90291 (1-310 827 2366).* **Open** Call for hours.

## Marina del Rey

An unsung aspect of LA life is its sailing. Many Los Angelenos keep boats, others live in them, at the **Marina del Rey Harbor**, a resort and residential complex just south of Venice in a contained area bounded by Washington Boulevard, Admiralty Way, Fiji Way and Via Marina. Conceived a century ago, finally completed in 1965, the Marina consists of a picturesque man-made harbour, with eight basins named to evoke the south seas (Tahiti Way, Bora Bora Way, Mindinao Way and so on) that are filled with 6,000 bobbing yachts, motor boats and flashy cruisers. This is surrounded by low- and high-rise apartment buildings and generic hotels, as well as many touristy restaurants. Perceived as a haven for swinging singles, the Marina is actually home to many retirees and young families for whom the complex is a reasonably priced and charming, if somewhat sterile place to live. It is livened up, however, by a motley crew of impecunious boat-dwellers. Simply to experience a pure 1970s period piece, the Marina is definitely worth seeing.

It's no place for culture vultures, however; except for a small public library, all the Marina's attractions are recreational. You can picnic, jog and cycle (the Marina is a link in the 21-mile coastal bike path) in the **Burton W Chace** and **Admiralty Parks** at the northern end; board a dock at the west end of the Burton W Chace or rent a boat to go ocean-fishing at Fisherman's Village, 13755 Fiji Way, at Lincoln Boulevard (Green Boathouse). You can also rent boats or join excursions at a number of charter companies located in the Marina: there's whale-watching in winter. If you want to park your own boat, contact the Visitor's Information Centre (*below*).

There are plenty of touristy shops, most of them concentrated in **Fisherman's Wharf**, a cheesy replica of a New England fishing town. The many eateries are to be recommended for their waterside charm rather than for their food, which does not rank among Los Angeles's best. The **Cheesecake Factory**, **Edie's Diner** and the ultimate beach supershack, **The Warehouse Restaurant** (go on a full stomach), on Admiralty Way are among the better ones to choose from.

At the south end of Marina del Rey (just north of LAX) is Playa del Rey, a predominantly residential beach neighbourhood and an artificial lagoon. **Tanner's Coffee Company** (200 Culver Boulevard) is one of the more lively local cafés in an area whose attractions are mainly beach-oriented. Playa del Rey is also a magnet for nature lovers and birdwatchers, who come to observe the great grey herons, white egrets and other winged and footed creatures that converge on the Ballona Wetlands, a natural sanctuary just east of Playa del Rey, in Playa Vista.

**Visitor's Information Center**
*4701 Admiralty Way, Marina del Rey, CA 90292 (1-310 305 9545).* **Open** 9am-5pm Mon-Fri.

## Pacific Palisades

Between Santa Monica and Malibu lies Pacific Palisades, a small, wealthy residential community that has managed to keep a lower profile than its neighbours. The perfect, clipped, shiny green lawns and large bungalows of Pacific Palisades are straight out of *Leave It To Beaver* – but contained within its Santa Monica Mountains location are some wonderful places to visit.

Don't miss the bizarre **Getty Museum**, J Paul Getty's Roman fantasy, at 17985 Pacific Coast Highway (unless you're going on foot or bus, call first to reserve a parking space, on 1-310 458 2003). For rugged nature, there's **Rustic Canyon Park** (1-310 454 5734), **Temescal Canyon Park** (1-310 459 5931) and **Will Rogers Historic State Park** (1-310 454 8212). The latter is the former home of famous American 'Cowboy Philosopher', trick roper, journalist and media personality Will Rogers. View his Western-style ranch, watch polo games and hike through magnificent parkland.

For a more manicured, but unbelievably lovely retreat, try the **Self-Realization Fellowship Lake Shrine** at 17190 Sunset Boulevard. You don't have to meditate to walk about and rest in this lakeside idyll, a meditation centre founded by Paramahansa Yogananda in 1920.

Will Rogers State Beach, it is rumoured, is one of the locations used for *Baywatch*. The production company doesn't give out filming schedules in advance, but if you do happen upon a shoot, you can rubberneck as much as you want. If you'd rather be part of the action, and have the requisite Barbie/Ken body, you could try asking Central Casting (1-818 562 2700) for work as an extra. By the way, the real male lifeguards are a lot hunkier than David Hasselhof, whose famously spindly legs are carefully kept out of the TV frame.

### Pacific Palisades Chamber of Commerce

*15330 Antioch Street, Pacific Palisades, CA 90272 (1-310 459 7963).* **Open** 9.30am-5pm Mon-Fri.
Visitor information and literature.

## Malibu

Joan Didion's famous pronouncement about LA, 'there's no there there', could equally be applied to Malibu. Malibu is not a place so much as a long stretch of the Pacific Coast Highway – 27 miles of it – which winds through some of Southern California's most magnificent coastal terrain. Parts of it are lined, on the ocean side, by beach houses of varying sizes and styles and, on the inland side, by largely mediocre commercial buildings which nestle against the Santa Monica Mountains.

The location is so desirable that residents are willing to live with the threat of seasonal, and often destructive fires and floods, and they form a cohesive community dedicated to preventing new development from marring a bucolic lifestyle. Malibu, finally incorporated as a city in 1990, is extremely wealthy (average income $150,000), due to its numerous entertainment industry residents, many of whom inhabit a private beachside street known as the Malibu Colony. But it also houses several trailer parks whose spectacular hillside locations make them the most enviable low-rent accommodation in the country. Malibu has neither major industry nor major culture. Its treats lie mainly in the beaches, restaurants, cafés and canyons (within yards of the entrance to one of the many canyon trails you can be completely out of view of the city).

Malibu eating experiences include top-notch California cuisine at Wolfgang Puck's **Granita** (23725 West Malibu Road), coffee and ornamental cakes at **Xanadu French Bakery** (3900 Cross Creek Road) and, if you prefer a grittier atmosphere, you can join bikers and surfers for burgers and all-day breakfast at the notorious **Malibu Inn & Restaurant** (22969 Pacific Coast Highway).

Students study business and other subjects at **Pepperdine University** (24255 Pacific Coast Highway, at Malibu Canyon Road). If you want to learn about conservation techniques for trees and flowers, take one of the bi-monthly Wednesday tours at La Diva Barbra's **Streisand Center for Conservancy Studies** (5750 Ramirez Canyon Road); book in advance on 1-310 589 2850, ext 301.

Malibu has a significant landmark, the **Adamson House**, a stunning 1929 Spanish-style house, which sits, together with the **Malibu Lagoon Museum**, in the **Malibu Lagoon State Park**. The Adamson House is adorned with decorative tiles manufactured at the once celebrated (and now closed) Malibu Tile Works. Visit the museum for more information about that and other Malibu historical artefacts.

### Malibu Chamber of Commerce

*Suite 100, 23805 Stuart Ranch Road, Malibu, CA 90265 (1-310 456 9025).* **Open** 9am-5pm Mon-Fri.
Visitor information and literature.

**Malibu**, *where the living is easy – for those who can afford it.*

# Westside: Inland

*Home to the nightlife of Sunset Strip and the daylight snobbery of Beverly Hills, this is the LA of popular imagination; a playground for the rich, the famous and the party crowd.*

## West Hollywood

The tiny city of West Hollywood (1.9 square miles) is the epicentre of gay and lesbian life in Los Angeles. It was formerly administered by LA County and somewhat neglected until 1984, when it became an independent city. Since then its problem has been not decay but growth. Its active nightlife centres predominantly around Santa Monica and Sunset Boulevards, where a string of restaurants, coffee bars and nightclubs are hopping nearly every night of the week.

One of the most lively parts of West Hollywood is the famous **Sunset Strip**. This is the stretch of Sunset Boulevard (one of the longest streets in LA) that runs approximately from Doheny Drive to Laurel Canyon in West Hollywood. Its development began in 1924 and by the 1930s it was Hollywood's playground, home to clubs like the Trocadero, Mocambo, The Players and Ciro's where performers such as Lena Horne and Edith Piaf belted out their sets. In the 1950s, Mickey Cohen and Bugsy Siegel called it home and in 1963 the **Whisky A-Go-Go** (still a club for breaking new acts) became the first discotheque on the West Coast. With Whisky's success, clubs such as Gazzarri's, the Zodiac, the Galaxy, Filthy McNasty's (named after a WC Fields movie) and The Trip opened. The Mamas and the Papas, the Byrds, the Doors and countless others played on The Strip, starting a musical revolution which ended in a riot in 1966, when young club-goers protested in the streets against the proposed redevelopment of such key venues as Pandora's Box.

In the 1970s the moguls moved in – David Geffen, Phil Spector, the disco giant Casablanca Records – and the Strip is still home to Geffen Island Records and other major record companies. Today, its glitzy, Las Vegas quality is kept alive by huge billboards – the Marlboro man, Absolut Vodka and murals of Elizabeth Taylor and James Dean painted on the sides of buildings. The **Comedy Store** helped break stars like Robin Williams, David Letterman and Whoopi Goldberg and still hosts comedic legends, and music clubs, such as the **House of Blues** and Johnny Depp's **The Viper Room**, continue to present the latest sounds. Restaurants such as **Chin Chin** (popular lunch place) and **Talesai** (great Thai food) and

hotels such as **Château Marmont** (where John Belushi died and Greta Garbo lived) and **The Mondrian**, which still brim with celebs help to keep the legend of the Strip alive. Bookstore **Book Soup** is well loved for its huge selection of literature, mags and late opening.

West Hollywood is one of the few districts that is easily walkable. Head a few blocks south of Sunset Boulevard to find exclusive restaurants such as **Morton's** on Melrose Avenue, **The Ivy** on North Robertson Boulevard (famed for its celebrity clientele and Hollywood deals), **Chaya Brasserie** on Alden Drive (more celebs and a good bar scene), **Le Colonial** on Beverly Boulevard (a restaurant/bar of the moment, jammed with celebs and famous for its 'list'), **Cicada** (music-biz hangout), a string of excellent French restaurants along La Cienega Boulevard, and **Tail-o'-the-Pup** on North San Vicente Boulevard, a landmark 1938 hot dog stand built in the shape of a huge hot dog.

**The Urth Café** on Melrose Avenue is popular place for its organic coffee, while next door **The Bodhi Tree** is a well-known Bhuddist bookstore and lecture room. The **Sunset Marquis** hotel (just south of Sunset Boulevard on Alta Loma Road) is a music celeb hangout, while over on Robertson Boulevard, **LunaPark** is a popular restaurant and eclectic nightclub. Tucked away at the northern end of Kings Road, the **Schindler House** and its garden, designed by RM Schindler, is an oasis of minimalist architecture, and over on Doheny Drive the **Lloyd Wright Home and Studio,** designed by Frank Lloyd Wright's eldest son, is a masterpiece of quirky architecture.

The **Pacific Design Center** (PDC) on 8687 Melrose Avenue at San Vicente Boulevard dominates West Hollywood's skyline. A gigantic blue and green glass building, it was designed by Cesar Pelli in 1975 to house outlets for the interior design trade. Fondly known as 'the blue whale', it is somewhat under-used for its size except when it hosts the bustling annual West Week design convention. South of the PDC on Beverly Boulevard and La Cienega Boulevard is the monstrous **Beverly Center** mall, a huge 'grey whale' as big as Pacific Design Center, housing the usual shopping outlets and where the Paul Mazursky film *Scenes from a Mall* was shot.

Dotted throughout the city are a scattering of art galleries, from Thomas Solomon's Garage (928 Fairfax Avenue) with its array of contemporary work to **Name That Toon Icons of Happiness** (8483 Melrose Avenue), an animation, clay, 3-D and computer art store. And if you're ever curious about American hardware, **Koontz** on Santa Monica Boulevard offers the best selection of fixtures and fittings in LA and very helpful staff.

## Beverly Hills

The city of Beverly Hills extends either side of Santa Monica and Sunset Boulevards, south-west of West Hollywood. All the clichés are true: expensively manicured and policed to within an inch of its so-called life, it comes on as a theme park for the rich, with shopping, eating and looking good in your car the major activities. It's brimming with lavish mansions and celebrities (Douglas Fairbanks and Mary Pickford were the first to move in, to their mansion Pickfair, in 1920), and is now populated by rich immigrants, with the second most spoken language being Farsi. The area is replete with lushly planted streets, lilac-flowering jacaranda trees that bloom in April and May and every architectural style imaginable.

The best way to experience the opulent living that is Beverly Hills is to drive around its residential streets that run north-south from Sunset to Santa Monica Boulevards, between Linden and Doheny Drives. Or check out the hillside houses in and around Benedict and Coldwater Canyons, north of Sunset. Just don't drive too slowly or the vigilant BH cops will be on your tail. For locations of celebrity landmarks, *see chapter* **Celebrity City**.

The Spanish Baroque-style **Civic Center**, which straddles Santa Monica Boulevard and Rexford Drive, is a unique reflection of the city's wealth, so carefully coiffed it looks like a movie set. In direct contrast is the Union 76 gas station (on the corner of Little Santa Monica Boulevard and Rexford Drive) with its magnificent 1950s cantilevered concrete canopy.

The real reason most people visit Beverly Hills is the 'Golden Triangle' – the shopping area bounded by Wilshire Boulevard, Canon Drive and Little Santa Monica Boulevard that includes Rodeo Drive, Dayton Way and Brighton Way and contains some of the most expensive shopping outlets in the world: Gucci, Armani, Ralph Lauren, Prada, Chanel, Cartier, Van Cleef & Arpels, among others. **Two Rodeo Drive**, a $200 million ersatz European cobbled walkway which boasts an even greater selection of exclusive stores, is always busy with both window-shopping tourists and serious spenders.

**Westwood Memorial Cemetary***'s most famous occupant. See page 96.*

*Beverly Hills: theme park for the rich.*

The recently refurbished **Beverly Hills Hotel** on Sunset Boulevard, aka 'the Pink Palace', was one of the first buildings to be built in the city and remains a popular celebrity hangout. Its bar, the Polo Lounge, is still the place for power-lunching and movie dealing. **The Peninsula Beverly Hills** on Little Santa Monica Boulevard is also a good place for celebrity-spotting, while next door stands the IM Pei-designed **CAA (Creative Artists Agency)** building, all minimalist white marble and cantilevered glass. The stretch of Beverly Drive south of Wilshire Boulevard to Pico Boulevard is a wonderful example of the kind of 1950s architecture that LA is renowned for.

**Nate & Al** (414 North Beverly Drive) is one of the best New York-style delis in the city, while upscale diner **Kate Mantilini** (9101 Wilshire Boulevard), named after a boxing promoter of the 1940s, is a feast of high-art architecture by noted firm Morphosis. The latest craze, cigar smoking, can easily be sampled, with several cigar hangouts – **Hamilton's**, **Philip Dane's** and **The Grand Havana Room** (a members-only club where the likes of Robert de Niro, Arnold Schwarzenegger and Andy Garcia keep their cigars in the club's beautiful humidor) – all within walking distance of each other.

Away from the shopping frenzy, **Greystone Mansion** (905 Loma Vista Drive), set in 18 landscaped acres, is an oasis of peace and quiet. Built

in 1927 by oil millionaire Edward L Doheny, the 55-room Tudor-style home has been used in such films as *The Witches of Eastwick* and *Indecent Proposal*. The gardens are open to the public.

## Westwood Village & UCLA

The University of California at Los Angeles – UCLA – is a sprawling 400-acre campus, originally built on a bean field in the city of Westwood in 1929. Diverse architectural styles blend together in beautifully landscaped grounds, highlighting the enormous wealth and influence of the school. The university is noted for its library holdings (which are among the largest in the world), its school of business administration, centre for health sciences and sports facilities. Due to the sheer size of the campus, students are always buzzing around and the 'Village' – one of the few walkable neighbourhoods in LA – is a good place for inexpensive food and, south of Wilshire, bookstores and good Persian cuisine. **Schoenberg Hall**, named after the composer who taught at the university in the 1940s, and **Royce Hall** are popular places for concerts.

**Westwood Memorial Cemetary**, on the edge of Westwood Village (1218 Glendon Avenue), is famous for its celebrity graves, including those of Marilyn Monroe and Natalie Wood, but the **Mormon Temple** (best seen from Santa Monica

Boulevard) is by far the most powerful presence in the area. The 257ft tower, crowned with a 15ft gold leaf statue of the angel Mormoni, is the largest temple of the Church of Jesus Christ of Latter Day Saints outside Salt Lake City, Utah. It is only open to church members but the beautifully green, manicured lawn and clean white stone building, which is lit up at night, is always an awe-inspiring sight.

**Rhino Records** and **Border's Books & Music** are both fine and famed outlets for music on Westwood Boulevard, south of Wilshire: the former for its knowledgeable, friendly staff and more eclectic selection of CDs and vinyl; the latter for the sheer volume of merchandise.

**Westside Pavilion** on Pico Boulevard is the epitome of the many 1980s shopping malls in LA; pastel colours juxtaposed with a glass-vaulted atrium and the obligatory selection of high-fashion stores that are in every other mall. However, it also houses the excellent **Samuel Goldwyn** four-screen cinema which often has exclusive runs of independent films. Also notable for its adventurous, independent movie screenings is the **Nuart**, one of LA's last surviving movie repertory houses, on Santa Monica Boulevard at Sawtelle Avenue in West LA (West LA is a loosely defined area that encompasses those areas on the Westside that are not independent cities or neighbourhoods but are in the western end of the city of Los Angeles).

Across the road from Westside Pavilion is **The Apple Pan** (10801 West Pico Boulevard), home of the homely American hamburger and waiters who have worked there 40 years or more. At No.10516 is **John O'Groats**, a Scottish-style eatery with great fish and chips and porridge (honest).

## Bel Air

A posh, sleepy hillside community between Brentwood and Beverly Hills, developed by Alphonzo E Bell in the early 1920s, Bel Air rapidly became a preferred location for stars and other celebrities who valued their privacy and a good view. There's not much for the outsider to see along the winding roads as the best houses are hidden from the street behind huge, imposing walls. Celebs who still inhabit the area include Joni Mitchell, Tom Jones, Barry Manilow, Elizabeth Taylor and Lionel Ritchie.

There's not much to do in Bel Air either, except take a jaunt to the **Hotel Bel-Air** on Stone Canyon Road. This ultra-expensive inn reflects the tranquil, dripping-with-money neighbourhood with its beautifully manicured gardens, a lake full of swans, herb garden, wood-burning fireplaces in the rooms and a cosy secluded bar. It has an expensive but delicious Sunday brunch and is also rumoured to entertain Prince Charles for a drink or two when he's in town. Grace Kelly lived here during her Hollywood years.

## Century City

This tiny city, between Beverly Hills and West LA, was once a movie backlot and the site of Tom Mix westerns. It was bought by Alcoa from 20th Century Fox in 1961 and today is still dominated by Fox studios and an overabundance of high-rise office buildings (8.6 million square feet of office space on only 176 acres). Amid these nondescript buildings, however, are the **Century Plaza towers**, two triangular towers designed by Minoru Yamasaki (who also designed New York's World Trade Center towers), and the **Century Plaza Hotel**, also designed by Yamasaki, a huge high-rise ellipse enlivened at night by orange lighting and a blue-lit fountain that sits in front of the hotel on the grandiose Avenue of the Stars.

**Century City Shopping Center** is a vast (18-acre), upscale mall with a bustling food court, Steven Spielberg's sub-oceanic themed restaurant Dive! and Houston's, a good place to grab a martini and a pizza after a film. It is also home to the **AMC Century 14**, reportedly the second largest movie theatre in the US and thus an excellent choice for blockbusters and very-big-screen entertainment.

*Earth to Planet LA... a forest of satellite dishes outside Sony Film Studios in Culver City.*

## Brentwood

Novelist Raymond Chandler wrote *High Window* and *Lady In The Lake* while living at 12216 Shetland Place, and Marilyn Monroe died a lonely death just down the road at 12305 Fifth Helena Drive. This exclusive residential neighbourhood west of Beverly Hills was farms and fields until 1915 when a real estate agent named Bundy developed them into streets. Landscape architects and engineers were commissioned to create 'flora, arbor and artistic park attractions'. Everything that suggested a formal city street was avoided, so Brentwood is like a small town and the main street, San Vicente Boulevard, has a line of coral trees (the official tree of LA) running down its centre.

The hills north of San Vicente are very rustic, very expensive and, needless to say, home to yet more celebrities. One in particular, OJ Simpson, has done much to put the neighbourhood on the map. Indeed, the condo of murdered Nicole Brown Simpson on Bundy Drive has become a regular tourist attraction and eating the same last meal that Nicole ate at **Mezzaluna** (11750 San Vicente Boulevard) has also become a rather sick pastime for some. The **Cheesecake Factory** has a busy bar scene, while **The New York Bagel Company**, designed by Frank Gehry, is the place to have breakfast. **Dutton's** on San Vicente Boulevard is one of the best bookstores in LA, sprawling its collection of books new and used over four requisitioned condo units.

Brentwood is also home to the soon-to-be-opened **J Paul Getty Center** on Getty Center Drive, an extension of the J Paul Getty Museum in Malibu. Set in the Santa Monica mountains, this complex will house everything but the Getty Trust's Greek and Roman collections, which will stay in Malibu.

## Culver City

An incorporated city with its own police force, Culver City, at the south-eastern crux of the I10/I405 intersection, is renowned for being safe – if boring. At one time it was the home of three major motion picture studios – Metro Goldwyn Mayer, Hal Roach Studios and Selznick International Studios – and produced half the films made in the US. MGM, which claimed to have 'more stars than there are in heaven', gave up its last piece of turf to the producers of *Dallas* and *Falcon Crest*. Now there is little else here. Sony Film Studios dominates the area and a host of art and photography warehouse conversions by some of LA's most progressive architects, such as the late Frank Israel and Eric Owen Moss, fill in the rest.

The old Helms Bakery building on Venice Boulevard now houses a collection of furniture stores, both contemporary and antique, as well as jazz venue **The Jazz Bakery** (3233 Helms Avenue). Further west at 10319 Venice Boulevard is **Versailles**, a cheap and cheerful Cuban restaurant worth visiting.

# Hollywood & Midtown

**Hollywood the word might exude glamour, but Hollywood the place singularly fails to. Console yourself with a visit to its more interesting neighbours.**

## Hollywood

Hollywood does not exist. A place that shares the name still continues to sputter along despite earthquakes, collapsing streets (due to subway construction mishaps) and general urban malaise, but the Hollywood that everyone imagines – the glittering, floodlit paradise of filmic immortality – is forever lost to the ages. Certainly, you can see glimpses of what Hollywood Boulevard used to be in the wonderfully overdone facades of **Mann's Chinese Theater** (6925 Hollywood Boulevard) and **El Capitan Theater** (6838 Hollywood Boulevard), but these days the famous street is just a profoundly depressing stretch of boarded-up storefronts, tacky souvenir shops and teenage runaways with mohawk haircuts.

The **Walk of Fame**, with its 2,000 star-shaped sidewalk plaques bearing the names of entertainment greats, still exists, but the bloom is well off the rose there, too; these days, anyone with $4,800 and a decent publicity agent can score a star of their own. The legendary intersection of **Hollywood and Vine**, once considered the heart of Hollywood, no longer buzzes with starlets and movie moguls – it's just another nondescript street corner.

Still, it's worth making a brief pilgrimage to the area's remaining landmarks. A first glimpse of the 50ft-high letters of the **Hollywood sign**, which stands on Mount Lee, about a mile to the east of Hollywood and Vine, is always a thrill. A good place to view it from is Paramount Studios at Melrose Avenue and Gower Street.

**Mann's Chinese Theater** – *struggling to keep the Hollywood dream alive.*

And any worth-his-salt music fan will experience a sense of wonder on seeing the **Capitol Records Building** at 1750 North Vine Street – it's shaped like a stack of records and topped with a stylus, allegedly the idea of songwriter Johnny Mercer and singer Nat King Cole – while the art deco interior of the **Pantages Theater** (6233 Hollywood Boulevard) is so beautiful and disorienting that it verges on the psychedelic. Anyone with a fetish for underwear or a taste for the camp should pay a visit to the Celebrity Lingerie Hall of Fame – an 'only in LA' exhibition of underwear worn by living and no-longer-living stars – at **Frederick's of Hollywood** (6608 Hollywood Boulevard). Underwear shop **Playmates of Hollywood** (at number 6438) occasionally holds transvestite lingerie shows that are not to be believed.

Unleash the tourist within and pay a visit to the **Hollywood Wax Museum** (6767 Hollywood Boulevard) or the **Guiness World of Records Museum** (at 6764), but make sure you leave the psychedelic drugs in your hotel room – both tourist traps contain exhibits that, if viewed in a fragile state of mind, could warp you for life. Those looking for a more reverent view of Hollywood history should check out the mini-museum of cinematic memorabilia on the second-floor mezzanine of the **Radisson Hollywood Roosevelt Hotel** (7000 Hollywood Boulevard), while memorabilia collectors and film fans should plan to drop some cash at the **Hollywood Book & Poster Co** (at number 6349), a store jammed to the rafters with obscure videos, rare lobby cards (promotional signs that used to be displayed in cinema lobbies) and stills from just about every movie ever made.

Sunset Boulevard east of Fairfax Avenue is pretty sleazy as well (Hugh Grant was nicked in this part of town), but it somehow seems a lot more vital than its counterpart to the north. Maybe it's the constant, furtive comings and goings from the hourly-rate motels or Sunset's equally busy string of guitar stores. Anyone interested in the latter should pay a visit to **Guitar Center** (7425 Sunset Boulevard): the selection of axes is dizzying in the extreme, and it's entertainment enough just to listen to the 'Hey, dude!' patois of the long-haired, be-spandexed shop assistants and customers.

**Crossroads of the World** (6671 Sunset Boulevard), a charming little outdoor shopping plaza built in 1936, predates Los Angeles' strip mall explosion by 50 years; unfortunately, its descendants chose to substitute poured concrete for the Crossroads' eye-pleasing fusion of French, Spanish and Italian architectural styles. Pity.

After Mann's Chinese Theater, the **Cinerama Dome** (6360 Sunset Boulevard) is the best place in town to see a movie, even if the wide-screen Cinerama process has long since thrown in the towel. Once you've experienced the gigantic screen and plush seats, you'll never want to go to your local multiplex again.

The buildings that comprise **A&M Studios** (1416 North La Brea Avenue) resonate not only with the sounds of the Rolling Stones and the Carpenters (among the thousands of other acts which have recorded here over the past few decades), but with cinematic history as well; the core of the complex was built in 1918 by Charlie Chaplin, who used it as his movie studio. Jazz musician Herb Alpert purchased the place for A&M in 1966, but concrete prints of Chaplin's feet are allegedly still visible outside studio 3.

**Moletown** (900 North La Brea Avenue) is a Hollywood landmark of an entirely different sort; it's *the* place to purchase memorabilia of current television hits, be it a *Friends* sweatshirt or an *NYPD Blue* baseball cap. Created by studio lighting whiz Peter Mole, Moletown is filled with mementos from his career, such as stills from his work with the Little Rascals (the group of child actors who appeared in the *Our Gang* films in the 1920s and 1930s) and a collection of lighting rigs. It's the one Hollywood attraction that's never crowded.

In the end (no pun intended), the best place to look for the Ghost of Hollywood Past is at **Hollywood Memorial Cemetary** (6000 Santa Monica Boulevard). Located just north of the **Paramount Pictures** lot (5555 Melrose Avenue), the cemetery serves as the final resting place for such limelit luminaries as Tyrone Power, Cecil B DeMille, Douglas Fairbanks Senior, Adolph Mejou, Nelson Eddy, studio mogul Harry Cohn (who wanted to be buried facing his beloved Columbia Studios), Peter Lorre, Peter Finch and Rudolph Valentino; legend has it that a mysterious 'Woman in Black' still stalks the cemetery, mourning for the latter. The grounds are incredibly peaceful, the decades-old monuments unique in design and, overall, it's much less of a downer than a stroll along Hollywood Boulevard. As the headstone of Mel Blanc – the voice of Porky Pig, Elmer Fudd et al – reads: 'That's all, folks!'

## Fairfax

Although Los Angeles's first major Jewish community settled in the East LA neighbourhood of Boyle Heights, the stretch of Fairfax Avenue between Beverly Boulevard and Melrose Avenue has been Los Angeles' main Jewish drag since the 1940s. (The neighbourhood's heavy Hassidic population makes it the safest place in LA to jog on a Friday evening.) If you're shopping for a new menorah or some cassettes of the latest in Israeli pop music, this is the place to go.

*The perfectly formed **MacArthur Park**.*
*See page 103.*

Kosher grocers, butcher's shops, restaurants and bakeries line the street, almost all of which are closed on Saturday. The exception to this is the legendary **Canter's** (419 North Fairfax Avenue), a World War II-era kosher restaurant, deli and bakery that's open 24 hours a day. The food is delicious and authentic (homesick New Yorkers eat here on a regular basis), and the portions are generous. Late-night diners are often treated to the spectacle of celebs such as Madonna or Sheryl Crow tucking into a plate of Jewish soul food. Another good lunch spot is **Eat-a-Pita** (No.465), a pleasant outdoor stand that serves some of the best Middle Eastern fast-food (falafel and so on) in town.

Just south of the Beverly-Fairfax intersection lies **CBS Television City** (7800 Beverly Boulevard), home to many a CBS game show and sit-com. Farther south along the same block is one of LA's most magical spots, the **Farmers' Market** (6333 West Third Street). Originating in 1934 as a place where local farmers could hawk their wares, the market has evolved over time into an enchanting outdoor maze of produce sellers, butcher's shops, restaurants and cheesy souvenir stands, patronised by the most integrated mix of humanity you'll see anywhere in the city. Grab an oyster po' boy from the Gumbo Pot, order a malted shake at Kokomo or just grab a stool at one of the market's two bars and watch the world go by.

## Miracle Mile & Midtown

Running 16 miles from Santa Monica to the eastern edge of Downtown, Wilshire Boulevard is essentially the spinal cord of Los Angeles. Taking a trip east along Wilshire from Fairfax Avenue to Alvarado Street is one of the few ways left to truly commune with the various phases of the city's history; much of it has gone missing, but various levels are still visible to the naked eye.

The **99 Cent Store**, on Wilshire Boulevard just west of Fairfax Avenue, was the source of much controversy when it opened in 1994. Local citizens' groups protested both the addition of the garish facade and the presence of the 'shady individuals' that such a bargain store would undoubtedly attract to their pristine neighbourhood; however, other than causing some traffic jams during evening rush hour, the store has had little adverse effect on the area. Besides, it's a great place for finding sweets that you haven't seen in 10 years. The neighbouring diner, **Johnie's** (6101 Wilshire Boulevard), is a rather rundown example of 1950s 'Googie' coffee shop architecture. It looks gorgeous when lit up at night, but is best viewed from the outside at all times; the food is not great.

The **Miracle Mile** district stretches along Wilshire Boulevard from Fairfax to La Brea Avenues. So named because of its tremendous commercial growth during the 1920s, the appellation

now seems somewhat ironic, given the rate at which resident businesses have been shutting their doors. The saga of the **May Co** department store (6067 Wilshire Boulevard) pretty much sums up the situation. Opened in 1940, the store was one of the commercial mainstays of the district, but the recent shift in consumer shopping habits (malls such as the Beverly Center now reign supreme) and the psychological residue of the 1992 LA riots (as far as most suburban shoppers were concerned, anywhere south of Ventura Boulevard was considered South-Central) forced it to close in 1993. The impressive facade, once slated for demolition, still stands, and the LA County Museum of Art supposedly has plans to renovate it, but it seems that it will be a while before the doors open again.

This stretch of Wilshire is also known as **Museum Row**, and for good reason. The **Los Angeles County Museum of Art** (5905 Wilshire Boulevard), the **Petersen Automotive Museum** (No.6060), the **Carole & Barry Kaye Museum of Miniatures** (No.5900), the **Craft and Folk Art Museum** (No.5800), and the **George C Page Museum of Tar Pit Discoveries** (No.5801) are all within easy walking distance of each other. The latter features the added attraction of the La Brea Tar Pits; a huge, bubbling swamp of primordial ooze, it remains, after millions of years, a great place to ruminate on the briefness of your existence.

The much-modernised **El Rey Theater** (5519 Wilshire Boulevard), built in 1936 in the Streamline Moderne style, regularly features live salsa bands. A few miles and many generic strip malls to the east, the **Wiltern Center** (at Western Avenue) is enjoying a similar renaissance. A breathtaking green art deco pile built in 1931, it lingered in a state of advanced decrepitude during much of the 1970s and 1980s, before being rescued from the wrecking ball and turned into a performing arts and commercial centre. Popular pop acts like Blur and Lenny Kravitz have recently strutted their respective stuffs inside the stunning **Wiltern Theater** on the corner of the Center. The neighbouring **Atlas Bar & Grill** (at 3760) is a must for California cuisine and cabaret in a deliciously camp interior.

Many of the small businesses along the stretch of Wilshire Boulevard between Western and Vermont Avenues have closed, due to traffic problems caused by recent Metro subway construction, giving this part of town a particularly bleak look. All is not lost, however. The **Ambassador Hotel** (3400 Wilshire Boulevard) – known to most as the site of Robert F Kennedy's assassination on the eve of the 1968 California primary elections – has reopened, and its adjoining nightclub, the **Coconut Grove**, is occasionally revived for lavish Hollywood parties. Restoration is also promised for the glorious **Bullock's Wilshire** (at 3050); one of the first department stores to open (in 1929) outside Downtown, it closed its doors after the 1992 riots.

Revitalisation is still light years away, however, for **Lafayette Park** (625 South Lafayette Park Place) and its larger neighbour, **MacArthur Park** (Wilshire Boulevard between Alvarado and Park View Streets). The latter, with its recently restored lake and 500ft high water spout, is an especially grand example of urban landscaping – that is, if you can ignore the crackheads, the drug dealers and the Central American gang members who populate it. It's a shame; even in its present state, it's still not difficult to see how the park could have inspired Jimmy Webb's epic ballad. But this time, the only thing left out in the rain is the park's resident encampment of homeless individuals.

## Hancock Park

A gorgeous residential neighbourhood dating back to 1910, Hancock Park is home to some of the most jaw-droppingly opulent mansions found outside of Beverly Hills and Bel Air. Bounded by Wilshire Boulevard and Van Ness, Highland and Melrose Avenues, Hancock Park is best toured by car – the local security services are apt to be suspicious of anyone on foot. Historically an Anglo enclave, it excluded blacks and Jews (who moved west) until 1948 when Nat 'King' Cole was the first African-American to live there. (Don't confuse this area with Hancock Park, an actual park west on Wilshire Boulevard.)

Stop for refreshment on the stretch of Larchmont Boulevard known as **Larchmont Village** (between Beverly Boulevard and First Street). This charming couple of blocks has a variety of restaurants – the Italian trattoria La Luna, at 113 North Larchmont Boulevard, is great –

antique shops and other small businesses, many of them housed in buildings built in the 1920s. The residents and neighbours of Larchmont Village take great pride in the area's period feel. At the time of writing, the only graffiti noticeable in the area was the spray-painted 'Go away!' on the walls of a newly constructed Blockbuster Video outlet.

## Koreatown

Torched during the 1992 riots, Koreatown – the Midtown neighbourhood roughly comprising the area south of Wilshire Boulevard, along Pico Boulevard between Western and Vermont Avenues – has made a remarkable comeback. Tensions between the Korean and African-American communities (and the area's Central American population) haven't exactly abated, but – for the shopowners, at least – things seem to be back to business as usual.

Korean banks, men's clubs and storefront grocers abound, especially along Pico and Olympic Boulevards, and there are even a couple of Korean car dealers. There are also loads of Korean eateries, of course. Although Korean cooking, with its heavier, meat-based dishes, hasn't quite caught on with non-Koreans, adventurous eaters should take the opportunity to have a spot of lunch in the area.

The pricey **Woo Lae Oak** (623 South Western Avenue) gets regular raves, while holes-in-the-wall like **Ham Hung** (809 South Ardmore Avenue) offer delicious but cheaper regional cooking. For a carnivorous (and non-Korean) experience, try **Taylor's Prime Steaks** (3361 West Eighth Street), a chop house with enormous buttoned-and-tufted booths and almost equally enormous steaks.

# Downtown

*It might be a skyscraper short of a skyline, but LA's downtown can offer a cross-section of Pacific Rim culture and some bonzo buildings besides.*

If Los Angeles has a centre, then it can be found in Downtown. Stretching south from the eastern end of Sunset Boulevard, it's the site of the original city and home to most of LA's political and financial institutions, many of its major historical landmarks and the Museum of Contemporary Art (MOCA). As the oldest part of the city, it's an area of contrasts: the faded, decaying elegance of early 1900s buildings alongside the monolithic skyscrapers of the 1980s. Admittedly, as US downtowns go, it's a little pathetic – small, lacking buzz and pretty much lifeless out of office hours – but it does have some impressive architecture, historic landmarks, the bustling Broadway, a Chinatown and, less than a mile away, Little Tokyo, the heart of LA's Japanese community.

After years of post-war decline, Downtown attracted a lot of investment in the 1980s, much of it from the Far East, and now it's packed during the week with commuting office workers, while the main drag, Broadway, is a buzzing Latino shopping zone, particularly at weekends. Every year,

on 5 May, Downtown plays host to the Cinco de Mayo celebrations: a parade down Olvera Street and then a fiesta commemorating the Mexican victory at the battle of Puebla.

Downtown is one of the few areas of LA where it's better to walk than drive. Everything can be seen in a day and DASH buses (*see chapter* **Getting Around**) serve the area at frequent intervals. Although it's not the best place in LA for star-spotting, you may well see film crews at work: it's a popular location for movies and TV shows. Most notably, perhaps, Ridley Scott immortalised Downtown's skyline and its landmark Bradbury Building in *Blade Runner*, a seminal LA movie.

No-one really knows how many people live in Downtown and it's certainly not a conventional residential area. It also attracts a considerable number of homeless people. Avoid walking round the area at night and, if you're arriving or departing from the Greyhound terminal on Seventh Street, be careful in its immediate vicinity.

*The glory days of the railroads are evoked by gracious* **Union Station** *(see page 105).*

### Los Angeles Convention & Visitors Bureau

*685 South Figueroa Street, LA, CA 90017 (1-213 689 8822).* **Open** 8am-5pm Mon-Fri; 8.30am-3pm Sat. Visitor information and literature.

## Chinatown

Located at the northern end of Downtown and starting where Broadway meets Sunset Boulevard, Chinatown has suffered in recent years from an exodus of residents to the San Gabriel Valley, now *the* place for Chinese food. Nevertheless, this small but busy neighbourhood is still home to an estimated 30,000 people and remains the spiritual centre of Los Angeles' Chinese community. North Broadway and North Spring Street are the main thoroughfares, the site of banks, businesses and traditional markets, while the streets running off them are also worth a look. Every February, giant dragons snake down North Broadway during celebrations for Chinese New Year.

There are plenty of restaurants in the area. **Ocean Seafood** (in the Chunsan Plaza at 747 North Broadway, between Ord and Alpine Streets), is good, but gets very busy at weekends. **Sam Woo's** (803 North Broadway, at Alpine Street) is also reasonable. Apart from eating, there's little to do here at night.

## Olvera Street

Just across Sunset Boulevard from Chinatown is **El Pueblo de Los Angeles Historical Monument** (622 North Main Street), a historic park and outdoor museum on the site of the original settlement of Los Angeles. In fact, the very first settlement was about half a mile from here, but there's now no trace of it. Consequently, LA's official birthday is 4 September 1781, the day that the first Spanish settlers began farming and building ranches on this site. The museum courtyard is occupied by taco stands and a gift shop. Next door is the **Old Plaza Church**. Established in 1784, it's the oldest Catholic church in LA, is still in use and has some impressive ceiling murals.

Cross Main Street and you reach the **Plaza**. With a bandstand in the middle, it's a popular place for performances by dancers and musicians and the trees offer some shade from the sun; in one corner is the **Mexican Cultural Institute**. The Plaza is the site of two annual festivals, the Blessing of the Animals at Easter and Las Posadas, just before Christmas. Running off the eastern side of the Plaza is **Olvera Street**, a small and narrow thoroughfare that's full of stalls selling postcards and Mexican handicrafts. Renovated in 1930 as a Mexican marketplace, it's now just a tourist trap but the **El Pueblo Gallery**, which shows local art, is worth checking out.

Olvera Street also contains **Avila Adobe**, the oldest house in Los Angeles. This small ranch-style house was built in 1818 and has now been restored, furnished with period pieces and operates as a museum. There are numerous Mexican restaurants along Olvera, all pretty average.

Visible from the Plaza and a short walk across Alameda Street is **Union Station** (800 North Alameda Street), one of the most accomplished structures in the city. Opened in 1939 on the site of the original Chinatown, which was consequently moved to its present location, it was the last of the great American train stations to be built and unified the three railroads that then served LA. With its distinctive, Spanish Mission-style exterior, marble floors and high ceilings, it's an evocative place at which to arrive in or depart from LA. Don't confuse Union Station with the imposing piece of colonial Spanish architecture that stands next to it: that's just the post office.

## Little Tokyo

Head south down Alameda Street for a few blocks, past Temple Street, and you reach the **Geffen Contemporary** wing of the **Museum of Contemporary Art** (152 North Central Avenue). Formerly known as the Temporary Contemporary, this is the second of MOCA's two sites, both in Downtown; the other is at California Plaza. If you buy a ticket for one site, it gets you into the other on the same day. The Geffen Contemporary is housed in an old warehouse converted by Frank Gehry. It's a more flexible space than the California Plaza site and concentrates mainly on post-World War II art. The always provocative exhibitions change frequently. A café and shop should be completed by early 1997.

Just down Central Avenue from MOCA, on the corner of First Street, is the **Japanese American National Museum** (369 East First Street). It's an appropriate place to start a tour of Little Tokyo, which begins at First Street and spreads west and north. The museum is dedicated to recording and relating the extensive history of the Japanese American community – Little Tokyo has been in existence for over a century – and mixes exhibits with films and, occasionally, performance art.

Cross First Street from the museum and you enter the **Japanese Village Plaza** (335 East Second Street), a two-storey mini-mall with restaurants, shops and karaoke bars. Pop into **Sushi and Teri** or the **Flying Fish** for something to eat. Restaurants here generally stay open later than most of LA's eating places and you can turn up after midnight and still get served.

At the end of the plaza is the **Fire Tower** with its distinctive tiled roof. Nearby is the **Japanese American Cultural and Community Center** (244 South San Pedro

Street). The centre has an art gallery and Japanese garden, and Kabuki performances and dance recitals are held in the **Japan America Theater** on the same site. Also in the area is the **Higashi Honganji Buddhist Temple** (505 East Third Street, at Central Avenue). With its subtle roof, it blends neatly into its very western surroundings. **St Vibiana's Cathedral** (114 East Second Street) is also nearby. Built in 1876 and in very poor condition, it's currently the subject of a battle between the diocese, which wants to tear it down and build a new one, and conservationists, who want to preserve it. If it's still standing, it's worth a look.

If you continue west past the Higashi Temple, you'll enter the Artists/Loft District – although the name is something of a misnomer: there are more homeless here than artists. During the 1980s, when both Downtown and the LA art scene were booming, artists began converting the derelict warehouses that are scattered throughout the area into studios and apartments. Developers quickly started doing the same thing in the hope of reproducing New York's SoHo on the West Coast, but the expected rush of tenants never materialised.

## Civic Center

A few blocks north of Little Tokyo along First Street is the area where many of LA's administrative and political institutions are based. The first you'll encounter is the **Times-Mirror Building**, home to the *Los Angeles Times* (202 West First Street, at Spring Street). The building is a slightly tatty example of 1930s architecture and the newspaper is the subject of derision for East Coasters, but it's an important LA institution, founded by the Chandler family, one of the elite WASP families that ran LA in the late 1800s and played a major part in the development of Downtown. Conveniently for *Times* reporters, **City Hall** (200 North Spring Street) is just across the road. Surrounded by uninspired modern office blocks, City Hall's graceful art deco lines have appeared in many movies and television shows. Until 1960 it was the tallest building in LA.

Nearby, in the Los Angeles Mall, an utterly soulless shopping area, is the **Los Angeles Children's Museum** (310 North Main Street). Partly designed by the ubiquitous Frank Gehry, it's an ambitious and fun museum with plenty of interactive exhibits and installations. Round the corner, on Aliso and Los Angeles Streets, is the **Metropolitan Detention Centre**, LA's newest prison. Hi-tech and designed to blend in with the office blocks around it, the structure looks nothing like a conventional jail. Local legend has it that a group of Japanese tourists once tried to check into it, thinking it was a hotel.

## Broadway

If you want a taste of what a real Mexican shopping street looks like, as opposed to the tourist tack of Olvera Street, then Broadway is the place to go. Running the whole length of Downtown, it's one of the most fascinating streets in the area – a place where old Los Angeles, in the shape of the once grandiose and now mostly decrepit buildings that line it, meets the new, increasingly Hispanic LA. Back in the 1920s and 1930s it was the most fashionable shopping and entertainment zone in the city, the place where developers vied with each other to put up stunning structures such as the 1893 **Bradbury Building** (304 South Broadway), where legendary impresarios like Sid Grauman (who was also responsible for Mann's Chinese Theater in Hollywood) built glittering palaces to show the movies that were beginning to dominate LA life, and where the stars came for the premieres of those movies.

The post-war decline of Downtown hit Broadway hard and many of the buildings are boarded up or in a state of disrepair, but there's a vitality to the street, particularly at the weekends, that you don't find anywhere else in LA. The stores sell mostly electronic goods, cut-price clothes – this is a good place to buy jeans – and jewellery (LA's jewellery district starts below Fifth Street and Broadway), but you don't come here for the shopping so much as the atmosphere.

Start at Second Street and Broadway and wander south. At the corner of Third Street and Broadway, there's the **Million Dollar Theater**, first opened by Sid Grauman in 1918 and now an evangelical church. Next door is **Grand Central Market** (317 South Broadway), an enclosed market in the Mexican tradition. It's one of the busiest places in Downtown, with a wide variety of fresh fruit stalls, butchers and fishmongers. If you want lunch and a beer, there are also plenty of taco stands, Chinese fast-food counters and pizza joints.

Further down Broadway, just past Sixth Street, is the **Los Angeles Theater** (615 South Broadway). The cinema was built in 90 days for the premiere of Chaplin's *City Lights* in 1930. It's now boarded up, but the extravagant facade is still visible. The only one of the old Broadway movie palaces that's still a working cinema is the huge **Orpheum** (842 South Broadway, between Eighth and Ninth Streets); built in 1926, it's a wacky blend of the colonial Spanish and French Gothic styles.

For a break from the hustle of Broadway, turn west at Fifth Street and head for **Pershing Square**. Named after the commander of the US Army in World War I, the square hosts free jazz, blues and salsa concerts during the summer and it's a good place to catch your breath. Dominating

# A river runs through it

The beleaguered LA River, infamous as a concrete-swathed storm drain, is regarded by most Angelenos as an embarrassing eyesore – but that's because few have ever stepped out of their cars for a close-up look. Even fewer know the secret spots where you can still find 125 species of birds, catch crayfish and walk riverbanks overgrown with lush vegetation, remnants of the river's past as an oasis draped in cottonwoods and sycamore, with steelhead trout leaping from its ponds.

The river was one of the main attractions for the original settlers, but it proved to have the rather disconcerting habit of changing its course. In the nineteenth century it discharged into Santa Monica Bay, now it meets the sea at Long Beach. Mid-century developers pinned it down in an ugly concrete channel for 46 miles of its 50-mile length. When film-makers needed a location that said 'urban wasteland', this is where they came: think the truck/bike chase in *Terminator 2* (pictured), the car race in *Grease*. So it takes a special sensibility to enjoy the contrasts afforded by mallards and great blue herons cheek by jowl with railyards, freeways and light industry.

## THE BRIDGES

Built between 1918 and the early 1930s, the bridges on the stretch of the LA River that curls round the east of Downtown represent some of the city's finest civic architecture. Created to address a traffic crisis early in the century, they form the major links between East LA, Little Tokyo, Chinatown and the Central Business District. Ranging from Beaux Arts to modern in style, these concrete arch structures are among the largest and most beautiful bridges in the US, a direct result of the turn-of-the-century 'City Beautiful' movement.

The bridges are best appreciated in twilight, when they are visible but also illuminated. From north to south, the more significant examples are at Glendale-Hyperion, North Broadway, Cesar Chavez Boulevard (previously Macy Street), Aliso Street (Main), First Street, Fourth Street, Seventh Street, Ninth Street (Olympic) and Washington Boulevard. There are also several freeway crossings.

The magnificent Glendale-Hyperion bridge, at the north end of the Silver Lake district, is the most frankly modern of the group and affords fine views of the Silver Lake and Glendale hills. Its wide, graceful arches, copper lamps and procession of octagonal pylons create a rhythmic impression as you cross.

Nearby is perhaps the easiest access for a walk along a stretch of the LA River that still follows its natural course, and has the wildlife to match. Park at Eatz café on the Atwater side of Los Feliz Boulevard and look for an opening in the fence some 15 yards upstream. You can walk one and a half miles upstream past stables and golf courses, availing yourself of a horse-crossing into Griffith Park. This is the site of the just-opened LA River bikeway, running north to the Gene Autry Western Museum and soon to continue south to Downtown.

Other bridge highlights include the beautiful, simple spandrels of the North Broadway bridge alongside Elysian Park. Cesar Chavez Avenue, with its Spanish Colonial twisted columns and triumphal arches, lies just beyond Union Station. The Fourth Street bridge is notable for its gothic arches and antique-styled lamps and Sixth Street impresses with its grand expanses. Furthest south, Washington Boulevard is decorated with terracotta friezes depicting tool-wielding workers engaged in the construction of a modern-day bridge.

## LOOKING AHEAD

Currently an LA River walk or bridge tour is likely to be a solitary experience, but change is afoot. Los Angeles is shifting its attitudes toward the river, joining a national movement for urban river restoration. Civic and environmental groups are calling for a 'greening' of the 58-mile long waterway, and Los Angeles County has just empowered a committee to make area-wide plans for watershed management that will promote naturalising the river wherever possible. With the push of its citizenry, it is likely that Los Angeles will once again have a river oasis, a source of pride and pleasure rather than embarrassment.

the western corner of the square is the **Biltmore Hotel**, built in 1923 and one of the grandest hotels in Los Angeles. Churchill used to stay here when he was in town.

## Financial District

A block west of Pershing Square and you enter the land of the skyscraper. The major banks have their huge, gleaming offices here and they dwarf everything around them. This neighbourhood used to be known as Bunker Hill and a century or so ago was where LA's rich built their houses, but most of those mansions are now long gone. The only remnant of that era is **Angels Flight**, the world's shortest railway (Hill Street, between Third and Fourth Streets). Opened in 1901, the funicular was designed to connect Bunker Hill with the business district that was then located around Hill and Spring Streets; it saved the residents from having to walk the steep slope back to their houses. It reopened in February 1996; a ride costs 25 cents and takes a mere two minutes (up and down).

A minute west of Bunker Hill and you reach the **Los Angeles Central Library** (630 West Fifth Street, between Grand Avenue and Flower Street). Completed in 1926 and recently refurbished after a fire, it's an excellent library and has a dramatic, tiled pyramid tower. Virtually opposite is the **Westin Bonaventure Hotel** (404 South Figueroa Street), the most distinctive skyscraper in Downtown. With its interior pools and bubble-shaped elevators, it's a refreshing change from the uniformity of most of the district's tall buildings.

If you feel the need to watch a movie while in the area, head for **Laemmle's Grande** (349 South Figueroa Street), a modern four-screen cinema that's rarely crowded. Also near here is the **Los Angeles Visitors & Convention Bureau** (685 South Figueroa Street), the main information centre for the city. The staff are very helpful.

Backtrack from the library down Fifth Street to Grand Avenue and then head north up the sharp little hill: the **Wells Fargo Centre** is on your left. Apart from being the headquarters of the Wells Fargo bank, it also houses the Wells Fargo History Museum, which tells the story of the bank founded in the heyday of the California Gold Rush. There's a 100-year-old stagecoach and gold nuggets on display.

Just up from the Wells Fargo Centre on the other side of the road is the other **MOCA** site (250 South Grand Avenue). Part of the billion-dollar California Plaza development, the museum is unmissable: there's a huge Swiss Army knife, designed by Claes Oldenburg, in front of it.

Carry on walking up Grand Avenue and on the left you'll come to the huge **Music Center** (at First Street). Gathered together in one complex are the Dorothy Chandler Pavilion, where the Oscars take place and the LA Philharmonic lives, the Mark Taper Forum and the Ahmanson Theatre, regarded as two of LA's better theatres. Guided tours are available.

*The world's shortest railway, **Angels Flight** (two minutes there and back).*

# East of Hollywood

**Generally run-down and seedy, this area is experiencing the glimmerings of a bohemian rebirth. If you want to go off the beaten track, it's the place to start.**

## East Hollywood

Ignored by most guidebooks, Hollywood east of the 101 freeway has, indeed, precious little to recommend it to your average tourist. Home to a number of film studios during the silent era – DW Griffith built his gigantic set for *Intolerance* at the north-east corner of Sunset Boulevard and Hillhurst Avenue – this urban wasteland of decaying buildings (many left unrepaired after the Northridge earthquake in 1994) and grimy strip malls is more than a few palm trees short of picturesque; nevertheless, it holds some pleasant surprises for the more adventurous traveller.

On the culinary side, your two best bets in this part of town are **Jitlada** (5233 West Sunset Boulevard, at Harvard Boulevard) and **Zankou Chicken** (No.5065). The former offers what may be Los Angeles' best Thai cuisine at extremely reasonable prices, while the latter serves up amazing Middle Eastern food with enough garlic to keep vampires at bay for weeks.

Visitors with a taste for the seedier side of life can pay a visit to the **Sunset Theater** at the corner of Sunset Boulevard and Western Avenue, one of the town's few remaining triple-X grind houses ('Free admission for ladies'), or grab a seat at **Jumbo's Clown Room** (5153 Hollywood Boulevard). One of Hollywood's most popular strip clubs, Jumbo's has found immortality as the joint where a pre-fame Courtney Love used to 'work the pole'. It's not unusual to spot members of visiting rock bands in the audience, nor is it out of the ordinary to witness occasional live music courtesy of local groups.

Just blocks away from Jumbo's, but at the opposite end of the cultural spectrum, is the lush oasis known as **Barnsdall Art Park** (4800 Hollywood Boulevard). Set on a hill high above the trash-strewn streets of East Hollywood, this peaceful, verdant park is home to the lovely **Hollyhock House** (built between 1917 and 1920, it was Frank Lloyd Wright's first Los Angeles commission), an art gallery and a number of arts and crafts centres,

all of which are overseen by the City of Los Angeles Department of Cultural Affairs. Though the once-delightful view of the city is now largely blocked by a nearby hospital complex, Barnsdall Art Park remains an enjoyable escape from the madness of the city.

## Griffith Park/Los Feliz

Just a few blocks north of Barnsdall Art Park lies the relative affluence of the Griffith Park/Los Feliz quarter. One of the few truly cohesive neighbourhoods in Los Angeles, Los Feliz has developed something of a reputation as a bohemian community, although sizeable populations of working-class Mexican-Americans and elderly pensioners still endure.

Stroll up Vermont Avenue, Los Feliz's main drag, and scope out the street's multicultural cocktail of vintage clothing shops, arcane book-stores – stop in at **Amok**, at number 1764, for a really impressive selection of books on self-mutilation – Spanish-speaking boutiques displaying elaborate communion dresses and, of course, coffeehouses. The most popular of the latter is **The Onyx** (number 1804), which does triple duty as a coffeehouse, art gallery (called The Sequel) and venue for local stand-up comedians and spoken-word artists, and is frequented by a trendy crowd of young bloods . Practically deserted by day, the fabulously upholstered bar **The Dresden Room** (No.1760) is another popular hangout, squeezing in the locals with a crowbar once the sun goes down.

Hike up Vermont Avenue past Los Feliz Boulevard for a look at the opulent houses which dot the 'Los Feliz Hills' in lower Griffith Park. The 4,000 acres of the park itself contain myriad attractions, be they the spectacular view from the **Griffith Park Observatory**, the animals at the **Los Angeles Zoo**, the Hollywood cowboy memorabilia at the **Gene Autry Museum**, the open-air concerts at the **Greek Theatre**, or Andy Gibb's burial slot at **Forest Lawn Cemetary**. Though the park is a perfect setting for hiking and picnicking, visitors would do well to bring some company; the park is also perfect for illegal firearm target practice and alfresco sexual trysts, and, well, you never know who you might bump into.

## Silver Lake

More tensely integrated and further down the economic totem pole than its neighbour to the north-west, Silver Lake – the area bounded by US101 to the south and I-5 to the north – boasts an equally vital mix of artists and labourers, with a small pocket of wealthier individuals ensconced in homes overlooking the **Silver Lake Reservoir**. A particularly sun-baked stretch of Sunset Boulevard forms the neighbourhood's backbone, offering a variety of junkstores, thrift shops and Mexican restaurants (the ornate **El Chavo**, at 4441 Sunset Boulevard, is particularly good) for your shopping and dining pleasure. Make sure you stop at **You've Got Bad Taste** (3816 Sunset Boulevard), a novelty boutique co-owned by Exene Cervenka, former vocalist of LA punk band X, where you can browse through stacks of obscure albums, choose from a large selection of mass-murderer paperbacks or stock up on his'n'her 'I Love Cock' T-shirts. Local bands sometimes give free shows here at weekends.

The best time to experience Silver Lake is during the annual **Sunset Junction** street fair in late August, when a mile of Sunset Boulevard is blocked off to traffic for three days, allowing celebrants to stroll the bazaar of craft stalls, ethnic food stands, live entertainment stages and beer trucks without incident. One of the few legitimate street fairs to be held in a city where pedestrians are generally regarded with suspicion, Sunset Junction offers a great opportunity for everyone from Latino gang members to outrageously camp transvestites to strut their stuff in a festive and friendly environment.

## Echo Park

While offering little for the tourist other than its beautifully landscaped, 26-acre namesake and close proximity to **Dodger Stadium** (1000 Elysian Park Avenue), home of the Los Angeles Dodgers baseball team, Echo Park – the area to the north of the Hollywood Freeway (US101) and east of Alvarado Street – can be a fine, if more than slightly funky place to set up housekeeping. Deployed as farmland by 19th-century settlers – Echo Park Lake originally served as a reservoir for neighbouring farmers – the area's winding hills still retain a rustic feel.

Although surrounded by some particularly dicey blocks, the 1300 block of **Carroll Avenue** is worth visiting for its painstakingly restored Victorian mansions, colourful remnants of the area's brief 1880s' incarnation as a popular suburb for the monied classes.

**Echo Park** itself, laid out in the 1890s by the architect Joseph Henry Taylor to resemble an English garden, serves during the summer as a focal point for various festivals presented by the neighbourhood's Cuban, Filipino, Vietnamese and Samoan communities.

*Los Feliz – as seen through the eyes of* **The Onyx** *coffeehouse and gallery (see page 109).*

# The Valleys

*More than mere suburban enclaves, LA's outlying valleys have much to offer, from the natural highs of the Santa Monica Mountains to the old-world appeal of Pasadena.*

Leave your hallucinogens at home before tackling the **Universal CityWalk**. See page 112.

Much of the charm and diversity of Los Angeles can be found in two interior valleys – the San Fernando Valley to the north, long renowned as the prototypical American suburb, and the San Gabriel Valley to the east, which has emerged as Los Angeles' true multicultural melting pot. At first glance, both valleys appear to be typical of suburban LA: hot, often smoggy and filled with unrelenting low-rise sprawl. Cut off from ocean breezes by the mountains, they can be 10-20°C hotter than LA proper in summer – and 10-20°C cooler in winter. Westsiders mock them, but natives wouldn't live anywhere else – and if tourists know where to look, they will understand why.

## San Fernando Valley

The history of the San Fernando Valley, presented in fictional form in the movie *Chinatown*, is one of the most colourful stories in US history. Early this century, LA's land barons hoodwinked voters into approving bonds for a water aqueduct and then diverted the water away from the city to the San Fernando Valley so they could cash in on the increased land values. Once an agricultural mecca, the San Fernando Valley has become known as the prototypical suburb, immortalised in the 1980s by the movie and song *Valley Girl*. The valley has some

1950s and '60s gems, including the Googie-style diner **Bob's Big Boy** in Burbank (4211 Riverside Drive, at Alameda Avenue; 1-818 843 9334).

Though still part of the City of Los Angeles, today the valley has more than 1.3 million inhabitants, and is also a business centre. It is home to California State University, Northridge, and was the epicentre of the massive Northridge earthquake in 1994 (most damage has since been repaired). The valley is accessible from Los Angeles via two freeways – US101 (also known as the Hollywood Freeway) and I-405 (San Diego Freeway) – and numerous winding canyon roads.

The San Fernando Valley is the gateway to the **Santa Monica Mountains**, one of the country's most beautiful and environmentally fragile urban mountain ranges. Separating the valley from the ocean, the Santa Monicas are covered with hiking and biking trails, and home to many ranches that once belonged to movie stars and studios. For more information, contact the Santa Monica Mountains National Recreation Area, 30401 Agoura Road, Suite 100, Agoura Hills, CA 90265 (1-818 597 1036).

One highlight of the Santa Monicas for tourists is **Paramount Ranch** (2813 Cornell Road, off Kanan Road, Agoura), where Paramount Studios' Western town set is still used today by the television series *Dr Quinn Medicine Woman*. The ranch is owned by t ie National Park Service and is open to the public.

The **Six Flags Magic Mountain** theme park (26101 Magic Mountain Parkway, just off I-5), is in Santa Clarita at the north end of the valley. The park has some of the region's biggest rollercoasters and an associated water park. For a glimpse of history along the way, make the easy detour to one of the earliest California missions, **Mission San Fernando Rey de España** (15151 San Fernando Mission Boulevard), which was founded in 1797.

Though Hollywood is 'over the hill', a good deal of Hollywood glitz (not to mention a thriving porn film industry) can be found in the San Fernando Valley – especially in Burbank and at Universal City, both located off US101 in the valley's east end. Warner Brothers, NBC and Walt Disney Studios are all located in Burbank's 'Media District' along Riverside Drive. Studio tours generally aren't available, but free tickets to the TV show tapings often are (*see chapter* **Comedy**). From Burbank, it's just a short drive on Barham Boulevard into Cahuenga Pass, home of the **MCA-Universal Studios** complex. The Universal Studios tour, formerly a homey tram trip across the back lot, has evolved into a theme park to rival Disneyland. The Universal site is also home to the Universal Amphitheater, a major cinema complex, and **Universal CityWalk** – an entertainment-oriented shopping mall that mimics the city around it with pint-sized version of local buildings.

Burbank and Universal are close to the **Los Angeles Zoo** (5333 Zoo Drive, east of Burbank, near the intersection of US134 and I-5; 1-213 666 4650).

## San Gabriel Valley

Modern settlement of the San Gabriel Valley, to the north and east of Downtown, originated with **Mission San Gabriel Archangel** (Mission and Junipero Serra Drives, San Gabriel). It's now perhaps LA's most diverse area, with Asian and Latino communities scattered throughout. Unlike the San Fernando Valley, the San Gabriel Valley is not part of the city of LA but is divided into many small suburban communities. It's accessible from LA via a series of east-west freeways, including I-210 (Foothill Freeway), I-10 (San Bernardino Freeway) and US60 (Pomona Freeway).

Older towns in the San Gabriel Valley, such as Pasadena, San Marino and La Verne, contain some of LA's most beautiful neighbourhoods. Pasadena was originally settled by wealthy retired farmers from the Midwest and remains one of the most charming towns in the area. The **Gamble House** (4 Westmoreland Place), designed by Charles and Henry Greene in 1908, is the leading example of Southern California's indigenous Craftsman bungalow, influenced – in typical Californian fashion – by both Japanese and Swiss architecture. **Old Town Pasadena** (centred on Colorado Boulevard and bounded by Arroyo Parkway, De Lacey

Avenue and Holly and Green Streets), is a revived 1920s retail district that has become a shopping and entertainment mecca. Colorado Boulevard is also the route of the annual **Rose Parade**.

Pasadena has a clutch of museums, including the **Norton Simon Museum** (411 West Colorado Boulevard), with a world-class collection of Renaissance and other art; the **California Institute of Technology**, or CalTech (1201 East California Boulevard); and the **Rose Bowl**, in Brookside Park.

Just to the south of Pasadena is the expensive suburb of San Marino, developed by land and railroad baron Henry Huntington. His former estate, now the **Henry E Huntington Library, Art Collections & Botanical Gardens** (1151 Oxford Road), houses a world-class collection of books and manuscripts and includes some of the most beautiful gardens in Southern California.

To the east of Pasadena is the lovely town of Arcadia, home of **Santa Anita Park** (285 West Huntington Drive), one of LA's best-known race tracks. Though dwarfed by a surrounding sea of suburbia, many older foothill communities along the Foothill Freeway, including Sierra Madre and Monrovia, contain charming early twentieth century downtowns. These communities lie in the shadow of the San Gabriel Mountains, one of the most geologically unstable mountain ranges in the world.

Further south in the San Gabriel Valley, modern suburbs blend in an undifferentiated mass, but some of them have a distinctive identity. Monterey Park, accessible from the Garfield Avenue and Atlantic Boulevard exits of the I-10, has become known throughout Asia as the leading Chinese-oriented suburb in the US. Most of the population is Chinese or Chinese-American, many of them immigrants from Taiwan and Hong Kong, while a significant minority is Latino. The commercial strips along Atlantic Street and Garfield Avenue may seem nondescript, but they contain some of the best Chinese restaurants anywhere in the US; local Chinese residents flock to them on Sunday mornings.

The San Gabriel Valley is also home to several majority universities, including **California State University** (515 State University Drive, off the I-10 in East LA), **California State Polytechnic University** in Pomona, a beautifully landscaped campus off the Kellogg Drive exit of the I-10, and the **Claremont Colleges**, a collection of six distinguished colleges near East Foothill Boulevard in Claremont. The town of Claremont and the campus offer shady streets and an academic setting reminiscent of East Coast Ivy League schools.

The eastern San Gabriel Valley is also home to the **Los Angeles County Fair**, held at the Fairplex (1101 West McKinley Avenue, at North White Avenue, Pomona) each year from mid-September to mid-October. LA County remains an important agricultural centre, and the county fair is one of the largest in the nation.

# Long Beach & the South Bay

**Trendy Westsiders seem to think Los Angeles stops at LAX. Their loss. Head south for some great beaches, diverse communities and an oceanside vibrancy.**

## The South Bay

### El Segundo, Manhattan Beach, Hermosa Beach & Redondo Beach

Just beyond the residential highrises of Marina del Rey, small-town **El Segundo** feels like another universe. There isn't a lot to do, so getting there really is half the fun. Vista del Mar, a beach-hugging road that starts just to the north in Playa del Rey, off Culver Boulevard at Dockweiler State Beach, is the most picturesque gateway to the South Bay. The best non-aquatic aspect of El Segundo, and true to its Everytown USA sensibility, is a real, old fashioned movie theatre. **The Old Town Music Hall** (140 Richmond Street, open weekends only) features pre-1960s film classics, a pipe organ and group singalongs.

But for the true flavour of the South Bay, continue south on Vista del Mar (which becomes Highland Avenue) until you reach **Manhattan Beach Boulevard**, then turn right towards the ocean. On sunny weekends, the Manhattan Beach Strand and pier are mobbed by bladers, cyclists and sun-worshippers. Cleaner than Venice, the seafronts in Manhattan and neighbouring Hermosa Beach offer similar people-watching pleasures.

Just back from the surf and sand, you can find good casual meals at **The Kettle** (1138 Highland Avenue), easily one of the best 24-hour restaurants in the LA area, café/bookstore **The Hungry Mind** (916 Manhattan Avenue), and **Negril's at the Beach** (900 Manhattan Avenue), which offers live reggae music and Caribbean cuisine.

The surfside flavour of Manhattan Beach continues on into **Hermosa** and **Redondo**

*Life's a beach....*

**Beaches**. As with Manhattan, the most chiselled bodies make their way along Hermosa's Strand and pier (end of Pier Avenue). Visitors might catch a pro beach volleyball championship – it's a centre for the sport – a surf festival or blading exhibition.

Those who prefer shade to sun can check out **The Lighthouse Café** (30 Pier Avenue), a watering hole since the 1950s, hangout of volleyball players and scenesters, and one of the best jazz clubs in LA; **The Comedy & Magic Club** (1018 Hermosa Avenue), where the likes of Jay Leno are said to try out new material; **Either/Or** (124 Pier Avenue), a well-stocked bookstore which Thomas Pynchon supposedly patronised when he lived nearby; **The World Famous Spot** (110 Second Street), a legendary vegetarian restaurant that is rumoured to be a hit with Paul McCartney; and **Ragin' Cajun** (422 Pier Avenue), an authentic Louisiana café.

Further south, Redondo Beach's **King Harbor**, at the end of Portofino Way – with its shops, eateries, fish markets and marina – is one of the most developed local piers. Some find it a bit naff, but it is the most family-oriented of these beaches.

## Palos Verdes & San Pedro

The loop around scenic Palos Verdes Peninsula is a candidate for the best ocean drive in Southern California. Take the Pacific Coast Highway south to Palos Verdes Boulevard, join Palos Verdes Drive West and then Palos Verdes Drive South. On the way, stop at the lovely **Wayfarers Chapel** (5755 Palos Verdes Drive South, between Western Avenue & Hawthorn Boulevard), the most visited building by architect Lloyd Wright (Frank's son), and the **South Coast Botanic Garden** (26300 South Crenshaw Boulevard), an 87-acre display of botanical beauty. Ironically, ritzy **Palos Verdes** shares the peninsula with one of LA's most colourful working-class communities, **San Pedro**, traditional home of fishermen, dockworkers, Navy staff and Mediterranean and East European immigrants. Gentrification and cuts in the defence budget have made their effects felt, but a walk along quaint Sixth Street and a Greek meal at **Papadakis Taverna** (301 West Sixth Street) or a Croatian one at **Ante's** (729 South Palos Verdes Street) will give you a feel for the area's past.

You get a spectacular view of the Pacific from nearby **Angels Gate Park** (3601 South Gaffey Street), also home to the giant Korean Bell of Friendship, a gift to the US from Korea. Below this bluff, **Point Fermin Park**, with its 1874 lighthouse, is a great picnic spot.

For families, the **Cabrillo Marine Aquarium**, housed in a Frank Gehry-designed building (3720 Stephen White Drive), and the **Los Angeles Maritime Museum** (Berth 84, at the end of Sixth Street) are both fun to explore.

## Long Beach

Drive over the majestic Vincent Thomas Bridge from San Pedro and you'll hit **Long Beach**, an old Navy port that's now a city with 500,000 inhabitants, a cosmopolitan mix of yuppies, artists, harbour workers, gays and students as well as a rainbow of races, including the largest Cambodian community outside Cambodia.

Yes, everyone knows about the **Queen Mary** in Long Beach Harbor (Pier J, at the end of the Long Beach Freeway), one of the largest passenger ships ever built, which has been turned into a hotel and restaurants – and it's magnificent.

Lesser known, but equally worth exploring, are the small but ambitious **Long Beach Museum of Art** (2300 East Ocean Boulevard); **Pine Avenue**, a once-blighted downtown street now home to such hip spots as restaurant and art gallery **System M** (No.213A), rock club **Blue Café** (210 Promenade) and cigar parlour-cum-dance club **Cohiba** (110 Broadway, entrance through Mum's Restaurant at 144 Pine Avenue); and eclectic **Broadway**, between Alamitos and Ximeno Avenues, which contains such remarkable restaurants as the 1920s bordello-themed **House of Madam Jo Jo's** (2941 East Broadway).

Fourth Street, near Cherry Avenue, is a funky strip of thrift stores, and Belmont Shore (along Second Street, from Park to Santa Ana Avenues) is where Cal State Long Beach students shop and bar-hop. Anaheim Street, between Atlantic and Cherry Avenues – unofficially known as Little Phnom Penh – is a struggling area that's home to many Cambodian shops and eateries, while **Naples** – actually three small islands in man-made Alamitos Bay – is an upscale district laid out around picturesque canals, similar to Venice up the coast but with none of the latter's decay.

In recent years, Long Beach has earned a rep for its rap scene. Snoop Doggy Dogg, Warren G, and Dove Shack are some of the local hitmakers. Unfortunately, many of these performers have left the city and there is now no hip-hop club as such. However, **VIP Records** (1012 East Pacific Coast Highway), an R&B/rap record store and studio where many of these acts got their start, is a good place to soak up the atmosphere, while at least one soul food restaurant in the old neighbourhood, **Margie's Kitchen** (1320 West Willow Street), has made a citywide reputation for itself.

But avoid Long Beach's beaches. Cleanliness is an issue in this industrial town and breakwaters were built years ago to hold back the waves. There are much nicer beaches elsewhere.

### Long Beach Chamber of Commerce

*1 World Trade Center, Long Beach, CA 90831 (1-310 436 1251).* **Open** 8am-5pm Mon-Fri.
Visitor information and literature.

# East LA

**A trek through the city's eastern environs shows how Mexican culture still flourishes despite centuries of US domination. Welcome to East LA, Mexico.**

'El Este' (the East Side), is a 50-square mile or so sprawl that extends, roughly, east from the Los Angeles River to just beyond Atlantic Boulevard, and north from Olympic Boulevard to the I-10. It consists of mainly residential working-class neighbourhoods with some light manufacturing in its southern environs and many commercial districts. The following is an overview of its more accessible, tourist-friendly areas.

Technically, East Los Angeles might start at the river, but the true spiritual starting point is **Olvera Street**, at the corner of Cesar E Chavez Avenue and Alameda Street in Downtown, pretty much all that remains from the days of Spanish, then Mexican rule. From here take **Cesar E Chavez Avenue** east to **Soto Street** in Boyle Heights. Stop off at this bustling intersection where diverse and vibrant murals depict the social, economic and political life of the Mexican people, from a march led by United Farm Workers union president Cesar Chavez (whom the avenue is named after) to a rendition of East LA neighbourhood scenes. For tours of these and other East Side murals, contact contact the Social and Public Art Resource on 1-310 822 9560 or Robin Dunnitz on 1-310 470 8864.

A burgeoning community of immigrant Latino street vendors thrives at the intersection, to the consternation of shop owners and the police. You'll find bargain silver and bootleg cassettes, as well as fresh mangoes and papayas. Chavez Avenue is also home to strolling musicians who will play a romantic bolero or two on their well-worn guitars for a reasonable fee as you dine at **La Parilla** (2126 East Cesar Chavez Avenue), **El Apetito** across the street, or some other enticing eaterie.

Head south on Soto Street, turn right on First Street and then right again onto Boyle Avenue and you'll find the **Mariachi Plaza**, one of the largest congregations of freelance mariachi musicians outside Mexico City's Garibaldi Square. Sporting traditional black *ranchero* outfits, they assemble at **Olympic Donut Shop** (1803 East First Street) and wait for passing drivers to hire them to play at social and family events. Along the way you can quaff a *cerveza* at **Red's Bar** (22 East First Street), a local lesbian haunt, or dine at **La Serenata di Garibaldi** (1842 East First Street), which specialises in Mexican haute cuisine.

Travel east again on First Street to **El Mercado** (3425 East First Street), a multi-level marketplace reminiscent of those found in Mexican cities. Upstairs are restaurants with duelling mariachi bands, each seeking to lure clientele from the others, while downstairs teems with stalls selling all manner of goods and produce.

Continue east on First Street to Gage Avenue, turn left onto Chavez Avenue and you'll find **Self-Help-Graphics** (3802 East Cesar Chavez Avenue), with its distinctive facade of multi-coloured pottery encased in plaster walls. The gallery specialises in the work of established and up-and-coming Latino artists and also runs community art workshops. The annual Dia de Los Muertos (Day of the Dead) celebration at the gallery in autumn has become an East LA tradition, presenting the cream of the Latino bohemian counter-culture crowd of poets, performance artists and agit-prop theatre groups and is a 'must be seen at' event for Latino and other local hipsters.

For breakfast or lunch, head west on Chavez Avenue to Evergreen Avenue and hang a right to the always crowded **El Tepeyac Café** (812 North Evergreen Avenue) to try a 'Hollenbeck Special', an oversized burrito that could choke a horse. Or amble south to **Ciro's** (705 North Evergreen Avenue) for more traditional Mexican food.

Continue west on Chavez Avenue, past the I-10, and turn right onto North Mission Road to reach **Lincoln Park** and **Plaza de la Raza** (3540 North Mission Road). The park has statues of Mexican revolutionary heroes and the plaza often hosts evenings of music, dance and theatre. From

*Taco trucks are endemic in East LA.*

**Olvera Street**, *the spiritual heart of East LA.*

Lincoln Park, take Main Street west to Avenue 19, and turn right to the **Bilingual Foundation of the Arts** (421 North Avenue 19), an award-winning theatre group that presents modern and classical productions, in both Spanish and English.

Take Main Street east, turn right onto Daly Street, cross North Mission Road (where Daly becomes Marengo), turn right onto Soto Street and head south until you reach **Whittier Boulevard**. Turn left and as you cross under the I-710 bridge you will encounter what some consider the unofficial 'capital' of East LA: 'The Boulevard'. This stretch of Whittier Boulevard, east to Atlantic Boulevard, offers a wealth of clothing shops, restaurants, department stores, botanicas selling healing herbs and incense, bakeries, nightclubs and bars and other commercial establishments.

On 29 August 1970, The Boulevard was the scene of a 'police riot' when a Chicano anti-war demonstration in a nearby park was attacked by police. Noted Chicano journalist Ruben Salazar was killed by a police tear gas pellet to the head in the Silver Dollar Café on Whittier Boulevard.

Salazar's death is thought by many to be retribution for his criticism of the Sheriffs' Department's abusive behaviour towards people of colour. The park was renamed **Salazar Park** (3864 Whittier Boulevard) in his honour and is a symbol of the 1970s Chicano Movement.

Taking Whittier Boulevard west to Eastern, and travel north to Ramona Boulevard in Monterey Park. Turn right and make your way to **Luminarias** (3500 Ramona Boulevard) or **Baby Doe's**, next door, for dinner and a night of salsa, merengue and more contemporary music. From their hilltop perch, both offer a splendid view of the San Gabriel Mountains to the north. The banda or norteño aficionado could try **La Zona Rosa** (1010 East Cesar Chavez Avenue).

Alternatively, for a feast of burritos and tacos, head east to Third Street, to **King Taco** (No.4504). Open 24 hours, it began as a solitary taco truck and is now a chain of restaurants (there's another branch on Chavez and Soto) and a cultural icon – and an early-morning stop for many an East Sider on their way home after a night of partying.

# South-Central

**It's got a reputation as a no-go area, but alongside inner-city communities struggling towards regeneration are thriving black suburbs.**

The term South-Central Los Angeles is an elusive one. Geographically, no two people agree on its boundaries, but it's generally used as a blanket term to indicate the areas of south LA that have a predominantly black community. Thus it includes Olympic Boulevard, above the I-10, as well as large swathes of the area below it, running down on either side of the I-110 south to Compton and Carson, east to Alameda Street and west to La Cienega Boulevard. Ironically, much of what's perceived as South-Central today is neither predominantly black nor technically in the City of Los Angeles at all.

At the turn of the century, the black community existed in what is now Little Tokyo. Following World War I, the population increased sharply as stories of the successes of local blacks circulated around the country. Thus began the steady migration of blacks west and south along the Central Avenue Corridor. **Central Avenue**'s significance in the history of black Los Angeles cannot be underestimated. It was the West Coast equivalent of Ellis Island to migrating blacks between the 1920s and the 1950s and home to some of the first financial enterprises, theatres, churches and social institutions established exclusively to serve blacks. Built in 1928 by a wealthy professional couple, the **Dunbar Hotel**, 4231 South Central Avenue, was the first hotel built by and for blacks. Along with several nightclubs in the area, including the now extinct Club Alabam, it brought to Central Avenue a universal reputation for its jazz scene. Modern-day Central Avenue is far less alluring – many of its buildings are vacant and in disrepair, but the Dunbar, now operated by the Dunbar Economic Development Corporation as low-income residential units, continues to be a centre of jazz culture.

*Spellbound at the* **Magic Johnson Theatres**.

(or WLCAC), 10950 South Central Avenue, about a mile from the Towers, a one-stop social and cultural centre. Victim of both the 1965 and '92 riots, it has now been completely rebuilt. The Center's public art piece, 'The Mother of Humanity', is the largest bronze sculpture of a black woman in the world. WLCAC showcases work by local inner-city artists, hosts live performances and houses the 'Mudtown Flats' exhibit, a re-creation of the final days of Dr Martin Luther King, Jr.

## Watts

After the jazz era, blacks continued their migration south along Central Avenue towards Watts, known primarily for the **Watts Towers** (*see chapter* **Sightseeing**) – designed, in fact, by an Italian but adopted as a symbol of black pride – and the rioting in 1965 and 1992. Though many areas are in neglect, Watts is cautiously re-emerging as a centre for black community pride, embodied by the **Watts Labor Community Action Committee**

## The Crenshaw District

The Crenshaw District is the area surrounding Crenshaw Boulevard south of the I-10 as far as Florence. It was the site of the 1932 Olympic village, now Village Green Apartments on Rodeo Road, near La Brea Avenue, and the first airport in LA. Though it's now one of the few predominantly black communities in Los Angeles County, the influence of earlier Japanese residents is still visible, notably in residential landscaping. **The Hills** – Baldwin, Windsor and View Park – are home to some of LA's most prominent upper middle-class and professional blacks. At the base of these well-manicured hills is an area known as the **Jungle**. Originally named for its lush tropical plantings, the Jungle is better known these days as a haven for illicit and gang activity.

In the 1940s, the first shopping plaza in the USA was built at the intersection of King (formerly Santa Barbara) and Crenshaw Boulevards. Now transformed into the **Baldwin Hills/Crenshaw Plaza**, it is the perfect place to park and see most of what's going on in this community.

Visit the **Magic Theatres** in the Plaza. Named for owner and basketball great Irvin 'Magic' Johnson, these cinemas have the friendliest staff in Los Angeles and show first-run films. For memorable soul food, leave your car in the lot and walk half a block east on King Boulevard to **M&M's Soul Food**, required eating for locals, and get in line. Or walk half a block west to **Boulevard Cafe**, 3710 King Boulevard, in the floundering Santa Barbara Plaza. The much touted **Dulan's Restaurant**, 4859 Crenshaw Boulevard, has a rear patio where regulars prefer to eat. (You'll need to drive or catch the Leimert/Slauson DASH bus.) Eateries in the Plaza itself include **Gagnier's**, for Louisiana style-cooking, **Joseph's on the Plaza** (live music some nights) and **Golden Bird Fried Chicken**. Don't, incidentally, expect the stellar service you received at the Magic Theatres. Some of these restaurants are well known for their rude, temperamental staff and less than attractive decor. Leave your diet behind. The food may be salty, and loaded with fat and calories, but worth every artery-clogging bite. If you have time, visit the **Black Gallery** (photography) in Santa Barbara Plaza and the **Museum of African American Art** (third floor of the Robinsons-May).

# All part of the service

A trip to black Los Angeles wouldn't be complete without a visit to a black church. They are considered to be the backbone of the black community for their commitment to outreach and activism, their outspoken, sometimes controversial ministers and their stellar choirs. Some big-name choices for visits are:

### First African Methodist Episcopal (FAME)
*2270 South Harvard Boulevard, between Adams Boulevard & Western Avenue, LA (1-213 735 1251).*
This highly influential church was started in the home of former slave Biddy Mason, but now inhabits an impressive building in the West Adams District, designed by celebrated black architect Paul R Williams. Minister Chip Murray is a big name on the scene and not afraid to be provocative.

### Crenshaw Christian Center
*7901 South Vermont Avenue, between Florence & Manchester Avenues, LA (1-213 758 3777).*
The home base of televangelist Reverend Fred Price, whose sermons are broadcast around the world, the Center holds 10,000 worshippers. Ed McMahon, Johnny Carson's sidekick, is often among them.

### West Angeles Church
*3045 South Crenshaw Boulevard, between Jefferson Boulevard & 30th Street, LA (1-213 733 8300).*
A bit of a celeb church, with a rapidly growing congregation that includes Denzel Washington and Magic Johnson. It's known for its choir and theatre productions. A new building is currently under construction; on completion, the church will move from its current building, known as the Golden Keyhole, and change its name to West Angeles Cathedral.

## Leimert Park

Leimert Park (pronounced Luh-murt), anchored by the Park itself and 43rd Street, is LA's most talked about black neighbourhood. In recent years, it has been experiencing the stirrings of cultural revolution, with art galleries, shops and restaurants beginning to replace the pawn shops and beauty salons that line the streets. Some notable stops include: the **Crossroads Arts Academy and Vision Theater Complex**, opposite the park on 43rd Place, owned by Marla Gibbs (Florence from the '70s sitcom *The Jeffersons*). For live jazz, visit **5th Street Dick's**, 3347 43rd Place. Along Degnan Boulevard, there are several art galleries and shops. Stop by **Phillip's Barbecue**, 4307 Leimert Boulevard, and prepare to wait in line for a take-out order of some of the best ribs in town. **Earle's Wieners**, 4326 Crenshaw Boulevard, has an assortment of hot dogs, links and vegetarian finger foods, or try **Coley's Kitchen**, 4335 Crenshaw, for Caribbean fare.

Most weekends you can find street fairs in the **Leimert Park** village, be they large, organised events or a band of self-proclaimed prophets talking to whoever will listen. Nearby is the **African Marketplace** (Rancho Cienega Park at Rodeo Road and King Boulevard), which celebrates diverse African cultures with a feast of foods, crafts and non-stop entertainment every August.

## Inglewood

Though outside the Los Angeles city limits, Inglewood is often considered a part of South Central. It is best known as the home of the **Great Western Forum** (Prairie and Manchester Boulevards), home to the Los Angeles Lakers basketball and Los Angeles Kings hockey teams. Just south of the Forum is the **Hollywood Park** racecourse (Prairie & Century Boulevards).

# Orange County

**Republicans, punk rockers, surfers and Disneyland. Yeah, they're all in Orange County – OC to the sun-struck natives – but wait, there's more....**

Seamlessly bordering Los Angeles County to the south east, Orange County is a major tourist destination in its own right, luring 40 million visitors a year with its amusement parks and copious coastline. Angelenos look down on it as a conservative white-collar suburb, with an element of justification. But if you make the trip to Disneyland, it's worth staying off the freeway for long enough to have a look round.

## The coast

**Seal Beach** and **Sunset Beach**, near the LA County border, begin the 50-mile expanse of beach bliss that is coastal Orange County. While these two beaches are unpretentious and fun, the real action starts just to the south in **Huntington Beach**, aka Surf City. It's easy to see how the city got its nickname by hanging out at the 1,800ft pier (Main Street, off Pacific Coast Highway). From dawn till dark, surfers are searching for the perfect wave. The best of them appear every summer in the Pro Surfing Championships. There's even a museum, the **International Surfing Museum** (411 Olive Avenue), devoted to the subject.

But there's a troubling undercurrent onshore. Main Street, recently redeveloped in a bland, modern style, has a reputation for attracting misfits and malcontents. Skinheads have roughed up 'undesirables' and Independence Day celebrations have sometimes veered out of control.

**Newport Beach** is something else altogether. From the multimillion-dollar homes overlooking Newport Harbor to the upscale outdoor **Fashion Island** mall (Newport Center Drive, at Pacific Coast Highway) and the **Newport Harbor Art Museum** (850 San Clemente Drive, which specialises in California art), Newport Beach is where the American leisure class can live out its life in sun-soaked splendour.

**Balboa Island** (Jamboree Road bridge and Pacific Coast Highway) and **Balboa Peninsula** (Balboa Boulevard and PCH) are both prime walking areas, and a ferry – terminals at Palm Street on the peninsula and Agate Avenue on the island – ushers visitors between the two. The island is covered with small shops, restaurants and houses, but perhaps the best activity is walking and browsing, not buying. On the peninsula, where everyone seems to be rollerblading or cycling, things are more downscale. **Balboa Pavilion** (at the beach end of Main Street), built in 1906 and once a Victorian bathhouse, is the jumping-off point for harbour and winter whale-watching tours as well as trips to Catalina Island (*see chapter* **Trips out of Town**). The bars and eateries along Balboa Boulevard are prime hangouts.

**Laguna Beach** began as an artists' colony and it's the home of the admired **Laguna Beach Museum of Art** (307 Cliff Drive), which also shows contemporary California art. Each summer the city's arts heritage is celebrated with the Laguna Festival of the Arts. This artistic lineage partly explains why this area is the most liberal in notoriously conservative Orange County. There's a sizeable gay community, which hangs out in such clubs as **The Boom Boom Room** (1401 South Coast Highway).

**Main Beach** (South Coast Highway and Broadway), with its pick-up basketball and volleyball games, is a must for people-watching. Scuba diving is also good here.

Further down the coast, **San Juan Capistrano** is famous for its swallows, which arrive each March from their winter haven to **Mission San Juan Capistrano** (Camino Capistrano and Ortega Highway) – even without the birds, the 1776-built mission is worth visiting. Across the way, the **San Juan Capistrano Regional Library** (31495 El Camino Real), built by postmodern architect Michael Graves, stages impressive world music concerts in its courtyard, while top-name rock shows come through **The Coach House** (33157 Camino Capistrano).

At the county's end, **San Clemente** has all the sun and waves but few of the crowds of its neighbours. Nixon's Western White House, a Spanish-inspired mansion called Casa Pacifica, can be seen from San Clemente State Beach.

## Central Orange County

**Costa Mesa** (which isn't on the coast) likes to bill itself as the city of the arts. It's the home of the **Orange County Performing Arts Center** (600 Town Center Drive), where symphonies and Broadway shows dominate. But it's really a city of development, thanks to **South Coast Plaza** (3333 Bristol Street, off the I-405), one of the largest shopping malls in the world, with more than 270 stores; **The Lab**, or 'the anti-mall' (2930 Bristol Street), a shopping mecca for the young and the pierced that includes two of OC's best eateries, the Gypsy Den café and Habana, a post-modern Cuban restaurant; and **Triangle Square** (Harbor and Newport Boulevards), a massive altar to consumerism that includes Nike Town and Virgin Megastore. **Memphis**, a proto-Southern restaurant with perhaps the best (perhaps the only) Indian fry bread in OC, sits next to The Lab. Not too far away is **Rock N Java** (1749 Newport Boulevard), a giant coffeehouse that proves that people here don't do anything in half measures.

Antiseptic **Irvine**, an early planned community, was so futuristic when it was built in the 1960s that *Planet of the Apes* was filmed there. It's home to the University of California at Irvine and the large **Irvine Spectrum** outdoor mall (junction of I-405 and I-5), with its 3-D IMAX cinema. However, the city does contain one of the county's most progressive dance clubs, **Metropolis** (4255 Campus Drive, in the Irvine Marketplace).

**Santa Ana** to the north gets a bad rap as Orange County's gangland. True, the heavily Latino city contains some of the county's toughest areas but it also has one of its most distinctive. Strolling along busy Fourth Street, between Ross and French Streets, with its colourful storefronts and constant hum of Spanish, is like being in a small city in Mexico. Not far away is the **Bowers Museum of Cultural Arts** (2002 North Main Street, at 20th Street), with its strong collection of Latin and African arts and crafts, and a budding artists' district (between Broadway and Bust, First and Third Streets), which, by the end of 1997, will house two contemporary art museums.

Another vital neighbourhood is **Little Saigon** in Westminster, the largest Vietnamese community outside Vietnam. However, this isn't a cosy, walking district. It sprawls across several miles of mini-malls but is well worth visiting, if only for the Vietnamese or Chinese food that's found at places such as **Seafood Paradise** (8602 Westminster Boulevard).

## Anaheim & inland

This area of Orange County is filled with some of the globe's best-known icons of middle Americana, of which **Disneyland** is the king. Compared to its new amusement park cousins, the Anaheim park (1313 Harbor Boulevard), built in 1955, is a bit down at heel but it's still the grandaddy of them all and has to be experienced.

The area around Disneyland is either kitschly camp or depressingly dreary, depending on your

*Walt opens the gates of **Disneyland** in 1955.*

views on cheap motels and bad food; no doubt Quentin Tarantino would feel right at home. Anaheim has little to recommend it but it does have **Linda's Doll Hut** (107 Adams Street, at Manchester Avenue), the cramped rock club where such OC bands as The Offspring got started.

For another slice of American pie, hop over to Beach Boulevard near La Palma Avenue in nearby Buena Park. Here are **Knott's Berry Farm**, a smaller, homier Disneyland, **Movieland Wax Museum** and **Medieval Times**, a knights-and-knaves eatery where food is beside the point.

Two other shrines to the American way of life deserve a visit, one spiritual, the other political. In Garden Grove, the **Crystal Cathedral** (12141 Lewis Street, at Chapman Avenue) – an all-glass house of worship designed by Philip Johnson for popular television evangelist Reverend Schuller – is an eye-popping marvel for its sheer excess. In Yorba Linda, about seven miles north of Anaheim, the **Richard M Nixon Library and Birthplace** (18001 Yorba Linda Boulevard) is, as these places generally are, a combination of library and propaganda machine.

### Anaheim/Orange County Visitor and Convention Bureau

*800 West Katella Avenue, CA 92802 (1-714 999 8999/ recorded information 1-714 635 8900).* **Open** 8am-5.30pm Mon-Fri.

# Eating & Drinking

Restaurants          **122**
Coffeehouses         **145**
Bars                 **149**

# Restaurants

**Still high on its restaurant renaissance, multicultural LA now ranks as one of the world's food capitals, and eating out as its prime leisure activity. From diner to designer, you'll find it here.**

Since the birth of talking pictures, restaurant-going in Los Angeles has had a greater significance than in any other city. Where the movers and shakers of the industry choose to show up, be seen and chow down is all-important. But which restaurant is hip changes as fast as the whims of the capricious stars who frequent it, making today's favourite flavour tomorrow's space for lease.

LA eateries were traditionally high on ambiance, but the food was ordinary. Then, in the early 1970s, Alice Waters revolutionised California cuisine. Following the opening of her famous Chez Panisse, LA chefs took Waters' philosophy of cooking with fresh seasonal produce and gave it a creative spin – New Californian cuisine became a distillation of a variety of cuisines, the foremost being French, Japanese and Italian, not necessarily together. During the 1980s a string of high-concept restaurants appeared in LA. Characterised by highly inventive and eclectic décor and presentation, places such as City Café, Michaels, Chaya Brasserie and Spago became events in themselves, and top chefs acquired a status equal to that of their celebrity clientele.

Superchefs have become big business. Spago creator Wolfgang Puck now owns Chinois on Main, Granita (a frozen pizza enterprise) and a chain of Wolfgang Puck Cafés, including one at LAX. Joachim Splichal's Patina has spawned four local spin-offs. Respected chef duo Mary Sue Milliken and Sue Fenniger of Border Grill host their own radio and television shows, spreading the word about good food.

Foodie mania has consumed Los Angeles. Farmers' markets selling organic produce are the hottest new shopping phenomenon. The healthy designer take-out, such as Tacone, is an emerging trend, and even fast-food chains are attempting to bump up their herb and vegetable content. LA also has its share of bargain ethnic restaurants, many of which you can find hidden in the most unexpected locations, including nondescript mini-malls.

## CODES OF BEHAVIOUR

The warm climate allows for a relaxed, anything-goes dress code in most establishments. Locals tend to eat early, usually 7-9pm. It's often advisable to valet park, rather than attempt to save $3.50, decipher the parking restriction signs and

invariably incur a fine. Tipping 15% is the norm, but if the service is exceptional, 20% isn't unusual. With the more fashionable restaurants, booking is essential. Smoking is often allowed on patios and sometimes at the bar of a restaurant; otherwise, don't even think about it. Bon appetit.

## Westside: beach towns

## Santa Monica

### Abiquiu

*1413 Fifth Street, at Santa Monica Boulevard, Santa Monica (1-310 395 8611). Bus 4, 304, Santa Monica 1, 3, 7, 10/I-10, exit Fifth Street north.* **Dinner** 6-9pm Mon-Thur, Fri; 6-11pm Sat. **Average** $35. **Credit** AmEx, MC, V.

A sweeping staircase (down which John Travolta slung the stunt man in *Get Shorty*), plenty of maple-coloured wood, black-and-white photos of Georgia O'Keefe and artefacts from the Southwest set the stage for drama. But the food is the real scene-stealer, designed by consummate showman John Sedlar, the creator of contemporary Southwestern cuisine and the facilitator for other influences – Asian, Greek, Italian – to roam subtly into the dishes. An appetiser might be ahi tuna zozobra, served with green chilli mashed potatoes, rock shrimp, wasabi and pickled ginger, followed by an entrée of braised halibut with lime, Patron tequila and black bean and corn salsa. Sadly, Sedlar has now left, but his staff are continuing valiantly and only time will tell what will become of this outstanding restaurant.
*Valet parking $3.50.*

### Border Grill

*1445 Fourth Street, at Broadway, Santa Monica (1-310 451 1655). Bus 4, 304, Santa Monica 1, 2, 3, 7, 8/I-10, exit Fourth Street north.* **Dinner** 5-10pm Mon-Thur; 5-11pm Fri; 4.30-11pm Sat; 4.30-10pm Sun. **Average** $30. **Credit** AmEx, DC, Disc, MC, V.

With its orange walls, vivid wall paintings, sharp margaritas, pulsating music, crowded bar and dining area and spicy New Mexican cuisine, this place is hot, hot, hot. Chef/owners Mary Sue Milliken and Sue Fenniger deserve their celebrity status (they host food shows on TV and radio); they have been instrumental in putting healthy, gourmet cuisine on the map, and this restaurant is a celebration of the joy of eating out. Recommended: everything.

### The Broadway Deli

*1457 Third Street Promenade, at Broadway, Santa Monica (1-310 451 0616). Bus 33, 304, 434, Santa Monica 2, 4/I-10, exit Fourth-Fifth Street north.* **Breakfast** 7am-3pm Mon-Fri; 8am-3pm Sat, Sun. **Lunch** 11am-5pm daily. **Dinner** 5pm-midnight Mon-Thur, Sun; 5pm-1am Fri, Sat. **Average** $18. **Credit** AmEx, MC, V.

A vast, airy deli with a long counter and many booths, which treats its New York Jewish fare with the same respect one would give to haute cuisine. We recommend the gravadlax and smoked salmon served with chewy country breads, and the herbed and honeyed roast chicken – but it's all good. *Valet parking $3.50.*

### Chez Jay

*1657 Ocean Avenue, between Pico Boulevard & Colorado Avenue, Santa Monica (1-310 395 1741). Bus 20, 33, 333, 320, 434, Santa Monica 1, 7, 10/I-10, exit Fourth-Fifth Street north.* **Breakfast** 9am-2pm Sat, Sun. **Lunch** noon-2pm Mon-Fri. **Dinner** 6-10.30pm Mon-Sat; 5.30-11pm Sun. **Average** $17. **Credit** AmEx, MC, V.

Ten tables (some booths), a dozen barstools, a massive schooner wheel, authentic portholes and sawdust on the floor. This is Chez Jay's, a beach-adjacent roadhouse in Santa Monica, frequented since owner Jay Fiondella opened the joint in 1959 by complete unknowns and a few celebrities in search of anonymity (Sean Penn, Warren Beatty, Marlon Brando, Henry Kissinger). It's low-key, downhome and funky. The simple fare (steak or fish in old-fashioned heavy sauces) isn't bad, either. There's also a great jukebox and free peanuts. Booking advised. *Valet parking $2.*

### Chinois on Main

*2709 Main Street, at Hill Street, Santa Monica (1-310 392 9025). Bus 33, 333, Santa Monica 1, 2, 10/I-10, exit Fourth Street south.* **Lunch** 11.30am-2pm Wed-Fri. **Dinner** 6.30-10.30pm Mon-Sat; 6.30-10pm Sun. **Average** $45. **Credit** AmEx, DC, Disc, MC, V.

Some people believe that this Wolfgang Puck eaterie is his pièce de résistance. The cuisine goes by the name of Pacific New Wave, which means a mélange of different ethnicities (Asian, French, Californian) rolled into one, sometimes creating confusion, other times delighting, all topped off with wife Barbara Lazaroff's absurdly over-the-top kitsch design and a slew of deliriously friendly waiting staff. Loud, sceney and fun. We suggest barbecued baby pork ribs in a honey-chilli sauce and Shanghai lobster in spicy curry. Book. *Valet parking $3.25.*

### Fritto Misto

*601 Colorado Avenue, at Sixth Street, Santa Monica (1-310 458 2829). Bus 434, Santa Monica 2, 3, 9/I-10, exit Fourth-Fifth Street north.* **Open** 11.30am-10pm Mon-Thur; 11.30am-10.30pm Fri, Sat; 5-9.30pm Sun. **Average** $13. **Credit** Disc, MC, V.

A popular, unpretentious neighbourhood pasta joint. Long queues, large portions, great prices, friendly service and a bustling atmosphere – but it's damned hard to find one's way down the long list of mix and match pasta and sauces.

### JiRaffe

*502 Santa Monica Boulevard, at Fifth Street, Santa Monica (1-310 917 6671). Bus 434, Santa Monica 2, 3, 9/I-10, exit Fifth Street north.* **Lunch** noon-2pm Tue-Fri. **Dinner** 6-10pm Tue-Fri; 5.30-11pm Sat; 5.30-9pm Sun. **Average** $16-$32. **Credit** AmEx, DC, MC, V.

**Abiquiu,** *sublime setting for* Get Shorty.

Young, goateed chefs Josiah Citrin and Raphael Lunetta have been buddies since they were 12, and have been cooking together for the past four years. Breathtaking dishes here include rock shrimp ravioli with tomatoes and green onions, and scallops with braised endive in a rich, dark gravy. The décor is simple, white and unpretentious. Booking advised. *Parking $3.50.*

### 1 Pico

*Shutters on the Beach, 1 Pico Boulevard, at Ocean Avenue, Santa Monica (1-310 587 1717). Bus 20, 33, 320, 434, Santa Monica 1, 7, 10/I-10, exit Fourth Street south.* **Dinner** 6-10.30pm daily. **Brunch** 11am-2.30pm Sun. **Average** $35. **Credit** AmEx, DC, Disc, MC, V.

Think ocean, sunsets and Ralph Lauren and you've got 1 Pico. Dip your toes in the sand before settling into a well-prepared meal, served with grace. We recommend brunch. *Parking $3.*

### Patrick's Roadhouse

*106 Entrada Drive, at Pacific Coast Highway, Santa Monica (1-310 459 4544). Bus Santa Monica 9/I-10, exit PCH north.* **Open** 8am-3pm Mon-Fri; 9am-3pm Sat, Sun. **Average** $15. **No credit cards.**

Funky beachside diner. Hot for breakfast (Billy Crystal likes his eggs 'Jewish-style' with salami) and burger-type lunches (Bill Clinton thinks they're among the best). Large on cholesterol and portions, long on queues, star-spotting and attitude. Short on sophistication. Don't even think about going at the weekend without a reservation, my dear.

### Rae's

*2901 Pico Boulevard, at 29th Street, Santa Monica (1-310 828 7937). Bus Santa Monica 7/I-10, exit Bundy Drive north.* **Open** 5.30am-10pm daily. **Average** $8. **No credit cards.**

Slick, turquoise-coloured classic 1950s diner, so popular there are often lines around the block. Breakfast is recommended.

### Remi

*1451 Third Street Promenade, at Broadway, Santa Monica (1-310 393 6545). Bus 33, 304, 434, Santa Monica 2, 4/I-10, exit Fourth-Fifth Street north.* **Lunch** 11.30am-2pm daily. **Dinner** 6-10pm Mon-Thur, Sun; 6-11pm Fri, Sat. **Average** $30. **Credit** AmEx, MC, DC, V.

Eat outside (and gander at the shoppers) or inside this upscale Italian restaurant, with its understated nautical theme (a gondolier logo, white walls, blue-and-white striped upholstery, brass railings and a porthole). Venetian dishes are the order of the day, including calves' liver with polenta or a simple rack of lamb, grilled with garlic and risotto. Finish with one of the encyclopedic list of grappas. *Valet parking $3.50.*

### Röckenwagner

*2435 Main Street, at Ocean Park Boulevard, Santa Monica (1-310 399 6504). Bus 33, 333, Santa Monica 1, 8, 10/I-10, exit Fourth Street south.* **Lunch** 11.30am-2.30pm Tue-Fri; 9am-2pm Sat, Sun. **Dinner** 6-10pm Tue-Fri; 5.30-10pm Sat, Sun. **Brunch** 9am-2pm Sat, Sun. **Average** $23. **Credit** AmEx, DC, MC, V.

The high-end restaurant that put German chef Hans Röckenwagner on the map. Located in trendy architect Frank Gehry's sculptural Edgemar Complex, Röckenwagner epitomises California cuisine in its marriage of eclectic and artistic food and décor. Most popular item is the crab soufflé with sliced mango and lobster-butter sauce. Book. *Valet parking $2.75.*

### Tlapazola Grill

*2920 Lincoln Boulevard, at Santa Monica Boulevard, Santa Monica (1-310 392 7292). Bus Santa Monica 3, 7/I-10, exit Lincoln Boulevard north.* **Lunch** 11am-3pm

Tue-Fri. **Dinner** 5-10pm Tue-Thur, Sun; 5-10.30pm Fri,
Sat. **Average** $12. **Credit** MC, V.
A 1950s diner meets Mexican cantina in this surprising
little restaurant on unloved Lincoln Boulevard. But it's
well worth trading the drab location for the delicious
authentic Mexican food – forget refried beans and salsa,
Tlapazola Grill serves mama's home cooking from the
Oaxaca region; try grilled salmon with pumpkin seed
sauce, or their speciality, pollo en mole negro – chicken
swamped in an extraordinary sauce of dark chocolate,
spices, nuts and chilli. Servings are very large, the prices
very reasonable.

### Typhoon

*Santa Monica Airport, 3221 Donald Douglas Loop South,*
*at 28th Street, Santa Monica (1-310 390 6565). Bus*
*Santa Monica 14/I-10, exit Bundy Drive south.* **Lunch**
noon-3pm Mon-Fri. **Dinner** 5.30-10.30pm daily. **Brunch**
11.30am-3pm Sun. **Average** $10-$25. **Credit** AmEx, DC,
Disc, MC, V.
This Pan-Asian restaurant sits right on the runway of Santa
Monica airport, providing a fabulous view of jet planes
taking off and landing, as well as the mountains and downtown LA. You can also sample excellent food from over 13
countries and scan for celebrities: Robert De Niro, Goldie
Hawn and Val Kilmer love this place. Very LA, but not in a
touristy way.

### Valentino

*3115 Pico Boulevard, at Centinela Avenue, Santa Monica*
*(1-310 829 4313). Bus Santa Monica 7/I-10, exit*
*Centinela Avenue south.* **Lunch** 11.30am-2.30pm Fri.
**Dinner** 5-11pm daily. **Average** $55. **Credit** AmEx, DC,
Disc, MC, V.
Piero Selvaggio has awards coming out of his ears for this,
his flagship restaurant, and endless praise for his wine col-
lection, too; some say it is the finest restaurant cellar in the
States. It's top-of-the-line Italian dining at its best and, if
you've got the money, splurge. Ask Piero to put together a
'tasting plate' for you. Booking required.
*Parking $3.*

### Zipangu

*802 Broadway, at Lincoln Boulevard, Santa Monica*
*(1-310 395 3082). Bus 4, 304, Santa Monica 1, 7, 9, 10/*
*I-10, exit Lincoln Boulevard north.* **Lunch** noon-2.30pm
Mon-Fri. **Dinner** 6-10.30pm Mon-Thur, Sun; 6-11pm Fri,
Sat. **Average** $15. **Credit** AmEx, MC, V.
Informal yet elegant and slightly off the beaten track,
Zipangu offers a combination of Italian and Japanese cook-
ing in a California style. The rare tuna steak served as a
starter or main course is a gem. Try the angel hair pasta with
seafood or vegetables or the fried calamari. Book.
*Parking $3.50.*

## Venice

### A Votre Sante

*1025 Abbot Kinney Boulevard, between Westminster*
*Avenue & Main Street, Venice (1-310 314 1187). Bus 33,*
*36, 333, Santa Monica 1, 2/I-10, exit Fourth Street south.*
**Open** 11am-10pm Mon-Fri; 9am-10pm Sat; 9am-9pm Sun.
**Average** $8. **Credit** AmEx, DC, Disc, MC, V.
Some people swear by this health-conscious, low-fat, vege-
tarian chain. The wraps – sandwiches using chapati bread
– are worth a try, as are the veggie burgers.

### Abbot Pizza

*1407 Abbot Kinney Boulevard, at California Avenue,*
*Venice (1-310 396 7334). Bus Santa Monica 2/I-10, exit*
*Lincoln Boulevard south.* **Open** 11am-11pm daily.
**Average** $2.50-$10. **Credit** MC, V.
Make sure you're not due for a dental visit and go gnaw on
a delicious bagel-crusted pizza.

### Capri

*1616 Abbot Kinney Boulevard, at Venice Boulevard,*
*Venice (1-310 392 8777). Bus 33, 33, 436/SR90, exit*
*Lincoln Boulevard north.* **Dinner** 6-10.30pm Mon-Thur,
Sun; 6-11pm Fri, Sat. **Average** $23. **Credit** AmEx, MC, V.
Capri is evidence that you don't have to spend big bucks on
décor or over-extend yourself on the menu to succeed. The
bare, whitewashed walls and cement floors somehow exude
romance while the brief menu of Venetian-inspired dishes
with a nouvelle slant are imaginative and make for a stress-
free ordering experience. Cocktail dresses are as welcome as
Bermuda shorts. Laid-back and on the money.

### The Fig Tree

*429 Ocean Front Walk, at Rose Avenue, Venice (1-310*
*392 4937). Bus Santa Monica 2/I-10, exit Fourth Street*
*south.* **Open** 9am-9pm daily. **Average** $15. **Credit**
AmEx, DC, MC, V.
Get front seats for the spectacle that is Venice Boardwalk
and eat healthily and heartily at the locals' fave oceanside
brunch hangout. All the vegetables are organic; cakes and
desserts are sweetened only with honey or fruit juice. Highly

recommended, if you go on an empty stomach, are the oat or cornmeal pancakes stuffed with blueberries or banana and served with apple butter and pure maple syrup. Yum.

## Joe's

*1023 Abbot Kinney Boulevard, between Westminster Avenue & Main Street, Venice (1-310 399 5811). Bus 33, 333, 436, Santa Monica 1, 2/I-10, exit Lincoln Boulevard south.* **Lunch** 11.30-2.30pm Tue-Fri. **Dinner** 6-11pm Tue-Sun. **Brunch** 11am-3pm Sat, Sun. **Average** $28. **Credit** AmEx, MC, V.

Joe's unassuming storefront stands wildly apart in this restaurant-heavy, artsy section of town. The place has a low-key feel but the Californian-French food is worth jumping up and down for. Try warm onion tart with salmon gravadlax and crème fraîche, followed by roasted pork tenderloin, potatoes, wild mushrooms and roasted garlic juice. There's a small bar, a small patio and a fixed-price menu, too. *Parking $2.50.*

## Rebecca's

*2025 Pacific Avenue, at North Venice Boulevard, Venice (1-310 306 6266). Bus Culver City 1/I-10, exit Fourth Street south.* **Dinner** 6-10pm Mon-Thur, Sun; 6-11pm Fri, Sat. **Average** $38. **Credit** AmEx, DC, MC, V.

This evening joint teems with hip, loud, young things who like to party. The food is nouvelle Mexican. There is a raw bar (oysters, clams and shrimp) and they serve great tropical drinks. Booking advised. *Valet parking $2.75.*

## Venus of Venice

*1202 Abbot Kinney Boulevard, between Westminster & California Avenues, Venice (1-310 392 1987). Bus Santa Monica 2/I-10, Lincoln Boulevard south.* **Open** 11.30am-8.30pm Mon-Fri; 9.30am-8.30pm Sat, Sun. **Average** $12. **No credit cards.**

This is a one-off affair, reminiscent of a Southern truckstop with its laissez-faire attitude, while eccentric owner Venus is a law unto herself. She whispers like Blanche Dubois, dresses usually in long pink numbers and serves up an array of home-made, vegetarian health food at a leisurely pace.

# Marina del Rey

## Aunt Kizzy's Back Porch

*4325 Glencoe Avenue, between Mindaneo Way & Maxella Avenue, Marina del Rey (1-310 578 1005). Bus 108, 220/US90, exit Mindanao Way north.* **Lunch** 11am-4pm Mon-Sat. **Dinner** 4-10pm Mon-Thur, Sun; 4-11pm Fri, Sat. **Average** $12. **Credit** AmEx.

Signed photos of black celebs line the walls of this cheerful, popular soul-food haunt tucked away in a mini-mall. If you're not cholesterol-conscious, it's a great place to sample comfort food, Southern-style. Try the fried chicken, ribs or pork chops.

## Benny's BBQ

*4077 Lincoln Boulevard, between Maxella Avenue & Washington Boulevard, Marina del Rey (1-310 821 6939). Bus Culver City 1, 2, Santa Monica 3, 7/SR90, exit Lincoln Boulevard north.* **Open** 11am-10pm Mon-Fri; noon-10pm Sat; 3-10pm Sun. **Average** $11. **Credit** AmEx, MC, V.

An institution providing the neighbourhood with smoky ribs and fab hot links (sausages) from a light oakwood barbecue. *Free parking at Brennan's next door.*

## Café del Rey

*4451 Admiralty Way, between Bali & Palawan Ways, Marina del Rey (1-310 823 6395). Bus 108, Santa Monica 3/SR90, exit Mindanao Way west.* **Lunch** 11am-2.30pm Mon-Sat. **Dinner** 5.30-10pm Mon-Thur; 5.30-10.30pm Fri, Sat; 5-10pm Sun. **Brunch** 10.30am-2.30pm Sun. **Average** $25. **Credit** AmEx, DC, Disc, MC, V.

A beautiful setting overlooking the Marina coupled with an excellent fusion of French and Pacific Rim cuisine by executive chef Katsuo Nagasawa. Many of the dishes surprise and prices are fair. Excellent choice for Sunday brunch, romantic dinner or when you're dropping someone at LAX. *Parking $3.*

## Killer Shrimp

*523 Washington Boulevard, at Ocean Avenue, Marina del Rey (1-310 578 2293). Bus 108, Culver City 1/SR90, exit Lincoln Boulevard north.* **Open** 11.30am-10pm Mon-Thur, Sun; 11.30am-11pm Fri, Sat. **Average** $13. **Credit** MC, V.

For some of the best shrimp west of the Bayou, get goin' to this chow house, one of a chain where you can eat shrimps, peeled or unpeeled, with Bayou butter or pepper sauce, served with bread, rice or spaghetti and on paper plates.

# Malibu

## Geoffrey's

*27400 Pacific Coast Highway, at Latigo Canyon Road, Malibu (1-310 457 1519). Bus 434/I-10, exit PCH north.* **Open** noon-10pm Mon-Thur; noon-11pm Fri; 11am-11pm Sat; 10.30am-10pm Sun. **Brunch** noon-4pm Sat, Sun. **Average** $25-$40. **Credit** AmEx, MC, V.

Dining on Geoffrey's cliffside deck, you could swear you're on the Riviera. But a look at the hearty, eclectic Californian menu, the California-heavy wine list and the Rayban-clad waiters soon set you straight. During the 1940s it was a motel as well, called The Holiday House (where it's rumoured Marilyn Monroe and JFK spent a weekend or two). The good food, exceptional view (featured in movies *The Player* and *Guilty By Suspicion*) and the harmonious service makes the distance worthwhile. Book. *Valet parking $3.*

## Gladstone's 4 Fish-Malibu

*17300 Pacific Coast Highway, at Sunset Boulevard, Malibu (1-310 454 3474). Bus 2, 434/I-10, exit PCH north.* **Open** 7am-11pm Mon-Thur, Sun; 7am-midnight Fri, Sat. **Average** $20. **Credit** AmEx, DC, Disc, MC, V.

Aka the busiest Greyhound refuelling stop on the PCH; both seagulls and tourists flock here for fresh seafood right on the beach. If you don't like having your name called over a megaphone and being treated like one of the hungry 3,000 (which is the average number of customers served per day), this isn't the place for you. *Parking $2.75.*

## Granita

*23725 West Malibu Road, at Webb Way, Malibu (1-310 456 0488). Bus 434/I-10, exit Webb Way.* **Lunch** 11.30am-2pm Wed-Fri; 11am-2pm Sat, Sun. **Dinner** 6-10pm Mon-Fri; 5.30-11pm Sat, Sun. **Brunch** 11am-2pm Sat, Sun. **Average** $32-$45. **Credit** MC, V.

The most recent addition to the Wolfgang Puck empire is slap-bang inside the Malibu Colony Plaza. The food is California-Provençal with Asian influences; the interior design beach-chic, styled, as always, by Puck's wife and partner Barbara Lazaroff. The open kitchen allows you to see new chef Lee Hefter prepare such amusements as crispy tempura softshell crab with radicchio-kaiware salad and pickled ginger and black bean vinaigrette or pan-roasted Maine monkfish with veal oxtail ravioli. Or you can entertain yourself at the bar, which has become beach-hip Central and a place to spy celebs from the Colony. Booking required.

## Inn of the Seventh Ray

*128 Old Topanga Canyon Road, at Topanga Canyon Boulevard, Topanga (1-310 455 1311). Bus 434/I-10, exit PCH north.* **Lunch** 11.30am-3pm Mon-Fri; 10.30am-3pm Sat; 9.30am-3pm Sun. **Dinner** 6-10pm daily. **Average** $13-$27. **Credit** AmEx, DC, Disc, MC, V.

You cannot leave LA without 'partaking of the angelic vibration of the violet ray' at this new age dining idyll. The drive through the Santa Monica Mountains and the Inn's gurgling creekside location are gorgeous while the karma-free, healthy dishes are eclectic and tasty, if a bit pricey. Booking required. *Valet parking $2.*

## Westside: inland

## West Hollywood & Melrose

### Barney's Beanery

*8447 Santa Monica Boulevard, off La Cienega Boulevard, West Hollywood (1-213 654 2287). Bus 4, West Hollywood A, B/I-10, exit La Cienega Boulevard north.* **Open** 10am-2am daily. **Average** $10. **Credit** AmEx, Disc, MC, V.

Funky West Hollywood haunt, now in its 76th year, where they serve a mean bowl of chilli and the biggest selection of beer in the city, maybe even the state – 37 on tap, 250 bottled brands. You can also practise your pool in this noisy, fun, late-nighter and even smoke a cigar.

### Book Soup Bistro

*8800 Sunset Boulevard, at Horn Avenue, West Hollywood (1-310 657 1072). Bus 2, 3, 105, 302, 429, DASH West Hollywood/I-10, exit La Cienega Boulevard.* **Open** noon-10pm Mon-Thur, Sun; noon-11pm Fri, Sat. **Average** $25. **Credit** AmEx, DC, Disc, MC, V.

Owner Glen Goldman opened this California-French bistro as a natural extension of Book Soup, his hip independent bookstore and newsstand. Wolf down a delicious plate of paglia e fieno with New Zealand mussels or prop up the long, wooden bar and pick on a crispy duck confit salad while shooting the breeze with the cocktail-shaking Harry. *Parking $1.25 per hour; free after 6pm and on weekends.*

### Café Med

*8615 Sunset Boulevard, at Sunset Plaza, West Hollywood (1-310 652 0445). Bus 2, 3, 302, 429/I-10, exit La Cienega Boulevard north.* **Open** 11.30am-midnight daily. **Average** $22. **Credit** AmEx, Disc, MC, V.

Possibly the least pretentious and most fun of these Sunset Plaza sidewalk restaurant/cafes, if it weren't for the pretentious Eurotrash clientele who inevitably lose their way to the neighbouring Le Petit Four. Try piadina bread with stracchino cheese and arrugala nope (herb seasoning), then the pasta al mare with a beautifully dressed insalata tricolore. *Parking free.*

### Caffè Luna

*7463 Melrose Avenue, between North Gardner Street & Vista Avenue, Melrose District (1-213 655 8647). Bus 10, 11/I-10, exit La Brea Avenue north.* **Open** 9am-3am Mon-Thur, Sun; 9am-5am Fri, Sat. **Average** $20. **Credit** AmEx, DC, Disc, MC, V.

Play with crayons, watch the insufferably skinny hipsters shop or luxuriate on the back patio, while waiting for the best halfway decent, well-priced Italian food on Melrose. If nothing else, it's open very late. *Parking $3.*

### Cava

*8384 West Third Street, at Orlando Avenue, West Hollywood (1-213 658 8898). Bus 14, 16, 105, 316, DASH Fairfax, West Hollywood/I-10, exit La Cienega Boulevard north.* **Breakfast** 6.30-11am, **lunch** 11.30am-

*Join the seagulls and tourists at*
**Gladstones 4 Fish**. *See page 125.*

4pm, **dinner** 4pm-midnight, daily. **Average** $22. **Credit** AmEx, DC, Disc, MC, V.

Hotel restaurants often cause yawns and sighs, but not so with Cava, a colourful bar and restaurant serving Spanish tapas-type food and more to a young crowd, often accompanied by live music upstairs. Check-out Steve Noriega's club night on Sundays. *Valet parking $2.50.*

### Chaya Brasserie

*8741 Alden Drive, at Robertson Boulevard, West Hollywood (1-310 859 8833). Bus 14, 16, 105, DASH Fairfax/I-10, exit La Cienega Boulevard north.* **Lunch** 11.30am-2.30pm Mon-Fri. **Dinner** 6-10.30pm Mon-Thur; 6-11pm Fri, Sat; 6-10pm Sun. **Late supper** 10.30pm-midnight Mon-Sat. **Average** $40. **Credit** AmEx, DC, MC, V.

This upscale but friendly restaurant serves excellent Mediterranean-French dishes with some Pacific Rim influences, in a pretty colonial-style setting, with large trees stretching to the high ceiling. It's been a mainstay of the neighbourhood for some time, attracting surgeons from nearby Cedars Sinai, film executives from New Line Cinema and Art and antique dealers from Robertson and Beverly Hills. The long bar has a healthy singles vibe, and offers some rather fine vodka drinks infused with pineapple. *Valet parking $3.50.*

### Chianti Cucina

*7383 Melrose Avenue, at Martel Avenue, Melrose District (1-213 653 8333). Bus 10, 11/I-10, exit Fairfax Avenue north.* **Open** *Chianti* 5.30-10.30pm Mon-Thur; 5.30-11pm Fri, Sat; 5.30-10pm Sun. *Cucina* 11.30am-11.30pm Mon-Thur; 11.30am-midnight Fri; Sat 4-11pm Sun. **Average** $15-$22. **Credit** AmEx, DC, MC, V.

Two restaurants that share the same kitchen. On the left is Chianti; opened in 1938, it's dark, formal, expensive and romantic, with a bar. On the right is Cucina, contemporary and airy. The food in both is outstanding contemporary northern Italian. *Parking $3.*

### Chin Chin

*8618 Sunset Boulevard, at Sunset Plaza Drive, West Hollywood (1-310 652 1818). Bus 2, 3, 105, 302, DASH West Hollywood/I-10, exit La Cienega Boulevard.* **Open** 11am-11pm Mon-Thur, Sun; 11am-midnight Fri, Sat. **Average** $15. **Credit** AmEx, MC, V.

California-Chinese restaurant with a café atmosphere, popular with those on a budget and for takeaways. We think the food can be haphazardly over-spiced, but some people are addicted to it.

### Cicada

*8478 Melrose Avenue, at La Cienega Boulevard, West Hollywood (1-213 655 5559). Bus 2, 3, 105, 302, DASH West Hollywood/I-10, exit La Cienega Boulevard north.* **Lunch** noon-2.30pm Mon-Fri. **Dinner** 6-10pm Mon-Sat. **Average** $35. **Credit** AmEx, DC, Disc.

Co-owner Bernie Taupin and wife Stephanie have created a wonderful sanctuary in West Hollywood, where the food is good and the atmosphere casually rarified. We suggest the gnocchi or the giant grilled portobello mushrooms. *Valet parking $3.*

### Citrus

*6703 Melrose Avenue, at Citrus Avenue, West Hollywood (1-213 857 0034). Bus 10, 11/I-10, exit La Brea Avenue north.* **Lunch** noon-2.30pm Mon-Fri. **Dinner** 6.30-10.30pm Mon-Fri; 6-11pm Sat. **Average** $30-$55. **Credit** AmEx, DC, MC, V.

One of LA's most imaginative menus (Californian-French) in a carelessly classy setting. Sit under white umbrellas (designed to put you in mind of the south of France) and

# Best for brunch

**Café del Rey** (Marina del Rey)

**The Fig Tree** (Venice)

**Four Oaks** (Bel Air)

**Granita** (Malibu)

**The House of Blues** (West Hollywood)

**Joe's** (Venice)

**1 Pico** (Santa Monica)

**The Polo Lounge** (Beverly Hills)

**The Source** (West Hollywood)

watch chef/owner Michel Richard create alongside chef de cuisine Alain Giraud in their glass kitchen. Try the wafer-thin onion rings and the chocolate mousse; Liz Taylor is said to pull up outside and send her driver in for several pots.
*Valet parking $3.50.*

### Duke's

*8909 Sunset Boulevard, at San Vincente Boulevard, West Hollywood (1-310 1-310 652 3100). Bus 2, 3, 105, 302/ I-10, exit La Cienega Boulevard north.* **Open** 7.30am-8.45pm Mon-Fri; 8am-3.45pm Sat, Sun. **Average** $6. **No credit cards.**
This 26-year-old greasy spoon was once housed in the old Tropicana Hotel, but nothing has changed since its relocation to the Strip where rock'n'rollers from nearby music venues Whiskey A-Go-Go and Rainbow Room slide in for emergency hangover breakfasts of apple hotcakes and omelettes, or for a fast lunch-time sandwich.
*Parking $1.*

### Eclipse

*8800 Melrose Avenue, at Robertson Boulevard, West Hollywood (1-310 724 5959). Bus 10, 11/I-10, exit Robertson Boulevard north.* **Dinner** 6-10.30pm Mon-Thur; 5.30-11.30pm Fri, Sat. **Average** $33. **Credit** AmEx, DC, Disc, MC, V.
A superswank Franco-American restaurant with a shiny steel open kitchen complete with brick oven, opened by former Spago maitre d' Bernard Erpicum, with some help from Steven Seagal, Joe Pesci and Whoopi Goldberg. Seafood is the speciality as are celebrities by the truckload. Dine on the patio or in the main restaurant, which looks as if somebody's mother chose the pink-peachy colour scheme.
*Parking $3.50.*

### Ed's Coffee Shop

*460 North Robertson Boulevard, between Dorrington & Melrose Avenues, West Hollywood (1-310 659 8625). Bus 220/I-10, exit Robertson Boulevard north.* **Open** 7am-3pm Mon-Fri; 7.30am-1pm Sat. **Average** $12. **No credit cards.**
Ed's reopened in May 1996 after a fire rendered it unserviceable for a year, but the menu, they say, is exactly the same. It's a low-key diner, popular with local tradesmen and Robertson designers alike. We recommend the huevos rancheros, the special burritos, the turkey quesadillas and the baked chicken – and we love the friendly service.

### The Gardens of Taxco

*1113 North Harper Avenue, at Santa Monica Boulevard, West Hollywood (1-213 654 1746). Bus 4, 304/I-10, exit La Cienega Boulevard north.* **Dinner** 4.30-11pm Mon-

Thur; 4.30pm-midnight Fri, Sat. **Average** $15. **Credit** AmEx, DC, MC, V.
One-of-a-kind Mexican dinner restaurant. The décor is on the tacky side but the atmosphere super hospitable. There are no menus so one of the family of owners will sing the entrees to you. Select chicken, pork, beef or shrimp and one of their special sauces are brought to your table in a red leatherette booth while a parade of starters are brought to your table and you are serenaded by live mariachi. The margaritas are lethal.
*Parking $1.50.*

### Gaucho Grill

*7980 Sunset Boulevard, at Crescent Heights Boulevard, West Hollywood (1-213 656 4152). Bus 2, 3, 105, 302, DASH West Hollywood /I-10, exit Fairfax Avenue north.* **Lunch** 11am-5pm Mon-Sat; noon-5pm Sun. **Dinner** 5-11pm Mon-Thur, Sun; 5pm-midnight Sat. **Average** $8. **Credit** AmEx, DC, MC, V.
Fun, economically priced Argentinian restaurant chain. This one is perfectly located for a bite before or after a movie at the adjacent Sunset 5 cinema complex or a browse around the Virgin Megastore. Lots of beef, plus chicken and salads.
*Parking free.*

### Georgia

*7250 Melrose Avenue, at Alta Vista Boulevard, Melrose District (1-213 933 8420). Bus 10, 11/I-10, exit La Brea Avenue north.* **Dinner** 6.30-11pm Mon-Sat; 5.30-10.30pm Sun.* **Average** $26. **Credit** AmEx, MC, V.
Brad Johnson, owner of the legendary Roxbury Club on Sunset Boulevard, created Georgia with backing from celebrities such as Denzel Washington and Eddie Murphy, so, inevitably, this pretty restaurant with a huge patio attracts a large movie star following. The Georgia peach daquiri is required drinking and the Southern food is down-home and health-oriented – imagine that.
*Parking $3.*

### Hirozen Gourmet

*8385 Beverly Boulevard, at Orlando Avenue, West Hollywood (1-213 653 0470). Bus 14/I-10, exit La Cienega Boulevard north.* **Lunch** 11.30am-2.30pm Mon-Fri. **Dinner** 6-10pm Mon-Sat; closed last Sat of the month.* **Average** $15. **Credit** AmEx, DC, Disc, MC, V.
Tucked inside a nondescript strip mall, known only to locals and clever people, sits Hirozen, a sublime gourmet Japanese restaurant and sushi bar. Owner/chef Hiro prepares delicate and unusual cooked dishes, good-looking salads and vegetable plates while his co-workers attend to some pretty smashing sushi. Be warned: it's small, and it fills up fast.
*Parking free.*

### The House of Blues

*8430 Sunset Boulevard, at Olive Drive, West Hollywood (concert hotline 1-213 650 1451/box office 1-213 848 5100). Bus 2, 429/I-10, exit La Cienega Boulevard north.* **Lunch** 11.30am-4pm daily. **Dinner** 4-11pm Mon-Thur, Sun; 4pm-midnight Fri, Sat. **Brunch** sittings at 9.30am, noon, 2.30pm Sun.* **Average** $15; brunch $24 adults, $12 4-12s. **Credit** AmEx, DC, Disc, MC, V.
This bizarre upstairs restaurant inside a well-styled new music venue serves hearty but refined Southern tucker and a wild 'Gospel Brunch' on Sundays. If you want to watch one of the many famous bands passing through the joint, get a front-of-house table and avoid the crush beneath.
*Valet parking $8.*

### Hugo's

*8401 Santa Monica Boulevard, at Kings Road, West Hollywood (1-213 654 3993). Bus 4, 304/I-10, exit La Cienega Boulevard north.* **Open** 7.30am-10pm daily; summer closes at 3pm Mon, Tue. **Average** $13. **Credit** AmEx, DC, JCB, MC, V.
An old favourite. Don't be fooled by the low-key atmosphere,

this American-Italian restaurant/café is a major power-breakfast and luncheon hangout. The breakfast pastas and pumpkin pancakes are heavenly.
*Parking free.*

### The Ivy

*113 North Robertson Boulevard, between Third Street & Beverly Boulevard, West Hollywood (1-310 274 8303). Bus 20, 21, 22, 220, 320/I-10, exit Robertson Boulevard north.* **Lunch** 11.30am-4.30pm, **dinner** 5-11pm, daily. **Average** $50. **Credit** AmEx, MC, V.
The service sometimes borders on rude or inattentive, but that doesn't seem to affect the status of this landmark California restaurant in a converted house with an adorably pretty patio. Real flowers and floral furnishings make you feel like you're at a summer wedding party. It's a great star-spotting place, especially at lunch-time, and they serve some excellent salads, crab cakes and fresh fish dishes. The white chocolate lemon/walnut cake covered in flowers and fruit is otherworldly.
*Valet parking $3.50.*

### Jones

*7205 Santa Monica Boulevard, between Poinsettia Place & Formosa Avenue, West Hollywood (1-213 850 1726/7). Bus 4, 212/I-10, exit La Brea Avenue north.* **Lunch** noon-4.30pm Mon-Fri. **Dinner** 7.30pm-1.30am daily. **Average** $24. **Credit** AmEx, Disc, MC, V.
Creators John Sidell and Sean MacPhearson have the trend thing down. Their 1930s retro restaurant-bar has the atmosphere of a nightclub and attracts the hippest younger set plus a spattering of celebs. Sit at the 'poodle table,' order the Caesar salad with a pizza and ignore the sometimes super-cilious attitude of the other diners.

### Joss

*9255 Sunset Boulevard, at Doheny Drive, West Hollywood (1-310 276 1886). Bus 2, 3, 429/I-10, exit La Cienega Boulevard north.* **Lunch** noon-3pm Mon-Fri. **Dinner** 6-10.30pm daily. **Average** $25. **Credit** AmEx, DC, MC, V.
At last, a restaurant where you can eat dim sum for lunch and dinner. An upscale, minimalist-designed celebrity hangout where the food is innovative and the atmosphere cool. Dinner is often quiet. If you're very lucky, you'll be served by tall maitre d' Martin Buckler, who will bend down to table level and help you order from an eclectic mix of Cantonese, Mandarin and Szechuan dishes. Lobster is a speciality.
*Parking $2.50.*

# Most fashionable

**Border Grill** (Santa Monica)

**Eclipse** (West Hollywood)

**Jones** (West Hollywood)

**Le Colonial** (West Hollywood)

**Le Deux Café** (Hollywood)

**The Mandarette** (West Hollywood)

**The Manhattan Wonton Company** (West Hollywood)

**The Newsroom Café** (West Hollywood)

**Manhattan Wonton Company.** *See p130.*

### Le Colonial

*8783 Beverly Boulevard, at Robertson Boulevard, West Hollywood (1-310 289 0660). Bus 14, 16, 220, DASH Fairfax/I-10, exit Robertson Boulevard north.* **Lunch** 11.30am-2pm daily. **Dinner** 5.30-11pm Mon-Wed, Sun; 5.30pm-midnight Thur-Sat. **Average** $25-$55. **Credit** AmEx, DC, MC, V.
Every town has to have one. And at the time of going to press, Le Colonial was it: the unsufferably hip place to be. Athough the designers have outdone themselves evoking a French/Vietnamese colonial joint, with a hip and inviting bar/lounge, some say it's quicker to order a pizza on your mobile phone; it will arrive long before the waitress does. However, if you can get a table outside, it's really very romantic and the banh cuon (Vietnamese ravioli stuffed with shrimp, chicken and mushroom) will take a long time to forget.
*Valet parking $3.50.*

### L'Orangerie

*903 North La Cienega Boulevard, between Melrose Avenue & Santa Monica Boulevard, West Hollywood (1-310 652 9770). Bus 4, 10, 11, 105, 304/I-10, exit La Cienega Boulevard north.* **Dinner** 6.30-11pm daily. **Average** $50. **Credit** AmEx, DC, Disc, JCB, MC, V.
The most seriously classic French cuisine in an aristocratic setting. Chef Ludovic Lefebvre's Provençal-inspired repertoire includes roasted lobster and potatoes confit with garlic and truffles or rack of lamb with goat's cheese and ratatouille risotto. A romantic, adult eating establishment. Make sure he remembers his pocket book and you, your jewels.
*Parking $3.50.*

### The Mandarette

*8386 Beverly Boulevard, at Orlando Avenue, West Hollywood (1-213 655 6115). Bus 14, 105/I-10, exit La Cienega Boulevard north.* **Open** 11am-10.30pm Mon-Fri;

*Sure, the food's good at **Barney Greengrass**, but the view's better. See page 132.*

2-11.30pm Sat, Sun. **Average** $15. **Credit** AmEx, DC, Disc, MC, V.

We love the Mandarette. It's a contemporary, high-ceilinged, reasonably priced neighbourhood Chinese, popular with a well-heeled young crowd looking for inspired food. The sort of joint where you can nibble from a cute list of appetisers, including onion pancakes or dumplings, or satisfy a yen for something heartier – maybe the colourful orange peel chicken or crispy sesame beef. You really can't go wrong here. *Parking $2.50.*

## Manhattan Wonton Company

*8475 Melrose Place, at La Cienega Boulevard, West Hollywood (1-213 655 6030). Bus 10, 11, 105, DASH Fairfax/I-10, exit La Cienega Boulevard north.* **Lunch** noon-2.30pm Mon-Fri. **Dinner** 6-10pm, **dim sum** 10-11pm, daily. **Average** $30. **Credit** AmEx, MC, V.

The new, hipper-than-hip, holier-than-thou, harder-than-hell-to-get-a-table place in town. No surprise that owner Paul Heller (nephew of scribe Joseph) is a former agent/producer, with every Tom, Dick and Harry of Hollywood whining and dining at his place. It's hard to decide where to sit – the pretty courtyard garden with a fountain and Philippe Starck ivory armchairs beckons as do the cosy rooms and the fireplace inside. The food is Brooklyn-Cantonese, nothing too refined, and the attitude is, well, all Californian. *Parking $3.*

## Marix Tex Mex Café

*1108 North Flores Street, at Santa Monica Boulevard, West Hollywood (1-213 656 8800). Bus 4, West Hollywood A, B/I-10, exit La Cienega Boulevard north.* **Lunch** 11.30am-4pm daily. **Dinner** 4-10.30pm Mon-Thur, Sun; 4pm-midnight Fri. **Average** $13. **Credit** AmEx, DC, Disc, MC, V.

This Santa Monica Boulevard-of-broken-dreams place positively jives, particularly on weekend nights. It's basically a tented patio. The margaritas are smooth and the prices are sweet. A favourite gay hangout. The food is like party food: fun and indigestible. *Parking $3.*

## Mexica Café

*7313 Beverly Boulevard, between Poinsettia Place & Fuller Avenue, West Hollywood (1-213 933 7385). Bus 14/I-10, exit La Brea Avenue north.* **Lunch** noon-3pm Mon-Fri. **Dinner** 5-10pm Mon-Thur, Sun; 5-11pm Fri, Sat. **Average** $15. **Credit** AmEx, MC, V.

Young pony-tailed guys and short-skirted girls frequent this contemporary Mexican find, which originally handled the overflow from not-too-faraway El Coyote. Now, it's the first choice for those with any tastebuds at all.

## Modada

*8115 Melrose Avenue, at Crescent Heights Boulevard, Melrose District (1-213 653 4612). Bus 10, 11/I-10, exit Fairfax Avenue north.* **Dinner** 6-11pm Mon-Sat. **Average** $35. **Credit** AmEx, DC, MC, V.

Sam Marvin was on a Dadaist tip when he tricked out his one-room restaurant. He cooks up some delicious, if weird-looking dishes; for example, 'erotic chicken – roasted boneless baby chicken stuffed with forest mushrooms on a flower of purple endive with a rose petal sauce'. The joint attracts a hip and eccentric crowd. And none of this comes cheap. *Parking $2.50.*

## Morton's

*8764 Melrose Avenue, at Robertson Boulevard, West Hollywood (1-310 276 5205). Bus 10, 11, 105, 220, West Hollywood A, B/I-10, exit Robertson Boulevard north.* **Lunch** noon-3pm Mon-Fri. **Dinner** 6-11.30pm Mon-Sat. **Average** $40. **Credit** AmEx, DC, MC, V.

Peter Morton (who created The Hard Rock Café and recently sold his shares in it) owns this upmarket restaurant – a bastion of the power-luncheon crowd and ever popular on Monday nights. Reminiscent of a cosy aircraft hangar, it offers a tranquil setting at tables masked by tall palms or at the bar, where Jack Martin (voted best bartender by *Los Angeles* magazine) will shake you up a cool martini while you gaze into the mirror overhead, slanted so you can spy on the diners. The American menu with a California twist isn't overly ambitious, but very serviceable. *Parking $3.50.*

### The Newsroom Café

*120 North Robertson Boulevard, at Beverly Boulevard, West Hollywood (1-310 652 4444). Bus 14, 220/I-10, exit Robertson Boulevard north.* **Open** 8am-10pm Mon-Wed, Sun; 8am-midnight Thur, Fri; 9am-midnight Sat. **Average** $12. **Credit** Amex, MC, V.

The new hot spot where you can eat health-conscious comfort food, such as chicken pot pie, five different kinds of Caesar salad and sugar-free, bluecorn blueberry waffles while watching the news and sports results or playing on the Internet. They also have a full-service fruit juice bar and offer 20 kinds of coffee and alcoholic beverages. Regulars include actors Sean Penn and Woody Harrelson and members of rock band the Red Hot Chilli Peppers.

### Orso

*8706 West Third Street, at Hamel Road, West Hollywood (1-310 274 7144). Bus 16, 27, 220, 316, 576, West Hollywood A, B/I-10, exit La Cienega Boulevard north.* **Open** 11.45am-11pm daily. **Average** $28. **Credit** MC, V.

Sitting on the back patio, you feel like you're taking a vacation from LA – if it weren't for all those celebrities. Regular Faye Dunaway is known to the waiting staff as Fadin' Away. Julia 'You'll never eat lunch in this town' Phillips likes this place because they *do* serve her. Timid Jennifer Jason Leigh chooses a corner table, close to the foliage. The house carafes of wine are excellent, the pizzas are thinner than the Los Angeleno girls that dine on them and the liver and onions is tremendous. The décor is a replica of the London and New York restaurants, but with less of a theatrical bent. *Parking $3.*

### Pane e Vino

*8265 Beverly Boulevard, at Sweetzer Avenue, West Hollywood (1-213 651 4600). Bus 14, 16/I-10, exit La Cienega Boulevard north.* **Open** 11.30am-11.30pm Mon-Sat; 5-10.30pm Sun. **Average** $25. **Credit** AmEx, MC, V.

Good northern Italian restaurant that's fashionable without being pretentious and always bustling. The acoustics aren't great inside; the pretty patio with tranquil fountains is where you want to be, but book ahead. Eat excellent thin-crusted pizzas cooked on the wood-burning fireplace, myriad fish and meat dishes cooked on the rotisserie or over charcoal, seafood pastas and exotic mushroom risottos. *Parking $2.75.*

### Pink's Hot Dogs

*709 North La Brea Avenue, at Melrose Avenue, Melrose District (1-213 931 4223). Bus 10, 11, 212/I-10, exit La Brea Avenue north.* **Open** 9.30am-2am Mon-Thur, Sun; 9.30am-3am Fri, Sat. **Average** $7. **No credit cards.**

This little hot dog stand has been pulling in the punters since Paul Pink started his business with a pushcart in 1939. His 'chilli dogs' went on to become the most popular in LA, drawing celebs along with a citywide clientele. It's one of LA's few late-night eateries and has a great night-time vibe. The burgers and dogs are OK, too.

### The Source

*8301 Sunset Boulevard, between La Cienega Boulevard & Fairfax Avenue, West Hollywood (1-213 656 6388). Bus 2, 3, 429, West Hollywood A, B/I-10, exit La Cienega Boulevard north.* **Open** 8am-midnight Mon-Fri; 9am-midnight Sat, Sun. **Average** $14. **Credit** AmEx, MC, V.

A diehard 1960s health nut joint, which Woody Allen joked about in *Annie Hall*. Best to go for Sunday brunch, sit on the front patio, order the special waffles or pancakes and sip freshly squeezed pineapple juice.

### Spago

*1114 Horn Avenue, at Sunset Boulevard, West Hollywood (1-310 652 4025). Bus 2, 3, 105, 302, 429/ I-10, exit La Cienega Boulevard north.* **Dinner** 6-11.30pm daily. **Average** $40. **Credit** DC, Disc, MC, V.

LA's most famous restaurant, where the chef is as celebrated as his customers. It's reassuring to know that normal people are allowed in, too. However, even if you book well in advance you will no doubt be relegated to some faraway table in the back, and you may be disappointed. The place has plastic chairs and the décor is tacky chic. This is the first of Wolfgang Puck's fast-growing empire of jumped-up pizza parlours-cum-eclectic California cuisine restaurants, with a menu sometimes inspired by one too many different ethnicities. However, many swear by his dishes of crispy Mandarin quail in a sweet orange-ginger sauce, lobster spring rolls or roasted duck with cracked black pepper sauce and sautéd pears. In spring 1997, he's relocating the whole kit and caboodle to take over the premises of Bistro Gardens 7, at 176 North Canon Drive, between Wilshire Boulevard and Clifton Way, Beverly Hills (1-310 652 4025). Booking essential. *Parking $2.75.*

### Tail-o'-the-Pup

*329 North San Vicente Boulevard, at Beverly Boulevard, West Hollywood (1-310 652 4517). Bus 14, 16, West Hollywood A, B/I-10, exit La Cienega Boulevard north.* **Open** 6am-5pm Mon-Sat. **Average** $7. **No credit cards.**

You don't visit Tail-o'-the-Pup for a gourmet experience. You visit it for a taste of the carefree, pre-cholesterol-conscious days of 1950s LA. This one is classic: a hot dog stand shaped like a giant hot dog, one of the few remaining examples of the buildings as signs that used to proliferate. The Mexican Olé chilli dog and the Baseball Special are recommended.

### Talesai

*9043 Sunset Boulevard, at Doheny Drive, West Hollywood (1-310 275 9724). Bus 2, 3, 429/I-10, exit La Cienega Boulevard north.* **Lunch** 11.30am-2.30pm Mon-Fri. **Dinner** 6-10.30pm Mon-Sat. **Average** $27. **Credit** AmEx, MC, V.

# LA landmarks

**Chez Jay**
Oceanside roadhouse (Santa Monica).

**Duke's**
Greasy spoon for after-hours rock'n'rollers (Hollywood).

**El Cholo**
Old-timer Mexican (Mid-Wilshire).

**The Ivy**
Celeb-heavy lunch-time haunt (West Hollywood).

**Musso & Frank Grill**
Old-fashioned film-biz hangout (Hollywood).

**Nat & Al**
The best deli in town (Beverly Hills).

**The Polo Lounge**
High-class hotel bar (Beverly Hills).

**Rex-Il Ristorante**
Art deco Italian (Downtown).

**Spago**
Wolfgang Puck's first and most famous (West Hollywood).

**Tail-o'-the-Pup**
1950s hot dog stand (West Hollywood).

**Yamashiro**
Japanese palace with an unparalleled view (Hollywood).

The city is jammed with bargain Thai restaurants and cafés but this is the upgraded gourmet version and it's well worth the trip to its cool and dark interiors. Order the Hidden Treasures (Thai versions of dim sum served in little clay covered pots), the pineapple fried rice and Phucket chicken.
*Parking $3.*

### Yujean Kang's
*8826 Melrose Avenue, at Robertson Boulevard, West Hollywood (1-310 288 0806). Bus 4, 220, West Hollywood A/I-10, exit Robertson Boulevard north.* **Lunch** noon-2.30pm, **dinner** 6-11pm, daily. **Average** $30. **Credit** AmEx, DC, Disc, MC, V.
The second startlingly good gourmet Chinese restaurant with a modern California twist from chef Yugean Kang, making Melrose and Robertson one of the hottest restaurant corners in West Hollywood. It's a cavernous contemporary space offset with antiques, including some opium beds in the waiting area.
*Parking $3.50.*

## Beverly Hills

### Barney Greengrass
*Barneys New York, Fifth floor, 9570 Wilshire Boulevard, at Camden Drive, Beverly Hills (1-310 777 5877). Bus 20, 21, 22/I-10, exit Robertson Boulevard north.* **Open** 8.30am-7pm Mon, Tue, Wed, Fri; 8.30am-9pm Thur; 9am-7pm Sat; 9am-6pm Sun. **Tea** 3-5pm daily. **Average** $25. **Credit** AmEx, MC, V.
There's nothing quite as uplifting as sitting atop exclusive department store Barneys of New York – in LA. The rooftop restaurant offers indoor and patio dining and one of the best views into Beverly Hills and the Hollywood Hills. The menu's big feature is smoked fish – everything from Nova Scotia salmon to hard-to-come-by sturgeon. The atmosphere is serene, elegant and privileged.

### Ed Debevic's
*134 North La Cienega Boulevard, at Wilshire Boulevard, Beverly Hills (1-310 659 1952). Bus 20, 105, 320, 322/I-10, exit La Cienega Boulevard north.* **Open** 11.30am-3pm Mon-Thur; 11.30am-midnight Fri, Sat; 11.30am-10pm Sun. **Average** $10. **Credit** AmEx, DC, Disc, MC, V.
Extremely loud and zany 1950s diner-cum-tourist-trap, plastered with fun memorabilia. Worth visiting just for the ridiculous waiting staff and their entertaining schtick, or if you have kids in tow. But it's probably best to eat first, unless you like burgers and fries served in a plastic basket, accompanied by a malt or a shake.
*Parking $2.50.*

### Il Cielo
*9018 Burton Way, at Doheny Drive, Beverly Hills (1-310 276 9990). Bus 27, 316, 576/I-10, exit Robertson Boulevard north.* **Lunch** 11.30am-3pm, **dinner** 6-10.30pm, Mon-Sat. **Average** $38. **Credit** AmEx, DC, Disc, MC, V.
One of the most terminally romantic restaurants in what was once an old house. Eat at one of the stone patios beneath twinkling lights and stars, smog permitting. The food is by no means the most original in town, but it's honest fare if a little pricey – and the friendly staff fall over themselves trying to make up for it.
*Valet parking $2.50.*

### Kate Mantilini
*9101 Wilshire Boulevard, at Doheny Drive, Beverly Hills (1-310 278 3699). Bus 20, 21, 22/I-10, exit Robertson Boulevard north.* **Breakfast** 7.30-11.30am, **lunch** 11am-5pm, Mon-Fri. **Dinner** 5pm-1am Mon-Thur; 5pm-2am Fri; 4pm-midnight Sat, Sun. **Brunch** noon-4pm Sat; 10am-4pm Sun. **Average** $30. **Credit** AmEx, MC, V.
A cavernous restaurant with some rather strange 1980s artworks suspended from the high ceiling. The large American

menu is nothing to write home about, but it's open late (by LA standards), they have some inviting wooden booths and, if you're careful what you order, you can have an enjoyable if overpriced meal, served by white-aproned, friendly staff.
*Valet parking $2.50.*

### Maple Drive
*345 North Maple Drive, at Burton Way, Beverly Hills (1-310 274 9800). Bus 27, Commuter Express 576/I-10, exit Robertson Boulevard north.* **Lunch** 11.30am-2.30pm Mon-Sat. **Dinner** 6-10pm Mon-Thur, Sun; 6-11pm Fri, Sat. **Average** $50-$65. **Credit** AmEx, DC, Disc, MC, V.
For years Maple Drive has been a lunch-time favourite for the entertainment crowd and a dinner-time choice for Beverly Hills residents. Sit in an intimate booth, listening to the jazz combo, chill out on the patio or loll at the long maplewood bar at happy hour where hors d'oeuvres are free and cigars can be puffed. Wherever you sit, you cannot fail to be impressed by Leonard Schwartz's fine New American cuisine. His crab cakes, happily more crab than cake, and accompanied by a sour cream dressing with golden caviar, will startle even the most jaded palette. You might yawn at the mention of another seared tuna but until you've sampled Leonard's, darling, you're just an ingénue.
*Valet parking $3.*

### Matsuhisa
*129 North La Cienega Boulevard, between Wilshire Boulevard & Clifton Way, Beverly Hills (1-310 659 9639). Bus 20, 21, 22, 105, 320/I-10, exit La Cienega Boulevard north.* **Lunch** 11.45am-2.15pm Mon-Fri. **Dinner** 5.45-10.15pm daily. **Average** $60. **Credit** AmEx, DC, MC, V.
Chef Nobuyuki Matsuhisa's fusion of Japanese and Peruvian cuisines attracts celebrities and expense-account eaters. Although traditional sushi is available, his additions of garlic, fresh chilli and special sauces are a shrewd delight. Try the squid 'pasta' with garlic sauce or sea scallops filled with black truffles and topped with caviar. Booking required.
*Parking $2.50.*

### Mr Chow's
*344 North Camden Drive, between Wilshire Boulevard & Brighton Way, Beverly Hills (1-310 278 9911). Bus 20, 21, 22, Beverly Hills BT/I-405, exit Wilshire Boulevard east.* **Lunch** noon-2.30pm Mon-Fri. **Dinner** 6-11.30pm daily. **Average** $40. **Credit** AmEx, DC, MC, V.
Breathe a sigh of relief as you enter the comforting cocoon that is Mr Chow. Started in London, opened in Manhattan, now the old-favourite, celebrity-popular Chinese dining spot is in upscale Beverly Hills. The night we were there, Steven

# Best budget

**Argentinian** Gaucho Grill (West Hollywood)

**Chinese** Chin Chin (West Hollywood)

**Cuban** Versailles (Culver City)

**Healthy** A Votre Sante (Venice)

**Italian** Fritto Misto (Santa Monica)

**Japanese** Noshi Sushi (Koreatown)

**Mexican** El Coyote (Park La Brea)

**Southern** Roscoe's House of Chicken 'N' Waffles (Hollywood)

**Thai** Lumpinee Thai (North Hollywood, San Fernando Valley)

Seagal and producer Joel Silver were chewing on some tender duck. The noodles prepared tableside are a big production piece. But be prepared to pay top dollar.
*Valet parking $3.50.*

## Mulberry Street Pizzeria

*347 North Canon Drive, between Brighton & Dayton Ways, Beverly Hills (1-310 247 8100). Bus 3, Beverly Hills BT, BD, RP/I-405, exit Santa Monica Boulevard east.* **Open** 11am-midnight Mon-Sat; 11am-11pm Sun. **Average** $16. **Credit** MC, V.
A no-frills pizza joint which looks like it might have been lifted from a Scorsese movie. The idea is not so far-fetched; owner is *Raging Bull* co-star Cathy Moriarty. The walls are covered in autographed photos of her celebrity friends and clientele and some days you may find Ms Moriarty herself, with sleeves rolled high, serving you some fine pizza or old-fashioned Sicilian favourites like spaghetti and meatballs. Sit at the counter, or at one of the few tables inside or out on the Beverly Hills sidewalk.

## Nate & Al

*414 North Beverly Drive, between Brighton Way & Little Santa Monica Boulevard, Beverly Hills (1-310 274 0101). Bus 4, 20, 27, Beverly Hills BT, RP/I-405, exit Santa Monica Boulevard east.* **Open** 7.30am-8.45pm daily. **Average** $13. **Credit** AmEx, MC, V.
Despite the tawdry exterior, this 50-year-old establishment is a big industry hangout, serving excellent, traditional Jewish deli fare. The blintzes are recommended.

## The Polo Lounge

*Beverly Hills Hotel, 9641 Sunset Boulevard, at Rodeo Drive, Beverly Hills (1-310 276 2251). Bus 2, 3, 429, 576/ I-405, exit Santa Monica Boulevard east.* **Breakfast** 7-11am, **lunch** 11am-4pm, **appetisers** 4-5.30pm, **dinner** 5.30-11pm, **late-night** 11pm-1.30am, daily. **Brunch** 11am-4pm Sun. **Average** $40. **Credit** AmEx, DC, MC, V.
A-not-to-be-missed piece of Old Hollywood where the power breakfast was first invented and being paged and having a telephone brought to your table was made a famous Hollywood tactic. The lounge was renamed after Darryl F Zanuck and his polo-playing buddies, such as Will Rogers, Tommy Hitchcock and Spencer Tracy. Although the hotel was recently overhauled, the lounge has been left intact and million-dollar deals are still sealed over eggs benedict.
*Parking $3.*

## Westwood & UCLA

### Asuka

*1266 Westwood Boulevard, at Wilshire Boulevard, Westwood (1-310 474 7412). Bus 20, 21, 22/I-405, exit Wilshire Boulevard east.* **Lunch** 11.30am-2pm Mon-Fri. **Dinner** 5.30-10pm Mon-Thur, Sun; 5.30-11pm Fri, Sat. **Average** $7.50-$17. **Credit** AmEx, DC, MC, V.
A consistent and friendly Japanese restaurant/sushi bar. A safe bet in none-too-noteworthy Westwood. The speciality is Japanese-style barbecue.
*Parking $2.*

### The Dynasty Room

*The Westwood Marquis Hotel, 930 Hilgard Avenue, at Weyburn Avenue, Westwood (1-310 208 8765). Bus 2, 21, 429, 576, Culver City 6, Santa Monica 1, 2/I-405, exit Wilshire Boulevard east.* **Lunch** 11.30am-2.30pm, **dinner** 5.30-10.30pm, daily. **Average** $48. **Credit** AmEx, DC, MC, V.
This part of town is a culinary desert, so booking is definitely recommended at this excellent restaurant. The food is innovative and the prices competitive. Ideal for a meal after a movie or an art opening at the Armand Hammer.

## The Gardens on Glendon

*1139 Glendon Avenue, at Lindbrook Avenue, Westwood (1-310 824 1818). Bus 21, Culver City 6/I-405, exit Wilshire Boulevard east.* **Lunch** 11.30am-3pm, **dinner** 6-11pm, daily. **Average** $30. **Credit** AmEx, MC, V.
One of the safer bets in student-happy Westwood, run by the creators of the Hamburger Hamlet chain. At lunch-time it caters to the business crowd with a casual menu of hearty salads and sandwiches, while in the evening a more refined California-style menu is served, accompanied by a piano player, to a more affluent crowd.
*Parking $2.50.*

## Shaharazad

*1442 Westwood Boulevard, at Ohio Avenue, Westwood (1-310 470 3242). Bus Santa Monica 1, 8, 12/I-405, exit Wilshire Boulevard east.* **Open** 11.30am-midnight Mon-Thur; 11.30am-4am Fri, Sat. **Average** $11. **Credit** AmEx, DC, Disc, MC, V.
Good Persian food at great prices – and it's open late. **Branch**: 138 South Beverly Drive, Beverly Hills (1-310 859 8585).

## Thai House

*1049 Gayley Avenue, at Kinross & Weyburn Avenues, Westwood (1-310 208 2676). Bus 2, 536, 573, 576, Commuter Express 431/I-405, exit Wilshire Boulevard east.* **Lunch** 11am-3pm Mon-Fri; noon-3pm Sat, Sun. **Dinner** 3-10pm Mon-Thur, Sun; 3-10.30pm Fri, Sat. **Average** $9. **Credit** MC, V.
Good, Thai cuisine in a clean contemporary setting.

# Bel Air, Brentwood & West LA

### Bombay Café

*12113 Santa Monica Boulevard, at Bundy Drive, West LA (1-310 820 2070). Bus 4, 304, Santa Monica 1, 10, 14/I-405, exit Santa Monica Boulevard west.* **Lunch** 11.30am-3pm Tue-Sun. **Dinner** 3-10pm Tue-Thur; 3-11pm Fri; 4-11pm Sat; 4-10pm Sun. **Average** $4-$15. **Credit** MC, V.
Expect queues at this highly popular Californian-Indian restaurant housed on the second floor of an unprepossessing mini-mall. Try the masala dosas (South Indian pancakes) or the Frankies (hand-made, egg-dipped tortillas filled burrito-style with chicken, lamb or cauliflower), accompanied by Indian beer or sweet chai (tea). Top it all off with rice pudding, or home-made mango or ginger kulfi.

### Chan Dara

*11940 West Pico Boulevard, at Bundy Drive, West LA (1-310 479 4461). Bus Santa Monica 7, 10, 14/I-10, exit Bundy Drive north.* **Lunch** noon-3.30pm Mon-Thur, Sun. **Dinner** 5-10.30pm Mon-Thur, Sun; 5-11.30pm Fri, Sat. **Average** $20. **Credit** AmEx, DC, Disc, MC, V.
The best of this very popular chain of rock'n'roll Thai restaurants. The food is excellent. Try the spicy garlic chicken and the Thai bouillabaisse with brown rice. Some joke that people come less for the good food and more for the pretty and provocatively dressed waitresses.
*Valet parking $3.35 .*

### The Chez

*Beverly Prescott Hotel, 1224 South Beverwil Drive, between Rodeo Drive & Pico Boulevard, West LA (1-310 772 2999). Bus 3, Santa Monica 5, 7, 13/I-10, exit Robertson Boulevard north.* **Breakfast** 7-11am Mon-Fri. **Lunch** 11.30am-2.30pm Mon-Fri. **Dinner** 5.30-10pm Mon-Thur; 5.30-11pm Fri, Sat; 5.30-9pm Sun. **Brunch** 8am-2.30pm Sat, Sun. **Average** $22. **Credit** AmEx, DC, MC, V.
The first Westside venture for South Bay restaurateurs Michael Franks and Robert Bell, with an eclectic menu.

At lunch-times, it's packed with execs from the nearby 20th Century Fox lot, while evenings are popular with locals from Cheviot Hills and leftovers from the studio. They also do a rollicking trade with the sixth-floor clients from the hotel, a floor given over exclusively to patients recovering from plastic surgery, for whom they offer 'soft' and 'hard' menus.

### Delmonico's Seafood Grille

*9320 West Pico Boulevard, between Beverly & Doheny Drives, West LA (1-310 550 7737). Bus Santa Monica 3, 5, 7, 13/I-10, exit Robertson Boulevard north.* **Open** 11.30am-10pm Mon-Sat; 5-10pm Sun. **Average** $25. **Credit** AmEx, MC, V.

While their sign 'If it swims we've got it' may not be entirely true, Delmonico's is dependable for a few fishy things. The Maine lobster is reliable and there are some good variations on grilled and sautéed fish, but too often the dishes are drowning in old-fashioned, rich sauces. A surprising number of meat dishes. A good wine list in a stately room, surrounded by beckoning booths. Booking recommended.
*Parking $2.50.*
**Branch**: 16358 Ventura Boulevard, Encino (1-818 986 0777).

### Four Oaks Restaurant

*2181 North Beverly Glen Boulevard, at Scenario Lane, Bel Air (1-310 470 2265). Bus 429, 578, 302/I-405, exit Sunset Boulevard east.* **Lunch** 11.30am-2pm Tue-Sat. **Dinner** 6-9.30pm daily. **Brunch** 10.30am-2pm Sun. **Average** $18-$28. **Credit** AmEx, MC, V.

Once a speakeasy, now a romantic hideaway cottage in rustic Beverly Glen Canyon, with chef Peter Roelant at the helm, formerly of L'Orangerie. The complex menu offers starters like lavender wood-smoked salmon cake with crisp potato and horseradish while main courses include white feather quails with pecan-apricot mushroom stuffing, port wine and shallot sauce. Indoor fireside dining or outside near the fountain.
*Valet parking $3.*

### Koutoubia

*2116 Westwood Boulevard, at Olympic Boulevard, West LA (1-310 475 0729). Bus 5, 8, 12/I-405, exit Santa Monica Boulevard east.* **Dinner** 6-10pm Tue-Thur; 6-11pm Fri-Sun. **Average** $21. **Credit** AmEx, DC, Disc, MC, V.

Laid-back Moroccan dinner restaurant with cushions and many courses.

### La Serenata Gourmet

*10924 West Pico Boulevard, at Westwood Boulevard, West LA (1-310 441 9667). Bus Culver City 3, Santa Monica 7, 8, 12, 13/I-10, exit Overland Boulevard north.* **Lunch** 11am-3.30pm Tue-Sun. **Dinner** 5-10pm Tue-Sun. **Average** $10. **Credit** AmEx, DC, MC, V.

The Westside version – less formal and less expensive – of the original upscale Mexican restaurant, La Serenata di Garibaldi, in East LA (*see below*). The speciality is still seafood dripping in some rather special sauces, but note they eschew lard and other heavy ingredients not commonly found in Mexican cuisine. Try the fish tacos and empanadas stuffed with pink shrimp. Be prepared to wait for your table, whether dining inside or out.
*Valet parking $2.*

### Mezzaluna

*11750 San Vicente Boulevard, at Gorham Avenue, Brentwood (1-310 447 8667). Bus 22, 322, Santa Monica 3/I-405, exit Wilshire Boulevard west.* **Open** 11.30am-10pm Mon-Fri; noon-10pm Sat; 5-10pm Sun. **Average** $25. **Credit** AmEx, DC, Disc, MC, V.

Reliable Italian in a popular shopping area. Good pizza if you like your crust thin and crisp; plus good pastas and a surprising array of carpaccio dishes. The one-room restaurant

is bright and airy, offering a good corner view of the busy high street. Nicole Brown Simpson ate her last meal here, thus prompting a wave of ghoulish types who want to sit at the same table and eat the same food.
*Valet parking $2.75.*

### VIP Harbor Seafood Restaurant

*11701 Wilshire Boulevard, at Barrington Avenue, West LA (1-310 979 3377). Bus 20, 329, Santa Monica 2/I-405, exit Wilshire Boulevard west.* **Lunch** 11am-3pm Mon-Fri; 10am-3pm Sat, Sun. **Dinner** 5-10pm Mon-Fri; 3-10pm Sat, Sun. **Average** $40. **Credit** AmEx, MC, V.

Popular Cantonese-style seafood restaurant with live tanks of lobster, crab, abalone and shrimp. Dim sum is served every day until 3pm.

## Century City

### Dive!

*Century City Shopping Mall, 10250 Santa Monica Boulevard, between Avenue of the Stars & Century Park West, Century City (1-310 788 3483). Bus 22, 27, 28, 316, 328, Santa Monica 5, Commuter Express 534, 573/I-405, exit Santa Monica Boulevard east.* **Open** 11.30am-11pm Mon-Thur, Sun; 11.30am-midnight Fri, Sat. **Average** $18. **Credit** AmEx, DC, MC, V.

A place for kids of all ages. Partly owned by Steven Spielberg, this theme park-styled restaurant serves fast food including ribs, pasta, pizza, burgers and salads, but, of course, specialises in submarine sandwiches – a super large hot-dog-style roll with any number of absurd fillings.
*Parking free first 2 hrs.*

### Houstons

*Century City Shopping Mall, 10250 Santa Monica Boulevard, between Avenue of the Stars & Century Park West, Century City (1-310 557 1285). Bus 22, 27, 28, 316, 328, Santa Monica 5, Commuter Express 534, 573/I-405, exit Santa Monica Boulevard east.* **Open** 11.30am-11pm Mon-Thur, Sun; 11.30am-midnight Fri, Sat. **Average** $25. **Credit** AmEx, MC, V.

It's a frenetic place, so relax, if you can, at the bar and wait for your pager to go off, signalling that your table is ready. The food is consistently good, upmarket fast-food-type fare. Try the very thin pizzas, hickory burgers or the BBQ ribs.
*Parking 2 hrs free with validation.*

### Yin Yang

*Century City Shopping Mall, 10250 Santa Monica Boulevard, between Avenue of the Stars & Century Park West, Century City (1-310 5576 3333). Bus 22, 27, 28, 316, 328, Santa Monica 5, Commuter Express 534, 573/I-405, exit Santa Monica Boulevard east.* **Open** 11.30am-9pm Mon-Thur, Sun; 11.30am-11pm Fri, Sat. **Average** $15. **Credit** AmEx, MC, V.

A high-energy restaurant with a good and interesting mix of different regional Chinese dishes. The Hong Kong-style dim sum is excellent.
*Parking 2 hrs free with validation.*

## Culver City

### Tucan

*9609 Venice Boulevard, at Hughes Avenue, Culver City (1-310 287 0130). Bus 33, 220, 333, 436, Santa Monica 12, Culver City 1, 4, 5/I-10, exit Overland Avenue south.* **Open** 10am-10pm daily. **Average** $12. **Credit** AmEx, DC, MC, V.

Good Mexican-Caribbean cooking with an emphasis on healthy (they only use olive oil) in a downhome setting. Sit on the patio and try the vegetarian plate – corn tamales, grilled vegetables, black beans and a small salad – or the salmon with black Indian pepper sauce.

## Versailles

*1415 South La Cienega Boulevard, at Pico Boulevard, Culver City (1-310 289 0392). Bus Santa Monica 5, 7, 12, 105/I-10, exit La Cienega Boulevard south.* **Open** 11am-10pm daily. **Average** $12. **Credit** AmEx, MC, V.
Well-known, funky, no-frills Cuban joint where the food is good, the prices great (even the LAPD can afford it) and the service to the point. Try the garlic chicken served with sweet raw onion and fried plantains on white rice and black beans. *Parking $2.50.*
**Branch**: Versailles Cuban Food, 10319 Venice Boulevard, Culver City (1-310 558 3168).

# Hollywood & Midtown

## Hollywood

### Hollywood Canteen

*1006 Seward Avenue, at Santa Monica Boulevard, Hollywood (1-213 465 0961). Bus 4, 420/I-10, exit La Brea Avenue north.* **Lunch** 11.30am-5.30pm Mon-Fri, Sun. **Dinner** 6-10pm daily. **Average** $20. **Credit** AmEx, MC, V.
Bang in the middle of Nowheresville, surrounded by film post-production houses, is this cool, retro grill. A simple counter greets you in the front while a more sophisticated collection of booths furnish the centre room, and there's also a small garden in the back, with a silver Airstream caravan for decoration. Good Caesar salads, pastas, chowders, steaks and fish.

### Hollywood Hills Coffee Shop

*6145 Franklin Avenue, between Gower & Vine Streets, Hollywood (1-213 467 7678). Bus 26, Community Connection 208/US101, exit Gower Street north.* **Open** 7am-4pm Mon, Sun; 7am-10pm Tue-Sat. **Average** $8. **Credit** AmEx, Disc, MC, V.
A banner outside alerts motorists to the 'Last cappuccino before the 101 freeway'. This non-greasy-spoon diner is favoured by celebs like Sandra Bullock, Quentin Tarantino and Tim Roth as a great meeting place or simply to read the morning paper with a terrific breakfast of blueberry pancakes or huevos rancheros. Conveniently located, this is an inexpensive and unassuming dive with enough charm and anti-fashion statement to suit Hollywood hipsters.

### Ita cho

*6775 Santa Monica Boulevard, between Highland & Las Palmas Avenues, Hollywood (1-213 871 0236). Bus 4, 304, 420, 426/I-10, exit La Brea Avenue north.* **Dinner** 6.30-11pm daily. **Average** $35. **Credit** AmEx, DC, Disc, MC, V.
Small and unusual Japanese restaurant with some out-of-the-ordinary cooked dishes and good sashimi, but absolutely no sushi. It's located in a mini-mall with some unsavoury characters in the vicinity, but worth the trip. Check out the spicy lotus root, Japanese jalepeno peppers, the aubergine with sweet miso paste and the dozen or so different sakes.

### Le Deux Café

*1638 Las Palmas Avenue, between Hollywood Boulevard & Selma Avenue, Hollywood (1-213 465 0509). Bus 26, 163, 181, 217/US101, exit Highland Avenue south.* **Breakfast** 8.30-11.30am, **lunch** 11.30am-3.30pm, **dinner** 6-11pm, Mon-Sat. **Average** $35. **Credit** AmEx, MC, V.
Michele Lamy, former manageress of Café des Artistes, has got her work cut out now she's opened her own small place in Hollywood. Despite its almost secret location (through the back of Grant's Parking; the attendent will lead you to the back garden entrance), she has attracted a madly fashionable crowd, so large that she's having problems seating them in this currently patio-only affair. French food. *Parking $2.*

### Lucy's Cafe El Adobe

*5536 Melrose Avenue, between North Beachwood Drive & North Windsor Boulevard, Hollywood (1-213 462 9421). Bus 10, 11/US101, exit Melrose Avenue east.* **Open** 11.30am-11pm Mon-Sat. **Average** $13. **Credit** AmEx, MC, V.
Opposite Paramount Studios, this has been a longtime haunt for movie stars and execs alike and photos of them adorn the walls. The food isn't the best Mexican in town, but the atmosphere is cool and the margaritas are strong. Enter via the 'Stage Door' in the parking lot behind.

### Musso & Frank Grill

*6667 Hollywood Boulevard, at Cherokee Avenue, Hollywood (1-213 467 7788). Bus 163, 180, 181, 212, 217, DASH Hollywood/US101, exit Highland Avenue south.* **Open** 11am-11pm Tue-Sat. **Credit** AmEx, DC, MC, V.
In 1919, Musso & Frank's opened its double doors on a what was just a muddy strip of Hollywood Boulevard. Everything about the neighbourhood has changed, but the old-style grill lives on with its original high-backed red leatherette booths, dark stained wood and faded hunting scene wallpaper, which have serviced three generations of Hollywood movers and shakers, including Valentino and Chaplin. If you're not deterred by the undertaker demeanour of the waiting staff nor a menu that hasn't changed in 70 years (lamb kidneys/ short ribs/sauerbraten), and you don't mind ruining your palette with a sidecar or a highball, this is a landmark must. Hollywood dining at its most textured and vintage.
*Parking 2 hrs free with valiadation.*

### Off Vine

*6263 Leland Way, at Seward Street, Hollywood (1-213 962 1900). Bus 2, 3, 210, 310, Commuter Connection 208/US101, exit Sunset Boulevard west.* **Lunch** 11.30am-2.30pm Mon-Fri. **Dinner** 5.30-11.30pm Fri; 5-11.30pm Sat; 5-10pm Sun. **Brunch** 11am-2.30pm Sun. **Average** $25. **Credit** AmEx, MC, V.
California-chic casual restaurant where the food is a mite ambitious, but the Arts and Crafts cottage hideaway setting (with a marlin through its roof) is just too cute to pass up. Perfect for special occasions or a lovers' tryst. The dessert soufflés are worth coming for alone.
*Parking $2.75.*

### Patina

*5955 Melrose Avenue, at Cahuenga Boulevard, Hollywood (1-213 467 1108). Bus 10, 11/US101, exit Melrose Avenue west.* **Lunch** noon-2.30pm Tue-Fri. **Dinner** 6-9.30pm Mon-Thur, Sun; 6-10.30pm Fri, Sat. **Average** $40. **Credit** AmEx, DC, Disc, MC, V.
Chef/owner Joachim Splichal cooks arguably some of the best food in town. But a glance at his menu tells you not to take his offerings too seriously. Tomatoes are not sun-dried but 'Hollywood roof-dried' and rabbit kidneys, liver and heart served with polenta gnocchi are termed 'everything from the rabbit'. Creative potato dishes are his signature. The setting is classy, without pretension, if a little noisy and austere. Splichal's wife/partner Christine takes care of business at the front of house.
*Parking $3.50.*

### Pinot Hollywood

*1448 North Gower Street, at Sunset Boulevard, Hollywood (1-213 461 8800). Bus 10, 11/US101, exit Gower Street south.* **Open** 11.30am-1am Mon-Fri; 5.30pm-1am Sat. **Average** $24. **Credit** AmEx, DC, Disc, MC, V.
Also owned by Joachim Splichal, this is a sparky upscale French bistro, with a great bar and patio dining. The only good food in the heart of Hollywood, and worth a visit even if you're not already on this side of town.

### Roscoe's House of Chicken 'N' Waffles

*1514 North Gower Street, between Selma Avenue &
Sunset Boulevard, Hollywood (1-213 466 7453). Bus 2, 3,
DASH Hollywood/US101, exit Gower Street south.* **Open**
9am-midnight Mon-Thur; 9am-3am Fri; 8.30am-3am Sat;
8.30am-midnight Sun. **Average** $9. **Credit** AmEx, MC, V.
One of a chain of funky Southern joints which people love
because they're open late, the prices are low and the down-
home dishes are reliable and tasty.

### Yamashiro

*1999 North Sycamore Avenue, at Franklin Avenue,
Hollywood (1-213 466 5125). Bus 1/US101, exit Highland
Avenue.* **Dinner** 5.30-10pm Mon-Thur, Sun; 5.30-11pm
Fri, Sat. **Average** $27. **Credit** AmEx, MC, V
You don't visit Yamashiro for the so-so Japanese food. You
visit it for the chance to consume cocktails and so-so Japanese
food in a truly magnificent setting: a hilltop Japanese palace
(it's a replica of a palace in Kyoto, complete with ornamental
gardens) with a spectacular, panoramic view of LA. A must
for new arrivals to the city. No shorts allowed.
*Valet parking $2.50.*

## Fairfax

### Canter's

*419 North Fairfax Avenue, at Oakwood Avenue, Fairfax
(1-213 651 2030). Bus 14, 217, DASH Fairfax/I-10, exit
Fairfax Avenue north.* **Open** 24 hours daily. **Average**
$12. **Credit** MC, V.
Visiting 65-year-old Jewish deli Canter's is a unique experience. The service can be charmless and the food tasteless,
but, hell, they are open 24 hours. They make their own pick-
les and sell some excellent chocolate-chip rugala and bagels
covered with melted cheddar and poppy seeds. After midnight, the restaurant becomes quite a scene of young 'atti-
tudinising' kids in search of sustenance after a night of
clubbing. There's also the Kibbutz Room, a bar which offers
nightly live entertainment.

### Du-par's

*Farmers' Market, 6333 West Third Street, at Fairfax
Avenue, Fairfax (1-213 933 8446). Bus 16, 217/I-10,
exit Fairfax Avenue north.* **Open** 10am-6.30pm daily.
**Average** $10. **Credit** AmEx, Disc, MC, V.
Good 1950s coffeeshop chain with old-fashioned service, gallons of free coffee refills and staple fare – pancakes, French
toast, pies and general breakfast stuff.

### Kokomo

*Farmers' Market, 6333 West Third Street, at Fairfax
Avenue, Fairfax (1-213 933 0773). Bus 16, 217/I-10,
exit Fairfax Avenue north.* **Open** 8am-6pm Mon-Sat;
9.30am-5pm Sun. **Average** $11. **Credit** MC, V.
Hip café with a counter and tables, which doubles as a tourist
trap and a meeting point for locals. The menu makes a vague
bid toward healthiness, but the best bets are the high-
cholesterol strawberry or banana pancakes. A popular place
to check out who's checking you out on a weekend at brunch
time, when there are often queues. No espresso served: get
your fix at another concession and bring it to your table.

## Miracle Mile & Park La Brea

### Al Amir

*5750 Wilshire Boulevard, at Courtyard Place, Mid-
Wilshire (1-213 931 8740). Bus 20, 21, 22, 320/I-10,
exit La Brea Avenue north.* **Open** 11.30am-10pm Mon-
Thur; 11.30am-1am Fri; 5.30pm-1am Sat. **Average** $23.
**Credit** AmEx, DC, Disc, MC, V.
Upscale Lebanese restaurant, housed in the courtyard of the
contemporary Museum Square office complex. Perfect for
supper after a browse in the LA County Museum opposite.
*Parking $3.*

### Atlas Bar & Grill

*3760 Wilshire Boulevard, at Western Avenue, Mid-
Wilshire (1-213 380 8400). Metro Wilshire/Western/bus
20, 21, 22, 207, 357/I-10, exit Crenshaw Boulevard north.*

*The heavenly* **Lumpinee Thai***: food from the gods, chairs from the dark side. See p141.*

**Lunch** 11.30am-3pm daily. **Dinner** 6-10pm Mon-Thur;
6-11pm Fri, Sat. **Average** $30. **Credit** AmEx, DC, MC, V.
Bar open until 2am nightly.

Atlas is the legacy of flamboyant restaurateur Mario
Tomayo, who died of AIDS in his early 30s after establish-
ing three highly successful restaurants in run-down neighbourhoods. Atlas followed the earlier, smaller Cha Cha Cha
(still going, *see below*) and Cafe Mambo (now closed) and
instantly attracted a mixed Midtown business and gay
crowd with its golden painted room the size of a tennis court,
super-camp décor and charming waiters. Its eclectic menu is
fine but not exceptional but, with cabaret most nights, dining here is more than just eating out, it's a total event.
*Valet parking $3.50.*

### El Cholo

*1121 South Western Avenue, between Pico & Olympic
Boulevards, Mid-Wilshire (1-213 734 2773). Bus 27, 28,
30, 207, 328, 357, Commuter Express 534/I-10, exit
Western Avenue north.* **Open** 11am-10pm daily.
**Average** $12. **Credit** AmEx, DC, MC, V.

There's very little to call contemporary in this LA landmark,
which opened in 1927. The service is old-style ceremonious
and the Mexican food is traditional.
*Valet parking $2.50.*

### El Coyote

*7312 Beverly Boulevard, between Poinsettia Place & Fuller
Avenue, Park La Brea (1-213 939 2255). Bus 14/I-10,
exit La Brea Avenue north.* **Open** 11am-10pm Mon-Thur,
Sun; 11am-11pm Fri, Sat. **Average** $10. **Credit** MC, V.

People usually don't come here for the food but to soak up
the carefree atmosphere and the margaritas. After 65 years in
business, it's an institution. Maybe it's the anti-snob factor.
*Parking $1.50.*

### Farfalla

*143 North La Brea Avenue, between First Street &
Beverly Boulevard, Park La Brea (1-213 938 2504). Bus
14, 212/I-10, exit La Brea Avenue north.* **Dinner** 5.30-
10.30pm Mon-Thur, Sun; 5.30-11.30pm Fri, Sat. **Average**
$25. **Credit** AmEx, MC, V.

Very popular Italian restaurant that attracts a hip thirtysome-
thing crowd. Sample the pizzas and the pastas, many of
which are home-made; especially good is the fusilli del-
l'aristocratico – truffle oil, roasted artichokes, shitake mushrooms and shaved ricotta. Live music upstairs some nights.
*Parking $3.*

### La Fonda

*2501 Wilshire Boulevard, at Carondelet Street, Westlake
(1-213 380 5055). Bus 21, 22, 29, 320/I-10, exit South
Vermont Avenue north.* **Lunch** 11am-2pm Mon-Fri.
**Dinner** 5pm-1am Mon-Thur; 5pm-2am Fri, Sat.
**Average** $17. **Credit** AmEx, DC, MC, V.

People have been frequenting La Fonda for 30 years. They
come principally to hear the famous mariachi musicians, Los
Camperos, but also to eat Mexican food. Fun for a party.
*Parking $5.*

### Maurice's Snack 'N' Chat

*5549 West Pico Boulevard, at Sierra Bonita Avenue,
Mid-Wilshire (1-213 931 3877). Bus Santa Monica 5, 7,
12, 13/I-10, exit Fairfax Avenue north.* **Open** 9am-10pm
daily. **Average** $12. **Credit** DC, Disc, MC, V.

Visit Maurice at her funky soul-food restaurant. She makes
the best home-fried chicken in town as well as great liver and
onions and smothered pork chops with brown sauce (cooked
with an eye to a low fat content).

### Red

*7450 Beverly Boulevard, at Vista Street, Park La Brea
(1-213 937 0331). Bus 14, DASH Fairfax/I-10, exit
Fairfax Avenue north.* **Breakfast** 7am-11.30am daily.

**Lunch** 11.30am-4pm Mon-Fri. **Dinner** 6-11pm Mon-
Thur, Sun. **Brunch** 7am-4pm Sat, Sun. **Average** $17.
**Credit** AmEx, MC, V.

A little restaurant-café with sidewalk tables. The salads are
OK, the whole roasted chicken is good and it's a fine spot to
observe the trendy young WeHo set who throng here.
*Valet parking $2.50.*

### Rita Flora Kitchens

*460 South La Brea Avenue, at Sixth Street, Park La Brea
(1-213 931 9900). Bus 16, 212, 316/I-10, exit La Brea
Avenue north.* **Open** 8am-11pm Mon-Sat; 8am-10pm Sun.
**Average** $13. **Credit** MC, V.

A café/restaurant in a florist. A novel idea, which goes down
well with the neighbourhood lunch crowd. Inventive salads,
sandwiches and saucy puddings.
*Parking $2.50.*

## Hancock Park

### Girasole

*225½ North Larchmont Boulevard, between Beverly
Boulevard & West First Street, Hancock Park (1-213 464
6978). Bus 14/US101, exit Melrose Avenue west.* **Lunch**
11.30am-3pm Mon-Sat. **Dinner** 6.30-10pm Thur-Sat.
**Average** $25-$50. **Credit** AmEx, MC, V

Outstandingly authentic Italian trattoria run by a northern
Italian couple. Ermanno takes care of things out front, while
Sonia cooks up a storm in the back. You can't go wrong, no
matter what you order, but the rigatoni with sausage, olives
and a slightly spicy tomato sauce is excellent.

### Prado

*244 North Larchmont Boulevard, at Beverly Boulevard,
Hancock Park (1-213 467 3871). Bus 14, 16/US101, exit
Melrose Avenue west.* **Lunch** 11.30am-3pm Mon-Sat.
**Dinner** 5-10pm daily. **Average** $23. **Credit** AmEx, DC,
Disc, MC, V.

Prado is split into two, with the themes of night and day
depicted on the walls and ceilings. But whichever side you
choose, your mood will be uplifted by the sophisticated cuisine
of the Americas. Try the Prado Sampler: moist corn tamales
served with sour cream, caviar and tomatillo sauce, shrimp in
black pepper sauce, crab cake with tartare sauce and a portion of Pacifico-style chile relleno. The tarte tatin is sublime.

## Koreatown

### Dong Il Jang

*3455 West Eighth Street, at Hobart Boulevard, Koreatown
(1-213 383 5757). Metro Wilshire/Western/bus 66, 67,
207, 357/I-10, exit Western Avenue north.* **Open** 11am-
10pm daily. **Average** $20. **Credit** AmEx, MC, V.

An upscale affair in the heart of Koreatown. You can dine at
the sushi bar, in a booth, or more privately, sitting on cushions on the floor. When it comes to traditional Korean BBQ,
we recommend the galbi-marinated beef short ribs, which
you cook at your table. These will arrive with myriad side
dishes, pickled vegetables, sweet potatoes, glass noodles and,
of course, rice. Soju, made from distilled sweet potato, will
certainly light you up, if the spicy food fails. Shika, made
from rice and sugar, is a good way to wash your palate at
the end of the meal.

### Noshi Sushi

*4430 Beverly Boulevard, at North Hobart Place,
Koreatown (1-213 469 3458). Bus 14, 207, 357/I-10,
exit Western Avenue north.* **Open** 11.30am-9pm Tue-Sun.
**Average** $10. **No credit cards.**

This is the perfect complement to an expensive day at The
Beverly Hot Springs, across the street. It's almost like a fast-
food sushi bar: basic, cheap and popular with the masses.
Try the halibut sushi in special sauce or spicy tuna handrolls.

## Woo Lae Oak

*623 South Western Avenue, between Wilshire Boulevard & Sixth Street, Koreatown (1-213 384 2244). Metro Wilshire/Western/bus 18, 20, 21, 22, 207, 320, 327/I-10, exit Western Avenue north.* **Open** 11.30am-10.30pm daily. **Average** $23. **Credit** AmEx, Disc, MC, V.

A traditional Korean BBQ restaurant, where you can barbecue a custom-made meal on your own 'hwaro' (table-top grill). Woo's sister restaurant in Beverly Hills serves near-psychedelic dishes culled from a mixture of French and Korean cuisines. We suggest the ke sal mari (crab and spinach crêpes), chap chae (fried glass noodles and assorted vegetables) and pajun (seafood and spring onion pancakes). **Branch:** 170 North La Cienega Boulevard, Beverly Hills (1-310 452 4187).

# Downtown LA

## Checkers

*Wyndham Checkers Hotel, 535 South Grand Avenue, between Fifth & Sixth Streets, Downtown (1-213 624 0000). Metro 7th Street/Metro Center or Pershing Square/bus 37, 78, 79/I-110, exit Sixth Street east.* **Lunch** 11.30am-2.30pm Mon-Fri. **Dinner** 5.30-10pm daily. **Brunch** 11am-2.30pm Sat, Sun. **Average** $45. **Credit** AmEx, DC, Disc, JCB, MC, V.

An elegant California-eclectic dining experience next to the the Music Center, MOCA and the newly restored Central Library, attracting suits, upscale travellers and celebrities such as Nicholas Cage, Bill Murray and Oprah Winfrey. *Parking free with validation.*

## Empress Pavillion

*Bamboo Plaza, Suite 201, 988 North Hill Street, at Bernard Street, Downtown (1-213 617 9898). Bus 45, 46, 83, 84, 85, 345/I-110, exit Hill Street east.* **Open** 9am-3pm, 3.30-9.45pm, daily. **Average** $20. **Credit** DC, MC, V.

Come with a crowd to this outstanding and vast Cantonese-style restaurant so you can flag down more of the dim sum waitresses. The rest of the menu is good, too.

## Mon Kee's

*679 North Spring Street, at Ord Street, Downtown (1-213 628 6717). Metro Union Station/bus 68, 76, 83, 84, 85, DASH B/I-110, exit Hill Street east.* **Lunch** 11.30am-3pm daily. **Dinner** 3-9.45pm Mon-Thur, Sun; 3-10.15pm Fri, Sat. **Average** $25. **Credit** AmEx, DC, Disc, MC, V.

Arguably the best Chinese seafood in the area. Pick out your own live Maine lobster or crab and have it cooked in garlic sauce, or get down and dirty with crispy whole shrimp served with a secret-recipe special sauce. *Parking $2.50.*

## Rex-Il Ristorante

*Oviatt Building, 617 South Olive Street, at Sixth Street, Downtown (1-213 627 2300). Metro Pershing Square or 7th Street/Metro Center/bus 444, 446, 447, DASH E, Foothill Transit 488, Santa Monica 10/I-110, exit Sixth Street east.* **Lunch** noon-2pm Thur, Fri. **Dinner** 6-10pm Mon-Sat. **Average** $43. **Credit** AmEx, DC, Disc, MC, V.

This Lalique-filled, art deco setting is one of LA's most elegant restaurants, serving state-of-the-art Italian food. If you can't afford dinner, take your date upstairs to the equally romantic bar and give her/him a twirl on the dancefloor. *Parking $3.50.*

## R23

*923 East Third Street, at Alameda Street, Downtown (1-213 687 7178). Bus 40, 436, 466/I-110, exit Third Street east.* **Lunch** noon-2pm, **dinner** 6-10.30pm, Mon-Sat. **Average** $25. **Credit** DC, MC, V.

The predominantly Japanese clientele testify to the worth of this sushi-lovers' sanctuary, tucked away in a back alley in Downtown's artist district. Understated chic is the flavour of R23 (Restaurant between 2nd and 3rd), a satisfying blend of delicate Japanese cuisine and a calmly minimalist interior.

## Tokyo Kaikan

*225 South San Pedro Street, between Second & Third Streets, Downtown (1-213 489 1333). Metro Civic Center/Tom Bradley or Pershing Square/bus 40, 436, 466/I-110, exit Third Street east.* **Lunch** 11.30am-2pm Mon-Fri. **Dinner** 6-10pm Mon-Fri; 5.30-10pm Sat. **Average** $20. **Credit** AmEx, JCB, MC, V.

Slip from one of the few shabu shabu (barbecue) bars in town into a sushi bar and then the old-fashioned cocktail bar. *Parking $2.*

## Yagura Ichiban

*Japanese Village Plaza Mall, 335 East Second Street, between San Pedro Street & Central Avenue, Downtown (1-213 623 4141). Metro Civic Center/Tom Bradley or Pershing Square/bus 10, 40, 42, 436, 445, 446, Commuter Express 430, 438, 448/I-110, exit Third Street east.* **Dinner** 5-10.30pm Mon-Sat. **Average** $20. **Credit** AmEx, MC, V.

Country-style Japanese food in Little Tokyo. *Parking free with validation.*

# East of Hollywood

## The Bodhi Garden

*1498 Sunset Boulevard, at Laveta Terrace, Silver Lake (1-213 250 9023). Bus 1, 2, 3, 4, 200, 302, 304/I-10, exit Alvarado Street north.* **Lunch** 10.30am-3pm, **dinner** 5-10pm, daily. **Average** $5. **No credit cards.**

No garden, no ambiance, no meat and no fortune cookies: just a hole-in-the-wall Vietnamese/Chinese place serving good food at low prices. Try the spicy tofu and the hot and sour soup.

## Cha Cha Cha

*656 North Virgil Avenue, at Melrose Avenue, Silver Lake (1-213 664 7723). Bus 10, 26/I-10, exit Vermont Avenue north.* **Open** 8am-10.30pm Mon-Thur, Sun; 8am-11pm Fri, Sat. **Average** $20. **Credit** AmEx, DC, Disc, MC, V.

Ten years' old in 1996: a festive place whose Latin American menu draws all the best people to the worst neighbourhood. *Parking $2.50.*

## Katsu

*1972 Hillhurst Avenue, at Finley Avenue, Los Feliz (1-213 665 1891). Bus 26, 180, 181/US101, exit Vermont Avenue north.* **Lunch** noon-2pm Mon-Fri. **Dinner** 6-10pm Mon-Thur; 6-11pm Fri, Sat. **Average** $28. **Credit** AmEx, DC, MC, V.

Upscale Japanese restaurant with minimalist décor. *Parking $3.*

## Millie's

*3524 West Sunset Boulevard, between Maltman Avenue & Griffith Park Boulevard, Silver Lake (1-213 664 0404). Bus 1, 2, 3, 4/US101, exit Silver Lake Boulevard north.* **Open** 8am-10pm Mon-Thur, Sun; 8am-midnight Fri, Sat. **Average** $7. **No credit cards.**

This quaint little all-American diner – complete with countertop jukebox that plays everything from Tony Bennett to Nick Cave – has gone through a lot of owners since it opened in 1926. Local eccentrics swarm here for home-made food at economical prices. Or is it because you can bring your own booze? Try the Eleanor R (for Roosevelt): two eggs over easy, cheddar, salsa and sour cream on rosemary potatoes.

## Hollywood Hills Coffee Shop *(top, see p135) and* Typhoon *(bottom, see p124).*

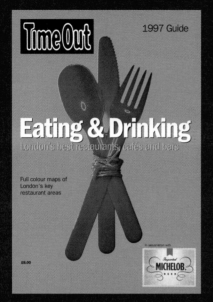

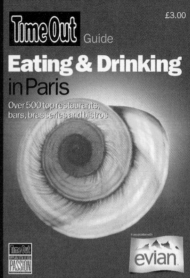

**Food
for the
thoughtful**

*A new day in the cigar-toting, beer-guzzling, pool-shooting* **Barney's Beanery**. *See p127.*

### Vida

*1930 Hillhurst Avenue, between Franklin & Clarissa Avenues, Los Feliz (1-213 660 4446). Bus 26, 180, 181/ US101, exit Vermont Avenue north.* **Dinner** 6-11.30pm daily. **Average** $29. **Credit** AmEx, DC, MC, V.
One of the new wave California-style restaurants that serves inventive, off-beat food. There is an array of different corners at which you can dine and a busy bar. The crowd is chic. *Parking $3.*

## The Valleys
## San Fernando Valley

### Art's Deli

*12224 Ventura Boulevard, at Laurel Grove Avenue, Studio City (1-818 762 1221). Bus 424, 425, 522, DASH Van Nuys/US101, exit Laurel Canyon Boulevard south.* **Open** 6.30am-10.30pm Mon-Thur; 6.30am-11.30pm Fri, Sat; 6.30am-10pm Sun. **Average** $10. **Credit** AmEx, DC, Disc, MC, V.
Many people think this is one of LA's best delis. Seating is mainly in booths, with large photos of their famous sandwiches on the walls: try the corned beef and pastrami. Also good blintzes, potato pancakes and bagels. *Valet parking $2.*

### Gladstone's

*Universal CityWalk, 1000 Universal Center Drive, Universal City (1-818 622 3474). Bus 420/US101, exit Universal Center Drive.* **Open** 11am-11pm Mon-Thur, Sun; 11am-midnight Fri, Sat. **Average** $18. **Credit** AmEx, DC, MC, V.
Reliable seafood served in gargantuan portions at this noisy tourist trap. *Parking $6.*

### Lumpinee Thai

*11020 Vanowen Street, at Vineland Avenue, North Hollywood (1-818 505 0761). Bus 152, 165/US101, exit Vineland Avenue north.* **Lunch** 11.30am-10pm daily. **Average** $6. **Credit** AmEx, MC, V .

A breathtaking find in an industrial part of town. It's cheap, and offers some unique Thai cuisine, with such dishes as Silver Crown, the Waterfall, the Volcano, Drunk Man with Meat and Tiger Crying. The cooks employ ancient recipes that supposedly bring therapeutic benefits to the eater.

### Saddle Peak Lodge

*419 Cold Canyon Road, off Piuma Road, Calabasas (1-818 222 3888). Bus 434/PCH, exit South Malibu Canyon Road north.* **Dinner** 6-10pm Wed-Fri; 5.30-10pm Sat; 5-10pm Sun. **Brunch** 11am-2pm Sun. **Average** $42. **Credit** AmEx, MC, V.
This is a fabulous escape from the city – it's only a 30-minute drive from Santa Monica to a rustic hunting lodge country setting, replete with fireplaces, waterfalls and Malibu views. Game is the speciality: antelope, kangaroo, buffalo, venison, pheasant and even ostrich are usually on the menu. It's an impossibly romantic hideout – if you don't mind being stared at by stuffed deer heads at almost every turn. Book. *Parking $2.50.*

### Surma Gate

*14611½ Ventura Boulevard, at Cedros Avenue, Sherman Oaks (1-818 788 9888). Bus 96, 236, 424, 425, 522, 561, DASH Van Nuys, Santa Clarita 798/I-405, exit Ventura Boulevard east.* **Lunch** 11.30am-2.30pm, **dinner** 5.30-10.30pm, daily. **Average** $12. **Credit** AmEx, DC, MC, V.
Bengali-run restaurant offering a great fish curry: Pacific salmon flavoured with mustard oil and pungent spices.

### Sushi Nozawa

*11288 Ventura Boulevard, between Tujunga & Vineland Avenues, Studio City (1-818 508 7017). Bus 420, 424, 522/US101, exit Vineland Avenue north.* **Lunch** noon-2pm Mon- Fri. **Dinner** 6-10pm Mon-Sat. **Average** $30. **Credit** MC, V.
The Valley's best-kept secret, hidden in a nondescript strip mall. Queue with others in-the-know who adore this no-frills café-style restaurant where they serve just one thing: sushi. Sushi so fresh it imperceptibly quivers on the plate. Above the somewhat taciturn chef's head is a large sign that brusquely announces 'No California Roll' and 'Tonight's Special: Trust Me'. Trust us: you will become a devotee.

## Call The World On Your Card.

Calling the world is easy using your card. You can do it from any telephone in the U.S. to over 100 countries. Just dial 1 800 CALL ATT® (1 800 225-5288) and a voice will tell you exactly what to do.

### Wolfgang Puck Café

*Universal CityWalk, 1000 Universal Center Drive, Universal City (1-818 985 9653). Bus 420/US101, exit Universal Center Drive.* **Open** 11am-10pm Mon-Thur, Sun; 11am-midnight Fri, Sat. **Average** $14. **Credit** AmEx, DC, MC, V.
Puck's downscaled Spago. You won't see any of the celebs, but the pizzas aren't dissimilar and the prices are cheap. However, it's one of a chain and the service is erratic. *Parking $6.*

## San Gabriel Valley

### Damon's Steakhouse

*317 North Brand Boulevard, between California Boulevard & West Lexington Drive, Glendale (1-818 507 1510). Bus 92, 93, 410, Glendale 1, 2/SR134, exit North Brand Boulevard south.* **Lunch** 11am-3pm Mon-Fri. **Dinner** 4-10.30pm Mon-Thur; 4-11pm Fri, Sat; 4-10pm Sun. **Brunch** 11am-3pm Sat, Sun. **Average** $18. **Credit** AmEx, DC, Disc, JCB, MC, V.
Tacky 1940s tiki lounge atmosphere, with steaks and Mai Tais.

### Harbor Village

*111 North Atlantic Boulevard, at Garvey Avenue, Monterey Park (1-818 300 8833). Bus 70, 260, Monterey Park 1, 2/I-10, exit North Atlantic Boulevard south.* **Lunch** 11am-2.30pm Mon-Fri; 10am-2.30pm Sat, Sun. **Dinner** 5.30-10pm daily. **Average** $14. **Credit** AmEx, DC, Disc, MC, V.
Possibly the best dim sum you'll eat outside of China or Hong Kong. Also recommended are the shark's fin soup, Peking duck and lobsters.

### The Market City Caffè

*33 South Fair Oaks Avenue, between Green Street & Colorado Boulevard, Pasadena (1-818 568 0203). Bus 180, 181, 188, 256, 402, 483/I-110, exit Colorado Boulevard west.* **Open** 11.30am-10pm Mon-Thur; 11.30am-midnight Fri, Sat. **Average** $16. **Credit** AmEx, DC, Disc, MC, V.
Reasonable Italian food (if you pay attention to what you're ordering); we liked the chicken in cream sauce with pasta. Eat outside in the marvellous garden. *Parking free with validation.*

### Pho Hoa

*410 South Atlantic Boulevard, at Newmark Street, Monterey Park (1-818 281 6123). Bus 70, 260, Monterey Park 3/I-10, exit Atlantic Boulevard south.* **Open** 9am-8pm daily. **Average** $5. **No credit cards.**
A cheap authentic bowl of satisfying Vietnamese noodles is the order of the day.

### The Raymond

*1250 South Fair Oaks Avenue, at Columbia Street, Pasadena (1-818 441 3136). Bus 188, 268, 483/I-110, exit Fair Oaks Avenue north.* **Lunch** 11.30am-2.30pm Tue-Fri; 11am-2.30pm Sat; 10am-3pm Sun. **Tea** noon-4pm Tue-Sun. **Dinner** 6-10pm Tue-Fri; 5.45-9.30pm Sat; 4.30-8pm Sun. **Average** $30. **Credit** AmEx, DC, Disc, MC, V.
This cutesy turn-of-the-century Craftsman house, with wood-panelled rooms, a bar and a patio draped with a bean vine, serves lunch, tea and dinner, all with a smile. The California-style food is good and the menu changes weekly. Even the most pedantic bon vivant could tickle their fancy here. A find.

## The South Bay

### Café Zoolu

*860 Glenneyre Street, at Thalia Street, Laguna Beach (1-714 494 6825). Bus Orange County Transit 1/I-405, exit SR133 (Laguna Canyon Road) west.* **Dinner** 5-11pm Wed-Sun. **Average** $25. **Credit** AmEx, DC, MC, V .
A small, busy local decorated with hints of the tropics. Tony Leech will seat you at one of the 11 tables or nine seats at the grill, where you can watch chef Michael Leech cook up a daily changing menu of eclectic Californian fare.

### Chez Melange

*Palos Verdes Inn, 1716 Pacific Coast Highway, between Prospect & Palos Verdes Avenues, Redondo Beach (1-310 540 1222). Bus 225, 232/I-405, exit Artesia Boulevard west.* **Breakfast** 7am-11.15am Mon-Fri; 7.30am-2.30pm Sat; 8am-2.30pm Sun. **Lunch** 11.30am-2.30pm Mon-Fri. **Dinner** 5-10pm Mon-Thur, Sun; 5-11pm Fri, Sat. **Average** $25. **Credit** AmEx, DC, Disc, MC, V.
In 1982, in the middle of the recession, Britisher Michael Franks and New Yorker Robert Bell walked into a bank with no collateral and came out with a $200,000 loan to build Chez Melange. They've parlayed that into five hugely successful restaurants to bring savvy food to the South Bay. The best at their flagship is nouvelle eclectic, but doesn't take itself too seriously – how could it, when it's housed in a late-1950s diner? There are also vodka, champagne and caviar bars. Other Franks and Bell establishments in the South Bay area are Depot (1250 Cabrillo Avenue, Torrance; 1-310 787 7501), an old train depot serving great California cuisine, and Descanso (705 Pier Avenue, Hermosa Beach; 1-310 379 7997), a bustling, seafood restaurant and bar with a bakery next door.

### L'Opera

*101 Pine Avenue, at First Street, Long Beach (1-310 491 0066). Bus 60, 232/I-710, exit Broadway east.* **Lunch** 11.30am-5pm Mon-Fri. **Dinner** 5-10pm Mon-Thur, Sun; 5pm-midnight Fri, Sat. **Average** $27. **Credit** AmEx, DC, Disc, MC, V.
Once a grand old bank, now the most elegant Italian restaurant in downtown Long Beach, replete with marble columns and a granite bar. The vaults are now used as a wine cellar. *Parking $3.*

### Reed's

*2640 North Sepulveda Boulevard, between Rosecrans Avenue & Imperial Highway, Manhattan Beach (1-310 546 3299). Bus 232/I-405, exit Imperial Highway or El Segundo Boulevard west.* **Lunch** 11.30am-2.30pm Mon-Fri. **Dinner** 5-10pm daily. **Average** $27. **Credit** AmEx, MC, V.
We highly recommend this New American French restaurant that serves up food from heaven, without pomp and circumstance. It's the child of Joe's in Venice (*see above*).

## East LA

### La Serenata di Garibaldi

*1842 East First Street, between State Street & Boyle Avenue, Boyle Heights (1-213 265 2887). Bus 30, 31/I-10, exit Boyle Avenue north.* **Open** 11am-10.30pm daily. **Average** $18. **Credit** AmEx, DC, MC, V.
Los Angeles is supposed to have great Mexican food but, for the most part, it doesn't. Here's the exception. In rundown Boyle Heights, it's a simple, small place that serves fresh fish in awesome sauces. Call ahead, get directions, park in the back and you'll dine at red-and-white checkered tables with Mexican families, mariachis and downtown artists. Or try the new branch, La Serenata Gourmet, in Midtown (*see above*).

## South Central

### Harold & Belle's

*2920 West Jefferson Boulevard, between Arlington Avenue & Crenshaw Boulevard, South Central (1-213 735 9023). Bus 38/I-10, exit Crenshaw Boulevard south.*

**Open** noon-10pm Mon-Thur; 1-11pm Fri, Sat; 1-10pm Sun. **Average** $18. **Credit** AmEx, Disc, MC, V.

If you ever find yourself in one of the city's dodgier neighbourhoods with a hankering for upscale Southern food, you're in luck. Once inside you are cosseted in elegance and, of course, good ol' Southern hospitality. Try breaded fish crowned with crayfish sauce, soft-shell crabs or Louisiana oysters. Book. *Valet parking $2.*

## Orange County/Anaheim

### Five Feet

*328 Glenneyre Street, at Forest Avenue, Laguna Beach, (1-714 497 4955). Bus Orange County Transit 1/I-5, exit SR133 (Laguna Canyon Road) west.* **Dinner** 5-10pm Mon-Thur, Sun; 5-11pm Fri, Sat. **Average** $40. **Credit** AmEx, DC, Disc, MC, V.

Some people have compared this place with Chinois on Main. The owners don't agree, although it attracts its share of star diners, including Robert De Niro, Al Pacino and Paul Reiser. It's a simple modern setting, with attention paid to small details, such as rose petals on the napkins.

### JW's

*Anaheim Marriott, 700 West Convention Way, at Harbor Boulevard, Anaheim (1-714 750 8000). Bus 43/I-5, exit Harbor Boulevard south.* **Dinner** 5-11pm daily. **Average** $35. **Credit** AmEx, DC, Disc, MC, V.

You have to see it to believe it. A French chateau, or a rather good fascimile thereof, slap-bang in the middle of the Marriott hotel. Seafood and game prepared in the French manner, with typical fussy hotel service. At least it's a safe haven from Disneyland.

### The White House

*887 South Anaheim Boulevard, at Vermont Street, Anaheim (1-714 772 1381). Bus 47/I-5, exit Harbor Boulevard north.* **Lunch** 11.30am-2pm Mon-Fri. **Dinner** 5-10pm daily. **Average** $40. **Credit** AmEx, DC, MC, V.

Only one and a half miles from Disneyland is this lovely turn-of-the-century white mansion where you can dine upstairs in northern Italian style in one of the four original bedrooms or sup in the more traditional reception rooms downstairs. *Valet parking $2.*

# Restaurants by cuisine

**American** Kate Mantilini (p132); Morton's (p130)
**Argentinian** Gaucho Grill (p128)
**BBQs & fast food** Barney's Beanery (p127); Benny's BBQ (p125); Dive! (p134); The Gardens on Glendon (p132); Houstons (p134)
**Californian** Geoffrey's (p125); The Ivy (p129); Jones (p129); The Raymond (p144); Red (p137)
**California-eclectic** Atlas Bar & Grill (p136); Book Soup Bistro (p127); Café del Rey (p125); Café Zoolu (p143); Chaya Brasserie (p127); Checkers (p138); The Chez (p133); Chez Melange (p143); Depot (p143); Descanso (p143); Eclipse (p128); Granita (p125); JiRaffe (p123); Maple Drive (p132); Modada (p130); Off Vine (p134); Röckenwagner (p123); Spago (p131); Vida (p141); Wolfgang Puck Café (p143)
**Californian-French** Citrus (p127); Joe's (p125); Patina (p134); Reed's (p143)
**Caribbean** Cha Cha Cha (p138)
**Chinese** Chin Chin (p126); Empress Pavillion (p138); Five Feet (p144); Harbor Village (p143); Joss (p129); The Mandarette (p129); Manhattan Wonton Company (p130); Mon Kee's (p138); Mr Chow's (p132); Yujean Kang's (p132); Yin Yang (p134)
**Cuban** Versailles (p135)
**Delis** Art's Deli (p141); The Broadway Deli (p122); Canter's (p136); Nate & Al (p133)
**Diners & grills** Chez Jay (p123); Damon's Steakhouse (p143); Duke's (p128); Du-par's (p136); Ed Debevic's (p132); Ed's Coffee Shop (p128); Hollywood Canteen (p135); Hollywood Hills Coffee Shop (p135); Millie's (p138); Musso & Frank Grill (p134); Patrick's Roadhouse (p123); Rae's (p123)
**Fish & seafood** Barney Greengrass (p132); Delmonico's Seafood Grille (p134); Gladstone's 4 Fish-Malibu (p125); Killer Shrimp (p124); VIP Harbor Seafood Restaurant (p134)
**French** JW's (p144); Le Deux Café (p135); Four Oaks Restaurant (p134); L'Orangerie (p128); Pinot Hollywood (p135)
**Game** Saddle Peak Lodge (p141)
**Healthy** A Votre Sante (p124); The Fig Tree (p126); Rita Flora Kitchens (p136); Inn of the Seventh Ray

(p125); Kokomo (p136); The Newsroom Café (p131); The Source (p131)
**Hot dogs** Pink's Hot Dogs (p131); Tail-o'-the-Pup (p128)
**Italian** Café Med (p127); Caffè Luna (p127); Capri (p124); Chianti Cucina (p126); Cicada (p126); Farfalla (p137); Fritto Misto (p123); Girasole (p137); Hugo's (p128); L'Opera (p143); The Market City Caffè (p143); Mezzaluna (p134); Orso (p131); Pane e Vino (p131); Remi (p122); Rex-Il Ristorante (p138); Valentino (p124); The White House (p144)
**Indian** Bombay Café (p132); Surma Gate (p141)
**International** The Dynasty Room (p133); 1 Pico (p122); The Polo Lounge (p133)
**Japanese** Asuka (p133); Hirozen Gourmet (p128); Ita cho (p135); Katsu (p138); Matsuhisa (p132); Noshi Sushi (p137); Sushi Nozawa (p141); Tokyo Kaikan (p138); Yagura Ichiban (p138); Yamashiro (p136)
**Japanese-Italian** Zipangu (p133)
**Korean** Dong Il Jang (p136); Woo Lae Oak (p138)
**Latin American** Cha Cha Cha (p138); Prado (p136)
**Mexican** Border Grill (p122); El Cholo (p137); El Coyote (p137); The Gardens of Taxco (p128); La Fonda (p137); La Serenata di Garibaldi (p143); La Serenata Gourmet (p134); Lucy's Café El Adobe (p134); Marix Tex Mex Café (p130); Mexica Café (p130); Rebecca's (p125); Tlapazola Grill (p123); Tucan (p134)
**Middle Eastern** Al Amir (p136); Koutoubia (p134); Shaharazad (p133)
**Pacific Rim** Chinois on Main (p123); Typhoon (p124)
**Pizza** Abbot Pizza (p124); Mulberry Street Pizzeria (p133)
**Spanish** Cava (p127)
**Southern** Aunt Kizzy's Back Porch (p125); Georgia (p128); Harold & Belle's (p143); The House of Blues (p128); Maurice's Snack 'N' Chat (p137); Roscoe's House of Chicken 'N' Waffles (p136); Venus of Venice (p125)
**Southwestern** Abiquiu (p122)
**Thai** Chan Dara (p132); Lumpinee Thai (p138); Talesai (p130); Thai House (p132)
**Vietnamese** The Bodhi Garden (p138); Le Colonial (p129); Pho Hoa (p143)

# Coffeehouses

**Forget alcohol. In this car-bound city, coffee is the drink of choice. Here's our guide to the crème de la crème of LA's caffeine-fuelled hotspots.**

Believe it or not, a quality cup of coffee used to be pretty hard to come by in Los Angeles. But having jumped on the bean and brew bandwagon, LA is now almost as steeped in the coffee culture as Seattle. And since driving is always a factor, the coffeehouse has to some degree eclipsed the bar.

There are three basic types of LA coffee bar: bohemian – dimly lit and furnished with old tables and couches, local art and/or shelves of second-hand books and alternative magazines; wannabe bohemian – as above but styled by an interior decorator; and establishment – streamlined counter, café tables, newspapers and a corporate identity, usually a franchise or part of a chain.

Of the chains, **Starbucks** is the most common; people may soon start calling coffee 'Starbucks' the way they call tissues Kleenex and vacuum cleaners Hoovers, so ubiquitous is the familiar

*Book yourself a table at **Novel Café**.*

green sign. The best thing about Starbucks is that you know exactly what you are going to get: every flavour, style, size and temperature of coffee imaginable, and average food. The company ideology is rather refreshing – all employees get full health benefits and stock options and the stores often donate leftover food to local charities. Call 1-800 782 7282 to find your nearest branch.

Other chains include the **Coffee Bean & Tea Leaf**, with almost 25 locations in and around LA. It also has a mail-order business (call 1-800 832 5323 for details) and reputedly serves the best iced coffee drinks in town. **Mani's Bakery** has four branches (in Santa Monica, Beverly Hills, West Hollywood and Studio City) and is best known for its incredible cakes and pies, many of them sugar-or fat-free. Call 1-800 996 6264 for location details.

However, not every LA neighbourhood is freckled with coffeehouses. In and around the beaches and through to Hollywood's eastern edges, there are many to choose from, but, as you go farther east, it's as if coffee didn't exist.

The major bookshop chains often have on-site cafés; for details, *see chapter* **Shopping & Services**.

## Westside: beach towns
## Santa Monica

### Interactive Café

*215 Broadway, at Second Street, Santa Monica (1-310 395 5009/e-mail: intrcafe@cafe.net). Bus 4, 33, 434, Santa Monica 7, 8, 10/I-10, exit Fourth Street north.* **Open** 6am-1am Mon-Thur, Sun; 6am-2.30am Fri, Sat. **Credit** MC, V.

Around the corner from Third Street Promenade, this spacious and airy café is furnished with cushy velvet sofas, Henry VIII-style chairs and flower arrangements that dwarf anyone under 5ft. Popular for its top-notch coffee, incredible fruit shakes, smoothies, home-made sandwiches and desserts, Interactive also sells cards, newspapers and mags.

### Novel Café

*212 Pier Avenue, at Main Street, Santa Monica (1-310 396 8566). Bus 33, 436, Santa Monica 1, 2, 10/I-10, exit Lincoln Boulevard south.* **Open** 7am-1am Mon-Fri; 7.30am-1am Sat, Sun. **Credit** AmEx, MC, V.

'This bookstore is dedicated with respect and humility to the Chinese god, Wei D'to, protector of books against fire, pillaging, decay and dishonest borrowers…' So reads the sign in the library room at this café/second-hand bookshop. The coffee and treats are nothing special, but the books and location – just off Main Street and a hop, skip and a jump from the beach – make up for such shortcomings in spades.

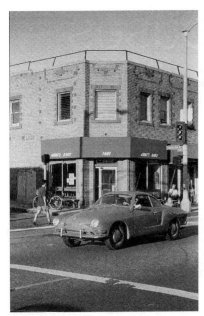

*Get the **Abbot's Habit** – for caffeine.*

# Venice

### Abbot's Habit
*1401 Abbot Kinney Boulevard, at California Avenue, Venice (1-310 399 1171). Bus Santa Monica 2, Venice 33/I-10, exit Lincoln Boulevard south.* **Open** 6am-9pm daily. **No credit cards.**
Abbot's Habit attracts a strange yet fascinating crowd of Venice locals, from yuppies who live on the canals to artists surviving on a shoestring. Local art is displayed on the walls; depending on the week and the artist, your morning coffee could be a soothing experience amid pastel abstracts or a rude awakening from huge, Munch-like faces. The muffins and other baked goods are delicious, even the fat-frees.

### Cyber Java
*1029 Abbot Kinney Boulevard, at Broadway, Venice (1-310 581 1300/e-mail: info@cyberjava.com). Bus 33, 436, Santa Monica 1, 2/I-10, exit Lincoln Boulevard south.* **Open** 7am-2am daily. **Credit** DC, Disc, MC, V.
Equipped with five top-of-the-line mainframes as well as fax, laser printing, photocopying and colour scanning services, this Internet café is usually packed, especially in the evenings. Use of a terminal costs $7.50 per hour or 50¢ per minute and workshops and Internet classes are also available. The coffee and food – salads, sandwiches, myriad desserts and baked goods – are delicious and good value.

### Van Gogh's Ear
*796 Main Street, between Rose Avenue & Abbot Kinney Boulevard, Venice (1-310 314 0022). Bus 33, 436, Santa Monica 1, 2/I-10, exit Fourth Street south.* **Open** 24 hours daily. **No credit cards.**
This colourful, slightly seedy, 24-hour coffeehouse – with a patio and upstairs porch – attracts Venice hippies as well as the buff and beautiful beach gang. Dishes with names like

the John Belushi (a seriously overstuffed omelette), the Pee-Wee Herman (a Cajun blackened-chicken 'samwitch'), and the Karen Carpenter (an almost calorie-free bowl of oatmeal and fruit) are creatively prepared and downright tasty. Don't miss the Fruit Fuck, made with, among other ingredients, fruit, spirilina, psyllium husk and brewer's yeast.

## Marina del Rey

### Cow's End
*34 Washington Boulevard, at Pacific Avenue, Marina del Rey (1-310 574 1080). Bus 108, Culver City 1, Commuter Express 437/I-10, exit Lincoln Boulevard south.* **Open** 6am-midnight daily. **No credit cards.**
With two floors and outdoor seating, the kitsch Cow's End is a prime spot for playing backgammon on the house boards or reading in an oversized, over-upholstered chair. Most of the cakes and sweet breads are home-made and worth the calories – especially the banana bread. Enjoy the small newsstand on the first floor and the cow paraphernalia.

### Also recommended
**The Bean Queen** *1513 Park Row, at Winward Avenue, Venice;* **Congo Square** *1238 Third Street Promenade, between Arizona Avenue & Wilshire Boulevard, Santa Monica;* **Prebica** *4325 Glencoe Avenue, at Mindanao Way, Maxella & Lincoln Boulevard, Marina del Rey.*

## Westside: inland
## West Hollywood

### The Abbey
*692 North Robertson Boulevard, at Santa Monica Boulevard, West Hollywood (1-310 289 8410). Bus 4, 10, 11, 105, 220/I-10, exit Robertson Boulevard north.* **Open** 8am-2am Mon-Thur; 8am-3am Fri-Sun. **No credit cards.**
This largely outdoor coffeehouse is smack-dab in the middle of West Hollywood's gay nightlife and offers the closest you can get to a pick-up scene at a café. Packed from morning till post-dark closing time, the Abbey is best for people-watching and eavesdropping. Good coffee drinks, salads and baked goods and a beautiful outdoor patio.

### Basix
*8333 Santa Monica Boulevard, at Flores Street, West Hollywood (1-213 848 2460). Bus 4, 304/I-10, exit La Cienega Boulevard north.* **Open** 7am-11pm daily. **Credit** AmEx, MC, V.
For connoisseurs of moist, home-made muffins, Basix is the place: try the pear nutmeg, banana bran or zucchini cinnamon flavours. Then move onto the pastas and mouth-watering salads, sandwiches and thin-crust pizzas. Although a little too popular for its own good this gay/mixed café has plenty of outdoor and indoor seating where you can enjoy the bustle of this pedestrianised area.

### Kings Road Café
*8361 Beverly Boulevard, at Kings Road, West Hollywood (1-213 655 9044). Bus 14/I-10, exit La Cienega Boulevard north.* **Open** 7.30am-11pm daily. **Credit** MC, V.
Although Kings Road Café seems to attract too many of the beautiful movers-and-shakers of LA – or at least those who think they are – its location is prime. A few blocks from the Beverly Center shopping mall, it offers large cups of well-brewed coffee, delicious muffins and cakes and popular breakfasts. However, like the egos of many of the customers (and the staff, come to that), prices are slightly inflated.

### Urth Caffè
*8565 Melrose Avenue, at Westmount Drive, West Hollywood (1-310 659 0628). Bus 10, 11, 105/I-10 east, exit La Cienega Boulevard north.* **Open** 6.30am-11pm Mon-Thur,*

Sun; 6.30am-midnight Fri, Sat. **Credit** AmEx, MC, V.
After two years of travelling throughout America and
Europe, visiting coffee roasters, companies, plantations and
tea importers, Urth's owners opened this, the first certified
organic coffee and tea store in the US. The delicious food
includes wholehearted savouries and desserts that will
forever change your tune about dieting; don't even think of
leaving without trying the famous three-layer cheesecake.
Complete with sprawling outdoor porch and relaxing music,
Urth offers coffeehouse life at its percolating best.

### Vienna Café/Melrose Baking Company
*7356 Melrose Avenue, at Fuller Avenue, West Hollywood
(bakery 1-213 851 8808/café 1-213 651 3822). Bus 10,
11/I-10, exit Fairfax Avenue north.* **Open** 7.30am-9pm
Mon-Thur, Sun; 7.30am-midnight Fri, Sat. **Credit** MC, V.
Set in trendy Melrose Avenue, Vienna Café is a quiet and
shady refuge from the hot sun and relentless shoppers.
Though somewhat overpriced, it serves delicious salads and
other creative dishes along with coffee drinks, baked fare
and sandwiches made with breads from the Melrose Baking
Company, which bakes the premises. We recommend olive
or walnut yam. A perfect spot for people-watching.

### Also recommended
**Buzz Coffee** *8000 Sunset Boulevard, at Crescent
Heights Boulevard, West Hollywood; 8200 Santa Monica
Boulevard, at Havenhurst Drive, West Hollywood; 7623
Beverly Boulevard, at Stanley Avenue, Fairfax;* **Melvin's**
*8205 Melrose Avenue, at La Jolla Avenue, West
Hollywood;* **Sweet Lady Jane** *8360 Melrose Avenue,
between Kings Road & Orlando Avenue, West Hollywood.*

## Beverly Hills

### Caffe Latte
*6254 Wilshire Boulevard, at Crescent Heights Boulevard,
Beverly Hills (1-213 936 5213). Bus 20, 21, 22/I-10, exit
La Cienega Boulevard north.* **Open** 7am-9pm Mon-Fri;
8am-3.30pm Sat, Sun. **Credit** AmEx, MC, V.
In a mall in one of LA's signature off-street mini-malls, spit-
ting distance from Miracle Mile, Caffe Latte is a favourite spot
for local residents and business people. It offers some boast-
worthy snacks such as cinnamon swirl french toast, the Jody

Maroni sausage sandwich and, of course, the home-brewed
coffees (beans roasted on the premises) and spirit-rejuve-
nating yogi teas (plain or with a halo of steamed milk). It
draws a big breakfast crowd, especially on the weekends.

### Michel Richard
*310 South Robertson Boulevard, between Third Street &
Burton Way, Beverly Hills (1-310 275 5707). Bus 27, 220,
316, 576/I-10, exit Robertson Boulevard north.* **Open** 8am-
10pm Mon-Sat; 9am-4pm Sun. **Credit** AmEx, DC, MC, V.
Started by popular chef Michel Richard (although he has long
since moved on), this fancy pastry shop – with a hedged-in
patio and spacious inside room – on fashionable Robertson
Boulevard brings in local regulars as well as film and music
industry bigwigs. It's no secret that someone was shot at a
patio table years back, but this doesn't deter the customers.

## West LA

### Lulu's Alibi
*1640 Sawtelle Boulevard, at Santa Monica Boulevard,
West LA (1-310 479 6007). Bus 4, 304, Santa Monica 1,
5/I-405, exit Santa Monica Boulevard west.* **Open**
8.30am-1am Mon-Thur, Sun; 8.30am-2am Fri, Sat.
**Credit** AmEx, MC, V.
If there is a story about Lulu's alibi, no one's telling, beyond
the fact that the original owner's name was Luanna. Choose
from a wide variety of coffee drinks as well as sandwiches,
salads, sweet breads, cookies and desserts – the most popular being tiramisu – and many Brazilian dishes, including
the hearty national dish, feijoada. With cosy indoor and outdoor seating, Lulu's attracts a vibrant crowd of all ages and
is a favourite with playgoers at the nearby Odyssey Theatre.

## Hollywood & Midtown

### Bourgeois Pig
*5931 Franklin Avenue, at Beachwood Drive, Hollywood
(1-213 962 6366). Bus 26, Community Connection 208/
US101, exit Gower Street north.* **Open** 9am-1.30am
daily. **No credit cards.**
Set in a quaint row of shops and restaurants at the bottom
of the Hollywood Hills at Beachwood Canyon, this dark and

# Coffeespeak

Don't just ask for a 'coffee': you must be specific to get what you want in LA's jargon-addict-
ed coffeehouses. Note that espresso-based drinks
can be ordered 'single', 'double' or 'triple', which
refers to the number of espresso shots.

**Americano** Espresso with added hot water.
**Macchiatto** Espresso with a touch of foamed milk.
**Red eye** Espresso combined with brewed coffee.
**Flat white** Espresso with steamed milk.
**Cappuccino** Espresso with steamed and foamed milk.
**Dry cappuccino** Espresso with only foamed milk.
**Wet cappuccino** Espresso with only steamed milk.
**2 per cent** Milk can be ordered whole, half-and-half (half
whole milk, half cream), 2 per cent fat, 1 per cent and non-
fat. Non-dairy eaters or vegetarians can opt for soy milk.
**Breve** Any drink made with half-and-half instead of reg-
ular cream.
**Cubano** Double shot of espresso with brown sugar added
first to the coffee grounds.

**Latte** Cappuccino with one-fifth espresso, three-fifths
steamed milk and one-fifth foamed milk. Often served
without the foam on top.
**Skinny** Latte with non-fat milk; for example, 'skinny latte'.
**No fun** Latte with non-fat milk and decaffeinated coffee.
**Mocha** Latte with cocoa, chocolate powder or chocolate
syrup and whipped cream on top.
**Iced** Any coffee drink can be ordered iced but there are
two versions: 'over ice' – a glass full of ice with drink
poured over it – or 'blended' – crushed ice is 'whipped in'
with the drink.
**Italian soda** Carbonated water over ice, with a shot of
flavoured syrup (kiwi, blackberry, peach, caramel, vanil-
la, almond and many, many more). Flavoured syrup can
be added to any of the coffee drinks (for example, strawberry mocha).
**French soda** Italian soda with half-and-half and a little
whipped cream.
**Short** New lingo for coffee sizes: if you want the smallest size, ask for a 'short'; for medium, ask for 'tall'; for
large, ask for 'grande'.

# The best for...

**Best latte** Urth Caffé
**Best yogi tea** Highland Grounds
**Best café to be seen without looking as if you want to be seen** The Living Room
**Best tiramisu** Interactive Café
**Best place to work on your screenplay** Insomnia Café if you want to be spotted in action; Novel Café if you really intend to weave plot and character; Cyber Java if you need a computer and don't have your own.
**Best iced mocha** Starbucks, which started the trend (but still uses too much sugar)
**Best place to sit and debate after a movie** Lulu's Alibi *(pictured)*
**Best muffins** Basix
**Best for live music** Horseshoe Coffeehouse

smoky café, furnished with elderly couches and chairs, has a pool table in the back room and a small newsstand next door. The coffee is good and comes in as many specifications as you could want.

## Highland Grounds
*742 North Highland Avenue, between Melrose & Waring Avenues, Hollywood (1-213 466 1507). Bus 10, 11/I-10 east, exit La Brea Avenue north.* **Open** *9am-12.30am Tue-Thur; 9am-1am Fri, Sat; 10am-9pm Sun.* **Credit** *MC, V.*
Moments after stepping inside this airy two-floor café or the adjacent patio, you forget you are in the middle of LA. Started by some of the founders of Caffe Latte, this family establishment serves exceptional food, ranging from hamburgers on grainy brown bread with thin French fries to guacamole and tortilla chips. The home-brewed coffee and teas are almost unbeatable (the yogi tea is the best in town) and the café now has a liquor license, which draws big crowds to its nightly music and entertainment scene.

## LA Insomnia
*7286 Beverly Boulevard, at North Poinsettia Place, Park La Brea (1-213 931 4943). Bus 14/I-10, exit Fairfax Avenue north.* **Open** *9am-4am daily.* **No credit cards.**
As coffeehouses are becoming more common and more creative in their presentation, Insomnia, with its grungy furniture and young, hip crowd, is no longer one of a kind.

However, both branches serve good coffee and baked goods and are open late enough for a post-club visit.
**Branch**: Melrose Insomnia *8164 Melrose Avenue (1-213 655 3960).*

## The Living Room
*112 South La Brea Avenue, between Beverly Boulevard & Third Street, Park La Brea (1-213 933 2933). Bus 16, 212/I-10, exit La Brea Avenue north.* **Open** *9am-midnight Mon-Thur, Sun; 9am-2am Fri, Sat.* **Credit** *AmEx, MC, V.*
In the beginning was the Living Room. The original 'poser café' that kicked off the whole coffeeshop craze in LA, the Living Room opened in 1986 and still draws a healthy crowd. However, since second-hand furniture, local art and coffee in vat-sized cups are nothing unusual these days, there's nothing particularly special about it now.

## Also recommended
Revival Café *7149 Beverly Boulevard, at Detroit Street, Park La Brea.*

# East of Hollywood

## Say Cheese
*2800 Hyperion Avenue, between Rowena Avenue & Griffith Park Boulevard, Silver Lake (1-213 665 0545). Bus 175/I-5, exit Los Feliz Boulevard west.* **Open** *8am-6.30pm daily.* **Credit** *AmEx, MC, V.*
Ignore the cutesy name: this is a peaceful coffeehouse and deli serving invariably fresh coffee in large café-au-lait cups. Fabulous deli sandwiches are made to order, hot or cold; one of the favourites is the California melt, made with cheese, turkey, onions, tomatoes and home-made dressing. One of the few coffeehouses – and a good one at that – in the area.

# The Valleys

## Boom Boom Room
*11651 Riverside Drive, at Colfax Avenue, North Hollywood (1-818 753 9966). Bus 96/US101, exit Laurel Canyon Boulevard north.* **Open** *8am-1am Mon-Thur; 8am-3am Fri; 9am-3am Sat; 9am-1am Sun.* **No credit cards.**
The perfect pitstop for an iced coffee to help recover from the opressive heat of the Valley. Decorated with old furniture and lamps with tasselled lampshades, it has the charm of a beloved and eccentric aunt's parlour. A great find in an area with limited coffee choices.

## Emerson's Coffeehouse & Gallery
*13203 Ventura Boulevard, between Coldwater Canyon & Fulton Avenue, Studio City (1-818 986 2233). Bus 424, 522/US101, exit Coldwater Canyon south.* **Open** *8am-1am Mon-Fri; 8am-2am Sat; 11am-2am Sun.* **No credit cards.**
Emerson's is the kind of coffeeshop where you'd expect to see a pair of pre-pubescents on a first date sharing a Coke with two straws. Although equipped with the latest milk-frothing and bean-brewing machinery and offering cakes, cookies, pastries and salads to rival the best, Emerson's presents a quaint, almost innocent atmosphere and draws a diverse clientele. Don't miss the 'elephant ear' pastries.

## Horseshoe Coffeehouse
*14568 Ventura Boulevard, at Cedros Avenue, Sherman Oaks (1-818 986 4262). Bus 424, 522/ US101, exit Van Nuys Boulevard south.* **Open** *8am-2am daily.* **Credit** *MC, V.*
Usually crowded indoors and out with the twentysomething crowd, what sets this café apart is its nightly music scene: soft love songs on Mondays, Hebrew/Mediterranean music on Tuesdays, big band on Wednesdays, jazz on Thursdays, world beat and reggae on Fridays, 1950s-1970s music on Saturdays and Euro hits and oldies on Sundays. Great food, plus board games, decks of cards and two pinball machines.

# Bars

*In a car-bound city, drinking for drink's sake is seldom on the menu – which makes the bar scene as close to a subculture as LA gets.*

Unlike Chicago and New York, where drinking is a way of life, going to a bar in Los Angeles is less an everyday occurrence than an event. Obviously, a city with lousy public transport does not exactly lend itself to drunken binges and most of the hip and happening places are too far apart to make it convenient to hop from one to another, but don't even expect to find much in the way of neighbourhood watering holes. Also, remember that LA is full of extremely hard-working people (hey, *somebody* has to put all those movies and TV shows together), many of whom have to go to work *very* early in the morning.

The current 'Lounge Revival' – a welcome result of the current vogue for easy listening sounds – has to a certain extent rekindled the idea of the bar as an altar to Dionysus; but in the main, darling, Los Angeles bars are places to see and be seen – not somewhere to get stinking drunk (note that the local police are extremely unsympathetic towards intoxicated motorists). If you must order something stronger than mineral water, be advised that most LA bartenders cannot mix a proper drink to save their lives; as with local restaurants, the majority of servers are actors killing time until their next job. Except where noted, your best bet is to stick with whatever beers or ales the establishment offers, though you shouldn't expect much in the way of micro-brews (real ales) – that vogue having somewhat passed LA by.

Helpful hint: most Angelenos seem to be unaware that it's proper etiquette to tip the bartender. As a result, the simple act of throwing your publican one or two dollars per round will win you a friend for life – or, at least, good service throughout the evening.

## BOOZE & THE LAW

All bars are subject to California's strict alcohol laws: you have to be over 21 to buy and consume the stuff (take photo ID even if you look older), and alcohol can be sold between the hours of 6am and 2am. Virtually every bar calls last orders at around 1.45am and technically staff are obliged to confiscate unconsumed alcoholic drinks after 2am.

Also, the Hollywood police department has, at the time of writing, been making a concerted effort to bust bartenders for 'overserving', even taking allegedly inebriated customers into custody as 'evidence'. Therefore, unless you feel like cooling your

heels down at the local precinct station, it would be wise to not make a show of your intoxication, regardless of how good a time you're having.

Many of LA's restaurants have bars with a scene in their own right – these include **Border Grill, Chaya Brasserie, Le Coloniale** and **Atlas** (*see chapter* **Restaurants**) – as do some hotels, notably **Shutters** and **Beverly Hills Hotel**, home of the happening Polo Lounge (*see chapter* **Accommodation**). For bars serving a specifically gay or lesbian clientele, *see chapter* **Gay & Lesbian**. Some bars have live music; if so, you may have to pay a cover charge of up to $5.

## Westside: beach towns

### Circle Bar

*2926 Main Street, at Pier Avenue, Santa Monica (1-310 392 4898). Bus 33, 333, Santa Monica 1, 2, 10/I-10, exit Lincoln Boulevard north.* **Open** noon-2am daily. **No credit cards**.

If you like your bars dark, poky and steeped in cigarette smoke, then this one's a must. The Circle Bar – literally an oval bar in a shoebox-sized room opening off Main Street – is one of the last bastions of seediness in Santa Monica, and, boy, are the locals proud of it.

### Father's Office

*1018 Montana Avenue, between 10th & 11th Streets, Santa Monica (1-310 451 9330). Bus 3, Santa Monica 3/ I-10, exit Lincoln Boulevard north.* **Open** noon-2am daily. **Credit** MC, V.

This amusingly named, no-frills Santa Monica bar is most notable for its extensive selection of hard-to-find microbrews; as such, it's popular with local professionals and residents.

### Ye Olde King's Head

*116 Santa Monica Boulevard, between Ocean Avenue & Second Street, Santa Monica (1-310 451 1402). Bus 4, 20, 22, 33, Santa Monica 1, 7, 8, 10/I-10, exit Fourth-Fifth Street north.* **Open** 11am-1.30am Mon-Thur; 10am-1.30am Fri-Sun. **Credit** AmEx, DC, MC, V.

Santa Monica's populous British contingent pretty much keeps this pub in business; with darts, fish and chips and stout in abundance, it makes a suitable home-away-from home. The best place in the area to watch televised World Cup soccer matches.

## Westside: inland

### Argyle Hotel Bar

*8358 Sunset Boulevard, between Sweetzer Avenue & La Cienega Boulevard, West Hollywood (1-213 654 7100). Bus 2, 3, 429, West Hollywood A, B/I-10, exit La Cienega Boulevard north.* **Open** 11am-1.30am daily. **Credit** AmEx, DC, Disc, MC, V.

Located in the breathtaking art deco structure now known as the Argyle Hotel (formerly the St James Club), this bar – which made a brief appearance in Robert Altman's *The Player* – has one of the finest selections of whisky in town. Dress to impress, as they say. Valet parking is usually $3.50.

## Bar Marmont

*8171 Sunset Boulevard, between Sweetzer Avenue & Crescent Heights Boulevard, West Hollywood (1-213 650 0575). Bus 2, 3, 429/US101, exit Highland Avenue south.* **Open** 6pm-1.30am daily. **Credit** AmEx, MC, V.
Located in an ugly, shanty-like structure (but with a luxurious interior) down the street from the hotel that gives it its name, Bar Marmont has become *the* place for Hollywood's élite (and those who wish they were) to lap up the prohibitively priced but nicely confected libations. Sunday nights often feature poetry readings by famous actors and actresses who should know better, which can be highly entertaining. *Parking $3.50 Mon-Wed, Sun; $5.50 Thur-Sat.*

# Tiki tacky

LA has a number of Polynesian-style (or 'tiki') bars, a trend dating back to the 1950s, when the US went through a serious infatuation with South Pacific island culture. Many of LA's Polynesian pleasure palaces have been destroyed or remodelled, but you can still catch a glimpse of the past at places like **Trader Vic's** and **Tiki-Ti**.

## Trader Vic's

*Beverly Hilton Hotel, 9876 Wilshire Boulevard, at Santa Monica Boulevard, Beverly Hills (1-310 274 7777). Bus 4, 20, 21, 22, 27/I-405, exit Wilshire Boulevard east.* **Open** 5pm-1am daily. **Credit** AmEx, DC, Disc, MC, V.
Renowned for both its absurdly overpriced Polynesian menu and its expensive-but-worth-it tropical drinks, Trader Vic's is an old-school tiki bar. Wizened old bartenders of South Sea Island descent create alchemical wonders with various liquors and fruit juices – ordering the ridiculously potent Tiki Puka-Puka will earn you their undying respect and admiration – while Hawaiian entertainer Don Ho's 1960s classic *Tiny Bubbles* seems to play at five-minute intervals. Extremely crowded with the young and beautiful of Beverly Hills at weekends, the place usually has a barstool or two free most nights of the week.

## Tiki-Ti

*4427 West Sunset Boulevard, between Hillhurst & Fountain Avenues, Silver Lake (1-213 669 9381). Bus 1, 2, 3, 26, 175/US101, exit Vermont Avenue north.* **Open** 6pm-2am Wed-Sat. **No credit cards.**
A tiny Polynesian gem in the shadow of Silver Lake's KCET television studios, the Tiki-Ti dares ask the inebriated question: how much Pacific Ocean-related junk can you pack into an outhouse-sized shack while still leaving room for a few customers? Despite the cramped conditions, dedicated sybarites come from near and far to sample such potent tropical concoctions as Ray's Mistake, Blood and Sand and The Stealth – although it's virtually impossible to drink more than two without throwing up, passing out or going into severe insulin shock.

## Barney's Beanery

*8447 Santa Monica Boulevard, at La Cienega Boulevard, West Hollywood (1-213 654 2287). Bus 4, West Hollywood A, B/I-10, exit La Cienega Boulevard north.* **Open** 10am-2am daily. **Credit** AmEx, Disc, MC, V.
This West Hollywood watering hole's reputation is still somewhat tainted by the distasteful memory of its former 'no gays allowed' policy, but the Midwest-style roadhouse does at least offer an unpretentious atmosphere and the choice of hundreds of beers from around the world. In the end, your comfort factor here will be determined less by your sexual preference than by your degree of affection for the lively décor, televised sports and the music of Bruce Springsteen. Service is more functional than sycophantic.

## bo kaos

*8689 Wilshire Boulevard, at South Hamel Drive, Beverly Hills (1-310 659 1200). Bus 20, 21, 22, 105/I-10, exit La Cienega Boulevard north.* **Open** 7pm-2am daily. **Credit** AmEx, MC, V.
A semi-exotic, dimly lit lounge on the eastern fringe of Beverly Hills, bo kaos is a regular site for record-release shindigs thrown by major labels. A cigar-chomping Matt Dillon has been sighted here.
*Valet parking $3.*

## Cava

*8384 West Third Street, at La Cienega Boulevard, West Hollywood (1-213 658 8898). Bus 14, 16, 105/I-10, exit La Cienega Boulevard north.* **Open** 6.30am-midnight daily. **Credit** AmEx, MC, V.
This Dali-esque establishment is known for its Spanish fare and easy-on-the-eyes clientele, but it also has an exceptionally comfortable bar on the second floor. Order a few delicious tapas plates to go with your drinks; they mix 'em strong here, and you'll need something in your stomach to soak up the excess alcohol.
*Valet parking $2.50.*

## Coronet Pub

*370 North La Cienega Boulevard, between Melrose Avenue & Beverly Boulevard, West Hollywood (1-310 659 4583). Bus 14, 105, DASH Fairfax/I-10, exit La Cienega Boulevard north.* **Open** 6am-2am daily. **Credit** MC, V.
Somewhat out of place in the shadow of the hulking Beverly Center shopping mall, this comfortable little joint seems to have been lifted directly from New York's Greenwich Village. It gets pretty crowded with playgoers before and after shows at the adjacent Coronet Theater, but is quite pleasant the rest of the time.

## Midtown/Hollywood

## Boardner's

*1652 North Cherokee Avenue, at Hollywood Boulevard, Hollywood (1-213 462 9621). Bus 1, 180, 181, 210, 212/US101, exit Highland Avenue south.* **Open** 11am-2am daily. **No credit cards.**
Welcome to Heavy Metal Has-been Central. Cheap beer and even cheaper entertainment – that is, if you find drunken former members of popular 1980s heavy metal acts entertaining – make a trip to this Hollywood mainstay worthwhile. Multiple bars and an airy back patio add to its frayed-at-the-edges appeal.

## Burgundy Room

*1621½ Cahuenga Boulevard, at Hollywood Boulevard, Hollywood (1-213 465 7530). Bus 1, 180, 210, 212/US101, exit Cahuenga Boulevard south.* **Open** 8.30pm-2am daily. **No credit cards.**
Once your eyes adjust to the darkness, you'll notice that this ragged-but-right Hollywood dive has an amazing jukebox –

The **Formosa Café**, *a long-running Hollywood classic.*

full of obscure punk and soul singles – and that it's in dire need of a good dusting. Motorcycle jackets are pretty much the required uniform.

## Cat & Fiddle Pub

*6530 Sunset Boulevard, between Highland Avenue & Cahuenga Boulevard, Hollywood (1-213 468 3800). Bus 2, 3, DASH Hollywood/US101, exit Sunset Boulevard west.* **Open** 11.30am-2am daily. **Credit** AmEx, MC, V.
This popular spot for expatriate Brits and visiting rock musicians, run by former Creation/Ashton Gardner & Dyke bassist Kim Gardner, offers good fish and chips as well as several English brews on tap. The back patio is an exceedingly pleasant place to enjoy a pint.
*Valet parking $2.75.*

## Coach & Horses

*7617 Sunset Boulevard, at Stanley & Curson Avenues, Hollywood (1-213 876 6900). Bus 2, 3, 429/US101, exit Highland Avenue south.* **Open** 11.30am-2am Mon-Thur; noon-2am Sat; 5pm-2am Sun. **No credit cards.**
Darts, a variety of lagers and a crew of unbelievably ill-tempered barmaids attract many of LA's British subjects to this tiny pub on Sunset's 'Guitar Row'. Billy Idol is often seen here, which may be a reason for avoiding/visiting the place, depending on your point of view.

## Formosa Café

*7156 Santa Monica Boulevard, at Formosa Avenue, Hollywood (1-213 850 9050). Bus 4, 212, West Hollywood A, B/I-10, exit La Brea Avenue north.*
**Open** 11.30am-2am daily. **Credit** AmEx, MC, V.
One of the few real remnants of Old Hollywood. The darkened interior of this charming Chinese box – which boasts the world's largest collection of Elvis decanters – is completely covered with autographed photos of movie stars who have imbibed here during the past six decades. Surprisingly, it's not that touristy, and still has a buzz. Take a seat at the bar or in an overstuffed red leather booth, order a drink and pretend you're a private detective or a matinee idol. Best steer clear of the food, however.
*Valet parking free with validation.*

## Frolic Room

*6245 Hollywood Boulevard, at Vine Street, Hollywood (1-213 462 5890). Bus 1, 180, 181, 217, 429/US101, exit Hollywood Boulevard west.* **Open** 10am-2am daily. **No credit cards.**
Stepping over the squatter overflow from the lobby of the neighbouring Pantages Theater will work up a thirst in even the hardiest of individuals, so refresh yourself with a visit to this hard-boiled relic from the 1940s.

## Lava Lounge

*1533 North La Brea Avenue, at Sunset Boulevard, Hollywood (1-213 876 6612). Bus 2, 3, 212, 302, 429/ I-10, exit La Brea Avenue north.* **Open** 9pm-2am daily. **Credit** Disc, MC, V.
Located in the middle of a fairly grim Hollywood strip mall, this relative newcomer updates the Polynesian pleasure palaces of the Eisenhower era with an attractive mirrors-and-bamboo look, while the triangle-backed leather barstools are the last word in bachelor pad luxury. Along with the usual beers and hard liquor, the bartenders mix a mean selection of tropical drinks.

## Molly Malone's Irish Pub

*575 South Fairfax Avenue, at Sixth Street, Park La Brea (1-213 935 1577/music hotline 1-213 935 2707). Bus 20, 21, 22, 217/I-10, exit Fairfax Avenue north.* **Open** 10.30am-2am daily. **Credit** AmEx, MC, V.
Irish to the nth degree, Molly's stout-brown walls are adorned with paintings of Brendan Behan, James Joyce and Ms Malone herself. A friendly and comfortable place to enjoy a pint of Guinness, the pub attracts an odd mix of musicians, twentysomething actors and actresses and incredibly aged Irishmen. Disparaging remarks about U2 are not tolerated.

## Musso & Frank Grill

*6667 Hollywood Boulevard, at Cherokee Avenue, Hollywood (1-213 467 7788). Bus 163, 180, 181, 212, DASH Hollywood/US101, exit Highland Avenue south.* **Open** 11am-11pm Tue-Sat. **Credit** AmEx, DC, MC, V.

Dinner at this remnant of Hollywood's golden age (it opened in 1919) can cost you an arm and a leg, but plenty of Angelenos come just to sit at the bar, sip martinis and soak up the wood-panelled atmosphere. Author and poet Charles Bukowski, in his relatively flush later years, ate and drank here regularly: what further recommendation do you need? *Parking 2 hrs free with validation.*

### Three of Clubs

*1123 Vine Street, at Santa Monica Boulevard, Hollywood (1-213 462 6441). Bus 4, 210, 420, 426/US101, exit Vine Street south.* **Open** 7pm-2am daily. **Credit** AmEx, MC, V.

Cloaked in anonymity on the edge of one of Hollywood's more dilapidated strip malls – look for the 'Bargain Clown Mart' sign overhead, or you'll miss it completely – the Three of Clubs is a cavernous wonder, complete with flocked velvet wallpaper and a ceiling decorated to look like a sparkling night sky. Although it looks (on the inside, at least) like the sort of place that Don Vito Corleone would hold court in, you're more likely to find beautiful twentysomethings packed into the dark booths, exchanging phone numbers to the sound of yesterday's easy-listening icons. Be warned: the bouncers can become rather surly at the slightest provocation.

## Downtown

### Hank's Bar

*840 South Grand Avenue, at Ninth Street, Downtown (1-213 623 7718). Metro 7th Street/Metro Center or Pershing Square/bus 40, 78, 79, 96, DASH C, E/I-110, exit Grand Avenue.* **Open** 10am-2am daily. **Credit** AmEx, MC, V.

If you're strolling around Downtown, be sure to stop in at this piece of Los Angeles history, a popular meeting place for policemen, reporters, and politicians since before World War II. Just about the only thing that's changed since then is the price of the drinks.

### Top of Five

*Westin Bonaventure Hotel, 404 South Figueroa Street, at Fourth Street, Downtown (1-213 624 1000). Metro 7th Street/Metro Center/bus 53, 60, 471, Montebello 40/US101 north, exit Third Street south.* **Open** 5.30-10pm daily. **Credit** MC, V.

If the idea of watching the sun set from a slowly revolving bar at the top of a Downtown hotel appeals to you, give this place a visit. The drinks are nothing special, but the view is – on a clear day, you get a panoramic eyeful of the city – and the rides in the glass elevator aren't bad, either.

## East Hollywood

### The Dresden Room

*1760 North Vermont Avenue, between Franklin Avenue & Hollywood Boulevard, Los Feliz (1-213 665 4294). Bus 26, 180, 181, Community Connection 203/US101, exit Vermont Avenue north.* **Open** 11am-2am Mon-Sat; 3pm-10pm Sun. **Credit** AmEx, MC, V.

This Los Feliz landmark has experienced something of a renaissance in the past few years, thanks to its eye-popping white leather and corkboard interior and regular appearances by Marty & Elayne, lounge duo extraordinaire. Gather around the white piano and request your favourites. *Valet parking $1.50.*

### Red Lion Tavern

*2366 Glendale Boulevard, at Silver Lake Boulevard, Silver Lake (1-213 662 5337). Bus 92/I-110, exit Silver Lake Boulevard west.* **Open** 11am-2am Mon-Fri; 10am-2am Sat, Sun. **Credit** AmEx, MC, V.

A popular hangout with Silver Lake's elderly German immigrant population, this restaurant/bar has also fallen into favour with the area's young hipsters, who revel in the unselfconscious cheesiness of the décor and annoy the regulars. Order a schnapps from a Mexican waitress in a Bavarian milkmaid outfit, take your pick from the Heino selections on the jukebox and ponder the deeper meaning of blutwurst.

**The Dresden Room** – *so naff it's hip again.*

# Shopping & Services

# Shopping & Services

*Want off-the-scale swank? The most personal of service? The quirky, kooky or just plain dorky? In the world capital of conspicuous consumption, you got it.*

Los Angeles is one of the US's largest manufacturing and retailing centres, and the design hub of the Pacific Rim. Automobiles, clothing and furniture designed here influence consumer markets worldwide. However, it's the 'I want, I need, I have to have it' mentality of the natives that makes LA a shoppers' heaven. The whole nation is, of course, primed to pander to consumerism. But the City of Angels, which blossomed largely as a result of the movie industry, with its emphasis on vanity and superficiality, excels in acquisition. Whether or not you want to partake personally, it's a great place just to marvel at others' frivolity, made more pleasant by the clement weather and well-planned shopping areas designed, of course, around the car. Note that Los Angeles County adds an 8.25% sales

tax on to the marked price of all merchandise and services; Orange County taxes at 7.75%.

## THE SHOPPING DISTRICTS

**Beverly Hills**, particularly the Rodeo Collection on **Rodeo Drive** – sometimes known as the 'Golden Triangle' – is for those with money to burn and less-than-radical taste. Hidden among the Chanels and Pradas, however, are the odd, one-off boutique and hip California designer. It's also home to some of the best department stores, such as Neiman Marcus and Barneys of New York. **Brentwood** has a range of upscale restaurants, bookshops, clothing boutiques and the petite Brentwood Gardens Mall. **Sunset Plaza** on Sunset Strip is another posh neighbourhood,

*Upscale heading for off the scale: swank unlimited at **Rodeo Drive**.*

scattered with high-end stores and sidewalk cafés, and great for a spot of people-watching.

**Melrose Avenue** is akin to the King's Road in London's Chelsea, once hip and avant-garde and now a somewhat tired-looking row of shops, cafés and restaurants that change hands quicker than a dealer at a poker table. However it's still popular with the young and a great place to spot young girls baring their pierced belly buttons.

**Robertson Boulevard** in West Hollywood is teeming with antique and design shops and is getting more fashionable by the nano-second, with a flurry of hip, upscale boutiques and shoe stores moving in. **Hollywood Boulevard**, not unlike the Venice Boardwalk, is fun and seedy, packed with one-off vendors selling T-shirts, trashy lingerie, cloned designer goods, sunglasses, bargain leather and naff gifts.

**Larchmont Village** is an oddity in LA – a four-block stretch of boutiques, shops and restaurants plonked slap bang in the middle of upscale residential Hancock Park – and not to be missed. **North La Brea Avenue** has re-emerged as an alternative trendy area with a mixture of clothing stores and restaurants. The **Farmers' Market** (6333 West Third Street, at Fairfax Avenue) is an unusual outdoor market full of tourist gift shops, fresh produce, cafés and Southwestern crafts.

**Westwood** offers the kind of shopping you would find in a mall, but without the structure. It used to be a popular place to roam, being close to the UCLA campus, open late, with a slew of bookshops, numerous cafés and fast-food restaurants, but its popularity has been usurped by **Third Street Promenade** in Santa Monica, which, rather like **Old Town Pasadena**, is a retro-fitted downtown area that emulates the mall experience. **Main Street** in Santa Monica is a revamped turn-of-the-century seaside resort, made into a delightful shopping experience with antique stores, fashion outlets, art galleries and speciality shops. On **Montana Avenue** you are spoilt for choice with furniture stores, antique and gift shops, restaurants, cafés, galleries, clothing shops and gourmet food stores. It's select, eclectic and has a good neighbourhood vibe.

**Downtown LA** is home to the garment district, jewellery trade centres, flower and funiture markets and the California Mart, the country's largest wholesale apparel centre. **Little Tokyo**, **Chinatown**, bustling Broadway and Mexican **Olvera Street** offer a good few hours of fun. **Seventh Street** has the city's largest collection of shoe stores and its original department stores.

**Universal CityWalk** in Universal City, sandwiched between two of LA's largest tourist attractions, Universal Studios and Universal City Cinema complex, has the feel of a futuristic shopping centre with a melange of shops and cafés. Parking is expensive, supposedly to discourage

gangs and hooligans. The sheer magnitude of the place and the wacky designs of the buildings make it well worth a visit.

## Department stores

### Barneys New York

*9570 Wilshire Boulevard, at Camden Drive, Beverly Hills (1-310 276 4400). Bus 20, 21, 22/I-10, exit Robertson Boulevard north.* **Open** 10am-7pm Mon-Wed, Fri, Sat; 10am-8pm Thur; noon-6pm Sun. **Credit** AmEx, JCB, MC, V.

A good facsimile of the now legendary New York store. It exudes exclusivity, while making more than a gesture toward hipness; even the underground car park is 'art directed' with subtle lighting and beautiful curves. Four floors then await to delight with cosmetics, jewellery, shoes, the best in designer clothes for both sexes, lingerie and home accessories. Atop sits more elegance: Barney Greengrass, a bar and first-rate rooftop restaurant with one of the best views into Beverly Hills. It also sells gourmet foodstuffs.

### Macy's

*Beverly Center, 8500 Beverly Boulevard, at La Cienega Boulevard, West Hollywood (1-310 854 6655). Bus 14, 104/I-10, exit La Cienega Boulevard north.* **Open** 10am-9.30pm daily. **Credit** AmEx, MC, V.

Having bought out all its competitors, Macy's is the 800lb gorilla of retail, offering sensible standards.

### Neiman Marcus

*9700 Wilshire Boulevard, at Roxbury Drive, Beverly Hills (1-310 550 5900). Bus 4, 20, 21, 22/I-10, exit Robertson Boulevard north.* **Open** 10am-6pm Mon-Fri; 10am-7pm Sat; noon-6pm Sun. **Credit** AmEx.

Although Neiman's is known as 'Needless Markups,' really nothing is overpriced here. It's simply that it's an upscale store selling top-of-the-line-goods that, naturally, retail for higher prices. It has one of the best women's shoe departments in town plus a fine confectionery counter and a good cosmetics department.

### Saks Fifth Avenue Beverly Hills

*9600 & 9634 Wilshire Boulevard, at Bedford Drive, Beverly Hills (1-310 275 4211). Bus 4, 20, 21, 22/I-405, exit Wilshire Boulevard east.* **Open** 10am-6pm Mon-Wed, Fri, Sun; 10am-8.30pm Thur; 10am-7pm Sat. **Credit** AmEx, MC, V.

Saks has been a part of Beverly Hills since 1938 and offers everything you could possibly want in upmarket glamour (Saks East) – and will offer even more when it opens the expanded store (Saks West) in the prime deco building that was formerly inhabited by I Magnin, to make Saks the largest Beverly Hills store. The new men's store, The 5th Avenue Club for Men, is claimed to offer the most comprehensive personal shopping service in the country.

### Sears

*5601 Santa Monica Boulevard, at Western Avenue, Hollywood (1-213 769 2600). Bus 4, 20, 175, 207, 357/US101, exit Santa Monica Boulevard west.* **Open** 10am-9pm Mon-Fri; 10am-8pm Sat; 10am-7pm Sun. **Credit** AmEx, Disc, MC, V.

Despite its ugly brown exterior, this is a useful department store for all domestic appliances and inexpensive utility items. A blue-collar kinda place.

## Shopping malls

Shopping malls sprang up in the 1950s and 1960s to encourage shoppers into the suburbs and away from what were becoming dangerous downtown

# Plastic fantastic

The Los Angeles mantra 'I see, I want, I must have' is often accompanied by 'I don't like, so I will change'. Plastic surgery, with its new technological advances, cheaper prices and shorter recovery time, is increasingly popular with common folk as with celebs. However, be forewarned that, as with most things, you get what you pay for. Just as the celebrities patronise the same small clique of fashion designers, so they rely on the same gang of plastic surgeons in Beverly Hills and environs for their nips, tucks, trims and sucks.

**Richard Ellenbogen** MD (1-310 276 3183) has a bachelor's degree in art, used to be a portrait painter in Miami and is one of LA's elite plastic surgeons. Patients that he can mention with immunity include the late Lana Turner and Kelly Kirkland. We took a representative page out of his diary, spanning one week, to ascertain what the most popular procedures currently are – six breast enlargements, one breast reduction, one breast uplift, two nose jobs, one upper and lower eyelid lift, one forehead lift, one full body lipo suction. One of those operations was on a man. The costs of those ops in the city vary wildly. Breast enlargement goes from $4,000 to $9,000; breast reduction $5,000-$10,000; nose job $2,500-$10,000; ears pinned back $2,500-$4,500; tummy tuck $5,000-$8,000. Then you've got to figure in the cost of the anaesthetist, the hospital (Ellenbogen uses his own surgery) and, of course, the post-op retreat.

If you're paying those prices, you might as well get the luxury of a five-star hotel. At the **Beverly Prescott Hotel**, the entire sixth floor is a nightmare of post-op victims and nurses, while, downstairs, The Chez restaurant offers guests culinary delights from a 'hard' or 'soft' menu. A suite at **The Peninsula Beverly Hills** is probably the most luxurious joint to recuperate in, but its high-profile status might prove inappropriate for those wishing to maintain a low profile (for both, *see chapter* **Accommodation**). The **Hidden Garden** (1-310 550 6855) is a Provençal-style villa often referred to as a 'spa retreat' on a client's invoices; it's so discreet that the address is the subject of some mystery.

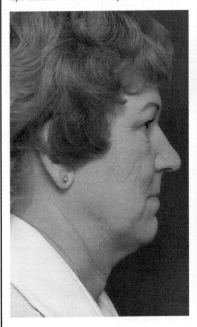 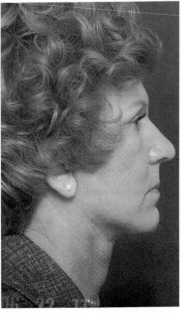

areas. In LA, the ultimate suburban sprawl, malls have all but taken over, and a visit to the mall often takes the place of other activities, since it combines dining, shopping, exercise, movie-going and driving in one experience.

The same stores and franchises appear again and again – Ann Taylor, Z Gallery, The Gap, The Limited, Express, Hold Everything, Crabtree & Evelyn, Victoria's Secret, Joan & David – usually anchored by a generic department store, adding to the general homegenous impression. They also usually house fast-food venues and cafés (with the occasional restaurant or individually owned store), movie theatres and often a large supermarket.

In West Hollywood sits the newly painted **Beverly Center** (8500 Beverly Boulevard, at La Cienega Boulevard; 1-310 854 0700), which has all you could possibly want in a mall, including two department stores, a good selection of shoe stores, an MAC Cosmetics, some high-end, one-off boutiques, a multi-screen cinema and The Hard Rock Café.

Across the street is **The Beverly Connection** (100 North La Cienega Boulevard; 1-213 651 3611), a smaller version of the same thing, with a Strouds, a Bookstar, Starbucks and a Sport Chalet. **Century City Shopping Center and Marketplace** (10250 Little Santa Monica Boulevard, between Avenue of the Stars & Century Park West; 1-310 277 3898) has an outdoor set-up and is comprehensive for both shopping and eating.

**Sherman Oaks Galleria** (15301 Ventura Boulevard, at Sepulveda Boulevard; 1-818 783 3550) is one of the original malls in LA and offers a real Valley experience in all its tackiness. **Westside Pavilion** (10800 West Pico Boulevard, at Westwood Boulevard, Culver City; 1-310 474 6255) has some good kids' toys and clothes stores, the only Nordstroms department store in the city (great for reasonably priced clothes), difficult parking and a good art-house cinema owned by Goldwyn.

**The Brentwood Gardens** (11677 San Vicente Boulevard, at Barrington Avenue; 1-310 820 7646) is a mini-mall with some excellent designer-filled boutiques. **The Glendale Galleria** (at Central & Broadway Avenues; 1-818 246 6737) has a Neiman Marcus, so we approve.

## Factory outlets

If you're willing to drive further afield, factory outlets offer factory seconds and some very good deals on major brand names such as Sony, Nike and Guess. However, some items are not returnable and may be out of date. For factory stores further out of LA, *see chapter* **Trips out of Town**.

### Citadel Factory Stores
*5675 East Telegraph Road, at Citadel Drive, City of Commerce (1-213 888 1220). Bus 462/I-5, exit Washington Boulevard north.* **Open** 10am-8pm Mon-Sat; 10am-6pm Sun.

### The Cooper Building
*860 South Los Angeles Street, at Ninth Street, Downtown (1-213 622 1139). Bus 27, 28, 40, 42, 83, 84, 85/I-110, exit Ninth Street east.* **Open** 8.30am-5.30pm Mon-Sat; 11am-5pm Sun.

## Acting classes

### Lee Strasberg Institute
*7936 Santa Monica Boulevard, at North Hayworth Avenue, West Hollywood (1-213 650 7777). Bus 1, 4, 17, 304/I-10, exit Fairfax Avenue north.*
You have to be interviewed. The shortest course runs for 12 weeks. They work recreating certain sensoral impulses, otherwise known as Method.

### Acting for Life Studio
*3435 West Magnolia, at Hollywood Way, Burbank (1-818 547 3268). Bus 163, 182/SR134, exit Pass Avenue north.*
Gene Bua – who has worked with actors Brad Pitt, Ted Danson and Drew Barrymore – runs an ongoing theatre workshop in a small space. He uses imagination techniques with his pupils rather than them relying on recalling old experiences and playing them out. For serious professionals only.

## Antiques
### Antique shops

### Blackman Cruz
*800 North La Cienega Boulevard, at Waring Avenue, West Hollywood (1-310 657 9228). Bus 105/I-10, exit La Cienega Boulevard north.* **Open** 10am-6pm Mon-Fri; noon-5pm Sat. **Credit** AmEx, MC, V.
Take a 14ft clock from the Waldorf Astoria that makes Big Ben look tired, or a 6ft alabaster floor lamp from Hearst Castle, or a duo of iron manhole cover and drain cover that Adam Blackman has turned into a little cigarette table with iron legs – they all hit the right nerve of the young, hip collectors of classic modern design. Blackman favours the large and luminous, while David Cruz has a penchant for extraordinary design. Together, they've got it covered.

### Ludy Strauss/The Quilt Gallery
*1025 Montana Avenue, at 10th & 11th Streets, Santa Monica (1-310 393 1148). Bus 3, Santa Monica 3/I-10, exit Lincoln Boulevard north.* **Open** 11am-5pm Mon-Sat. **Credit** MC, V.
Ludy collects North American quilts and hooked rugs (both 1800-1940) and American folk art, furnishings and paintings.

### Modernica
*7366 Beverly Boulevard, at Martel Avenue, Melrose District (1-213 933 0383). Bus 14/I-10, exit Fairfax Avenue north.* **Open** 11am-6pm Mon-Sat; noon-5pm Sun. **Credit** MC, V.
Owned by brothers Frank and Jay Novak from Nebraska, this store specialises in Modernist furniture (1929-1960), particularly Southern California design. They also replicate items, have three franchises in Japan and have just opened a store in New York.

### Off the Wall
*7325 Melrose Avenue, at Fuller Avenue, Melrose District (1-213 930 1185). Bus 10, 11/I-10, exit La Brea Avenue north.* **Open** 11am-6pm Mon-Sat. **Credit** AmEx, MC, V .
Antiques and weird stuff. Currently in stock is a 22ft animated neon sign from a movie drive-in, depicting a 1950 Cadillac with two girls waving, their blonde hair blowing and the wheels of the car turning. Also, Frank Lloyd Wright furniture, phenomenal chairs by Bugatti and a fibreglass menagerie of barnyard animals.

### Thanks For The Memories

*8319 Melrose Avenue, between Sweetzer Avenue & Kings Road, Melrose District (1-213 852 9407). Bus 10, 11/ I-10, exit La Cienega Boulevard.* **Open** noon-6pm Mon-Sat. **Credit** AmEx, Disc, MC, V.

Probably one of the most comprehensive collections of art deco and Streamline Moderne in the city. Johnny Depp purchased an oversized, burled walnut, 1930s Austrian cabinet; Patricia Arquette bought some Murano glass for husband Nic Cage to add to his collection; Diane Keaton bought some Mexican silver jewellery as gifts for friends.

### Wells

*2209 Sunset Boulevard, at Mohawk Street, Silver Lake (1-213 413 0558). Bus 1, 2, 3, 4, 200, 304/US101, exit North Alvarado Boulevard north.* **Open** 11am-6pm Mon-Sat. **Credit** AmEx, MC, V.

Probably the largest collection of Southern Californian antique tiles and pottery from the turn of the century to the 1940s. Colourful, geometric tiles with Moorish overtones; early Bauer, Catalina, Batchelder and Hillside pottery; architecturally interesting garden pieces.

### The Yellow Room

*511 North Robertson Boulevard, between Melrose & Rangely Avenues, West Hollywood (1-310 274 3190). Bus 10, 11, 105, 220/I-10, exit Robertson Boulevard north.* **Open** 10am-6pm Mon-Sat. **Credit** AmEx, MC, V.

Jonathan Blackman brings possibly the largest collection of antique world globes on the West Coast, once made for kings and cardinals, to ordinary folk with a sense of chic. Prices start at $150 for an illuminated glass globe from the 1930s and soar into thousands for an early 1800s celestial. Also scientific instruments, and along with partner Paul Marra, eclectic furniture from the 20th century.

## Antique malls

### Cranberry House

*12318 Ventura Boulevard, between Whitsett & Laurel Grove Avenues, Studio City (1-818 506 8945). Bus 424, 522/US101, exit Laurel Canyon south.* **Open** 11am-6pm daily.

Some 15,000sq ft of antique clothing, furniture and accessories on two floors of a 1930s building. The ambiance and service is markedly welcoming. Gift wrapping.

### Pasadena Antique Center

*444 & 480 South Fair Oaks Avenue, between Del Mar & California Boulevards, Pasadena (1-818 449 7706). Bus 177, 256, 483/I-110, exit Colorado Boulevard west.* **Open** 10am-6pm daily.

More than 130 booths and showcases.

### Santa Monica Antique Market

*1607 Lincoln Boulevard, between Colorado Avenue & Olympic Boulevard, Santa Monica (1-310 314 4899). Bus Santa Monica 9/I-10, exit Lincoln Boulevard north.* **Open** 10am-6pm Mon-Sat; noon-5pm Sun.

This 20,000sq ft mall has 200 different dealers selling quality antiques and collectibles.

## Flea markets

### Pasadena City College

*1570 East Colorado Boulevard, between South Hill & Bonnie Avenues, Pasadena (1-818 585 7123). Bus 181, 188, 401, Foothill Transit 187/I-110, exit Colorado Boulevard east.* **Open** 8am-3pm first Sun of the month. **Admission** free.

A manageable-sized market selling furniture clothing, jewellery and nostalgia items.

*Old clothes never die at* **Greenspan's**, *p165.*

### The Rose Bowl

*1001 Rose Bowl Drive, at Arroyo Boulevard, Pasadena (1-213 588 2727). Bus 177/SR134, exit Orange Grove Boulevard north.* **Open** 9am-4.30pm second Sun of the month; early admission at 6am. **Admission** $5; early $10.

The best flea market in town.

### Long Beach Veteran's Memorial Stadium

*5000 Lew Davis Street, at Conant Street, Long Beach (1-213 655 5703). Bus Long Beach Transit 112/I-405, exit Lakewood Boulevard north.* **Open** 6.30am-3pm third Sun of the month & first Sun in Nov; early admission at 5.30am. **Admission** $4.50; early $10.

The largest antiques and collectibles market in the West.

## Art supplies

### Aaron Brothers Art Mart

*1645 Lincoln Boulevard, between Colorado Avenue & Olympic Boulevard, Santa Monica (1-310 450 6333). Bus Santa Monica 9/I-10, exit Lincoln Boulevard north.* **Open** 9am-9pm Mon-Sat; 10am-6pm Sun. **Credit** AmEx, Disc, MC, V.

The Westside's biggest art supply store. Discount prices.

### The Art Store

*7301 West Beverly Boulevard, at Poinsettia Place, West Hollywood (1-213 933 9284). Bus 14/I-10, exit La Brea Avenue north.* **Open** 9am-8pm Mon-Fri; 9am-6pm Sat; 11am-5pm Sun. **Credit** AmEx, MC, V.

Everything from frames, portfolios, oils, pastels, clay, faux finishes and easels to cards and art books.

## Astrology

### Star Power

*Yoga West, 1535 South Robertson Boulevard, between Cashio & Pickford Streets, Beverly Hills (1-310 552 4647). Bus 220/I-10, exit Robertson Boulevard north.* **Open** 24-hour answerphone. **No credit cards.**

Proprietor Anita Sands Hernandez is the Wal-Mart of Wizardry. She will give you a palm, tarot and astrological reading in one hour for $25.

## Bookshops

Angelenos are not the illiterates that the rest of the world likes to pigeonhole them as. Although, in the main, they haven't the same opportunities to read on trains and buses as other urbanites, publishers do a a very brisk trade in Southern California. Bookstores have remade themselves into coffeehouses, entertainment centres with author readings and book groups, and meeting places – the 1990s version of the aerobics class – safe places to encounter interesting people.

There are three main bookshop chains, with branches all over town, many with on-site cafés. Phone one branch to find the nearest to you: **Barnes & Nobles** (Westwood branch: 1-310 475 4144); **Border's Books & Music** (Santa Monica branch: 1-310 393 9290); and **Brentano's** (West Hollywood branch: 1-310 652 8024). Below are the best of the independents.

### Bodhi Tree Bookstore

*8585 Melrose Avenue, at Westbourne Drive, West Hollywood (1-310 659 1733). Bus 10, 11, 105, DASH Fairfax, West Hollywood/I-10, exit La Cienega Boulevard north.* **Open** 10am-11pm daily. **Credit** MC, V.

---

# Dating agencies

It's a favourite pastime of Angelenos to find a mate for recently singled friends, but should this fail, there's always the classifieds; we recommend the *LA Weekly*. It can be a fun way to meet people over the phone, but we advise absolute caution if you plan to get together in person. There are also professional matchmakers and video-dating services, which are usually time-consuming, exorbitantly priced and often disappointing.

You could try **The Meeting Pointe** (1901 Avenue of the Stars, Century City; 1-310 556 8700), which is probably the safest and most effective new dating game in town. It's a private club, offering a café with a full bar, patio dining, mixer parties and nightly entertainment. They also have voicemail systems and a video library.

---

Once a place frequented only by underground mystics, hippies and some pretty odd people and mentioned in Shirley Maclaine's first book *Out on a Limb*, the Bodhi Tree is now recognised as the best metaphysical bookstore in town, and attracts many international questers. It hosts alternative workshops, poetry readings and seminars. The annex at 606 Westbourne Drive sells second-hand books.

### Book Soup

*8818 Sunset Boulevard, at Horn Avenue, West Hollywood (1-310 659 1733). Bus 2, 3, 105, 302, 429, DASH West Hollywood/I-10, exit La Cienega Boulevard north.* **Open** noon-10pm Mon-Thur; noon-11pm Fri; 11.30am-11pm Sat; 11.30am-10pm Sun. **Credit** AmEx, DC, MC, V.

If you only have time to visit one bookstore in LA, Book Soup is definitely the most pleasurable place to dip your nose into the delicious smell of fresh print, whether your penchant is for Raymond Chandler in paperback or the photos of Bruce Weber in hardback, or if you just want to lose track of time at its extensive domestic and international newsstand. Readings and signings are held. Visit Book Soup Bistro for a cappuccino or a full meal.

### Bookstar

*The Beverly Connection, 100 North La Cienega Boulevard, between Beverly Boulevard & Third Street, West Hollywood (1-310 289 1734). Bus 14, 105, DASH Fairfax/I-10, exit La Cienega Boulevard north.* **Open** 9am-midnight daily. **Credit** AmEx, Disc, MC, V.

Part of Barnes and Noble, this is an unusually large and well-supplied bookstore with helpful staff.

### Cook's Library

*8373 West Third Street, between Kings Road & Orlando Avenue, West Hollywood (1-213 655 3141). Bus 16, DASH Fairfax/I-10, exit La Cienega Boulevard north.* **Open** 1-5pm Mon; 11am-6pm Tue-Sat. **Credit** MC, V.

Salivate over owner Ellen Rose's 4,000-plus collection of books on food and wine from around the world.

### Elliot Katt – Books on the Performing Arts

*8570½ Melrose Avenue, at Westmount Drive, West Hollywood (1-310 652 5178). Bus 10, 11, DASH Fairfax, West Hollywood/I-10, exit La Cienega Boulevard north.* **Open** 11am-5.45pm Mon-Sat. **Credit** AmEx, MC, V.

An extensive collection of books on any and every aspect of the performing arts in the US. Movie studios, production companies, directors, producers and stars pop in and out on a daily basis. Prices range from $20 to $20,000.

### Every Picture Tells A Story

*7525 Beverly Boulevard, at Sierra Bonita Avenue, Mid-Wilshire, LA (1-213 932 6070). Bus 14, DASH Fairfax/I-10, exit Fairfax Avenue north.* **Open** 10am-6pm Tue-Sat. **Credit** AmEx, MC, V.

Children's books and framed illustrations, and characters in doll or stuffed-animal form.

### Larry Edmunds Cinema & Theater Bookshop

*6644 Hollywood Boulevard, between Whitely & Cherokee Avenues, Hollywood (1-213 463 3273). Bus 1, 163, 180, 181, 212, 217, DASH Hollywood/US101, exit Cahuenga Boulevard south.* **Open** 10am-6pm Mon-Sat. **Credit** MC, V.

Cinema and theatre books, movie magazines, scripts, posters, and memorabilia.

### Mysterious Bookshop

*8763 Beverly Boulevard, between Robertson & San Vicente Boulevards, West Hollywood (1-310 659 2959). Bus 14, 16, 220/I-10, exit La Cienega Boulevard north.* **Open** 10am-6pm Mon-Sat; noon-5pm Sun. **Credit** AmEx, Disc, MC, V.

LA's oldest and largest mystery bookstore, selling new, used and rare mystery, spy, detective, crime books and thrillers. Come here for a dose of LA noir.

## Samuel French Theater & Film Bookshop

*7623 Sunset Boulevard, at Stanley Avenue, West Hollywood (1-213 876 0570). Bus 2, 3, 429/I-10, exit Fairfax Avenue north.* **Open** 10am-6pm Mon-Fri; 10am-5pm Sat. **Credit** AmEx, Disc, MC, V.
Just about every film script in print, a myriad of theatre scripts and many books about drama and film.
**Branch:** 11963 Ventura Boulevard, Studio City (1-818 762 0535).

## Thomas Brothers Maps & Travel Bookstore

*521 West Sixth Street, between Grand Avenue & Olive Street, Downtown (1-213 627 4018). Metro Pershing Square or 7th Street/Metro Center/bus 442, 444, 446, 447, Foothill 488, Montebello 40, Santa Monica 10/I-110, exit Sixth Street east.* **Open** 9.30am-5.30pm Mon-Fri. **Credit** AmEx, Disc, MC, V.
Like the name says. A browsing favourite for Downtown workers out on their lunch break.

## Vroman's

*695 East Colorado Boulevard, between El Molino & Oak Knoll, Pasadena (1-818 449 5320). Bus 180, 181, 188, 256, 401/I-110, exit Colorado Boulevard east.* **Open** 9am-9pm Mon-Thur; 9am-10pm Fri. **Credit** AmEx, Disc, MC, V.
Vroman's is the largest independent bookstore in Southern California with a 32,000 sq ft shop floor stuffed with books. It's 102 years old and still going strong. Books, magazines, stationery and paper goods, audio books and rentals and, soon, a coffee bar.

*Film and TV togs end up at* **It's a Wrap**, *p165.*

## W&V Dailey Rare Books

*8216 Melrose Avenue, between Harper & La Jolla Avenues, Melrose District (1-213 658 8515). Bus 10, 11/I-10, exit Fairfax Avenue north.* **Open** 11am-5pm Tue-Sat. **Credit** AmEx, MC, V.
Rare and wonderful books and first editions. William Dailey also does book appraisals and recently completed the late Timothy Leary's archive.

## Cameras & electronics

The large electronic chainstores can be intimidating, but the sheer volume of merchandise allows them to offer the best bargains. One store will often make a promise to match another store's lower price, so check the Sunday papers to see who's offering the top deal in town.

### Frank's Camera

*5715 North Figueroa Street, at Avenue 57, Highland Park, (1-213 255 0123). Bus 81, 176, 256, DASH A/I-110, exit South Avenue 52 north.* **Open** 10am-5.30pm Mon-Sat. **Credit** MC, V.
In business for 28 years, Frank sells new and used cameras and will also process your film, send your camera out for repair and rent you a video camera.

### The Good Guys

*100 North La Cienega Boulevard, between Beverly Boulevard & Third Street, West Hollywood (1-310 659 6500). Bus 14, 205, DASH Fairfax/I-10, exit La Cienega Boulevard north.* **Open** 24 hours daily. **Credit** AmEx, Disc, MC, V.
The place for all your personal electronic, mobile, home audio and visual needs. Watch for the specials and the shop's promise to match the prices of any other store in town.

### Harry's Camera & Video

*11851 Ventura Boulevard, at Carpenter Avenue, Studio City (1-818 763 9750). Bus 230, 424, 522/US101, exit Laurel Canyon Boulevard south.* **Open** 9am-6pm Mon-Sat. **Credit** AmEx, MC, V.
Sales, rentals and repairs. Also film processing.

### Samy's Camera

*200 South La Brea Avenue, between Second & Third Streets, Mid-Wilshire (1-213 938 2420). Bus 16, 212, 316, DASH Fairfax/I-10, exit La Brea Avenue north.* **Open** 8am-8pm Mon-Fri; 9.30am-6pm Sat. **Credit** AmEx, Disc, MC, V.
Some 20,00sq ft of photographic heaven (including digital and video rentals and sales) for both amateurs and professionals. Also processing and repairs.

## Catering

### On Location Catering

*Coleen Stewart (1-310 396 3015/1-310 399 6678).*
Coleen and her helpful staff feed hungry film-makers and film stars on movie sets and also cater for private parties. Clients have included George Clooney and Drew Barrymore.

## Complementary medicine

### East-West Medicine Center

*300 South Beverly Drive, No 105, at Dayton Way, Beverly Hills (1-310 278 1905). Bus 3, 328, DASH Beverly Hills/I-10, exit Robertson Boulevard north.* **Open** 10am-8pm Mon-Sat. **No credit cards.**

*Dishes of the day at* **New Stone Age**, *p166.*

If you want to drop a few pounds, give up smoking or drinking, quieten your mind, rid yourself of asthma, depression or any physical pain, Shlomit will dive into her white pockets and come up with another tiny disposable needle (virtually painless) to acupuncture your pains away. She does house calls and also practises the full range of traditional Chinese medicine: herbs, nutrition, massage therapy and yoga.

### Gurutej Kaur Khalsa

For information, call 1-310 273 9266.
When you're out of sync, Gurutej, who is Sikh and has been a Kundalini yoga teacher for 26 years, will heal you with Raj Yog, using external sound (gongs and bells), vibrations (colour and light), warm chakra pillows and essential oils to change energy flow and release old patterns that contribute to stress and disease.

### Healing Waters

*136 North Orlando Avenue, between First & Third Streets, Park La Brea (1-213 651 4656). Bus 14, 16, DASH Fairfax/I-10, exit La Brea Avenue north.* **Open** 1-5pm Mon-Sat. **No credit cards.**
At this cute shop where terracotta angels adorn the windows and glass windchimes hang from the door, you can get either a Bach Flower or an Aura-Soma Color consultation by appointment. Both will rejuvenate your mind and spirit.

### Kartar Khalsa

*PO Box 67354, LA, CA 90067 (1-310 559 0055).* **Open** daily, by appointment only. **No credit cards.**
Feng shui practioner Kartar Khalsa will come to your home and tell you if your house is contributing to a health problem, impeding your love life or undermining your financial success. Then she'll tell you how to fix it. 'Every building has its own personality and relationship with the people who live or work there,' says Kartar.

### Ron Teagarden's Herbal Emporium

*9001 Beverly Boulevard, at Weatherly Drive, West Hollywood (1-310 205 0104). Bus 14/I-10, exit la Cienega Boulevard north.* **Open** 1-7pm Mon; 11am-7pm Tue-Sat; noon-5pm Sun. **Credit** AmEx, MC, V.
When you're suffering from *une crise de nerves*, run to the Teagarden to buy Shen Chinese herbs. If your libido is lacking, purchase extract of deer antler.

### Unity Health & Medical Center

*8805 Santa Monica Boulevard, between Huntley Drive & San Vicente Boulevard, West Hollywood (1-310 855 7546). Bus 2, 10, 11, 14, 105, 220, DASH West Hollywood/I-405, exit Santa Monica Boulevard east.* **Open** 10am-7pm Tue, Thur; 1-7pm Wed; 10am-4pm Sat. **No credit cards.**
This friendly, upbeat centre, run by vivacious Lily, offers acupuncture, Chinese herbology, meditation and yoga therapy. The centre also has a dermatologist, masseuse, chiropractor, internist (specialist in the diagnosis and treatment of internal disorders that do not require surgery) and skincare professional.

### Dr Richard Schachter PhD

*PO Box 11295, Beverly Hills, CA 90213 (1-310 275 0666).*
After a day of compulsive shopping in LA, repent with human behaviour specialist Dr Richard Schachter. He has worked with many a celebrity shopaholic and is available for private consultations; call for more information.

## Computers

### Computer City

*337 South La Cienega Boulevard, at San Vicente Boulevard, West Hollywood (1-310 289 1330). Bus 28, 105, 328/I-10, exit La Cienega Boulevard north.* **Open** 10am-9pm Mon-Fri; 9am-9pm Sat; 11am-6pm Sun. **Credit** AmEx, MC, V.
Superstore with leading brand names, software and games.

### Egghead Software

*7162 West Beverly Boulevard, between Formosa & La Brea Avenues, Mid-Wilshire (1-213 937 0401). Bus 14/I-10, exit La Brea Avenue north.* **Open** 9am-9pm Mon-Fri; 10am-7pm Sat; 10am-6pm Sun. **Credit** AmEx, DC, Disc, MC, V.
Good selection of mainstream computer software and games.

### Fry's

*3600 Sepulveda Boulevard, at Rosecrans Avenue, Manhattan Beach (1-310 364 3797). Bus 125, 232/I-405, exit Rosecrans Avenue west.* **Open** 8am-9pm Mon-Fri; 9am-8pm Sat; 9am-7pm Sun. **Credit** Disc, MC, V.
A dizzying array of computers, software and gadgetry.

## Carwashes

### Handy J

*14311 Ventura Boulevard, at Beverly Glen Boulevard, Sherman Oaks (1-818 788 3011). US101, exit Woodman Avenue south.* **Open** 8am-6pm Mon-Sat; 8.30am-5.30pm Sun. **Credit** AmEx, MC, V.
Moderate prices and the best detailing in town.

### Sunset Carwash

*7955 Sunset Boulevard, at Hayworth Avenue, West Hollywood (1-213 656 2777). I-10, exit Fairfax Avenue north.* **Open** 8.30am-7pm Mon-Sat; 9am-5pm Sun. **Credit** AmEx, MC, V.
Drink free coffee or iced tea, play a video game, get your shoes shined or simply watch as at least three guys make your automobile sparkle.

## Dance supplies

### Capezio Dance-Theater Shop

*1777 Vine Street, at Yucca Street, Hollywood (1-213 465 3744). Bus 163/US101, exit Hollywood Boulevard west.* **Open** 10am-6pm Mon-Fri; 10am-5pm Sat. **Credit** MC, V.
If you need your first pair of point shoes or jazz booties or a new leotard, this is where to come.

## Dry cleaners

### Effrey's

*8917 Melrose Avenue, between Robertson Boulevard & Doheny Drive, West Hollywood (1-310 858 7400). Bus 4, 220/I-10, exit Robertson Boulevard north.* **Open** 8am-5.30pm Mon-Fri; 8am-1pm Sat. **Credit** AmEx, MC, V.
For the ultimate in dry cleaning. They won't hurry and it will cost the earth, but for those treasured items go somewhere else at your peril.

### Michael Faeth Studio Cleaners

*10800 Washington Boulevard, between Midway & Overland Avenues, Culver City (1-310 838 1801). Bus Culver City 1, 3/I-10, exit Overland Avenue south.* **Open** 24 hours daily. **No credit cards**.
This outfit services many of the film studios' costume departments; they cleaned up on *Batman and Robin* and *Waterworld*.

## Fashion

If you think fashion begins and ends with Paris, London and New York, think again, cookies. LA has its own distinctive style. Anything goes. The climate often dictates. So do the stars. Status labels have always carried their weight here but you should check out LA's rising young designers, including John Eshaya, St Vincent and Anna Hueling for women and The Fever label for men. Fred Segal and Barneys are excellent places to catch the scene. *See also above* **Department stores**.

### Easy Rider

*7450 Melrose Avenue, at Vista Street, Melrose District (1-213 658 8817). Bus 10, 11/I-10, exit Fairfax Avenue north.* **Open** 11am-9pm Mon-Sat; noon-7pm Sun. **Credit** AmEx, MC, V.
For all your biker needs. Leathers, flannels, and T-shirts embossed with the image of Harleys.

### Fred Segal/Ron Herman Melrose

*8100 Melrose Avenue, at Crescent Heights Boulevard, Melrose District (1-213 651 4129). Bus 10, 11/I-10, exit La Cienega Boulevard north.* **Open** 10am-7pm Mon-Sat; noon-6pm Sun. **Credit** AmEx, MC, V.
Fred Segal is the answer to one-stop fashion shopping for those with style, taste and money. A cornucopia of stores under one roof with everything from hip casual wear to upscale designer gear for men, women and small children, plus gifts, some furniture and beauty goods.
**Branch**: **Fred Segal Santa Monica** 500 Broadway, Santa Monica (1-310 393 4477).

### Harari

*110 North Robertson Boulevard, between Alden Drive & Beverly Boulevard, West Hollywood (1-310 275 5521). Bus 14, 20, 21, 22, 220, 320, DASH Fairfax/I-10, exit Robertson Boulevard north.* **Open** 11am-7pm Mon-Sat; noon-6pm Sun. **Credit** AmEx, MC, V.
Funky, stylish womenswear in flowing silk and cotton prints.

### Jay Wolf

*517 North Robertson Boulevard, at Melrose Avenue, West Hollywood (1-310 273 9893). Bus 10, 11, 220/I-10, exit Robertson Boulevard west.* **Open** 11am-7pm Mon-Fri; 10.30am-6pm Sat. **Credit** AmEx, MC, V.
Expect a very personal service in this boutique, which carries Hugo Boss, Joseph Abboud and Paul Smith for men and Paul Smith and Margaret Howell for women.

### J Crew

*3 Colorado Boulevard, at Fair Oaks Avenue, Pasadena (1-818 568 2739). Bus 180, 181, 188, 256, 402, 483, Foothill Transit 187/I-110, exit Fair Oaks Avenue north.* **Open** 10am-9pm Mon-Sat; 10am-7pm Sun. **Credit** AmEx, MC, V.
One of the few shops for this high-quality catalogue designer: the ultimate in preppie-style casual clothing for both sexes.

### Jonathan A Logan

*8336 Melrose Avenue, between Sweetzer Avenue & Kings Road, Hollywood (1-213 653 9155). Bus 10, 11/I-10, exit La Cienega Boulevard north.* **Open** 8am-7pm Mon-Fri; 10am-5pm Sat. **Credit** AmEx, MC, V.
Custom-designed leather. Their film credits include *Street Fighter II* and *Time Cop*.

### Madison

*106 South Robertson Boulevard, between West Third Street & Alden Drive, West Hollywood (1-310 275 1930). Bus 20, 21, 22, 220, 320/I-10, exit Robertson Boulevard north.* **Open** 11am-7pm Mon-Sat; noon-5pm Sun. **Credit** AmEx, MC, V.
An eclectic mix of hip clothes for sophisticated women by Product, Calvin Klein and Alberta Ferretti and shoes by Costume National, Miu Miu and Patrick Cox.

### Marshalls

*11239 Ventura Boulevard, between Vineland & Tujunga Avenues, Studio City (1-818 753 1301). Bus 96, 166, 424, 522/US101, exit Vineland Avenue south.* **Open** 10am-9pm Mon-Sat; 11am-7pm Sun. **Credit** AmEx, Disc, MC, V.
This discount store sells clothes, gifts and household stuff. The best place to buy bargain Calvin Klein undergarments.

### Maxfields

*8825 Melrose Avenue, at Robertson Boulevard, West Hollywood (1-310 274 8800). Bus 10, 11, 220/I-10, exit Robertson Boulevard north.* **Open** 11am-7pm Mon-Sat. **Credit** AmEx, DC, Disc, MC, V.
The Sistine chapel of upscale designer gear and accessories for cutting-edge men and women: Gigli, Gucci, Prada, Comme des Garçons, Yamamoto, Jill Sander. Enjoy the personal service and drink the store's own-label designer water while you mix and match.

### Scott Hill

*100 South Robertson Boulevard, at Alden Drive, West Hollywood (1-310 777 1190). Bus 20, 21, 22, 220, 322/I-10, exit Robertson Boulevard north.* **Open** 11am-6pm Mon-Sat. **Credit** AmEx, MC, V.
Scott Hill will put together a whole wardrobe for you and catalogue and coordinate your existing one. Donna Karan, Calvin Klein, Armani. Business and casual menswear.

### Shauna Stein

*No 679, The Beverly Center, 8500 Beverly Boulevard, at La Cienega Boulevard, West Hollywood (1-310 652 5511). Bus 14, 104/I-10, exit La Cienega Boulevard north.* **Open** 10am-9pm Mon-Fri; 10am-7pm Sat; 11am-6pm Sun. **Credit** AmEx, DC, Disc, MC, V.
A potpourri of upscale designer women's wear, including Rifat Ozbek, Moschino and Dolce & Gabbana, for women with money to burn.

## Spike's Joint West

*7263 Melrose Avenue, between Poinsettia Place & Alta Vista Boulevard, Melrose District (1-213 932 7064). Bus 10, 11/I-10, exit La Brea Avenue north.* **Open** 11am-8pm Mon-Sat; noon-6pm Sun. **Credit** AmEx, Disc, MC, V.
Sporty street clothes designed by Mr Spike Lee, among others.

## The Swell Store

*126 North La Brea Avenue, between First Street & Beverly Boulevard, West LA (1-213 937 2096). Bus 14, 212/I-10, exit La Brea Avenue north.* **Open** 11am-8pm Mon-Sat; noon-7pm Sun. **Credit** AmEx, MC, V.
Check out the huge Hush Puppy on top of the store. Venture inside for clothes for the young and hip club crowd.

## Syren

*7225 Beverly Boulevard, between Alta Vista Boulevard & Formosa Avenue, West Hollywood (1-213 936 6693). Bus 14, 212/I-10, exit La Brea Avenue north.* **Open** 11am-6pm Tue-Sat. **Credit** AmEx, MC, V .
Punk rock and fetish rubber clothing. They designed the suit for *Batman.*

## Worn Out West

*645 North Martel Avenue, at Melrose Avenue, West Hollywood (1-213 653 5645). Bus 10, 11/I-10, exit La Brea Avenue north.* **Open** 11.30am-7pm Mon-Sat; noon-7pm Sun. **Credit** AmEx, Disc, MC, V.
Renowned for its large selection of used Levi's, cowboy boots, work shirts and military outfits.

## X-Large & X-Girl

*1766 North Vermont Avenue, between Hollywood Boulevard & Franklin Avenue, Los Feliz (1-213 666 3483). Bus 1, 180, 181, 204, 217, 354, Community Connection 203/US101, exit Vermont Avenue north.* **Open** noon-7pm Mon-Sat; noon-6pm Sun. **Credit** AmEx, MC, V.
Two lines of action wear clothes for grown-up boys and girls. The shop also carries other hip designers, including Sophia Coppola's Milk Fed line.

# Designer

## Agnès B

*100 North Robertson Boulevard, at Alden Drive, Beverly Hills (1-310 271 9643). Bus 20, 21, 22, 220, 320, 322/I-10, exit Robertson Boulevard north.* **Open** 11am-7pm Mon-Sat; noon-6pm Sun. **Credit** AmEx, MC, V.
Modern-day classics for men and women and a new line for teenagers, entitled Lolita.

## Ann Taylor

*357 North Camden Drive, between Wilshire Boulevard & Brighton Way, Beverly Hills (1-310 858 7840). Bus 20, 21, 22/I-405, exit Wilshire Boulevard east.* **Open** 10am-7pm Mon-Fri; 10am-6pm Sat; noon-5pm Sun. **Credit** AmEx, MC, V.
Well-priced sensible day and evening wear for women.

## Betsey Johnson

*7311 Melrose Avenue, between Poinsettia Place & Fuller Avenue, Melrose District (1-213 931 4490). Bus 10, 11/I-10, exit La Brea Avenue north.* **Open** 11am-7pm Mon-Sat; noon-6pm Sun. **Credit** AmEx, MC, V.
Hip, sexy, affordable fashion for women with little girls' hearts. Everything from polyester minis to Lurex trousers.

## Chanel

*400 North Rodeo Drive, at Brighton Way, Beverly Hills (1-310 278 5500). Bus 4, 20, 21, 22, 320/I-10, exit Robertson Boulevard north.* **Open** 10am-6pm Mon-Sat; noon-5pm Sun. **Credit** AmEx, DC, JCB, MC, V.

It's like stepping into Coco's original salon in Paris. Don't you remember, cherie? La Rue Cambon?

## Christian Dior

*Two Rodeo, 230 North Rodeo Drive, between Wilshire Boulevard & Dayton Way, Beverly Hills (1-310 859 4700). Bus 20, 21, 22/I-10, exit Wilshire Boulevard east.* **Open** 10am-6pm Mon-Sat. **Credit** AmEx, JCB, MC, V.
Clothing, cosmetics, accessories, menswear.

## Emporio Armani

*9533 Brighton Way, between Rodeo & Camden Drives, Beverly Hills (1-310 271 7790). Bus DASH Beverly Hills/I-10, exit Robertson Boulevard east.* **Open** 10am-6.30pm Mon-Wed, Fri, Sat; 10am-8pm Thur; noon-5pm Sun. **Credit** AmEx, MC, V.
Three floors of the slightly more affordable Armani stuff for men and women.

## Giorgio Armani

*436 North Rodeo Drive, between Brighton Way & Little Santa Monica Boulevard, Beverly Hills (1-213 271 5555). Bus 4, 20, 21, 22, 320/I-405, exit Santa Monica Boulevard east.* **Open** 10am-6pm Mon-Sat. **Credit** AmEx, Disc, MC, V.
Much sought-after upscale wear for men and women.

## Gucci

*347 North Rodeo Drive, between Brighton & Dayton Ways, Beverly Hills (1-310 278 3451). Bus 4, 20, 21, 22, 320, DASH Beverly Hills/I-405, exit Wilshire Boulevard east.* **Open** 10am-6pm Mon-Sat; noon-5pm Sun. **Credit** AmEx, JCB, MC, V.
Handbags, women's and men's apparel, luggage and gifts, all marked with that famous insignia.

## Hermès

*343 North Rodeo Drive, between Dayton & Brighton Ways, Beverly Hills (1-310 278 6440). Bus 4, 20, 21, 22, 320, DASH Beverly Hills/I-405, exit Wilshire Boulevard east.* **Open** 10am-6pm Mon-Sat. **Credit** AmEx, MC, V.
One of the first Hermès stores, with an abundance of cherrywood, housing the slightly lighter merchandise, oriented toward the clement California climate.

## Laura Urbinati

*8667 Sunset Boulevard, at Sunset Plaza Drive, West Hollywood (1-310 652 3183). Bus 2, 3, 429/I-10, exit La Cienega Boulevard north.* **Open** 10am-7pm Mon-Fri; 10am-6pm Sat; noon-5pm Sun. **Credit** AmEx, MC, V.
Two floors of Urbinati wear, including her famed bathing suits in earth-toned cottons and knitwear, along with a few other classy, wearable, designers-with-edge such as Helmut Lang, Costume National and Martin Margiela.

## Prada

*9521 Brighton Way, between Rodeo & Camden Drives, Beverly Hills (1-310 276 8889). Bus DASH Beverly Hills/I-405, exit Wilshire Boulevard east.* **Open** 10.30am-6.30pm Mon-Sat; noon-5pm Sun. **Credit** AmEx, MC, V.
You're almost nothing in this town if you don't carry a Prada bag on your shoulder, and genuine, mind – no cheap market trash. The shop also sells an equally high-priced line of women's clothing.

## Product

*7374 Beverly Boulevard, between Martel & Fuller Avenues, Melrose District (1-213 932 1958). Bus 14, DASH Fairfax/I-10, exit La Brea Avenue north.* **Open** 11am-7pm Mon-Sat; noon-6pm Sun. **Credit** AmEx, MC, V.
As the name suggests, the place is simple, sexy clothing for the sharp, modern woman, from designer Elaine Kim.

# California theming

Forty-one years after the creation of Disneyland in Anaheim, now undergoing renovation, the insidious legacy of Walt has reached what seems to be its apotheosis in the current pervasiveness of theming. Once confined to theme parks and other leisure centres, theming has broken into the commercial world and is now the rage in retailing. Themed malls are in and they're going global.

The notion of the themed mall appears to have originated here in Los Angeles with the opening of CityWalk, a private 'street' within the MCA/Universal lot that consists of a terrace of violently coloured and decorated renditions of existing LA buildings, a circular plaza filled with carefully vetted 'street' performers, a variety of themed and entertainment industry stores and a general bombardment of surround-sound music, neon and colour. It also has its own police sub-station.

The themed mall is today's answer to the suburban mall of the 1960s and 1970s, the vaunted solution to blighted inner city commercial districts. Shopping as entertainment within a controlled, non-threatening, pedestrianised environment. Entertainment is the magnet and all such malls have huge multiplex cinemas or an IMAX, and restaurants, often themed along the lines of Planet Hollywood, Fashion Café and the Hard Rock Café. Also essential is a vast accompanying parking structure – you drive in order to walk.

**CityWalk** was designed by Venice-based architect Jon Jerde. Jerde has established himself as the guru of the medium, having breathed new life into distressed neighbourhoods with such shopping extravaganzas as **Horton Plaza** in San Diego and the **Fremont Street Experience** in Las Vegas (for both, *see chapter* **Trips out of Town**), as well as the **Westside Pavilion** in Culver City (10800 West Pico Boulevard, at Westwood Boulevard; 1-310 474 6255) and several similar complexes in cities in South-east Asia.

His concept – essentially, to create a pumped-up, high-intensity amalgam of all the components of public urban life that were becoming anathema to Modern America, such as walkable streets, squares, cafés, street performers and so on – have been applied to the revitalisation of shopping neighbourhoods in Santa Monica (**Third Street Promenade**), Pasadena (**Pasadena Old Town**) and in new themed centers like the recently opened **Irvine Spectrum** in Irvine (Irvine Entertainment Center, where the 1-5 & 1-405 meet; 1-714 450 4900), a 21-screen cineplex in an open mall that is intended to capture the essence of a Moroccan casbah. The most extreme example of theming to date is **Caesars Forum Shops** at Caesars Palace in Las Vegas, where you shop in an evocation of Rome under an artificially changing sky (*see chapter* **Trips Out of Town**).

## Todd Oldham

*7386 Beverly Boulevard, at Martel Avenue, Melrose District (1-213 936 6045). Bus 14, DASH Fairfax/1-10, exit La Brea Avenue north.* **Open** 11am-7pm Mon-Sat; noon-6pm Sun. **Credit** AmEx, MC, V.

This fantasy store designed by Texan design king Oldham is a mosaic of coloured glass chandeliers, real shells embossed on surfaces and myriad leaves from a thousand books pasted on the floor. It's worth a visit to scope out the decor even if you don't have a yen (or a pound, or a dollar) for his hip, brightly coloured clothes.

## Tyler Trafficante

*7290 Beverly Boulevard, between Poinsettia Place & Alta Vista Avenue, Melrose District (1-213 931 6769). Bus 14, DASH Fairfax/1-10, exit La Brea Avenue north.* **Open** 10am-6pm Mon-Fri; 11am-6pm Sat. **Credit** AmEx, MC, V.

Although Tyler Trafficante doesn't actively discourage off-the-street business (if you ring the bell they should let you in, unless you're completely disreputable), staff here do spend most of their time with by-appointment clients known to include Julia Roberts, Brad Pitt and Seal, who comes for his signature ballgowns and fine tailored suits. It's more of an atelier, really – all very Melrose.

## Discount

### Loehmans

*333 South La Cienega Boulevard, between Olympic & Wilshire Boulevards, Mid-Wilshire (1-310 659 0674). Bus 28, 105, 328/1-10, exit La Cienega Boulevard north.* **Open** 10am-9pm Mon-Sat; 11am-7pm Sun. **Credit** Disc, MC, V.

Discount women's clothes and shoes. Be sure to check out The Back Room, devoted to more upscale designer names, including Perry Ellis and Bill Blass.

### Wilson Leather Outlet Store

*3117 Magnolia Boulevard, between Fairview & California Streets, Burbank (1-818 841 7789). Bus 183/SR134, exit Buena Vista Street north.* **Open** 10am-7pm Mon-Sat; noon-6pm Sun. **Credit** AmEx, MC, V.

Overstocked and returned coats, jackets, dresses and skirts. Good prices, conservative designs.

### Ross Dress for Less

*1751 Westwood Boulevard, at Santa Monica Boulevard, Westwood (1-310 477 1707). Bus 4, 304, Santa Monica 1, 8, 12/1-405, exit Wilshire Boulevard east.* **Open** 9.30am-9pm Mon-Sat; 9.30am-7pm Sun. **Credit** AmEx, MC, V.

Men's and women's clothing and accessories.

### Saks SFO

*652 North La Brea Avenue, between Clinton Street &*
*Melrose Avenue, Melrose District (1-213 939 3993). Bus*
*10, 11, 212/I-10, exit La Brea Avenue north.* **Open**
11am-8pm Mon-Fri; 11am-7pm Sat, Sun. **Credit** MC, V.
Many a bargain for men, women and children.
**Branch**: 9608 Venice Boulevard, Culver City (1-310 559
5448).

## Vintage & second-hand

### American Rag

*150 South La Brea Avenue, between First & Second*
*Streets, Park La Brea (1-213 935 3154). Bus 212/I-10,*
*exit La Brea Avenue north.* **Open** 10am-10pm Mon-Sat;
noon-7pm Sun. **Credit** AmEx, DC, MC, V.
One of the largest collections of vintage clothing in LA, in a
relaxed, warehouse-sized setting.

### Aardvarks

*7579 Melrose Avenue, between Curson & Sierra Bonita*
*Avenues, Melrose District (1-213 655 6769). Bus 10, 11/*
*I-10, exit Fairfax Avenue north.* **Open** 11am-9pm Mon-
Sat; 11am-7pm Sun. **Credit** AmEx, Disc, MC, V.
An old favourite, offering funky 1950s to 1970s clothing.
**Branch**: **Aardvark's Odd Ark** 85 Market Street,
Venice (1-310 392 2996).

### Deja Vu USA

*7600 Melrose Avenue, at Curson Avenue, Melrose District*
*(1-213 653 8252). Bus 10, 11/I-10, exit La Brea Avenue*
*north.* **Open** 11am-8pm daily. **Credit** AmEx, MC,V.
For the perfect pair of used jeans, look no further.

### Greenspan's

*3422 Tweedy Boulevard, at Long Beach Boulevard,*
*South Gate (1-213 566 6964). Bus 117/I-105, exit Long*
*Beach Boulevard north.* **Open** 10.30am-6pm Mon-Thur;
10.30am-7pm Fri, Sat. **Credit** AmEx, Disc, MC, V.

In 1928, Edward Greenspan started to buy up unfashionable
men's and boys' wear, at bargain prices. People thought
that he was crazy. Now movie studios and rappers
collide in their quest for authentic clothing from the 1930s
to the present day — workwear, inner city and dress wear
and hats. Much of it is still in the original packaging.

### It's a Wrap

*3315 West Magnolia Boulevard, at California Street,*
*Burbank (1-818 567 7366). Bus 183/SR134, exit Pass*
*Avenue north.* **Open** 11am-8pm Mon-Fri; 11am-6pm Sat,
Sun. **Credit** MC, V.
Film wardrobe purchases and sales. You could find yourself
(almost) wearing Bruce Willis' trousers from *Die Hard* or
Elizabeth Berkley's get-up from *Showgirls*.

### Re-Mix

*7605½ Beverly Boulevard, between Curson & Stanley*
*Avenues, Park La Brea (1-213 936 6210). Bus 14,*
*DASH Fairfax/I-10, exit Fairfax Avenue north.* **Open**
noon-7pm Mon-Sat; noon-6pm Sun. **Credit** AmEx, MC, V.
Unworn shoes for both genders from the 1930s to the 1970s.
Also some clothing, still in its original packaging.

### Time After Time

*7425 Melrose Avenue, between Martel Avenue & Vista*
*Street, Melrose District (1-213 653 8463). Bus 10, 11/*
*I-10, exit Fairfax Avenue north.* **Open** noon-6pm Mon-
Fri; 11am-7pm Sat; 1-6pm Sun. **Credit** AmEx, MC, V.
Vintage bridal and evening gowns from the mid-1800s onward.

## Children's clothes

*See also chapter* **Children**.

### 98% Angel

*No 5A, Malibu Country Mart, 3835 Cross Creek Road,*
*off Pacific Coast Highway, Malibu (1-310 456 0069). Bus*
*434/I-10, exit Pacific Coast Highway north.* **Open** 10am-
6pm Mon-Sat; 11am-5pm Sun. **Credit** AmEx, MC, V.

*Go down Mexico way at* **Grand Central Market**. *See page 169.*

A hip store for all your little darlings' wardrobe needs, over-looking a sandbox in a cute shopping plaza in the heart of Malibu. Brands carried include Mini Man, Metropolitan Prairie and Cacharel.

### Pixie Town

*400 North Beverly Drive, at Brighton Way, Beverly Hills (1-213 272 6415). Bus 3, 4, 14, 20, 21, 22, DASH Beverly Hills/I-10, exit Robertson Boulevard north.* **Open** 10am-6pm Mon-Sat. **Credit** AmEx, MC, V.
Pricey designer clothing and shoes for upwardly mobile new-borns and kids up to age 15.

### Pom D'Api

*9411 Brighton Way, between Beverly & Canon Drives, Beverly Hills (1-310 278 7663). Bus DASH Beverly Hills/I-10, exit Robertson Boulevard north.* **Open** 10am-6pm Mon-Sat; noon-5pm Sun. **Credit** AmEx, MC, V.
A smörgåsbord of chic French footwear from 'Smellies' (scented plastic beach sandals) to jester-style slippers for chil-dren and teens.

### Tartine & Chocolat

*1410 Montana Avenue, between 14th & 15th Streets, Santa Monica (1-310 656 1166). Bus Santa Monica 3, 11/I-10, exit 26th Street north.* **Open** 10am-7pm Mon-Fri; 10am-6pm Sat; noon-6pm Sun. **Credit** AmEx, MC, V.
This delightful French store inspires you to spend money, even if you don't have a newborn or a kid under 12.

## Dress hire

### One Night Affair

*2370 Westwood Boulevard, between Tennessee Avenue & West Pico Boulevard, West LA (1-310 652 4334). Bus Culver City 3, Santa Monica 7, 8, 12, 13/I-10, exit Santa Monica Boulevard east.* **Open** 11am-7pm Tue-Fri; 9am-6pm Sat. **Credit** AmEx, Disc, MC, V.
Women's designer wear, from cocktail dresses to wedding gowns, by Gianni Versace to Bill Blass. By appointment only.

### Tuxedo Center

*7360 Sunset Boulevard, at North Martel Avenue, Hollywood (1-213 874 4200). Bus 2, 3, 429/I-10, exit La Brea Avenue north.* **Open** 9am-6pm Mon-Fri; 9am-5pm Sat. **Credit** AmEx, MC, V.
Traditional formal wear for men.

## Fashion accessories

## Jewellery

### Harry Winston

*371 North Rodeo Drive, at Brighton Way, Beverly Hills (1-310 271 8554). Bus 4, 20, 21, 22, 320, DASH Beverly Hills/I-405, exit Wilshire Boulevard north.* **Open** 10am-5.30pm Mon-Fri; 10am-5pm Sat. **Credit** AmEx, DC, JCB, MC, V.
This is where the Oscar nominees get their shinies for the big night. It's been in business for over 100 years, supplying the rarest and finest diamonds, rubies, sapphires and emer-alds in traditional settings. Prices run from $800 to several million dollars for one piece.

### Michael Dawkins

*8649 Sunset Boulevard, between Horn Avenue & La Cienega Boulevard, West Hollywood (1-310 652 4964). Bus 2, 3, 429/I-10, exit La Cienega Boulevard north.* **Open** 10am-6pm Mon-Sat. **Credit** AmEx, MC, V.
Inventive local designer who works in silver and gold and seems to adore pearls.

### New Stone Age

*8407 West Third Street, at North Orlando Avenue, West Hollywood (1-213 658 5969). Bus 16, DASH Fairfax/I-10, exit La Cienega Boulevard north.* **Open** 11am-6pm Mon-Sat; noon-5pm Sun. **Credit** MC, V.
Hip jewellery from over 20 different designers, costing from $20 to $400. Also ceramics in a colourful, folky setting.

## Lingerie

### Frederick's of Hollywood

*6608 Hollywood Boulevard, at Schroeder Avenue, Hollywood (1-213 466 8506/1-800 323 9525). Bus 1, 26, 310, DASH Hollywood/US101, exit Hollywood Boulevard west.* **Open** 10am-6pm Mon-Thur; 10am-9pm Fri; 10am-6pm Sat; noon-5pm Sun. **Credit** AmEx, Disc, MC, V.
This legendary store has survived earthquakes, riots and even the subsidence caused recently by the building of the Metro subway. Don't forget to visit the Celebrity Lingerie Hall of Fame in the back.

### Heidi Wear

*1247 Third Street Promenade, between Wilshire Boulevard & Arizona Avenue, Santa Monica (1-310 394 7488). Bus 20, 320, 322, Santa Monica 2, 3, 8, 9/I-10, exit Fourth-Fifth Street north.* **Open** 11am-9pm Mon-Fri; 11am-11pm Sat, Sun. **Credit** MC, V.
Was a service, is now a shop. Madame Heidi Fleiss has turned her designs to boxers, T-shirts, sweat pants and pyja-mas, all emblazoned with her name in 'real big red' letters.

### Pixie Town

*400 North Beverly Drive, at Brighton Way, Beverly Hills (1-213 272 6415). Bus 3, 4, 14, 20, 21, 22, DASH Beverly Hills/I-10, exit Robertson Boulevard north.* **Open** 10am-6pm Mon-Sat. **Credit** AmEx, MC, V.
Pricey designer clothing and shoes for upwardly mobile new-borns and kids up to age 15.

### Trashy Lingerie

*402 North La Cienega Boulevard, at Oakwood Avenue, West Hollywood (1-310 652 4543). Bus 14, 104/I-10, exit La Cienega Boulevard north.* **Open** 10am-7pm Mon-Sat. **Credit** MC, V.
Drew Barrymore and Elizabeth Berkley frequent this shop full of leather, lace, made-to-measure corsets and G-strings. You have to become a member to shop; it's to keep out the riff-raff and is only a formality.

## Shoes, luggage & repairs

### Artistic Shoe Repair

*9562 Dayton Way, at Rodeo Drive, Beverly Hills (1-310 271 1956). Bus 4, 20, 21, 22, 320/I-10, exit Robertson Boulevard north.* **Open** 8.30am-5.30pm Mon-Fri; 8.30am-3pm Sat. **No credit cards.**
John Yegeyan and Mike Shadoian have been repairing shoes for the Beverly Hills set for over 15 years.

### Beverly Hills Luggage

*404 North Beverly Drive, at Brighton Way, Beverly Hills (1-310 273 5885). Bus 4, 20, 27, DASH Beverly Hills/I-10, exit Robertson Boulevard north.* **Open** 9.30am-6pm Mon-Fri, Sun; 9.30am-5.30pm Sat. **Credit** AmEx, MC, V.
The store's over 100 years old, sells all the major brands of luggage and will repair anything you bring in.

*Opposite: Getting horny at* **Necromance**.
*See page 170.*

## Charles David

*The Beverly Center, 8500 Beverly Boulevard, at La Cienega Boulevard, West Hollywood (1-310 659 7110). Bus 14, 104/I-10, exit La Cienega Boulevard north.* **Open** 10am-9pm Mon-Fri; 10am-8pm Sat; 10am-6pm Sun. **Credit** AmEx, MC.

You can rely on this US shoe store that manufactures in Italy and Spain to provide an excellent selection of up-to-the-moment designs in a good array of colours and materials.

## Cole Haan

*Two Rodeo, 260 North Rodeo Drive, between Dayton Way & Wilshire Boulevard, Beverly Hills (1-310 859 7622). Bus 20, 21, 22/I-10, exit Wilshire Boulevard east.* **Open** 10am-7pm Mon-Sat; noon-5pm Sun. **Credit** AmEx, DC, JCB, MV, V.

Solidly traditional US designs to complete your uptown prep-pie look. Its signature loafers and moccasins have become quite a status symbol and are particularly popular in Australia and Germany.

## Delvaux

*8647 Sunset Boulevard, between La Cienega & San Vicente Boulevards, West Hollywood (1-310 289 8588). Bus 2, 3, 429/I-10, exit La Cienega Boulevard north.* **Open** 10am-6pm Mon-Sat. **Credit** AmEx, MC, V.

Exclusive, exclusive, exclusive. Founded in 1829, Delvaux was once the licensed supplier of quality luggage to the Belgian Court. It now makes scarfs, handbags, briefcases and gloves; this is its only US store and there is a feeding frenzy for its limited stock of haute couture designs.

## Kenneth Cole

*8752 Sunset Boulevard, between San Vicente & La Cienega Boulevards, West Hollywood (1-310 289 5085). Bus 2, 3, 105, 429, West Hollywood A, B/I-10, exit La Cienega Boulevard north.* **Open** 10am-7pm Mon-Thur, Sat; 10am-8pm Fri; noon-5pm Sun. **Credit** AmEx, MC, V.

This New York-based shoe company offers designer shoes, briefcases and outer wear at affordable prices. Outside the store are footprints in the concrete, including those of Richard Gere, Liz Taylor and Matthew Modine, and on their respective birthdays, 10 per cent of the shop's proceeds that day go to the star's choice of AIDS charity.

## Maraolo

*9546 Brighton Way, between Rodeo & Camden Drives, Beverly Hills (1-310 274 8181). Bus DASH Beverly Hills/I-10 exit Robertson Boulevard north.* **Open** 10am-6pm Mon-Sat; noon-5pm Sun. **Credit** AmEx, MC, V.

This Neopolitan company has its own line of shoes and handbags and also manufactures for Armani, Donna Karan and Polo Ralph Lauren.

## Richard's Luggage & Handbags

*1416 Third Street Promenade, between Santa Monica Boulevard & Broadway, Santa Monica (1-310 451 8539). Bus 4, 33, 333, Santa Monica 2, 3, 7/I-10, exit Fourth-Fifth Street north.* **Open** 10am-10pm Mon-Thur; 10am-11pm Fri, Sat; 11am-9pm Sun. **Credit** AmEx, Disc, MC, V.

Everything from small tote bags to hardwearing Xero Halliburton luggage. Repairs, too.

Film memorabilia

## Chick A Boom

*6817 Melrose Avenue, between Orange Drive & Mansfield Avenue, Melrose District (1-213 931 7441). Bus 10, 11/I-10, exit La Brea Avenue north.* **Open** 11am-6pm Mon-Sat. **Credit** AmEx, Disc, MC, V.

Toys, magazines, ads, movie posters and bumper stickers from the 1930s to the 1970s .

## Cinema Collectors

*1507 Wilcox Avenue, at Sunset Boulevard, Hollywood (1-213 461 6516). Bus 1, 163, 180, 181, 212, 217/US101, exit Fairfax Avenue south.* **Open** 10am-6pm Mon-Sat. **Credit** AmEx, MC, V.

Posters and photographs.

## Florists

To order flower deliveries in the US and internationally, call 1-800 736 3383.

## Campo dei Fiori

*648 Martel Avenue, between Clinton Street & Melrose Avenue, West Hollywood (1-213 655 9966). Bus 10, 11/I-10, exit Fairfax Avenue north.* **Open** 10am-8pm Mon-Fri; 10am-5pm Sat. **Credit** AmEx, MC, V.

Fashion-conscious florist selling everything from country-cottage garden arrangements with hydrangeas and wild roses to exotic tropicals.

## LA Flower Market

*754 Wall Street, between Seventh & Eighth Streets, Downtown (1-213 622 1966). Bus 10, 11, 20, 21, 22, 48, 51, DASH D/I-110, exit Ninth Street east.* **Open** 8am-noon Mon, Wed, Fri; 6am-noon Tue, Thur, Sat.

The smell is intoxicating and the bustle of the city's retailers buying their blooms at wholesale prices is worth the trip. From midnight to dawn.

## The Woods

*11711 Gorham Avenue, between San Vicente Boulevard & Barrington Avenue, Brentwood (1-310 826 0711). Bus 22, 322, Santa Monica 3, 14/I-405, exit Wilshire Boulevard west.* **Open** 8am-8pm Mon-Thur; 8am-9pm Fri, Sat; 9am-7pm Sun. **Credit** AmEx, MC, V.

A spectacular contemporary florist. All the arrangements are an expression of the beauty of all things growing – not just flowers, but fruit, vegetables and herbs, too. Meg Ryan favours the luscious garden roses, grown especially for the store; John Travolta likes to buy arrangements flowing in customised silver treasure chests; and Jim Belushi is always using The Woods to express his thanks to various women in his world.

## Food & drink

### Bakeries

## Mani's Bakery

*519 South Fairfax Avenue, between Fifth & Sixth Streets, Park La Brea (1-213 938 8800). Bus 217/I-10, exit Fairfax Avenue north.* **Open** 6.30am-midnight Mon-Thur; 6.30am-1am Fri; 7.30am-1am Sat; 7.30am-midnight Sun. **Credit** AmEx, Disc, MC, V.

Back-to-basics, hip bakery. They use only fruit juice to sweeten, and organic flour. You can sup coffee and cake (fat-free, of course) on the premises.

**Branches:** 8801 Santa Monica Boulevard, West Hollywood (1-310 659 5955); 2507 Main Street, Santa Monica (1-310 396 7700); 3960 Laurel Canyon Boulevard, Studio City (1-818 762 7200).

## Michel Richard

*310 South Robertson Boulevard, at Burton Way, Beverly Hills (1-310 275 5707). Bus 27, 220, 316, 576, DASH Fairfax/I-10, exit Robertson Boulevard north.* **Open** 8am-10pm Mon-Sat; 9am-4pm Sun. **Credit** AmEx, MC, V.

Munch warm, buttery croissants and slurp a lazy cappuccino at this patisserie's coveted sidewalk tables.

### Noah's Bagels

*200 South Beverly Drive, at Charleville Boulevard, Beverly Hills (1-310 550 7392). Bus 3/I-10, exit Robertson Boulevard north.* **Open** 6.30am-7pm Mon-Fri; 7am-6pm Sat, Sun. **No credit cards.**
Set to become the McDonald's of bagels, there a Noah's in almost every shopping area, selling a wild variety of bagels and some inventive smears.

### Sweet Lady Jane

*8360 Melrose Avenue, at Kings Road, West Hollywood (1-213 653 7145). Bus 10, 11/I-10, exit La Cienega Boulevard north.* **Open** 8.30am-11.30pm Mon-Sat. **Credit** AmEx, MC, V.
One of the best cake and dessert shops in town.

## Beer & wine

### Wally's

*2107 Westwood Boulevard, between Mississippi Avenue & Olympic Boulevard, West LA (1-310 475 0606). Bus Santa Monica 5, 8, 12/I-405, exit Santa Monica Boulevard east.* **Open** 9am-8pm Mon-Sat; 10am-6pm Sun. **Credit** AmEx, MC, V.
One of the best wine and beer stores in town, with a great selection of grappas, cognacs and single malts, and a full-service gourmet deli. Also gift baskets and delivery.

### Du Vin

*540 North San Vicente Boulevard, between Melrose & Rangely Avenues, West Hollywood (1-310 855 1161). Bus 10, 11, 105, 220, West Hollywood A, B/I-405, exit Santa Monica Boulevard east.* **Open** 10am-7pm Mon-Sat. **Credit** AmEx, MC, V.
If the monk sign is out on the street, Du Vin is open. Enter through a cobblestoned courtyard that seems more European than West Hollywood and through Du Vin's portals – it looks like someone's personal, albeit large wine cellar, full of sophisticated Italian, French and Californian wines. Renee and David will offer advice if needed.

## Farmers' markets

One of the joys of LA are the Farmers' Markets: a collection of (often organic) farmers selling fresh fruit and veg and purveyors of eggs, honey, jam, flowers, plants and fish, who set up stalls in a specially cordoned-off area. You should be able to find a market going on somewhere in the city on any given day of the week; two of the most notable are the Hollywood Farmers' Market on Ivar Street, between Hollywood Boulevard and Sunset Boulevard (8.30am-1pm Sun; 1-213 963 4151), and the Santa Monica Farmers' Market at the intersection of Arizona Avenue and Third Street (8.30am-noon Sat; 1-310 458 8712).

## Gourmet supermarkets

### Gelsons Market

*Century City Shopping Center, 10250 Santa Monica Boulevard, between Little Santa Monica & Constellation Boulevards, Century City (1-310 277 4288). Bus 22, 27, 28, 316, 328, Santa Monica 5, Commuter Express 534, 573/I-405, exit Santa Monica Boulevard east.* **Open** 9am-10pm Mon-Sat; 9am-9pm Sun. **Credit** AmEx, Disc, MC, V.
First-rate gourmet market. You dream it up, they deliver it. Other branches dotted around town include Marina del Rey, Pacific Palisades and the Valley.

### Trader Joe's

*7304 Santa Monica Boulevard, at Poinsettia Place, West Hollywood (1-213 851 9772). Bus 4, DASH Hollywood/ I-10, exit La Brea Avenue north.* **Open** 9am-9pm daily. **Credit** AmEx, Disc, V.
Angelenos swear by this market which sells many dry goods with a health bent and fantastic pre-packed meals at bargain prices. Many locations to choose from: call 1-800 746 7857, punch in your zip code and they'll tell you the nearest branch.

## Natural food stores

### Beverly Hills Juice Bar

*8382 Beverly Boulevard, at Orlando Avenue, Beverly Hills (1-213 655 8300). Bus 14/I-10, exit Robertson Boulevard north.* **Open** 8am-6.30pm Mon-Fri; 10am-6pm Sat.
**No credit cards.**
Wonderful fruits and veggies squeezed daily into delightful drinks to go. Combination drinks include hot tomato tonic and apple ginger drinks. Also smoothies and a dairy-free ice-cream called Banana Manna.

### Erewhon Natural Foods

*7660 Beverly Boulevard, at Stanley Avenue, Park La Brea (1-213 937 0777). Bus 14, DASH Fairfax/I-10, exit Fairfax Avenue north.* **Open** 9am-9pm Mon-Fri; 9am-8pm Sat, Sun. **Credit** Disc, MC, V.
Organic produce, grains, food supplements, cosmetics and a deli counter, but short on fresh chicken and fish.

### Wholefoods

*239 North Crescent Drive, between Clifton & Dayton Ways, Beverly Hills (1-310 274 3360). Bus 20, 21, 22, 320, 322, DASH Beverly Hills/I-10, exit Wilshire Boulevard east.* **Open** 9am-9pm daily. **Credit** AmEx, Disc, MC, V.
Arguably the best in natural gourmet food shopping. Great fish and meat counter.

## Speciality outlets

### Aristoff Caviar & Fine Foods

*321 North Robertson Boulevard, at Rosewood Avenue, West Hollywood (1-310 271 0576). Bus 14, 220/I-10, exit Robertson Boulevard north.* **Open** 9.30am-5pm Mon-Fri; 10am-noon Sat. **Credit** AmEx, DC, MC, V.
Purveyors of fine caviar: beluga and sevruga or American paddle fish, which savvy Jack Nicholson, not known for his extravagance, plumps for, at half the price.

### Beverly Hills Cheese Store

*Rodeo Collection, 421 Rodeo Drive, between Little Santa Monica Boulevard & Brighton Way, Beverly Hills (1-310 278 2855). Bus 4, 20, 21, 22, 320, DASH Beverly Hills/ I-10, exit Santa Monica Boulevard east.* **Open** 9.30am-6pm Mon-Sat. **Credit** AmEx, MC, V.
Every cheese known to man, fresh cornichons, olives, baguettes, foie gras, pâté and saucissons, wines and balsamic vinegars and olive oils housed in an old worldy setting, served by men in long blue pinnies.

### Divine Pasta Company

*615 North La Brea Avenue, between Clinton Street & Melrose Avenue, Park La Brea (1-213 939 1148). Bus 10, 11, 212/I-10, exit La Brea Avenue north.* **Open** 11am-8pm Mon-Sat. **Credit** AmEx, MC, V.
An extraordinary array of fresh pasta, home-made sauces, and all the things that accessorise them.

### Grand Central Market

*317 South Broadway, between Third & Fourth Streets, Downtown (1-213 624 2378). Metro Pershing*

Square/bus 1, 2, 4, 45, 92, 93, 345, 410, 418, Commuter Express 413, 423/I-110, exit Third Street east. **Open** 9am-6pm Mon-Sat; 10am-5pm Sun. **No credit**. Landmark bustling market that puts one in mind of a Moroccan bazaar. Great Latin American produce.

### Greenblatt's Delicatessen

*8017 West Sunset Boulevard, between Crescent Heights Boulevard & Laurel Avenue, West Hollywood (1-213 656 0606). Bus 1, 2, 3, 217, 302, 429/I-10, exit Fairfax Avenue north.* **Open** 9am-2am daily. **Credit** AmEx, MC, V.
Deli and wine shop with a small cafeteria-style eating area.

### Homarus Lox

*9340 West Pico Boulevard, between Edris & Beverly Drives, West LA (1-310 273 3004). Bus Santa Monica 7, 13/I-10, exit Robertson Boulevard north.* **Open** 10am-6pm Mon-Fri; 8am-6pm Sat; 8am-4pm Sun. **Credit** AmEx, MC, V.
The only outlet for this New York-based company, specialising in flavoured lox – lemon-dill, rosemary-mint and jalapeno-cilantro.

### Al Gelato

*806 South Robertson Boulevard, between Olympic Boulevard & Whitworth Drive, Beverly Hills (1-310 659 8069). Bus 28, 220, 328/I-10, exit Robertson Boulevard north.* **Open** 10am-midnight daily. **No credit cards**.
Forget Häagen-Dazs, this is ice-cream heaven: a wicked selection of intense and exotic flavours.

### Phil's Fish and Poultry

*11640 San Vicente Boulevard, at Barrington Avenue, Brentwood (1-310 820 5853). Bus 22, 322, Santa Monica 2, 3, 5/I-10, exit Wilshire Boulevard west.* **Open** 9am-6.30pm Mon-Fri; 9am-5.30pm Sat. **Credit** MC, V.
The best and most exotic fish and meat. Give them a day's notice for fresh bunnies, Muscovy ducks, whatever.

## Gifts & stationery

### Artissimo

*7378 Beverly Boulevard, at Martel & Fuller Avenues, West Hollywood (1-213 933 2778). Bus 14/I-10, exit La Brea Avenue.* **Open** noon-5.30pm Mon-Fri; noon-4pm Sat. **Credit** AmEx, MC, V.
Contemporary crafts in ceramic, glass, metal, wood and fibre, mainly by California designers.

### Geary's

*351 North Beverly Drive, between Dayton & Brighton Ways, Beverly Hills (1-310 273 4741). Bus 4, 20, 27, DASH Beverly Hills/I-405, exit Wilshire Boulevard east.* **Open** 10am-6pm Mon-Wed, Fri, Sat; 10am-8pm Thur. **Credit** AmEx, MC, V.
Important and expensive gifts come from Geary's: Baccarat, Wedgewood and Lalique.

### General Wax and Candle Company

*6863 & 6858 Beck Avenue, between Lankershim Boulevard & Van Owen Street, North Hollywood (1-818 765 5800). Bus 165/US101, exit Laurel Canyon Boulevard exit north.* **Open** 9am-5pm Mon-Fri; 9am-2pm Sat. **Credit** AmEx, MC, V.
Forget 12in tapers, the fanciful candles here might be in the shape of a baby's bottle, could smell like coffee and could be designed to float in your bathtub.

### Goat

*306 South Edinburgh Avenue, at West Third Street, Park La Brea (1-213 651 3133). Bus 16, 212, 316, DASH Fairfax/I-10, exit Fairfax Avenue north.* **Open** 11am-6pm daily. **Credit** MC, V.
An eclectic, fun gift store, for people with a bohemian bent.

### Hammacher Schlemmer

*309 North Rodeo Drive, between Brighton & Dayton Ways, Beverly Hills (1-310 859 7255). Bus 4, 20, 21, 22, 320, DASH Beverly Hills/I-10, exit Robertson Boulevard north.* **Open** 10am-6pm Mon-Wed, Fri, Sat; 10am-7pm Thur; noon-5pm Sun. **Credit** AmEx, DC, Disc, MC, V.
Hi-tech gadgetry and non-essential gift items for people with an excess of greenbacks – for example, the world's smallest camera and a posture feeder for dogs with back conditions.

### Necromance

*7220 Melrose Avenue, between Alta Vista Boulevard & Formosa Avenue, West Hollywood (1-213 934 8684). Bus 10, 11/I-10, exit La Brea Avenue north.* **Open** noon-7pm Mon-Thur; noon-8pm Fri, Sat; 1-7pm Sun. **Credit** MC, V.
Owner Nancy calls her gaff a natural history store. She sells animal and human skulls and bones, mounted insects, beetles and butterflies, jewellery made from teeth and bones, and antique medical and funerary tools and products.

### Panpipes Magickal Marketplace

*1641 Cahuenga Boulevard, between Selma Avenue & Hollywood Boulevard, Hollywood (1-213 462 7078). Bus 1, 163, 180, 181, 212/US101, exit Cahuenga Boulevard south.* **Open** 11am-7pm Mon-Sat. **Credit** MC, V.
LA's oldest full-service occult store, selling everything from voodoo dolls and mojo bags (for casting spells) to crystal balls. The place to visit if you want to improve your love life or your bank account.

### Planet Blue 1 & 2

*Malibu Country Mart, 3835 Cross Creek Road, off Pacific Coast Highway, Malibu (1-310 317 9964). Bus 434/I-10, exit PCH north.* **Open** 9.30am-6.30pm Mon-Fri; 9.30am-11pm Sat; 9.30am-7pm Sun. **Credit** AmEx, MC, V.
Two organic stores: one has everything to do with beds and beauty products and the other has organic clothes.

### The Pleasure Chest

*7733 Santa Monica Boulevard, between Genesee & Stanley Avenues, West Hollywood (1-213 650 1022). Bus 4, West Hollywood A, B/I-10, exit Fairfax Avenue north.* **Open** 10am-midnight Mon-Thur, Sun; 10am-12.45am Fri, Sat.* **Credit** AmEx, MC, V.
The best in naughty, erotic and X-rated toys, and said to be Madonna's favourite store. Worth a visit if only to view the limos parked in the lot and the oddly dressed folk inside.

### The Sharper Image

*9550 Santa Monica Boulevard, at Camden Drive, Beverly Hills (1-310 271 0515). Bus 4, 27, 304, DASH Beverly Hills/I-10, exit Santa Monica Boulevard east.* **Open** 10am-7pm Mon-Fri; 10am-6pm Sat; noon-5pm Sun. **Credit** AmEx, DC, Disc, MC, V.
Electronic gadgets and gifts for adults who already have everything: an $8,000 juke box that plays CDs, Bang & Olufsen stereos, and massage chairs.

### The Soap Plant/Wacko/Zulu

*7416 Melrose Avenue, at Martel Avenue, West Hollywood (1-213 651 5587). Bus 10, 11/I-10, exit La Brea Avenue north.* **Open** 11am-10pm Mon-Thur; 11am-midnight Fri, Sat; noon-7pm Sun. **Credit** AmEx, MC, V.
Something between an old-fashioned head shop, quirky gift store and magic shop. It's been around forever.

### Soolip

*8646 Melrose Avenue, at Norwich Drive, West Hollywood (1-310 360 0545). Bus 10, 11/I-405, exit Santa Monica Boulevard east.* **Open** 11am-7pm Mon-Sat; noon-5pm Sun. **Credit** MC, V.
Scented ink, exotic ribbons, notepaper made of bamboo, a huge array of cards, exquisite wrapping paper, a calligraphy service and wedding invitations printed on a letter press.

## Health & beauty

## Shops

### Fred Segal The Apothia

*8100 Melrose Avenue, at Crescent Heights Boulevard,
Melrose District (1-213 651 0239). Bus 10, 11, DASH
West Hollywood/I-10, exit Fairfax Avenue.* **Open** 10am-
7pm Mon-Sat; noon-6pm Sun. **Credit** AmEx, MC, V.
Part of the Fred Segal empire, this is a beauty paradise for
spoilt princesses, carrying a rainbow of skin, body and hair-
care products, including Kiehls, Jean Laporte, Comptoir Sud
Pacifique, Thymes Ltd and Molton Brown.

### Larchmont Beauty Centre

*208 North Larchmont Boulevard, at Beverly Boulevard,
Hancock Park (1-213 461 0162). Bus 14/I-10, exit La
Brea Avenue north.* **Open** 8.30am-7pm Mon-Sat. **Credit**
AmEx, MC, V.
Everything you could ever want to pretty yourself up:
high-end hair and skincare products by Decleor, Thymes
Ltd, JF Lazartigue and Neal's Yard as well as aromather-
apy products by Aroma Vera, Tisserand and Essential
Elements.

### Palmetto

*1034 Montana Avenue, between 10th & 11th Streets,
Santa Monica (1-310 395 6687). Bus 3, Santa Monica 3/I-
10, exit Lincoln Boulevard north.* **Open** 10am-6pm
Mon-Sat; noon-5.30pm Sat; 10am-5pm Sun. **Credit** AmEx,
MC, V.
This 18-year-old store can barely contain its vast stock of
wondrous, almost exclusively natural and sometimes hard-
to-find skin, hair and bodycare products.

### The Sharper Image Spa

*316 North Beverly Drive, between Wilshire Boulevard &
Dayton Way, Beverly Hills (1-310 273 7144). Bus 3, 20,
21, 22/I-405, exit Wilshire Boulevard east.* **Open** 10am-
7pm Mon-Fri; 11am-6pm Sat; noon-5pm Sun. **Credit**
AmEx, Disc, JCB, MC, V.
High-end goods to rejuvenate your mind and body and make
you look and feel good – from skincare products and aro-
matic candles to massage tables and exercise equipment.

## Hairdressers

### Art Lunar Salon

*8930 Keith Avenue, at Robertson Boulevard, West
Hollywood (1-310 247 1383). Bus 4/I-10, exit Robertson
Boulevard north.* **Open** 9am-6pm Tue-Sat. **Credit** MC, V.
Enter a quaint garden, dripping with exotic blooms, and go
through a white wooden door to a 1940s cottage. This is Art
Luna's workplace and, unlike most hair salons, is a tranquil
refuge. Angelica Huston, Michelle Pfeiffer and Winona
Ryder are among his loyal followers.

### Louis Licari Color Group

*450 North Canon Drive, between Santa Monica Boulevard
& Brighton Way, Beverly Hills (1-310 247 0855). Bus 3,
4, 14, 27, 304/I-10, exit Santa Monica Boulevard east.*
**Open** 8am-6pm Mon-Sat. **Credit** AmEx, MC, V.
Otherwise known as the King of Color, this New Yorker
who trained as a painter is now using his palette of colours
on women's hair. Natural light and white flowers abound
in his two-floor Beverly Hills salon, with a delightful small
terrace.

### The Magnificent Brothers

*4267 Crenshaw Avenue, between Stocker & West
43rd Street, Leimert Park (1-213 299 0223). Bus 42,
105, 210, 310, DASH Crenshaw, Leimert-Slauson/I-10,*
*exit Crenshaw Boulevard.* **Open** 9am-7pm Mon-Thur;
8am-8pm Fri, Sat. **No credit cards.**
Old-fashioned barber's specialising in African-American
hair. Come for the ambiance and to catch up on the local gossip as much as for a cut or shave.

### Pickford

*8940 Keith Avenue, at Robertson Boulevard, West
Hollywood (1-310 276 3926). Bus 4/I-10, exit Robertson
Boulevard north.* **Open** 9am-5pm Tue-Sat. **Credit** MC, V.
On the grounds of Mary Pickford's silent studio lot, hidden
amid trees, sits this low-profile salon, owned by Cornishman
Christopher Koch, one of Vidal Sassoon's myriad protégés.
Need a chop, see Christopher. Want a change of colour, book
with Nick Eastman.

### Prive

*8458 Melrose Place, at La Cienega Boulevard, West
Hollywood (1-213 651 5045). Bus 10, 11, 105, DASH
Fairfax/I-10, exit La Cienega Boulevard north.* **Open**
10am-4pm Mon; 9am-7pm Tue-Sat. **Credit** AmEx, MC, V.
Everything here starts with an 'L' for Eduardo Laurent. Even
the lampshades are imprinted with his stamp. And why not
– the Biarritz native is one of the best hairdressers in town.
He gave Melrose Place starlette Josie Bisset her gamine short
coiffe and tends Sophia Loren's locks. If you sit in front of
the famous Laurent long mirror, in his leopardskin chair, you
too can get imprinted with his inimitable style. Also request
Eduardo's customised organic scalp treatment, part science
and part his grandmother's secret recipe.

## Make-up artists

### The Cloutier Agency

*1026 Montana Avenue, between 10th & 11th Streets,
Santa Monica (1-310 394 8813). Bus 3, Santa Monica 3/
I-10, Lincoln Boulevard north.* **Open** 9am-5.30pm Mon-
Fri. **No credit cards.**
Some of Chantal Cloutier's top make-up artists, usually
booked out for several thousand dollars per day on com-
mercials and fashion shoots, are now available to paint your
face. Go glamour, girl!

## Manicure & pedicure

### Kimberly's Nails

*8046 West Third Street, at Crescent Heights Boulevard,
West Hollywood (1-213 653 5342). Bus 16, DASH
Fairfax/I-10, exit La Cienega Boulevard north.* **Open**
9am-10pm Mon-Sat; 10am-5pm Sun. **No credit cards.**
You can get a basic manicure and pedicure for $14, a full set
of acrylics for $25, wraps for $30 and the ever-popular French
manicure for $8. Ask for Christina.

## Massage

### Hamn's Rejuvenation Center

*8474 West Third Street, Suite 204, at La Cienega
Boulevard, Beverly Hills (1-213 966 4141). Bus 16,
DASH Fairfax/I-10, exit La Cienega Boulevard north.*
**Open** 9am-9pm daily. **Credit** AmEx, MC, V.
Experience the most uplifting 55 minutes in LA with the
blind Korean master of shiatsu massage, Suk Hamn. Follow
with a sizzling steambath, bracing body scrub.

### Kenny Nakaji

*1611 Montana Avenue, between 16th & 17th Streets,
Santa Monica (1-213 599 1935). Bus Santa Monica 3,
11/I-10, exit 26th Street north.* **Open** times vary. **No
credit cards.**
Open up your meridians and let chi flow freely with shiatsu-
anma massage and reflexology by Kenny Nakaji.

# Don't bogie that stogie

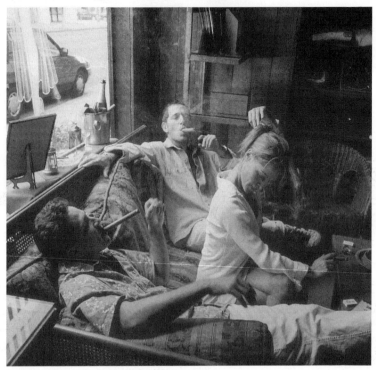

*Stoke up a smoke at **Philip Danes Cigar Lounge**.*

Despite California's stringent anti-smoking laws, there has been a revival of cigar culture, which involves sitting with a fine hand-rolled stogie, sipping cognac or single malt scotch and being all-round pretentious. **The Grand Havana Room** in Beverly Hills offers the ultimate in this experience, but unless you're tight with Jack (Nicholson) or Arnold (Schwarzenegger), you'll need a miracle to get into this members-only joint – and at $2,000 for a locker in the humidor, who really cares anyway? Some more realistic alternatives follow.

### Bloom's General Store

*714 Traction Avenue, at Hewitt Street, Downtown (1-213 687 6571). Bus 16, DASH A, Montebello 40/I-110, exit Fourth Street east.* **Open** 8am-11pm Mon-Thur, Sun; 8am-11.30pm Fri-Sat. **No credit cards.**
Quite possibly the coolest place in LA to fire up a stogie,

Bloom's carries over three dozen brands of hand-wrapped cigars, and even hosts a 'Cigar Night' (8pm Tuesdays).

### Hamilton's Wine Bar

*9713 Little Santa Monica Boulevard, between Linden & Roxbury Drives, Beverly Hills (1-310 278 0347). Bus 4, 27, 20, 21, 22/I-405, exit Santa Monica Boulevard east.* **Open** 4pm-2am Mon-Sat. **Credit** AmEx, MC, V.
A sartorial wine bar, where people come to schmooze, booze and cruise (and smoke some fine stogies).

### Philip Danes Cigar Lounge

*9669 Little Santa Monica Boulevard, between Roxbury & Bedford Drives, Beverly Hills (1-310 285 9945). Bus 4, 20, 21, 22, 27/I-405, exit Santa Monica Boulevard east.* **Open** 11am-2am Mon-Fri; noon-2am Sat; 9.30am-12.30am Sun. **Credit** AmEx, Disc, MC, V.
Hip, happening and unpretentious in Beverly Hills, with a cool humidor and nightly entertainment. Cute girls in mini-skirts provide helpful service with drinks and cigars. Harry Dean Stanton plays harmonica on Thursdays.

# Skin & body care

## Aida Thibiant's European Day Spa

*449 North Canon Drive, at Little Santa Monica Boulevard, Beverly Hills (1-310 278 7565). Bus 3, 4, 14, 27/I-405, exit Santa Monica Boulevard east.* **Open** 9am-6pm Mon-Wed, Fri, Sat; 9am-8pm Thur. **Credit** AmEx, Disc, MC, V.

An upscale, totally aesthetic experience. Purified air and an 18ft waterfall are some of the bonuses here, as well as the usual range of face and body treatments. You might run into Michelle Pfeiffer, Ali MacGraw or Rachel Hunter.

## Esthetica

*931½ North La Cienega Boulevard, between Santa Monica Boulevard & Waring Avenue, West Hollywood (1-310 659 5152). Bus 105/I-10, exit La Cienega Boulevard north.* **Open** 10am-6pm Mon-Wed, Fri, Sat; 10am-9pm Thur; and by appointment. **Credit** AmEx, MC, V.

In a secluded, quaint cottage above a garage, ex-model Brandy provides facials, body treatments (including herbal steam body wraps and bust treatments), waxing and tinting, for men and women.

## Georgette Klinger

*131 South Rodeo Drive, at Wilshire Boulevard, Beverly Hills (1-310 274 6347). Bus 3, 20, 21, 22/I-10, exit Robertson Boulevard north.* **Open** 9am-6pm Mon, Tue, Thur-Sat; 9am-8.30pm Wed. **Credit** AmEx, DC, MC, V.

It's pristine, well-designed without too many frills and professionally run without the sycophantic pandering which one comes to expect with Beverly Hills' beauty joints. Hell, Mrs Hilary Clinton likes it! There's a separate area for men.

# Spas

For more on spas and retreats further out of Los Angeles, *see chapter* **Trips out of Town**.

## Beverly Hot Springs

*308 North Oxford Avenue, between Oakwood & Beverly Boulevards, Mid-Wilshire (1-213 734 7000). Bus 14, 207, 357/I-10, exit Western Avenue north.* **Open** 9am-9pm daily. **Credit** AmEx, MC, V.

In the middle of the hurlyburly that is LA sits BHS, the city's only natural spring. Spend the day jumping from hot to cold baths, relaxing in a funky artificial grotto, steam rooms, massage rooms and facial rooms, or get the full body treatment – lie naked and be scrubbed, hosed down and anointed with milk and cucumber ($50 plus $3-$4 entrance).

## The Regent Beverly Wilshire

*9500 Wilshire Boulevard, between Rodeo & El Camino Drives, Beverly Hills (1-310 275 5200). Bus 3, 20, 21, 22/I-405, exit Wilshire Boulevard east.* **Open** 6am-9pm daily. **Credit** AmEx, Disc, MC, V.

This classic hotel has a delightful spa facility. As well as the usual run-of-the-mill manicure, facial and massage treatments, you can enjoy the gym, the patio deck with a pool (designed along the lines of Sophia Loren's in Italy), two hot tubs, heated at different temperatures, and a sauna. It's open to non-residents so long as you have a treatment.

# Sports trainer

## Xavier Carrica

*816 Westmount Drive, LA, CA 90069 (1-310 652 3712).* **Open** daily, by appointment only. **No credit cards.**

When Xavier's over-sized black Bronco truck shows up, you know you're in for one helluva workout. It's not that he eschews regular fitness instruction, it's more that he's willing to go out on a limb, and often out of the gym environment, to motivate his clients. He's been known to inspire scuba-diving, speed-cycling and kayaking to get his clients into shape. He's also a licensed sports masseur.

# Tattooing & body piercing

## Body Electric

*7274½ Melrose Avenue, at Poinsettia Place, Melrose District (1-213 954 0408). Bus 10, 11/I-10, exit La Brea Avenue north.* **Open** noon-8pm Wed-Sun. **Credit** AmEx, MC, V.

Riley Baxter is one of four tattoo artists that work out of this parlour above Angeli's Italian restaurant. Prices $45-$100.

## The Gauntlet

*8722 Santa Monica Boulevard, at Huntley Drive, West Hollywood (1-310 657 6677). Bus 4, 304/I-10, exit La Cienega Boulevard north.* **Open** noon-7pm Mon-Sat; noon-5pm Sun. **Credit** AmEx, MC, V.

Some claim this is one of the best body piercing facilities in the city. Prices start at $15.

# Household & furniture

## Crate & Barrel

*Century City Shopping Center, 10250 Santa Monica Boulevard, between Century Park West & Avenue of the Stars, Century City (1-310 551 1100). Bus 22, 27, 28, 316, 328, Santa Monica 5, Commuter Express 534, 573/I-405, exit Santa Monica Boulevard east.* **Open** 10am-9pm Mon-Fri; 10am-6pm Sat; 11am-6pm Sun. **Credit** AmEx, Disc, MC, V.

Home accessories so beautifully displayed you want 'em all.

## Diva

*8802 Beverly Boulevard, at Robertson Boulevard, West Hollywood (1-310 278 3191). Bus 14, 220/I-10, exit Robertson Boulevard north.* **Open** 9.30am-6pm Mon-Sat. **Credit** AmEx, MC, V.

High-style contemporary furnishings and accessories, especially light fixtures.

## Imagine That

*8906 Melrose Avenue, between Almont Drive & Santa Monica Boulevard, West Hollywood (1-310 247 1270). Bus 4, 10, 11/I-405, exit Santa Monica Boulevard east.* **Open** 10am-5.30pm Mon-Sat. **Credit** MC, V.

Custom-made children's furniture, so cute you yearn to buy it for yourself, regardless of the diminutive measurements.

## Shabby Chic

*1013 Montana Avenue, between 10th & 11th Streets, Santa Monica (1-310 394 1975). Bus Santa Monica 3/I-10, exit Lincoln Boulevard north.* **Open** 10am-6pm Mon-Sat; noon-5pm Sun. **Credit** AmEx, MC, V.

Furniture and accessories that are a hybrid of English countryside and California beach, with a client list that includes Bruce Springsteen and Tracey Ullman.

## Williams Sonoma

*317 North Beverly Drive, between Brighton & Dayton Ways, Beverly Hills (1-310 274 9127). Bus 4, 20, 27, DASH Beverly Hills/I-10, exit Robertson Boulevard north.* **Open** 10am-6pm Mon-Fri; 10am-8pm Thur; 10am-6.30pm Sat; noon-5pm Sun. **Credit** AmEx, Disc, MC, V.

Fabulous upscale kitchen accessories almost – but not quite – too good looking to use.

## Musical instruments

### The Guitar Center
*7425 Sunset Boulevard, between North Martel Avenue & North Vista Street, Hollywood (1-213 874 1060). Bus 2, 3, 429/I-10, exit La Brea Avenue north.* **Open** 10am-9pm Mon-Fri; 10am-6pm Sat; 11am-6pm Sun. **Credit** AmEx, Disc, MC, V.
Most musical instruments and vintage guitars.

## Opticians

### Joe Roberts Optical
*3507 West Magnolia Avenue, between Avon & Cordova Streets, Burbank (1-818 842 0666). Bus 163, 183/ SR134, exit Pass Avenue north.* **Open** 9am-5pm Tue-Fri; 9am-noon Sat. **No credit cards.**
Dispensing optician, custom gold soldering and difficult repairs. Often you can have your specs back the same day.

### Oliver Peoples
*8642 Sunset Boulevard, at Sunset Plaza, West Hollywood (1-310 657 2553). Bus 2, 3, 429/I-10, exit Sunset Boulevard north.* **Open** 10am-7pm Mon-Fri; 10am-6pm Sat. **Credit** AmEx, MC, V.
A candy store of machine age inspired opthalmic frames and full-service opticians. Designs by Paul Smith, Elton John and Ollie Peoples (for children) plus one-of-a-kind vintage frames.

## Pets

### The Clip Joint
*348 North La Cienega Boulevard, between Beverly Boulevard & Oakwood Avenue, West Hollywood (1-310 289 1729). Bus 14, 104/I-10, exit La Cienega Boulevard north.* **Open** 8am-4.30pm Tue-Sat and by appointment. **No credit cards.**
All-purpose grooming joint for pets.

### The Limehouse Vetinary Clinic
*10742 Camarillo Street, between Cartwright & Vineland Avenues, North Hollywood (1-818 761 0787). Bus 152, 166, 420/SR134, exit Vineland Avenue north.* **Open** 9am-1pm, 2pm-6pm, Mon-Thur; 9am-1pm Fri; and by appointment. **Credit** MC, V.
Holistic vets, whatever next. Acupuncture, homeopathy, herbals and musculo-skeletal manipulation is what pets flock here for, but there's a three-month waiting list.

### The Kennel Club
*5325 West 102nd Street, between Aviation Boulevard & Concourse Way, LAX District (1-310 338 9166). Bus 117/I-405, exit SR42 (Manchester Boulevard) west.* **Open** 8am-6pm Mon-Fri; 8am-2pm Sat; noon-6pm Sun. **Credit** AmEx, Disc, MC, V.
Upmarket kennels. Services include limo drop-off and pick-up, pool time (aka 'yappy hour'), customised theme cottages with names like Gone with the Wind and Country Farm, with (of course) TVs. Your dog will never want to come home again.

## Records, tapes & CDs

### A-1 Record Finders
*5639 Melrose Avenue, at Larchmont Boulevard, Hollywood (1-213 732 6737). Bus 10, 11, 210, 310, 426/US101, exit Melrose Avenue west.* **Open** noon-6pm Mon-Sat. **Credit** AmEx, MC, V.
A-1 will scour the earth for your hard-to-find penchant, but only on vinyl. Of course, they may already have it in stock.

### Tower Records
*8801 West Sunset Boulevard, at Horn Avenue, West Hollywood (1-310 657 7300). Bus 2, 3, 429/I-10, exit La Cienega Boulevard north.* **Open** 9am-midnight daily. **Credit** AmEx, MC, V.
It's an institution, but the last few times we went in search of nothing too obscure, they were out of stock, and we were forced to flee to the nearby Virgin Megastore.

### Virgin Megastore
*8000 Sunset Boulevard, at Crescent Heights Boulevard, West Hollywood (1-213 650 8666). Bus 2, 3, 217, 302, 429/I-10, exit La Cienega Boulevard north.* **Open** 9am-midnight Mon-Thur, Sun; 9am-1pm Fri, Sat. **Credit** AmEx, Disc, MC, V.
Richard Branson proves himself once again. Not only well-stocked sections from soul to classical, an in-house DJ, easy access and free parking but a whole floor dedicated to movies, videos, laserdiscs and computer games.

## Sports & adventure

### Adrenalin
*131 Broadway, between First & Second Streets, Santa Monica (1-310 260 1440). Bus 20, 22, 33, 320, 322, 434, Santa Monica 1, 7, 10/I-10, exit Fourth-Fifth Street north.* **Open** 11am-8pm daily. **Credit** AmEx, JCB, MC, V.
Surfwear by Billabong, Rusty and Gotcha; skatewear by Girl, World Industries and Chocolate; snowboarding wear by Avalanche and Division 23; and street fashion by Kik Wear, BC Ethic, Counter Culture and Split. They also carry the hard goods for these sports.

### Adventure 16
*11161 West Pico Boulevard, between Sepulveda Boulevard & I-405, West LA (1-310 473 4574). Bus Santa Monica 7, Culver City 6/I-10, exit Overland Boulevard north.* **Open** 10am-8pm Mon-Fri; 10am-6pm Sat; 10am-6pm Sun. **Credit** AmEx, MC, V.
The best outward bound store in the city. Helpful staff cater for your every camping need, and there's a great selection of travel books.

### Sports Chalet
*920 Foothill Boulevard, at Angeles Crest Highway, La Canada Flintridge (1-818 790 9800). Bus Foothill Transit 187/I-210, exit Angeles Crest Highway north.* **Open** 9.30am-7pm Mon-Fri; 10am-7pm Sat; 10am-6pm Sun. **Credit** AmEx, MC, V.
You have to change freeways maybe three times, but it's only 25 minutes from Downtown LA in good traffic and is worth every one of them, because this is the ultimate sports store. Diving, mountaineering, boating – whatever your sport, Sports Chalet has the goods. Branches in West Hollywood and Marina del Rey.

## Ticket agencies

### Absolut Tickets
*129 North Larchmont Boulevard, between First Street & Beverly Boulevard, Hancock Park, (1-213 957 6699). Bus 14/I-10, exit La Brea Avenue north.* **Open** 9am-6.30pm Mon-Fri; 10am-5pm Sat. **Credit** AmEx, Disc, MC, V.
These guys sell tickets for sports, concerts and theatre events. They usually have the first 15 rows in the house.

*Opposite: Staff at **Body Electric** have designs on your skin. See page 173.*

*Festive flora at the* **LA Flower Market.** *See page 168.*

## Toys

*See also chapter* **Children.**

### Toys-R-Us

*402 Santa Monica Boulevard, at Fourth Street, Santa Monica (1-310 451 1205). Bus 4, Santa Monica 1, 2, 3, 7, 8/I-10, exit Fourth Street north.* **Open** *9.30am-9.30pm Mon-Sat; 10am-7pm Sun.* **Credit** *AmEx, Disc, MC, V.*
One of the largest branches of this toy store chain. There are others in Culver City (1-310 398 5775) and West Hollywood (1-310 558 1831).

### FAO Schwarz

*Beverly Center, 8500 Beverly Boulevard, at La Cienega Boulevard, West Hollywood. Bus 14, 104/I-10, exit La Cienega Boulevard north.* **Open** *10am-9pm Mon-Fri; 11am-8pm Sat; 11am-6pm Sun.* **Credit** *AmEx, Disc, MC, V.*
The famous New York toy store.

## Travel agents

### Travel 21

*1108 Abbot Kinney Boulevard, at Westminster Avenue, Venice (1-310 399 9137). Bus Santa Monica 2/I-10, exit Lincoln Avenue south.* **Open** *9am-6pm Mon-Fri; 11am-3pm Sat.* **Credit** *AmEx, MC, V.*
All-purpose travel company. No fuss, no special service, but they'll work hard to find the bargains. We recommend Jodine.

## Video rental

To find out your nearest branch of the ubiquitous Blockbuster chain, call 1-800 800 6767.

### Vidiots

*302 Pico Boulevard, at Third Street, Santa Monica (1-310 392 8508). Bus Santa Monica 1, 2, 3, 7, 8/I-10, exit Lincoln Boulevard north.* **Open** *10am-11pm Mon-Thur, Sun; 10am-midnight Fri, Sat.* **Credit** *AmEx, Disc, MC, V.*
Foreign and hard-to-find stuff plus regular commercial fare.

### Rocket Video

*726 North La Brea Avenue, between Melrose & Waring Avenues, Hollywood (1-213 965 1100). Bus 10, 11, 212/I-10, exit La Brea Avenue north.* **Open** *11am-10pm Mon-Thur, Sun; 11am-11pm Fri, Sat.* **Credit** *AmEx, MC, V.*
The cinephile's video store: Rocket is likely to have that obscure masterpiece when no one else does.

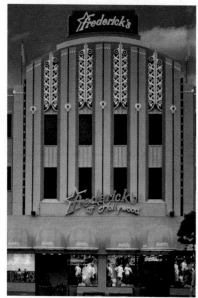

*Legendary lingerie at* **Frederick's,** *p166.*

# "Cygnet"

36" x 46"

## Sunny Leigh Designs
270 Lafayette Street 1206
New York, NY 10012
212-219-1493

# Arts & Entertainment

| | | | |
|---|---|---|---|
| Media | **180** | Film | **199** |
| Active LA | **184** | Museums & Galleries | **205** |
| Comedy | **193** | Music | **212** |
| Dance Clubs | **195** | Theatre & Dance | **221** |

# Media

**It's a fast-moving city, and if you're not in touch, you'll be left behind. Here's all you need to know to turn on and tune in.**

## Newspapers & magazines

Los Angeles, for the most part, is not an excessively literate town; part of the problem is that most travelling is by car rather than public transport. Where citizens of San Francisco, Chicago and New York do much of their newspaper and magazine reading while commuting, Angelenos tend to get most of their information from television and radio. Films, of course, occupy the highest echelon of all LA-based media. Given the sheer number of actors, directors, producers and screenwriters running around this town, it makes a twisted sort of sense that whatever happens on the big screen is much more important than the news of the day – unless the news of the day happens to be a local disaster.

For information on specialist business publications, *see chapter* **Business**, and for gay magazines, *see chapter* **Gay & Lesbian**.

## Dailies

With the demise of the *Herald Examiner* a few years ago and the *Free Press* many years before that, the **Los Angeles Times** (35¢) is secure in its position as the only major daily newspaper in town. While extensive in its coverage of worldwide and local events, this centrist publication's lack of estimable competition is evident in its unbelievably sloppy editing and fact-checking; you can amuse yourself for hours playing 'Spot the Typo'. The paper's Calendar section devotes a lot of space to arts coverage, with a predictable emphasis on Hollywood films, while its music coverage is strictly middle-of-the-road.

The **Wall Street Journal** (75¢) and **New York Times** ($1) are both widely available, while the **Washington Post** ($1.85) can be harder to track down. For British newspapers, head for the newsstand on Santa Monica's Third Street Promenade (*see below* **Outlets**). A myriad foreign-language dailies – including **La Opinion** (25¢), published in LA and the largest Spanish newspaper in the country – are also available at newsstands and drop-boxes throughout the city.

## Free weeklies

To get a sense of what's actually going on in Los Angeles on any given week, the city's free weeklies are your best bet, and you can pick them up at just about every magazine stand, bookshop or record store in the city. The **LA Weekly**, which belongs to the same company that owns New York's *Village Voice*, offers a *Voice*-like combination of dreadfully PC features (read by few) and detailed arts listings (read by everyone). As most of the city's live music venues advertise in the paper's music section, the *Weekly* remains *the* publication to pick up when planning an evening of club (or theatre or gallery) hopping.

Newest on the scene is the **New Times Los Angeles**, one in a series of 'alternative' weeklies published by the Phoenix, Arizona-based corporation New Times Inc, which generated a lot of local bad will in 1996 when it gutted weeklies the *LA Reader* and Westwood's *Village View* to make way for its new recruit. Avoid, if only to protest the continuing corporate zombification of the American media.

**Entertainment Weekly**, a sort of a bargain-basement *People Magazine*, is also available on newsstands free of charge. Also worth mentioning is **BAM**, a free music magazine published twice monthly. While the nature of its publishing schedule means that its listings are usually somewhat outdated, *BAM* is filled with profiles of up-and-coming local bands, which makes it of interest to anyone looking to get a whiff of LA rock'n'roll.

## Tabloid weeklies

If celebrity sightings are your thang, you would do well to pick up one of the many weekly gossip magazines that reside next to the cash registers at grocery stores. Although the focus isn't strictly local, and the stories can be somewhat dubious, they often reveal helpful clues as to the latest Tinseltown hotspots. For instance, even if George Clooney and Sandra Bullock weren't actually 'spotted on a date' at a certain Sunset Strip bistro, the mention of said eatery usually means that it's a happening place for watching famous folks, and that commandeering a table there might just provide a bonanza of star sightings – provided you can get a table, of course. Of the many tabloids, **The Star** ($1.29) is definitely the most Hollywood-intensive, and usually the most accurate; during the OJ Simpson murder trial, it regularly broke related stories weeks ahead of the *LA Times*.

*Read all about it at* **World Book & News**.

The mother of them all is **World Book & News** at 1652 North Cahuenga Boulevard, at Hollywood Boulevard, Hollywood (1-213 465 4352); nearly a full city block in length, the stand matches its overwhelming selection of international periodicals with an equally overwhelming selection of paperback books, including the entire published oeuvre of ghetto novelist Iceberg Slim.

On the Westside, a plethora of publications can be found at the newsstand on **Third Street Promenade**, at Arizona Avenue.

## Monthlies

**Buzz** ($3) is the hippest of the city's monthly mags (it also has a weekly supplement, available from Virgin Megastores). While offering the same sort of celebrity profiles that are every mainstream LA publication's bread and butter, *Buzz* at least features some talented regular columnists – and the magazine's restaurant, club and events listings can be handy in a pinch. The venerable **Los Angeles** ($2.95) is also undergoing a makeover, having been purchased by Cities, and is attempting to position itself as the West Coast's answer to *Vanity Fair* and the *New Yorker* rolled into one. **Venice** ($1.50) is a lower-budget composite of *Buzz* and *Los Angeles*, but with better coverage of what's going on in its titular 'hood.

## Outlets

Considering that no one here actually seems to read, Los Angeles has a surprising number of newsstands. One of the best is the stand outside West Hollywood's **Book Soup** bookstore at 8818 Sunset Boulevard (1-310 659 3110), which carries an impressive array of US, British and French periodicals. **Circus of Books**, 4001 Sunset Boulevard, at Sanborn Avenue, Silver Lake (1-213 666 1304), also stocks just about whatever you require.

## Television

You want to watch *television*? Are you kidding? Let's face it: if you've seen American television before, LA television isn't going to offer much in the way of anything new. Certainly, the argument could be made that, if you can only truly understand Homer by reading him in Greece, then you can only fully comprehend *Baywatch* or *CHiPS* by watching them in Los Angeles, even though television here generally sticks to the same mind-rotting morning-news-into-game-show-into-soap-opera-into-chat-show-into-evening-news-into-evening-soap-opera mantra as it does in the rest of the country. If, however, you can't get through the day without bathing in cathode rays, there are plenty of channels to keep you off the streets.

For comprehensive information about what's on the box, pick up the ever-popular **TV Guide** ($1.19), which has a handy table telling you which channel each cable station can be found on. The *LA Times* also prints daily TV listings.

### The Networks

Like most American cities, Los Angeles has affiliates of the three major networks: **CBS** (KCBS, channel 2), **NBC** (KNBC, channel 4) and **ABC** (KABC, channel 7). The top three are being given a serious run for their ratings by **Fox TV** (KTTV, channel 11), and the fledgling **Warner Brothers** network (KTLA, channel 5) is also beginning to chip away at their respective hold on Angelenos.

Some of the more popular programmes include news shows *60 Minutes* (CBS, 7pm Sun), *Today* (NBC, 7am Mon-Fri) and *Good Morning America* (ABC, 7am Mon-Fri); comedies *The Nanny* (CBS, 8pm Mon), *Friends* (NBC, 8pm Thur) and Seinfeld (NBC, 9pm Thur); and the late-night chat shows of David Letterman (CBS, 11.30pm Mon-Fri) and Jay Leno (NBC, 11.30 Mon-Fri). *The X-Files* appears on Fox, 9pm Fri. (Times, of course, may change.)

### Cable TV

Although watching cable television requires a monthly fee, many Angelenos subscribe as a means of improving both reception and choice of programmes. At present, there are 38 cable channels (with more planned), including **CRT** (Court TV, showing live trial footage; **ESPN** (sports); **CNN** (24-hour quality international news coverage); the **Discovery Channel** (anthropological and zoological documentaries); and the **Home Shopping Network** – which enables you to order ugly jewellery and useless appliances from the privacy of your own home. Public access cable features anything from religious puppet shows to experimental films.

The problem is that, due to a lack of regulation, different cable companies provide different services to different neighbourhoods, resulting in a confusing state of affairs: channel 43 may be MTV in your neighbourhood, but it could be the Disney Channel on the other side of town. Some cable networks, such as **Comedy Central** (24-hour comedy), **E! Entertainment Television** (a pop- culture mix of celebrities and movie news) or the **Sci-Fi Channel**, are limited to half-day programming (or aren't aren't available at all) in various parts of the city, and each cable company publishes a different monthly schedule.

Most hotels worth their nightly rates offer cable as a standard feature, but if your room doesn't have a copy of your neighbourhood's cable guide, your best bet, sorry to say, is to do your best with a copy of *TV Guide* or to channel-surf until you find what you're looking for.

## Public TV

**KCET** (channel 28) is Los Angeles' local Public Broadcasting Service affiliate, providing all the ponderous, self-important programming we've come to expect from public television. Now that the government has almost completely slashed PBS funding, the ungodly fundraisers seem to occur even more frequently than before.

## Tapings

It's often much more interesting to watch a show being recorded than to watch the show itself on TV, though you should bear in mind that a half-hour sitcom can sometimes take up to five hours to complete. Free tickets for tapings can be obtained at **CBS Television City** (7800 Beverly Boulevard, Fairfax, 1-213 852 2624); **NBC Television Studios** (3000 West Alameda Avenue, at Olive Avenue, Burbank, 1-818 840 3537); **Fox Television Center** (1999 South Bundy Drive, at La Grange Avenue, West LA, 1-310 584 2000); and **Paramount Television Studios** (860 North Gower Street, Hollywood, 1-213 956 5575).

**Audience Associates** (1-213 467 4697) and **Audiences Unlimited** (1-818 753 3470) also provide tickets for tapings, so give them a call, too.

## Radio

Although the city has long been a major player in the history of American music, Los Angeles' present radio situation is pretty dire. With the decline of heavy metal as LA's chief musical export, most of the city's rock stations have become clones of each other, rotating an ever-shrinking playlist of so-called alternative bands and puerile tag-team morning shows in an attempt to curry favour with the 18-25 demographic of MTV viewers. Limited mostly to right-wing blowhards, the local talk radio is more entertaining, if not particularly inspiring (*see box* **LA Talk radio**). A great many Angelenos seem to listen to the radio solely for traffic reports, which you can hear at regular intervals on almost every station during the morning and evening rush hours.

## Classical

**KUSC-FM 91.5**, **KCSN-FM 88.5** and **KKGO -FM 105.1** – while not strictly round-the-clock classical – all offer the music of dead European males on a regular basis. KUSC's Schickele Mix, (6-7pm, Sun), is hosted by Peter 'PDQ Bach' Shickele and is highly recommended.

## Jazz

On the off-chance that you're spending a Friday evening by the radio, **KLON-FM 88.1**'s Jazz on the Latin Side, hosted by Jose Rizo, will have you samba-ing in your seat from 8pm to midnight. **KCLU-FM 88.3**, **KPCC-FM 89.3** and **KCRW-FM 89.9** also feature jazz in various time slots.

## Dance & hip-hop

LA's two major dance and hip-hop stations are **KKBT-FM 92.3** and **KPWR-FM 106.3**; the latter sticks to more of a hits-based playlist while the former gravitates towards harder and deeper grooves. Unlike most local stations, both insert a high percentage of local acts and artists into their daily rotation.

## Rock & pop

**KROQ-FM 106.7** is probably the most influential alternative rock station in America; when they add a song to their playlist, similarly formatted stations across the country follow suit. Check out Rodney Bingenheimer's Rodney on the ROQ show (10pm-1am, Sun) for a highly enjoyable mix of American indie, Britpop and classic punk. **KSCA-FM 101.9** specialises in 'adult alternative' music, which means it's a good place to hear the talented likes of kd lang, Lyle Lovett and Elvis Costello. **KLOS-FM 95.5** is the place to turn to for your daily dose of grunge, while **KIIS-FM 102.7** is doubtless a godsend to the city's Mariah Carey fans. **KACE-FM 103.9** rolls out a wide array of soul and funk hits from the 1960s and 1970s; **KBIG-FM 104.3** and **KRLA-AM 1110** spin pop oldies from the 1950s and 1960s; and **KOST-FM 103.5** serves up anthems of co-dependency for all you lovers out there.

## College & public radio

Loyola Marymount's **KXLU-FM 88.9** provides noisy and nice indie sounds, although its weak signal can make it hard to find. USC's **KUSC-FM 91.5** features heavy doses of classical and talk, while public stations **KCRW-FM 89.9**, **KPFK-FM 90.7** and **KPCC-FM 89.3** serve up the usual eclectic mix of talk shows, news, world music, alternative rock, jazz and classical.

Supported by a dedicated subscriber audience KCRW is the standout public radio station, featuring excellent news programming and original music shows. Morning Becomes Eclectic (9am-noon, Mon-Fri), is especially popular with the Westside's yuppie contingent; host Chris Douridas has been described as the American John Peel, although he falls short of Mr Peel's wit or depth of knowledge. However, Jason Bentley, whose Metropolis show airs on KCRW at 8pm Mon, Wed-Fri, is *the* LA DJ for cutting-edge dance music from around the world.

## Internet sites

### http://www.at-la.com
Hooks you up with an enormous guide to LA-related websites. With over 7,000 links in 1,000 categories at last check, it's a good place to start.

### http://artscenecal.com/index.html
A comprehensive guide to what's on view in the area's galleries and museums.

### http://www.ladining.com
Feeling hungry? Then browse here for LA restaurant listings by cuisine and location.

### http://www.campgrounds.com/ctpa/ca /ca.htm
A handy guide to good camping spots (for both tents and RVs) throughout California.

### http://www.latimes.com/home/destLA /beaches2/
Is the surf up? Is the sun out? Has your beach of choice been closed due to shark attacks? Find out at the *LA Times'* beach guide website.

### http://felix.scvnet.com:80/~highlites/ grim/
The Los Angeles Grim Society's website, 'dedicated to the least savoury aspects' of local history and lore, is the place to go if the names Fatty Arbuckle, John Holmes and Angelyne mean anything to you.

# Los Angeles talk radio

Despite the popularity of car phones, French elocution tapes and Dove AudioBooks, talk radio is the real LA rush-hour experience. The more abundant and entrenched of LA talk radio is still of Conservative mettle: despite the post-Oklahoma City backlash against right-wing radio, talkmeisters **Bob Heckler** (9am-noon Mon-Fri, KMPC-AM 710), **Bill 'The Man' Handel** (5am-9am Mon-Fri, KFI-AM 640), and **Rush 'The Fat Idiot' Limbaugh** (9am-noon Mon-Fri, KFI-AM 640) continue to deliver their dubious blend of fear-mongering and vaudeville – albeit with tamer tongues.

A more moderate sage is **Larry Elder** (3-7pm Mon-Fri, KABC-AM 709), who is black, conservative and determined to return a bit of dignity and intelligence to drive-time 'politalk' (for roundtable discussions on affirmative action, he consults his mother). For the more liberal, pipe-smoking contingent, there's urbane, British-bred **Michael Jackson** (9am-noon, Mon-Fri KABC-AM 790), or the gracious **Warren Olney**, whose 'Which Way LA?' (1-2pm Mon-Fri, KCRW-FM 89.9) is probably the best issues-forum radio program in California. In more limited doses, there's victims'-rights

lawyer/OJ Simpson nemesis and tireless self-promoter **Gloria Allred** (7-9pm Sun KABC-AM 790), and even the fringe ramblings of former 'Gov. Moonbeam' **Jerry Brown** (4-5pm Mon-Fri, KPFK-FM 90.7). But if you are truly attracted to the perversity, cruelty, and cynicism of American shock radio then 'King of All Media' **Howard Stern** (6-10am Mon-Fri, KSLX-FM 97.1) and his smeared-carbon-copy competition, **The Mark and Brian Show** (6-10am Mon-Fri, 95.5 KLOS-FM), deliver in droves; however, we urge you to take the high road and punch up **The Tilden and Minyard Show** (5am-9am Mon-Fri, KABC-AM 790), which would sound like a couple of white guys (they are) sittin' around reading the newspapers (they do) – except that Peter Tilden is downright hilarious. And Tilden's ex-partner, husky-voiced, 'recovering Catholic' **Tracey Miller** (5.30-9am Mon-Fri, KMPC-AM 710), offers incisive deconstructions of current events that don't leave such a bad taste in your mouth.

If straight news is what you're after, **KNX-AM 1070**, **KFWB-AM 980**, **KNNS-AM 1260** and **KNNZ-AM 540** all offer 24-hour, up-to-the-minute coverage.

# Active LA

***Its considerable natural resources, plus the desire to be the fittest and the thinnest, make LA the perfect place for outdoor – and indoor – pursuits.***

## The great outdoors

Angelenos are spoilt by the natural resources on their doorstep, and they use their beaches, marinas and mountains with enthusiasm and imagination. Whatever trips your wire, from climbing to wind skating, walking to snowboarding, you can bet you'll find somewhere to do it here.

## Adventure games

LA is home to many, let's say, alternative sports. These include anything from war games to virtual reality to bungee jumping. Make sure you bring a friend as a witness, otherwise no one back home will believe you.

### Close Encounters

*22400 The Old Road, Newhall (1-805 255 5332/24-hour infoline 1-213 656 9179). I-5, exit Roxford Street west.* **Rates** $30-$60. Call for opening times.
You play paintball on the 60-acre main field, which can accommodate up to 300 people; private parties can rent one of the three other fields. Individuals and groups are welcome and equipment rental and instruction are provided.

### Gamesmith

*PO Box 2133, El Segundo, CA 90245 (1-310 322 0924). Contact Jeff Siadek (1-310 322 0924/E-mail: Jsiadek@ delphi.com).*
These unusual role-playing games require groups of at least 8-20 people. The play involves a whodunnit mystery in a vast array of genres (eg sci-fi, Casablanca, Wall Street). The whole game takes about 90 minutes and costs anywhere from $100-$200. Jeff Siadek provides the props and location (if required). Individuals can join scheduled groups.

### Laser Storm

*22535 Hawthorne Boulevard, at Sepulveda Boulevard, Torrance (1-310 373-8470). Bus 444, Torrance Transit 2, 4, 7, 8, 9/I-405, exit Hawthorne Boulevard south.* **Open** 3-10pm Mon-Thur; 3pm-midnight Fri; 10am-midnight Sat; 10am-10pm Sun.
Laser Tag is a convenient alternative to paintball. Most people play as individuals in a room that holds up to 25 people. Each person is given a light-sensitive chest protector, a gun and complete freedom to annihilate the opponent. Each round costs $3 or $4.

### Malibu Castle Park

*2410 Marine Avenue, at Inglewood Avenue, Redondo Beach (1-310 643-5166). Bus 126, 215, Lawndale*

The **Rose Bowl**, Pasadena, home to soccer and American football. See page 191.

*Transit West/I-405, exit Inglewood Drive north.* **Open**
11am-11pm Mon-Thur, Sun; 11am-midnight Fri, Sat.
Multi-game complex with an arcade, baseball batting cages,
miniature golf and water slides. The North Hollywood location also has go-kart racing, at $3.50 a lap.
**Branch**: 12400 Vanowen Street, at Whitsett Avenue,
North Hollywood (1-818 765 4002).

### Malibu Grand Prix

*17871 Castleton Street, at Stoner Creek Road, City of
Industry (1-818 965 3933). Bus Foothill Transit 482, 495/
SR60, exit Fullerton Road south.* **Open** 11am-10pm daily.
Race against the clock in mini-speedsters ($10-$20).

### Virtual World

*1 Colorado Boulevard, at Fair Oaks Avenue, Old Town
Pasadena (1-818 577 9896). Bus 180, 181, 188, 256,
402, Foothill Transit 187, 690/I-110 to Arroyo Parkway,
exit Colorado Boulevard west.* **Open** 11am-11pm Mon-
Thur, Sun; 10am-1am Fri, Sat.
Step into a pod and blast other players to smithereens.
Networks enhance the latest versions of BattleTech and Red
Planet. Individuals can play, either against a computer or
other players. Games cost $7-$9.

## Aviation

Although introductory flights are mainly promotional ploys
by small flying schools to get you to join, they're also a great
chance to fly small aircraft without any previous experience.
At Santa Monica Airport, try **American Flyers** (1-310 390
2099; $99 for 1 hour in the air) or **Justice Aviation
Services** (1-310 313 6792; introductory flights from $35). At
Van Nuys Airport, the **Van Nuys Flight Centre** (1-818
994 7300) offers introductory flights for $49.

### Air Combat USA

*230 North Dale Place, at Artesia Boulevard, Fullerton
(1-800 522-7590). Bus Orange County Transit 25/I-5,
exit Artesia Boulevard east.* **Open** 7am-6pm daily.
This is not a flight simulator. Air Combat allows you to take
control of a SF-260 Nato Attack Fighter and engage in a real-
life dogfight. The $695 price includes a video. You leave from
Fullerton Municipal Airport (about an hour's drive from LA)
and all dogfights take place over the channel between
Catalina Island and the mainland.

### Orbic Helicopters

*16700 Roscoe Boulevard, between Balboa Boulevard &
Woodley Avenue, Van Nuys (1-818 988 6532). Bus 152,
236, 418, Commuter Express 573, 574/I-405, exit
Roscoe Boulevard west.* **Open** 8am-8pm daily.
Operating out of Van Nuys Airport, demo flights cost $65-
$85 for 25 minutes; tours $80 per person.

## Bungee jumping

### Mega Bungee

*1119 Queens Highway, Pier J, at the Queen Mary, Long
Beach (1-310 435 1880). Metro Transit Mall/bus Long
Beach Transit Roundabout C/I-405, exit I-710 south.*
**Open** 10am-6pm Wed-Sun.
The tallest freestanding bungee tower (220ft) on the conti-
nent. A jump costs $85.

## Cycling & mountain biking

It's easy to bike long distances in LA, so take the necessary
precautions: plenty of water and some sunscreen. Riding off-
road isn't actually legal in Los Angeles, but there haven't
been any efforts to stop the hundreds of cyclists that weave
through the Santa Monica Mountains, home to the most popular and most accessible MTBing areas. Here, numerous fire

trails jut off Mulholland Boulevard from Beverly Hills to
Topanga and Malibu. You may have to squeeze under a gate
or two, but keep pedalling until you reach the peaks.
**Topanga State Park** (20825 Entrada Road, off Topanga
Canyon Boulevard, Topanga; 1-310 455 2465) and **Malibu
Creek** (28754 Mulholland Highway, off Malibu Canyon
Road, Agoura; 1-818 880 0367) may seem a little out of the
way, but they're well worth it. **Torrance** has an easy, scenic
ride that starts at Del Cerro Park and ends at Crenshaw
Boulevard in the Palos Verdes Estates; you can ride there
and back in less than three hours. You can get a map of
**Santa Monica** with marked bike trails from the Visitor's
Information Center just north of Santa Monica Pier. All bike
paths, except MTB routes, are paved.

### BIKE PATHS

**Griffith Park**: over 14 miles of bike trails; can be hilly.
Contact Woody's Bicycle World (3157 Los Feliz Boulevard,
Griffith Park; 1-213 661 6665) for information about the park
and rentals.
**Kenneth Hill Bikeway**: Starts at Arroyo Boulevard,
Pasadena, and heads to Arroyo Seco and the Rose Bowl.
**San Vincente Boulevard to Ocean Boulevard**: Start
at San Vicente Boulevard and Barrington Avenue and go
west to Ocean Boulevard and Santa Monica Beach.
**South Bay Bicycle Trail**: Extends 22 miles from Will
Rogers State Beach south to Torrance. There are many
places to rent bikes along Ocean Front Walk in Venice.
**Sepulveda Basin Recreation Area**: 17015 Burbank
Boulevard, at Woodley Avenue, Encino (1-818 784 5180). Flat
bicycle paths for nine miles. Best during the winter.

### BIKE RENTALS

Oceanfront stalls can rent you half-decent clunkers for cruising the beach paths, but for anything more serious, go to a
proper bicycle shop.

### Bicycle Ambulance

*1423 Sixth Street, between Broadway & Santa Monica
Boulevard, Santa Monica (1-310 395 5026). Bus 4, 304,
Santa Monica 1, 7, 10/I-10, exit Fourth-Fifth Street
north.* **Open** 9am-6pm daily.
Mountain bikes cost $15 a day; 21-speeds $20 a day.

### Spokes 'n' Stuff

*7614 Santa Monica Boulevard, at Spaulding Avenue,
West Hollywood (1-213 650 1076). Bus 4, DASH West
Hollywood/I-10, exit Fairfax Avenue north.* **Open**
10.30am-6.30pm Thur-Sun.
Mountain bikes cost $22 a day, RockShox $30 a day, road
bikes $14-$30 a day. Huge selection.
**Branches**: 175 Admiralty Way, Marina del Rey (1-310
306 3332); Loews Hotel, 1700 Ocean Avenue, Santa
Monica (1-310 395 4748).

## Golf

There are some distinguished private clubs in the LA, such
as the Riviera Club, which hosts the LA Open, but also a
good number of public courses. An LA reservation card
(available from any public course), allows you to book in
advance. Ask at a pro-shop for details of other courses.

### Griffith Park Golf Course

*4730 Crystal Springs Drive, Griffith Park (course 1-213
663 2555/shop 1-213 664 2255). Bus 96/I-5, exit Crystal
Springs Drive north.* **Open** 6am-6pm daily.
Two 18-hole championship courses within Griffith Park. You
can rent equipment at the pro-shop. A round costs $17 week-
days, $22 at weekends. Carts are $20.

### Rancho Park Golf Course

*10460 West Pico Boulevard, between Motor & Patricia
Avenues, Rancho Park (1-310 838 7373). Bus Culver*

*City 3, Commuter Express 431, Santa Monica 7, 13/I-10,
exit Overland Avenue north.* **Open** 6am-6.30pm daily.
Rancho Park (18-hole, par-71) claims to have more traffic
than any other course in the world, which means that a) it's
one of the nicest courses in LA and b) it's one of the hardest
to get on. It costs $20-$25 to play.

### Sepulveda Golf Complex

*Balboa & Encino courses: 16821 Burbank Boulevard, at
Balboa Boulevard, Encino (1-818 995-1170). Bus 154,
236, 573, Commuter Express 574/US101, exit Balboa
Boulevard south.*
*Woodley Lake course: 6331 Woodley Avenue, at Victory
Boulevard, Van Nuys (1-818 780 6886). Bus 164, 236/
I-405, exit Burbank Boulevard west.*
*Both* **Open** 6.30am-7pm daily.
Balboa is an 18-hole, par-70 course, and both the Encino and
Woodley courses are 18-hole, par-72. A round costs $17
weekdays, $22 weekends. Equipment and carts available.

## Hang-gliding

### Windsports International

*16145 Victory Boulevard, between Havenhurst &
Woodley Avenues, Van Nuys (1-818 988 0111). Bus 164,
236/I-405, exit Victory Boulevard west.* **Open** 10am-6pm
Tue-Fri; 9am-noon Sat.

Locations vary, depending on wind direction, but you'll
always launch from sloping hills where the wind turbulence
is more predictable, not from cliffs. Introductory lesson $99.

## Horseriding

*See also chapter* **Sightseeing**.

### Los Angeles Equestrian Center

*480 Riverside Drive, at Main Street, Burbank (office
1-818 840 9066/stables 1-818 840 8401). I-5, exit
Alameda Avenue west.* **Open** 8am-7pm Mon-Fri; 8am-
4pm Sat, Sun. **Horses** $15 1 hour; $24 1½ hours;
$28 2 hours; $15 refundable deposit; no under-12s.
LAEC is a public stables on the northern tip of Griffith Park,
which has 54 miles of horse trails.

### Malibu Riding & Tennis Club

*33905 West Pacific Coast Highway, between Decker Road
& Mulholland Highway, Malibu (1-310 457 9783). Bus
434/I-10, exit PCH north.* **Open** 7am-5pm Tue-Sun.

## Rock climbing

There aren't many locations for outdoor climbs in LA but
indoor walls have caught on in a big way – climbing provides an excellent workout.

# Trail mix

Nobody walks in LA (except in popular shopping
districts) but those in the know hike. Blessed with
an amazing variety of wilderness, the sprawling
metropolis offers mountain, ocean and desert
landscapes – often minutes away from bustling
city streets. None of the hikes below require spe-
cialised gear – a decent pair of sneakers and a bottle of water will do – but you'll need a car to reach
them. Most trails are hot in the summer, so it's
best to hike in the early morning or late afternoon.
Watch out for snakes and avoid shiny, tri-leafed
foliage; it may be poison oak.

## Hollywood Hills

This portion of the Santa Monica Mountains
extends from Griffith Park to Beverly Hills and
includes notable city views.

### Griffith Park Observatory to Mount Hollywood
**(3½ miles, easy)**
From Vermont Avenue, north of Los Feliz Boulevard, follow signs to the Observatory. From the north end of the
parking lot, follow a wide sandy track across a bridge and
continue for 1 mile around curves that offer a good view
of the Hollywood sign. At the fork, bear medium left (not
hard, uphill left) and continue on the main road for ½ mile
to Dante's View, a beautiful garden oasis that offers magical views of Downtown. A few feet beyond, enjoy views
of Burbank, Glendale and the San Gabriel Mountains.
Continue bearing left ¼ mile to Mt Hollywood for a 360°
view of the LA basin. Reverse to return, or try other paths,
always keeping the Observatory in sight. The Griffith
Park/Sierra Club Guided Night Hikes (1-213 387 4287)

meets at the upper merry-go-round parking lot, 7pm Tue
& Thur, year round.

### Bronson Canyon and Bat Caves
**(3-4 miles, initially steep)**
Park at the end of Bronson Avenue (north of Franklin
Avenue). Ascend the fire road for about one mile. At the
top, find a beautiful 'road to nowhere' with Hollywood and
city views. Head left towards the Hollywood sign or right
towards the Griffith Park Observatory. Return the same
way. Just below the parking lot, ¼ mile along a dirt road,
you will find a group of freestanding caves probably
familiar from the *Batman* TV series. This eerie, magical
setting recalls cowboy shoot-'em-ups and affords an excellent view of the Hollywood sign for non-hikers.

### Hollywood Sign **(3½ miles, steep)**
Park at the northern end of Beachwood Drive (north of
Franklin Avenue). Walk right on Hollyridge Drive 75ft to
the dirt track on the left. Ascend (ignoring the downhill trail
to stables) for ½ mile to a fork. Turn left uphill and continue to an asphalt road. Turn right and continue all the way
up to the radio towers. This hike offers canyon, city and
San Fernando Valley views, including the Burbank film
studios and Forest Lawn cemetery. At the top, you'll find
yourself behind and above the famed sign, observing that
the letters have corrugated backs, with Madonna's house
and Lake Hollywood in the near distance. Don't attempt to
climb down; it's dangerous and illegal.

### Runyon Canyon **(2-3 miles, moderate)**
Park at the northern end of Fuller Avenue (north of
Franklin Avenue) and enter through 'The Pines' park
gates. Head left uphill at the fork for the longer fire-road
route or right for an easy ascent to a plateau and a more
difficult ridge route to the top. Once the grounds of a
notable Hollywood estate mistakenly attributed to Errol

## Natural High Adventures

*19528 Ventura Boulevard, Suite 507, between Corbin & Shirley Avenues, Tarzana (1-818 704 0590). Bus 424/ US101, exit Tampa Avenue south.* Instruction, equipment and guides for outdoor climbs. Classes range from $65-$145. Call for details.

## Rocreation

*11866 La Grange Avenue, at Bundy Drive, West LA (1-310 207 7199). Bus Santa Monica 9, 10, 14/I-10, exit Bundy Drive north.* **Open** 11am-10pm Mon, Wed; 6am-10pm Tue, Thur; 11am-8pm Fri; 9am-7pm Sat, Sun. $15 per session (plus gear hire $5); classes (with gear) are $37.

## Rollerhockey

Despite gaining in popularity, especially among die-hard rollerbladers, inline hockey is still in its pick-up game stage. It can be tricky to find a location with frequent games, but there always seem to be players at the beach parking lot just north of **Ocean Park**, in south Santa Monica and at **West Hollywood Park & Recreation Center** (647 North San Vicente Boulevard, West Hollywood; 1-213 848 6534).

### Venice Roller Works

*7 Westminster Avenue, at Speedway, Venice (1-310 450 0669). Bus Santa Monica 2/I-10, exit Lincoln Boulevard south.* **Open** 10am-6pm Mon-Fri; 9am-6.30pm Sat, Sun. Rent skates, pads and helmet ($10), sticks ($15) and balls ($2).

## Scuba diving

The best places to dive are off **Leo Carillo State Beach**, **Laguna Beach**, **Redondo Beach** and **Palos Verdes**, but if you're really serious, head to **Catalina Island** (*see chapter* **Trips Out of Town**). Most of LA's coastline consists of miles of sloping sand, but Catalina has rocky shores inhabited by kelp beds, fish and even shipwrecks.

### Just Add Water Sports

*1803 Lincoln Boulevard, Suite A, at Michigan Avenue, Santa Monica (1-310 581 2717). Bus Santa Monica, 3, 7/ I-10, exit Lincoln Boulevard south.* **Open** 10am-7pm Mon-Fri; 9am-5pm Sat, Sun.
The $250 PADI certification course takes place over two weekends and includes two beach dives and one boat dive. Students must have their own gear – mask, fins, snorkel, boots, gloves and hood – which can cost $200-$250.

### Splash/Dive

*2490 Lincoln Boulevard, between Venice & Washington Boulevards, Venice (1-310 306 6733). Bus Santa Monica 3, 7, 8/I-10, exit Lincoln Boulevard south.* **Open** 10am-6pm Mon-Sat; 11am-5pm Sun.

---

Flynn, the canyon grounds contain scattered ruins that are fun to explore. Enjoy the evening social hour at the 'bench', with great ocean sunsets and Downtown views.

**Fryman Canyon (3 miles, moderate)**
Start at Fryman Road, off Laurel Canyon Boulevard, just to the south of Studio City. Begin this pretty walk at the Wilacre Park sign. The fire-road trail is among the greenest in springtime, offering San Fernando Valley views and a chance to visit the Tree People Nature Preserve at the top. Like Runyon Canyon, this is very popular with dog walkers as an 'off-leash' spot. Alternatively, start from above, at the intersection of Coldwater Canyon Boulevard and Mulholland Drive.

## Santa Monica Mountains

While the Hollywood Hills are technically part of this range, these hikes represent the West LA section, from Brentwood to Malibu.

**Sullivan Canyon (2-4 miles, easy)**
Follow Sunset Boulevard 2½ miles west from the I-405 and turn right onto Mandeville Canyon Road. Turn left onto Westridge Road, then left onto Bayliss Road, then left onto Queensferry Road, go ¼ mile and park at the end. The asphalt road at the left leads to a cement flood-control apron. Turn right to enter this lovely, quiet canyon and amble through shady oak and sycamore groves with frequent creek crossings. Retrace your steps at will.

**Malibu Creek State Park (3½-4½ miles, easy)**
From the Pacific Coast Highway, head 6½ miles inland on Malibu Canyon Road, or, from the US101, take Las Virgenes Road 4 miles south, to the park entrance. From the parking lot, follow the fire road to a fork. Take the high road right over a bridge and follow the Gorge Trail

upstream to a spectacular volcanic gorge recognisable from Tarzan movies. When you're done frolicking in the water, continue on the high road, bearing left towards Century Lake, taking in valley views and weird rock outcrops. End here, or continue on the fire road to the site of the former *M\*A\*S\*H* set.

**Solstice Canyon (1½-6 miles, easy to moderate)**
From the Pacific Coast Highway, turn right at Corral Canyon Road. At the first bend, turn left into the park and proceed to the visitor centre parking lot (1-310 456 5046) Take one of the free maps and choose any route, or just walk along an old dirt road, following a beautiful wooded creek to the Grotto Waterfalls and ruins of the old Roberts ranch house. For excellent views, return along one of the ridge trails.

## Out of Town

### Devil's Punchbowl
Take the I-5 north to the SR14 and take the Little Rock turn-off to the east (Pearblossom Highway). Just beyond the town of Pearblossom, take route N6 south, following signs to the park. The drive will take about 1¼ hours. A one-mile loop hike lets you get up close and personal with earthquake country at this bowl-shaped intersection of several fault-lines. Take in Mojave Desert views, explore wildly tilting rocks, play in the creek at the canyon bottom or join the climbers who use this site to rehearse their moves.

### Vasquez Rocks County Park
Take the I-5 north to the SR14, exit at Agua Dulce and follow signs to the park: about a 45-minute drive. Follow any trail to examine an otherworldly rockscape familiar from old cowboy movies and *Star Trek* episodes. Scramble up giant sandstone slabs and look for the caves that once sheltered famed bandit Tiburcio Vasquez.

As well as offering gear rental (to certified divers only), Splash runs a two-week certification course costing $250 for the weekend format, $275 for weekdays.

## Skateboarding & inline skating

Believe it or not, skateboarding is a crime in Los Angeles. There used to be a number of skateparks, but now only **Temecula** and **Huntington Beach** have areas sanctioned specifically for skateboarders. That doesn't stop them from weaving in and out of traffic on **Venice Beach**, where a good place to watch skateboarders do tricks is near the basketball courts. Inline skating (rollerblading), on the other hand, is everywhere. The best and safest places to skate are **Ocean Front Walk** along Venice Beach and **Griffith Park**. If you want to check out that 1970s roller-disco vibe, try Wednesday nights at **Moonlight Rollerway** (5110 San Fernando Road, Glendale; 1-818 241 3630), where they've been rollerdancing since the 1950s.

### ZJ Boarding House
*2619 Main Street, at Ocean Park Boulevard, Santa Monica (1-310 392 5646). Bus 33, Santa Monica 1, 2, 8, 10/I-10, exit Lincoln Boulevard south.* **Open** 9am-9pm daily.
Top-of-the-line skateboards and accessories for rent. Also snowboards ($25 a day), boots ($10), boot-and-board package ($30), surfboards ($25 a day, $15 a half-day) and wetsuits ($10 a day, $5 a half-day).

## Skiing & snowboarding

Angeles National Forest offers skiing at **Mount Baldy** (1-909 981 3344) and **Mount Waterman** (1-818 790 2002), both only 45 minutes to an hour's drive from LA. However, Big Bear,

---

# Gun clubs

Make no mistake, LA is gun-country. Angelenos haven't shed their Wild West roots yet, and gun sales continue to soar. It's easy to rent guns at any of the shooting ranges, but unless you've had adequate experience in handling a firearm, gun clubs won't allow you to shoot. Most clubs offer instruction in the basics of safety and shooting.

### Beverly Hills Gun Club
*12306 Exposition Boulevard, at Centinela Avenue, West LA (1-310 826 6411).*
Beginner group classes (usually 10am-1pm Sun) cost $68 per person (with gun rental). Private lessons are $89 an hour.

### Firing Line
*17921 Jamestown Lane, off Brookshire Lane, at Talbert Avenue, Huntington Beach, Orange County (1-714 841 2100).*
Instructions and rentals.

### Survival Shooting
*11664 National Boulevard, Suite 357, at Barrington Avenue, Santa Monica (1-310 398 4942).*
Dusty Morean is a good person to ring with any questions. He also gives private lessons that include discounts on equipment and legal representation (God forbid) for £100 an hour.

---

about two and a half hours out of LA, is considered superior (*see chapter* **Trips Out of Town**): the three most popular resorts are **Bear Mountain** (1-909 585 2519), **Snow Valley** (1-909 867 2751) and **Snow Summit** (1-909 866 5766). For 24-hour snow reports, call 1-310 828 5115 or ZJ Boardinghouse (*see above* **Skateboarding & inline skating**).

### Sandy's Ski and Sport
*4110 Lincoln Boulevard, at Washington Boulevard, Marina del Rey (1-310 822 9203). Bus Santa Monica 3, 7, 8/I-10, exit Lincoln Boulevard south.* **Open** 10am-8pm Mon-Sat; 10am-6pm Sun.
Reasonable prices – $14 per day for skis, boots and poles, $25 for a snowboard and boots – and friendly staff.

### Val Surf & Sport
*4810 Whitsett Avenue North, between Huston Street & Riverside Drive, Hollywood (1-818 769 6977). Bus 96/US101, exit Laurel Canyon Boulevard north.* **Open** 9am-8pm Mon-Fri; 9am-6pm Sat; 10am-5pm Sun.
Snowboard rental $25 per day; ski rental $20 per day.

## Skydiving

### Perris Valley Skydiving School
*2091 Goetz Road, Perris, Riverside County (1-800 832 8818). I-215, exit D south-east (one-way).* **Open** 9am-7pm daily.
A two-hour drive south-east of LA. Dives cost about $160.

### California City Skydiving Center
*5999 Curtiss Place, California City (1-800 258 6744). SR14, exit California City Boulevard east.* **Open** 8am-4.30pm Mon-Thur; 8am-6.30pm Fri-Sun.
A 90-minute drive north of LA. Costs range from $144-$300.

## Watercraft

### Action Water Sports
*4144 Lincoln Boulevard, between Maxella Avenue & Washington Boulevard, Marina del Rey (1-310 306 9539). Bus Santa Monica 3, 7, 8/I-10, exit Lincoln Boulevard south.* **Open** 10am-6pm Mon-Sat; 11am-5pm Sun.
Surf-style kayaks cost from $35 a day to rent. Jet skis are $70-$90 for 90 minutes.

### Malibu Ocean Sports
*22935 West Pacific Coast Highway, at Malibu Pier, Malibu (1-310 456 6302). Bus 434/I-10, exit PCH north.* **Open** 10am-6pm Mon-Thur, Sun; 9am-7pm Fri, Sat.
Kayak tours are $49 per person, 'moonlight paddles' $39.

### Marina Boat Rentals
*Fisherman's Village, 13719 Fiji Way, Marina del Rey (1-310 574 2822). Bus 220/I-10, exit Lincoln Boulevard south.* **Open** 11am-5pm Mon-Fri; 10am-6pm Sat, Sun.
Wave runners ($65 per hour), sailboats ($25 first hour, $15 every hour after), kayaks ($10 single, $15 double), electric boats ($45 per hour).

### Nature Tours
*1666 Euclid Street, at Olympic Boulevard, Santa Monica (1-310 453 8754). Bus Santa Monica 9, 11/I-10, exit Lincoln Boulevard south.* **Open** 8am-6pm daily.
Wave runner and jet ski rentals ($55 per hour) and tours.

## Watersports

Be warned – learning to surf is difficult. It can take weeks just learning to sit on the board properly, let alone negotiating the white-wash, and, sadly, windsurfing is even harder. Most novices opt for the easier-to-learn alternatives: boogie-boards (aka body-boards), bodysurfing and skimboarding.

If you're learning to surf, choose a wide-open beach break such as **Zuma Beach** (1-310 457 9891), **Will Rogers State Beach** (1-310 451 2906) – the surfing is best where Sunset Boulevard meets the PCH – **Santa Monica Beach** (1-310 458 8311), or **El Porto** (at Manhattan Beach). Excellent beach breaks for intermediate surfers can be found at **Manhattan**, **Hermosa**, **Redondo** and **Huntington Beaches**. Only experienced surfers should test their skill at the competitive, surfers-only point breaks, such as **Topanga State Beach**, near the intersection of the PCH and Topanga Canyon Road, **Malibu Lagoon State Beach**, by the inter-section of the PCH and Cross Creek Road, just north of Malibu Pier (one of the most famous surf breaks in the world), and **The Wedge** (a very dangerous surf break) located at the end of Balboa and Ocean Boulevards at the top of the Balboa Peninsula, Orange County. If you surf between October and May, you'll need a wetsuit. Call ZJ Boardinghouse (*see above* **Skateboarding & inline skating**) for a complete report on surf conditions. Malibu Ocean Sports (*see above* **Watercraft**) also rents gear.

### ET Surfboards

*904 Aviation Boulevard, between Ocean Drive & Pacific Coast Highway, Hermosa Beach (1-310 379 7660). Bus 225, 232/I-405, exit SR91 (Artesia Boulevard) west.* **Open** 10am-8pm Mon-Fri; 10am-7pm Sat; 10am-6pm Sun. All boards in stock, including snowboards.

## Wind skating

### WindSkate, Inc

*Beach parking lots at Ocean Park & Santa Monica (1-310 453 4808).* Call for an appointment.
Jamie Budge doesn't have an actual store but relies on demonstrations near Santa Monica Beach to attract custom. If you see someone clutching a hand-held sail device that pro-pels them on their skateboard or rollerblades, it's probably a WindSkate. The sails cost $7 an hour or $25 a day.

## Participation sports

## Beach volleyball

In this mecca for volleyball, the best courts are on **Santa Monica Beach**, just south of the pier. **Will Rogers State Beach** has courts south of the Santa Monica Canyon, near the parking lot. A good resource is the **Volleyball Organization in Los Angeles** (VOILA), 8424A Santa Monica Boulevard, West Hollywood; contact Lance on 1-213 656 4319.

## Bowling

There are plenty of places to bowl in the LA area; for details, call the **Southern California Bowling Proprietors Association** on 1-818 972 1112.

**Dodger Stadium**. *See page 192.*

### Bay Shore Bowl

*234 Pico Boulevard, between Fourth & Main Streets, Santa Monica (1-310 399 7731). Bus 20, 33, 434, Santa Monica 1, 7, 8/I-10, exit Fourth Street south.* **Open** 9am-midnight Mon-Thur, Sun; 9am-1am Fri, Sat.

## Ice skating & hockey

Surprisingly, California has produced champion figure skaters, but ever since Wayne Gretsky came to the LA Kings, Angelenos have found a new interest: ice hockey. It's easy to get in on a game – the only problem is that no one really knows how to play except for displaced East Coasters.

### Culver City Ice Arena

*4545 Sepulveda Boulevard, at Braddock Drive, Culver City (1-310 398 5719). Bus Culver City 6/I-405, exit Sawtelle Boulevard south.* Call for opening times.
From 12.30-5pm Mon-Fri, it costs $6 to skate ($2 skate rental). There are pick-up games on Wednesday and Thursday nights ($18; goalies play free).

## Pool & billiards

You'll find a pool table in most bars and bowling alleys. But if you want the freedom to play as long as you like, try these:

### Breakshot Billiard Club

*11970 Venice Boulevard, at Inglewood Boulevard, Mar Vista (1-310 391 3435). Bus 33, 436/I-10, exit Lincoln Boulevard south.* **Open** 11.30am-2am Mon-Thur, Sun; 1.30pm-4am Fri, Sat. **Pool** $2-$12 per hour.

### Gotham Hall

*1431 Third Street Promenade, between Broadway & Santa Monica Boulevard, Santa Monica (1-310 394 8865). Bus 4, 304, Santa Monica 1, 2, 3, 8/I-10, exit Fourth Street north.* **Open** 4pm-2am Mon-Fri; 3pm-2am Sat, Sun. **Pool** $7-$14 per hour.
A very swanky establishment. Dress up and bring a cigar.

### Yankee Doodles

*1410 Third Street Promenade, between Broadway & Santa Monica Boulevard, Santa Monica (1-310 394 4632). Bus 4, 304, Santa Monica 1, 2, 3, 8/I-10, exit Fourth Street north.* **Open** 11am-2am daily. **Pool** $6-$12 per hour.
Sports bar Yankee's has 30 pool tables, four foosball tables, a free-throw and football toss. There are also 42 monitors and eight big-screen TVs showing satellite sports all day.

## Tennis & racquetball

You can find tennis and racquetball courts at most gyms and recreation centres. Book a couple of days in advance.

### Marina Tennis Center

*13199 Mindanao Way, at Glencoe Avenue, Marina del Rey (1-310 822 2255). Bus 108, 220, Commuter Express 437/SR90, exit Mindanao Way north.* **Open** 8am-10pm Mon-Fri; 8am-6pm Sat, Sun. **Courts** $12-$14 per hour.

### Rustic Canyon Recreation Center

*601 Latimer Road, between Brooktree & Hiltree Roads, Santa Monica (1-310 454 5734). Bus 2, 576, Commuter Express 430, Santa Monica 9/I-405, exit Sunset Boulevard west.* **Open** 9am-9.30pm Mon-Thur; 9am-5.30pm Fri; 9am-5pm Sat; 10am-5pm Sun.

### The Tennis Place

*5880 West Third Street, at Cochran Avenue, Mid-Wilshire (1-213 936 9900). Bus 16, DASH Fairfax/I-10, exit La Brea Avenue north.* **Open** 7am-11pm daily. **Courts** $13-$15 per hour.

## YMCAs

For details of other locations, call 1-800 872 9622.

### Santa Monica Family YMCA

*1332 Sixth Street, between Santa Monica Boulevard &
Arizona Avenue, Santa Monica (1-310 393-2721). Bus 4,
304, Santa Monica 1, 7, 10/I-10, exit Fifth Street north.*
**Open** 6am-10pm Mon-Fri; 7am-7pm Sat; 11am-7pm Sun.
Racquetball and handball courts, free weights, boxing,
aerobics, lap pool, spa, pick-up basketball and volleyball, and
a running track on the roof. Non-members pay $10 a day.

### Stuart M Ketchum Downtown YMCA

*401 South Hope Street, at Fourth Street, Downtown
(1-213 624 2348). Bus Commuter Express 423, 430,
437/I-110, exit Ninth Street east.* **Open** 5.30am-9.30pm
Mon-Fri; 8am-4.30pm Sat; 9am-3.30pm Sun.
Indoor lap pool, running track, squash, racquetball and tennis courts. Non-members pay $10-$15 a day.

## Fitness

YMCAs often have gyms; *see above* **Participation sports**.

## Circuit sculpting

### Dove's Bodies

*4010 Colfax Avenue, at Ventura Boulevard, Studio City
(1-818 980 7866). Bus 424, 522/US101, exit Laurel
Canyon Boulevard south.* Call for opening times.
An inspired, customised yet ever-evolving, workout class
that will melt fat, firm, tone and define.

## Dance classes

Classes vary, so call for details of times and prices.

### Arthur Murray Studio

*262 North Beverly Drive, between Dayton & Wilshire
Boulevards, Beverly Hills (1-310 274 8867). Bus 4, 20,
21, 22, 27, DASH Beverly Hills/I-10, exit Robertson
Boulevard north.*
Conservative dance studio that will teach you just about any
step from ballroom to swing. However, they'll want you to
sign up for a whole course and it can get costly.

### Delane Vaughn's Jazz Class

*Alley Kat Studios, 1455 Gordon Street, at Sunset
Boulevard, Hollywood (1-213 462 1755). Bus 2, 3, 210,
212/US101, exit Vine Street south.*
The most inventive dance class in LA. Just listen to Delane's
funky music selections and imitate his jaguar-like moves.
Call first to check this is still the venue for Delane's classes.

### Lichine Ballet Academy

*405 North Foothill Road, between Burton Way & Civic
Center Drive, Beverly Hills (1-310 276 5202). Bus 4, 14,
27, 576/I-10, exit Robertson Boulevard north.*
Darling, old-fashioned, one-room dance studio in Beverly
Hills offering Russian ballet to all ages and levels.

## Gyms

Many people see Angelenos as obsessive about fitness – and
they're right. Gyms have sprouted here faster than Starbucks
and Blockbuster combined. These are open to non-members:

### Family Fitness Center

*9911 Pico Boulevard, Floor A, between Roxbury Drive &
Century Park East, Century City (1-310 553 7600). Bus
Santa Monica 7, 13/I-405, exit Santa Monica Boulevard
east.* **Open** 24 hours daily.

*Surfers at Hermosa Beach.*

Weights, aerobics and even cardio-kickboxing. Non-members pay $10 a day.
**Branches**: 1500 Rosecrans Avenue, Manhattan Beach
(1-310 536 9300); 465 North Halstead Street, Pasadena
(1-818 351 2222)

### Future Shape

*13288 Fiji Way, at Lincoln Boulevard, Marina del Rey
(1-310 821 1920). Bus Santa Monica 3/I-10, exit Lincoln
Boulevard south.* **Open** noon-8pm Mon-Fri; 10am-4pm Sat.
So you want to exercise but can't get off your bum? Then
you'll love EMS (Electric Muscle Stimulation), a way to workout while lying in a lounge chair and watching TV. Small
electrodes are placed on certain muscles of your body and,
with each controlled shock, your muscle flexes and contracts.
$15 for a 50-minute session.

### Golds Gym

*360 Hampton Drive, at Rose Avenue, Venice (1-310 392
6004). Bus 33, 436, Santa Monica 1, 2/I-10, exit Lincoln
Boulevard south.* **Open** 4am-midnight Mon-Fri; 5am-
midnight Sat, Sun.
'The mecca of bodybuilding' is how this truly impressive
Temple of the Bod bills itself. $15 a day or $50 a week.

### Hollywood Gym and Fitness Center

*1551 North La Brea Avenue, between Hawthorne Street
& Sunset Boulevard, Hollywood (1-213 845 1420). Bus
107, 212/US101, exit Highland Avenue south.* **Open** 24
hours daily.
Yoga, boxing, Nautilus/free weights, aerobics, sauna and chi-
ropractic facility. A day pass is $10; kickboxing $15 a class.

### Marina Athletic Club

*12980 Culver Boulevard, between Lincoln Boulevard &
SR90, Marina del Rey (1-310 301 2582). Bus 220, Santa
Monica 3/SR90, exit Mindanao Way.* **Open** 5am-
midnight Mon-Fri; 6.30am-9pm Sat, Sun.

Lap pool, track, spinning cycles, volleyball/basketball gym, step aerobics, yoga, Jacuzzi – all within a cool, industrial-style aeroplane hangar. A day pass costs $10.

## Pilates

### Live Art
*1100 South Beverly Drive, Suite 20, between Olympic & Pico Boulevards, Beverly Hills (1-310 277 9536). Bus 3, Santa Monica 5, 7, /I-10, exit Robertson Boulevard north.*
Angels, towers, erotica (exercises), transformers, magic circles and wands (equipment) make up pilates, a meditative, low-impact form of exercise designed to lengthen as much as strengthen. It was invented in the late 1920s and has been practised for years by dancers. Siri Dharma Galliano's clients at Live Art have included Glenn Close, Dennis Quaid and Jessica Lange. Call for an appointment.

## Spinning

### Sharon's Fitness Domaine
*8475 Holloway Drive, between La Cienega & Santa Monica Boulevards, West Hollywood (1-213 656 1254). Bus 4, 105, 304, DASH West Hollywood/I-10, exit La Cienega Boulevard north.* **Open** 8am-noon, 3pm-8pm, daily.
Spinning is the new fitness regime that is LA's latest fad. You sit on a stationary Schwinn bike, listen to inspirational music and your teacher while he/she takes you on a journey over hills and dales, in a simulation of a real ride, as you alter your bike's resistance accordingly.

## Yoga

### Crunch
*8000 Sunset Boulevard, at La Cienega Boulevard, West Hollywood (1-213 654 4550). Bus 2, 3, 302, 429, 105, DASH West Hollywood/I-10, exit La Cienega Boulevard north.* **Open** 5am-11pm Mon-Fri; 8am-8pm Sat, Sun.
Candles, soothing music, yoga and martial arts combine in the fashionable genre of power yoga. Detractors say this is yoga for aerobics enthusiasts.

### Iyengar Yoga Institute of LA
*8233 West Third Street, between La Jolla & Orlando Avenues, West Hollywood (1-213 653 0357). Bus 16, DASH Fairfax/I-10, exit Fairfax Avenue north.*
Start your class with an incantation and ease into Iyengar, which involves various props including ropes, tables and walls. A type of meditation in action. Call for class times.

### Yoga Center West
*1535 South Robertson Boulevard, at Cashio Street, Mid-City (1-310 552 4647). Bus 220/I-10, exit Robertson Boulevard north.* **Open** 10am-8pm daily; call for classes.
Specialists in Kundlani, the yoga of awareness. Try Gurutej's class; she's been teaching for 26 years.

## Spectator sports

LA fans have a reputation for being fickle and there's no doubt that Angelenos like to see their teams winning, but the city has always taken sport seriously: it hosted the 1932 and 1984 Olympics and, more recently, the 1994 soccer World Cup Final was played at the Rose Bowl in Pasadena. There's a lot of support for LA's glamour teams: the Dodgers (baseball), the Lakers (NBA basketball) and the Galaxy (soccer), although there's no American football team. This is an embarrassment both to the National Football League and to the city: until recently there were two teams, the Rams and the Raiders. The Rams went to St Louis and no one really minded because they never won; more shocking was the return of the Raiders to Oakland, their original home, for the 1995 season. Football fans now only have the college teams at UCLA and USC to root for.

## INFORMATION & TICKETS
The sports section of the *LA Times* is one of the better parts of the paper. The calendar lists the team fixtures and broadcast schedules for the day. There are magazines and papers for every sport; *Sports Illustrated* is well written and the coverage of US sports is excellent. The best place to go for tickets are the teams' own box offices. Ticket agencies

# Football crazies

Soccer is no longer the mystery it once was to most Americans: kids play it at school and the launch of Major League Soccer in 1996 has further increased awareness about the great game. But this doesn't mean that Americans are prepared to give up their allegiance to US sports. In LA though, there's an intriguing situation where there's no professional American football team but the Galaxy, LA's soccer team, attracts 20,000-plus crowds to its home games in the Rose Bowl in Pasadena. It's the unique ethnic mix that makes LA the premier soccer city of the US. Immigrants from Mexico and Latin America brought 'futbol' culture with them and provide the base for homegrown efforts, while many of the million or so expat Europeans in the area also support the game, as do increasing numbers of Americans. The result is a bewildering number of amateur teams and leagues, often organised by country, that can be seen in action at the high schools, sports grounds and parks of LA, the Valleys and Orange County. Griffith Park is popular for Saturday games; during the 1994 World Cup, an unofficial amateur version was held here.

### The Los Angeles Galaxy
*The Rose Bowl, 1001 Rose Bowl Drive, at Arroyo Boulevard, Pasadena (1-818 577 3100). Bus 177/SR134, exit Orange Grove Boulevard north.* **Tickets** $10-$30.
In their first season, the Galaxy were the best team in the country – which means they're equivalent to a competent English First Division club. Watch for Jorge Campos, the Mexican national keeper who also likes to play up front, and winger Cobi Jones, a Valley boy and US international.

charge booking fees, but sometimes it's the only way to get a ticket (look in the *Yellow Pages* under Ticket). Or take your chances with touts (known in the US as scalpers); they don't take credit cards.

## American football

The only options are **UCLA** (tickets 1-310 825 2101) and **USC** (tickets 1-213 740 4672). Both are strong college teams and the season runs from September to November.

### UCLA Bruins

*The Rose Bowl, 1001 Rose Bowl Drive, at Arroyo Boulevard, Pasadena (1-818 577 3100). Bus 177/SR134, exit Orange Grove Boulevard north.*

### USC Trojans

*Los Angeles Memorial Coliseum, 3911 South Figueroa Street, at Martin Luther King Jr Boulevard, Downtown (1-213 747 7111). Bus 40, 42/I-110, exit Martin Luther King Jr Boulevard west.*

## Auto racing

The main event is the Indy car **Long Beach Grand Prix** (1-310 981 2600), which takes place on a street circuit in Long Beach every April. Between April and September there's motocross every Friday at the Orange County Fairgrounds (1-714 708 3247). In mid-1997, the California Speedway in Fontana, 90 minutes from LA, is scheduled to open and will become the focal point for auto sports in the Southland.

## Baseball

LA is a big baseball town and the **LA Dodgers** (1-213 224 1500) are the main attraction. Playing in the National League, they were twice winners of the World Series in the 1980s and are the most famous franchise in US sport after the Yankees. They had a long and venerable history as the Brooklyn Dodgers before coming to LA 35 years ago. The **California Angels** (1-714 937 7200) play in Anaheim in Orange County; they're one of the weaker teams in the American League, but Disney has bought a controlling interest in the team, so that might change (along with their name). The season runs from April to October.

### Dodgers Stadium

*1000 Elysian Park, at Stadium Way, Echo Park (1-213 224 1400). Bus 1, 2, 3, 4/I-110, exit Dodger Stadium north.* **Open** 8.30am-5.30pm Mon-Sat & days of games. **Tickets** $6-$11. **Credit** MC, V.

### Anaheim Stadium

*2000 State College Drive, between Katella & Orangewood Avenues, Anaheim, Orange County (1-714 254 3000/ ticket information 1-714 663 9000). Bus Orange County Transit 49, 50/I-5, exit Katella Avenue east.* **Open** 8.30am-5pm Mon-Fri & days of games. **Tickets** $5-$14.50. **Credit** AmEx, Disc, MC, V.

## Basketball

A tale of two teams: the terminally hip **Lakers** (1-310 412 5000), with their all-star supporters led by Jack Nicholson, and the **Clippers** (1-310 673 6003), one of the NBA's cinderella teams. The season runs from October to April.

### Great Western Forum

*3900 Manchester Boulevard, at Prairie Avenue, Inglewood (1-310 673 1300). Bus 115, 211, 315, 442/I-405, exit Manchester Boulevard east.* **Open** box office 10am-6pm Mon-Fri & days of games. **Tickets** $21-$110.

*Work that body at **Muscle Beach**.*

### LA Sports Arena

*3939 South Figueroa Street, at Martin Luther King Jr Boulevard, Exposition Park, Downtown (1-213 748 6131). Bus 81, 102, 200, 442, 444/I-110, exit Exposition Boulevard west.* **Open** box office 10am-6pm Mon-Fri and days of games. **Tickets** $10-$275.

## Horse racing

There are three tracks in the LA area, as well as at La Jolla, a couple of hours down the coast. They all feature flat racing and are closed for part of the year. Call for post times.

### Hollywood Park Race Track

*1050 South Prairie Street, between 90th Street & Century Boulevard, Inglewood (1-310 419 1500). Bus 115, 211, 315, 442/I-405, exit Manchester Boulevard east.* **Admission** $6.
The Breeders Cup, one of the big US races, takes place here in late 1997. There's also a casino.

### Los Alamitos Race Course

*4961 Katella Avenue, at Walker Street, Los Alamitos, Orange County (1-714 995 1234). Bus Orange County Transit 50/I-5, exit Katella Avenue west.* **Admission** $3.

### Santa Anita Park

*285 West Huntington Drive, between Baldwin & Santa Anita Avenues, Arcadia (1-818 574 7223). Bus 79, 188, 268 Foothill Transit 184/I-210, exit Baldwin Avenue south.* **Admission** $4.

## Ice hockey

The **Los Angeles Kings** (1-310 673 6003) have seen their play and support slump after the 1996 transfer of Wayne Gretsky, the ageing superstar of the National Hockey League. In contrast, the three-year-old **Mighty Ducks** (1-714 704 2700), another Disney-owned franchise, are booming down in Anaheim. The **Ice Dogs** (1-213 683 1640) play in the NHL's feeder league.

# Comedy

**As a testing ground for big-name mega-comics and a breeding ground for tomorrow's talent, Tinseltown takes the laughter business seriously.**

Los Angeles is the centre of the US comedy machine. Despite the laid-back attitude that pervades Southern California, the entertainment industry is anything but – it's wired, it's hungry and it's always looking for the next mega-star comedian. Consequently, the cream of American comics are in heavy rotation in LA, refining their 'quality minutes' and hoping for that elusive television or film deal.

In addition to the numerous touring comics who swing though LA, big names flex their new material in surprise appearances around town. On any given night, you might catch Jerry Seinfeld dropping into The Laugh Factory to try out some new gags or Robin Williams sitting in with a local improv group. Many television comedy writers use the clubs to stay sharp, and there are always countless newcomers waiting for their chance and working the various open-mike shows around town.

Many of the clubs that used to feature only stand-up comedians are now broadening their offerings to include sketch and improvised comedy. While the number of venues in LA may have decreased over the past five years, there has at least been a consistent increase in the quality of the comedy.

Check the comedy section of the *LA Weekly* for up-to-date listings.

*Go improv crazy at* **TheatreSports**.

## Venues

### Acme Comedy Theater

*135 North La Brea Avenue, between Beverly Boulevard & First Street, Hollywood (1-213 525 0202). Bus 14, 212/I-10, exit La Brea Avenue north.* **Shows** 8pm, 10.30pm Fri, Sat; 7.30pm Sun. **Admission** $10-$14. **Credit** AmEx, MC, V.

On a very happening thoroughfare (great bars and restaurants within laughing distance), this brand new theatre has three in-house performing sketch companies that provide a consistently good comedy product. The theatre also hosts Acme Unplugged (10.30pm, Fri) – a jam of LA's top improvisers from comedy groups such as the Groundlings, TheatreSports and Second City, hosted by Fred Willard. *Booking advisable.*
*Valet parking $2.75.*

### Comedy Act Theater

*3339 West 43rd Street, at Degnan Boulevard, Crenshaw (1-310 677 4101). Bus 40, 105, DASH Crenshaw/I-10, exit Crenshaw Boulevard south.* **Shows** 8.30pm Thur,

Fri; 9pm Sat. **Admission** $10; 2-drink minimum. **No credit cards**.

Located in the rather dodgy Crenshaw district of LA, this predominantly black club is off the typical tourist track, and you may find it's best to go there with some locals. The late Robin Harris (Sweet Dick Willie in Spike Lee's *Do The Right Thing*) is one of the many notable talents to have called this thrumming venue home. It draws high-calibre talent as well as providing a great testing ground for an endless stream of new comics. Similar to New York's Apollo Theatre in atmosphere, the black audience is most definitely part of the act and the energy in the place is quite amazing.

### The Comedy Store

*8433 Sunset Boulevard, at La Cienega Boulevard, West Hollywood (1-213 656 6225). Bus 2, 3, 429/I-10, exit La Cienega Boulevard north.* **Open** 7.30pm-2am daily; shows vary. **Admission** $8-$12; 2-drink minimum. **Credit** AmEx, MC, V.

Owned by Mitzi Shore, mom of Pauly Shore (the current king of the adolescent B-movie wave), this ancient warhorse of a comedy club, in the heart of Sunset Strip, has three rooms whose offerings run from A-list stand-up talent such as Roseanne and Richard Pryor to sketch and comedy fledglings. It has been the birthplace of such mega-stars as Robin Williams, David Letterman and Sam Kinison, among others. The regular rota of stand-up showcases includes The Clean Comedy Show and The Gay and Lesbian Show. A good first stop.
*Parking $6.*

## Groundlings Theater

*7307 Melrose Avenue, at Poinsettia Place, Hollywood (1-213 934 9700). Bus 2, 3, 429/I-10, exit Fairfax Avenue north.* **Shows** 8pm Thur; 8pm, 10pm Fri, Sat; 7.30pm Sun. **Admission** $10-$17.50. **Credit** AmEx, MC, V.

Located on hip-and-happening Melrose Avenue, this sketch comedy and improv company is a hot ticket. The Groundlings have been around for over 20 years and still manage to produce sketch comedy that hits the mark with stunning consistency. Their ranks have spawned top talents such as Julia Sweeney, Jon Lovitz and Paul Reubens (aka Pee Wee Herman). On their improv jam night Cookin' with Gas (8pm, Thur), you might find any number of celebrity guests riffing with the regulars. Booking advisable.

*Valet parking at Tommy Tang's, 7473 Melrose Avenue, $3.50.*

## The Ice House

*24 North Mentor Avenue, at Colorado Boulevard, Pasadena (1-818 577 1894). Bus 181, 188, 256, 401/I-110 to Arroyo Parkway, exit Colorado Boulevard east.* **Shows** 8.30pm Tue-Thur; 8.30pm, 10.30pm Fri; 7pm, 9pm, 11pm Sat; 8pm Sun. **Admission** $8.50-$12.50; 2-drink minimum. **Credit** AmEx, MC, V.

One of the oldest comedy venues in LA, this club has two rooms; the Ice House (stand-up) and the Ice House Annex (sketch). Talent ranges from the ridiculous to the sublime; usually, the sublime is to be found in the stand-up room. Enough said.

## IThe Improvisation

*8162 Melrose Avenue, between Kilkea Drive & La Jolla Avenue, West Hollywood (1-213 651 2583). Bus 10, 11, DASH Fairfax/I-10, exit La Cienega Boulevard north.* **Shows** 8pm Mon-Thur, Sun; 8pm, 10pm Fri; 8.30pm, 10.30pm Sat. **Admission** $8-$11. **Credit** AmEx, MC, V.

Celebrity haunt and industry watering hole, this club is one of the highest rungs on the Hollywood comedy ladder. Deals and drinks are made at the bar nightly. Booking advised.

*Valet parking $3.50.*

## LA Connection

*13442 Ventura Boulevard, between Woodman Avenue & Coldwater Canyon Avenue, Sherman Oaks (1-818 784 1868). Bus 424, 522, DASH Sherman Oaks/US101, exit Coldwater Canyon Avenue south.* **Shows** 9pm Thur; 8pm, 9pm, 10.30pm Fri; 7.30pm, 9pm, 10.30pm Sat; 3.30pm (improv for kids), 7pm, 8pm, 9pm Sun. **Admission** $7-$12. **Credit** MC, V.

The long-running LA Connection is a company of comics known for their live dubbing of B-movies. They offer numerous improv and sketch shows, which are funny but pretty predictable. Book in advance.

## The Laugh Factory

*8001 Sunset Boulevard, at Crescent Heights Boulevard, West Hollywood (1-213 656 1336). Bus 26, 163, 212, 217/I-10, exit Fairfax Avenue north.* **Shows** 8pm Mon-Thur, Sun; 7.30pm, 10pm Fri, Sat. **Admission** $8-$10; 2-drink minimum. **Credit** MC, V.

Another premier stand-up club with plenty of industry connections and big-time celebrity surprise appearances. Many comics who appear on the *Tonight Show*.

*Parking $3.*

## LunaPark

*665 North Robertson Boulevard, at Santa Monica Boulevard, West Hollywood (1-310 652 0611). Bus 4, 10, 220, West Hollywood A, B, N/I-10, exit Robertson Boulevard north.* **Open** *restaurant* 6.30-11pm Tue-Thur, Sun; 6.30pm-midnight Fri, Sat; *club* 6.30pm-2am daily; shows vary. **Admission** $5-$12. **Credit** AmEx, MC, V.

An upscale venue known for its live music, LunaPark has recently embraced alternative comedy with the addition of the Un-Cabaret (7.30pm, Sun); where comedy meets performance art. A great alternative for those tired of traditional stand-up clubs.

*Parking $3.*

## TheatreSports

*1713 North Cahuenga Boulevard, at Hollywood Boulevard, Hollywood (1-213 469 9689). Bus 163, 180, 181, 212/US101, exit Cahuenga Boulevard south.* **Shows** 8pm Mon, Thur; box office open 7.30pm. **Admission** $8-$10. **No credit cards**.

This critically acclaimed company is 100% improv. Running for the past eight years in infamous B-movie director Ed Wood's old theatre in the heart of Hollywood, they offer unique improv formats and consistent, dangerous fun. The group also hosts visiting improvisers from around the world.

*Parking $3.*

## Upfront Comedy

*123 Broadway, between Ocean Boulevard & Second Avenue, Santa Monica (1-310 319 3477). Bus 20, 23, 424, Santa Monica 1, 7, 10/I-10, exit Fourth-Fifth Streets north.* **Shows** 8pm Tue, Wed; 8pm, 10pm Thur-Sat. **Admission** $10. **No credit cards**.

The westernmost outpost of graduates from Chicago's Second City club (former home of Dan Akroyd, John Belushi et al), this venue brings together a host of improv groups and sketch comedy acts. A great place to see veteran improvisers work out.

# Tape heads

An alternative comedy experience – and one unique to Los Angeles – is to watch a live television sitcom, such as *Roseanne* or *Seinfeld*, being recorded. Being a member of the audience is a great opportunity to see TV stars in action, but, be warned, sometimes these tapings can take over three hours. It's common for a local stand-up comedian to warm up the audience, occasionally giving away show merchandise to keep people happy and in their seats. For a schedule of tapings, send an SAE to **Audiences Unlimited** (which handles the bookings for over 50 sitcoms including *Mad about You* and *Cybill*) at 100 Universal Plaza, Building 153, Universal City, CA 91608 (1-818 753 3470). Tickets are free and should be booked, if possible, 30 days in advance.

# Dance Clubs

*It's a work-hard city, so all-night playgrounds are hard to find. But the club scene compensates with bags of diversity and energy. Party on.*

The dance club scenes in Los Angeles are as varied as the ethnic groups that comprise the city's population. From the East LA clubs where the house music hybrids incorporate the local Latino vibe to Leimert Park's proving ground for rising rappers to Hollywood's beautiful-people playpens, the city offers it all. All except quality public transport, that is, making clubbing an involved proposition in terms of getting there and back. This means that the private car and the seldom-seen taxi become necessary, and clubbing begins a couple of hours earlier than the past-midnight norm of other cities. But an early start need not mean an early night – plan your club-going strategically and you can see the evening through till dawn.

Most of LA's serious clubbers refer to the early 1990s as a halcyon era for the dance music scene, before bad drugs swept through and top DJs took flight northwards for the cosy environs of San Francisco or the Pacific Northwest. Still, LA's clublife has mutated to survive. The underground scene has become a hit-and-run, one-off operation featuring top international table-talent, with the flier and the phone as its modes of communication.

The counters of most hip shops on Melrose Avenue are stacked with fliers for upcoming events, and the folks at **Beat Non Stop** record shop (7262 Melrose Avenue, at Poinsettia Place; 1-213 930 2121) are in the know on where to go. A particularly good source of fliers is the vinyl-wear superstore **Mondorama** (1756 Vermont Avenue, between Melbourne and Prospect Avenues; 1-213 953 6635); while you're there, you might as well see if they've got any at the **X-Large** clothing store next door. The free *LA Weekly* newspaper is the only steady source of up-to-date club listings, while on the newsstands, *URB* – a one-time smudgy local 'zine and now a slick national mag – drops a few hot hints in its DA Scoop column.

At Hollywood clubs, no-dance gawkers and uptight wallflowers are as common as those reckless souls who take heedlessly to the dancefloor. This means that some clubs resemble spectator-sport stadiums, but that's what happens when everyone who's not an obvious liability gets let in. Few clubs have tough door policies, nor do many clubs feel stiflingly exclusive once you're inside.

Which is not to say that it's not a fashion-conscious scene – even the most loose-limbed LA clubbers are trying to cultivate a look (don't let them tell you otherwise) and overdressed is a rarely used word in the clubland vocabulary (still, always remember to wear sensible shoes). Also, there is an abundance of clubs in Hollywood that get involved with promotions by movie studios keen on pushing their new films; hence, free posters, passes and dress-like-a-film-star contests are the norm – but then, this *is* Hollywood.

You have to be 21 to drink in California; clubs will 'card' punters (ask to see ID) at the door and issue over-21s with a stamp or wrist band which will allow them to get served at the bar. A few places don't admit under-21s at all. Note that few dance clubs accept credit cards.

## Arena

*6655 Santa Monica Boulevard, at Los Palmas Avenue, Hollywood (1-3 462 0714). Bus 4, 420/US101, exit Santa Monica Boulevard west.* **Open** 9pm-4am Tue, Thur-Sun. **Admission** $8-$10.

Thursday and Friday are prime nights – this former ice-house packs them in by the thousands for floor-filling house, techno and disco. But don't worry about the crowds – at 22,000sq ft, the club has room to spare. Getting in can require an hour in an immigration-length queue, but the chatty, happy, cha-cha darlings that compose Arena's core crowd are more than content to swap lipstick and hair gel application tips to pass the time. On Sundays, the club takes on a distinctly Latin vibe, as live bands take over and the ostensibly 'family' night ends at 2am.

## Checca

*7323 Santa Monica Boulevard, at Fuller Avenue, West Hollywood (1-213 850 7471). Bus 4, DASH Hollywood/1-10, exit La Brea Avenue north.* **Admission** free if dining; otherwise $5-$10.

With two rooms whose décor lets slip that this is a French-Italian restaurant by day, Checca has long been home to the on-again, off-again hip-hop club B-Side on Wednesday nights, where the leave-your-gun-at-home-and-throw-your-hands-in-the-air party vibe prevails. Thursdays means the recently established Café Bleu, filled with LA's sporty, Brit-pop obsessives. Small and social, Checca's full bar contributes to its reliable status.

## Cherry

*Upstairs at the Love Lounge, 657 North Robertson Boulevard, between Melrose Avenue & Santa Monica Boulevard (1-213 896 9099). Bus 4, 10, 11, 220, DASH Hollywood/1-10 exit Robertson Boulevard north.* **Open** 10pm-2.30am Fri. **Admission** over-21s only; $10.

One of LA's longest running serial clubs, operating beneath an alternative-new-wave-glam-punk banner, Cherry is heavy

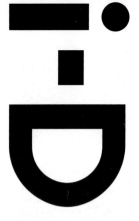

# SUBSCRIBE
## TO THE WORLD'S FINEST FASHION MAGAZINE

# 12 MONTHS OF GOOD i-DEAS FOR £27!
# AND GET A FREE i-DENTITY T-SHIRT WORTH £1

- - - - - - - - - - - - - - - - - - - - - - - - - - - - - -

**subscription rates** for 12 i-Ds per year plus free i-Dentity T-shirt

uk      europe     world [airmail]
☐ (£27.00)  ☐ (£36.00)  ☐ (£58.00)

**Value of order £** _____

**Access/Visa number:**

☐☐☐☐☐☐☐☐☐☐☐☐☐☐

**Signature:** _____

**Expiry date:** _____

**Yes please, this offer is** (i-D)ea

**Name:** _____

**Address:** _____

_____

_____

**Tel:** _____ **Date:** _____

**Print name and address very clearly. Please write your name and address on the back of your cheque or postal order.** For US subs information please dial: 1-800-544-6
Send a cheque/postal order in POUNDS STERLING made payable to Levelprint Ltd., or send details of credit card number, expiry date, name and address of cardholder to: i-D Magaz
Universal House, 251-255 Tottenham Court Road, London, W1P 0AE or telephone 0171 813 6170. All prices are inclusive of postage and packing. Allow 28 days for delivery (in UK or

*The entrance to Johnny Depp's **Viper Room** (see page 198), where River Phoenix died.*

on sweaty bodies singing along to floor-filling tunes from the not-too distant past. Regular theme nights such as Warhol's Factory give the go-go dancers a reason to climb atop their pedestals, while the inevitable rock-star sighting is eagerly awaited by those who never make it down from the balcony. Lucky girls get tapped for free entrance to the after-hours Girl Bar at the back of the building, where many a top model has been known to writhe.

### Club los Globos

*3040 West Sunset Boulevard, at Descanso Drive, Silver Lake (1-213 663 6517). Bus 1, 2, 3, 4, 201/US101, exit Silver Lake Boulevard north.* **Open** 8pm-2am daily. **Admission** $10.

The dazzling neon exterior is indicative of the sheen of joy flying off the fun-loving, slightly older, Spanish-speaking crowd. Salsa and merengue are the orders of the night, as live bands alternate with DJs. If you don't have a lucky partner to show you how, watching and nursing a Cerveza Montezuma is indeed the next best thing.

### Club Mambo

*11620 Wilshire Boulevard, between Barrington & Federal Avenues, West LA (1-310 837 3775). Bus 20, 320, Santa Monica 2, 3/1-405, exit Wilshire Boulevard west.* **Open** 8pm-2am Sun. **Admission** $8.

Salsa-lovers unite! Free lessons by salsa pro Ron Arciaga at 8pm give you the technique to click the night away. Live bands perform at 9.30pm, and rare Latin and Cuban videos complete the visual feast.

### Crush Bar

*1743 North Cahuenga Boulevard, at Hollywood Boulevard, Hollywood (1-213 461 9017). Bus 163, 180, 181, 212/US101, exit Cahuenga Boulevard north.* **Open** 9pm-2am Fri, Sat. **Admission** 21 and over only; $8-$10.

Setting out its stall with a white-on-black Hollywood-hero mural on its outside walls, the Crush Bar is not the youngest or the hippest Hollywood club, but it still makes a bid for being one of the most fun. The heady scents of excessive

perfume and musk mix with the delicious smells of the pizzas ordered from Greco's next door. After a hot slice, wriggle your greasy belly to well-known soul, 1970s disco and house classics. Come-as-you-are casual.

### Florentine Gardens

*5951 Hollywood Boulevard, between Bronson Avenue and North Gower Street, Hollywood (1-213 464 0706). Bus 1, 180, 181, 217, 429/US101, exit Hollywood Boulevard west.* **Open** 9pm-3am Fri; 9pm-5am Sat. **Admission** $8 Fri; $12 Sat.

Where many hardened clubbers got their start, this cavernous danceteria is consistently packed with stylish kids (many of them Latino) who welcome the mix of funk, hip-hop, disco and techno. While the volume of the crowd transforms the free buffet into a mess-hall chow line, the eagerness of the tireless youth infuse the atmosphere with energy long after the most carefully constructed hairdo has wilted. Expect to queue to get in, and dress to impress to make sure you do.

### The Garage

*4519 Santa Monica Boulevard, at Virgil Avenue, Silver Lake (1-213 683 3447). Bus 4, 26, 304/US101, exit Santa Monica Boulevard east.* **Open** 5pm-3am Mon-Sat; 4-8pm Sun. **Admission** 21 and over only; $3-$8.

What this single nondescript room lacks in ambience is made up for by a fun-loving hipster clientele and cheap full bar. Call ahead to find out what's on offer; possibilities range from a grrrl-band agit-fest to a strictly dancehall knees-up to Saturday night's fierce house club. Sunday afternoons are a hoot, featuring local Silver Lake bands performing live, plus punk, alternative and indie tunes, with the venerable Dr Vaginal Cream Davis. We recommend a late-night snack from Jay's Jaydogs or Jayburgers on the opposite corner.

### Louis XIV

*606 North La Brea Avenue, between Clinton Street & Melrose Avenue, Hollywood (1-213 934 5102). Bus 10, 11, 212/1-10, exit La Brea Avenue.* **Open** 6pm-midnight Mon-Thur, Sun; 6pm-1am Fri, Sat. **Admission** $5.

Another venue that's a restaurant by day, where the sounds and styles are decidedly Euro. Best treated as a meeting place or a stop in between spots, Louis XIV's saving graces are its two floors, which invite wandering, and its fresh-air front patio. A surprisingly small amount of dancing gets done considering the volume of what sounds like a compilation of last year's European house and techno hits playing in a continuous loop.

## Martini Lounge

*5657 Melrose Avenue, between Gower Street & Larchmont Boulevard, Hollywood (1-213 407 4058 4068). Bus 10, 11/1-10, exit La Brea Avenue north.* **Open** 9pm-2am daily. **Admission** $5.

As much a bar as a dance club. You can chew on a mid-priced salad or sandwich mid-week as none-too-serious live bands rock out on the small stage. Come Saturday and Sunday, the hip-hop brings in a bigger crowd that does indeed dance.

## McInerneys House of Entertainment & Supper Club

*2020 Wilshire Boulevard, at 20th Street, Santa Monica (1-310 449 1300). Bus 20, 320, Santa Monica 1, 2/1-10, exit 26th Street north.* **Call for details of opening times and admission.**

This may well turn into the newest and hippest kid on the block by virtue of the fact that actor Sean Penn is one of the primary investors. The club offers nightly live entertainment and a large dancefloor. The décor is upmarket and elegant. *Parking $2.50.*

## The Palace

*1735 North Vine Street, at Hollywood Boulevard, Hollywood (1-213 462 3000). Bus 163, 180, 181, 212, 217/US101, exit Hollywood Boulevard west.* **Open** 10pm-2am Thur-Sat. **Admission** $10.

Located across the street from the landmark Capitol Records building, this cavernous blue edifice can – and does – hold a couple of thousand youngsters from all over the metropolitan area who file in as the rock crowd is leaving the gig just finished. With a 20,000 watt (translation: really loud) sound system at full power and a laser show, the Palace is anything but intimate. An upstairs balcony provides a refuge for smoking and the odd grope. The music is provided by radio station DJs, so the fare is predictably commercial club cuts, new-wave classics and alternative floor-fillers.

## The Probe

*836 North Highland Avenue, between Waring & Willoughby Avenues (1-213 461 8301). Bus 10, 11/US101, exit Highland Avenue south.* **Open** 9pm-3am daily. **Admission** $5-$10.

On Sundays, The Probe hosts Club 70s: the name says it all. Expect to queue to get in, but your kitsch dish will be piled high with music of every genre from 'the decade that lives forever'. Arms remain thrown in the air all night while culture boundaries abound – if you've never seen the *Brady Bunch* TV show, the look-alike contest might be lost on you. Dress in 1970s garb for full participatory effect. Thursdays are downright gloomy, which is to say that the Helter Skelter club delivers on its promise of being Hollywood's premier goth joint.

## Project Blowed

*4343 Leimert Boulevard, at 43rd Street, Leimert Park (1-213 759 8373). Bus 4, 105, 210, DASH Crenshaw/Leimert Station/1-10, exit Crenshaw Boulevard South.* **Open** 8pm-midnight Thur. **Admission** $4.

Although strictly speaking not a dance club, heads still bob at this hip-hop spot, where an open-mic policy means the whole spectrum of LA's MCs takes a turn (the cream of the talent has been gathered on the double album 'Project Blowed'). The young black crowd can be insular to outsiders and a degree of antagonism has seeped in after a police raid provoked a peaceful crowd to riot in early 1996. Worth doubling up with a trip to venerable jazz club 5th Street Dick's (*see chapter* **Music**), located a few doors away on West 43rd Place.

## Roxbury

*8225 Sunset Boulevard, between Sweetzer Avenue & Havenhurst Drive, West Hollywood (1-213 656 1750). Bus 2, 3, 429/1-10, exit La Cienega Boulevard north.* **Open** 10pm-2am daily. **Admission** $10.

Plenty of hair products in evidence at this slick, upscale club on the Sunset Strip for people who dress like their paycheck depends on it. Three levels provide house, hip-hop and 1970s styles. There are a whopping five full bars where you can drink your fill when you get in – you'll have plenty of time waiting in line to work up the appropriate thirst.

## Take Five

*6114 Sunset Boulevard, at Gower Street, Hollywood. Bus 2, 3, DASH Hollywood/US101, exit Gower Street South.* **Open** 10pm-2am Thur. **Admission** $5.

Located across the street from huge rock venue the Hollywood Palladium and on the same block as the Denny's where Martin Landau eats his grilled cheese, Take Five is yet another venue for omnipresent LA DJs Mike Messex, Sean Perry and Big Daddy Carlos to do their groovy thing. As much lounging and pool playing as dancing will go down to the rap, soul and retro classics. If you want to get in free, wear a Hawaiian shirt or claim you're a pal of Beastie Boy Mike D (his clothing company X-Large sponsors the event).

## The Viper Room

*8852 Sunset Boulevard, at Larrabee Street, West Hollywood (1-310 358 1880). Bus 2, 3, 105, 302, 429, DASH B/1-10, exit La Cienega Boulevard north.* **Open** 9pm-2am daily. **Admission** $10-$15.

The teeth-gnashing wait and surly doormen set the scene for the Johnny Depp-owned club that will always be most famous for hosting River Phoenix's death. An uninviting, low-ceilinged sweatbox that specialises in funk and disco favourites while packing in Valley Girls and the guys who love them. The prime motive for going is having the right to truthfully proclaim 'I went to The Viper Room' – and spotting members of Duran Duran and the Sex Pistols fresh from their tanning-bed sessions.

## The West End

*1301 Fifth Street, at Arizona Avenue, Santa Monica (1-213 656 3905). Bus 4, 304, Santa Monica 1, 2, 3, 8/1-10, exit 4th/5th Street north.* **Open** 10pm-3am daily. **Admission** 21 and over only; $5-$10.

If you've spent the day on the Westside at the beach, and brought a change of clothes, this nearby club is a worthwhile bet. Sundays are pure house music with reliable DJs Doc Martin and Steve Loria while a particularly well-scrubbed crowd gets flirtatious. Other nights include reggae (Thur), disco (Fri) and live bands (phone for details). Saturdays start at 4pm, when you can relive the 1980s until 2am.

## The World

*7070 Hollywood Boulevard at North Sycamore Avenue, Hollywood (1-213 467 7070). Bus 1, 180, 181, 212/US101, exit Highland Avenue South.* **Open** 10pm-3am daily. **Admission** $7-$15.

Once you realise that The World hosts clubs formerly held in a shopping mall, you'll understand the scented, weekend collegiate crowd. The most musically progressive night is Wednesday, where the mid-week devotees revel in the light and sound of the large main room. Gothic-tinged Thursdays is the night for the club Perversion, where the black-clad go to see the more-goofy-than-titillating bondage show (real, nonetheless) and dance to industrial and techno in the aptly-named, ambience-heavy Velvet Lounge.

# Film

**Sorry, no tips on how to become a movie star. But plenty of advice on celluloid choice in the film capital of the world.**

## HOLLYWOOD: THE BEGINNINGS

The old film-makers liked to say that it was the perfect shooting weather that brought them to Hollywood in 1912, but the reality was more prosaic: Los Angeles was a long way from New York and the tough patent laws that controlled film-making there. The sunshine was an added advantage though, as was the close proximity of Mexico, just in case the patent boys came west. By the beginning of World War I, Hollywood was jammed with film companies operating out of old barns and warehouses.

Among the infant, micro-studios churning out ever more films to satisfy a worldwide market that kept growing and growing were the prototypes of Paramount and Universal Studios, while the value of stars became swiftly apparent, notable among them Charlie Chaplin and Mary Pickford. Pickford, as well as being 'America's Sweetheart', was a shrewd judge of her own worth and in 1919, along with Chaplin, Douglas Fairbanks and DW Griffith, cinema's first great director, she formed United Artists to distribute their own work, becoming, in the process, one of the richest women in America. Hollywood's first golden age began. Before the smog and traffic came and long before the prying eyes of the press got too close, LA became a playground for the movie people.

But by the mid 1920s things were changing. The great studios – MGM, Paramount, Universal and Columbia – were up and running and the legendary studio bosses such as Sam Goldwyn, Louis B Mayer and Carl Laemmle weren't going to let the actors run things. Helped by the first public outcry at the immorality of Hollywood – sparked by the murder of a British director and fuelled further by the involvement of the very popular comedian Fatty Arbuckle in the death of an actress – the studios began to take control of the fledgling industry.

The arrival of sound further consolidated the studios' power; the new technology meant immediate pay cuts for the silent stars, who had to prove they could make the transition to talkies. Not all of them did, but by now American talent was being bolstered increasingly by new arrivals from Europe. The Brits had been here since the beginning, but the rise of Hitler prompted much of the German film industry, the artistic powerhouse of world cinema in the 1920s, to up and move to Hollywood. LA was now the world capital of film-making, its lure so powerful that even Eisenstein, the great Russian communist director, stopped by in 1932 for a brief visit.

## THE PRODUCTION LINE

The 1930s saw Hollywood's second golden age. The studios now controlled every aspect of movie-making, locking the talent into long-term contracts that granted them extravagant salaries while ensuring they had no control over what they did. The studios were literally movie factories: actors and directors were assigned to projects whether they liked them or not, writers clocked in every day at the writers' building and an army of technicians kept the cameras rolling. This new corporate atmosphere displeased many of the actors and film-makers, but the sheer number of movies being produced meant there was work for everyone, and some films were enormously accomplished.

The moguls were also busy working on Hollywood's somewhat dissolute public image. Nearly all were immigrants from Eastern Europe, but they determined to make the film industry as American as baseball. Scandals were kept quiet, donations were made to political parties and the outbreak of World War II provided Hollywood with the chance to show that it could wave the flag better than anyone. After the war, the dark side of this studied patriotism emerged: the blacklist that condemned hundreds of writers, directors and actors to years of unemployment, as the studios hastily complied with McCarthy's mission to root out communist sympathisers in public life.

The 1940s also saw the first cracks in the studio system and by the end of the 1950s, competition from television and the stars' desire to control their own destinies appeared to signal their demise. But after some lean times in the 1960s and 1970s, they have bounced back. Even though they no longer have the stars on a string and are now owned by the Japanese, the banks and, in the case of 20th Century Fox, by Rupert Murdoch, the studios are still here. In a town with a short history, they act as a reassuring constant and they're growing more powerful through their non-movie interests: merchandising, running theme parks and owning sports teams. And the flow of hopefuls has never stopped. Tens of thousands of people pitch up in LA every year, pulled by the same dreams that have been drawing the star-struck since 1912.

## TINSELTOWN TODAY

All this history and expectation conspires to make LA film-obsessed. If people don't work in the industry, they know – or want to know – someone who does, and at LA parties there's always one room where the occupants are talking movies. Opening nights for the big new releases are always packed and every premiere is shown live on TV. In terms of actual cinema-going and film-related activities, this translates into a huge range of choices. There are film programmes aplenty at UCLA, USC and just about every college in and around the city (*see chapter* **Students**), a couple of film festivals every month, workshops everywhere, and, if you stay here for any length of time, you're almost certain to happen on a location shoot.

## HOW TO BE AN EXTRA

Back in the 1930s it was easy to get yourself into a feature film as an extra. You simply rolled up to the Central Casting building at Hollywood Boulevard and Western Avenue, where they took your particulars and sent you home to wait for their call. David Niven got his start this way. Nowadays, however, things are different. Central Casting is no more and extras are normally recruited from agencies that charge a registration fee before they send you out on a job. Check the *LA Weekly*'s classified section for ads for these agencies and look in the actors' trade papers, *Drama-Logue* and *Back Stage West* (both $1.85), available at most newsstands.

## TICKETS & INFORMATION

The best sources for listings, reviews and ticket information are the *LA Times* and *LA Weekly*. The *Times* reviewers can be erratic; the *Weekly* is more reliable. Check also for festivals and tributes. Buy tickets from the individual venues and bear in mind that first nights are very popular.

Not surprisingly, there are literally thousands of screens in LA; we have listed a selection of the most interesting. For bog-standard local multi-screens, again check the papers.

## The cinemas

Los Angeles isn't the greatest place to catch the latest European releases: only the big hits make it over and, although a lot of European cinema is shown in LA, it's mostly screened in the context of tributes, retrospectives and special seasons. Luckily, there are a lot of these and they're not just restricted to art-house cinemas.

## Classic, new & experimental

### American Cinematheque

*Information 1-213 466 3456.*
Specialising in tributes and retrospectives, the Cinematheque has a growing reputation for innovative programming. Screenings are held at various locations; phone for information.

### American Film Institute

*Information 1-213 856 7600 9am-5pm Mon-Fri.*
Dedicated to preserving and advancing the moving image, the AFI also runs the LA International Film Festival and sometimes organises screenings for the general public.

### 4 Star Theater

*5112 Wilshire Boulevard, between Highland & La Brea Avenues, Miracle Mile (1-213 936 3533). Bus 212, 320, 322/I-10, exit La Brea Avenue north.* **Open** varies; call for schedule. **Tickets** $5 adults; $3 senior citizens; $2 children. **No credit cards.**
Operating on the weekends, the 4 Star mainly revives classic American movies.

### IMAX

*700 State Drive, at Figueroa Street & Exposition Boulevard, Exposition Park, Downtown (box office 1-213 744 2014). Bus 81, 200, 442, 444, DASH E/I-110 north, exit Martin Luther King Jr Boulevard west.* **Open** *box office* 9.45am-9pm daily. **Tickets** $6.25 adults; $5 13-17s; $4.25 senior citizens; $4 4-12s. **Credit** MC, V.
The five-storey high and 70ft wide screen at the IMAX Theatre is perfectly suited to capturing vast landscapes and showing off the natural world – and documentaries on these subjects is what the theatre mostly screens.

### Industry Cyber Café

*3191 Cahuenga Boulevard, at Barham Avenue, Hollywood (1-213 845 9998). Bus 420/US101, exit Barham Avenue west.* **Open** 8am-8pm Mon-Thur; 8am-midnight Fri; 10am-midnight Sat; 10am-10pm Sun. **Credit** AmEx, Disc, MC, V.
Designed as a meeting place and resource centre for resting actors and aspiring film-makers, the Cyber Café has a free Sunday night showcase (7pm) for short films and videos. The results can be mixed – but at least they serve a decent cup of coffee.

### LA County Museum Of Art

*5905 Wilshire Boulevard, between La Brea & Fairfax Avenues, Miracle Mile (1-213 857 6010). Bus 20, 21, 22, 320/I-10, exit Fairfax Avenue north.* **Open** *box office* 10am-5pm Tue-Thur; 11am-9pm Fri; 11am-6pm Sat, Sun; *shows* 7.30pm Fri, Sat; 1pm Wed. **Tickets** $6 adults; $4 senior citizens, students. **No credit cards.**
The museum regularly runs short seasons and tributes at the Leo S Bing Theater and on Wednesday afternoons screens classic movies for the bargain price of $1. One of Martin Scorsese's favourite rep venues.

### Museum Of Contemporary Art (MOCA)

*250 South Grand Avenue & 251 North Central Avenue, Downtown (1-213 626 6222/box office 1-213 626 6828). Metro Pershing Square/bus DASH A, B/I-110, exit Fourth Street east.* **Open** *box office* 11am-5pm Tue-Sun; call for show times. **Tickets** $6 adults; $4 senior citizens, students. **No credit cards.**
Both the MOCA sites screen experimental and classic films and videos as part of exhibitions.

### Silent Movie

*611 North Fairfax Avenue, at Melrose Avenue, Hollywood (1-213 653 2389). Bus 10, 11, 217, DASH Fairfax/I-10, exit Fairfax Avenue north.* **Open** *shows* 8pm Wed, Fri-Sun. **Tickets** $6 adults; $4 children. **No credit cards.**
Possibly the only cinema in the world devoted solely to

**The Los Angeles Theater** – *no longer showing films, but a damn fine building. See page 202.*

showing silent movies, this theatre is definitely worth a visit if you want to see a silent in an authentic environment, with, of course, an organist playing the accompaniment live.

### Tales Bookshop/Café

*667 South La Brea Avenue, at Wilshire Boulevard, Miracle Mile (1-213 933 2640). Bus 20, 21, 22, 212, 320, 322/I-10, exit La Brea Avenue north.* **Open** *shows* 7.30pm Mon, Thur; 7.30pm, 9.30pm, 7.30pm, 7.30pm, 9.30pm, Sat, Sun. **Tickets** $4. **Credit** MC, V.
Half book store and half coffeehouse, Tales presents weekly screenings of classic 16mm prints. Since the screen is so large it doesn't matter if you sit in the bookshop or the café: you can always see. Tales specialises in film noir.

### UCLA Film & Television Archive

*UCLA Campus, 405 Hilgard Avenue, Westwood (admin 1-310 206 8013/box office 1-213 206 8365/recorded information 1-213 206 3456). Bus 2, 21, 429, 576, Culver City 6, Santa Monica 1, 2, 3/I-10, exit Sunset Boulevard east.* **Open** *admin* 9am-6pm Mon-Fri; *box office* 1 hour before show; call for more details. **Tickets** $6 adults; $4 senior citizens, students. **No credit cards**.
UCLA's huge archives are a treasure trove of little-seen silents, classics from the 1930s heyday of Hollywood, newsreels and documentaries. As films are restored by the archive they're screened, mostly here at the Melnitz Theatre, but screenings aren't just limited to what comes out of the archive; in any given week there's normally something for everyone. There are screenings throughout most of the year.

## Drive-ins

The rise of the multiplexes has only hastened the decline of the drive-in, once a cherished part of the American movie-going experience. Because everyone lives near a mall, and hence a multiplex, the drive-ins have been squeezed out and there are now only four in the Greater Los Angeles area. They all show current releases and, for obvious reasons, screenings start at dusk. Tickets cost $5 and credit cards are not accepted.

### Los Altos Drive-In

*2800 North Bellflower Boulevard, at 28th Street, Los Altos, Long Beach (1-310 421 8831). Bus Long Beach 91, 93/I-405 exit Bellflower Boulevard east.*

### Van Nuys Drive-In

*15040 Roscoe Boulevard, between Noble & Kester Avenues, Van Nuys (1-818 786 3500). Bus 152, 418/I-405, exit Roscoe Boulevard east.*

### Vermont Drive-In

*17737 South Vermont Avenue, at Artesia Boulevard, Gardena (1-310 323 4055). Bus 130, 444, Torrance 1, 2/SR91 west, exit Vermont Avenue south.*

### Winnetka Drive-In

*9300 Winnetka Avenue, at Plummer Street, Chatsworth (1-818 349 6808). Bus 167, 243/I-405, exit Nordhoff Street west.*

## Laemmle chain

The **Laemmle** chain of cinemas (named after Carl Laemmle, the founder of Universal Studios), frequently has miniseasons and tributes to individual directors. There are eight Laemmle cinemas scattered across LA and the Valley, including **Sunset 5** (8000 Sunset Boulevard, at Crescent Heights Boulevard, West Hollywood; 1-213 848 3500); **Laemmle's Monica 4-Plex** (1332 Second Street, between

Santa Monica Boulevard & Arizona Avenue, Santa Monica; 1-310 394 9741); **Laemmle's Royal** (11523 Santa Monica Boulevard, between Butler & Colby Avenues, West LA; 1-310 477 5581); and **Laemmle's Music Hall** (9036 Wilshire Boulevard, at Doheny Drive, Beverly Hills; 1-310 274 6869).

## Movie palaces

There are some extravagant movie palaces in Los Angeles, dating from the early glamour days of the industry. The most famous of these is **Mann's Chinese Theater** at 6925 Hollywood Boulevard, at Highland Avenue; a bizarre re-creation of a Chinese temple, but also a good place to see a film. Almost opposite it is the elegant **El Capitan Theater** at Hollywood Boulevard and Highland Avenue (1-213 467 7674), a favourite spot for premieres. In Downtown, the 2,000-seat **Orpheum** (842 South Broadway, at Eighth Street; 1-213 239 0937) is the last of the great 1920s Broadway theatres still to operate as a cinema; the **Los Angeles Theater** at 615 South Broadway is still worth a look, though.

Other notable cinemas include the **Cinerama Dome** (6360 Sunset Boulevard, at Ivar Avenue, Hollywood; 1-213 466 3401), with its giant screen and spectacular sound system; the very comfortable six-screen **GCC Hollywood Galaxy** (7021 Hollywood Boulevard, at Sycamore Avenue, Hollywood; 1-213 957 9246), the pleasant **Vista** (4473 Sunset Drive, at Sunset Boulevard, Los Feliz; 1-213 660 6639), the **AMC Century 14** (in the Century City Shopping Mall, Santa Monica Boulevard, at the Avenue of the Stars; 1-310 553 8900) and the 18-screen **Universal City 18 Cinemas** at Universal CityWalk (1-818 766 4317). The **Mann Theaters**, all in Westwood, are frequently used for big-name premières (Mann Village Theater, 961 Broxton Avenue, 1-310 208 5576; Mann Bruin Theater, 950 Broxton Avenue, 1-310 208 8998; Mann National Theatre, 950 Broxton Avenue, 1-310 208 4366; all at Weyburn Avenue).

## Repertory

Bear in mind that many of the cinemas listed above also act as rep venues.

### New Beverly Cinema

*7165 Beverly Boulevard, at North Detroit Street, Park La Brea (1-213 938 4038). Bus 14, 212/I-10, exit La Brea Avenue north.* **Open** box office 1½hour before show; call for schedule. **Tickets** $5 adults; $4 students; $2.50 senior citizens. **No credit cards**.
One of the more popular cinemas in LA, the New Beverly is an utterly standard cinema that shows recent releases at bargain rates immediately after they've come off general release. It also revives older movies.

### Nuart

*11272 Santa Monica Boulevard, at Sawtelle Avenue, West LA (1-310 478 6379). Bus 4, 304, Santa Monica 1, 5/I-405, exit Santa Monica Boulevard west.* **Open** box office from 5pm daily; call for show times. **Tickets** $7.50 adults; $4.50 senior citizens. **No credit cards**.
The best rep house on the Westside, the Nuart is a good place to catch independent and foreign movies. It also programmes rep classics like *The Rocky Horror Picture Show* (midnight, Sun) and hosts midnight screenings.

### Rialto

*1023 Fair Oaks Avenue, at Oxly Avenue, South Pasadena (1-818 799 9567). Bus 176, 483/I-110, exit Fair Oaks Avenue south.* **Open** box office from 4pm Mon-Fri; from noon Sat, Sun **Tickets** $7 adults; $4 senior citizens. **No credit cards**.
Another place to catch *The Rocky Horror Picture Show* (midnight, Sat), alongside the latest art-house releases. A stand-by if you're ever in Pasadena – and a decent cinema to boot.

# And the winner is...

*Of the all the stars that Hollywood has immortalised on screen, LA itself has played the biggest role. We are proud to announce our own Tosca (Time Out Salutes the City of Angels) winners.*

*A raging Michael Douglas in* Falling Down.

## BEST APOCALYPTIC SCENARIO

**Blade Runner** (Ridley Scott, 1982)
Ridley Scott's seminal vision of LA in 2019, complete with androids and the Bradbury Building.
**Highly commended**: Earthquake, Escape from LA, Independence Day, Miracle Mile, 1941, Strange Days, The Terminator, Terminator 2: Judgment Day, Them!

## EXORCISE THAT ZEITGEIST

**LA Story** (Mick Jackson, 1991)
Rollerskates, road rage, therapy, colonic irrigation – all the LA clichés are bundled into one unexpectedly charming package. With Steve Martin.
**Highly commended**: Down and Out in Beverly Hills, Grand Canyon, Into the Night, Scenes from the Class Struggle in Beverly Hills, Short Cuts, Welcome to LA

## BIGGEST AIRHEADS

**Clueless** (Amy Heckerling, 1995)
Alicia Silverstone is the Beverly Hills babe with a wardrobe the size of the Hollywood Bowl and an even bigger heart.
**Highly commended**: Airheads, Earth Girls Are Easy, Encino Man, Pretty Woman

## COPS & ROBBERS

**Heat** (Michael Mann, 1995)
The ritual dance between cop and criminal (Pacino and De Niro) played out against the vast, soulless city. Check those night-time shots and the Downtown shootout.
**Highly commended**: Beverly Hills Cop, Colors, Die Hard, Internal Affairs, Reservoir Dogs, To Live and Die in LA

## HOLLYWOOD ON HOLLYWOOD

**Sunset Boulevard** (Billy Wilder, 1950)
Failed screenwriter meets faded starlet in this classic satire on Hollywood.

**Highly commended**: Barton Fink, The Big Picture, California Suite, The Day of the Locust, Ed Wood, Get Shorty

## CLASSIC NOIR

**Double Indemnity** (Billy Wilder, 1944)
Dark, paranoid thriller with Barbara Stanwyck and Fred MacMurray teaming up for a spot of insurance fraud
**Highly commended**: The Big Sleep (1946), DOA (1950), Farewell My Lovely (1944), Kiss Me Deadly

## NEW NOIR

**Chinatown** (Roman Polanski, 1974)
Water supply/real estate shenanigans in 1930s LA starring a nose-plastered Jack Nicholson.
**Highly commended**: Devil in a Blue Dress, The Long Goodbye (1973), Mulholland Falls, The Two Jakes, Who Framed Roger Rabbit?

## THE URBAN EXPERIENCE

**Boyz N the Hood** (John Singleton, 1991)
A teenage boy tries to survive with integrity intact in a community ravaged by crack, poverty, police harassment and guns.
**Highly commended**: El Norte, Falling Down, South Central

## FASTEST MOVERS

**Point Break** (Kathryn Bigelow, 1991)
They surf, they run really fast and they skydive without parachutes. Keanu Reeves and Patrick Swayze play Malibu Macho.
**Highly commended**: Lethal Weapon (1, 2 & 3), Speed, White Men Can't Jump

Strange Days *for Ralph Fiennes.*

*Yet another essential LA moment: the drive-in cinema.*

## Private screenings

As you'd expect, there are endless industry and press screenings in LA, but gaining access to them isn't easy unless you know someone on the inside. However, on most weekends there are people outside the big multiplexes offering free tickets to previews and test screenings of soon-to-be released movies. Try the **Laemmle's Monica 4-Plex** and the **AMC Century 14** (*see above*); if you're aged under thirty you might just get asked inside.

You may be asked to fill in a report card on the movie: the studios use these to decide whether the film should be changed before it goes out on general release – your chance to influence a blockbuster. The **Bruin** (948 Broxton Avenue, near the UCLA campus; 1-310 208 8998) is often used for sneak previews of upcoming movies; they're advertised in advance in the *LA Times* and *LA Weekly*.

## Film festivals

Film festivals are held every month in Los Angeles; check the *LA Weekly* for upcoming events. The **Los Angeles International Film Festival** (1-213 856 7707) is the main one for independent and foreign movies; run by the AFI and now in its 10th year, it's held for two weeks in October and always attracts big crowds. **Outfest: The Los Angeles Gay and Lesbian Film Festival** (1-213 951 1247) is one of the most comprehensive of its kind in the world and runs for a fortnight every July.

## Studio tours

The **Universal Studios** tour (*see chapter Sightseeing*) is justly famous for its spectacular rides, but if you want a tour that shows something of how a studio operates then you have to go to either **Paramount** or **Warner Brothers**.

The two-hour Paramount tour is good value for the $15 admission, spinning you round not only the oldest and most attractive studio, but also the only one still located in Hollywood. The Warners tour is almost double the price – $29 – for the same amount of time and its lot doesn't have the historical resonance of Paramount's, which has been in the same place, give or take a few hundred metres, since 1915. Both tours promise to try to get you onto any soundstages they can, so you can actually see a film shooting – but don't expect to be shaking hands with Arnold Schwarzenegger. If you're lucky, you'll get to see a few vaguely familiar faces being whisked around on the golf carts that serve as transport on the lots.

Numbers are limited on both tours, so book a few days ahead. Children under ten are not allowed on either tour.

### Paramount Studios

*5555 Melrose Avenue, at Gower Street, Hollywood (1-213 956 1777). Bus 10, 11/US101, exit Gower Street south.* **Open** 9am-2pm Mon-Fri; tours every half-hour. **Tickets** $15. **No credit cards.**

### Warner Brothers Studios

*4000 Warner Boulevard, at Hollywood Way & Olive Avenue, Burbank (1-818 954 1744). Bus 96, 152, 163/ SR134, exit Pass Avenue south.* **Open** 9am-4pm Mon-Fri; tours on the hour. **Tickets** $29. **Credit** AmEx, MC, V.

# Museums & Galleries

**Yes, it's got lots of kooky collections, but LA also has some serious cultural and scientific institutions that give the lie to its airhead reputation.**

Now is an exciting time to be museum-hopping in LA. The newly built Getty Center will be opening in autumn 1997, at about the same time as the remodelled California Science Center; the Hollywood Entertainment Museum should be open by the time this guide is published; and recently opened museums include the Museum of Tolerance, the Skirball Cultural Center and the Museum of Television & Radio.

It is best to plan excursions with a map since museums are usually clustered near one another. For example, the **Museum Mile** (aka Miracle Mile) section of Wilshire Boulevard is home to LACMA, the George C Page Museum, the Petersen Automotive Museum and the Museum of Miniatures, while **Exposition Park** in Downtown LA houses the Natural History Museum, the California Science Center and the California Afro-American Museum. **Pasadena** also has a clutch of heavyweights, including the Norton Simon Museum of Art and the Pacific Asia Museum.

If you take the subway, don't forget to check out the permanent projects commissioned by the MTA: Jim Isermann designed the Fifth Street station on the Blue Line and Jonathon Borofsky has a piece at Civic Center on the Red Line. Call MetroArts (1-213 922 4278) for information about self-guided tours and temporary projects.

# Museums

## Art & culture

### Barnsdall Park
*4800 Hollywood Boulevard, at Vermont Avenue, Los Feliz. Bus 1, 180, 181, 204, 217, Community Connection 203/US101, exit Sunset Boulevard east.*
Barnsdall Park is home to the Frank Lloyd Wright-designed Hollyhock House (1-213 913 4157), the Junior Arts Center (1-213 485 4474), which holds art classes for kids, and the LA Municipal Art Gallery (12.30-5pm Wed, Thur, Sat, Sun, 12.30-8.30pm Fri; $1.50 adults; 1-213 485 4581), where exhibitions are often interesting, with an emphasis on the work of Southern California artists. The gallery also hosts films, concerts and readings.

### California African-American Museum
*600 State Drive, at Figueroa Street, Exposition Park, Downtown (1-213 744 7432). Bus 81, 200, 442, 444, 445, DASH C/I-110, exit Exposition Boulevard.* **Open** 10am-5pm Tue-Sun. **Admission** free; donation requested.
Research library and museum focusing on the cultural and historical achievements of African-Americans, with permanent exhibits of sculpture, landscape painting and African tribal art. Past shows have included a survey of African puppetry, black music in 1960s LA and the history of illustration for African-American children's books. *Parking $5.*

### Craft & Folk Art Museum
*5800 Wilshire Boulevard, at Curson Avenue, Miracle Mile (1-213 937 5544/recorded information 1-213 243 0469). Bus 20, 21, 22, 320/I-10, exit La Brea Avenue north.* **Open** 11am-5pm Tue-Sun. **Admission** $4 adults; $2.50 children, senior citizens. **Credit** AmEx, MC, V.
Modestly sized exhibition space showcasing examples of ceramics, textiles and other craft and folk art from around the world, including Japan, Mexico and India. Every October, the International Festival of Masks is held in Hancock Park, on the other side of Wilshire Boulevard. Parking is free here.

### Geffen Contemporary at MOCA
*152 North Central Avenue, at First Street, Downtown (1-213 626 6222). Bus 30, 31, 40, 42, 436, 445, 466, DASH A, D/US101, exit Alameda Avenue south.* **Open** 11am-5pm Tue, Wed, Fri-Sun; 11am-8pm Thur. **Admission** $6 adults; $4 students, senior citizens; free under-12s; free 5-8pm Thur. **Credit** AmEx, MC, V.
Long known as the Temporary Contemporary, this satellite building of the Museum of Contemporary Art (*see below*) has recently become more permanent on account of its new name and the sizeable donation from Dreamworks mogul David Geffen that went along with it. The cavernous warehouse interior, redesigned by Frank Gehry, plays host to changing exhibitions as well as selections from the museum's permanent collection, and has a reading room and small bookstore. *Parking $2.50.*

### The Henry E Huntington Library, Art Collections & Botanical Gardens
*1151 Oxford Road, second entrance at corner of Orlando Road & Allen Avenue, San Marino (1-818 405 2100/ recorded information 1-818 405 2141). Bus 79/I-110, exit Arroyo Parkway to California Boulevard east.* **Open** *winter* noon-4.30pm Tue-Fri; 10.30am-4.30pm Sat, Sun; *summer* 10.30am-4.30pm Tue-Sun. **Admission** $7.50 adults; $6 senior citizens; $4 students; free first Thur of the month. **Credit** MC, V.
Scholars and other researchers can use the vast library here, which contains six millions items, including a Gutenberg

Bible and the earliest known edition of Chaucer's *Canterbury Tales*. Regular citizens are free to wander the vast (130 acres) and gorgeous gardens, marvel at the fantastic varieties of cactus in the 12-acre Desert Garden and tour the museum, which includes English and French paintings from the eighteenth and nineteenth centuries, furniture and items from the library. An enchanting place to spend an afternoon; wear a silly flowered dress and a sun hat and have tea in the gazebo.

### Japanese American National Museum

*369 East First Street, at Central Avenue, Downtown LA (1-213 625 0414). Bus 30, 31, 40, 42, 436, 445, 466, DASH A, D/I-110, exit Fourth Street east.* **Open** 10am-8pm Mon; 10am-5pm Tue-Sun. **Admission** free; donation requested.

This recently opened museum has many exhibitions relating to Japanese American culture. Past exhibits have included depictions of life in Japanese internment camps and the history of Kona Coffee (a gourmet coffee grown and harvested by Japanese-American emigrés since 1813).

### The J Paul Getty Museum at the Getty Villa

*17985 Pacific Coast Highway, at Pacific Coast Highway, Malibu (1-310 458 2003). Bus 434/I-10 west, exit PCH north.* **Open** 10am-5pm Tue-Sun. **Admission** free; book parking 7-10 days in advance. **Credit** AmEx, MC, V.

### The J Paul Getty Center for the Fine Arts

*1200 Getty Center Drive, at the I-405, Brentwood. Bus 561/I-405, exit Getty Center Drive.* **Open** Tue-Sun (hours to be decided). **Admission** free; book parking 2 weeks in advance. **Credit** AmEx, MC, V.

Scheduled to open in autumn 1997, the grandiose new $733 million Getty Center in Brentwood, set on a 110-acre 'campus' and designed by Richard Meier, promises to provide a suitable home for the Getty Trust's impressive collection of Western painting from the thirteenth to nineteenth centuries, European decorative arts and furniture, illuminated manuscripts and photographs and much much more. It will also house other branches of the Trust – the Getty Research Institute for the History of Art and the Humanities, the Getty Conservation Center, the Getty Grant Program – plus a restaurant, two cafés, a 450-seat auditorium, a large library and gardens designed by artist Robert Irwin. Phew.

Just before the Getty Center opens, the Getty Museum in Malibu – modelled after the Villa de Papyri, a luxurious first-century Roman villa that stood in Pompeii – will close for a renovation that will transform it into the 'Getty Villa', reopening in 2000 as the home for the Trust's extensive collection of Greek and Roman antiquities. If you come by bus, ask the driver for a special museum pass.

### Los Angeles County Museum of Art (LACMA)

*5905 Wilshire Boulevard, between Fairfax & La Brea Avenues, Miracle Mile (1-213 857 6000). Bus 20, 21, 22, 320/I-10, exit Fairfax Avenue north.* **Open** 10am-5pm Tue-Thur; 10am-9pm Fri; 11am-6pm Sat, Sun. **Admission** $6 adults; $4 students, senior citizens; $1 6-17s; free second Wed of the month. **No credit cards.**

The largest museum complex in LA is housed in five buildings around a central courtyard, each with a different focus. With twentieth-century masterpieces, textiles, Indian and Southeast Asian art, contemporary art and Pre-Columbian art, LACMA has a bit of everything. The Pavilion for Japanese Art is impressive, while the Contemporary Sculpture Garden features nine large-scale outdoor sculptures. Recent exhibitions have included the retrospectives of Los Angeles artists Lari Pittman and (by adoption, at least) David Hockney. There are lectures and films and jazz in the courtyard on Friday nights. Parking is free after 5pm on Friday.

*Parking $5 Wilshire Boulevard & Spaulding Avenue.*

*Cutting-edge art at **MOCA**.*

### Museum of Contemporary Art (MOCA)

*250 South Grand Avenue, at Third Street, Downtown (1-213 626 6222/Patinette restaurant 1-213 625 1178). Metro Civic Center/Tom Bradley or Pershing Square. Bus 30, 31, 40, 42, 436, 445, 466, DASH A, D/I-110, exit Fourth Street east.* **Open** 11am-5pm Tue, Wed, Fri-Sun; 11am-8pm Thur. **Admission** $6 adults; $4 students, senior citizens; free under-12s; free 5-8pm Thur. **Credit** AmEx, MC, V.

MOCA is the city's leading venue for contemporary art, hosting travelling exhibitions as well as those organised by its own curators. Its light, flexible and airy galleries were designed by Japanese architect Arata Isozaki and a huge Swiss Army knife by Claes Oldenburg stands outside. Recent shows have included local superstars photographer Uta Barth and architect Frank Israel, a retrospective of Bruce Nauman and photos by Sigmar Polke. The museum also has a small gourmet café, Patinette (an offshoot of Patina on Melrose Avenue) and a well-stocked bookshop.

### The Museum of Television & Radio

*465 North Beverly Drive, at Little Santa Monica Boulevard, Beverly Hills (1-310 786 1000). Bus 14/I-10, exit Robertson Boulevard north.* **Open** noon-5pm Wed-Sun; noon-9pm Thur. **Admission** $6 adults; $4 students, senior citizens; $3 under-12s. **No credit cards.**

The permanent collection consists of 75,000 TV and radio programmes, easily accessible via a computer catalogue – and exactly the same as the holdings of the Museum of Television and Radio in New York. It also hosts changing exhibitions on such subjects as the costumes and make-up from *Star Trek*.

*Parking $1 per hour; free 2hrs with validation.*

### Museum of Tolerance at the Simon Weisenthal Center

*9786 West Pico Boulevard, at Roxbury Drive, West LA (1-310 553 8403/Simon Weisenthal Center 1-310 553 9036). Bus 7/I-10, Robertson Boulevard exit south.* **Open** 10am-5pm Mon-Thur; 10am-3pm (Nov-Mar 10am-1pm) Fri; 11am-5pm Sun. **Admission** $8 adults; $6 senior citizens; $5 students; $3 3-12s. **Credit** AmEx, MC, V.

This multimedia museum concentrates on the disastrous effects of intolerance. The permanent exhibition area is divided into two parts. One confronts contemporary America's racism, with exhibits about the 1992 Los Angeles riots, the Civil Rights movement, hate groups and racial stereotypes; the other, more extensive area guides visitors through the Holocaust, with dioramas, photos and stories. At the beginning of this section, you get a 'passport' with a child's photograph on it; their fate is revealed to you at the end of the tour. Upstairs, in the Multimedia Learning Center, you can explore the subject further by computer. We recommend that you book in advance.

*Free parking.*

# Picture this

You might expect to find a plethora of modern art in LA, but there is also a surprisingly large amount of pre-twentieth century and classical work. Here are some masterpieces to look out for.

### Irises by Van Gogh

Painted in the garden of the asylum at Saint-Remy, this frieze-like rendering depicts a garden of irises with Van Gogh's characteristic bold brush strokes and striking colour schemes of purple, green, yellow and red.
*The J Paul Getty Center for Fine Art*

### The Pavilion for Japanese Art

Oklahoma oilman and art collector Joe D Price donated over 300 scrolls and screens from the Edo period (seventh century) to LACMA, and built a new pavilion to house them – just to make sure they were correctly lit. Edo art, unlike the austere religious art that preceded it, centres on exotic, vivid and colourful celebrations of nature.
*LACMA*

### The Blue Boy by Thomas Gainsborough

This portrait by the father of the eighteenth-century British landscape school is easily one of the most recognisable paintings in any LA museum. The gallery also houses the eerily similar 'Pinkie' by Sir Thomas Lawrence, depicting the youthful aunt of Elizabeth Barrett Browning.
*Henry E Huntington Art Gallery*

### Still Life with Oranges, Lemons and a Rose by Francisco de Zurbaran

One of the great masterpieces of European painting is also the only signed and dated still life from this Spanish master, whose art was devoted to religious portraits of saints. The Norton Simon also holds Rodin's 'Burghers of Calais' and the famous Galka Scheyer collection of paintings by Klee, Jawlensky, Feininger and Kandinsky.
*Norton Simon Museum of Art*

### The Honore Daumier Collection

Over 10,000 works by the French caricaturist, painter, sculptor and satirist is the highlight of this oft-maligned museum's collection of late nineteenth-century art. Van Gogh's disturbing 'The Hospital at Saint-Remy', painted a year before he died, is also here.
*UCLA Armand Hammer Museum of Art*

## Norton Simon Museum of Art

*411 West Colorado Boulevard, at Orange Grove Boulevard, Pasadena (1-818 449 6840). Bus 177, 180, 181/I-110, exit Colorado Boulevard west.* **Open** noon-6pm Thur-Sun. **Admission** $4 adults, $2 students, senior citizens. **No credit cards.**
This important and modern museum houses mostly European art, from the Renaissance to the mid-twentieth century, in a pleasant, usually uncrowded setting near Old Town Pasadena's shopping area. Highlights include the Impressionist collection and works by Rembrandt, Goya, Degas and Picasso.
*Free parking.*

## Pacific Asia Museum

*46 North Los Robles Avenue, at Colorado Boulevard, Pasadena (1-818 449 2742). Bus 180, 181, 256, 267, 401, 402/I-110, exit Colorado Boulevard east.* **Open** noon-5pm Wed-Sun. **Admission** $4 adults; $2 students, senior citizens. **No credit cards.**
Art and artefacts from Asia and the Pacific Rim (plus events for kids and families) in the historic Grace Nicholson Building, a recreation of a Northern Chinese palace, with a charming Chinese Garden Court to match.
*Free parking.*

## Santa Monica Museum of Art

*2437 Main Street, between Hollister Avenue & Ocean Park Boulevard, Santa Monica (1-310 399 2801). Bus 33, 333, Santa Monica, 1, 8, 10/I-10, exit Lincoln Boulevard south.* **Open** 11am-6pm Wed, Thur, Sat, Sun; 11am-10pm Fri. **Admission** $4 adults; $2 students; $1 under-12s. **Credit** AmEx, MC, V.
Based in a Gehry-designed outdoor mall, SMMA shows a mixed bag of LA artists and out-of-towners in a fairly large main space and a smaller, more experimental project room. Ever the community-minded institution, the museum also hosts 'Friday night salons' with discussions usually relating to the current exhibition. An added bonus is the Ben & Jerry's ice-cream store, 20 feet from the museum's entrance.
*Parking free for 1hr.*

## Skirball Cultural Center & Museum

*2701 North Sepulveda Boulevard, at the I-405, West LA (1-310 440 4500). Bus Culver City 6/I-405, exit Skirball Center/Mulholland Drive south.* **Open** 10am-4pm Tue, Wed; 10am-9pm Fri; noon-5pm Sat; 10am-5pm Sun. **Admission** $6 adults; $4 students, senior citizens. **Credit** MC, V.
Opened in 1996, this offshoot of Hebrew Union College has exhibitions, lectures and events relating mostly to the experience of Jewish Americans, including a reconstruction of a Middle East archeological dig, a room-size exhibit devoted to religious decorative arts and a collection of art that chronicles Jewish emigration to America.
*Free parking.*

## Southwest Museum

*234 Museum Drive, at Avenue 43, Highland Park (1-213 221 2164). Bus 81, 83, DASH A/I-110, exit Avenue 43 north.* **Open** 11am-5pm Tue-Sun. **Admission** $5 adults; $3 students, senior citizens; $2 7-18s. **No credit cards.**
Located in an impressive building atop a tranquil hill in Mount Washington, the Southwest displays selections from its huge collection of Native American art and artefacts, as well as old-fashioned dioramas. The unusual entrance tunnel, originally installed in 1920 after the first director had a heart attack and died while climbing the hill, has recently been reopened and a new elevator installed.
*Free parking.*

## UCLA Armand Hammer Museum of Art & Cultural Center

*10899 Wilshire Boulevard, at Westwood Boulevard, Westwood (1-310 443 7000). Bus 20, 21, 22, 320, 322, 429, Santa Monica 1, 2, 4, 8, 12/I-405, exit Wilshire Boulevard east.* **Open** 11am-7pm Tue, Wed, Fri, Sat; 11am-9pm Thur; 11am-5pm Sun. **Admission** $4.50 adults; $3 students, senior citizens; $1 UCLA students; free 6-9pm Thur. **Credit** AmEx, MC, V.
Management of this medium-sized Westwood museum has recently become the responsibility of UCLA. Selections from the permanent collection, including Impressionist and Post Impressionist paintings, are on view along with more topical exhibitions of contemporary art. Recent shows have included 'Sexual Politics', a survey of feminist art.
*Parking $2.75 first 2 hours; $1.50 each additional 20 minutes; $20 maximum.*

## UCLA Fowler Museum of Cultural History

*UCLA Campus, between the Dance Building & Royce Hall, Westwood (1-310 825 4361). Bus 2, 21, 302, 561, Santa Monica 2, 8, 12/I-405, exit Sunset Boulevard east.* **Open** noon-5pm Wed, Fri-Sun; noon-8pm Thur.
**Admission** $5 adults; $3 students, senior citizens; $1 UCLA students. **Credit** MC, V.

Tucked away on the UCLA campus, this museum has changing exhibitions about various ethnographical topics: European and US silver from the seventeenth to nineteenth centuries; a collection of warpath-ritual fabrics from Borneo; and quilts and photos from an Amish community.
*Parking $5.*

## Science

### California Science Center

*700 State Drive, between Figueroa & Menlo Street, Exposition Park, Downtown LA (1-213 744 7400). Bus 81, 102, 200, 442, 444, 445, 446, 447/I-110, exit Exposition Boulevard.* **Open** 10am-5pm daily.
**Admission** *museum* free; *IMAX* $6 adults; $4.75 18-21s; $4 children, senior citizens. **Credit** (IMAX only) MC, V.
Scheduled to open in 1997, the Science Center (containing the former California Museum of Science and Industry and Aerospace Museum) will consist of four themed wings: World of Life, Creative World, World of the Pacific and Worlds Beyond. The first to open will be World of Life, which includes a 50ft long transparent human body, and Creative World, which will focus on the adaptability of human beings and their relationship with technology. You can also look forward to the newly improved, seven-storey 3-D IMAX cinema.
*Parking $5.*

### The George C Page Museum of La Brea Discoveries

*5801 Wilshire Boulevard, between La Brea & Fairfax Avenues, Miracle Mile (information 1-213 936-2230/museum 1-213 857 6311). Bus 20, 21, 22/I-10, exit La Brea Avenue north.* **Open** 10am-5pm Tue-Sun.
**Admission** $6 adults; $2 5-10s; $3.50 students, senior citizens; free first Tue of month. **Credit** AmEx, Disc, V.
Inside the half-underground Page museum, check out the old bones found in the surrounding La Brea Tar Pits, along with reconstructed, lifesize skeletons of mammoths, wolves, sloths and eagles and an animatronic saber-toothed tiger. Walk around the park and look for stray puddles of oozing black tar, still seeping from the ground. In the summer, you can see paleontologists at work in the ongoing excavation of Pit 91 and smell the tang of tar in the air. A giant recreation of a mastodon sinking into a pit as his 'wife' and child look on is heart-rending.
*Parking $7.50.*

### Griffith Park Observatory & Planetarium

*2800 East Observatory Road, Griffith Park (1-213 664 1181/recorded information 1-213 664 1191/Laserium 1-818 901 9405). Bus 96/I-5, exit Los Feliz Boulevard west.* **Open** *summer* 12.30-10pm daily; *winter* 2-10pm Tue-Fri; 12.30-10pm Sat, Sun. **Admission** *Planetarium shows* $4 adults; $3 senior citizens; $2 children; *Laserium shows* $7 adults; $6 senior citizens, children; under-5s not admitted. **Credit** MC, V.
Magnanimous landowner Griffith J Griffith donated Griffith Park to the city of Los Angeles, stipulating in his will that a public observatory be built. 'If every person could look through that telescope,' he declared, 'it would revolutionise the world'. Though Griffith himself became embroiled in scandal (beg someone at the information desk for details), the observatory that bears his name continues to be a favourite destination, and for good reason. Besides the free public telescope (open on cloudless nights), the building has science exhibits, a

Planetarium and Laserium, a Foucault pendulum and a Tesla coil. During comets and eclipses, local astronomy clubs set up 'scopes on the lawn and talk shop to anyone who will listen. The formidable 1934 deco modern building has been featured in many films, from the acclaimed (*Rebel Without a Cause, Terminator 2*) to the disdained (*Flesh Gordon*). Plenty of people come just for the view – on a clear day, you can see from the mountains to the ocean, and when it's smoggy, you really get a perspective on that famous brown cloud.

### Los Angeles County Museum of Natural History

*900 Exposition Boulevard, between Hoover & Menlo Streets, Exposition Park, Downtown (1-213 744 3414/recorded information 1-213 744 3466). Bus 81, 102, 200, 442, 444, 445, 446, 447/I-110, exit Exposition Boulevard west.* **Open** 10am-5pm Tue-Sun. **Admission** $8 adults; $5.50 12-17s; $2 5-12s. **No credit cards.**
This is one of the few museums in the area that actually feels like a 'proper' museum. The huge Spanish-Renaissance building opened in 1913 and is the third largest natural history museum in the US, its 35 halls and galleries packed with stuffed birds, mammals, gems, a Tyrannosaurus Rex skull and Native American pottery, textiles and baskets. Don't forget to visit the Insect Zoo, full of stick insects, Madagascan hissing cockroaches, scorpions, tarantulas and a load of ants.
*Parking $3.*

### Museum of Jurassic Technology

*9341 Venice Boulevard, at Bagely Avenue, Culver City (1-310 836 6131). Bus 33, 220, 333, 436, Culver City 1, 4, 5/I-10, exit Robertson Boulevard south.* **Open** 2-8pm Thur; noon-6pm Fri-Sun. **Admission** free; $4 donation requested.
The MJT is more a museum about curiosity than a collection of curiosities. Displays range from the factually whimsical to the downright fantastic, from an actual human horn to obscure theories concerning human memory processes. A simple description of this place could never do it justice. A visit is absolutely mandatory.

## Presidential libraries

The Los Angeles area is home to two presidential libraries, more than any other US city. They are open for research but public interaction is mainly via the museums. Displays detail the lives of the presidents, with full-scale reproductions of their offices, gifts they have received and dresses worn by their wives. The tone of the two is very different: Reagan's banks on sentimentality while Nixon's focuses more on the intellectual rigour required of a president. Both libraries are some way out of LA, in opposite directions.

### Richard M Nixon Library & Birthplace

*18001 Yorba Linda Boulevard, at Rose Drive, Yorba Linda, Orange County (1-714 993 5075). Bus Orange County Transit 26/SR90 (Imperial Highway), exit Yorba Linda Boulevard west.* **Open** 10am-5pm Mon-Sat; 11am-5pm Sun. **Admission** $5.95 adults; $3.95 senior citizens; $2 8-11s. **Credit** AmEx, Disc, MC, V.
Located in the out-of-the-way suburb where Nixon was born, the library provides an overview of his presidency as well as a tour of his first modest house. Exhibits chronicle his political life, including the many scandals that threatened to end his career. The gifts section includes a gun from Elvis Presley and a rock in the shape of Nixon's profile from Barry Goldwater, as well as the usual assortment of buckles and paintings. Richard and Pat Nixon are buried in the gardens.
*Free parking.*

## Ronald Reagan Presidential Library & Museum

*40 Presidential Drive, at Madera Road, Simi Valley, Ventura (1-805 522 8444). Train Metrolink Simi Valley/US101 to SR23 north, exit Olsen Road north.* **Open** 10am-5pm daily. **Admission** $4 adults; $2 students, senior citizens. **No credit cards**.

Simi Valley has gained an unglamorous infamy in recent years as the site of the (first) LAPD trial that set off the 1992 riots. It's also home to this library; great for fans of the Gipper, but liberal types will probably see red. The museum has a CD-Rom display containing his most endearing quips, photos of him as a young lad with a football, a re-creation of the Oval Office plus awesome gifts received over the years, such as the longest zipper in the world, a beaded gown given to Nancy by Imelda Marcos and a White House-shaped Kleenex box made from white yarn.

# Only in LA

## The Autry Museum of Western Heritage

*4700 Western Heritage Way, opposite LA Zoo, Griffith Park (1-213 667 2000). Bus 96/I-5, exit Los Feliz Boulevard west.* **Open** 10am-5pm Tue-Sun. **Admission** $7 adults; $5 students 13-18s, senior citizens; $3 under-12s. **Credit** AmEx, MC, V.

Angelenos are often accused of confusing the Hollywood version of the world with the real thing. Nowhere is this more evident than at the Autry Museum, where the real history of the West is presented side by side with images and props from the various silver screen interpretations – such as a lifesize bronze sculpture of Gene Autry (aka 'The Singing Cowboy') and his horse, Champion.

*Borofsky's ballerina, public art in Venice.*

## Frederick's of Hollywood Celebrity Lingerie Hall of Fame

*6608 Hollywood Boulevard, at Hudson Avenue, Hollywood (1-213 466 8506). Bus 1, 163, 180, 181, 210, 212, 217/US101, exit Highland Avenue south.* **Open** 10am-6pm Mon-Sat; noon-5pm Sun. **Admission** free.

This 'museum' is made up of a few rooms in the back of a well-known lingerie emporium. On display, next to an oil painting of founder Mr Frederick, are brassieres with names like the 'peek-a-boo' and the 'depth charge'. Madonna's black-and-gold sequinned bustier can be found here, along with the bra Marilyn Monroe wore in *Let's Make Love*, and, inexplicably, a bra that was thrown on stage during a Kiss concert. Still as trashy as ever, the rest of the store is almost a museum itself. Amazing shoes, too.

## Hollywood Entertainment Museum

*7021 Hollywood Boulevard, at Sycamore Avenue, Hollywood (1-213 469 9151). Bus 1, 180, 181, 217/I-10, exit Highland Avenue south.* **Open** 10am-6pm Tue-Sun. **Admission** $7.50 adults; $4.50 students, senior citizens; $3 children. **Credit** AmEx, DC, MC, V.

Not yet open at time of writing, this museum promises to thrill with exciting and fascinating Hollywood memorabilia, such as the *Cheers* bar, and educational exhibits relating to the local entertainment industry. It has also taken over the collection of the now-defunct Max Factor Museum of Beauty, including film stars' wigs and cosmetics. *Parking $2.*

## International Surfing Museum

*411 Olive Avenue, between Main & Fifth Streets, Huntington Beach, Orange County (1-714 960 3483). Bus Orange County Transit 29/I-405, exit Beach Boulevard south.* **Open** *summer* noon-5pm daily; *winter* noon-5pm Wed-Sun. **Admission** $2 adults; $1 students. **Credit** AmEx, MC, V.

Various exhibits honour Duke Kahanamoku, the father of surfing, celebrate surf music and showcase the women of surfing and the heroes of surf lifesaving. This small museum is staffed with friendly volunteers full of stories – ask to hear about Dick 'King of the Surf Guitar' Dale's guitar, which was stolen from the museum's original building and now hangs in the rear gallery. Head for the beach if you want a taste of contemporary beach culture.

## Carole & Barry Kaye Museum of Miniatures

*5900 Wilshire Boulevard, between Ogden Drive & Spaulding Avenue, Miracle Mile (1-213 937 6464). Bus 20, 21, 22, 320/I-10, exit Fairfax Avenue north.* **Open** 10am-5pm Tue-Sat; 11am-5pm Sun. **Admission** $7.50 adults; $6.50 senior citizens; $5 students; $3 children. **Credit** MC, V.

*Die Rich and Tax Free* author Barry Kaye and his wife Carole began collecting miniatures in 1989. Their seemingly undiscerning taste has led to this mishmash of fabulous tiny things and outright kitsch. Revel in the intricate perfection of 'Alexander's Siege Tent at Halicarnassus' and reel before the smaller-than-life depiction of the OJ Simpson trial, complete with anonymous jurors. *Parking $3.60 ($1.80 with validation).*

## Museum of Neon Art (MONA)

*Grand Hope Park, 501 West Olympic Boulevard, between Hope Street & Grand Avenue, Downtown (1-213 489 9918). Metro Pico Street or 7th Street/Metro Center/bus 27, 28, 38, 96, 327, 328/I-110, exit Ninth Street east.* **Open** 11am-5pm Wed, Fri, Sat; 11am-8pm Thur; noon-5pm Sun. **Admission** $5 adults; $3.50 students, senior citizens. **Credit** AmEx, MC, V.

A celebration of the many uses of neon, including signage and fine art. Permanent exhibits on show at MONA include works by kinetic-art pioneers Lili Lakich and Candace Gawne and a rather fine neon interpretation of the Mona Lisa. *Free parking.*

## The Nethercutt Collection

*15200 Bledsoe Street, at San Fernando Road, Sylmar (1-818 367-2251). Bus 94/I-5, exit Roxford Street east.* **Open** by appointment. **Admission** free.

Within an innocuous building in an even more innocuous industrial suburb to the north of LA, heirs to the fortune of a cosmetic company Dorothy and JB Nethercutt have assembled a huge collection of functional objects, all of which somehow fit into their very personal concept of beauty. Their agenda also dictates that everything on the premises must be in working order; the impressive Rolls-Royces are all driven to a picnic once a year and the gargantuan Mighty Wurlitzer Pipe Organ can be enjoyed during scheduled recitals. Visitors are also treated to a huge collection of Stueben Glass hood ornaments, nickelodeons, French furniture, clocks and watches and a ceiling mural depicting the members of the immediate family as cherubs. You must book for the two-hour tour (10am and 1.30pm, Tue-Sat) and the dress code prohibits shorts and jeans out of respect for the stuff. It's about a 30-minute drive from West LA.

## Petersen Automotive Museum

*6060 Wilshire Boulevard, at Fairfax Avenue, Miracle Mile (1-213 964 6315/recorded information 1-213 930 2277). Bus 20, 21, 22, 217, 320, 322/I-10, exit Fairfax Avenue north.* **Open** 10am-6pm Tue-Sun. **Admission** $7 adults; $5 students, senior citizens; $3 5-12s. **Credit** AmEx, MC, V.

A very tasteful, up-ended, monster pick-up truck marks the entrance to LA's version of the car museum. Inside, lifesize dioramas of supermarkets, garages and restaurants recreate the early days of the drive-in lifestyle, complete with a full range of classic automobiles parked out front. Upstairs, changing exhibitions showcase various aspects of car culture, from cars of the stars to fancy racing machines; even motorcycles are not overlooked. In the lobby, there's an AM/PM mini-market to satisfy your craving for highway cuisine; have a beer and a spicy hot dog and ruminate about lacquer and chrome. *Parking $5.*

# Galleries

Art galleries are sprinkled liberally throughout virtually every neighbourhood in LA, making a thorough exploration possible only for a caped crusader. However, with planning and a decent map, the diligent art-viewer can see plenty in a short time. For listings by location, try the *LA Weekly*. The *Art Now Gallery Guide*, available at most galleries, has exhaustive listings and easy-to-read maps. For reviews and cultural criticism, try local art magazine *Art Issues*, available at bookstores or newsstands. NY-LA free art 'zine *Coagula* is full of irresponsible gossip and unpopular opinions, and can be found anywhere ballsy enough to give it away. Venues and phone numbers are constantly changing, so always ring first to save a wasted trip.

## The galleries

Santa Monica has the biggest concentration of galleries, mainly clustered in 'art malls'. The recently opened **Bergamot Station** (2525 Michigan Avenue, at Cloverfield Boulevard; 1-310 829 5854), has brought together several of the city's well-known art dealers under one

corrugated steel roof. **Shoshana-Wayne** (1-310 453 7535), **Burnett Miller** (1-310 315 9961), **Rosamund Felsen** (1-310 828 8488), **Track 16** (1-310 264 4678) and **Patricia Faure** (1-310 449 1479), among others, can be found here, alongside a small café and a resale shop that looks inviting but has odd hours.

Down the street is **Yong's Complex** (aka 'Baby Bergamot' or 'Bergamette', at Nebraska Avenue & Berkeley Street). Don't miss the whippersnappers at **Acme** (1800B Berkeley Street; 1-310 264 5818) and **Dan Bernier** (3026½ Nebraska Avenue; 1-310 264 4882). If you're interested in fresh-brazen-contemporary-neo-conceptual, these galleries also make a good starting point to find off-the-map art events. Pump friendly gallerists Bob or Randy at Acme for information on where to head next; if they don't know about it, it's probably not worth going to.

Also in the neighbourhood are **Christopher Grimes** (916 Colorado Avenue, between Ninth and Tenth Streets; 1-310 587 3373) and photo gallery **G Ray Hawkins** (908 Colorado Avenue; 1-310 394 5558). A few blocks away is **Blum and Poe** (1-310 453-8311), located in the **Broadway Complex** (2042 Broadway, between 20th Street and Cloverfield Avenue).

Nearby Venice also has its share of art spaces. **LA Louver** (45 North Venice Boulevard, at Pacific Avenue; 1-310 822 4955) has a spectacular space and shows relatively well-known artists, while **Angles** (2230/2222 Main Street; 1-310 396 5019), across the street from the Santa Monica Museum of Art, shows post-minimal work. Don't miss Jonathon Borofsky's outdoor sculpture of a giant, clown-faced ballerina, tutu and all, on Main Street, across the street from the Rose Café.

In Beverly Hills, a pair of newly opened New York galleries, **PaceWildenstein** (9540 Wilshire Boulevard, between Camden & Rodeo Drives; 1-310 205 5522) and **Gagosian** (456 North Camden Drive, at Santa Monica Boulevard; 1-310 271 9400), near other NY imports Barneys New York and Saks Fifth Avenue, are very chi-chi spaces showing blue-chip artists.

In West Hollywood, the **Margo Leavin Gallery** (812 North Robertson Boulevard, at Santa Monica Boulevard; 1-310 273 0603) shows established, mostly Los Angeles artists; **Regen Projects** (629 North Almont Drive, between Melrose Avenue & Santa Monica Boulevard; 1-310 276 5424) has a mix of NY-LA hipsters; while **Kohn Turner** (454 North Robertson Boulevard, between Rangely & Dorrington Avenues; 1-310 854 5400) shows a mixed bag of work.

On Hollywood Boulevard, down the street from Frederick's of Hollywood, between Schroeder & Wilcox Avenues, are two non-profit-making galleries: **Los Angeles Contemporary Exhibitions** (LACE; 1-213 957 1777) at number 6522 and, next door, the **Los Angeles Center for Photographic Studies** (LACPS; 1-213 466 6232). Both spaces host shows by (usually) local artists, which range from awe-inspiring to flat-out awful. Los Angeles Contemporary Exhibitions also presents performance art, theatre, dance and video events.

## Underground events

For a while, it was all the rage to open a gallery in your own living room or garage; most have gone completely legit or out of business but occasional 'underground' events can still be ferreted out. There is no sure way to find out about such happenings since they are often not listed by major publications, so the best method is to ask around.

**Bliss House** (825 North Michigan Avenue, between Mountain Street & Orange Grove Boulevard; 1-818 398 0855), the Pasadena house of LA artist Kenneth Riddle, has been holding shows for a number of years and still does so sporadically. The recently opened **Art Center Auxiliary** (1033 Palm Court, South Pasadena (1-818 403 9727) is another living room venue while **The Hatchery** (1308 Factory Place, Studio 2D, Downtown; 1-213 689 0198) holds events in the hallway of this artist's loft building.

*Well, it's one way to cope with the traffic at the **Petersen Automotive Museum**.*

# Music

*From classical spectaculars at the Hollywood Bowl to hardcore rock'n'rolling on Sunset Strip, LA offers a magical musical tour.*

## TICKETS & INFORMATION

Big-name concerts – both classical and rock – often sell out, so buy tickets in advance if you can. It's always worth checking with the box office on the day of the show as the promoters sometimes release excellent seats at that time. Whenever possible, try to get tickets directly from the venue in order to save on credit card booking charges. At smaller venues, you can usually pay on the door.

Alternatively, you can buy tickets through mega-service **Ticketmaster**, whose many (cash-only) outlets can be found in Blockbuster Music, Tower Records, Robinsons-May and Ritmo Latino stores. Tickets for selected shows are also available for no service charge at the Ticketmaster Box Office (6243 Hollywood Boulevard, between Vine & North Gower Streets; 10am-6pm Mon-Sat). For credit card bookings (AmEx, Disc, MC, V), call 1-213 480 3232 or 1-714 740 2000; note that the 'convenience' charges are fairly high.

The most comprehensive music listings can be found in *LA Weekly*, while the *Los Angeles View* and the *LA Times'* Sunday Calendar section are also good sources. For record and CD shops, *see chapter* **Shopping & Services**. For radio stations, *see chapter* **Media**.

# Classical

Although there may have been a time when it was appropriate to call the Los Angeles classical musical landscape a cultural wasteland, things have changed for the better. In the early 1970s, the Los Angeles Philharmonic metamorphosed into a world-class orchestra under the baton of Zubin Mehta, breaking the city into the elite ranks of US orchestras led by Cleveland and Chicago. The Phil, currently led by young Finnish music director Esa-Pekka Salonen, has expanded, hydra-like, into a multi-tiered organisation responsible for the majority of classical performances in LA. Most of these are staged in the Music Center at the **Dorothy Chandler Pavilion** (Oct-May) and at the **Hollywood Bowl** (June-Sept).

Other notable ensembles include the **Los Angeles Chamber Orchestra**, the **Pasadena Symphony** and the **Long Beach Symphony**,

all of which are capable of competent music-making and the occasional inspired performance. Quality classical programming can also be found at a number of educational institutions, notably UCLA's **Veterans Wadsworth Theater** (*see below* **Rock, Roots & Jazz: Major venues**).

## Major venues

### Dorothy Chandler Pavilion

*Music Center, 135 North Grand Avenue, at First Street, Downtown (1-213 972 7200/LA Philharmonic 1-213 972 7300/LA Opera 1-213 972 7219/LA Master Chorale 1-213 972 7282). Metro Civic Center/Tom Bradley/bus 78, 79, 96, 379, 427, Commuter Express 423/I-110 north, exit Fourth Street east.* **Open** box office 10am-6pm Mon-Sat. **Tickets** $6-$120. **Credit** AmEx, MC, V. *Parking evenings & weekends $7; weekdays $2.50 per 20 mins ($15 dollar maximum); valet parking $17.*

The grand dame of the city's concert scene and the largest hall in town devoted almost solely to classical music, the Pavilion is probably best known internationally for the one night each year that it hosts the Academy Awards. Movie stars in tuxes aside, the home of the LA Opera, the Los Angeles Philharmonic and the Los Angeles Master Chorale is the place to go for an evening of high culture.

Built in the early 1960s after a fund drive by Dorothy 'Buff' Chandler, wife of *LA Times'* publisher Norman, the Pavilion sits at the south end of the LA County-operated Music Center, a stone and marble edifice it shares with the Mark Taper Forum and the Ahmanson Theater. Sandwiched between the Criminal Courts Building and the Department of Water and Power, the Center provides an oasis in what can be a fairly dodgy corner of Downtown. Further south from the Pavilion is the future site of the Disney Concert Hall, designed by Frank Gehry, a long-planned project currently on hold pending a major fund-raising effort.

The Pavilion's comfortably plush house seats 3,200 amid dark wood panelling, muted colours and iridescent crystal chandeliers. Sound quality, acceptable everywhere in the building, is best on the upper floors, though the view from the top balcony can be vertigo-inducing. During the interval, stroll on the terrace that circles the building for an interesting view of Downtown.

### LA Opera & Los Angeles Philharmonic

Having given its first performance in 1987, the LA Opera is one of the newest of the city's major arts companies. It specialises in high-concept stagings of familiar operas featuring international stars such as Maria Ewing, Placido Domingo and Galina Gortchakova, but has also been a welcoming home to the Peter Sellars/Salonen production of *Pelléas et Mélisande* and the famous David Hockney-designed *Tristan und Isolde*.

*Opposite:* The Dorothy Chandler Pavilion, dispenser of Oscars and classical music.

Owing to the leanings of its youthful music director, Esa-Pekka Salonen, the Philharmonic's programming consists of an unusually large contemporary repertoire, often side by side with the standard warhorses. A few people invariably walk out on such explorations, but the more tolerant are often rewarded with the startling results. When the dashing Salonen is not in town, one might find a heralded young newcomer or an established top gun wielding the baton. Sir Simon Rattle, Pierre Boulez and Zubin Mehta have especially strong relationships with the orchestra and appear regularly. For more insight into the evening's programme, the Philharmonic offers Upbeat Live!, a free pre-concert lecture in the Pavilion's Grand Hall starting half an hour before every performance.

### Hollywood Bowl

*2301 North Highland Avenue, at Odin Street, Hollywood (1-213 850 2000). Bus Hollywood Bowl/US101, exit Highland Avenue/Hollywood Bowl.* **Open** June-Sept; *box office* 10am-9pm Mon-Sat; noon-8pm Sun; *rehearsals* 9.30am-12.30pm day of performance. **Tickets** *bench seats* $1-$24 Tue, Thur; $3-$26 Fri, Sat; *box seats* $61-$75 Tue, Thur; $69-$90 Fri; $75-$95 Sat; other ticket prices vary; call to check. **Credit** AmEx, Disc, MC, V.
*Parking Hollywood Bowl $10-$24.20; park and ride $5 round trip; shuttle $2.50 round trip.*

A perennial favourite with both locals and tourists, this world-famous jewel of an outdoor amphitheatre has hosted concerts since its first LA Philharmonic performance on Easter morning 1921. Nestled in an aesthetically and acoustically blessed fold in the Hollywood Hills, the Bowl, it is said, was once a gathering spot for the area's Native American tribes. One of the theatre's first shells was designed by Lloyd Wright (son of Frank); much later it was given a going-over by Frank Gehry. It is a deceptively large venue, with a capacity of almost 18,000.

A balmy summer night at the Bowl is the quintessential LA experience and can bring out the romantic in even the terminally cynical. Closer to ritual than concert-going, the evening starts for most with an alfresco dinner consumed in the stands or one of the many picnic areas in the grounds. The Patio and Deck restaurants (both 1-213 851 3588) serve pre-concert meals, and dinner picnic baskets can also be ordered.

**Events**

The Bowl is the summer home of the LA Philharmonic and, since 1991, conductor John Mauceri's pops-oriented Hollywood Bowl Orchestra, which has taken over on most weekends, often joined by big-name talents like Natalie Cole or Carol Burnett. Look for the frequent performances that are capped off by a firework display synchronised to the music of Sousa, Tchaikovsky or Handel. Jazz concerts are held frequently and several rock concerts each summer feature superstars like Elton John, Tom Petty and Rod Stewart.

The Bowl is a country park and thus open to the general public during the day. In the summer, orchestra rehearsals (open to the public) are held several mornings a week. For details of the Hollywood Bowl Museum, *see chapter* **Museums & Galleries**.

**Tickets**

The prized box seats at the front, sold by subscription for the classical and jazz series, are often handed down from generation to generation, making them virtually unobtainable. If budget isn't a limitation, check with the box office on the day of performance, as these prime seats sometimes become available. Don't worry if you're seated a long way from the stage, as the sound system is updated virtually every year. Time-delay speakers deliver fortissimos and pianissimos evenly to the entire audience, making the $1 ($3 Fri, Sat) seats at the top, complete with enchanting vistas, a great bargain.

## Other orchestras

### The Da Camera Society's Chamber Music in Historic Sites

*Information 1-310 440 1351.* **Tickets** $18-£60. **Credit** MC, V.
First-rate chamber ensembles and soloists presented in some of the city's architecturally more interesting premises. Many performances sell out in advance to subscribers, but try your luck and you may end up listening to Bach violin partitas in the Tiffany glass-crowned music room of the Doheny Mansion or a Mozart piano sonata in an ultra-modern house on the edge of the Pacific in Malibu.

### Long Beach Symphony

*Information 1-310 436 3203.* **Tickets** $9-$55. **Credit** AmEx, MC, V.
Tickets are available from the above number or from the Long Beach Convention Center on 1-310 436 3661.

### Los Angeles Baroque Orchestra

*Information 1-310 458 0425.* **Tickets** $18-$24. **Credit** MC, V.
This authentic period-instrument orchestra appears in various churches and small halls around town, playing the music of Bach, Mozart, Beethoven and others of the era. Call for a schedule.

### Los Angeles Chamber Orchestra

*Information 1-213 622 7001.* **Tickets** $12-$42. **Credit** AmEx, MC, V.
LA's foremost ensemble devoted to the chamber orchestra repertoire from the 17th to the 20th century performs at the Veterans Wadsworth Theater, Westwood, and the Alex Theater, Glendale. Call for details.

## Other venues

### Bing Theater

*Los Angeles County Museum of Art, 5905 Wilshire Boulevard, between La Brea & Fairfax Avenues, Miracle Mile (box office 1-213 857 6010/Sundays at Four 1-213 485 6873). Bus 20, 21, 22, 320/I-10, exit Fairfax Avenue north.* **Open** *box office* 10am-5pm Tue-Thur; 10am-9pm Fri; 11am-6pm Sat, Sun.
Inside the museum, the intimate and well-appointed Bing hosts Sundays At Four, a series of free concerts featuring chamber ensembles and soloists. Evening concerts (8pm, Mon, Wed) are also held, but admission is charged ($7-$15).

### Japan America Theater

*244 South San Pedro Street, between Second & Third Streets, Downtown (1-213 680 3700). Bus 16, Commuter Express 438, DASH A/I-110, exit Fourth street east.* **Open** *box office* noon-5pm daily. **Tickets** $10-$100. **Credit** MC, V.
Modelled in the shape of a Japanese fan, this intimate theatre (capacity 840) hosts the best of Japanese performing arts, from traditional Kabuki, Noh, Kageboschi (shadowplay) and Bunraku (puppet theatre) to contemporary music, comedy and dance.

### Pasadena Civic Auditorium

*300 East Green Street, at Euclid Avenue, Pasadena (1-818 449 7360/Pasadena Symphony 1-818 793 7172). Bus 180, 181, 188, 256, Foothill Transit 187/I-110, exit Green Street east.* **Open** *box office* 10am-5pm Mon-Sat. **Credit** AmEx, MC, V.
The Pasadena Symphony shares this facility with several musicals a year and the Emmy Awards. The auditorium also contains a 1920s Moeller organ, the largest of its kind west of the Mississippi.
*Parking $5.*

## College venues

Call for information on concerts and ticket prices.

### Bovard Auditorium at USC

*3551 Trousdale Park Way, near Gate 1 on Exposition Boulevard, Downtown (1-213 740 4211/USC box office 1-213 740 7111). Bus 102, Dash C/I-110, exit Exposition Boulevard south.* **Open** *box office 9am-6pm Mon-Fri.* **Credit** Disc, MC, V.

### Gindi Auditorium at the University of Judaism

*15600 Mulholland Drive, at Casiano Road, Bel Air (1-310 476 9777). Bus 561/I-405, exit Mulholland Drive north.*

### Harriet & Charles Luckman Fine Arts Complex at Cal State LA

*5151 State University Drive, at Eastern Avenue, Cal State University (1-213 343 6600). Bus 256, 483, 485, 487, 489/I-10, exit Eastern Avenue.* **Open** *box office 1.30-4.30pm Mon, Wed, Fri.* **Credit** AmEx, MC, V.

### Schoenberg Hall at UCLA

*405 Hilgard Avenue, at Sunset Boulevard, Westwood (1-310 825 2101). Bus 2, 21, 429, 561, 576/I-405, exit Sunset Boulevard east.* **Open** *box office 9am-5pm Mon-Fri.* **Credit** AmEx, MC, V.

Also at UCLA, **Royce Hall** (1-310 825 8989) is currently closed due to renovations following earthquake damage; it is scheduled to re-open in autumn 1998.

# Rock, Roots & Jazz

Los Angeles is acknowledged as the music industry capital of the United States – and, by inference, the world. Although not a 'jazz town' like New York or a 'blues town' like Chicago, LA is still an important stop on any touring artist's itinerary and the city can hold its own when it comes to the quality and quantity of jazz and blues performances. As for more ethnic and experimental music-making, the sheer size and diversity of the city's populace ensures that all the world's musics are represented, for better or worse. It is the lasting rock'n'roll mythology of the city, however, that plays itself out every day in a very visible fashion, especially along the legendary Sunset Strip.

As has been the case since the 1960s, when bands like the Doors, the Byrds and the Buffalo Springfield were new, cutting-edge acts, most important gigs and related socialising happens in Hollywood. Some clubs, like the venerable **Whisky A-Go-Go** and **Troubadour**, have survived, while others have been reincarnated or fallen by the wayside. A good bet for exploring up-to-date rock sounds (the quality of which can be subjective) is the Hollywood club **Dragonfly**.

Scenes also develop sporadically in other (usually Hollywood-adjacent) neighbourhoods, such as East Hollywood, known for the rootsy, punk-tinged sound pioneered by the classic, now-defunct LA band X, the funk, sex and rock'n'roll of the Red Hot Chili Peppers (still in operation) and the hard-edged psychedelic rock of Jane's Addiction (also broken up, but semi-reformed as Porno for Pyros). Currently, the Silver Lake area is getting itself a name for its quality bands and resulting record company attention. The hub of this action is the coffee-shop-cum-glittery-rock-dive **Spaceland**, where you might see and hear the dislocated musings of local hero Beck, the critically lauded alternative-country roar, twang and moan of the Geraldine Fibbers or the witty melodic crunch of up-and-coming trio Velouria.

Although gangsta rap originated in neighbouring Compton and LA is home to the successful Death Row and Ruthless rap record labels, don't count on seeing much of this urban African-American artform live in Los Angeles. Based on past history and current stereotypes, promoters and their liability insurers are hesitant to get involved. Paradoxically, but in keeping with their commitment to Black music, the corporate-run **House of Blues** has almost single-handedly kept rap and hip-hop in front of LA audiences.

One of the best ways to experience Los Angeles' diverse Latino culture is through its music. The significant amount of Latin music activity in town certainly isn't limited to mariachis. Well-known Latin pop stars appear frequently at mainstream venues such as the **Universal Amphitheatre**, as well as more obscure locales such as the **Pico Rivera Sports Arena** (11003 Rooks Road, Pico Rivera; 1-310 695 0509). Some weekends, merengue dances take place at the **Hollywood Palladium**. The salsa crowd does its thing weekly at the tiny

*LA's finest – local hero Beck.*

El Floridita (1253 North Vine Street, Hollywood; 1-213 871 8612) and at other clubs. The emerging Roc en Espanol movement (passionate guitar-heavy rock'n'roll, sung in Spanish) convenes periodically at **The Palace** in Hollywood and various smaller clubs. Many of these shows are not publicised at all in the English-speaking media. More assimilated, a talented contingent of East LA-based bands play multi-faceted music all over town, including world music hangout **LunaPark**. Up-and-coming acts include sophisticated Chicano rock outfit Quetzal and the ska-inflected Latin swingers Yeska.

Free shows of everything from roots to reggae to pop to world music take place during the summer at the Santa Monica Pier and at California Plaza, Downtown. For year-round festival information, contact the City's Department of Cultural Affairs (1-213 485 2433).

Take photo ID to every music venue. This will not only enable you to drink (if you are 21 or over), but in many cases allow you through the door. Some shows are open to 18s and over, depending on the venue's alcohol-licensing arrangement.

## Major venues

### Great Western Forum

*3900 Manchester Boulevard, at Prairie Avenue, Inglewood (1-310 673 1300/LA Lakers 1-310 412 5000/LA Kings 1-310 673 6003). Bus 115, 211, 315, 442/I-405, exit Manchester Boulevard east.* **Open** *box office* 10am-6pm Mon-Fri; varies Sat, Sun. **Admission** varies. **Credit** AmEx, MC, V.

The Lakers play basketball and the Kings play hockey at this acoustically challenged classic in the concrete arena tradition. Superstar rock and pop attractions such as Van Halen and Gloria Estefan have played here and although the venue has an undeniable energy when 18,000 souls are packing it, the flipside is that concert-goers shouldn't expect to be able to see the act's facial features.
*Parking $7.*

### Greek Theater

*2700 North Vermont Avenue, at Los Feliz Boulevard, Griffith Park (1-213 665 1927/box office 1-213 665 5857). Bus Community Connection 203/US101, exit Vermont Avenue north.* **Open** June-Oct; *box office* noon-6pm Mon-Fri; 10am-4pm Sat, Sun; until 9pm night of shows. **Admission** varies. **Credit** MC, V.

This bucolic open-air 6,000-seater in Griffith Park is a great place to catch pop and rock perennials such as Sting, Lyle Lovett or the Allman Brothers. You won't hear anything really daring, but the setting is perfect for bravura spectacles, such as Chicano rockers Los Lobos' annual homestand. One drawback: the intractable stack parking.
*Parking $6-$25.*

### Henry Fonda Theater

*6126 Hollywood Boulevard, at Gower Street, Hollywood (1-213 468 1700). Bus 1, 180, 181, 212, 217/US101, exit Vine Street south.* **Open** *box office* from 2pm day of show. **Admission** varies. **Credit** AmEx, MC, V.

Occasional shows by adult-oriented acts like the Charlie Watts' Quintet or Ray Davies are a treat in this intimate Hollywood theatre (capacity 800). It suffered earthquake damage in 1994 and hasn't been very busy since.
*Parking $6.*

### Hollywood American Legion Hall

*2035 North Highland Avenue, between Franklin Avenue & Hollywood Boulevard, Hollywood (1-213 960 2035). Bus 420/US101, exit Highland Avenue south.* **Opening times** and **admission** vary; call for schedule. **No credit cards**.

Reminiscent of a Masonic lodge, the 1,000-capacity American Legion is owned by war veterans and is leased out now and then by enterprising young promoters for shows by next-big-things like Portishead and No Doubt. The concrete bunker of a room wasn't made for loud music, but acoustic draping has helped resolve some of the sound problems.

### Hollywood Palladium

*6215 Sunset Boulevard, between Argyle & El Centro Avenues, Hollywood (1-213 962 7600). Bus 2, 3, 210, 212/US101, exit Vine Street south.* **Opening times** and **admission** vary; call for schedule. **No credit cards**.

Mosh pits are common at this venue, which has the tightest door policy in town; even pens and chewing gum are banned. Recently refurbished (not that you can tell), the faded ballroom, once ruled by the sounds of Glenn Miller and Tommy Dorsey, has now been claimed by successful high-energy, alterna-punk-style bands like The Foo Fighters and Fugazi.
*Parking $5-$7.*

### House of Blues

*8430 Sunset Boulevard, at Olive Drive, West Hollywood (concert hotline 1-213 650 1451/box office 1-213 848 5100). Bus 2, 429/I-10, exit La Cienega Boulevard north.* **Open** *box office* 10.30am-midnight daily. **Admission** $10-$50. **Credit** AmEx, DC, Disc, MC, V.

Brainchild of a Hard Rock Café founder, the flagship operation of the wildly successful House of Blues chain of club-music-hall-restaurants is to the blues what McDonald's is to the hamburger. While the bands in this Disneyesque juke joint are extremely diverse and mostly of top quality, the poor sightlines, cramped standing room, parking problems and surly staff may give you the blues.
*Valet parking $8.*

### John Anson Ford Theater

*2580 Cahuenga Boulevard East, at Vine Street, Hollywood (1-213 466 1767). Bus 163, 420/US101, exit Cahuenga Boulevard north.* **Open** 4 hours before show; call for schedule. **Admission** varies. **Credit** (advance only) Disc, MC, V.

The LA County-sponsored Summer Nights at the Ford series is the mainstay at this small (1,200 capacity) but enchanting outdoor amphitheatre, which presents everything from local choreographer and dance diva Naomi Goldberg's stunning Los Angeles Modern Dance & Ballet programmes to a samba-crazed Brazilian festival.
*Parking $5.*

### The Palace

*1735 North Vine Street, at Hollywood Boulevard, Hollywood (1-213 462 3000). Bus 163, 180, 181, 212, 217/US101, exit Hollywood Boulevard west.* **Open** 9pm-4am Thur-Sun; shows vary, so call for schedule. **Admission** varies. **Credit** AmEx, MC, V.

In the heart of Hollywood, this small 1927 theatre holds 1,200 fans for shows mainly of the alternative rock variety. The upstairs balcony provides an escape from the downstairs crush, but don't expect the sound to be clear anywhere. It turns into a disco at 10.30pm from Thursday to Saturday, so shows on those evenings start punctually.

### Pantages Theater

*6233 Hollywood Boulevard, between Vine Street & Argyle Avenue, Hollywood (1-213 468 1700). Bus 180, 181, 212, 217/US101, exit Vine Street south.* **Opening times** and **admission** vary; call for schedule. **Credit** AmEx, MC, V.

Another smallish (2,200 capacity) theatre with an art deco design, the Pantages is a great place to see established acts.

*The Red Aunts kick it at **Spaceland** (see page 218).*

However, largely due to construction for the Metro subway, it isn't currently very active, apart from some musicals and a few award shows. It costs $6 to park.

### Universal Amphitheater

*100 Universal City Plaza, Universal City (1-818 777 3931/recorded information 1-818 622 4440). Bus 420/ US101, exit Universal Center Drive.* **Open** *box office* 1pm-9pm Mon, Tue, Thur-Sun. **Admission** varies. **Credit** AmEx, MC, V.

This slick, semi-circular room for major pop, rock, R&B and Latin acts is probably not what God had in mind when he invented rock'n'roll. But clean sightlines and good acoustics (except for below the balcony) make this a popular spot for underage Valley girls and other music lovers.
*Parking $6.*

### Veterans Wadsworth Theater

*Veterans Administration Grounds, at Wilshire & San Vincente Boulevards, Westwood (1-310 825 2101). Bus 20, 320, Santa Monica 2, 3/I-405, exit Wilshire Boulevard west.* **Opening times** and **admission** vary; call for schedule. **Credit** AmEx, MC, V.

Located on the VA's Westwood grounds and run by UCLA, the 1,400-seater Wadsworth presents many of the university's performing arts series programmes, ranging from classical recitals to ethnic dance performances to world music shows as well as the occasional pop concert.
*Parking $5.*

### Wiltern Theater

*3790 Wilshire Boulevard, at Western Avenue, Mid-Wilshire (1-213 380 5005). Metro Wilshire/Western/bus 20, 21, 22, 207, 357/I-10, exit Western Avenue north.* **Open** *box office* noon-6pm Mon-Sat; 3 hours before show. **Admission** varies. **Credit** MC, V.

An art deco gem renovated and energised 10 years ago by the late rock impresario Bill Graham, the Wiltern draws a mostly older crowd for the likes of Lou Reed, Liz Phair and the occasional dance troupe or musical. The venue's comfortable seating and human scale make up for the crummy surrounding neighbourhood. The lobby is a well-known hangout for music industry professionals.
*Parking $5.*

## Rock

### Alligator Lounge

*3321 Pico Boulevard, at Centinela Avenue, Santa Monica (1-310 449 1844). Bus Santa Monica 7/I-10, exit Bundy Drive north.* **Opening times** and **admission** vary; call for schedule. **No credit cards.**

This is the most adventurous room on the Westside, booking local bands and lesser-known national acts of all stripes and colours, from rootsy Zydeco outfits such as CJ Chenier to guitarist Nels Cline's experimental Monday 'new music' nights. Worth scanning the listings for.

### Al's Bar

*305 South Hewitt Street, between Alameda & Traction Streets, Downtown (1-213 625 9703). Bus 16, DASH A, Montebello 40/I-10, exit Alameda Street east.* **Open** 6pm-2am Mon-Thur, Sat, Sun; 3pm-2am Fri; shows 9pm daily. **Admission** $3-$7. **No credit cards.**

Al's has been a favourite of loft-living bohemians and low-living alcoholics for years. Some might find the deep Downtown location and heavy vibe a tad scary, but many of LA's more compelling bands have done time in its spartan digs. For those that take their beer drinking, pool playing and arty hard rocking seriously.

## Billboard Live

*9039 Sunset Boulevard, at Doheny Drive, West Hollywood (1-310 274 5800). Bus 2, 3, 429/I-10, exit La Cienega Boulevard north.* **Open** 7pm-2am Wed-Sun; *box office* 10am-1am daily. **Admission** usually $10-$15. **Credit** AmEx, MC, V.

Named for the trade magazine that is the music industry's bible, Billboard Live is the latest entrant (opened August 1996) in the Sunset Strip club game. Boasting a 'low-tech plush' interior and huge TV screens out front, it books up-and-coming recording artists, especially those appearing in the magazine's charts, as well as old standbys such as James Brown and Tony Bennett.
*Valet parking $7.*

## Coconut Teaszer

*8117 Sunset Boulevard, at Crescent Heights Boulevard, Hollywood (1-213 654 4773). Bus 2, 3, 429/I-10, exit La Cienega Boulevard north.* **Open** 6.30pm-2am daily. **Admission** $10. **Credit** AmEx, MC, V.

Many bands that play the Teaszer would probably kill their own grandmothers for a record deal, which gives the place an air of desperation to accompany its painful decibel levels. Downstairs, the Crooked Bar showcases mostly talented unknowns playing acoustic sets.
*Parking $3-$5.*

## Dragonfly

*6510 Santa Monica Boulevard, at Wilcox Avenue, Hollywood (1-213 466 6111). Bus 4, 420/I-10, exit La Brea Avenue north.* **Open** 9pm-2am daily. **Admission** $1-$5. **Credit** AmEx, MC, V.

A Hollywood rock emporium masquerading as a Middle Eastern harem, Dragonfly plays host to at least one band with a heavy music industry buzz pretty much every night, thus attracting record company talent scouts and scenesters alike. Between sets, cool off by the fountain on the back patio.
*Parking $3.50.*

## Genghis Cohen Cantina

*740 North Fairfax Avenue, between Melrose & Waring Avenues, West Hollywood (1-213 653 0640). Bus 10, 11, 217, DASH Fairfax/I-10, exit Fairfax Avenue north.* **Open** *shows* varies Mon; 8.15pm Tue-Thur; 9pm Fri, Sat; 8.30pm Sun. **Admission** $4-$7. **Credit** AmEx, MC, V.

Come for the tunes, not the food, at this small music room, and restaurant where singer-songwriters earnestly plug away in an acoustic setting, hoping for that publishing deal.
*Valet parking $2.50.*

## Jabberjaw

*3711 West Pico Boulevard, between Crenshaw Boulevard & Fourth Avenue, Crenshaw (1-213 732 3463). Bus 30, 31, 209/I-10, exit Crenshaw Boulevard north.* **Open** *shows* 10pm daily. **Admission** $5. **No credit cards.**

When you think about it, it kinda makes sense that a mid-city coffeehouse is one of LA's premier indie music venues. Lo-fi, thrash and trash sounds assault a caffeine-loaded crowd of misfits and underground scenemakers. There's no alcohol served, so under-21s are welcome.

## LunaPark

*665 North Robertson Boulevard, at Santa Monica Boulevard, West Hollywood (1-310 652 0611). Bus 4, 10, 220, West Hollywood A, B, N/I-10, exit Robertson Boulevard north.* **Open** *shows* usually 8pm daily. **Admission** $7-$12. **Credit** AmEx, MC, V.

Impresario Jean-Pierre Bocarra has for the past several years presented an incredibly wide array of music – as well as comedy and performance art – to a mixed crowd in this comfortable club. Enter through the restaurant and either go downstairs to the low-ceilinged cabaret or make your way to the main room in the back. Bookings have included female belters Alanis Morissette and Joan Osborne, but usually tend more towards world music and thinking man's pop.
*Parking $3.*

## The Roxy

*9009 Sunset Boulevard, between San Vincente Boulevard & Doheny Drive, West Hollywood (1-310 276 2222). Bus 2, 3, 105, 302, 429 /I-10, exit La Cienega Boulevard north.* **Open** 8pm daily; call for show times. **Admission** $10-$15. **Credit** AmEx, DC, Disc, MC, V.

One of the Strip's few survivors from the 1970s, the Roxy has a history of career-making performances by top names such as Bob Marley, Neil Young and Bruce Springsteen. Nowadays, most shows of note are nouveau-punk bands booked by alternative promoter Goldenvoice. Unless you're industry-connected, get there early to snag a table or it's more than likely that you'll be standing the whole time. The sound system has been much improved recently, but beware: on many nights it emanates the sounds of starry-eyed locals participating in the hateful (if common) 'pay-to-play' scheme.
*Parking $5.*

## Spaceland

*1717 Silver Lake Boulevard, at Effie Street, Silver Lake (1-213 413 4442/infoline after 8pm 1-213 661 4380). Bus 201/US101, exit Silver Lake Boulevard north.* **Open** *shows* 9pm daily. **Admission** $5-$8. **Credit** AmEx, MC, V.

*The* venue of the moment. Decorated in space-age retro bowling-alley style, Spaceland is friendly, laid-back, and sports some of the coolest bands around. Things can get crazy here.

## The Troubadour

*9081 Santa Monica Boulevard, at Doheny Drive, West Hollywood (1-310 276 6168/recorded information 1-310 276 1158). Bus 4, DASH A, West Hollywood/I-405, exit Santa Monica Boulevard east.* **Open** 1.30pm-2am Mon-Fri; 3pm-2am Sat, Sun. **Admission** $5-$12. **No credit cards.**

Elton John made his US debut at the Troub in 1970 during the club's salad days, when it nurtured the careers of neo-folkies Jackson Browne, Linda Ronstadt and David Crosby. Resurrected fairly recently from the depths of metaldom, the venue (which looks like an Alpine ski lodge) once again hosts acts of taste and substance.
*Valet parking $3.50.*

## The Viper Room

*8852 Sunset Boulevard, at Larabee Street, West Hollywood (1-310 358 1880). Bus 2, 3, 105, 302, 429, DASH B/I-10, exit La Cienega Boulevard north.* **Open** 9pm-2am daily. **Admission** $10-$15. **Credit** AmEx, MC, V.

Actor Johnny Depp's place, The Viper Room is more notorious for its celebrity overdoses (most famously, River Phoenix) than the whimsical and varied selection of talent it presents.
*Parking $5.*

## Whisky A-Go-Go

*8901 Sunset Boulevard, at Clark Street, West Hollywood (recorded information 1-310 535 0579/office 1-310 652 4202). Bus 2, 3, 105, 429/I-10, exit La Cienega Boulevard north.* **Open** 8pm-2am daily; *office* 10am-7pm Mon-Fri. **Admission** $7-$15. **Credit** AmEx, DC, Disc, V.

Still crazy after all these years – the Doors were at one time the house band and virtually all the significant pop acts of the past three decades have played this landmark club at one time or another. While nationally known talent appears regularly, the majority of the venue's fare is promising young bands, many of whom can be heard for free on Monday nights. Open to all ages; parking $5.

*Opposite: The legendary* **Whisky-A-Go-Go.**

The Whisky

THU    I MOTHER EARTH
TONIC      GODS CHLI

Candlebox

Lucy

## Roots & blues

### BB King's Blues Club
*Universal CityWalk, 1000 Universal Center Drive,*
*Universal City (1-818 622 5464). Bus 420/US101, exit*
*Universal Center Drive.* **Open** 5pm-1am Mon-Thur, Sun;
5pm-2am Fri, Sat. **Admission** $6 Mon-Thur, Sun; $12
Fri, Sat. **Credit** AmEx, DC, Disc, MC, V.
Local guitar slingers and the odd national R&B name ply
their trade at the LA branch of blues master King's Memphis
supper club. This is the most down-to-earth joint on
Universal City's hideously commercial and plastic CityWalk.
*Parking $6.*

### The Derby
*4500 Los Feliz Boulevard, at Hillhurst Avenue, Los Feliz*
*(1-213 663 8979). Bus 180, 181/US101, exit Sunset*
*Boulevard east.* **Open** 4pm-2am Mon; 11am-2am Tue-
Sun. **Admission** $3-$5. **Credit** AmEx, MC, V.
Slick back your hair and groom your goatee because swing's
the thing for hep cats and sweet kittens at The Derby.
*Parking $3.50.*

### Fais Do-Do
*5257 West Adams Boulevard, at Cloverdale Avenue,*
*Culver City (1-213 954 8080). Bus 37/I-10, exit La Brea*
*Avenue south.* **Open** 7pm-midnight Tue, Wed, Sun; 7pm-
2am Thur-Sat. **Admission** $5. **Credit** MC, V.
Specialising in the New Orleans sound, Fais Do-Do can be
counted on for a friendly, funky clientele grooving to the
music and enjoying the good selection of tap beers.
*Valet parking $3 Fri-Sat.*

### Harvelle's
*1432 Fourth Street, between Broadway & Santa Monica*
*Boulevard, Santa Monica (1-310 395 1676). Bus 4, 304,*
*Santa Monica 1, 2, 3, 7, 8/I-10, exit Fourth-Fifth Street*
*north.* **Open** 8pm-2am daily. **Admission** $3-$8.
**No credit cards.**
Santa Monica's self-styled 'home of the blues' is smokin'
seven nights a week in a comfortable bar/lounge setting.

### Jack's Sugar Shack
*1707 Vine Street, at Hollywood Boulevard,*
*Hollywood (1-213 466 7005). Bus 1, 163, 180, 181,*
*212/US101, exit Gower Street south.* **Open** 11.30am-
2am, *shows* 9pm, daily. **Admission** free-$15. **Credit**
AmEx, Disc, MC, V.
Retaining the Polynesian tiki house look of its former location, Jack's serves up a healthy dose of blues and rockabilly
as well as indie/alternative acts.
*Valet parking $3.50.*

### McCabe's
*3101 Pico Boulevard, at 31st Street, Santa Monica*
*(1-310 828 4497). Bus Santa Monica 7/I-10, exit*
*Centinela Avenue south.* **Open** 10am-10pm Mon-Thur;
10am-6pm Fri, Sat; 1-5pm Sun. **Admission** $10-$20.
**Credit** AmEx, DC, Disc, MC, V.
By day a guitar shop, by night (usually at the weekends)
McCabe's intimate back room is renowned for acoustic
pickin' and singin' by country-folk rock types like Rosanne
Cash and Jorma Kaukonen.

### The Mint
*6010 West Pico Boulevard, at Crescent Heights*
*Boulevard, Midtown (1-213 954 9630). Bus Santa*
*Monica 5, 7, 12/I-10, exit La Cienega Boulevard north.*
**Open** 8pm-2am daily. **Admission** $5-$15. **Credit**
AmEx, MC, V.
Re-opened in autumn 1996 with an enlarged capacity, The
Mint's blues, jazz and roots intensive line-up satisfies the urge
for those looking for some good, honest, downhome jams.
*Valet parking $3.*

## Jazz

### The Baked Potato
*3787 Cahuenga Boulevard West, at Lankershim*
*Boulevard, North Hollywood (1-818 980 1615). Bus 96,*
*152, 420, 424, 425/US101 north, exit Lankershim*
*Boulevard south.* **Open** 7pm-2am, *shows* 9.30pm,
11.30pm, daily. **Admission** $10; 2-drink minimum.
**Credit** AmEx, Disc, MC, V.
Musician and owner Don Randi's pint-sized room spawned
the LA jazz fusion sound in the 1970s and is still the site of
many a synth-driven romp. Don't miss the menu full of –
you'd never guess it from the name – spuds.

### Baked Potato Pasadena
*26 East Colorado Boulevard, between Fair Oaks &*
*Raymond Avenues, Old Town Pasadena (1-818 564*
*1122/booking & information after 5pm 1-818 564*
*1720). Bus 180, 181, 256, 483, Foothill Transit 187/*
*I-110 to Arroyo Parkway, exit Colorado Boulevard west.*
**Open** 7pm-2am, *shows* 9pm, 11pm, Tue-Sun.
**Admission** $5-$10. **Credit** AmEx, DC, Disc.
Younger and bigger brother of the original Potato, with more
varied bookings, but still focusing on contemporary jazz.
*Parking $4.*

### Catalina Bar & Grill
*1640 North Cahuenga Boulevard, at Hollywood*
*Boulevard, Hollywood (1-213 466 2210). Bus 1, 163,*
*180, 181, 212/US101, exit Cahuenga Boulevard south.*
**Open** 7pm-1am, *shows* 8.30pm, 10.30pm, daily.
**Admission** $10-$20. **Credit** AmEx, Disc, MC, V.
Catalina Popescu consistently pulls jazz's heaviest hitters
into her highly civilised, peach-shaded establishment.
With the venue's bent toward be-bop, a residence here is de
rigueur for old-guard names such as McCoy Tyner and
Pharoah Sanders as well as the new crop of jazz men typi-
fied by the likes of Branford Marsalis and Joshua Redman.
We suggest you leave the cooking to the players; though
dining here isn't recommended.
*Parking $3.*

### 5th Street Dick's Coffeehouse
*3347½ West 43rd Place, at Degnan Boulevard, Leimert*
*Park (1-213 296 3970). Bus 40, 105, 210, 310, DASH*
*Crenshaw/I-10, exit Crenshaw Boulevard south.* **Open**
4pm-2am Mon-Thur; 4pm-5am Fri; 1pm-5am Sat; 1pm-
2am Sun; *shows* 9pm Mon-Thur; 9pm, 1am Fri, Sat;
5.30pm Sun. **Admission** $5. **No credit cards.**
Traditional jazz workouts last into the wee hours upstairs
at 5th Street Dick's as some of the city's most skilled practi-
tioners hone their chops, usually for free. Dick's Sock-It-To-
Me cake alone is worth the trip. Note the late opening hours;
they're few and far between.

### Jazz Bakery
*3233 Helms Avenue, at Venice Boulevard, Culver City*
*(1-310 271 9039). Bus 33, 436, Culver City 1, 4/I-10,*
*exit La Cienega Boulevard south.* **Open** *shows* 8.30pm
Mon-Fri; 4pm, 8.30pm, Sat, Sun. **Admission** $10-$20.
**No credit cards.**
Mostly jazz of the straight-ahead variety from members of
the pantheon, such as Ahmad Jamal and Dave Gruisin.

### St Mark's
*23 Windward Avenue, at Pacific Avenue, Venice (1-310*
*452 2222). Bus Culver City 1, Santa Monica 2, DASH*
*Venice/I-10, exit Lincoln Boulevard south.* **Open** 7pm-
2am, *shows* 9pm, Tue-Sun. **Admission** $5-$15. **Credit**
AmEx, DC, MC, V.
A relaxed beachside spot for contemporary jazz and R&B,
with an active (straight) pick-up scene at the bar.
*Parking $3.*

# Theatre & Dance

*Even in Celluloid City live artforms do exist – you just have to look a little bit harder than in most places.*

## Theatre

Because of the nature and influence of Hollywood, LA theatre is born of an environment where the stage is not considered of primary importance; where extremely small and often experimental stage works simply provide a workout for actors, writers, and directors otherwise employed by television and film. Even so, those who take theatre – and the arts of acting, writing, and directing – seriously have created some world-class shows here.

Theatres vary from the big, Broadway wannabes to small black boxes. Part of the fun of LA theatre is experiencing the architecture and use of space as integral parts of a show. You might see Brecht in an old warehouse, Shakespeare outside under sycamores or Kushner amid the reds and golds of a turn-of-the-century style opera house.

The best way to discover what's on is to pick up a copy of the *LA Times* or the *LA Weekly*. For tickets and general information for most theatres, call either **Theatix** (1-213 466 1767) or **Telecharge** (1-800 233 3123).

## Major venues

### Henry Fonda Theater

*6126 Hollywood Boulevard, at Gower Street, Hollywood (1-213 468 1700). Bus 1, 180, 181, 212, 217/US101, exit Vine Street south.* **Credit** AmEx, MC, V.
Located in a depressed neighbourhood, the Henry Fonda often houses touring shows such as *And The World Goes Round*, *The Kathy and Mo Show* and the gay musical *Party*. *Parking $6.*

### James A Doolittle Theater

*1615 North Vine Street, between Hollywood Boulevard & Selma Avenue, Hollywood (1-213 462 6666). Bus 1, 26, 180, 181, 212, 429, Community Connection 208/US101, exit Vine Street south.* **Credit** AmEx, MC, V.
Serious drama or knee-jerking fun – from *Angels in America* and *Woman Warrior* to Leiber and Stoller's musical cabaret *Smokey Joe's Café* – the Doolittle is a class act.

### John Anson Ford Amphitheater

*2580 Cahuenga Boulevard East, at Vine Street, Hollywood (1-213 466 1767). Bus 163, 420/US101, exit Cahuenga Boulevard north.* **Credit** (advance only) Disc, MC, V.
A landmark since the 1930s, the Ford is grand yet surprisingly intimate. It presents a variety of works, including experimental productions from the Mark Taper Forum (shown in the Taper, Too space, inside and under the main stage), Summer Nights at the Ford (works by some of LA's most original artists) and the annual Shakespeare Festival LA, held in July. *Parking $5.*

*The rather lovely* **Pantages Theater**.

### Music Center of Los Angeles

*Music Center, 135 North Grand Avenue, at First Street, Downtown (1-213 972 7211). Metro Civic Center/Tom Bradley/bus 78, 79, 96, 379, 427, Commuter Express 423/I-110 north, exit Fourth Street east.* **Tickets** $6-$120. **Credit** AmEx, MC, V.
The Music Center is LA's premier performing arts centre, housing the Dorothy Chandler Pavilion (*see chapter* **Music**), the **Ahmanson Theater** and the **Mark Taper Forum**. Big is the name of the game at the Ahmanson. So huge you need super-powered binoculars to see the actors, it's right up there with the biggest of the big theatres on Broadway, presenting shows such as *Miss Saigon*, *Phantom of the Opera*, *Kiss of the Spider Woman* and *Carousel*. The smaller and less populist Mark Taper has presented the likes of *Three Tall Women*, *Psychopathia Sexualis* and *Black Elk Speaks*. *Parking evenings & weekends $7; weekdays $2.50 per 20 mins ($15 dollar maximum); valet parking $17.*

### Pantages Theater

*6233 Hollywood Boulevard, between Vine Street & Argyle Avenue, Hollywood (1-213 468 1700). Bus 180, 181, 212, 217/US101, exit Vine Street south.* **Credit** AmEx, MC, V.

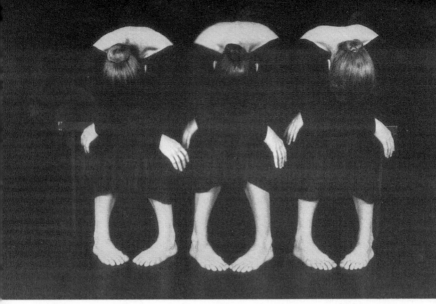

*Local innovators the **Lewitzky Dance Company** in 'Episode #1 (Recuerdo)'. See **Dance**.*

A sumptuous theatre: art deco with a marble and bronze entranceway and a majestic vaulted lobby bookended with ballroom-type staircases and guarded by statues of a movie director and an aviatrix, it was built in 1929 as a movie palace. Between 1949 and 1959, the Pantages was best known for hosting the Academy Awards. In 1967, the theatre transformed into a venue for Broadway musicals and later for concerts and other shows – some of the latest including *Joseph and the Amazing Technicolor Dreamcoat* and David Byrne with his Brazilian band. Legend has it that eccentric millionaire Howard Hughes' ghost still roams the Pantages; he owned it for a few years in the early 1950s. *Parking $6.*

### Schubert T Theater

*2020 Avenue of Stars, at Constellation Boulevard, Century City (1-800 233 3123). Bus 22, 27, 28, 316, 328, Santa Monica 5, Culver City 3/I-405, exit Santa Monica Boulevard east.* **Credit** AmEx, DC, Disc, MC, V.
With its red carpets, and glowing candy and drink bar, the Schubert oozes nostalgia. Long-running shows have included *Beauty and the Beast* and *Sunset Boulevard*.

## 99-seat theatres

Under the 99-Seat Equity Waiver Agreement, small theatres (with fewer than 99 seats) are exempt from having to pay Equity (acting union) rates. This has a two-fold effect: major players often get involved at grass-roots level, and 'fringe' productions, in the 'let's put on a show' sense, flourish.

In addition to the theatres listed below, the area known as Theater Row, in a rather scruffy neighbourhood in Hollywood, has several small spaces often used for short one-off runs, where quality ranges from dismal to inspirational. Look out for shows at the **Complex** (6472 Santa Monica Boulevard), the **Attic Theatre Centre** (Attic 2, 6562½ Santa Monica Boulevard) and the **Hudson**

(6539 Santa Monica Boulevard), among others. The area can be spooky to visit, but sometimes you'll hit the jackpot with, for example, the likes of Jenifer Lewis' one-woman show *The Diva Is Dismissed* or the play of the OJ trial, which changed daily to reflect events in the courtroom.

### The Actors' Gang

*6209 Santa Monica Boulevard, at El Centro Avenue, Hollywood (1-213 465 0566). Bus 4, 210, 310, 304, 420, 426/US101, exit Vine Street south.* **Tickets** available though Theatix. **Credit** AmEx, Disc, MC, V.
Formed in 1981 by artistic director Tim Robbins and a group of energetic theatre souls, the Actors' Gang has become something of an institution in this celluloid-obsessed city. The Gang, which loosely bases much of its work on the rules and form of Commedia dell'Arte, produces inventive new works and daring adaptations of classic plays. Memorable shows include classics *The Oresteia, Peer Gynt* and *Woyzeck* and original works *Hysteria, Klub* and *Asylum*.

### The Evidence Room

*3542 Hayden Avenue, between Steller Drive & National Boulevard, Culver City (1-310 841 2799). Bus Culver City 1, 4, 5, Community Express 438/I-10, exit National Boulevard south.* **Tickets** $15. **No credit cards.**
Started two years ago by a group of college friends, the Evidence Room requires its audience to think. The space, a cleverly employed, cavernous warehouse, houses plays – from Harry Kondoleon's *The Houseguests* to Simon Donald's *Life of Stuff* – that may be disturbing, but never dull.

### Geffen Playhouse

*10886 Le Conte Avenue, at Tiverton Avenue, Westwood (1-310 208 6500/box office 1-310 208 5454). Bus 2, 21, Santa Monica 1, 2, 8, 12, Culver City 6, Commuter Express 431, 576/I-405, exit Wilshire Boulevard east.* **Credit** AmEx, MC, V.
Producing director Gil Cates said of the Geffen's inaugural season: 'These are passionate works. They deal with the passions found in the human spirit, the quest for freedom of

expression and the search for simple truth.' A varnished and beautiful little theatre, the Geffen Playhouse has featured the works of Terrence McNally, John Patrick Shanley, Doug Wright and Robert Brustein.
*Parking $2.*

## Highways Performance Space

*1651 18th Street, at Olympic Boulevard, Santa Monica (1-310 453 1755/tickets 1-213 660 8587). Bus Santa Monica 9/I-10, exit Cloverfield Avenue north.* **Credit** (advance only) AmEx, MC, V.
Presenting over 200 performances annually, Highways works toward promoting the development of contemporary, socially involved artists and art forms. From solo dramatic artists and small dance companies to visual art shows and spoken word presentations, Highways is more about the process of art than the finished product. It also organises educational and residency programmes.

## The MET

*1089 North Oxford Avenue, at Santa Monica Boulevard, Los Angeles (1-213 957 1741). Bus 4, 175, 207, 304, 420/I-10, exit Western Avenue north.* **Credit** MC, V.
An adventurous and inspired theatre south-east of Hollywood, the MET, founded by actors Amy Madigan, Ed Harris, Holly Hunter and Beth Henley among others, invariably means quality work. The company hosts actor/director/writer workshops, out of which came writer/director Susan Emshwiller's *Brush Strokes*, a compilation of six short plays inspired by the paintings of Edward Hopper.
*Parking $3.*

## A Noise Within

*234 South Brand Boulevard, at Colorado Street, Glendale (1-818 546 1924). Bus 92, 93, 177, 183, 410, Glendale Transit B/SR 134, exit Central Avenue south.* **Credit** AmEx, MC, V.
Founded in 1992, this classical theatre company is housed in a former Masonic Temple Building in Glendale. It has gained an enviable reputation for its productions (Shakespeare, Shaw, Molière, Chekhov and classic US playwrights, among others). One of the few US theatres with a resident acting company performing in rotating repertory, it also offers year-round conservatory classes, the annual Summer with Shakespeare programme for teens and an ambitious and successful Student Outreach Program.
*Free parking.*

## Odyssey Theater Ensemble

*2055 South Sepulveda Boulevard, at Mississippi Avenue, West LA (1-310 477 2055). Bus Culver City 6/I-405, exit Santa Monica Boulevard east.* **Credit** AmEx, MC, V.
The essence of this 27-year-old theatre is summed up in an award it received in 1982 for '...demonstrating a continual willingness to experiment provocatively in the process of theatre'. A large blue building in West LA housing three theatres, the Odyssey continues to present innovative versions of classical and original works, including *Caucasian Chalk Circle*, *Accidental Death of an Anarchist* and *The Bacchae*.
*Parking $2.50.*

## Pasadena Playhouse

*39 South El Molino Avenue, between Colorado Boulevard & Green Street, Pasadena (1-818 792 8672). Bus 180, 181, 188, 256, 401, Foothill Transit 187/I-110 to Arroyo Parkway, exit Colorado Boulevard east.* **Credit** AmEx, MC, V.
Opened at the turn of the century and in its present site since 1925 (although it stayed dark for almost 20 years between 1969 and 1986), the Pasadena Playhouse is a landmark. Drawing audiences from over 300 zip codes – along with the blue-haired subscribers who make up a good portion of the Playhouse's audiences – this architectural wonder presents six plays a year. Some of its most popular long-runners have

included *Sisterella*, *Mail*, *Bus Stop*, *Other People's Money* and *Steel Magnolias* (spot the cinema connection).
*Parking $4.*

## Will Geer Theatricum Botanicum

*1419 North Topanga Canyon Boulevard, at Cheney Drive, Topanga (1-310 455 3723). Bus 434/I-10, exit PCH north.* **Tickets** $15 adults; $8.50 students, seniors. **No credit cards.**
Founded by actor Will Geer (best known as Grandpa in the TV series *The Waltons*) as a haven for blacklisted actors, artists, and musicians in the 1950s. Attending a Botanicum show is an outdoor adventure, as the open-air amphitheatre is built under the giant sycamore trees in Will Geer's backyard. The company concentrates on Shakespeare.

## The Tiffany

*8532 Sunset Boulevard, at La Cienega Boulevard, West Hollywood (1-310 289 2999). Bus 2, 3, 429/I-10, exit La Cienega Boulevard north.* **Credit** AmEx, MC, V.
Quality drama is on the bill at this Sunset Boulevard theatre. Plays often feature names in film and theatre; past successes include *Marvin's Room* and *Kindertransport*.
*Parking $3.*

## Also of note:

**The Matrix Theater** 7657 Melrose Avenue, between Spaulding and Stanley Avenues, Melrose District (1-213 852 1445).
**California Cottage Theater** 5220 Sylmar Avenue, Van Nuys (1-818 990 5773).
**Canon Theater** 205 North Canon Drive, at Wilshire Boulevard, Beverly Hills (1-310 859 2850).
**Coast Playhouse** 8325 Santa Monica Boulevard, between Kings Road and Sweetzer Avenue, West Hollywood (1-213 650 8507).

## Outside LA

For those who will travel to see a show, outside LA lie several legendary Tony award-winning theatres:
**La Jolla Playhouse** 2910 La Jolla Village Drive, at Exposition Boulevard, La Jolla (1-619 550 1010).
**Old Globe** Balboa Park, San Diego (1-619 239 2255).
**South Coast Rep** 655 Towne Center Drive, between Anton & Sunflower Avenues, Costa Mesa (1-714 957 4033).

## Dance

Dance in Los Angeles reflects the cultural diversity of the city. The city plays host to most of the touring ballet and modern companies, but the scene also fizzes with the energy of vibrant non Euro-American forms – from flamenco to Taiko drumming, from classical Indian dance to the shamanistic ritual dances of Korea. The annual **Festival of Masks** (1-213 937 5544) in Hancock Park in October and **Music and Dance in the Grass** (1-310 206 1786) at UCLA in May are two festivals not to be missed. For listings try the Calendar section of the *LA Times*, *Dance News* ($20 from the Dance Resource Centre; 1-213 622 0815), *Dance West* or *LA Dance and Fitness Magazine*.

Exciting multicultural work takes its place alongside local and experimental independent work in the smaller spaces. Worth looking out for are the **Lewitzky Dance Company** (1-213 580 6338); **Loretta Livingston and Dancers** (1-213

627 4684; and **Naomi Goldberg's Los Angeles Modern Dance & Ballet** (1-213 655 8759). 'Hyper-dance' – a risk-filled, acrobatic and daring form of movement – originated on the West Coast. Look out for **Mehmet Sander** and **Jacques Heim** and his company **Diavolo Dance Theatre**. The experience is breathtaking. Hyper-dance is often on the bill at **Highways** (*see above* **99-seat theaters**.

## Major venues

The **Dorothy Chandler Pavilion** at the Music Center in Downtown (*see above* **Theatre**) is the place to catch touring ballet companies, including the Joffrey Ballet and American Ballet Theater.

### Harriet & Charles Luckman Fine Arts Complex at Cal State LA

*5151 State University Drive, at Eastern Avenue, Cal State University (1-213 343 6600). For full listings, see chapter* **Music/Classical***.*
A state-of-the art theatre dedicated to presenting local artists and multicultural performers from around the world.

### UCLA Center for the Performing Arts

*405 Hilgard Avenue, at Sunset Boulevard, Westwood (1-310 825 2101). Bus 2, 21, 429, 561, 576/I-405, exit Sunset Boulevard east.* **Credit** *AmEx, MC, V.*
The centre hosts many out-of-town performers. During term time watch out for the artists-in-residence programme, which offers a series of free lectures, masterclasses and open rehearsals. **Royce Hall** (1-310 825 8989), the grandest of the two main venues on the campus (the other is Schoenberg Hall), will remain out of commission until 1998, because of damage incurred in the 1994 earthquake.

### Veterans Wadsworth Theater

*Veterans Administration Grounds, at Wilshire & San Vincente Boulevards, Westwood (1-310 825 2101). For full listings, see chapter* **Music/Rock, Roots & Jazz***.*
Although the small stage can make larger companies look cramped, this theatre plays host to some of the leading international names in dance. Recent talents to have graced its boards include STOMP and Lines Dance Company.

## Regional venues

### Cerritos Center for the Performing Arts

*12700 Centre Court Drive, at Bloomfield Avenue, Cerrito (1-310 916 8500). Bus 130 Norwalk Transit 3/SR 91, exit Bloomfield Avenue south.* **Credit** *AmEx, Disc, MC, V.*
Ballet and multicultural performances.
*Free parking.*

### Irvine Barclay Theater

*4242 Campus Drive, at Bridge Drive, Irvine, Orange County (1-714 854 4646). OC Transit 65, 74, 76, 175, 382/I-405, exit Jamboree Road west.* **Credit** *AmEx, MC, V.*
Larger-scale national touring companies appear here, including Stephen Petronio and Paul Taylor.
*Parking $3.*

### Orange County Performing Arts Center

*600 Town Centre Drive, between Bristol Street & Sunflower Avenue, Costa Mesa, Orange County (1-714 556 2787). OC Transit 53, 55, 57, 59, 74/I-405, exit Bristol Street north.* **Credit** *AmEx, MC, V.*
Definitely worth the trip. A wide-ranging programme includes ballet, a musical or the Samulnori Drummers and Dancers of Korea.
*Parking $6.*

## Smaller spaces

### The Fountain Theatre

*5060 Fountain Avenue, at Normadie Avenue, Hollywood (1-213 663 1525). Bus 175, 206 DASH Hollywood/US101, exit Normandie Avenue north.* **Credit** *AmEx, MC, V.*
Like the outdoor John Anson Ford Theater (*see above*), a place to find home-grown talent and multicultural performers. Absolutely the best place to see flamenco.
*Parking $1.*

### Keck Theatre

*Occidental College, 1600 Campus Road, at Alumni Avenue, Eagle Rock (1-213 259 2737). Bus 83, 84/Calif2, exit Verdugo Road south.* **Credit** *MC, V.*
If the Lewitzky Company could call anywhere home, then it would be here at Eagle Rock, out towards Pasadena. A hyper-dance venue.
*Free parking.*

# Community performers

The riots of 1992 may be the stuff of legend but in Los Angeles, racial tensions are the stuff of everyday life, and the city is as famous for its social problems as it is for its film industry. Many artists in LA have made the pressing social issues of the city both the subject and the sphere of their art. Two such artists to look out for are John Malpede and Lula Washington.

**John Malpede** founded LAPD (Los Angeles Poverty Department; 1-213 413 1077) in 1985. Then a New York performance artist, he was appalled to see the homeless being 'cleared up' by the LAPD (his company's name is a take on this acronym) in preparation for the 1984 Olympic Games. His response was to establish the first theatre company in the US to consist entirely of homeless and formerly homeless people. Expect mayhem, laughter and grit. You can see performances all over town – and that means *all* over.

**Lula Washington** grew up in housing projects. In 1980 she founded her own Afro-centric dance company (1-213 678 6250) to provide a creative outlet for young people in South Central, and has since worked with other youth and children's dance ensembles. The company's home was damaged in the 1994 earthquake and she is currently planning a new, custom-built venue, but you can still see the troupe in venues around town.

# In Focus

| Business | 226 |
| Children | 228 |
| Gay & Lesbian | 231 |
| Students | 236 |

# Business

**The lowdown on how and where to do business in LA, from hiring a cellular phone to 24-hour copyshops.**

In general, doing business in Los Angeles is, in some form or another, related to the film and entertainment industry. Perhaps partly because of this, the perception, especially if you come from the East Coast, is that LA is somehow less aggressive than New York and that Southern Californians (whether native or imported) just don't have the same drive to get things done. Don't be fooled. Angelenos actually work very hard. The city's schedule has been somewhat dictated by the film industry's need to start shooting as soon as it is light and finish when the light fades. Hence, many start and finish work early and, because everyone has to drive, few drink at lunch or dinner.

Don't worry if your business meeting is postponed several times before you actually get to the table; this is normal. The common LA affliction of 'flaking' (making and then rescheduling appointments) occurs in business as well as socially; it's nothing personal. Once you finally get to meet, the bargaining is as ruthless as anywhere else.

Because Los Angeles is such a vast city, you will probably need both a car and a good street map to get to that business meeting on time (*see chapter* **Getting Around**). Angelenos will always take time to tell you the best way to get to where you're going, but planning your route in advance always helps. A cellular phone helps, too. No serious business person in this town is without one – it adds pose points if nothing else.

Don't be afraid to sell your wares. Americans love the sound of success, and the louder and longer you can trumpet yours, the better. Don't be shy about celebrity name-dropping, if you have those kind of contacts. A relationship with a celebrity, however tenuous, gives great kudos and can open many doors. And don't be ashamed to talk about money. You may not want to show all your proverbial cards at the beginning of your meeting, but anything left unspoken, especially money, will only leave you stiffed later. As California is a sue-happy state, always get everything in writing.

## Business information centres

### Los Angeles Convention & Visitors Bureau
*685 South Figueroa Street, LA, CA 90017 (1-213 689 8822/fax 1-213 624 9746).* **Open** 8am-5pm Mon-Friday; 8.30am-3pm Sat.

Offers extensive services for business travellers and tourists, including Destination Los Angeles ($5), containing updated entertainments, special events and hotel and dining listings.

### Los Angeles Area Chamber of Commerce
*350 South Bixel Street, LA, CA 90017 (1-213 580 7500/ fax 1-213 580 7511).* **Open** 8.30am-5pm Mon-Fri.
Similar to the Visitors Bureau, providing a wide range of information and referral services.

## Services

### Cellular phones

#### Shared Technology Cellular
*(1-800 933 3836).* **Open** 24 hours daily. **Credit** AmEx, DC, Disc, MC, V.
Daily, weekly and monthly cellular phone rentals available. The phones themselves are free; you pay for the air time ($1.95 per metered minute, including domestic long-distance calls and calls outside your own area code).

### Couriers

#### DHL Worldwide Express
*(1-800 225 5345).* **Open** usually 8am-8pm Mon-Fri. **Credit** AmEx, Disc, MC, V.
Air courier service with overnight delivery in the US. Pick-up at your location or a local DHL office; call for details. Like most courier services, there is no pick-up service after about 4pm, depending on the office location.

#### Express Connection
*Suite 522, 12121 Wilshire Boulevard, at Bundy Drive, West LA (1-310 447 8000).* **Open** 24 hours daily. **Credit** AmEx, Disc, MC, V.
One of the fastest and most reliable courier services, Express will phone to tell you when your package was delivered. It can deliver anywhere in the US and has a 24-hour pick-up service. This is the main office; branches throughout LA.

#### Federal Express
*(1-800 463 3339).* **Open** 9am-6pm Mon-Sat. **Credit** AmEx, DC, Disc, MC, V.
One of the largest courier services with drop-off locations all over the city and pick-up available. Worldwide.

#### UPS
*(1-800 742 5877).* **Open** 24 hours daily. **Credit** (air courier service only) AmEx, MC, V.
No drop-off facilities but pick-up and delivery (in those famous brown vans) guaranteed. Worldwide.

### Message services

#### American Answering Service
*(1-310 277 7000).* **Open** 24 hours daily. **Credit** MC, V.
Live and voicemail answering service, with private, local and 1-800 numbers.

## Mail Boxes Etc

*(1-800 789 4623/1-213 656 7788).* **Open** 9am-6.30pm
Mon-Fri; 10am-5pm Sat. **Credit** AmEx, Disc, MC, V.
One of the numerous mail receiving and forwarding services
in the city, with 90 locations in LA. Also offers an array of
shipping and business services.

## Office services

For other copy shops, consult the *Yellow Pages.*

### Kinko's

*7630 Sunset Boulevard, at Stanley Avenue, Hollywood
(1-213 845 4501). Bus 2, 3, 429/I-10, exit Fairfax Avenue
north.* **Open** 24 hours daily. **Credit** AmEx, Disc, MC, V.
Kinko's light, bright and efficient copy houses offer everything you will need from faxing and computing (including
dtp; e-mail due to come on line by 1997) to photocopying and
even video-conferencing. Branches throughout the city; ring
1-800 743 2679 for details.

## Contacts/reference

### Film & entertainment

### ASCAP

*(1-213 883 1000).* **Open** *office* 9am-5.30pm Mon-Fri;
*index* 9am-noon, 2-5pm, Mon-Fri.
ASCAP protects intellectual properties, collecting royalties
for artists, composers and publishers, and licensing venues
for PA systems or jukeboxes, as well as providing quick reference, publishing and agency contact information.

### Directors Guild of America

*7920 Sunset Boulevard,West Hollywood, CA 90046
(1-310 289 2000/fax 1-310 289 2029).* **Open** 9am-
5.30pm Mon-Fri.

# Dress to impress

In a city where image is everything, it's not surprising that what you wear is all-important.
However, don't assume that a suit always
equals power: sometimes the CEO will be the
guy in tennis shoes and a baseball cap while
his assistant will be wearing the starched silk
shirt and Italian shoes. In general, Angelenos
tend to dress casually – open-necked, button-
down shirt; jeans; tennis shoes; sunglasses (a
must) – but it is a deceptive casualness: the
jeans cost $200, the tennis shoes are imported
from Spain and the shades are by Armani.
Women tend to dress better than men.

Some hints for those who want to dress to
impress: 'power colours' include beige, cream,
black, taupe, olive, grey and pale peach;
Richard Tyler is a favoured designer for
women, Armani for men (Ralph Lauren is
considered too 'suburban'); don't wear bright
colours or gold and white because this will
make you (heaven forbid) look like a tourist.

---

The Directors Guild protects the artistic and economic rights
of directors as well as offering training and mentor programmes, seminars and workshops to its 10,000 members.

### The Margaret Harrick Library at the Center for Motion Picture Study

*333 South La Cienega Boulevard, at Olympic Boulevard,
Beverly Hills (1-310 247 3035/quick reference 247 3020).
Bus 28, 105/I-10, exit La Cienega Boulevard north.*
**Open** 10am-5.30pm (phone reference 9am-3pm) Mon,
Tue, Thur, Fri.
A reference library only, but you can sit in extremely pleas-
ant surroundings and search for anything and everything
related to film, including press clippings, stills and scripts.

### Screen Actors Guild

*5757 Wilshire Boulevard, Miracle Mile, CA 90036
(information 1-213 954 1600/agents & PR 1-213 549
6737).* **Open** 9am-5pm Mon-Sat.
An essential contact for getting the phone number of any
actor's publicist or agent.

### Writers Guild of America-West

*8955 Beverly Boulevard, West Hollywood, CA 90048
(1-310 550 1000/fax 1-310 550 0322).* **Open** 10am-5pm
Mon-Fri.
Essentially a union for writers, the WGA monitors, collects
and distributes millions of dollars in residuals. Its research
library contains more than 3,000 film scripts, 500 videos
(including seminars, interviews and conferences) and 500
volumes about writers and writing.

## Libraries

### LA County Law Library

*301 West First Street, at Broadway, Downtown (1-213
629 3531). Bus 4, 96, 420, 424/US101, exit Broadway
south.* **Open** 8.30am-10pm Mon-Thur; 8.30am-6pm Fri;
9am-5pm Sat.
The third largest law library in the US, offering complete
services for law research on any topic you can think of, both
national and international.

### Los Angeles Central Library

*630 West Fifth Street, between Grand Avenue & Flower
Street, Downtown (general information 1-213 228 7000/
business 1-213 228 7100). Bus 16, 18, 78, 79, 96,
Foothill 492, DASH E/I-110 north, exit Sixth Street east.*
**Open** 10am-5.30pm Mon, Thur-Sat; noon-8pm Tue, Wed;
1-5pm Sun.
The most comprehensive library in the city, with excellent
facilities and a very knowledgeable reference staff.

## Publications

The *Hollywood Reporter* and *Daily Variety* (both
dailies costing $1.50) are Hollywood's twin bibles,
with the latest scoop on industry manoeuverings
and projects in production. *Billboard* (weekly, $5.50)
is the music industry equivalent. On the newspaper
front, the *Los Angeles Times* (35¢) is an overstuffed
but nevertheless important broadsheet; the *Los
Angeles Daily News* (25¢) is its main competitor.

The *Los Angeles Daily Journal* ($2) provides
California legal news while *Investors Business
Daily* ($1) and *Los Angeles Business Journal* ($2.50)
are business-focused newspapers. Upmarket busi-
ness magazines include *Barron's* ($3), *Business
Week* ($3.50), *Forbes* ($5), *Fortune* ($4.50) and
*Money* ($3.50). *See also* chapter **Media**.

# Children

**Endless sandy beaches, a glut of theme parks and all the facilities of a big city – even the most level-headed kid will feel thoroughly spoiled after a stay in LA.**

## Babysitters

### Babysitters Agency of Santa Monica
*1105 Garfield Avenue, Marina del Rey, CA 90291 (1-310 306 5437).* **Open** 9am-5pm Mon-Sat. **Average** $8 per hour with 4-hour minimum. **No credit cards.**
Babysitters aged at least 21 will take the kids out for a bike ride, a swim or other activities. They need 24 hours' notice and charge $8 per hour (4 hours minimum) plus transport.

### Babysitters Guild
*Suite 812, 6399 Wilshire Boulevard, Los Angeles, CA 90048 (1-213 658 8792/1-213 852 1422 fax).* **Open** 9.30am-4pm Mon-Fri; 11am-1pm Sat. **Average** $9 per hour plus $4 gas fee. **No credit cards.**
In business for nearly 50 years, the Guild employs babysitters aged 40 to 60, who speak English, have CPR (cardiopulmonary recusitation) training and drive. They serve hotels all over the city at a cost of $9 an hour for one child, $2 an hour for each additional child, plus transportation and parking, with a four-hour minimum.

### Mount St Mary's College – Student Placement Office
*Chalon Campus, 12001 Chalon Road, Los Angeles, CA 90049 (1-310 471 9883).* **Open** 8am-5pm Mon-Fri.
The Student Placement office will provide a list of college students who babysit. You make the arrangements yourself. Fees are normally $5-$10 an hour.

## Shopping

*See also chapter* **Shopping & Services**.

### Books & toys

### Allied Model Trains
*4411 South Sepulveda Boulevard, at Braddock Drive, Culver City (1-310 313 9353). Culver CityBus 5, 6/I-405, exit Culver Boulevard east.* **Open** 10am-6pm Mon-Thur; 10am-7pm Fri; 10am-6pm Sat. **Credit** AmEx, Disc, MC, V.
Housed in a replica of Union Station, this is the store where you will find trains, trains, trains and any accessories to do with trains. Makes include Thomas the Tank Engine, Brio and Playmobile for small children and Fleishmann, LGB, Lionel and others for the serious enthusiast.

### Children's Book World
*10580 3/4 West Pico Boulevard, between Prosser & Manning Avenues, Culver City (1-310 559 2665). Bus Culver City 3, Santa Monica 7, 13, Commuter Express 431/I-10, exit Overland Avenue north.* **Open** 10am-5.30pm Mon-Fri; 10am-5pm Sat. **Credit** MC, V
A huge children's bookstore with devoted and knowledgeable staff. There's storytelling three Saturdays a month.

### Imaginarium
*Century City Shopping Center, 10250 Santa Monica Boulevard, Between Century Park West & Avenue of the Stars, Century City (1-310 785 0227). Bus 22, 27, 28, 316, 328, Santa Monica 5, Commuter Express 534, 573/I-405, exit Santa Monica Boulevard east.* **Open** 10am-9pm Mon-Fri; 10am-6pm Sat; 11am-6pm Sun. **Credit** AmEx, Disc, MC, V.
Like a child's bedroom, toys are strewn everywhere, ready for play. Kids can entertain themselves for hours with computers, trains and playhouses – and make friends in the process. There's no pressure to buy, but you probably will.

### Lakeshore Learning Materials
*8888 Venice Boulevard, at National Avenue, Midtown (1-310 559 9630). Bus 33, 220, 333, 436, Santa Monica 12/I-10, exit National Avenue south.* **Open** 9am-6.30pm Mon-Fri; 9am-5pm Sat; 11am-5pm Sun. **Credit** AmEx, Disc, MC, V.
This is the place where teachers buy those wonderful, stimulating, politically correct toys and manipulatives that children play with at school.

### Clothes

### Flap Happy
*2330 Michigan Avenue, at Cloverfield Avenue, Santa Monica (1-310 453 3527). Santa Monica 9/I-10, exit Cloverfield Avenue north.* **Open** 10am-5pm Mon-Sat. **Credit** Disc, MC, V.
The retail outlet for this Venice-based clothing manufacturer: colourful patterned cotton clothes for up to fives.

### Flap Jack's
*2462 Overland Avenue, at Pico Boulevard, Rancho Park, LA (1-310 204 1896). Bus Santa Monica 7, Culver City 3, Commuter Express 431, 13/I-10, exit Overland Avenue north.* **Open** 10am-6pm Mon-Sat. **Credit** MC, V.
A huge selection of second-hand clothes for up to tens.

### Gap Kids
*409 North Beverly Drive, between Brighton Way & Little Santa Monica Boulevard, Beverly Hills (1-310 273 1685). Bus 4, 20, 27, DASH Beverly Hills/I-10, exit Robertson Boulevard north.* **Open** 10am-8pm Mon-Fri; 10am-7pm Sat; 11am-6pm Sun. **Credit** AmEx, Disc, MC, V.
Reasonably priced small versions of the clothes Gap makes for adults. You can find Gap Kids in shopping malls all over the city. Call for details of your nearest.

## Entertainment

For listings of theme parks, beaches and other family attractions, *see chapter* **Sightseeing**. For more entertainment suggestions, refer to the Calendar section of the Sunday *Los Angeles Times*, *LA Weekly* and the monthly *LA Parent*, which can be found in any location that caters for kids.

On weekdays during July and August, **Open House at Hollywood Bowl** (*see chapter* **Music**) lays on performances and workshops of all varieties for children aged between three and twelve.

# Circuses & shows

### Disney on Ice
*LA Sports Arena, 3939 South Figueroa Street, at Martin Luther King, Jr. Boulevard, Exposition Park, Downtown (1-213 748 6131). Bus 81, 102, 200, 442, 444, 445, 446, 447/I-110, exit Exposition Boulevard west.* **Tickets** $10.50-$30. **Credit** MC, V.
Plugged into the Disney marketing machine, stories from the animated features are skated out in costume on ice. A big, good-natured spectacle that kids love, for four days in winter.

### LA Circus
*For information, call 1-213 751 3486.*
Sponsored by the Los Angeles Cultural Affairs Office, this delightful one-ring circus sets up in the inner city parks for a one- or two-day show and runs children's circus workshops as well. At the time of writing this happens eight times a year. Call for a performance schedule.

### Ringling Brothers and Barnum & Bailey Circus
*LA Sports Arena, 3939 South Figueroa Street, at Martin Luther King Jr Boulevard, Exposition Park, Downtown LA (1-213 748 6131). Bus 81, 102, 200, 442, 444, 445, 446, 447/I-110, exit Exposition Boulevard west.* **Tickets** $10.50-$30. **Credit** MC, V.
The Ringling Brothers and Barnum & Bailey three-ring spectacle is the epitome of the US circus. This one's as big, loud and lavish as they come and is in town for 7 days in June.

# Music

From October to May, Open House at the Music Center schedules a concert and workshop series for children aged from three upwards at the **Dorothy Chandler Pavilion** (*see chapter* **Music**).

### Pasadena Symphony Musical Circus
*Pasadena Civic Auditorium, 300 East Green Street, at Euclid Avenue, Pasadena (1-818 449 7360/1-818 793 7172 Pasadena Symphony). Bus 180, 181, 188, 256 Foothill Transit 187/I-110, exit Green Street east.* **Credit** AmEx, MC, V.
Musicians and teachers help children aged 4-11 discover the joy of music-making through a hands-on session with a variety of orchestral instruments, an event that relates to the theme of that evening's concert.
*Parking $5.*

### Will Geer Theatricum Botanicum
*1419 North Topanga Canyon Boulevard, at Cheney Drive, Topanga (1-310 455 3723/1140). Bus 434/I-10, exit PCH north.*
This rustically located open-air theatre welcomes children's performers on Sundays at 11am from June through August.

# Restaurants

With child-friendly fast-food joints and family dining chains, such as Denny's, endemic, the problem won't be where you can feed your kids, but how to get them out of there.

### DC-3
*2800 Donald Douglas Loop North, at 28th Street, Santa Monica (1-310 399 2323). Santa Monica 8/I-10, exit Bundy Drive south.* **Lunch served** 11.30am-2.30pm

Mon-Fri. **Dinner served** 6pm-10pm Tue-Thur; 6pm-11pm Fri-Sat. **Credit** AmEx, Disc, MC, V.
The city's most fashionable restaurant back in the late 1980s, DC-3 offers a service from Tuesday-Thursday whereby kids are entertained and fed while you eat. The children are taken care of by babysitters (activities include museums, movies, and rides on the flight simulator) while the parents eat (main courses $17-$24; a fixed-price three-course meal costs $21). The average price of meal on the children's menu is $5.95. Children must be out of nappies and walking.

# Theatre/puppets

Comedy club **LA Connection** runs a improvisation show, inspired by your suggestions, for children at 3.30pm on Sundays (*see chapter* **Comedy**).

### Bob Baker Marionette Theater
*1345 West First Street, at Glendale Boulevard, Downtown (1-213 250 9995). Bus 14/I-110, exit Third Street west.* **Tickets** $10 adults; $8 seniors. **Credit** AmEx, MC, V.
Original marionette productions are staged at 2.30pm Saturday and Sunday, and 10.30am Tuesday to Friday.
*Booking essential. Free parking.*

### Santa Monica Playhouse
*1211 Fourth Street, between Arizona Avenue & Wilshire Boulevard, Santa Monica (1-310 394 9779). Bus 20, 320 Santa Monica 2, 3, 8, 9/I-10, exit 4th Street north.* **Tickets** $8. **Credit** MC, V.
Five or six original family musicals are staged each year by the Playhouse's Actors' Repertory Theatre Company.

# Libraries

Most of the public libraries in and around Los Angeles have regular storytelling and workshops. To learn about other performances and events, ask for the *Children's Activities* pamphlet available free at most branches.

### Los Angeles Central Library
*630 West Fifth Street, between Flower Street & Grand Avenue, Downtown (1-213 228 7000/1-213 228 7055 children's tour reservation line/1-213 228 7250 children's library). Metro 7th Street/Metro Center/bus 16, 18, 78, 79, 96, DASH E, Foothill Transit 492/I-110 north, exit Sixth Street east.* **Open** 10am-5.30pm Mon, Thur-Sat; noon-8pm Tue, Wed; 1-5pm Sun.
The children's library here is well equipped and very active. The Ronald McDonald multimedia centre features eight interactive workstations. To locate books, children can refer to Kid Cat, a computer catalogue system that uses icons – so there's no need to spell! The KLOS Story Theater seats 60 people for programmes that alternate between music and dance, storytelling and puppet shows (2pm Sat). On any given day you will find storytelling, dancing, music, crafts and more throughout the library and its grounds.

# Museums

Of LA's general musuems, children will be particularly entertained by the **California Science Center**, where they can experience a simulated earthquake, watch chicks hatch, design a bicycle and go to a workshop in rocketry; the **Natural History Museum**, which has a 6,000sq ft interactive gallery and a giant ant farm; the Discovery

Center at the **Skirball Cultural Center**, where young archaeologists can play at being Indiana Jones; the **George C Page Museum of La Brea Discoveries**, where woolly mammoths still roam the earth; and the **Petersen Automotive Museum**. For all, *see chapter* **Museums**.

### Angels Attic Museum

*516 Colorado Boulevard, between 5th & 6th Street, Santa Monica (1-310 394 8331). Bus 434, Santa Monica 2, 3, 9/I-10, exit 5th Street north.* **Open** 12.30-4.30pm Thur-Sun. **Admission** $4 adults; $3 seniors; $2 under-12s. **Credit** MC, V.

Doll lovers can covet more than 60 antique dollhouses and dolls from around the world.

### Los Angeles Children's Museum

*310 North Main Street, at Temple Street, Downtown (1-213 687 8801/1-213 687 8800 recorded information). Metro Civic Center/Tom Bradley/bus 434, 436, 439, 442 DASH D/US101, exit Los Angeles Street south.* **Open** 9.15am-1pm Tue-Sat; 10am-5pm Sat-Sun by reservation only. **Admission** $5 adults, children; ¹⁄₂-price for parties of 10 or more. **No credit cards.**

Children can record a song in a professional recording studio, make a TV show, learn about recycling, make an animated cartoon and more. The theatre hosts performances and related workshops by storytellers, musicians, dancers, actors, artists, animal handlers and writers.

*Parking $3.30 per hour weekdays; free with validation after two hours; $3.30 per day weekends.*

### Kidspace Museum

*390 South El Molino Avenue, between California & Del Mar Boulevards, Pasadena (1-818 449 9144). Bus 267/I-110 to Arroyo Parkway, exit California Boulevard east.* **Open** *May-Sept* 1pm-5pm Wed, Sun; 10am-5pm Sat; *June-Aug* 1pm-5pm Mon-Thur, Sun; 10am-5pm Fri, Sat. **Admission** $2.50 1-2s; $3.50 seniors; $5 over-3s. **Credit** MC, V.

Curious kids can visit a simulated beach, shop in a mini supermarket, make masks, observe animal and insect habitats and ecosystems, play with computers and a fire truck, be a TV news anchor and study California's night skies. *Free parking.*

### Museum of Flying

*2772 Donald Douglas Loop North, at 28th Street, Santa Monica (1-310 392 8822). Santa Monica 8/I-10, exit Bundy Drive south.* **Open** 10am-5pm Wed-Sun. **Admission** $7 adults; $5 seniors; $3 children. **Credit** AmEx, MC, V.

There are more than 40 aircraft in and around this Santa Monica museum. Embryonic aviators can clamber into cockpits, attend workshops, watch videos and learn about designing and flying aircraft.

## Outdoors

The rolling hills of **Griffith Park** (*see chapter* **Sightseeing**) make a great one-stop outdoor experience for children. There are picnic areas, miles of trails for hiking or horseback riding, the Travel Town Railroad and Museum (5200 Zoo Drive; 1-213 662 9678), the Griffith Park Merry-Go-Round, built in 1926 and operated daily during the summer and at weekends, the **Los Angeles Zoo** (*see below*) and the **Griffith Park Observatory and Planetarium** (1-213 664 1191); *see chapter*

*Sightseeing*). On clear nights, the twin refracting telescope is open for the public to view the night sky.

### TreePeople Tours

*12601 Mulholland Drive, at Coldwater Canyon, Beverly Hills (1-818 753 4620)/US101, exit Coldwater Canyon Boulevard south.* **Tours** Wed, Thur, Fri at 10am. **Admission** $4.50 per child. **Credit** MC, V.

Spend a delightful, politically correct day with TreePeople. This non-profit group plants and cares for native and exotic trees while enlightening the Los Angeles community about protecting the environment. It's located in the 45-acre Coldwater Canyon Park, where visitors can enjoy guided walks and educational displays at the centre. Children can garden, learn about conservation and explore the recycling area. Booking is essential for the tours.

## Flora & fauna

### Cabrillo Marine Aquarium

*3720 Stephen White Drive, at Pacific Avenue, San Pedro (1-310 548 7562). Bus 446 MAX 3/I-110, exit Harbor Boulevard west.* **Open** 10am-5pm Tue-Sun. **Admission** free.

This 60-year-old aquarium is dedicated to California marine life. It's home to a jellyfish farm, a hands-on tide pool exhibit and 30 ocean-life tanks that line the walls of the 20,000sq ft facility. Special events include two-hour whale-watching trips, guided walks to the tide pools at Point Fermin Marine Life Refuge and grunion runs (special trips made during this small, pencil-sized fish's migrating season – an opportunity to catch and eat the grunion, but not for the seasick). *Parking $6.50.*

### Hydrosphere

*# D-3, 860 Via De La Paz, Pacific Palisades, CA 90272 (1-310 230 3334).* **Open** office 9am-5pm Mon-Fri. **Admission** $15. **Credit** MC, V.

This three-hour ocean adventure boards at Long Beach and heads towards sea, where all manner of sea life, and the Southern California kelp forest, can be seen via a live video feed from Hydrosphere divers. You can speak to the divers while they are underwater, and on-board naturalists give information and answer questions. If you have all day to spare, there are also shark and sea lion tours.

### Los Angeles Zoo

*5333 Zoo Drive, Griffith Park, LA (1-213 666 4650). Bus 96/SR134, exit Victory Boulevard south.* **Open** 10am-5pm daily. **Admission** $8.25 adults, over-13s; $5.25 seniors; $3.25 under-13s. **Credit** AmEx, Disc, MC, V.

Home to more than 1,600 animals in lushly landscaped settings, the highlights include a reptile house, a koala house, gorilla and tiger exhibits and animal shows. The Safari Shuttle, a tram that travels to many of the environments, takes the pain out of the zoo's steep slopes. Phone for details of special workshops where children can accompany zoo keepers as they breed breakfast to the animals and sleepovers where children can have a night-time stroll with the keepers. *Free parking.*

### Sebastian Rainforest

*6109 DeSoto Avenue, at Erwin Street, Woodland Hills (1-800 829 7322). Bus 243, Santa Clarita 796/US101, exit DeSoto Avenue north.* **Open** 8am-5pm Mon-Fri. **Admission** free.

Experience a miniature rainforest created inside the Sebastian haircare product corporation's building in the San Fernando Valley. The exhibit features artefacts made by rainforest inhabitants, a small aquarium, a rain sculpture and displays of rainforest animals and products. A trained guide gives a 30-60 minute tour (booking advised). *Free parking.*

# Gay & Lesbian

*It may be overshadowed by its northern neighbour San Francisco, but gay LA can more than hold its own. Whatever – or whoever – turns you on, you'll find it here.*

The Los Angeles region, a sprawling megalopolis of 15 million people, as many as a half a million of whom may be gay or lesbian, holds every imaginable configuration of gay and lesbian life, from tall, tan, tattooed beach bunnies to low-riding cholos, from two-stepping cowgirls to dykes on bikes, from homebound couples with dogs, gardens and kids in Gap clothes to ultra smooth all-night-dancers with pierced nipples. Let this be your ticket in.

Gay Los Angeles is concentrated in West Hollywood, Hollywood and Silver Lake, with a few interesting outliers in the Valleys, at the beaches and in the central city area. The City of West Hollywood, incorporated in 1985, is for many the gayest city in the world, where hundreds of gay men and lesbians live their daily lives with the same reckless abandon as the hetero-majority.

Los Angeles continues to be devoured by AIDS. Many thousands of gay people (as well as thousands of non-gay people) become infected each year with HIV here. Don't fuck without condoms. If this is a problem for you or if you would like information about prevention programmes call Sex Essentials at AIDS Project Los Angeles (1-213 993 1636).

Most of the places listed here are relatively easy to find and well worth the trouble. Don't let the driving distances scare you: buckle up, tune in to KCRW (89.9 FM) and enjoy Gay Los Angeles.

### International Gay Travel Association
*Box 4974, Key West, FL 33041 (1-800 448 8550/fax 1-304 296 6633).*
A consortium of over 900 travel companies provides comprehensive information and referrals to gay-friendly travel agents, tours and accommodation.

### LA Gay & Lesbian Center
*1625 North Schrader, at Hollywood Boulevard, West Hollywood 90028 (1-213 993 7600/1-213 993 7430 recorded information).* **Open** 9am-9pm Mon-Sat.
An essential, and central place for connecting with other same-gender-loving folks. Appointment recommended.

# Gay

## Books/media

There are many free gay-themed mags, most available at the venues listed in this book. Look out for these: *Frontiers, Edge, Sex Vibe, Forefront, Night Life.*

### A Different Light Bookstore
*8853 Santa Monica Boulevard, at San Vincente Boulevard, West Hollywood (1-310 854 6601).* **Open** 10am-midnight daily. **Credit** AmEx, MC, V.
The largest selection of gay and lesbian literature in town. Readings (practically) nightly, a good selection of magazines and cards and super-friendly service.

### Circus of Books
*8230 Santa Monica Boulevard, between Harper & La Jolla Avenues, West Hollywood (1-213 656 6533).* **Open** 6am-2am daily. **Credit** Disc, MC, V.
There are two of them. They're sleazy and can be a lot of fun. Get a porno-mag, some lube and maybe a date. **Branch**: 4001 Sunset Boulevard, at Sanborn Avenue, Silver Lake (1-213 666 1304).

## Body & mind

In Los Angeles the body is king. While you're here grab your sceptre and join the parade. Check the free gay magazines for hundreds of ads, from legit massage to sex dates and everything in between.

### AIDS/HIV
*See also chapter* **Survival**. For referrals to 40 or so locations where you can get free anonymous or confidential HIV tests, call 1-800 922 2537.

### AIDS Activism
*AIDS Programs Office of the County of Los Angeles, 600 South Commonwealth Avenue, 6th floor, Los Angeles, CA 90005 (1-213 351 8000).* **Open** 8am-5pm Mon-Fri.
Ask for the current meetings list.

### The Mountain AIDS Project
*610 Santa Monica Boulevard #217, Santa Monica (1-310 394 0562).* **Open** 11.30am-4.30pm Mon-Thur.
Spiritual retreats, support groups and drop-in center for anyone affected by HIV/AIDS. Call first.

### Fitness classes/gyms

LA's fitness gurus have mastered the workout class. Try these listed here, they cost just $10 each and you'll leave LA thinner and fitter: spinning at **Todd Tramp** (624 North La Cienega Boulevard, at Melrose Avenue, West Hollywood; 1-310 657 4140); **Super Sculpt** at Martin Henry (1106 North La Cienega Avenue, at Holloway Drive, West Hollywood; 1-310 659 9200); **High Impact** at Voight by the Sea (1919 Broadway, between 19th & 20th Streets, Santa Monica; 1-310 453 4350). The city is also packed full of gyms. Three that are guaranteed to pump you and make you hard are: **Gold's** in Hollywood (1016 Cole Avenue, at Santa Monica Boulevard, Hollywood; 1-213 462 7012); **The Sports Connection** (8612 Santa Monica Boulevard, at La Cienega Boulevard, West

Hollywood; 1-310 652 7440); **World Gym**, 8560 Santa Monica Boulevard, at La Cienega Boulevard, West Hollywood (1-310 659 6630).

## Hair

Remember, LA is the land where fantasies come true and you're only as good as your last haircut.

### Clark Nova

*8118 West Third Street, at Crescent Heights Boulevard, West Hollywood (1-213 655 1100).* **Open** 1pm-6pm Tue-Wed 10am-8pm Thur-Fri 9am-6pm Sat.
Have Eusebio trim you up. The best in the business.

### Doyle Wilson

*8006 Melrose Avenue, between Edinburgh & Laurel Avenues, West Hollywood (1-213 658 6987).* **Open** 9am-5pm Tue, Sat 9am-8pm Wed, Thur, Fri.
The talk in here is cheaper than the haircut, but you may end up getting a rinse next to Faye Dunaway, or hearing about the 'horrible nightmare it was on the set of so-and-so's last movie'. And you'll leave looking fabulous.

## New age

### Bodhi Tree

*8585 Melrose Avenue, at Westbourne Drive, West Hollywood (1-310 659 1733).* **Open** 10am-11pm daily.
Get your aura cleansed. This LA institution has been aligning chakras, smudging sage, clearing crystals, and brewing tea for decades.

## Psychotherapy

### Keith Rand, MFCC

*(1-213 251 3844).*
For some one-on-one attention, or a men's group. Everyone in LA needs a therapist. How does that make you feel?

## Tattoos & body piercing

### The Gauntlet

*8722 Santa Monica Boulevard, between La Cienega & San Vincente Boulevards, West Hollywood (1-800 746 4728/1-310 657 6677).* **Open** noon-7pm Mon-Sat; noon-4pm Sun.
You own it, they'll mark it up and pierce it.

## Entertainment

## Bars & clubs

Los Angeles has a whole set of clubs that change venues regularly and attract thousands weekly. **Temple** comes and goes, call 1-213 243 5221 for current information; **Rudolpho's** (1-818 576 0720) always has something happening; **House of Blues** (1-213 653 2699) sometimes has a Sunday tea dance.

### WEST HOLLYWOOD

The West Hollywood strip tends to attract a cleaner, younger, fresh-from-the-gym crowd more interested in vertical communication than horizontal boot-banging.

### Motherlode

*8944 Santa Monica Boulevard, between Robertson & San Vincente Boulevard, West Hollywood (1-310 659 9700).* **Open** noon-2am daily.
Friendly place with guys playing pool and making smalltalk. Everyone's favourite beer bust on Sunday afternoons.

### Rage

*8911 Santa Monica Boulevard, at San Vincente Boulevard, West Hollywood (1-310 652 7055).* **Open** 1.30pm-2am Mon-Fri; 2pm-2am Sat, Sun. **Cover** $6-$8.
Newly renovated quintessential West Hollywood gay dance club. Daily happy hour on the sidewalk (1.30pm-8pm).

### Revolver

*8851 Santa Monica Boulevard, at Larrabee Street, West Hollywood (1-310 659 8851).* **Open** 4pm-2am daily.
Video bar. Lots of guys having a good time watching each other have a good time. Cover is $5-$10, Fri and Sat only.

### HOLLYWOOD

Hollywood bars and clubs attract an entirely different crowd. The music's better, the haircuts shorter, the muscles look bigger in the bad lighting and the nights start and end later.

### The Probe

*836 North Highland Avenue, between Waring & Willoughby Avenues, Hollywood (1-213 461 8301).* **Open** 9pm-3am nightly. **Cover** $5-$10.
Take your disco nap beforehand because you're going to be up late. Arrive after midnight to see turned-on muscle queens with their shirts off. There's a door scene some Saturdays. Everyone has to go at least once.

### Spike

*7746 Santa Monica Boulevard, at Genesee Avenue, Hollywood (1-213 656 9343).* **Open** noon-2am Sun-Thur noon-4am Fri-Sat. **Cover** $2 Wed; $3 Fri, Sat after 1.30pm.
The Levis/leather bar on the Westside. Always an interesting crowd: cruisey guys with sex on their minds.

### The Study

*1723 Western Avenue, between Hollywood Boulevard & Russell Avenue, Hollywood (1-213 464 9551).* **Open** 11am-2am daily.
A friendly local bar with a pool table.

### Tempo

*5520 Santa Monica Boulevard, at Western Avenue, Hollywood (1-213 466 1094).* **Open** 9am-2am Mon-Thur 8pm-2am Fri-Sun. **Cover** $6 Fri & Sun; $7 Sat.
Rooftop patio with music from south of the border. Popular after-hours, too. Security parking.

**Clark Nova** – *hair-stylist par excellence.*

No pain, no gain – but you can always just watch. **Gold's** gym, see page 231.

## SILVER LAKE

Silver Lake bars and clubs come in as many shapes and sizes as the clientele. Tattoos, piercings, facial hair, and leather; if you're into it, you'll find it.

### Cuffs

*1941 Hyperion Avenue, at Fountain Avenue, Silver Lake (1-213 660 2649).* **Open** 4pm-2am Sun-Thur; 4pm-4am Fri, Sat. **Cover** $3.
Quintessential Silver Lake. Nobody leaves empty-handed.

### Faultline

*4216 Melrose Avenue, at North Vermont Avenue, Silver Lake (1-213 660 0889).* **Open** 4pm-2am Mon-Fri; 2pm-2am Sat, Sun.
Leather ethic; video; Wayne's LeatherRack on premises. Sunday beer bust is always a kick in the rubber parts.

### Salsa Con Clase

*Rudolpho's, 2500 Riverside Drive, at Fletcher Drive, Silver Lake (1-213 669 1226).* **Open** 8pm-2am nightly.
On the first and third Sunday of the month you can rumba, merengue and cha cha to your heart's content.

## Beaches

### Will Rogers

This beach is north of Santa Monica Pier, on Pacific Coast Highway at Chatauqua, in front of the Beach Club in Santa Monica. On sunny weekend days it's packed, it's fun, it's free, it's got tons of guys playing volleyball and it all lasts till sunset. Down-sides are iffy water quality and a scarcity of parking: bring your $6, park in the lot and save some aggravation. Patrick's Roadhouse is across the street.

### Venice

Head for the stretch where Windward Avenue meets the beach, next to the wall, just down from Muscle Beach and in front of the boardwalk. This beach attracts them all. After, you could check out Roosterfish (1302 Abbot Kinney Boulevard; 1-310 392 2123), a friendly neighbourhood bar.

### South Laguna Beach

It's a long drive down to Laguna from LA, but the water is clean and the beach is hot. It's especially nice on a weekday. The gay section is on Pacific Coast Highway, just past the pier. Look for the gay flag (it's easy to miss), park on the side of the road and take the stairs down. Stop at Wahoo's Fish Tacos (1133 South Pacific Coast Highway; 1-714 497 0033) for the best in the business, or the Boom Boom Room *(see chapter* **Bars***)*.

## Bathhouses/sex clubs

The sex club/bathhouse world is alive and kicking. Take your own condoms.

### The Hollywood Spa

*1650 Ivar Street, between Hollywood Boulevard & Selma Avenue, Hollywood (1-800 772 2582 recorded information/1-213 464 0445).* **Open** 24 hours daily. **Rates** $16-$20.
Twenty four hour bathhouse with a DJ every night. They'll give you the towel.

### Splash

*8054 West Third Street, at Crescent Heights Boulevard, West Hollywood (1-213 653 4410).* **Open** 11.30am-4am daily. **Rates** $17.50-$50 per hour.
18 private, spic and span jacuzzi suites boast 'water so clean you can drink it'. Yeah, well.... Reservations recommended.

### The Vortex

*1090 Lillian Way, between Eleanor Avenue & Santa Monica Boulevard, Hollywood (1-213 465 0188).* **Open** 8pm-5am Mon-Fri; 2pm-5am Sat, Sun. **Cover** $3-$8.
Stand-up sex club. Levis, leather and lots of sweat.

### Zone

*1037 North Sycamore Avenue, between Romaine Street &*
*Santa Monica Boulevard, Hollywood (1-213 464 8881).*
**Open** 7pm-5am Mon-Sat; noon-5am Sun. **Cover** $5-$11.
Stand-up sex club for the glamour boy in you. Private mem-
bers only (membership $15 LA natives, $8 non-natives).

## Coffeehouses

### The Abbey

*692 North Robertson Boulevard, at Santa Monica*
*Boulevard, West Hollywood (1-310 289 8410).* **Open** 8am-
2am Mon-Sat; 8am-2am Fri-Sun.
A nice alternative to the nightly bar scene in West Hollywood.
The coffee and desserts may leave you wanting, but the fresh
air and the general ambiance cannot be beat.

### Buzz

*8000 Sunset Boulevard, at Crescent Heights Boulevard,*
*West Hollywood (1-213 650 7742).* **Open** 7am-midnight
Mon-Thur, Sun; 7am-2am Fri, Sat.
The coffee's mediocre, the art is even worse, but they're
always busy.

### Starbucks

*8595 Santa Monica Boulevard, West Hollywood (1-310 659*
*1856).* **Open** 5.30am-10pm Mon-Fri; 6am-10pm Sat, Sun.
Like they need more business. But it's hopping with homos.

### Tsunami Coffee House

*4019 Sunset Avenue, at Sanborn Avenue, Silver Lake*
*(1-213 661 7771).* **Open** 10am-10pm Tue-Sun.
Artwork, baked goodies, and the proceeds go to the Sunset
Junction Youth Program.

## Drag shows

### Mugi

*5221 Hollywood Boulevard, between Hobart Boulevard &*
*Kingsley Drive, Los Feliz (1-213 462 2039).* **Open** 8pm-
2am nightly. No cover.
Thursday night drag show.

### Queen Mary

*12449 Ventura Boulevard, at Whitsett Avenue, Studio City*
*(1-818 506 5619).* **Open** 11am-2am Wed-Sun. **Cover** $7 Fri-
Sat $2 Sun.
A Valley tradition. Female impersonators nightly.

## Restaurants

### Angeli Caffe

*7274 Melrose Avenue, between Alta Vista Boulevard &*
*Poinsettia Place, Hollywood (1-213 936 9086).*
Excellent Italian food. Best bread in town, big portions, rea-
sonable prices. Go for lunch and say hi to Ted. Cookbooks,
T-shirts and speciality items for sale, too.

### California Chicken Cafe

*6805 Melrose Avenue, at Mansfield Avenue, Hollywood*
*(1-213 935 5877).*
Roast chicken and salads. Cheap, no frills. But the lines are out
the doors and the boys from the gym are there carbo-loading.

### Cha Cha Cha

*656 North Virgil Avenue, at Melrose Avenue, Silver Lake*
*(1-213 664 7723).* Booking advised.
Mario Tamayo's legacy lives. The flamboyant restaurateur
died of AIDS a couple of years back, but you can still eat and
drink to his memory at the restaurant he made famous. The
Caribbean jerk chicken is excellent and so is the chicken sandwich. Tuesday night is Homo Happy Hour.

# Car cruising

Cruising around the block for the 38th time
and still wondering if the guy in the striped
shirt noticed you in your rented convertible?
If this sounds like you, the next section will
drive you wild. Cruising in LA in a car is a
favourite pastime. The only rules are don't hit
anyone or anything. And remember: public
sex/lewdness is still a crime in LA.

### Vaseline Alley

The City of West Hollywood created this cruiser's
wet dream with several one-way and no-left-turn
signs creating a loop-of-love sure to keep you busy
for hours. It's the alley behind the West Hollywood
Circus of Books (at La Jolla and Santa Monica
Boulevard). The cruisey neighbourhood nearby is
the logical extension of Vaseline Alley into the residential neighbourhood below. Park your car and
walk. Before you know it, you'll have many new
friends.

### The Silver Lake stretch

This place starts hopping around 12.30am and will
keep you coming around again. Cruise along Griffith
Park Boulevard from near where Fountain ends all the
way up to Hyperion. Turn around and try it again.

### Griffith Park

Enter Griffith Park off Vermont north of Los Feliz
Boulevard and turn right to the tennis courts any day
of the week. Or for a special treat on Sunday afternoons,
head to the 'circle' north of Los Feliz Boulevard, just
east of Western on Fern Dell Drive. It'll be up on your
right after the concession stand. Que bueno.

### French Quarter (at French Market)

*7985 Santa Monica Boulevard, between Edinburgh &*
*Hayworth Avenue, West Hollywood (1-213 654 0898).*
The food is only OK but it's a gay LA institution.

### Tango Grill

*8807 Santa Monica Boulevard, at San Vincente*
*Boulevard, West Hollywood (1-310 659 3663).*
Argentinian cuisine plus grilled chicken. Cheap. Try
the mashed potatoes. Sit for hours and watch the parade
go by.

## Rollerskating

### Moonlight Rollerway

*5110 San Fernando Road, at West Harvard Street,*
*Glendale (1-818 241 3630).* **Open** 3.30-5.30pm Wed;
10am-noon, 1.30-4pm Sat, Sun.
Gay rollerskating every Sunday and Thursday, 8-10.30pm.

## Theatre

### Celebration Theater

*7051 Santa Monica Boulevard, at La Brea Avenue,*
*Hollywood (1-213 857 8085).* **Tickets** $15-$20. **Credit**
AmEx, MC V.
Constantly changing series of high quality gay- and lesbian-
themed plays.

# Lesbian LA

Los Angeles has several lesbian scenes, from the culturally diverse Long Beach to the cigar dykes of West Hollywood. **The Valley** has lots of dance clubs: salsa, house and techno music are the favourites of dyke DJs in this neck of the woods. If you love latin beauties, you'll find an abundance here, but plan your adventure at night to avoid the well-known heat of the Valley communities. **West Hollywood**, specifically Santa Monica Boulevard between Fairfax and Robertson Boulevards, is coffeehouse heaven. Here is an array of spots like Little Frieda's, Starbucks, Buzz's and Manni's Bakery where female same-gender love is in the majority. Entertainment varies from LA's hottest lesbian poets and comics to screenings of gay films, board games and pool. West Hollywood is the city of lipstick lesbians, flat-tops, white T-shirts and blue jeans. The newest lesbian hobby in WeHo, as its residents call it, is cigar smoking; the calibre of a woman is determined by the price of the cigar on which she is toking. How do you know the price? By the fragrance of the smoke, of course.

**Silver Lake** is another gay and lesbian metropolis; **South-Central** Los Angeles houses one of the oldest and most popular gay clubs in town, Jewel's Catch One Disco. You haven't visited LA's lesbian scene until you pass through the doors of Jewel's. **LBC** (Long Beach City) is culturally diverse. Predominantly African-American and Latino, the gay women's community here has an abundance of theatres, coffeehouses and great beaches at its disposal.

Last but certainly not least is, yes, you got it, the famous **Hollywood**, that huge melting pot of every kind of Los Angeleno. The LA Gay & Lesbian Center (*see above* **Gay**), the largest gay community center in the world, is bang in the middle, right off the Strip. Drop by the lobby to pick up a copy of *Lesbian News* magazine. For bookshops selling lesbian literature, *see above* **Gay**.

## Accommodation

The following hotels are lesbian/bisexual/transsexual friendly. Try also **Le Montrose Suite Hotel** (*see chapter* **Accommodation**).

### Malibu Beach Inn

*22878 Pacific Coast Highway, between Carbon Canyon & Cross Creek Roads, Malibu (1-800 462 5428 reservations/ 1-310 456 6444 front desk/).* **Rates** $130-$275.
Expensive but worth every dime – south-facing rooms have an ocean view and there's a secluded beach nearby.

### Ramada Inn

*8585 Santa Monica Boulevard, at La Cienega Boulevard, West Hollywood (1-310 652 6400 front desk/1-800 845 8585 reservations).* **Rates** $90-$115.
It's on the Strip, you can get a room for under a hundred bucks and there's a pool. What more could a girl need?

## Entertainment

### Clubs & bars

#### Girl Bar at Axis

*652 North La Peer Avenue, at Santa Monica Boulevard, West Hollywood (1-213 460 2531).* **Open** 9pm-2am nightly. **Cover** $5-$8 .
LA's lesbian mecca. All kinds of women who love women, go-go dancers, live performers – GB has it all.

#### Jewel's Catch One

*4067 West Pico Boulevard, at 12th Avenue, Mid-City (1-213 737 1159).* **Open** 5pm-2am Mon-Thur, Sun; 5pm-5am Fri, Sat.
The focus of LA's African-American lesbian scene. Thursday is ladies' night, with strippers, lip-sync show and dancing. Arrive early on Saturday for good seats and safe parking; leave before 2am. There's a $4-£8 cover charge.

#### The Palms

*8572 Santa Monica Boulevard, at La Cienega Boulevard, West Hollywood (1-213 652 6188).* **Open** 1pm-2am daily.
Sisters of all races party here, on the Strip. It's a jeans and T-shirt crowd; the DJ plays mainly house music.

#### Rudolpho's

*Rudolpho's, 2500 Riverside Drive, at Fletcher Drive, Silver Lake (1-213 669 1226).* **Open** 8pm-2am nightly.
On Fridays and Saturdays, this is the spot if you love to salsa. Mostly Latino sisters; live performers; dancing to house.

#### The Lodge

*4923 Lankershim Boulevard, at Camarillo Street, North Hollywood (1-818 769 7722).* **Open** noon-2am daily.
Nights and cover charge vary: call for info. Wednesday is black female night. Dress casual. A slightly older crowd.

#### Executive Suite

*3428 East Pacific Coast Highway, at Redondo Avenue, Long Beach (1-310 597 3884).* **Open** 9pm-2am daily.
On Friday or Saturday there's dancing to hip-hop, house, and R&B. It gets crowded, so get there early. Lots of lesbians of colour. **Cover** $5-$8.

### Restaurants

In West Hollywood, after the party, everybody goes to the **House of Pancakes** (7006 Sunset Boulevard; 1-213 466 8370) for American fanfare, dinner or breakfast. It's crowded, so prepare yourself for a short wait. Dine on American and continental food with LA's outest women at the good-value **French Quarter** (*see above* **Gay**). If you're in star-spotting mood, visit Hollywood's **Hot Wings Cafe** (7011 Melrose Avenue; 1-213 930 1233) for mainly chicken with a few vegetarian dishes. Dress Melrose, punk rock or '90s sporty. If fried food isn't your scene, swing by **Simply Wholesome** (4508 Slauson Avenue, Windsor Hills; 1-213 294 2144) for a full veggie menu, sugar-free desserts and health drinks. For fine dining, take her to the **Odyssey** in the Granada Hills/Valley area (15600 Odyssey Drive; 1-818 366 6444). It has a 16ft salad bar loaded with everything from tofu to caviar – and it don't come cheap. **Gladstones 4 Fish-Malibu** (17300 Pacific Coast Highway; 1-310 454 3474) is a big seafood spot with a mixed crowd.

### Coffeehouse

#### Little Frida's

*8730 Santa Monica Boulevard, between La Cienega & San Vincente Boulevards, West Hollywood (1-310 854 5421).* **Open** 8am-midnight Mon-Thur, Sun; 8am-1am Fri, Sat.
Mainly white sisters hang out here, but the cultural events draw a more diverse crowd. Poetry, pool and patio dining, plus hot and cold sandwiches, salads and great coffee.

# Students

**There's more to education in LA than the stereotypes of Beverly Hills 90210. Here's the lowdown on the city's academic institutions.**

Contrary to all you may have heard, intelligent life does exist in Los Angeles. Co-existing with the glitter of Tinseltown are numerous colleges and universities offering world-class instruction. Between them they have spawned a wealth of award-winning film-makers and scientists, powerful politicians, famous (and infamous) athletes (think OJ Simpson) and renowned academics.

LA's major colleges and universities are either public (state-funded) or private – a distinction rarely noticeable in the quality of instruction and only in tuition costs if you're a legal resident of California (residents pay considerably lower fees at public schools than non-residents). However, California's enduring fiscal crisis has left public institutions (such as UCLA) short on facility and equipment upgrades and with a high student-to-instructor ratio. Wherever you choose to go, expect to pay $10,000-$25,000 (including tuition and basic living expenses) for a year of full-time study.

Remember that you will have to prove your source of financial support when applying for a visa. Financial aid for foreign students – usually in the form of scholarships or 'work-study' (working for the school) – varies among institutions, so investigate the options early with their Financial Aid Officers to learn how to qualify. Scholarships are usually scarce and competition is always fierce.

Each college's version of an International Students Office should be well informed of issues pertaining specifically to foreign students. Contact the college's Admissions Office for application materials and specifics on prerequisites: you may have to take an admission test – for example, the Scholastic Achievement Test (SAT) or Graduate Record Exam (GRE). Non-English speaking students should expect to take a TOEFL (Test of English as a Foreign Language) or equivalent.

## ACADEMIC LIFE

Political activism on local campuses has been recently focused on the threatened repeal of Affirmative Action legislation – which applies mandatory quotas for minority groups – and its significance to Californian universities' admission and hiring practices. This state-wide debate is well suited to LA's highly multicultural campuses set within a city of complex, highly charged race relations. Most schools, in fact, pride themselves on the diversity of their students (including many

from abroad) and have a bewildering array of organisations and social events to celebrate the differences and similarities between groups. LA's geographical sprawl does, however, force the schools themselves to sit miles apart, resulting – ironically – in infrequent mixing between their student bodies and highly spirited rivalries, most palpable during team sports events (college men's American football and basketball are particularly popular and competitive).

## Where to study

### Art Center College of Design

*1700 Lida Street, at Linda Vista Avenue, Pasadena, CA 91103 (1-818 584 5000/admissions 1-818 396 2373/fax 1-818 405 9104). Bus 177/I-110, exit Orange Grove Boulevard north.*
The private and very stylish Art Center calls upon the 'new generation of hungry, creative student minds' to propel art and commercial and industrial design into the twenty-first century. Also has a location in La Tour-de-Peilz, Switzerland.

### California Institute of Technology

*1201 East California Street, at Hill Avenue, Pasadena, CA 91125 (1-818 395 6811/admissions 1-818 395 6341/fax 1-818 795 1547). Bus 177/I-110, exit California Boulevard east.*
Science students can't do much better than 'CalTech'. This is particularly true for the maths, physics and chemistry departments, even though electrical engineering is the most popular major. This private college counts more than 20 Nobel laureates among its alumni and past and present faculty. This is also where the local news turns for information on California earthquake activity.

### Loyola Marymount University

*7101 West 80th Street, between McConnell Avenue & Fordham Road, LA, CA 90045 (1-310 338 2700/admissions 1-310 338 2750/fax 1-310 338 2797). Bus 115/I-405, exit La Tijera Boulevard west.*
Overlooking Marina del Rey and founded by Jesuits, the private Loyola Marymount is primarily an undergraduate institution but also offers advanced degrees in law, education and business administration. The successor to the oldest college in Southern California (St Vincent's, established in 1865), its library holds extensive materials on early Los Angeles.

### Occidental College

*1600 Campus Road, at Alumni Avenue, LA, CA 90041 (1-213 259 2500/admissions 1-213 259 2700/fax 1-213 259 2958). Bus 83, 84/SR2, exit Verdugo Road south.*
You'll get a glimpse of 'Oxy' on *Beverly Hills 90210* whenever those perky TV teens hang out at 'California University'. But in addition to a filming location, this is also a fine (private) liberal arts college with a remarkably large number of students from ethnic minorities given the school's small size (about 1,600 students).

## Santa Monica College

*1900 Pico Boulevard, between 16th & 20th Streets, Santa Monica, CA 90405 (1-310 450 5150/admissions 1-310 452 9381/fax 1-310 399 1730). Bus Santa Monica 7, 11/I-10, exit Cloverfield Boulevard.*

A community college (state-funded and providing students with the first two years of the four-year bachelor's degree), SMC was founded in 1929 and ranks first among 107 California community colleges in the number of transfers to the esteemed University of California system. Its large enrolment includes over 2,000 students from 99 countries. The college radio station, KCRW, is the leading public radio station in Southern California.

## Southern California Institute of Architecture

*5454 Beethoven Street, at Jefferson Boulevard, LA, CA 90066 (1-310 574 1123/admissions 1-310 574 3625/fax 1-310 574 3801). Bus 110/SR90, exit Centinela Ave south.*

'SCI-Arc' (yes, you must learn to abbreviate if you want to speak Los Angelese) may look like a modest warehouse from the outside but it has been one of the leading architecture schools in the country since its establishment in 1972. Urban theorist Mike Davis (author of bestseller *City of Quartz*) is among this private school's distinguished faculty, which, alongside its goal 'to produce architects who are truly artists and thus inherently subversive', makes SCI-Arc a top choice for both undergraduates and graduates in architecture. It also has a terrific public lecture series.

## University of California-Los Angeles (UCLA)

*405 Hilgard Avenue, at Sunset Boulevard, LA, CA 90095 (1-310 825 4321/admissions 1-310 825 3101/fax 1-310 206 1206). Bus 2, 21, 29, 576, Culver City 6, Santa Monica 1, 2, 3, 8/I-405, exit Sunset Boulevard east.*

Located in Westwood, across the street from the mansions of Bel Air, UCLA is a public research university highly regarded for its undergraduate and graduate courses in the liberal and fine arts, as well as the sciences (biology is the most popular major) and professional programmes. It carries one of the largest library collections in the world and the athletic programme consistently cultivates championship sports teams. Both the Olympic Games of 1984 and the Northridge quake 10 years later gave the campus much-needed structural and cosmetic improvements.

# So you wanna be in the movies?

Let's face it: there's no better place to study the technical, creative, commercial and critical aspects of the movies than Los Angeles. So if you think you might be the next Orson Welles, Louis B Mayer or Pauline Kael, but are not yet ready to swim with the sharks, you'll do best by first attending an accredited institution with a strong reputation in film studies. Fortunately, Los Angeles offers several.

Be warned: don't waste your money on a course you saw on a random flier. Instead, think about the country's first film school, **USC School of Cinema-TV** (1-213 740 2235), whose generous alumni, among them George Lucas, have helped keep the equipment state of the art and the teaching supreme. UCLA's **Department of Film and Television** (1-310 825 5761) also has some of the best directing and producing courses in the country as well as a first-rate critical studies division. The **American Film Institute** (AFI) at 2021 North Western Avenue, LA, CA 90027 (1-213 856 7628), the **Art Center College of Design** (*see above* **Where to study**) and the burgeoning graduate programme at **Chapman University's School of Film and Television** in the neighbouring city of Orange (333 North Glassell Avenue, Orange, CA 92866; 1-714 997 6765/fax 1-716 997 6700) are also smart choices for prospective film students.

If the financial and time commitment of enrolling on a degree course are prohibitive, consider taking part in these schools' Extension Programs, which provide the same quality of instruction – including talks by some of the industry's most respected players – but on a fee-per-class basis. These schools also have excellent resources for finding a range of internships, in which the 'currency of experience' is supposed to (and often does) make up for the fact that you'll work very hard for free.

## Libraries & research facilities

UCLA's **Archive Research and Study Center** (ARSC; 1-310 206 5388) and USC's **Warner Brothers Archives** (1-213 748 7747) can prove important resources for serious film scholars, but a more beautiful facility and holder of many rare, film-related materials is the **Margaret Herrick Library** at the **Academy of Motion Picture Arts and Sciences** (333 South La Cienega Boulevard, Beverly Hills; 1-310 247 3000). It also has a phone reference service (1-310 247 3020), where operators research the answer to your most vexing movie trivia question. The recently opened **Museum of Television & Radio** (465 North Beverly Drive, Beverly Hills; 1-310 786 1000) has a large collection of TV shows and news footage on video which you can view. Finally, the **Los Angeles Central Library** (1-213 228 7000) not only holds films and recordings in its vast data banks but is also architecturally splendid and has a top-rated restaurant in the grounds, Café Pinot (1-213 239 6500), well worth a splurge after a long, hard day of head-down research.

*Be like Barton Fink and get an education in screenwriting. See box page 237.*

### University of Southern California (USC)

*University Park, bounded by Figueroa Street, Exposition & Jefferson Boulevards, Vermont Avenue, LA, CA 90089 (1-213 740 2311/admissions 1-213 740 8899/fax 1-213 740 6364). Bus 38, 81, 102, 200, DASH C/I-110 south, exit Exposition Boulevard west.*

USC (or, to abbreviate further, SC) is the largest private, non-denominational university on the West Coast. Undergrads live amid a huge fraternity 'scene' where sports (the Trojans) matter almost more than life itself (OJ went here). USC's best known undergraduate fields are in the pre-professional areas of journalism, business, theatre, architecture and communications. Many of the graduate programmes are also strong, the most celebrated being the School of Cinema-TV's film production course.

### Visas & ID cards

Once you are accepted by a school and agree to attend, you will be sent an I-20 form to act as certification of your eligibility for a student visa (an F-1 or M-1, depending on your course). Apply for the visa at your home country's US consulate or embassy. Your ability to prove that you can support yourself for nine months will be key to the success of your application, as you will not be allowed to take paid employment (after nine months you may be able to work part-time). Exchange students (those who are 'trading places' with a US student) should receive an IAP-66 form instead, which will enable them to apply for a J-1 visa, also issued to students on vacation work exchange programmes such as those run by BUNAC (16 Bowling Green Lane, London EC1R 0BD; 0171 251 3472). Individuals interested in visiting schools in Los Angeles prior to applying or accepting an offer of admission are eligible for a B-2, a 'prospective student' visa.

Once in LA, if you have any questions about visa regulations, contact your school's International Students Office (or its equivalent) before tackling the bureaucracy of the INS (Immigration and Naturalization Service, 300 North Los Angeles Street, LA, CA 90012; 1-213 526 7647).

If you want to open a bank account, write a cheque or drive a car during your stay, you will have to visit one of the numerous branches of the Department of Motor Vehicles (DMV) to apply for a California driver's licence or a California ID card (expect to wait a month for each), either of which are guaranteed to make your life much easier than having just a passport and a college ID card. While most students find their college ID affords them all the types of discounts available with an International Student Identity Card, you can buy an ISIC ($19) at the Los Angeles branch of the Council on International Educational Exchange, 10904 Lindbrook Drive, LA, CA 90024 (1-310 208 3551).

### Student accommodation

Most students live in dormitories, houses or apartments, alone or with roommates. Some live on campus for convenience, others choose cheaper rents (prices tend to be higher closer to the school) and a 'real world' environment and put up with a commute to class.

For accommodation advice, contact your school's Housing Office or International Students Office. Staff there will be able to provide you with everything from lists of people looking for roommates to a bill of rights for renters. Short-term housing needs may be met by the low-cost **Hostelling International/American Youth Hostel** in Santa Monica (1436 Second Street, between Santa Monica Boulevard and Broadway; 1-310 393 9913); *see also* the **Hostels & B&B** section of our **Accommodation** chapter.

# Trips Out of Town

# Trips Out of Town

**With scorching deserts, snow-covered peaks and spectacular beaches competing for attention, LA is the ideal jump-off point for exploring southern California and beyond.**

With its benign climate, spectacular terrain and diverse neighbourhoods and activities, Los Angeles offers so much that it hardly seems necessary to go out of town. However, even Lotus Land can get wearying and when you feel you've overdosed on traffic jams and concrete, you can do what Angelenos have always done: retreat to the relatively unspoiled natural environments and interesting cities just a few hours away. This being the Golden State, there is, of course, an abundance of choice: arid and semi-arid, high and low deserts to the east; alpine vistas, mountain lakes and skiing in the nearby San Gabriel mountains; quaint, ocean-fresh coastal towns on Catalina Island; and Las Vegas, San Diego and the Mexican border just, by US standards, a short drive away.

This is the land of the automobile, so the easiest – sometimes the only – way to get to the places listed below is by car. On some trips, such as those up US101 towards San Francisco or through the Mojave desert, the drive itself is the experience. All the destinations described involve a drive of an hour and a half upwards. It is also possible to travel by plane, train and bus to larger destinations such as Palm Springs, Santa Barbara, Las Vegas and San Diego. Check the ads in the 'Travel & Adventure' section of *LA Weekly* for bargain fares or consult a travel agent. Call Amtrak (1-800 872 7245) for information on trains, which you catch at Union Station, 800 North Alameda Street, Downtown LA, CA 90012. Greyhound (1-800 231 2222) offers a first-come, first-served bus service (no booking) at its crowded Downtown terminus at 1716 East Seventh Street.

## General information

All good bookstores (*see chapter* **Shopping & Services**) have shelves of travel guides to Southern California. Sunday's *LA Times* has a travel section that includes a Weekend Escape feature.

### California Trade & Commerce Agency Office of Tourism
*Suite 1600, 801 K Street, Sacramento, CA 95814 (1-916 322 3424).*

## Accommodation

### California Association of Bed & Breakfast Innkeepers (CABBI)
*2715 Porter Street, Soquel, CA 95073 (1-408 464 8159).*

### California Hotel & Motel Association
*PO Box 160405, Sacramento, CA 95816 (1-916 444 5780).*

## Camping & outdoors

### California Department of Parks & Recreation
*PO Box 2930, Sacramento, CA 94296 (1-916 653 6995).*

### California Department of Fish & Game
*12th Floor, 1416 Ninth Street, Sacramento, CA 95814 (1-916 653 7664).*

### State Park Campground reservations
*Mistix 1-800 444 7275; Destinet 1-800 444 7275.*

### National Park Service Western Region Information Center
*Building 201, Fort Mason, San Francisco, CA 94130 (1-415 556 0560).*

### US Forest Service Appraiser's Building
*630 Sansome Street, San Francisco, CA 94111 (1-415 705 2874/camping reservations 1-800 283 2267).*

## Driving

### CalTrans Highway Information Network
*1-800 427 7623/1-916 445 1534.*
Recorded information on road conditions of major California State highways.

### Automobile Club of Southern California
*2601 South Figueroa Street, Los Angeles, CA 90007 (1-213 741 3686).* **Open** 9am-5pm Mon-Fri.
The Triple A (American Automobile Association) provides excellent maps, guidebooks (with accommodation and restaurant recommendations) and campground listings – and they won't cost you a penny if you're a member of the British AA. Branches everywhere.

# Alpine experience

You've no doubt heard the claim that in LA you can ski in the morning and surf in the evening. Well, at the right time of year, and if you are prepared to get up early enough, you can get to Big Bear or Lake Arrowhead for the snow and back to the coast for the waves in one day. These resorts are under two hours away from LA in the San Bernardino Mountains north-east of the city, a drive that takes you east on the I-10 through Downtown and various uninteresting suburbs until you get to the other side of San Bernardino. There you are engulfed by looming mountains and transported into a winding drive up slopes that go from arid and brush-covered to alpine. Though close to each other, the two are different

# Santa Catalina Island

It's hard to imagine anywhere in Southern California where the golf cart would replace the automobile as the preferred mode of street transport, but this is the case on Catalina. The Prisoner would have felt at home on this small, impossibly cute island, about 20 miles from San Pedro, with its clean beaches and clear water, undulating pastures, natural bay and twee town named Avalon; all of which is almost entirely owned by one outfit, the Santa Catalina Island Company (1-310 510 2000), which maintains strict limits on cars and growth. In the early part of this century, Catalina was an offshore playground for movie stars. In 1919, it was purchased by William Wrigley Jr, heir to the chewing gum fortune, who built the impressive art deco Avalon Theater and Casino, now the **Santa Catalina Island Museum** (1 Casino Way, Avalon; 1-310 510 2414), dedicated to the island's history. A herd of buffalo (aka American bison) were brought to the island in 1924 for the filming of Zane Grey's *The Vanishing American*. They are now the main attraction on Catalina, some 86% of which is a nature reserve.

As well as buffalo, you can see pigs, goats, deer, native ground squirrel, quail, foxes, rattlesnakes, the reinstated bald eagle, swordfish, tuna and numerous other species of flora and fauna. You can examine cacti, succulents and local plants at the **Wrigley Memorial and Botanical Garden** (1400 Avalon Canyon

Road; 1-310 510 2288), check out fine Arabian horses at **El Rancho Escondido** and kayak, snorkel, jet-ski, scuba-dive or fish at **Two Harbors**, a resort village on the north-west of the island, and at some of the other beaches. The island's climate and topography are similar to that of LA but the air is much fresher.

Shopping, restaurants, hotels and other tourist attractions are mainly to be found in the picture-postcard, white-stucco, bayside town of **Avalon**. With a population of about 3,000 (with a jump to 6,000 in summer and 10,000 at weekends), it is the largest residential community on Catalina.

You can tour the island on foot, by sightseeing bus or rented bicycle, horse or golf cart. To hike, you need a permit, available free of charge from the Catalina Island Conservancy (125 Claressa Avenue, Avalon; 1-310 510-1421).

### Getting there

**By boat**: Catalina Channel Express (1-310 519 1212) runs a regular, one-hour, $36 round-trip service from Long Beach and San Pedro Harbors, while Sail Catalina (1-310 592 5790) offers a 75-minute trip on a catamaran from Huntington Harbor ($48.50 round trip). Catalina Cruises (1-800 228 2546) offers a two-hour leisure cruise from Long Beach Harbor ($23 round trip). Catalina Flyer (1-714 673 5245) is a 75-minute catamaran service from Newport Beach ($33 round trip).
**By air**: Island Express (1-310 510 2525) offers a 15-minute helicopter flight from San Pedro and Long Beach Harbors ($121 round trip) while Super Shuttle (1-310 782 6600) and Best Shuttle (1-310 670 7080) run airport shuttle services from all LA airports to Catalina Island sea and air terminals.

### Where to stay

You can camp on Catalina, though you must get a permit and book in advance. For the Hermit Gulch Campground in Avalon Canyon call 1-310 510 8368; for other sites, contact Catalina Island Camping, PO Box 5044, Two Harbors, Catalina Island, CA 90704 (1-310 510 0303). For hotels, contact the Chamber of Commerce.

### Tourist information

**Catalina Island Chamber of Commerce & Visitors Bureau**
*1 Green Pier, Avalon, Catalina Island, CA 90704 (1-310 510 1520/fax 1-310 510 7506).*

in character. Lake Arrowhead is prettier, affluent and more artsy, while the focus at Big Bear is on mountain sports.

## Lake Arrowhead

At an altitude of 5,000ft (1,000ft higher than Ben Nevis) Lake Arrowhead is another world: an artificial lake in an alpine setting of pine and oak forests and crystal-clear air, with the neo-Bavarian **Arrowhead Village** and various smaller tourist and residential communities tucked discreetly away in the woods. Snow-covered in winter and desert-hot in the summer, it is, like many such delightful places, overrun with tourists (best to go off-season or on a weekday).

This being the States, however, and not Bavaria, the tourists can't let go of the internal combustion engine; the lake is speed-boat heaven and, sadly, churned into a (doubtless) oily, unswimmable froth. You can swim – if you want to join loud, white America at play – at the nearby, smaller **Lake Gregory**. More pleasant is the hiking and fishing, or you could walk the three-mile circumference of the lake and tackle the gym apparatus en route. In winter, the focus is on cross-country skiing and skating – there's a big ice-rink in Blue Jay village. The restaurant food is nothing to write home about; your best bet is to buy picnic supplies at Jensen's Market in Blue Jay Village, halfway round the lake from Arrowhead Village.

### Getting there

**By car**: Take the I-10 east to the I-215 (heading east), then take the SR30 east for one mile to the SR18 (Waterman Avenue exit). Follow the SR18 up the mountain and take the Lake Arrowhead turn-off.
**By train**: Mountain Area Rapid Transit Authority (MARTA) offers daily round trips through Arrowhead and San Bernardino (1-909 584 1111) for $7.50 (round trip).

### Where to stay

There are numerous inns, hostelries and camping sites to choose from in Arrowhead. For information contact the Lake Arrowhead Village Chamber of Commerce (*see below*).

### Tourist information

**Crestline/Lake Gregory Chamber of Commerce**
*23840 Lake Drive (inside Vineyard Bank), Crestline, CA 92325 (1-909 338 2706/1-909 338 5022 fax)*
**Lake Arrowhead Village Chamber of Commerce**
*PO Box 219, Lake Arrowhead, CA 92352 (above Subway restaurant) (accommodation 1-800 337 3716/1-909 337 3715/marketing & tourism 1-909 336 1547/fax 1-909 336 1548).*

## Big Bear

Under snow, Big Bear is very inviting. In high summer, it is less so – an exposed, windy and downmarket version of Arrowhead. But it has a large lake for watersports and offers some of the best downhill and cross-country skiing in the

*Mountain biking in* **Big Bear**.

region. At 8,805ft, **Bear Mountain** is the highest ski area, with 11 lifts and a 1,665ft vertical drop. **Snow Summit** is the other choice slope. In summer, the snow melts away and the mountains become the site for downhill bike races, hiking and horse riding, while the lake is used for windsurfing, sailboarding, water-skiing, jet-skiing and fishing.

### Getting there

**By car**: Go east on the I-10 to join the SR30 in Redlands. Follow the SR30 to the SR330, then join the SR18, heading west. Turn right across the dam to Big Bear Lake.
**By air**: Big Bear Shuttle (1-909 585 5514) offers a door-to-door air service to Ontario and LAX airports and also a van service that can carry bikes, skis and snowboards ($70).
**By train**: As for Arrowhead; *see above.*

### Where to stay

**Apples Bed & Breakfast Inn**
*42430 Moonridge Road, Big Bear Lake, CA 92315 (1-909 866 0903)*. **Rooms** $145-$185.
**Truffles**
*43591 Bow Canyon Road, Big Bear Lake, CA 92315 (1-909 585 2772)*. **Rooms** $115-$140.
**Moonridge Manor**
43803 Yosemite Drive, Big Bear Lake, CA 92315 (1-909 585 0457). **Rooms** $50-$175.
**Windy Point Inn**
*39015 North Shore Drive, Fawnskin, CA 92333 (1-909 866 2746)*. **Rooms** $125-$195.
There are also several campsites in Big Bear; for more information, contact the Visitor Center (*see below*).

### Tourist information

**Big Bear Resort Association**
*630 Bartlett Road, Big Bear, CA 92315 (1-909 866 7000).*

## Idyllwild

If you want alpine without the skiing, an alternative destination is Idyllwild, a pleasant artsy community at the crest of the San Jacinto Mountains above Palm Springs. For information on getting there via the Palms Springs Aerial Tramway, *see below* **Palm Springs**. Alternatively, come off the I10 at the junction with SR243 and follow it south.

# Just deserts

Las Vegas and Palm Springs may seem like they are here to stay but yank their water supply and they would dematerialise, becoming once more part of the arid bone-bare landscape that is the Mojave Desert. This forbidding dry moat encircles most of Los Angeles, extending east to the state border. It is magnificent, humbling, weird – and not to be missed.

The desert consists of mile upon mile of subtly hued, near-naked mountain ridges and plains, dotted with the vestiges of human habitation: dead mining towns, abandoned gas stations and diners on the old Route 66; shiny new towns with their surreal golf courses and swimming pools; and the ubiquitous US military with its vast, sinister bases. The wilderness is inhabited by strange creatures of the four- and two-feet variety: coyotes and roadrunners, gun-toting rednecks and UFO believers. Don't expect California cuisine and gay rights once you cross the San Bernardino Mountains; the desert is another world.

## CLIMATE

In the Los Angeles basin it is easy to forget that you're on the same latitude as North Africa. The cold Pacific acts as a giant air-conditioner for the coast, but inland, during summer, is like the Sahara, with temperatures regularly reaching upwards of 110°C. In winter, after dark, it can plummet below freezing. The best time to visit the desert is during temperate February and March, when most years it bursts, briefly but spectacularly, into spring bloom.

## DESERT SAFETY

Sunstroke and heat exhaustion are the two dangers to watch for in the desert. Horror stories abound about what happened to those who did not prepare themselves properly. If you are visiting in the hot season – April to October – wear a hat, plenty of sunscreen and cover up. Hike early in the morning or late in the day; don't even think of going out at noon – and never go hiking alone. Take plenty of water. A half pint of Evian isn't going to cut it for a day out in Joshua Tree in July – a gallon a day per person is the recommended intake. In summer, high winds blow at 30 or 40mph and a lip salve is essential.

Make sure your vehicle is up to the trip, too. If it starts to overheat, turn the air-conditioning off, open the windows and turn the heating full on to let heat escape from the engine. If you park for any length of time, leave a window slightly open.

## SUGGESTED ITINERARY

Palm Springs and Las Vegas are destinations in themselves but they are also in the midst of striking desertscapes. One way to enjoy them is to take a three-day (or more) road trip taking in Palm Springs, Joshua Tree National Monument, Anza-Borrego Desert State Park, Mojave National Preserve, Las Vegas, Death Valley National Park and the Ridgecrest/Edwards Airforce Base area.

The following is one of many possible routes: head east on the I-10 to Palm Springs, Anza-Borrego and environs. From Palm Springs, take the SR62 north and east to Joshua Tree National Park and Twentynine Palms. Then follow the SR247 to Barstow and head east through the Mojave National Preserve; either via the I-15, which continues to Las Vegas, or via the I-40 or the remaining stretch of Route 66 (from Ludlow to Essex) to the more southerly town of Needles (from there, take the US95 north to Las Vegas). From Vegas, take the CR160 to Pahrump, then the CR372 and the SR178 into Death Valley National Monument. Drive through Death Valley and take the SR178 south to the US395. Join the SR14 and head south, taking in the Mojave/Ridgecrest area and drop back down into LA.

## Palm Springs

The highway to Palm Springs heads east through sprawling San Bernardino and Riverside Counties,

# Factory outlets

The icing on the cake of a trip out of Los Angeles is the chance to stock up on cut-price designer goods from one of the many factory outlet centres in Southern California. You can save 25-40% on gear from Esprit, Eddie Bauer, Charles David Shoes, the Luggage Factory, Vans and many more retailers at the bland-looking factory outlets located near to freeway exits outside several cities; keep your eyes skinned for signs. Here are a few in the Los Angeles region:

### Factory Outlet Center

*2552 Mercantile Way, at Lenwood Road, Barstow (1-619 253 7342). I-15, exit Lenwood Road.* **Open** 9am-8pm daily.

### San Diego Factory Outlet Center

*4498 Camino de la Plaza, San Ysidro, CA (1-619 690 2999). I-5, exit Camino de la Plaza west.* **Open** 10am-8pm Mon-Fri; 10am-7pm Sat; 10am-6pm Sun.
Next to the the San Ysidro International Border with Tijuana, Mexico.

### Desert Hills Factory Stores

*48400 Seminole Road, Cabazon (1-909 849 6641). I-10 to west of Palm Springs, exit Apache Trail.* **Open** 10am-8pm Mon-Tur, Sun; 9am-8pm Sat.

passing near the city of Fontana, site of the world's largest truckstop. Development finally peters out at the Banning Pass, which cuts through the sparse San Jacinto Mountains. From there the hills are covered in whirring wind farms. This eloquent Christo-like composition of man and nature is followed by the surreal green carpet in a parched desert valley that is Palm Springs.

Sheltered from the smog and haze of the LA basin by the bulk of Mount San Jacinto, this affluent, amply irrigated and manicured desert town is the home of retired movie stars, amateur golfers and former mayor, now US senator, Sonny Bono. In addition to touristy shops and restaurants on **Palm Canyon Drive**, there are some great scenic spots. Take the Palm Springs Aerial Tramway (1-619 325 1391; $17 adults; $11 children) to the crest of San Jacinto for a total change of ecosystem. From this alpine spot you can walk a mile to **Idyllwild**, a mountain retreat housing a small artsy community and school (*see above* **Alpine**). Visit **Agua Caliente Indian Reservation**, with its lush hiking trails through three canyons; call the Tribes Council Office (110 North Indian Canyon Drive; 1-619 325 5673) for more information. Don't miss the 3,000 varieties of desert plants at the eccentric **Moorten Botanical Garden** (1701 South Palm Canyon Road; 1-619 327 6555).

*Strange but true – a Joshua tree.*

There are many lodgings in Palms Springs but the most interesting is Korakia Pensione (257 South Patencio Road, Palm Springs, CA 92262; 1-619 864 6411), a Greco-Moorish-style villa. It's very popular with trendy Angelenos, so book ahead.

### Getting there

By car: Take the I-10 east all the way to Palm Springs: 103 miles, about 2 hours.
By air: From LAX on American Eagle (1-800 433 7300; $176 round trip), Sky West (1-800 453 9417; $160 round trip) or United Express (1-800 241 6522; $196 round trip). Estimated flight time 50 minutes.
By bus: Greyhound operates 12 buses a day. Cost: $20 round trip. Estimated journey time 3-4 hours.

### Tourist information

Palm Springs Visitors Information Center
2781 North Palm Canyon Drive, 92262 (1-800 347 7746/1-619 778 8418).

## Anza-Borrego Desert State Park

The drive to Anza-Borrego from Palm Springs takes you south, past the San Jacinto Mountains, through the new, bland desert cities of Cathedral City and Rancho Mirage – all the rage with retirees – and the ancient **Living Desert** (1-619 346 5694), a 1,200-acre wildlife and botanical park in Palm Desert, 1.5 miles south of SR111.

Anza-Borrego (1-619 767 5311) is a huge, 600,000-acre state park 100 miles south-east of LA. It has everything: 8,000ft high mountains, palm-lined canyons in Borrego Palm Canyon, ancient fossils, scrubby, sandy wastes and a few oases. You can hike, mountain bike, camp open or in one of two campgrounds (1-800 444 7275 for reservations) or stay in a motel in the small town of **Borrego Springs**, which has one of the few roundabouts in the US, charmingly named Christmas Circle. There is a visitor centre, built into the earth, 1.7 miles west of the town on Palm Canyon Drive (1-619 767 4205; open daily Oct-May, weekends and holidays only June-Sept). The spring wildflower bloom peaks in March, covering the desert in sunflowers, June primroses and other exotica, depending on the year. From Anza-Borrego you can head east into the Imperial Valley and see the salty **Salton Sea**, a large but shallow inland lake formed when the Colorado River burst its banks early this century.

## Joshua Tree National Monument

To the north of Palm Springs, the desert valley gives way to massive granite monoliths, scrub and, as far as the eye can see, strange, jagged trees with spiky blooms. These are Joshua trees, actually a form of cactus, and thousands grow in the amazing Joshua Tree National Monument, which you can enter from the north via the SR62 and Twentynine Palms or from the south via the I-10. Admission is $5 per vehicle and there are two

*The bizarre desert landforms at Zabriskie Point,* **Death Valley**. *See page 249.*

visitors' centres, one at each entrance. The main one is at 74485 National Park Drive, Twentynine Palms, CA 92277; 1-619 367 7511).

There are nine campgrounds in the park (but only two have water) and plenty of motels in Twentynine Palms. As well as Joshua trees and other desert flora and fauna, the area has spectacular rock formations that are very popular with climbers. The wildlife in the desert tends to be shy and nocturnal; early mornings and evenings are the best times to see coyotes or roadrunners. It is rumoured that Byrds musician Gram Parsons has a secret burial site somewhere in the park.

While in Joshua Tree plan on staying at the delightful, quirky Twentynine Palms Inn (73950

*The abandoned* **Kelso Depot**.

Inn Avenue, Twentynine Palms, CA 92277; 1-619 367 3505), a destination in itself in the otherwise uninteresting small town of **Twentynine Palms**, which services a marine base in the flat desert north of Joshua Tree. The twenty-nine palms, and more, grow thanks to a real oasis, now full of ducks. The Inn is a last staging post before the empty expanses of the East Mojave; it has been in the same family for four generations and present owner Jane Smith is a mine of information.

## Mojave National Preserve

En route to Las Vegas you will drive for several hours through the unrelieved reddish-brown plains and hills of the high desert. Signs of life are few – the uninteresting desert town of **Barstow** is the biggest staging post. Stop at its factory stores mall (*see box* **Factory Outlets**) and the informative California Desert Information Center (831 Barstow Road; 1-619 256 8313). More fun is tiny **Baker**, which boasts the tallest thermometer in the world and the eccentric delights of The Mad Greek diner, and is the northern gateway to the Mojave National Preserve. Home to two campsites, plenty of Joshua trees, sand dunes, the abandoned Spanish-style **Kelso** train depot and the former health resort of **Soda Springs** at Zzyzx (run by early radio evangelist Curtis Howe Springer), the preserve is crisscrossed with roads (many unpaved). For more information, contact the Mojave Desert Information Center (72157 Baker Boulevard, CA 92309; 1-619 733 4040), beneath the thermometer in Baker.

The cluster of casinos at the state border is a brief desert bloom that signals your arrival in the gambling state of Nevada. When you finally arrive in the Las Vegas Valley, the city emerges from the nothingness like Shangri La dipped in neon.

You've arrived in the capital of kitsch; several mind-blowing miles of neon extravaganzas, over-the-top fantasy hotels, magic shows, sex shows, free drinks and all-you-can-eat buffets, all enticing you to part with your cash. It's horrendous and fabulous at the same time. Find a hotel, drop everything and join the party. The gambling never stops – which is exciting at night, depressing by day – and nor will you, until the adrenaline rush is over and you want to pass out or get out.

## The Strip

To get the biggest thrill out of Vegas, try to arrive at night, and head for **Las Vegas Boulevard** (aka the Strip). Most of the action in Vegas takes place in the new themed casino-hotels that line the four-mile Strip, and on **Fremont Street** in downtown. Apart from their deluxe suites and private gaming rooms, hotel rooms and casinos are pretty generic; the difference is in the theming, the betting odds and stakes and the quality of the cheap food. So pick one, stay there and visit the rest. Casinos in Vegas change faster than the seasons; by the time you read this another kitsch colossus will have appeared. But the following essential casinos should be still standing.

### Caesars Palace

*3570 Las Vegas Boulevard South, at Flamingo Road, Las Vegas, NV 89109 (1-800 634 6661 reservations/1-702 731 6636 fax).* **Rooms** $129-$299. **Suites** $550-$750. **Credit** AmEx, DC, Disc, MC, V.

How can you not love a place where, at one time, you could literally ask the waitress to peel you a grape? Caesars is the ultimate Vegas casino – low, dark velvet ceilings hung with crystal prisms and staff clad in Roman costume. Make sure you check out the outsize version of Michelangelo's David – this one, unlike the original, is uncircumcised – and the surreal Caesars Forum Shops, an enclosed Rome-themed shopping mall (90 shops) complete with trompe l'oeil sky and programmed lighting that simulates a transition from dawn to dusk every hour on the hour.

### The Mirage

*3400 Las Vegas Boulevard South, between Flamingo Road and Spring Mountain Road, Las Vegas, NV 89109 (1-800 944 7444 reservations/1-702 791 7414 fax).* **Rooms** $99-$349 **Suites** $300-$950. **Credit** AmEx, DC, Disc, MC, V.

Created by local casino tycoon Steve Wynn, this was the first of the massive themed casinos. It draws the crowds with its elaborate Polynesian theming, an erupting volcano on the street and its hugely successful show by bizarre illusionists Siegfried and Roy and their white tigers.

Also owned by Steve Wynn is neighbouring **Treasure Island** (3300 Las Vegas Boulevard South; 1-702 894 7111), which offers the best spectacle in town, Buccaneer Bay. For no expense you can join thousands of other pedestrians to watch pirates and the British navy duke it out amid much pyrotechnic canonballing until a full-scale frigate disappears underwater. At **Excalibur** (3850 Las Vegas Boulevard South; 1-800 937 7777/1-702 597 7777) Wagner meets King Arthur and a flaming dragon in this confused medieval-themed cartoon

*A sphinx guards the portals of* **Luxor** *casino. See page 248.*

# On the mission trail

'With the best theological intentions in the world,' argues late LA historian Carey McWilliams in his seminal book *Southern California: An Island on the Land,* 'the Franciscan padres eliminated Indians with the effectiveness of Nazis operating concentration camps'. During the Spanish conquest of California, the Spanish missionary monks, led by Father Junipero Serra, founded a string of 21 missions from San Diego in the south to Sonoma, about 40 miles north of San Francisco. The first, San Diego de Alcala in Mission Valley in San Diego (pictured), was established in 1769, the last, San Francisco Solano, in 1823; by 1848 the mission system came to an end.

The aim behind the missions was to convert the primitive tribal peoples and to establish self-sustaining communities. The missions succeeded in creating productive, wealthy farms and a reputation for hospitality for all who passed by. They also managed to deplete the numbers of the forced American Indian converts who died in thousands from a combination of depression, disease and malnutrition.

The missions were viewed with contempt until the late nineteenth century, when California boosters reinvented the mission as an icon of long-standing tradition, solid values and romance. For the overzealous Spanish padres had also left a legacy of mission buildings, whose white, sometimes Moorish-style buildings with bougainvillaea-shaded quadrangles and simple, solid interiors with hand-crafted furnishings stood for simple elegance and serenity, seen as missing in the rest of modern California culture. This spawned Mission-style or themed architecture and decor, a popular and influential branch of California design.

It is possible to tour the California missions, many of which have been renovated or reconstructed and now function as Catholic parishes. The 21 missions are all located near US101, which loosely follows the old El Camino Real (The Royal Road), named in honour of the Spanish monarchy which financed the colonising expeditions. The stretch of the 101 from San Diego to Los Angeles is now the I-5.

In San Diego you can see the first mission to be founded, **San Diego de Alcala** (10818 San Diego Mission Road; 1-619 281 8449), and, a few miles north, just east of Oceanside on SR76, the 18th, **San Luis Rey de Francia** (4050 Mission Avenue, San Luis Rey; 1-619 757 3651). The remains of **San Juan Capistrano** (1-714 248

2049), in the shape of a cross, lie at Camino Capistrano in San Juan Capistrano, about 40 miles south of Long Beach. Every year, on 19 March, this mission celebrates the return of the cliff swallows from Argentina.

In LA County itself you can visit **San Gabriel Archangel** (537 West Mission Drive, San Gabriel; 1-818 457 3035), formerly one of the wealthiest missions with a copper baptismal font from King Carlos III of Spain and priceless altar statues. **San Fernando Rey de Espana** (15151 San Fernando Mission Boulevard, Mission Hills; 1-818 361 0186), in the north-west of the LA urban area, is the largest freestanding adobe structure in California. Just north of LA, in Ventura, is **San Buenaventura** (225 East Main Street, Ventura; 1-805 648 4496).

If you tour the Central Coast (*see* **Heading North**) you can visit **Santa Barbara** (2201 Laguna Street, Santa Barbara; 1-805 682 4713); **Santa Ines** (1760 Mission Drive, Solvang; 1-805 688 4815); and **La Purisima Conceptión** (2295 Purisima Road, Lompoc; 1-805 733 3713), which is the most completely reconstructed mission in the state.

**San Luis de Obispo de Tolosa**, whose chapel was built of logs, is further north in San Luis Obispo (782 Monterey Street; 1-805 543 6850); yet further north is **San Miguel Archangel** (775 Mission Street, San Miguel; 1-805 467 3256); then **San Antonio de Padua** (Mission Creek Road, Jolon; 1-408 385 4478), followed by **Nuestra Senora de la Soledad** (36641 Fort Romie Road, Soledad; 1-408 678 2586). The Moorish **San Carlos Borromeo de Carmelo** is at 3080 Rio Road in Carmel (1-408 624 3600) and the last in the Central Coast region is **San Juan Bautista** (Second & Mariposa Streets, San Juan Bautista; 1-408 623 4528).

castle. Inside it is light and bright and the ceilings are higher than in some of the other casinos. At new resort **New York New York** (3790 Las Vegas Boulevard; 1-800 693 6763/1-702 740 6969), the Manhattan skyline rises out of the desert. NYNY is next door to the fin-de-siècle-styled **Monte Carlo** (3770 Las Vegas Boulevard South; 1-800 311 8999/1-702 730 7777), the other new kid on the block.

The gargantuan **MGM Grand** (3799 Las Vegas Boulevard South; 1-800 929 1111/1-702 891 1111), the largest hotel in the world with 5,005 rooms, lures you in with a giant gold-green lion and a not-so-great theme park. The family entertainment is better at the slightly shabby **Circus Circus** (2880 Las Vegas Boulevard South; 1-702 734 2268), in which acrobats turn somersaults above the slot machines. For Egyptian theming plus Segaworld, a mini-Manhattan and a better-than-average buffet, head for the **Luxor** (3900 Las Vegas Boulevard South; 1-800 288 1000/1-702 262 4000), a 30-storey pyramid in sleek black glass at the south end of the Strip. Towering over the Strip, at the north end, is the retro sci-fi tower of the **Stratosphere Hotel and Casino** (2000 Las Vegas Boulevard South; 1-800 998 6937/1-702 380 7777). There, the term 'high roller' is being applied to the hair-raising roller-coaster zooming around the 'pod' 1,000ft above the Strip at the top of the tower. Even more terrifying is the 'Big Shot', a ride that propels you 160ft into the air at 45mph – as if gambling wasn't exciting enough. Visit the tower; forget the mediocre hotel.

## Fremont Street

If you are starting to feel that your gambling dollars might be funding all these extravagant spectacles, take yourself to **El Cortez** (600 East Fremont Street; 1-800 634 6703/1-702 385 5200). The nicotine-stained walls, smoke-filled, jammed gaming room and sour, ageing cocktail waitresses are a welcome relief after all the razzmatazz of the Strip. The El Cortez also has the 'loosest' slots in Vegas and single-deck and two-dollar blackjack tables. It is one the few remaining outposts of seediness on Fremont Street, formerly Las Vegas' tawdry 'Glitter Gulch', now the Fremont Street Experience. Four street blocks are enclosed in a barrel vault, illuminated, on the hour, by a stupendous 'light spectacular'. Don't miss it.

You can play high-stake poker at the famous **Binion's Horseshoe** (128 Fremont Street; 1-800 237 6537/1-702 382 1600), host of the annual World Poker Tournament, and take a good meal at **The Golden Nugget** (129 East Fremont Street; 1-800 634 3454/1-702 385 7111), also owned by Steve Wynn and the snazziest casino-hotel on Fremont.

## Off-Strip

You don't have to be on the Strip to gamble. Join locals at the popular **Rio Suite Hotel and**

*Will you strike gold at* **Treasure Island***?*

**Casino** (3700 West Flamingo Road; 1-800 888 1808/1-702 252 7777) for gaudy Latin-American theming, waitresses in teeny thongs and the best casino food in Vegas, or mingle with Angeleno media and movie folk at the **Hard Rock Casino and Hotel** (4455 Paradise Road; 1-800 473 7625/1-702 693 5000). With 1950s Miami styling and only 340 rooms, this is a somewhat precious homage to the glamorous, adults-only Vegas of old.

## Sightseeing

Also of interest in Vegas is the very kitsch **Liberace Museum** (1775 East Tropicana Avenue; 1-702 798 5595). Here, the queen of showmanship's toys are divided up by category: massive costumes suitable for the heads of Ruritanian monarchs in one wing, be-rhinestoned pianos and Rolls Royces in another, and everywhere photos of the relentlessly grinning tinkler. From the ridiculous to the sublime: 30 miles from the city is the engineering marvel that made Vegas possible – the extraordinary **Hoover Dam**. Head south on US93 to get to this monument to FDR's Depression-era public works programme. It is a monolith of 40 million cubic yards of concrete and art deco styling, in a stunning Lake Mead setting – marred only by a veritable forest of pylons and power lines.

### Getting there

**By car**: Take the I-10 east to the I-15 north through the desert until you reach Las Vegas: 286 miles, 5-6 hours. **By air**: From LAX on American Eagle (1-800 433 7300; $198 round trip), Southwest (1-800 435 9792; $100-$150 round trip), United Express (1-800 241 6522; $56-$99 round trip) or America West (1-800 235 9292; $56-$130 round trip). Estimated flight time 1 hour 15 minutes. **By train**: At 10.45am on Tue, Thur and Sun, you can take the Amtrak for $77 (round trip). Estimated time 7 hours. **By bus**: 12 Greyhound buses per day. Cost: $74.

### Where to stay

The casino-hotels above tend to fall into the medium to expensive range (though they all offer massive off-peak discounts, usually Sun-Thur). There are numerous cheaper lodgings. Contact the Visitor Center (1-702 892 7576) for comprehensive hotel listings and the latest discount information.

### Tourist information

**Visitor Information Center**
*3150 Paradise Road, Las Vegas, NV 89109 (1-702 892 7576).*

## Death Valley National Monument

Whether you travel to Death Valley on the way back from Las Vegas or from Los Angeles, you'll be traversing desolate plains and mountain ranges, punctuated here and there with pitstops offering little more than gas and junk food. This barren otherworldliness is the attraction of the trip, however, and the essence of Death Valley, one of the hottest places in the world. Its stillness belies a varied terrain riddled with diverse plant and animal life, whose beauty lies in the subtle colours and geological formations of the undulating rock, dunes and dry, below-sea-level salt lake bed. Despite killer temperatures of 120°C (170°C at ground level) during the summer, and little water, humans have tried to inhabit Death Valley, leaving such landmarks as **Scotty's Castle**, a 1920s Spanish-Moorish mansion, and the **Harmony Borax Works** ruins. There are many dramatic vistas, but if you've seen Antonioni's sexy *Zabriskie Point*, you won't want to miss that spot.

### Getting there

Death Valley has several approach roads, leading from the US395 on the California side and the US95 from Nevada. The California approaches are probably the most breaktakingly scenic, particularly the SR190.

### Where to stay

There are several campgrounds (you can book at the Furnace Creek and Texas Spring Group Campground on 1-619 786 2331 or 1-800 365 2267), and three lodgings: Furnace Creek Inn and Ranch (both at 1-619 786 2345) and Stovepipe Wells Village (1-619 786 2387). Out of season – ie summer – some of these close. It costs $5 (per vehicle) to enter the monument.

### Tourist information

**Death Valley Visitors Center**
*Death Valley National Park, SR190 at Furnace Creek, Death Valley, CA 92328 (1-619 786 2331).*

## Mojave & Ridgecrest

Moving south on the SR178 and then the SR14 towards Los Angeles from Death Valley, you'll be descending through the Mojave/Ridgecrest area; from red-brown desert into flat, whitish salt lakes, largely occupied by military bases. See the erosion-carved formations in **Red Rock Canyon State Park**, made famous in *Jurassic Park*, and **Trona Pinnacles**, also a popular movie location.

Just before you enter Lancaster on the edge of the LA region, stop at the famous **Edwards Airforce Base**, home of *The Right Stuff* and occasional site of space shuttle landings. There is a museum on the base, open five days a week, which has planes and memorabilia from over 50 years of flight testing. Once a year, usually in October, there is an open day when the public can see a display of the latest USAF technology in action (1-805 277 1110 for details).

# Heading north

The drive from Los Angeles to San Francisco along the Pacific Coast Highway is one of the great American Road Trips. At some point you'll press the pedal to the metal and realise that hitherto you had experienced only a pale imitation of happiness. But every now and then you'll need to get out of the car, and there are plenty of great places to stop. This trip takes you on SR1 and US101 through the **Central Coast**, the coastal region that stretches from the northern end of Malibu for about 400 miles to just south of Santa Cruz, through terrain that goes from the sunny white beaches of the Santa Barbara coastline in the south through the rugged, misty mountain ranges of Big Sur. You can do it in two days or more, depending on how long you choose to rest.

The Pacific Coast Highway (SR1, more familiarly known as Highway One) starts in Santa Monica (head west on the I-10 and it becomes the PCH) and wends its way through the hilly coastline of Malibu and to the agricultural flatlands of the small towns of Oxnard and Ventura. They serve as a jumping-off point for the **Channel Islands National Park**, a wildlife sanctuary on an archipelago of five islands, reachable by boat or plane from Oxnard's Channel Islands Harbor or Ventura Harbor (for more information, contact the Ventura Visitors and Convention Bureau, 89C South California Street, Ventura, CA 93001; 1-805 648 2075/1-805 648 2150 fax).

After Ventura, it's well worth taking a detour inland on the SR33 to idyllic **Ojai**, a small community in a semi-arid valley of oaks and orange groves nestled at the foot of the imposing Topa Topa Mountains. (Ojai is a destination in itself, and if you go direct from LA, try to enter from the east, on SR150, for a staggering drive through mountains into the seemingly hidden valley.)

The town is charming, a combination of leftover hippiedom and a provincial arts community which has spawned such treats as the annual, and much respected, **Ojai Music Festival** in early summer, and **Barts Books** (302 West Matillija Road; 1-805 646 3755), an open-air second-hand bookstore that has bookshelves on the exterior walls; if you visit out of hours, choose your book and drop the requisite cash in the slot.

Ojai also has natural attractions, the most wondrous being the Wheeler Hot Springs (*see box* **Spas & retreats**). For more on Ojai, contact the Ojai Valley Chamber of Commerce, 150 West Ojai, Ojai, CA 93023; 1-805 646 8126/1-805 646 9762 fax).

After Ojai, you can head west along SR150 and rejoin US101 for a pleasant drive through sparkling, south-facing mountainous coastline leading into Montecito and Santa Barbara.

Santa Barbara is California's Riviera. Ninety miles north of LA, situated by the sparkling ocean (marred only by offshore oil rigs) in a fertile valley hugged by the lush Santa Ynez Mountains, Santa Barbara is the seaside getaway of choice for affluent Angelenos. They inhabit the hillside community of Montecito and have brought gentrification and exclusiveness to a town that also has great surf – at **Rincon Beach**, between Carpinteria and Santa Barbara, and **Muscle Shoals**, about 10 miles south of Santa Barbara – and a laid-back beach community. It was once home to the Spanish, who left a firm imprint in the shape of Mission Santa Barbara (*see box* **On the mission trail**) and some of the best Mission-style architecture in this region. There's only one tall edifice, the El Encanto

# Wine country

Though overshadowed by San Francisco in terms of wine tours, LA has its share of top wineries within easy reach. In fact, it's not uncommon to come across extensive vineyards within the burbs themselves; recently, some ancient Italian vines were discovered near Ontario, just east of Pomona, where the local Italian community had been using the grapes for their own jug wine. But for touring and tasting, the most accessible wineries are to the north in Santa Barbara County.

Sweltering on the beach, with a vista of shimmering gas rigs poking out of the hazy blue, it's hard to believe you're within a half-hour drive of vineyards, harder still to believe this is classified as a 'cool' wine region. Fat, ripe watermelons perhaps, juicy tomatoes even, but rows of Sauvignon Blanc? The answer, of course, is in the water. It's icy cold, and cold water means unhappy surfers but happy winemakers. Cool breezes and, more importantly, blankets of fog in the summer help temper the excesses of summer heat. What makes this wine region unique is that the main valleys (Santa Ynez, pictured, Los Alamos and Santa Maria) run west to east – most other California wine regions run on a north to south axis – and it has the geographical anomaly of being the only viticultural region lying to the west of the coastal range. The result? Vineyards regularly shrouded in fog – and some stunning wines.

Santa Barbara is the starting point for vineyard tours. If you're short of time, the **Santa Barbara Winery** (202 Anacapa Street, Santa Barbara, CA 93101; 1-805 963 3633) is in the middle of downtown and does daily tours and tastings. The **Wine Cask** (813 Anacapa Street, at Canon Perdido Street; 1-805 966 9463) is one of the best wine shops (and restaurants) in Southern California, with over 1,000 different labels listed. Owner Doug Margerum prices all the wines in the restaurant at $10 above retail, which makes it well worth trading up to the more expensive stuff. Don't be surprised if you should find a Nuit-St-Georges or a Chassagne-

Montrachet sitting on the wine-by-the-glass list. The Santa Barbara Convention and Visitors Bureau (1-805 965 3021) has information on the two-day Vintners Festival (April), the Harvest Celebration (October) and the Santa Barbara Wine Auction (May).

Driving north from Santa Barbara, into the Santa Ynez Valley, you can almost choose which grape variety to taste according to which side of US101 the winery is on. Turn off to the west and sip elegant Chardonnay and Pinot Noir at **Sanford Winery** (7250 Santa Rosa Road, Buellton, CA 93427; 1-805 688 3300); turn east, away from the coast, and the warmer temperatures bring gum-staining Cabernet Sauvignon and Merlot. Try both at **Firestone Vineyard** (5017 Zaca Station Road, Los Olivos, CA 93441; 1-805 688 3940) – run by the family that moved from tyres to rootstock – which has one of the best visitors' centres in the area.

Further north is the **Santa Maria Valley**, where many of the big wine guns (Mondavi, Kendall-Jackson) source grapes. Maison Deutz Winery (453 Deutz Drive, Arroyo Grande, CA 93420; 1-805 481 1763) is worth visiting for its excellent sparking wine, while **Zaca Mesa Winery** (6905 Foxen Canyon Road, Los Olivos, CA 93441; 1-800 350 7972) is experimenting with Rhône grape varieties. A glass of Californian Viognier, anyone?

Hotel; the rest are white-stucco, red-tiled buildings. There are also some historic adobe structures.

Park in any of the municipal car parks (first 90 minutes free) and take a walk through 12 blocks of downtown, up busy State Street, lined with cafés and pleasant, useless shops, from Gutierrez Street to Victoria Street and back down Anacapa Street, to see some stunning Spanish-style architecture and plazas. The Moorish-style **Santa Barbara Courthouse** between Anapamu Street and Figueroa Avenue is a marvel. Then drive the official Scenic Route for a climb through the bountiful surrounding hill communities, a stop at the Mission, and, from Alameda Padre Serra Road, a spectacular view over town and ocean. The **Botanical Gardens** and **Hot and Cold Springs Trails** are among many natural stand-outs.

Being a celeb city, Santa Barbara has many restaurants on a par with those of LA. However, the unmissable, totally affordable gourmet experience is to be had at **La Super Rica Taqueria** (622 Milpas Street, 1-805 963 4940), between Cota and Ortega Streets, where, for under $10, you can eat some of the best Mexican food this side of Oaxaca. Get great coffee at the **Santa Barbara Roasting Company** (1-805 962 0320) at the south end of State Street.

### Getting there

**By car**: For the scenic route, head north on the SR1 (Pacific Coast Highway) and join the US101, which goes direct to Santa Barbara: 96 miles; about a 2-hour drive.
**By air**: From LAX on American Eagle (1-800 433 7300; $88-$284 round trip), Sky West (1-800 453 9417; $88-$218 round trip) or United Express (1-800 241 6522; $88-$207 round trip). Estimated flight time: 40 minutes.
**By train**: Amtrak (1-800 872 7245) schedules eight trains per day. Fares: $29; between 2.5 and 3 hours.
**By bus**: Greyhound (1-800 231 2222) has 11 buses daily for a 24 hour journey. Fares: $24; 2 hours.

### Where to stay

If you can afford it, stay at the luxurious Biltmore Hotel in Montecito (1260 Channel Drive, Santa Barbara, CA 93108; 1-800 332 3442 reservations/1-805 969 4682 fax). Otherwise, there are numerous B&Bs, including the The Cheshire Cat (36 West Valerio Street, Santa Barbara, CA 93101; 1-805 569 1610) and Sycamore Cottage (646 North Hope Avenue, Santa Barbara, CA 93110; 1-805 687 7055). Run by Saral, a massage therapist and minister, and David, a screenwriter, this secluded, woodsy retreat has only one (large) room.

### Tourist information

**Santa Barbara Visitor Information Center**
*1 Santa Barbara Street, Santa Barbara, CA 93101 (1-805 965 3021).*
**Santa Barbara Chamber of Commerce**
*12 East Carrillo, Santa Barbara, CA 93101 (1-805 965 3023/1-805 966-5954 fax).*

## The wild coast

After Santa Barbara you'll be back on US101 for a 30-mile coastal stretch until you turn inland to the curious Danish-American town of **Solvang**, with preserved Nordic architecture alongside the Mission Santa Ines. The road then passes, to the west, the flower fields of **Lompoc**, which burst into radiant bloom in June and July, towards **San Luis Obispo**. The must-see in this mission town,

*Fancy a dip? The Neptune Pool at **Hearst Castle**. See page 252.*

fittingly, is a Madonna – but a secular one: the unbelievable Madonna Inn (100 Madonna Road, off the US101, San Luis Obispo, CA 93405; 1-800 543 9666 reservations/1-805 543 9666 fax). Created and decorated by road builder Alex Madonna and his wife Phyllis, the Madonna Inn leaves all other themed and kitsch environments at the starting block. The hotel's 110 rooms are all different; elaborate fantasies based on a palette of blue, green or, predominantly, pink, pink, pink. Ask for one of the rock-themed suites or just take tea in the frou-frou dining room. Also in San Luis Obispo are the Sycamore Hot Springs (*see box* **Spas & retreats**).

After San Luis Obispo, you can rejoin the coastal SR1, passing charming **Cambria** in a wooded valley, until you enter the open, rolling hills of **San Simeon**. There, set back from the sea, is the extraordinary and completely over-the-top **Hearst Castle**. Designed by celebrated California architect Julia Morgan for newspaper tycoon William Randolph Hearst, the Castle is a monument to Hearst's excess (and the model for Xanadu in *Citizen Kane*). It can be visited only by guided tour – make sure get on one that includes the swimming pools. For more information, contact Hearst San Simeon State Monument, 750 Hearst Castle Road, San Simeon, CA 93452 (1-805 927 2093).

After San Simeon, the road hugs the coast, passing along the cliffs of the Santa Lucia range; you'll see stunning vistas of forested headlands and huge kelp beds in the water, and, from one of the many stopping points, you can watch for seals and sea otters. You then reach the **Julia Pfeiffer Burns State Park**, where an 80ft waterfall drops onto the beach, in spectacular **Big Sur**. Sometimes compared to the Scottish highlands, Big Sur is a stunning stretch of coastline, with fog-swathed redwood forests and winding cliffs that drop sharply down to chilly beaches. A mecca for well-to-do new agers who flock to the Esalen Institute educational centre and spa, it is also home to the Henry Miller Library. If you can afford it, stay at the Post Ranch Inn for hippie luxury (Highway 1, PO Box 219, Big Sur, CA 93920; 1-800 527 2200 reservations/1-408 667 2824 fax); if not, try Ripplewood Inn (Highway 1, Big Sur, CA 93920; 1-408 667 2242). For more information, call Pfeiffer Big Sur State Park (1-408 667 2315).

After this, you'll be on the road to **Carmel** – a well-preserved, pretty town most famous for its one-time mayor Clint Eastwood – and then the **Monterey Peninsula**, a 17-mile scenic drive through rocky coastline on a toll road (the fee changes with the season) that passes through the famous Pebble Beach Golf Course.

**Monterey**, site of John Steinbeck's *Cannery Row*, used to be a large fishing port. These days, the fish are confined to the Monterey Bay Aquarium (886 Cannery Row; 1-408 648 4888), which claims the world's largest plate glass win-

*Rocky views from Highway One.*

dows in its million-gallon tank. Steinbeck is remembered in the Spirit of Monterey Wax Museum on Cannery Row, itself metamorphosed into a shopping mall with piscine-themed restaurants.

From here it is another 100 or so miles, via the surfing town of **Santa Cruz**, to **San Francisco** and its environs, covered in the *Time Out Guide to San Francisco*.

## Returning to LA

### Route 5

The fastest route from San Francisco back to LA is along the inland I-5. This whips you through California's central valley, mile upon mile of fruit-growing and cattle-rearing plains. The cattle farms, where miserably thin cows are jammed together in arid, open fields, are not a pretty sight, nor smell. The fruit farms, acres of uniform orchards worked by Mexican immigrants, dotted with small, dusty towns, offer an insight into the underbelly of the California dream. It's not unscenic, though, and makes a welcome contrast to the heat and dust of the LA region.

### Route 99

Alternatively, you can deviate from the I-5 onto the more inland SR99, which stretches for some 500 miles from Red Bluff in Northern California to just south of **Bakersfield** – centre of the agricultural industry and California's country music capital – just over 100 miles north of LA. From here, rejoin the I-5 to Los Angeles. The SR99 takes you through the irredeemably awful **Fresno**, which appears to have only chain stores and fast-food restaurants, but is a necessary staging post on the way to the Sierra Nevada mountains further east, where you will find more natural wonders in the shape of Yosemite, Kings Canyon and Sequoia National Parks and Mammoth Lakes ski area.

# Heading south

## San Diego

San Diego is wholesome America by the sea. The fact that the Republican Party's annual convention was held here in 1996, and that it has the largest US navy base on the West Coast, should give you some idea of its character. But it's certainly a pleasant place to visit and worth a day's sightseeing – or even two, if you want to take in its abundance of cultural institutions and historical districts. Its beaches and animal attractions also make it great for children. The climate is wonderful; like LA but cooler and less smoggy, with sea breezes blowing in to its stunning bayside location. It's also a mere 25 miles from gutsy – and unmissable —Tijuana on the Mexican border.

The second largest city in California, with a population of about two million, San Diego's economy was built on the defence industry; the losses resulting from cuts in federal expenditure are now being recouped through its growing tourist, biomedical, telecommunications and high-tech industries (it's sometimes referred to as Silicon Valley South).

You can still get a sense of the might of the US navy if you take the two-mile long Coronado Bay Bridge (which swoops over the harbour from downtown to the 'island' of **Coronado**, actually a peninsula); you get a dramatic view of the cruisers, aircraft carriers, destroyers and other vessels anchored in the bay. Coronado is home to the North Island Naval Air Station and the Naval Amphibious Base, and you can visit the historic Victorian **Hotel del Coronado** (scene of shenanigans in *Some Like It Hot*), now a resort complex that specialises in organising family reunions (1500 Orange Avenue, San Diego, CA 92118; 1-800 463 3533 reservations/1-619 522 8262 fax).

If you stay out of the poorer, rougher neighbourhoods on the fringes and to the south, the San Diego you will see is thoroughly spruce and well organised. It consists of distinct neighbourhoods loosely knit together by freeways. Although, as is usual in Southern California, the car is the most efficient way to take it all in, you can get around the metropolitan area on San Diego Transit Corporation buses, or use the San Diego Trolley between downtown and Old Town to the north or Tijuana to the south.

The heart of the city is downtown, a combination of sparkling high-rise business district and commercial core. Head for **Horton Plaza**, a complex of shops and restaurants on six lavishly decorated open-air levels named after Alonzo Horton, the founder of 'New Town', now downtown; this vibrant, highly coloured collage of buildings, conceived by Los Angeles architect Jon Jerde, is a

*San Diego's **Mission Bay** – 17 miles of beaches. See page 254.*

forerunner of his more recent themed mall, CityWalk at MCA-Universal Studios. Next to Horton Plaza is the historic, 16-block **Gaslamp Quarter**, a nineteenth-century district now transformed into San Diego's hottest place for shopping and eating. At present the emphasis is on Italian cuisine – there are numerous good restaurants. Also in downtown, by the waterfront, is the maritime-themed **Seaport Village**. You can stay – or just have afternoon tea – at the grand **US Grant Hotel** (326 Broadway, San Diego, CA 92101; 1-800 237 5029 from California/1-800 237 5029 elsewhere) on the corner of Fourth Avenue and Broadway.

From the commercial centre you can head northeast to the expansive **Balboa Park**. Stimulated by the 1915 and 1936 International Expositions, Balboa Park is a monument to the improving zeal of the WASP. Encompassing 1,200 acres of landscaped gardens and cultural monuments, it houses three theatres and 13 museums covering the fine arts and sciences, among them the **Reuben H Fleet Space Theater and Science Center** (1-619 238 1233) and the **Old Globe Theatre** (1-619 231 1941/1-619 239 2255 ticket services), the West Coast's oldest residential theatre (San Diego is a West Coast theatrical hub) – and the ornate 200ft high **California Tower**, as well as the famous **San Diego Zoo** (2920 Zoo Drive; 1-619 234 3153). Here, wild environments are simluated in contrived climate zones, such as Gorilla Tropics, Tiger River and the Polar Bear Plunge. You can see animals in a more natural habitat in the Zoo's **Wild Animal Park** (15500 San Pasqual Valley Road; 1-619 747 8702), a preserve 30 miles north of downtown (get a pass and directions from the zoo). Both of these are best visited early in the morning.

More animals, this time of the trick-playing marine variety, can be seen at **Sea World** (1720 South Shores Drive, 1-619 226 3901), in the Mission Bay neighbourhood. Sea World is part of **Mission Bay Park**, a vast aquatic resort; it encompasses 17 miles of glistening beaches, and all the usual watersports. Mission Bay is also home to **Belmont Park**, which features The Plunge, reportedly the largest indoor swimming pool in Southern California, and the Giant Dipper, a restored 1925 wooden rollercoaster.

Known as the Golden Triangle, **La Jolla** is a pretty, unspoilt cliffside village north of downtown, the site of **the Museum of Contemporary Art** (700 Prospect Street; 1-619 454 3541), on boutique-lined Prospect Street, the **Torrey Pines State Reserve** and **Torrey Pines Golf Course** (11480 Torrey Pines Road, 1-619 552 1784), as well as winding cliff and beach walks. You can study more fish at the **Stephen Birch Aquarium-Museum** (2300 Expedition Way; 1-619 534 3474) or worship at the shrine of a master architect and master scientist, the **Salk Institute for Biological Studies** (10010 North Torrey Pines Road; 1-619 453 4100), Louis Kahn's serene research retreat built for the institute's founder, Jonas Salk. La Jolla has several domestic-scale lodgings including the reasonably priced Bed and Breakfast Inn at La Jolla (7753 Draper Avenue, La Jolla, CA 92037; 1-619 456 2066), a converted Cubist-style house designed by celebrated architect Irving Gill.

San Diego offers a dose of its pre-Anglo history in the form of **Point Loma**, west of downtown, and **Mission Valley** and **Old Town**, north of downtown. From the Cabrillo National Monument at the southern tip of Point Loma, you get a panoramic view of San Diego as seen by Portuguese explorer Juan Rodriguez Cabrillo when he 'discovered' the West Coast in 1542. The Mission San Diego de Alcalla (*see box* **On the mission trail**) that founded San Diego was moved from here in 1774, but some of San Diego's remaining Spanish settlement has been preserved in the six-block **Old Town State Historic Park**; the subsequent transition to US rule is recorded in the adjacent **Heritage Park**.

Get a taste of 1950s and 1960s San Diego in the downtown part of the **Hillcrest** neighbourhood; there's a bevy of vintage cafés and shops, as well as the 1950s-themed, and very popular, **Corvette Diner Bar & Grill** (3946 Fifth Avenue; 1-619 542 1001), where you can view a high-sheen 1954 Corvette and eat some classic diner food.

Last but not least, San Diego is a mecca for sports; specialities include great surfing at Ocean Beach and sports fishing at Point Loma. You can watch the races at the Del Mar Thoroughbred Club (Jimmy Durante Boulevard, at Via de la Valle; 1-619 755 1141) in the emerging Del Mar suburb in north San Diego, polo at the San Diego Polo Club (14555 El Camino Real; 1-619 481 9217) and football at the Jack Murphy Stadium (9449 Friars Road; 1-619 280 2121), site of the Super Bowl in 1997.

## Getting there

**By car**: From downtown LA, take the I-5 south. From west LA, take the I-405 south and then join the I-5. The built-up LA region seems to go on and on – as far as San Clemente. After this you'll be driving through rolling hills and inaccessible shoreline, much of which is taken up by Camp Pendleton marine corps. Watch for people running across the freeway (there are road signs to warn you of the danger spots); this area is notorious for illegal immigrants trying to make a runner from boats that have sailed up from Mexico. From LA, the trip takes about 3 hours.

**By air**: From LAX on American Eagle (1-800 433 7300; $176-$146 round trip), Sky West (1-800 453 9417; $160-$292 round trip) or United Express (1-800 241 6522; $122-$380 round trip) to San Diego International Airport Lindbergh Field. Estimated time: 50 minutes.

**By train**: Amtrak operates ten trains per day, sometimes more. Cost: $33 round trip. Estimated time: 2 hrs, 40 min.

**By bus**: Greyhound has 31 buses a day; the journey takes 2-4 hours. Cost: $19.

## Where to stay

**San Diego Hotel Reservations**
*1-800 728 3227*

There is a huge choice of hotels and lodgings in San Diego; call this outfit for information and reservations.

## Tourist information

**Conventions & Visitor's Bureaux International Visitor Information Center**
*11 Horton Plaza, at F Street & First Avenue, San Diego, CA 92101 (1-619 236 1212).*

**Balboa Park Visitors Center**
*House of Hospitality, 1549 El Prado, San Diego, CA 92101 (1-619 239 0512).*

**The California Concierge Activity Line of San Diego**
*1-619 294 7100.*
An interactive phoneline giving information on attractions and services.

**The Transit Store**
*449 Broadway, San Diego, CA (1-619 234 1060).*
Public transport information, plus tokens, passes ($5-$15), timetables, maps and brochures. Alternatively, for bus route info call 1-619 233 3004; for trolley info 1-619 231 8549.

# Spas & retreats

You won't have fully experienced the laid-back West Coast lifestyle until you have soaked in a hot tub. Native Americans in this region knew that the secret of life lay in the therapeutic mineral waters that bubble up from the ground all over California – and so do some of their successors. Wallow in warm waters or hot mud, in natural surroundings, enclosed spas or redwood tubs; the sophistication scale extends in both directions. For transport and driving directions, contact the individual resorts.

## Greater Los Angeles

### Glen Ivy Hot Springs Spa

*25000 Glen Ivy Road, at Temescal Canyon Road, Corona, CA 91719 (1-909 277 3529/1-800 454 8772). I-15 south, exit Temescal Canyon Road west.* **Open** 10am-6pm daily. **Rates** $19.50 Mon-Thur; $25 Fri-Sun. **Credit** MC, V.
Otherwise known as Club Mud, this spa in nearby Riverside County is a fave with those who want to wallow in the ooze, on a budget. For a mere $19.50 (weekdays) you can enjoy day-long use of the mineral sulphur baths (the rotten egg smell soon disappears) and a good lathering in soft red clay.

## Between LA & San Francisco

### Wheeler Hot Springs

*16825 Maricopa Highway, at SR33, Ojai, CA 93023 (1-805 646 8131). US101, exit SR33 north.* **Open** *Spa* 9am-9pm Mon-Thur; 9am-10pm Fri-Sun. *Restaurant* dinner 9am-5.30pm Thur-Sun; **brunch** 10am-2.30pm Sat, Sun. **Mineral bath** $10 per 30 mins. **Massages** $36-$85. **Credit** AmEx, MC, V.
Enjoy low-key and rustic but nonetheless hedonistic luxury at this magical health resort six miles north of Ojai. Pay by the half hour for the private redwood tub rooms, with a range of body scrub and other therapeutic and cosmetic treatments on demand. Follow this up with a delicious lunch at the spa's restaurant, serving good-value Modern European cuisine, sometimes accompanied by live jazz. A popular destination for ailing East Coasters in the nineteenth century, Wheeler lost its original overnight cabins to fire and flood, but new rooms are planned.

### Sycamore Hot Springs

*1215 Avila Beach Drive, at US101, San Luis Obispo, CA 93405 (1-805 595 7302). US101, exit Avila Beach Drive west.* **Open** *restaurants* 7.30am-9.30pm daily,

*spa* 24 hours daily. **Massages** $40-$85 50. **Rooms** $109-$215. **Credit** AmEx, MC, V.
It's worth driving the 200 miles north to San Luis Obispo (make it a stop on your coastal trip to San Francisco) to soak in a secluded open-air redwood tub under a tree. Twenty such spas dot the sycamore- and oak-lined hillside at this 100-year-old resort; the balcony of each bedroom in the hotel also has a private tub, if you choose to stay overnight.

### Tassajara Buddhist Meditation Center

*Tassajara Springs, Carmel Valley, CA 93924 (booking: day 1-408 659 2229/overnight 1-415 431 3771). SR1, then east on G16.* **Prices** call for details.
Between 1 May and Labor Day, members of the public have access to this wooded mountainside retreat with two spring-fed pools, south-east of Monterey. Book in advance and check your brakes; the road is steep.

## Desert

### Deep Creek Hot Springs

*Hesperia, CA.*
**Getting there**: Take the Hesperia exit off the I-15 between LA and Barstow, then follow Hesperia's Main Street until it veers right, when you make a smooth left turn. Continue until you come to a left turn with a 15mph sign; take that, then the first right. Follow signs for Bowen Ranch, where the parking attendant will give you a hiking map.
There is no phone and no good road to Deep Creek; instead, you will have a 45-minute drive over increasingly bad roads until you park your car at Bowen's Ranch, and then a steep 2.5-mile hike. But the soak is that much sweeter when you finally arrive at the river at the base of the dramatic San Bernardino Forest Canyon, with its 'clothing optional' hot spring pools at different levels on the rock face. Best time to visit is during the week (weekends can be hectic) in late spring after the rains, when the river is high and the weather mild.

### Two Bunch Palms

*67425 Two Bunch Palms Trail, Desert Hot Springs, CA 92240 (1-619 329 8791). I-10, exit Palm Drive north.* **Suites/villas** $135-$570. **'Relaxation services'** $50-$150. **Credit** AmEx, MC,V.
The soak of choice for celebs; this is where Tim Robbins took a mud bath in *The Player*. He could equally have chosen a herbal or salt steam or a lounge in the steamy spa swimming pool, an oasis in this desert paradise of bungalows and palm trees. If you can't afford the rates at Two Bunch Palms, then try one of the many other hotels or motels in Desert Hot Springs, Palm Springs' neighbour; many of them have Jacuzzis or swimming pools that use natural mineral waters.

# Tijuana

After squeaky-clean San Diego, Tijuana smacks you in the face like a strong margarita. It's loud, it's messy, it's gaudy – and it's great. On the one hand, Tijuana is a busy business city of almost two million inhabitants; on the other, it remains true to its origins as a high-kicking border town. Noisy American students descending on the Avenida Revolución for weekend drinking binges (alcohol is not sold to under-21s in California) are the latter-day incarnation of northerners who, since the time of prohibition, have escaped to Tijuana for drink, gambling and cheap sex.

The city is also a first, intoxicating taste of the vibrant, yet impoverished land that is Baja California and Mexico. Although Tijuana feels totally different from the US, it is an easy place to visit. You can stay there without a visa for up to 72 hours, but take your passport – you will need it to get back into the US. You can pay in dollars, which will go a long way; the recent devaluation of the peso means you get more for your buck. And while speaking Spanish is obviously an asset, you will get by with English.

Local spectacles in Tijuana include bullfighting, which takes place from May to September at the **El Toreo de Tijuana** (Boulevard Agua Caliente, at Avenue Cuauhtémoc; 01152-66 85 22 10/86 15 10), dog racing at the famous **Agua Caliente Racetrack** (Boulevard Agua Caliente, at Avenida Salinas; 01152-66 88 05 55) and Jai Alai (a fast game involving throwing and catching a ball in a long wicker basket) at the **Jai Alai Palace** (Avenue Revolución, at 7th Street; 01152-66 85 25 24). Otherwise, the main attraction for the day visitor is the tourist-oriented **Avenida Revolución**, a pulsating strip of vividly decorated discos, clubs, shops and street vendors selling everything from religious kitsch, leather goods and Mexican pottery to cheap cigarettes (buy the Mexican-made US brands to avoid trouble with customs), alcohol (best bargains are the Mexican tequilas, brandies and beers; customs allow you to bring one litre back into the US) and pharmaceutical drugs (this is where prescription drug-addicted Americans come to stock up on products they can't get over the counter at home). There are some 30 bars and nightclubs on the street as well as numerous hole-in-the-wall eateries selling adequate Mexican and ethnic foods.

If you want to go where the Mexicans go, head to the newer **Zona Rio** district east of Avenida Revolución. There, at the bars on the old-style **Plaza Fiesta**, you can eat tapas with the locals. Or go to **Señor Frogs** (Paseo Tijuana, between Avenida Alfonso Reyes & Puente Mexico) in the Pueblo Amigo shopping centre by the border, a bar that's particularly popular after Sunday bullfights. For good Mexican food, try **Guadalajara Grill** at 19 Avenida Diego Rivera or **La Casa del Mole**, near

the Lucerna Hotel on Paseo de los Heroes. For excellent seafood, Tijuana's speciality, try **El Faro de Mazatlan** at 9542 Sanchez Taboada Boulevard.

## Getting there

**By car**: Take the I-5 or I-805 south from San Diego for 25 miles until you reach the San Ysidro International Border. There you can park for a minimal fee at one of the many border parking lots and walk, bus or taxi the short distance into Tijuana. You could drive in, but most US rental cars are not insured for Mexico and the traffic is chaotic. Remember that in Mexico it is illegal to turn right on red.
**By bus**: Take the San Ysidro South Line trolley (1-619 233 3004) from downtown San Diego, destination San Ysidro. It runs every 15 minutes from 5am-midnight.

## Getting back

Retrace your steps (look for 'To USA' signs) until you get to US customs. Be prepared to wait up to 15 minutes if you are on foot, up to an hour in a car. Unless you are a Mexican trying to make a break for the border, the customs officials will probably give you no trouble. You can bring in $400 worth of incidental purchases, a litre of alcohol and 200 cigarettes.

## Where to stay

Try La Villa de Zaragoza (1120 Avenida Madeo, Zona Centro; 01152-66 85 18 32/36) or the Hacienda del Rio (10606 Sanchez Taboada Boulevard; 01152-66 84 86 44).

## Tourist information

There are two information centres at the border and two in the downtown area, one at 8206 Avenida Revolución, at Calle 1 (01152-66 88 16 85/85 84 72), the other on Revolución between Calles 3 and 4 (01152-66 88 05 30). A general information number is 01152-66 84 05 37/38.

# Survival

# Survival

*The help pages – how to deal with daily life and cope in a crisis.*

## Emergencies

For police, fire or ambulance, dial 911 (free from pay phones). Other emergency numbers include:

**American Red Cross**
*1-213 739 5200. 24-hour disaster information.*

**California Missing Children Hotline**
*1-800 222 3463.*

**Coast Guard**
*1-310 980 4400. Search and rescue emergencies.*

**Federal Bureau of Investigation**
*1-310 477 6565.*

**Poison Information Center**
*1-800 777 6476.*

## Cars

Car trouble is a sad fact of life in Los Angeles. Make sure your insurance coverage is adequate, whether on your domestic policy or through the rental company (you are advised to take out both a damage waiver and liability insurance). Should you break down or have an accident in a rental car, call the rental company immediately. Also be sure to get the other party's driving licence number, address and insurance details.

Should you lock yourself out of your car, rental companies will sometimes assist you, sometimes not. It might be worth borrowing a slim jim from a garage and trying to do it yourself. Failing that, call a locksmith on 1-800 300 6807.

The LAPD suggests that you keep the rental lease agreement with you at all times in case your car gets towed or stolen (most people stick it in the glove compartment; bad idea). If you do get towed, call the nearest police precinct to find out which impound lot the car has ended up in (there are 10 in the LA area). Precinct phone numbers are in the front of the phone book in the City Government listings. To reclaim your car, you'll need your rental papers, your passport or international driving licence and a wad of cash to pay for the parking ticket, the cost of towing ($70) and a day's storage (usually $12). You'll also need to know the licence plate number – if you don't have the rental agreement to refer to, you should find it on the car keys.

*In LA, the nearest spiritual healer or tie-dyed T shirt is never far away. See page 264.*

# Parking

Los Angeles is a city of drivers, which means parking in popular areas can be frustrating and sometimes downright impossible. If you see numerous spaces in busy areas, beware: parking restrictions vary enormously from area to area and street to street, and the signs detailing them are far from straightforward. Most streets have street-cleaning days when parking is illegal, while many allow permit parking only after 6pm and at weekends. Read all parking signs at least twice as parking enforcement officers lie in wait and pounce mercilessly. All parking tickets accrued while in a rented vehicle are your responsibility. And don't think the car hire company will never track you down once you're back home. They always do. Even worse, fines double if not paid within 30 days. Fortunately, parking meters and free or cheap car parks are plentiful. Most parking meters take quarters (25 cents), dimes (10c) and nickels (5c).

## Car parks

Many of these car parks allow two hours free parking before 6pm. Car parks for major shopping complexes are free or cheaper if you validate your ticket at the checkout. Don't feel you have to buy something to have your ticket validated.

### Beverly Hills

241 North Canon Drive, between Clifton & Dayton
461 North Bedford, at Little Santa Monica
440 North Camden, at Little Santa Monica
438 North Beverly Drive, at Little Santa Monica
Beverly Center (corner of La Cienega & Beverly): three hours parking for a dollar.
Beverly Connection (corner of La Cienega & Beverly, directly opposite Beverly Center): 90 mins free parking with Belverly Center validation

### West Hollywood

Sunset Boulevard, between Crescent Heights & Laurel Avenue
8383 Santa Monica Boulevard, at Kings Road
8700-block of Melrose Avenue, at Robertson Boulevard

### Santa Monica

Public parking structures stand virtually side by side on Second and Fourth Streets between Broadway and Wilshire Boulevard. The beach and shops are easily accessible from any of these.

## Consumer advice

### Department of Consumer Affairs

*Consumer Information Hotline 1-800 344 9940/1-916 322 1700 for deaf callers only.*
Investigates complaints and gives information/referrals for over 42 state agencies on what actions and rights are available to consumers.

### Better Business Bureau

*1-714 527 0680.*
Good for filing complaints against businesses. Also provides information on reliable businesses in your area.

## Disabled

### DIRECT LINK for the disABLED

*1-805 688 1603*
Information on disability-related needs and referrals to local, state, and national resources for over 7,000 disabilities.

### Dial-A-Ride

1-800 431 7882
Refers mobility-impaired people and senior citizens to door-to-door transportation services.

### Metropolitan Transit Authority

Disabled Riders Information 1-800 621 7828

## Foreign consulates

For problems with passports and other emergencies, call your consulate office. Only the countries listed below have offices in LA; nationals of other coutries should call their consulate in Washington. To find the number, call directory assistance for Washington on 1-202 555 1212.

**Australia** *1-213 469 4300.*
**Canada** *1-213 346 2700.*
**Commission of the European Community** *1-800 852 0262.*
**Germany** *1-213 930 2703.*
**Spain** *1-213 938 0158.*
**United Kingdom** *1-310 477 3322/1-213 856 3755 (24-hour emergency number).*

## Health & medical

It is often rumoured that if you have no medical insurance, some of LA's hospitals – and emergency rooms in particular – may turn you away. This is, in fact, illegal. ERs are allowed to turn you away only if your injury is not considered an emergency, though they will do all they can to make you pay up. Taking out full medical cover is still imperative, ideally with a large and reputable company which will pay upfront rather than reimbursing you later. Treatment for a broken finger, for example, in the tourist-inhabited parts of Los Angeles might set you back $5,000, a broken leg $25,000. A visit to an emergency room to treat an allergic reaction may cost as much as $1,000. If your medical problem is not an emergency and you do not have health insurance, try the LA Free Clinic (8405 Beverly Boulevard, at Orlando Avenue, West Hollywood; 1-213 653 1990), but don't expect an immediate appointment.

## Hospitals

Hospitals listed below all have emergency rooms.

### Cedars-Sinai Medical Center

*8700 Beverly Boulevard, at George Burns Road, West Hollywood (1-310 855 2000). Bus 14, 16, 27, 83, 40/I-10, exit La Cienega Boulevard north.* **Open** 24 hours daily.
Cedars-Sinai is the hospital of the rich and famous and may cost you an arm and a leg. It is, however, conveniently located for West Hollywood and Beverly Hills.

### St Joseph's Medical Center
*501 South Buena Vista Street, at Alameda Avenue, Burbank (1-818 843 5111). Bus 96, 152/SR 134, exit Buena Vista Street north.* **Open** 24 hours daily.

### Century City Hospital
*2080 Century Park East, between Constellation & Olympic Boulevards, Century City (1-310 553 6211). Bus 28, 328, 573, Commuter Express 534, Culver CityBus 3/I-405, exit Santa Monica Boulevard east.* **Open** 24 hours daily.

### Children's Hospital of Los Angeles
*4650 West Sunset Boulevard, at Vermont Avenue, Los Feliz (1-213 660 2450). Bus 2, 3, 204/US101, exit Vermont Avenue north.* **Open** 24 hours daily.

### St John's Hospital & Health Center
*1328 22nd Street, at Santa Monica Boulevard, Santa Monica (1-310 829 5511). Bus 4, Santa Monica 1/I-10, exit 26th Street north.* **Open** 24 hours daily.

## AIDS/HIV

### AIDS Healthcare Foundation Clinic
*West Hollywood Cedar-Sinai Medical Office Towers, 8631 West Third Street, Suite 740-E, West Hollywood (1-310 358 5541). Bus 16, 27, 44, 105/I-10, exit La Cienega Boulevard north.* **Open** 8.30am-5pm Mon-Fri.
HIV/AIDS medical provider offering quality care regardless of ability to pay.

### Jeffrey Goodman Special Care Clinic
*1625 Schrader Boulevard, at Hollywood Boulevard, Hollywood (1-213 993 7500). Bus 1, 26, 163, 180, 181,*

# Hot lines

LA Smog Report: 1-800 242 4022
LA Convention & Visitors Bureau
events hotline: 1-213 689 8822
Freeway conditions: 1-213 628 7628
Weather report: 1-213 554 1212
Los Angeles Surf & Weather Report:
1-310 578 0478
Wildflower Hotline: 1-818 3533
ZIP code information: 1-213 586 1737
INFO LINE Los Angeles: 1-800 339 6993
Movie Phone (cinema info and booking):
1-213 777 3456/1-310 777 3456

*210, 212/ US101, exit Cahuenga Boulevard south.* **Open** 9.30am-8pm Mon-Fri; 9.30am-1.30pm Sat.
Free anonymous AIDS testing.

## Abortion/contraception

### Family Planning Associates Medical Group
*12304 Santa Monica Boulevard, between Bundy Drive & Centinela Avenue, West LA (1-310 820 8084). Bus 4, Santa Monica 1, 10, 14/I-405, exit Santa Monica Boulevard west.* **Open** 8am-4.30pm Mon-Fri; 8am-2pm Sat.
*6000 West San Vincente Boulevard, at Fairfax Avenue & Olympic Boulevard, West Hollywood (1-213 937 1390). Bus 27, 28, 217/I-10, exit Fairfax Avenue north.* **Open** 8am-4.30pm Mon-Fri; 8am-2pm Sat.

## Complementary medicine
See chapter **Shopping & Services**.

## Dentists

### Los Angeles Dental Society
*1-213 380 7669.*
Referrals to approved practices.

### Western Los Angeles Dental Society
*1-310 641 5561.*
A phone referral service that provides locations and phone numbers of dentists who keep emergency hours.

## Drugstores
For round-the-clock drugstores *see below* **Late**.

## Opticians
See chapter **Shopping & Services**.

## Psychiatric emergency

### Los Angeles County Department of Mental Health
*1-213 738 4961/1-800 854 7771 24 hours daily.*
Information and referral.

## Sexually transmitted diseases

### LA Free Clinic
*8405 Beverly Boulevard, at Orlando Avenue, West Hollywood (1-213 653 1990). Bus 14/I-10, exit La Cienega Boulevard north.* **Open** 9am-7.45pm Mon-Thur; 9am-4.45pm Fri.
Call first to book an appointment.

### California Self-Help Center
*1-310 825 1799.*
A central agency that refers callers to an appropriate support group for their particular needs.

### AIDS Project Los Angeles
*1313 North Vine Street, at Fountain Avenue, Hollywood (1-213 993 1600/1-800 922 2437 24-hour hotline in English/1-800 922 2438 24-hour multilingual hotline.* **Open** 9am-5pm Mon-Fri.
An outreach organisation for people with AIDS/HIV.

### Alcoholics Anonymous
*1-213 936 4343.*

### Child Care Information & Referral
*1-213 413 0777.*

### LA Suicide Prevention Hotline
*1-213 381 5111.*

### Southern California HIV/AIDS Hotline
*1-213 876 2437/1-800 922 2437.*
A helpline offering information and support, including referrals to reputable test centres.

### Late

An early start to the working day, a generally healthy vibe, no real drinking culture – all these combine to make LA the city that sleeps quite well, actually. Although there's no shortage of 24-hour gas stations, mini-marts, supermarkets or fast-food outlets, all entertainment tends to cease at the early end of the small hours, and there are no bars open after 2am.

### Cinemas

Lots of the multiplexes have midnight showings on Friday and Saturday; if you're interested in something less mainstream, try:

### New Beverly Cinema
*7165 Beverly Boulevard, at North Detroit Street, Park La Brea (1-213 938 4038). Bus 14, 212/I-10, exit La Brea Avenue north.* **Tickets** $5 adults; $4 students; $2.50 seniors. **No credit cards.**
Revival house for older movies. At press time, *Reservoir Dogs* was in the cult Saturday midnight slot.

### Nuart
*11272 Santa Monica Boulevard, at Sawtelle Avenue, West LA (1-310 478 6379). Bus 4, 304, Santa Monica 1, 5/I-405, exit Santa Monica Boulevard west.* **Tickets** $7.50 adults $4.50 seniors. **No credit cards.**
Midnight screenings at weekends, with the Rocky Horror Picture Show firmly ensconced on Saturdays.

## Coffeehouses

### Van Gogh's Ear
*796 Main Street, between Rose Avenue & Abbot Kinney Boulevard, Venice (1-310 314 0022). Bus 33, Santa Monica 1, 2/I-10, exit Fourth Street south.* **Open** 24 hours daily. **No credit cards.**
Colourful, slightly seedy, 24-hour coffeehouse, with a patio and upstairs porch.

### LA Insomnia
*7286 Beverly Boulevard, at North Poinsettia Place, Park La Brea (1-213 931 4943). Bus 14/I-10, exit Fairfax Avenue north.* **Open** 9am-4am daily. **No credit cards.**
Good coffee and cakes and a late-night buzz. There's a branch at 8164 Melrose Avenue (1-213 655 3960).

## Couriers

### Express Connection
*Suite 522, 12121 Wilshire Boulevard, at Bundy Drive, West LA (1-310 447 8000). Open 24 hours daily.*
**Credit** AmEx, Disc, MC, V.
Express has a 24-hour pick-up service. This is the main office; there are branches throughout LA.

## Dance clubs

The majority of dance clubs call it a night at 2am; notable exceptions are Arena, Florentine Gardens and the Probe (*see chapter* **Dance Clubs**).

### 5th Street Dick's
*3347½ West 43rd Place, at Degnan Boulevard, Leimert Park (1-213 296 3970). Bus 40, 105/I-10, exit Crenshaw Boulevard south.* **Open** 4pm-2am Mon-Thur; 4pm-5am Fri; 1pm-5am Sat; 1pm-2am Sun. **Shows** 9pm Mon-Thur, 9pm, 1am, Fri-Sat; 5.30pm Sun. **Cover** $5. **No credit cards.**
Not a dance club per se, but you will see a lot of bobbing heads, tapping fingers and whistles of amazement at this all-night jazz club, where the 'cooking sessions', featuring some of the LA jazz world's pride and joy, go on till daybreak.

## Drugstores

### Rexall Square Drugs
*8490 Beverly Boulevard, at La Cienega Boulevard, West Hollywood (1-213 653 0880). Bus 14, 16, 105/I-10, exit La Cienega Boulevard north.*
A health superstore open 24 hours a day.

### Sav-on Drugs
*1-800 627 2866.*
24-hour pharmacy and drugstore. Call for nearest location.

## Money

There are no late-night bureaux de change, but since most shops/restaurants/gas stations will break a travellers cheque, this shouldn't be much of a problem.

## Office services

### Kinko's

*7630 Sunset Boulevard, at Stanley Avenue, Hollywood (1-213 845 4501). Bus 2, 3, 217/I-10, exit Fairfax Avenue north.* **Open** 24 hours daily. **Credit** AmEx, Disc, MC, V.
These light, bright and efficient copy houses offer all the services you could need, from faxing and computing to photocopying and even video-conferencing. There are branches throughout the city; ring 1-800 743 2679 for details of your nearest.

## Post office

*LAX branch, 5800 West Century Boulevard, at Airport Avenue, Inglewood (1-310 337 8840).* **Open** 24 hours daily.

## Restaurants

Late-opening restaurants listed in our Restaurants chapter include Canter's (page 136), Kate Mantilini (page 132) and Caffe Luna (page 127).

### Benito's Original Taco Shop

*8001 West Third Street, at Fairfax Avenue, West Hollywood (1-213 938 7427). Bus 16, 217/I-10, exit Fairfax Avenue north.* **Open** 24 hours daily. **Average** $5. **No credit cards.**
Tacos, burritos, enchiladas... Cheap, hot and good.

### Damiano's

*412 North Fairfax Avenue, at Beverly Boulevard, Hollywood (1-213 658 7611). Bus 217/I-10, exit Fairfax Avenue north.* **Open** 10.30am-6am daily. **Average** $15. **Credit** AmEx, MC, V.
More pizza-pie combinations than Michael Eisner has suits; good for that late-night, alcohol-fuelled hunger that hits without warning.

### Jerry's Famous Deli

*8701 Beverly Boulevard, at San Vincente Boulevard, West Hollywood (1-310 289 1811). I-10, exit La Cienega Boulevard north.* **Open** 24 hours daily. **Average** $15. **Credit** AmEx, MC, V.
Not-so-bad deli most notable for its bustling dining area, central location and star-spotting potential.

### Original Pantry Cafe

*877 South Figueroa Street, at Ninth Street, Downtown (1-213 972 9279). Bus 20, 21, 22, 27, 81/I-110, exit Ninth Street east.* **Open** 24 hours daily. **Average** $17. **Credit** MC, V.
Over 75 years old and counting, this LA standby piles up the carbohydrates and proteins in its famously large portions of food. The Mayor of Los Angeles, Richard Riordan, is the owner of the place.

### Pacific Dining Car

*1310 West Sixth Street, at Witmer Street, Downtown (1-213 483 6000). Bus 18/110, exit Third Street west.* **Open** 24 hours daily. **Average** $25. **Credit** AmEx, MC, V.
A succulent, marblised steak at 3.30am? Sure, why not. As a bonus, breakfast is served all through the night.
**Branch:** 2700 Wilshire Boulevard, at 27th Street, Santa Monica (1-310 453 4000).

### Swingers

*8020 Beverly Boulevard, at Laurel Avenue, West Hollywood (1-213 653 5858). Bus 217/I-10, exit Fairfax Avenue north.* **Open** 6.30am-2am Mon-Thur, Sun; 6.30am-4am Fri-Sat. **Average** $12. **Credit** AmEx, DC, Disc, MC, V.
1950s-style diner; good omelettes, pies, and sandwiches.

## Shopping & services

### Pavilions

*8969 Santa Monica Boulevard, between Robertson & San Vincente Boulevards, West Hollywood (1-310 273 0977). Bus 4/I-10, exit La Cienega Boulevard north.* **Open** 24 hours daily.
A good place to pick up gourmet eats.
**Branches:** 9467 Olympic Boulevard, at Beverly Drive, Beverly Hills (1-310 553 5734); 802 Montana Avenue, at Lincoln Boulevard, Santa Monica (1-310 395 1682); 11750 Wilshire Boulevard, at Barrington Avenue, West LA (1-310 1-310 479 5294/pharmacy 1-310 473 6138).

### World Book & News

*1652 North Cahuenga Boulevard, at Hollywood Boulevard, Hollywood (1-213 465 4352). Bus 1, 180, 181/US101, exit Cahuenga Boulevard south.* **Open** 24 hours daily.
World-class newsstand.

### Greenblatt's

*8017 West Sunset Boulevard, between Crescent Heights Boulevard & Laurel Avenue, West Hollywood (1-213 656 0606). Bus 1, 2, 3/I-10, exit Fairfax Avenue north.* **Open** 9am-2am daily. **Credit** AmEx, MC, V.
Full service deli, cafeteria and wine shop.

### Pix

*211 South La Brea Avenue, between 2nd & 3rd Streets, Park La Brea (1-213 936 5183). Bus 16, 20, 212/I-10, exit La Brea Avenue north.* **Open** 24 hours daily. **Credit** AmEx, Disc, MC, V.
Camera repair and rentals all day and all night.

## Left luggage

Los Angeles International Airport (known as LAX) has storage lockers, but note that Union Station doesn't. If you wish to store something for more than a few days, call Public Storage on 1-800 447 8673 for your nearest location. The company has storage facilities all over Los Angeles. Minimum charges are for one month's storage.

## Legal problems

Los Angeles is a sue-happy city and however frivolous or unlikely you may think it, being sued is a common occurrence. If you bump into someone's car at 15mph, they may try to sue you for thousands. So, if in doubt, consult an attorney. There are hundreds listed in the Yellow Pages. If you think you have a claim against someone else, also consult an attorney. Though legal fees are high, most attorneys will work for a percentage – usually one-third – of any settlement.

If you are arrested and held in custody, call your insurer's emergency number for legal advice. Uninsured Brits can call the 24-hour emergency number at the consulate (*see above*).

# Site seeing: Los Angeles on line

*http://www.clublink.com*
Club listings
*http://www.calendar.com*
Concert listings
*http://www.dnai.com/~lmcohen/lacd.html*
Jazz and blues clubs listings
*http://www.lacma.org*
LA Opera
*http://www.paranioa.com/faq/Los Angeles.txt*
Sex/adult entertainment listings
*ftp://ftp.netcom.com/pub/jc/jclark/web/wehoweb.
html*
Guide to West Hollywood
*http://www.mapper.com*
California Map & Travel Center bookstore
*http://rt66.com/ftp/usr2/lazlo/LosAngeles.Recor
dShops*
Guide to LA CD and record shops
*http://www.ca.gov*
California State home page
*http://www.defense@artscenecal.com*
Art Museum Guide to LA.
*http://www.stagenet@stagenet.com*
Internet Stage & Screen Resources
*http://www.emmys.org*
Academy of TV Arts & Sciences
*http://walrus.wr.usgs.gov*
US Geological Survey home page
*http://www.scientology.org*

L Ron Hubbard's Church of Scientology home
page
*http://www.at-la.com*
Over 8,700 links to websites about and for Los
Angeles and California
*http://www.earthquakes.com*
'A Decade of Notable California Earthquakes'
*http://www.knowtribe.com*
News and works from some of LA's emerging
artists
*http://www.neo.com/Monk/LosAngeles/essay.
html*
A hip, underground travel/culture guide to LA
*http://www.laweekly.com*
*LA Weekly* home page
*http://www.fountainhead.com*
Los Angeles Visitor's Information
*http://graffiti.org*
City Walls: LA: A graffiti guide to Los Angeles
*http://latino.sscnet.ucla.edu/murals/dunitz/street
– G.html*
Guide to East LA street murals
*http://www.fountainhead.com/livecam.html*
Live camera view of Santa Monica beach
*http://www.rfx.com/hollywood*
Live camera of Hollywood sign
*http://www.lapl.org*
Los Angeles Public Library
*http://www.latimes.com*
The *LA Times* site

## Lost property

If you think you've lost something at Los Angeles International Airport, first try your airline, then the general lost property number (1-310 417 0440). Los Angeles is not the world's most honest city but if you really think an honest soul may have handed in your beloved lost property, the best place is the local police department (listed at the front of the phone book in the City Government section).

## Lost credit cards/cash crisis

To report lost or stolen credit cards call 1-800 556 5678 (Mastercard and Visa), 1-800 992 3404 (American Express), 1-800 347 2683 (Discover) or 1-800 234 6377 (Diner's Club). The numbers for travellers cheques are 1-800 227 6811 (Visa) and 1-800 221 7282 (American Express).

If you need to have money wired to you, this can be done almost immediately via Moneygram. Call 1-800 926 9400 for the nearest agent. The centrally located American Express Travel Office at 8493

West Third Street, at La Cienega Boulevard, West Hollywood (1-310 659 1682), offers this facility.

## Post offices

For more information on post offices, *see chapter* **Essential Information**. Here are some of best-located branches

### West Hollywood
*1125 North Fairfax Avenue, at Santa Monica Boulevard, West Hollywood (1-213 654 6902).* **Open** 8.30am-5pm daily.

### Brentwood
*200 South Barrington Avenue, at Sunset Boulevard, West LA (1-310 476 3065).* **Open** 7.30am-5pm Mon-Fri 7.30am-2pm Sat.

### Beverly Hills
*325 North Maple Drive, at 3rd Street, Beverly Hills (1-310 247 3400).* **Open** 8.30am-5pm Mon-Fri.

### Santa Monica
*1248 Fifth Street, at Arizona Avenue, Santa Monica (1-310 576 2626).* **Open** 9am-6pm Mon-Fri 9am-1pm Sat.

## Post restante

If you need to receive mail but don't know what your address will be, have it sent to: General Delivery, [your name], Los Angeles, CA 90086/9999, USA. You can then pick it up at the main Downtown post office: 760 North Main Street, Downtown (1-213 617 4421).

## Public toilets

There is a dearth of public restrooms in LA. Big shopping malls have them, as do cinema complexes. Santa Monica and Venice beaches have plenty, though they're functional at best. You may find yourself having to buy a coffee or a drink simply to use a restroom.

## Reference libraries

### Los Angeles Central Library

*630 West Fifth Street, between Grand Avenue & Flower Street, Downtown (1-213 228 7000). Bus 16, 18, 78, 79, 96, Foothill 492, DASH E/I-110 north, exit Sixth Street east.* **Open** 10am-5.30pm Mon, Thur-Sat; noon-8pm Tue, Wed; 1-5pm Sun.
The most comprehensive library in the city with excellent facilities and a very knowledgeable reference staff.

## Religion

Los Angeles is a veritable melting pot of religions: if it exists, then it's here. Cults also proliferate. Recruiting can take place in the unlikeliest setting, so beware of eager young things approaching with a clipboard and invitations to 'special guest events'. These cults are usually more interested in your wallet than your spiritual wellbeing.

## Places of worship

### St Mary of the Angels Anglican Church
*4510 Finley Avenue, Los Feliz (1-213 660 2700).*

### American Buddhist Congress
*4267 West Third Street, Hancock Park (1-213 386 8139).*

### First Baptist Church of Hollywood
*6682 Selma Avenue, Hollywood (1-213 464 7343).*

### First Southern Baptist Church of Hollywood
*1528 North Wilton Place, Los Angeles (1-213 466 9631).*

### St Monica's Roman Catholic Church
*725 California Avenue, Santa Monica (1-310 393 9287).*

### All Saints Episcopal Church
*504 North Camden Drive, Beverly Hills (1-310 275 0123).*

### Hope Lutheran Church of Hollywood
*6720 Melrose Avenue, Los Angeles (1-213 938 9135).*

### Islamic Cultural Centre
*434 South Vermont Avenue, Hollywood (1-213 384 5753).*

### Beverly Hills Presbyterian Church
*505 North Rodeo Drive, Beverly Hills (1-310 271 5194).*

### Westwood United Methodist Church
*10497 Wilshire Boulevard, Westwood (1-310 474 4511).*

### Aatzei Chaim Synagogue
*8018 West Third Street, Park La Brea (1-213 852 9104).*

### Congregation Beth Israel Synagogue
*8056 Beverly Boulevard, West Hollywood (1-213 651 4022).*

## Tipping

At most hotels and restaurants, tip 15% (20% for superb service, or if the place is very fancy and expensive, or if you're drunk). Be forewarned that some of the snazzier establishments will include the tip in the final tally. Following is a brief list of tip requirements:

**Electrolysis** 15%-35% ($1 minimum)
**Beautician** 10%-20%
**Bartender** 10%-15% (50¢ minimum)
**Chambermaid** 50¢-$1 per night
**Manicurist/pedicurist** 15%-35% ($1 minimum)
**Doorman** $1-$2 (more for special services)
**Cloakroom attendant** $1 (per item)
**Valet parking attendant** $1-$2 (depending on speed of car delivery)
**Hairdresser/barber** 15%-20%
**Shoeshine** 50¢-$1
**Porters** $1-$4 for unloading, $1 per bag
**Taxi driver** 15%

Don't bother tipping cinema ticket-takers or ushers, fast-food employees, department store clerks or supermarket bag-packers.

## Women

In terms of safety, Los Angeles is no different from any other major US city – it's as dangerous as you want it to be. A single woman in Compton, a gang stronghold, would certainly be at risk; a single sensible woman in the main Los Angeles areas of interest – Hollywood, West Hollywood, Beverly Hills, Century City, Westwood, Santa Monica, Venice and Malibu – should be at no more risk than if she were taking the tube in London. That said, a street in Los Angeles that may be deemed a safe area could be minutes from a notoriously bad area, so assume the worst.

Women who will be driving extensively and alone would be well-advised to use a good local map (the *Thomas Guide* is expensive but indispensable) and rent a mobile phone. Though calls are not cheap, local hire is. In fact, some car hire companies offer free phone rental.

### LA Commission on Assaults Against Women Rape Hotline
*Central LA 1-213 626 3393; LA County 1-310 392 8381.* **Open** 24 hours daily.

### AIDS Clinic for Women
*3860 West Martin Luther King, Jr. Boulevard, LA (1-213 295 6571).* **Open** 8am-4.30pm Mon-Fri.

### Shelter for Victims of Domestic Violence
*1-213 268 7564.* **Open** 24 hours daily.

### Women Helping Women Talkline
*1-213 655 3807.* **Open** 10am-1pm Mon-Thur; 6pm-8pm Tue, Wed.

## Visas

Under the Visa Waiver Scheme, citizens of Japan, the UK and all West European countries (except Ireland, Portugal, Greece and the Vatican City) do not need a visa for stays of less than 90 days for business or pleasure, as long as they have a passport that is valid for the full 90-day period and a return or onward journey ticket (an open standby ticket is acceptable).

Some restrictions, such as for those who have previously been turned down for a visa or have infectious diseases, may apply. For British citizens, the US Embassy in London provides a reasonably comprehensive recorded message for all general visa enquiries (0898 200290).

Canadians and Mexicans do not need visas, but they may be asked for proof of their Canadian or Mexican citizenship. Travellers from American Samoa, Guam, Puerto Rico and the US Virgin Islands are US citizens and do not require visas.

All other travellers, including those from Australia and New Zealand, must have visas. Full information and visa application forms can be obtained from your nearest US embassy or consulate. If you're visiting on business or pleasure no inoculations are necessary.

## Working in LA

Fancy staying on a little longer and getting a job to boost your holiday spending money? Unless you're a US citizen or hold a Green Card or work visa, forget it. Labour laws are incredibly strict with any company hiring illegal aliens facing substantial fines. A few years ago, it was occasionally possible to work for 'tips only'. Those days are long gone. If you wish to consult an excellent immigration attorney, however, call the Law Offices of Ralph Ehrenpreis (1801 Century Park East, Suite 450, Century City, LA 90067; 1-310 553 6600).

# Size conversion chart for clothes

| Women's clothes | | | | | | | | | |
|---|---|---|---|---|---|---|---|---|---|
| British | 8 | 10 | 12 | 14 | 16 | • | • | • | • |
| American | 6 | 8 | 10 | 12 | 14 | • | • | • | • |
| French | 36 | 38 | 40 | 42 | 44 | • | • | • | • |
| Italian | 38 | 40 | 42 | 44 | 46 | • | • | • | • |
| **Women's shoes** | | | | | | | | | |
| British | 3 | 4 | 5 | 6 | 7 | 8 | 9 | • | • |
| American | 5 | 6 | 7 | 8 | 9 | 10 | 11 | • | • |
| Continental | 36 | 37 | 38 | 39 | 40 | 41 | 42 | • | • |
| **Men's suits/overcoats** | | | | | | | | | |
| British | 38 | 40 | 42 | 44 | 46 | • | • | • | • |
| American | 38 | 40 | 42 | 44 | 46 | • | • | • | • |
| Continental | 48 | 50/52 | 54 | 56 | 58/60 | • | • | • | • |
| **Men's shirts** | | | | | | | | | |
| British | 14 | 14.5 | 15 | 15.5 | 16 | 16.5 | 17 | • | • |
| American | 14 | 14.5 | 15 | 15.5 | 16 | 16.5 | 17 | • | • |
| Continental | 35 | 36/37 | 38 | 39/40 | 41 | 42/43 | 44 | • | • |
| **Men's shoes** | | | | | | | | | |
| British | 8 | 9 | 10 | 11 | 12 | • | • | • | • |
| American | 9 | 10 | 11 | 12 | 13 | • | • | • | • |
| Continental | 42 | 43 | 44 | 45 | 46 | • | • | • | • |
| **Children's shoes** | | | | | | | | | |
| British | 7 | 8 | 9 | 10 | 11 | 12 | 13 | 1 | 2 |
| American | 7.5 | 8.5 | 9.5 | 10.5 | 11.5 | 12.5 | 13.5 | 1.5 | 2.5 |
| Continental | 24 | 25.5 | 27 | 28 | 29 | 30 | 32 | 33 | 34 |

**Children's clothes**

In all countries, size descriptions vary from make to make, but are usually based on age or height.

# Further Reading

## Non fiction

**Richard Alleman** *The Movielover's Guide to Hollywood*
Famous sites and tales.
**Alternative Press of America** *Inside the LA Riots*
Compendium of opinions on the 1992 riots.
**Kenneth Anger** *Hollywood Babylon*
The dark side of the Tinseltown myth.
**Reyner Banham** *Los Angeles: The Architecture of Four Ecologies*
Architectural history and paean to life in the fast lanes.
**Leon Bing** *Do or Die*
General history of and observations on LA gang culture.
**Al Clark** *Raymond Chandler in Hollywood*
An account of the career of the author who made 'noir' and 'LA' synonymous.
**Carolyn Cole & Kathy Kobayashi** *Shades of LA: Pictures from Ethnic Family Albums*
Beautifully rendered scrapbook of the ethnic family in LA.
**John & LaRess Caughey, eds.** *Los Angeles: Biography of a City*
Anthology of essays on the city.
**Mike Davis** *City of Quartz*
Exhilarating Marxist critique of LA's city 'planning'.
**David Gebhard & Robert Winter** *Los Angeles – An Architectural Guide*
Walking tour through some well-known (and not so well-known) architectural landmarks.
**William A Gordon, ed.** *The Ultimate Hollywood Tour Guide*
Walking/driving tour of Hollywood past.
**Steve Harvey** *The Best of Only In LA*
Collection of absurdities from the popular *LA Times* columnist.
**Barney Hoskyns** *Waiting for the Sun: Strange Days, Weird Scenes, and the Sound of LA*
The music scene in LA from the 1960s to the present.
**Charles Moore, Peter Becker & Regina Campbell** *The City Observed: Los Angeles, A Guide to its Architecture & Landscapes*
Geographical and architectural study of the LA area.
**Carey McWilliams** *Southern California: An Island on the Land*
A history of LA's sinfulness and its scandals. Yeah!
**Leonard Michaels, David Reid, and Raquel Scher, eds.** *West of the West*
Superb collection of essays on LA and California by such authors as Joan Didion, Rudyard Kipling, MFK Fisher, Amy Tan, Jack Kerouac, Aldous Huxley and Octavio Paz.
**Marry Ovnick** *LA: At the End of the Rainbow*
Apparently 'architecture sums up the civilizations it enshrines'.
**Julia Phillips** *You'll Never Eat Lunch in This Town Again*
No-holds barred exposé of Hollywood bitchery and excess.
**David Reid, ed.** *Sex, Death & God in LA*
Wonderful, navel-gazing essays from authors like Eve Babitz, Ruben Martinez, Mike Davis and David Thomson.
**Luis J Rodriguez** *Always Running*
Autobiography of a Latino gang member.
**Richard Romo** *East Los Angeles*
A fascinating, scholarly history of the Barrio from the turn of the century to the Depression.
**Sanyika Shakur** *Monster: Autobiography of an LA Gang Member*

A look inside the LA gangs by one who lived to tell the tale.
**Tim Street-Porter** *The Los Angeles House*
Astute, fascinating history of LA residential architecture.
**Stuart Swezey, ed.** *Amok Journal: A Compendium of Psycho-Psychological Investigations*
From LA's Amok bookstore comes an anthology of the macabre and grotesque. Not for the squeamish.
**Paul Theroux** *Translating LA*
Around the neighbourhoods with the great traveller.
**Jeffery Toobin** *The Run of His Life: The People v. OJ Simpson*
Solid overview of the Trial of the Century.
**Zagat Survey**
Comprehensive annual restaurant guide.

## Fiction

**T Coraghessan Boyle** *The Tortilla Curtain*
Post-Proposition 187 drama about prejudice, immigration and cultural barriers seen through the eyes of a white 'liberal' and a Mexican illegal immigrant couple.
**Charles Bukowski** *Hollywood*
The legendarily drunk poet's musings on making a movie in Tinseltown.
**James M Cain** *Double Indemnity, Mildred Pierce*
Classic 1930s/'40s noir.
**Raymond Chandler** *The Big Sleep, The Long Goodbye*
Meet the private dick to whom all others have to measure up: Philip Marlowe in *the* classic hard-boiled detective novels.
**Bret Easton Ellis** *Less Than Zero*
1980s, coke-spoon chic novel about being young and fast on both coasts.
**James Ellroy** *The Black Dahlia, The Big Nowhere, LA Confidential, White Jazz*
His LA Quartet is a masterpiece of contemporary *noir*.
**John Fante** *Ask the Dust*
Depression-era Los Angeles as seen by an Italian émigré.
**David Fine, ed.** *Los Angeles in Fiction*
Anthology of writers such as Walter Mosley, Norman Mailer, Hysaye Yamamoto, Thomas Pynchon, James M Cain, Oscar Zeta Acosta, et al.
**F Scott Fitzgerald** *The Pat Hobby Stories*
Short stories about living and working in Hollywood from a Great American Writer who died there.
**Elmore Leonard** *Get Shorty*
Miami loan shark turns movie producer in gutsy thriller.
**John Miller, ed.** *Los Angeles Stories*
Collection of fiction and essays on the city by Henry Miller, F Scott Fitzgerald, Raymond Chandler, et al.
**Walter Mosley** *The Easy Rawlins Mystery Series*
The heir apparent to Philip Marlowe, Mosley's Easy Rawlins is an African-American who turns his hand to detection in post-war LA.
**Budd Schulberg** *What Makes Sammy Run?*
Furious attack on the studio system from one of its employees.
**University of California Press** *California Fiction Series*
Reissues of novels that explore the culture and history of California include *Fat City* by Leonard Gardner, *Golden Days* by Carolyn See and *Continental Drift* by James Houston.
**Bruce Wagner** *I'm Losing You*
Biting Hollywood satire.
**Nathanael West** *The Day of the Locust*
Classic, apocalyptic raspberry flung at the movie industry.
**Evelyn Waugh** *The Loved One*
Hilarious and accurate satire on the American way of death.

# Index

**Note:** *Numbers in bold indicate the
section giving key information on the
topic; italics indicate illustrations.*

Abiqulu 122, *123*
Academy Awards 47, 108
accommodation **15-32**
    hostels/B&Bs 31-32, 240
    lesbian 235
    out of town **240**, 241-256
    rented 32
    student 238
    *see also* hotels
adventure games 184-185
advertisements 80, *81*
African-American LA 69, 117-118
    history 60, 61-62, 65
    Marketplace/Cultural Fair 49
    museums 118, 120, 205
Agua Caliente Reservation 244
AIDS/HIV 231, 260, 261, 265
Air Combat USA 185
air quality 5
air travel
    airlines 9
    internal flights 242, 244, 248,
        251, 254
airports
    LAX 9, *11*
    Santa Monica 90
    transport to and from 9
alcohol laws 7-8, 149, 195
Alcoholics Anonymous 261
Ambassador Hotel 86, 102
ambulance 3
American Express 3
American Film Institute 200
American football 192
Anaheim 31, **120**, 144
Anaheim Stadium 192
Angels Attic Museum 230
Angels Flight 63, 108, *108*
Anza-Borrego Desert 244
aquariums 114, 252, 254
aqueducts 58, 61
Arcadia 112
architecture 41, **75-78**, 253, 254
    by area 89, 91, 95, 96, 97, 98,
        100, 102, 106, 110, 119
    Craftsman 112
    Googie/1950s **78**, 80, 95, 96,
        102, 111
    Institute 237
    LA Conservancy Tours 46
    *see also* Gehry, Frank
Argyle hotel *15*, **20**, 149
Arrowhead Village 242
art
    advertising as 80, *81*
    African-American 118, 120, 205
    College of Design 236
    festivals 48, 119
    galleries 95, 105, 109, *110*,
        114, 205, **210**

Latino 115, 120
    masterpieces **207**
    museums of 112, 114, 118,
        119, 120, **205-208**
    noir 61
    public 91, 115, 117, *209*
    supplies 158
    Venice artists 91
astrology 159
ATMs (Automated Teller
    Machines) 3
attitude 3
Automobile Club of Southern
    California 240
Autry Museum of Western Heritage
    **209**
aviation 59, 90, 149, 185, 230, 249

babysitters 228
Baker 245
bakeries 168-169
Balboa Island/Peninsula 119
Ballona Wetlands 92
banks 3
Barney Greengrass *130*, 132
Barney's Beanery 127, *141*
Barneys New York 83, 84, **155**
Barnsdall Park 109, **205**
    Hollyhock House 76, *77*, 109, 205
bars 109, **149-152**
    celebrity haunts 84-85, 152
    gay/lesbian 232-233, 235
    Polynesian ('tiki') 150
Barstow 245
baseball 192
basketball 192
bathhouses, gay 233
*Baywatch* 92-93
beach volleyball 114, **189**
beaches **33-34**, 89-93, 113-114, 119
    gay 233
    Internet information 183
    out of town 249-253
beauty treatments 85, **171-173**
    hotel salons 17, 20-23, 28
Bel Air 41, **97**, 134
    Hotel *17*, **22**, 97
Belushi, John 21, 86, 94
Beverly Hills 40, **95-96**, *96*
    bars/coffee houses 147, 150
    hotels 20-24, *25*
    museums/galleries 78, 206, 210
    restaurants 132-133
    Rodeo Drive 40-41, 154
Beverly Hills Hotel **20**, 96
    Polo Lounge 85, 96, **133**
Big Bear 242
Big Sur 252
*Billboard* 227
billiards 189
Biltmore Hotel **27**, 59, 108
Blessing of the Animals 48
boats/boating 92, 188
body piercing 173, *175*

Borrego Springs 244
bowling 189
Bradbury Building **75**, *75*, 106
Bradley, Tom 64
Brazilian Summer Festival 49
breakfast 122, 123, 127, 129, 132,
    133, 135, 137, 143
Brentwood 82, **98**, 134, 154
    *see also* Getty Center for the
        Fine Arts
bridges 107
Broad Beach 82
Broadway 106
Buddhism
    American Buddhist Congress 264
    The Bodhi Tree 94, 232
    Higashi Honganji Temple 106
    Self-Realization Fellowship 46, 92
    Tassajara Meditation Center 255
Buena Park 120
Bullocks 80, 102
bungee jumping 185
Bunker Hill 63
Burbank 112
bureaux de change 3
    in hotels 19-31
burgers 80, 97
buses **9-11**, **12**
    Greyhound 11
business services **226-227**
    hotel facilities 17-32
    information/complaints 259
*Buzz* 181

CAA (Creative Artists Agency) 96
Cadillac, The **19**, *20*, 25
cafés 90, 91, 92, 98, 120
    celebrity haunts **85**
    Patinette (in MOCA) 206
    *see also* coffeehouses
California Department of Fish &
    Game 240
California Department of Parks &
    Recreation 240
California Science Center 208
California Trade & Commerce Agency
    Office of Tourism 240
CalTech (California Institute of
    Technology) 53-54, 112, **236**
CalTrans Highway Information
    Network 240
Cambodian community 114
camping **32**, **240**, 241, 242, 244,
    245, 249
    Internet guide to 183
canyons 92, 93, 186-187, 230
Capitol Records Building 100
Carmel 252
Carole & Barry Kaye Museum of
    Miniatures 209
cars and driving 9, **12-13**, 58,
    **79-81**, **258**
    in the desert 243
    freeways **12**, 61, 62, **63**, 79

licences 80, 238
lowriders 72, *73*
in Mexico 256
museum collections 210, *211*
out of town **240**, 242-256
Pacific Coast 43, 114, 249
parking **12-13**, 80, **259**
rental **13**, 81
safety advice 8
suggested scenic routes **43**
carwashes 80, **161**
cashpoints *see* ATMs
Catalina *see* Santa Catalina Island
catering 160
cathedrals
  Crystal **78**, 120
  St Vibiana's 106
caviar 169
celebrity spotting 25, **82-86**, 94,
    97, 123, 124, 131, 133, 135
  graves 86, *95*, 96, 100, 109, 245
  tours 46
cemeteries **86**, *95*, 96, 100, 109
  Forest Lawn **45**, 86, 109
Central Avenue 117
Century City 21, 83, **97**, 190, 222
  restaurants 134
Chamber of Commerce **226**
Chandler, Raymond 61, 98
Channel Islands National Park 249
Chaplin, Charlie 19, 86, 100
Château Marmont **21**, 94
chemists 261
Chemosphere 77
Chez Jay 123
children **228-230**
  care advice 260
  Junior Arts Center 205
  missing 258
  Nursery Nature Walks 46
Children's Museum, LA 106, **230**
Chinatown **105**
Christmas 48, 50, 105
churches **264**
  black **118**
  evangelical 106
  Methodist 118, 264
  Old Plaza 105
  Wayfarers Chapel 114
  *see also* cathedrals; missions
cigar smoking 96, 114, **172**
Cinco de Mayo **48**, 72
cinemas 60, 97, 99, 100, 108,
    112, 118, 120, **200-202**
  drive-ins 202, *204*
  information/booking 200, 260
  late night 261
  private screenings 8
  vintage palaces *76*, 76, 77, 113
  *see also* Mann's Chinese Theater
circuses 229
Civic Center/City Hall 106
Claremont 112
Clarion Hollywood Roosevelt
    Hotel **24**, 86
climate **3-5**, 111
  desert 243
clubs 94, 109, 116
  comedy 193-194
  gay/lesbian 119, 232-233, 235
  dance **195-198**, 261
coast guard 258
Coca-Cola Bottling Plant 77
coffee, types of 147

coffeehouses 78, 109, **145-148**
  gay/lesbian 234, 235
  Googie **78**, 102, 111
  late-night 261
Coldwater Canyon Park 230
colleges 236-238
comedy 94, 109, **193-194**
Comedy Store 94, **193**
conservation 93, 230
consulates 259
consumer advice 259
contraception 260
Convention & Visitors Bureau,
    LA 105, 108, 226
Costa Mesa 119-120
couriers **226**, 261
cowboys 46, 48, 209
Craft & Folk Art Museum 205
Crawford, Joan 86
credit cards **5**
  stolen 263
Crenshaw District 117-118
crime **8**, 68-69
Crystal Cathedral **78**, 120
Culver City **98**, 164, 208
  Ice Arena 189
  restaurants 134-135
  theatres/venues 220, 222
currency **5-7**
  *see also* bureaux de change
customs 7
cycling **13**, 92, 111, **185**
  mountain *242*, 242, 244
  rental 19, 28, 185

*Daily Variety* 227
dance **223-224**
  classes 91, 190
  supplies 162
dance clubs **195-198**, 261
*Dancing Clown* 91
DASH 9-11
dating agencies 159
Daumier, Honore 207
Day of the Dead **49**, 115
Dean, James 86
Death Valley 249
dentists 260
desert **243-249**
  information centers 245, 249
Devil's Punchbowl 187
Didion, Joan 61, 63, 93
Diez y Seis de Septiembre 72
diners 80, 111, **144**
Directors Guild of America 227
disabled services **7**, **259**
  hotels with access 17-32
Disney Animation Building 78
Disney on Ice 229
Disneyland **39**, 62, 120, *120*
  hotels 31
Dodgers Stadium 62, *189*, **192**
domestic violence shelter 265
Dorothy Chandler Pavilion **212**, *213*
Downey, Robert, Jr 66, *71*
Downtown 27-28, **41**, **104-108**, 155
  museums 205, 206, 208, 209
  restaurants/bars 138, 152
*Dr Quinn Medicine Woman* 111
drag racing 72
drag shows 234
dress 227

dress hire 166
driving *see* cars and driving
drugstores 261
dry cleaners 162
Duke's 128
Dunbar Hotel 117

Eames House 77, *78*
earthquakes **53-54**, 60, 64
  Northridge (1994) 109, 111
  survival advice **53**
East Hollywood 109
East LA **115-116**, 143
Easter 48, 105
Echo Park 110
  Dodgers Stadium 62, *189*, **192**
  Lotus Festival 49
Edwards Airforce Base 249
El Capitan Theater 76, 202
El Cholo 137
El Matador beach 34
El Pueblo de Los Angeles Historical
    Monument 56, **105**
El Segundo 113
electricity 7
Ellroy, James 61
emergencies 8, 258
Ennis-Brown House 76, **77**
Esalen Institute 252
estates, gated 70
exercise *see* fitness
Exposition Park 205, 208

Fairfax **100-102**, 136
FBI 258
festivals and events **47-50**, 105,
    110, 119, 205, 223, 249, 250
film and entertainment industry 59
  casting 200
  catering 160
  contacts/information **227**
  dry cleaners 162
  history **199-200**
  memorabilia168
  publications 159, 160, 227
  schools/research **237**
  second-hand costumes *160*, 165
  *see also* cinemas; studios; film
film festivals 49, 204
film locations 77, 104, 106, 107,
    **203**, 208, 236, 249
  *Blade Runner* 75, 104
  *Get Shorty* 122
  *Guilty by Suspicion* 125
  *Indecent Proposal* 96
  *Jurassic Park* 249
  *Planet of the Apes* 120
  *The Player* 125, 150, 255
  *The Poseidon Adventure* 39
  *Pretty Woman* 22
  *Prizzi's Honor* 23
  *Scenes from a Mall* 94
  *Some Like it Hot* 253
  *Speed* 79
  *The Vanishing American* 241
  *Witches of Eastwick* 96
film noir 61
Financial District 108
Fire Tower 105
fires 54-55

emergency number 8
Fisherman's Wharf 92
fishing 92, 240, 241, 242
fitness **190-191**
 *see also* sports
Fleiss, Heidi 166
floods 55
florists 168, *177*
football *see* American football;
 soccer
Forest Lawn Memorial Parks **45**,
 86, 109
Formosa Café *151*, 151
Four Seasons at Beverly Hills **21**, 85
Fred Segal 83
Frederick's of Hollywood
 Celebrity Lingerie **166**, *177*
 Hall of Fame **209**
freeways **12**, 61, 62, **63**, 79

Gable, Clark 86
Gamble House 75-76
games, role-playing 184, 185
gangland culture 68-69
gardens 114, 205, 241, 244, 251
 *see also* Henry E Huntington
 Library
gay LA 94, 119, 130, 146, **231-234**
 car cruising 234
 festivals 49
Geffen Contemporary at MOCA 77,
 105, **205**
Gehry, Frank 77-78, 89-90, 91, 98,
 105, 106, 114, 123, 205, 207
George C Page Museum 208
Getty Center for the Fine Arts,
 J Paul **43**, 78, 98, **206**, 207
Getty Museum, J Paul (Getty Villa)
 43, 78, 92, **206**
ghosts 24, 25
Gladstone's 4 Fish 125, *126*
golf courses **185-186**, 252, 254
Googie style **78**, 102, 111
Grant, Hugh 86
Graumans Chinese Theater *see*
 Mann's Chinese Theater
Great Western Forum 216
Griffith Park **45**, 106, **109-110**, 230
 Autry Museum **209**
 golf course 185
 Greek Theater 216
 Observatory/Planetarium 45, **208**
Guiness World of Records 100
gun clubs 188
gyms 91, **190-191**
 gay and lesbian 231-232
 Golds Gym 84-85, 91, 190, *233*

hairdressers 85, **171**, 232
Hallowe'en 49
Hancock Park **103**, 137
 Larchmont Village 103, 155
hang-gliding 186
health **259-260**
 complementary treatments
 **160-161**, 171, 191
 Poison Information Center 258
health food 169
Hearst Castle *251*, 252
helicopter tours/demos 46, 185

helplines 260-261
Henry E Huntington Library, Art
 Collections & Botanical Gardens
 **37**, *37*, 112, **205**, 207
Henry Fonda Theater 216, **221**
Hermosa 113-114
hiking 111, 241, 242, 244
 in the desert 243
 trails **186-187**
history **56-65**, 111, 199, 247
 Hollywood 199-200
 key events 65
 1990s 65, 66-71
Hockney, David 19, 24, 206
holidays, national 47
Hollyhock House 76, *77*, 109, 205
Hollywood 59, 82, **99-100**
 bars/clubs 149-152, 195-198
 Chinese Theater/Walk of Fame
 **37**, *40*, *57*, 99, *99*, 202
 coffeehouses 147-148
 Gym & Fitness Center 190
 hotels/hostels 24-27, 31
 Industry Cyber Café 200
 museums/galleries 100, 209, 210
 restaurants 135-136
 Ripley's Believe It or Not 39
 theatres/venues 216, 221-222
 Wax Museum **37**, 100
 *see also* film and entertainment
 industry; West Hollywood
Hollywood Boulevard **41**, 155
Hollywood Bowl **34**, **214**
Hollywood Hills 46, **186-187**
Hollywood News Calendar 82
*Hollywood Reporter* 227
Hollywood Reservoir and Dog
 Park 46
Hollywood Sign **41**, 99, 186
Hoover Dam 248
horse racing 112, **192**
horse riding 46, **186**
hospitals **259-260**
hostels **31-32**, 238
hot rods 50
hot springs 251, 255
Hotel Figueroa *17*, 27
hotels **15-31**, 45, 62, 94, 108
 budget 19, 24-25, 28, 31-32
 chains 21
 first class 17-19, 20-23, 24,
 27, 28-31
 former Hollywood haunts 86
 mid-range 19, 23-24, 27-28, 31
 prices and services 15-17
 *Queen Mary* **39**, 114
House of Blues 216
houses, celebrity **83**, **86**, 91
houses, historic **75-78**
 Adamson House 93
 Avila Adobe 105
 Greystone Mansion 96
 Venice Beach House *32*, 32
 *see also* Hollyhock House
Huntington Beach 119
Hydrosphere 230

ice cream 170
ice hockey 189, 192
ice skating **189**, 242
ID cards, student 238
Idyllwild **242**, 244

immigration 7
Independence Day 49
Indians *see* native Americans
Inglewood 118
insurance 7
 car 13
Internet sites 183, **263**
 café (Cyber Java) 146
Irvine **120**, 164, 224
Islamic Cultural Centre 264
Ivy, The 129

James A Doolittle Theater 221
Japanese LA 61-62, **105-106**
 festival 49
 National Museum 105, **206**
 Pavilion of Art 206, **207**
 theater 106, **214**
Jewel's Catch One 235
Jewish LA **100-102**
 food 102, 122, 133, 136, 141
 169, 170
 museums 206, 207
John Anson Ford Amphitheater
 216, **221**
Joplin, Janis 86
Joshua Tree National Monument
 *244*, **244-245**
Julia Pfeiffer Burns State Park 252

kayaks 188
Kennedy, Robert F 86
kennels 174
Kidspace Museum 230
King, Rodney *64*, 65, 66
Knott's Berry Farm **40**
Korean Bell of Friendship 114
Koreatown **103**, 137-138

La Brea Tar Pits **37**, 208
La Jolla 254
*LA Weekly* 180, 195
LACMA *see* Los Angeles County
 Museum of Art
Laguna Beach 119, 144
Lake Arrowhead 242
Lake Gregory 242
language 5
Larchmont Village 103, 155
Las Vegas 164, **246-248**
Laser Storm 184
late-night LA **261-262**
 coffeehouses 145-149, **261**
 Comedy Store 94, **193**
 gyms 190
 live music 217-220
Latino LA 61, 65, **72-74**, 120
 festivals 49, 50
 music 50, 74, 102, 195, 197
 215-216
 *see also* Mexican LA
legal information 227, 262
Lawford, Peter 86
Leimert Park 118
lesbian LA 49, **235**
 Red's Bar 115
Lewitzky Dance Company *222*, 223
Liberace Museum 248

libraries 119, **227**
 film and TV 227, 237
 LA Central 76, 77, 108, 227,
   229, 237, **264**
 Presidential 120, **208-209**
 *see also* Henry E Huntington
   Library
limousines **12**, 81, 84
Lincoln Park 115-116
listings 180, 195, 210, 212
 Internet 263
Little Tokyo 62, **105-106**
Live Art 191
Living Desert 244
Long Beach **114**
Los Angeles County Fair 112
Los Angeles County Museum of Art
 (LACMA) **45**, 200, **206**
 Bing Theater 214
 Pavilion of Japanese Art 207
Los Angeles County Museum of
 Natural History **208**
*Los Angeles Daily News* 227
Los Angeles Galaxy 191
Los Angeles Grim Society 183
Los Angeles Theater 106, *200*, **202**
*Los Angeles Times* 106, 180, 227
Los Feliz **109-110**, *110*, 152, 220
 restaurants 138, 141
 *see also* Barnsdall Park; Griffith
   Park
lost property 263
luggage
 left- 262
 shops/repairs 166-168
Lumpinee Thai *136*, 141
LunaPark 218

MacArthur Park *101*, 103
McPherson, Aimee Semple 59
Macy's 155
magazines **180-181**
 gay and lesbian 231
Magic Johnson Theaters *117*, 118
mail boxes 8, 227
Main Beach 119
make-up artists 171
Malibu 19, **93**, *93*, 125-127, 206
 beaches **34**
 campsites 32
 sports facilities 184-185, 186
 *see also* Getty Museum
Malpede, John 224
Manhattan Beach 113
Manhattan Wonton Co *129*, 130
manicures and pedicures 171
Mani's Bakery 145, **168**
Mann's Chinese Theater **37**,
 *40*, *57*, 99, *99*, 202
Mansfield, Jayne 86
Manson, Charles 64
maps 160
marathon 48
mariachi 50, 115, 137
Marina del Rey **92**, **92**, 125, 146
 Athletic Club 190
markets
 African 118
 Farmers' **34**, 102, 155, **169**
 flea 158
 Grand Central 106, *165*, **169**
Marley, Bob 50, 218

massage 171
MCA-Universal *see* Universal
 City/Studios
meditation *see* retreats; yoga
Melrose Avenue **41**, 155
mental health 232, 260
message services 226-227
Metro **11**, 68
MetroArts 205
Mexican LA 37, 56, 60, 61, 69,
 72, **105**, 106, **115-116**
 festivals 50
 *see also* Latino LA; mariachi
Midtown **102**, 147-148, 150-152
 hotels 24-27
 restaurants 135-136
Million Dollar Theater 60, 106
Miracle Mile **102**, 136-137, 200
 museums 102, 205, 206, 209, 210
Mission Bay *253*, 254
missions 56, 112, **247**
MOCA *see* Museum of
 Contemporary Art
Mojave Desert **243-249**
 information centers 245
 Kelso Depot *245*, 245
 National Preserve 245
Mondrian Hotel **22**, 94
Monroe, Marilyn 22, 24, 86, 98, 209
 grave 86, *95*
Monterey 252
Monterey Park 112
Mormon Temple 96-97
motor racing 192
motorcycling
 clothes 162
 rental 13
movie palaces *see* cinemas
MTA 9-11, 12, 79
mudslides *52*, 55
Mulholland Drive 45
Museum of African American Art 118
Museum of Contemporary Art (MOCA)
 **45**, 108, *206*, **206**
 cinemas 200
 Geffen Contemporary 77, 105, **205**
 Store 90
Museum of Flying 90, **230**
Museum of Jurassic Technology 208
Museum of Neon Art 209
Museum of Television & Radio 78,
 **206**, 237
Museum of Tolerance 206
museums 43-35, 102, **205-210**
 art 112, 114, 118, 119, 120,
   **205-208**
 aviation 90, 149, 230
 cars 210, *211*
 children's 106, 229-230
 Hollywood 100, **209**
 Internet listings 183
 Malibu 93
 maritime 114
 out of town 241, 248, 255
 science 208
 surfing 119, 209
 Wells Fargo 108
music, classical 119, **212-215**
 children's workshop 229
music, rock, roots & jazz **215-220**
 *BAM* magazine 180
 current scene 215-216
 jazz venues 98, 114, 117, 118,
   206, **220**

Latin 50, 74, 102, 195, 197
 major venues 216-217
 mariachi 50, 115, 137
 1960s and Sunset Strip 94
 punk/indie 110, 197
 reggae/rap 50, 113, 114
 rock venues 102, 119, 120, 198,
   **217-218**
 roots/blues venues 119, **220**
Music Center of LA 108, **221**
 Dorothy Chandler Pavilion
   **212**, *213*
music festivals 48, 49, 50, 249
Musso & Frank Grill 135

Nate & Al 133
native Americans
 festival 48
 history 56, 89, 247
 reservations 244
Necromance *167*, 170
Nelman Marcus 155
Nethercutt Collection 210
New Age centres and shops 91,
 94, 159, 170, 232, 252
 *see also* Buddhism; retreats
New Stone Age *161*, 166
New Year festivals 48, 50
Newport Beach 119
newspapers **180-181**
 business 227
Nixon, Richard 120, 208
noir culture 61
Norton Simon Museum 112, **207**

observatory 45, **208**
office services **227**, 262
oil industry 58, 60
Ojai 249
Oldenburg, Claes 78, 91, 206
Olvera Street **37**, 56, **105**, 115, *116*
Olympic Games 60, 64
Onyx, The 109, *110*
opening hours 8
opera 212
opticians 174
Orange County 28, 68, **119-120**,
 144, 208, 209, 224
 Crystal Cathedral **78**, 120
 Knott's Berry Farm **40**
 *see also* Disneyland
Orpheum 106, 202
Oscars 47, 108

Pacific Asia Museum 207
Pacific Coast Highway **43**, 114, 249
Pacific Design Center 94
Pacific Palisades **82**, 92-93
paintball 184
Palm Canyon 244
Palm Springs 242, **243-244**
Palos Verdes 114
Pantages Theater 100, 216, *221*,
 **221-222**
parades 49-50
Park La Brea 137
parks **45-46**, 92, 93, 103, 110,
 114, 115-116

Pasadena 28, 75, 112, 185, 202, 220
  Antique Center 158
  Civic Auditorium 214
  Gamble House **75-76**
  museums/galleries 205, 207, 210
  Old Town **41-43**, 164
  parades *47*, 49-50, 57, 112
  Playhouse 223
  Rose Bowl *184*, 191
Pasadena Freeway 79
Peninsular Beverly Hills **22**, 96
Pershing Square *3*, 78, 106-108
pet services 174
Petersen Automotive Museum
  **210**, *211*
Phoenix, River 86
photography
  gallery 118
  shops/processing 160
pilates 191
planetarium 208
plastic surgery 156
Playa del Ray 92
Poison Information Center 258
police department (LAPD) 69-70
  emergencies 8
  and minorities 63-64
pollution 55
pool 189
population 67
post offices 8, **263**
  late-night 262
post restante 263
pregnancy 260
Presley, Elvis 86
prisons 68-69, 106
'Proposition 187' 74
pub, Irish 151
Puck, Wolfgang 122, 123, 125,
  131, 143
puppet theatre 229

**q**

*Queen Mary* **39**, 114

**r**

racecourses 112, **192**
racism 61-62, 63-64, 65
racquetball 189
radio 81, **182-183**, 237
  museum 78, **206**, 237
Radisson Huntly Hotel 45
railways **12**, 63
  funicular 63, 108
  history 57
  *see also* Union Station
Ramona Pageant 48
ranches 92, 111, 241
Rape Hotline 264
Reagan, Ronald 64, 66-68, 209
real estate 56-58
record industry 23, 100
Red Cross **53**, 258
Red Rock Canyon State Park 249
Redondo Beach 113-114
religion *see* churches; *and*
  *individual religions*
restaurants **122-144**
  by area 89-98, 100, 103, 105,
    109, 110, 113-116, 118, 120,
    **122-144**, 254
  background/etiquette 122

budget 132
celebrity haunts **83-84**, 85, 89
children's specialities 229
by cuisine (index) **144**
  drive-through 80
  gay/lesbian 234, 235
  Internet listings 183
  late-night 262
  vegetarian 114, 124, 125
  Cambodian 114
  Caribbean 113, 144
  Chinese 105, 112, 120, 144
  Croatian 114
  Cuban 120, 144
  Greek 114
  Japanese 45, 105, 144
  Jewish 102, 122, 133, 136, 141
  Mexican 45, 105, 110, 115, 116,
    144, 251, 256
  Polynesian 150
  soul food 114, 118
  southern 114, 118, 120, 144
  Vietnamese 120, 144
retreats 46, 92, 255
Rex-Il Ristorante 138
Ridgecrest 249
Ripley's Believe It or Not 39
river (bridges and walks) 107
Riverside County Fair & National
  Date Festival 48
rock climbing 187, 245
rollerhockey 187
rollerskating (gay) 234
Rose Parade *47*, **50**, 57
Roxy, The 218
Rustic Canyon Park 92

**s**

Saks Fifth Avenue 155
Salton Sea 244
San Bernadino Mountains 241-242
San Clemente 119
San Diego 164, 223, **253-255**
  Factory Outlet Center 243
  mission 247, *247*
San Fernando Valley 58, **111-112**
  restaurants/cafés 141-143, 148
  Sebastian Rainforest 230
San Gabriel Valley 112, 143
San Jacinto Mountains 242, 244
San Juan Capistrano 119
San Luis Obispo 247, 251-252
San Marino 112
  *see also* Henry E Huntington
    Library
Santa Ana 120
Santa Barbara 247, **250-251**
Santa Catalina Island 241
Santa Monica 12, **89-90**, 155
  Antique Market 158
  bars/coffeehouses 145, 149
  beach **34**
  Fourth Street Steps *89*, 89
  galleries 90, **210**
  hotels/hostel 17-19, 31-23
  Museum of Art 90, **207**
  restaurants 122-124
  Third Street Promenade **43**,
    155, 164
  Twilight Dance Series 49
Santa Monica Mountains 111-112,
  187
Santa Ynez valley 250, *250*

Sawdust Festival 48
Schindler House **76-77**, 94
Schwarzenegger, Arnold 89
Screen Actors Guild 227
scuba diving 119, **187-188**
Sebastian Rainforest 230
Self-Realization Fellowship Lake
  Shrine **46**, 92
sex clubs 109, 198, 233-234
sexually-transmitted diseases 260
Shangri-La Hotel **19**, 89
shoe repairs/shops 166-168
shops 83, **154-177**
  by area 41, 89-91, 94-95, 97, 98,
    100, 102, 106, 109, 110, 114,
    116, 120, **154-155**, 244
  art supplies 158
  books/periodicals 91, 94, 98,
    100, 109, 114, 145, **159-160**,
    *181*, 181, 202, 228, 231, 249
  cameras/electronics **160**, 170
  children's 159, 165-166, 177, 228
  clothes size conversion 265
  computers 161
  department stores 155
  factory outlets 157, **243**
  fashion **162-168**, 195
  fetish/sex 163, 170
  film/TV memorabilia 100, 168
  florists 168
  food/drink 82-83, **168-170**, 251
  gifts/stationery 170
  guitars/instruments 100, **174**
  health/beauty 171-173
  household/furniture 98, **173**
  large sizes 163
  late-night 262
  leather 162, 164, 166-168
  lingerie 100, **166**, *177*, 209
  records/tapes/CDs 97, 110, 114,
    120, **174**, 195
  second-hand/antiques **157-158**
  sports 120, **174**
shopping malls 94, 97, 100, 119,
  120, **155-157**
  themed **164**
Siegel, Bugsy **86**, 94
Silver Lake **110**, 138, 148
  bars/clubs 150, 152, 218, 233
Simon Wiesenthal Center 206
Simpson, OJ 65, 66, 68-69, 98
Sinclair, Upton 60
Six Flags California **40**, 112
skateboarding 188
skating
  ice **189**, 242
  inline 188
  roller (gay) 234
  wind 189
skiing **188**, 242
Skirball Cultural Center 207
skydiving 188
smog information 5
smoking 8
  cigars 96, 114, **172**
snowboarding 188
soccer 191
Soda Springs 245
South Bay **34**, **113-114**, 143
South Central 60, 61, **117-118**,
  143-144
Spadena House 39
Spago 131
spas 17, 19, 85, **173**, 252, **255**

Spelling, Aaron 66, 82
Spielberg, Steven 82, 134
spinning (exercise) 191
sports **184-192**
  bars 149, 150
  shops 173
  spectator 191-192
  trainer/masseur 173
  *see also individual sports*
Starbucks 145
stars *see* celebrity spotting
statistics 67
Steinbeck, John 60, 252
Streisand Center for Conservancy
  Studies 93
stock exchange 60
students 236-238
studios, film 98, 109, 111, 112, 199
  Paramount 112, 204
  tours **204**
  Warner Brothers 204, 237
  *see also* Universal City/Studios
studios, recording 23, 100
subway *see* Metro
suicide prevention 261
Sunset Boulevard **43**, 100
Sunset Strip **43**, 94, 154-155
sunstroke prevention 243
supermarkets 82-83
Surf & Weather Report 260
surfing 119, **188-189**
  museum 119, **209**
  US Open & Exposition 48
synagogues 264

Tail-o'-the-Pup 131
tattoo artists 173
tax, sales 154
taxis **12**
  airport 9
telephones **8**
  answering services 226
  cellular 226
  useful codes/numbers 8
television **181-182**
  CBS 102
  live shows 182, **194**
  memorabilia 100
  museum 78, **206**, 237
  schools and research 237
Temescal Park 92
Temporary Contemporary Museum
  *see* Geffen Contemporary at MOCA
tennis courts 189
theatre 99, 108, **221-223**, 254
  acting classes 157
  bookshops 159, 160
  children's 229
  comedy 193-194
  festival 49
  gay 234
  Japanese 106
  Latino 74, 116
TheatreSports *193*, **194**
theme parks **39-40**, 112, 120
  *see also* Disneyland
ticket agencies 174, 191-192, 212
Tijuana **256**, *256*
time, local 8
Times-Mirror Building 106
tipping 264
toilets 264

Torrey Pines 254
tourist information **8**
  out of town **240**, 241-256
tours **46**
  architecture 75
  art 91
  conservation 93, 230
  East LA 115
  *Self-Guided Tours* (MTA) 9
  studios 204
transport **9-13**, 63
  out of town **240**, 241-254
  to and from airports 9
travel passes 11
tuxedos 166
Twentynine Palms 244-245

UCLA (University of California
  Los Angeles) 96, **237**
  archives 202, 237
  Bruins 192
  libraries 78, 96
  museums 207, 208
  Schoenberg Hall 96, **215**
  theatres **217**, 224
Union Station 63, 77, *104*, 105
Universal City/Studios **35**, *111*,
  112, 155, 202, 220
  Amphitheater 217
  CityWalk **40**, *111*, 112, 164
  Sheraton Universal 28
universities 93, 112, 120, **236-238**
  concert venues 215, 224
USC Trojans 192

Vasquez Rocks Country Park 187
Venice **43**, *90*, 90-91, *91*, 146, *209*
  beach **34**
  Chamber of Commerce 92
  galleries 210
  Golds Gym 84-85, 91, **190**, *233*
  hotels/inns 19, *20*, *32*, 32
  restaurants 124-125
  St Mark's (jazz venue) 220
Ventura 209, **249**
Veterans Wadsworth Theater **217**,
  224
veterinary clinic 174
video rental 177
Vietnamese community 120
views **45**
vineyards *see* wineries
Viper Room 86, 94, *197*, 198, **218**
Virtual World 185
visas **265**
  student 238
Visitors Information Centres **8**, 90

walking **13**
  tours 46
  *see also* hiking
Washington, Lula 224
water supply 58
watersports **188-189**, 241, 242, 254
  *see also individual sports*
Watts **117**
Watts Towers *39*, **39**, 76, 77
wax museums 37, 120, 252

weather forecasts 5, 260
Wells Fargo Center 108
West Hollywood 20-23, **94**, 146-147
  restaurants 127-132
  shopping areas 83, 155
West LA 133-134, 147, 223
Westin Bonaventure Hotel **27**,
  *28*, 108, 152
Westside
  beach towns 17-20, **89-93**,
    122-127, 145-146, 149
  inland 20-24, **94-97**, 127-135,
    146-147, 149-150
  *see also individual areas*
Westwood 23, 24, **96-97**, 133,
  155, 202, 207, 222
  *see also* UCLA
whales **50**, 92, 119, 230
Whisky A-Go-Go 94, **218**, *219*
Whittier Boulevard 116
wildlife 92, 107, 119, 230, 241,
  244, 245, 249
  conservation 93, 230
  marine 230, 252
  Nursery Nature Walks 46
Will Geer Theatricum Botanicum
  49, **223**
Will Rogers Historic State Park **46**
Wilshire Boulevard **43**, 102
Wiltern Theater *76*, 76, 102, **217**
wind skating 189
wine
  auctions 250
  festivals 48, 250
  shops 169
wineries 250
Witch's House *see* Spadena House
women's welfare 264-265
work 265
Wright, Frank Lloyd 76, 77, 109,
  205
Wright, Lloyd (son of FL) 94, 114
writers 60, 61, 74, 152, 252
Writers Guild 227

Yamashiro **45**, 136
YMCA 31, 190
yoga 89, **191**

zoos
  LA 109, 112, **230**
  San Diego 254
Zuma Beach 34

# Los Angeles Guide
## Advertisers' Index

Please refer to the relevant sections for addresses/telephone numbers

Benihana — **Inside Front Cover**

### Essential Information
Hollywood Metropolitan Hotel — **Page 2**
Western Union — **Page 2**
Bloomingdale's — **Page 4**
The Groundlings Theatre — **Page 6**

### Getting Around
Bloomingdale's — **Page 10**

### Accommodation
Days Inn — **Page 14**
Marina Pacific Hotel — **Page 14**
Super 8 Motel — **Page 16**
Westlake Plaza Inn — **Page 18**
Hollywood 8 Motel — **Page 30**

### Sightseeing
Hertz — **Page 36**
World Cricket League — **Page 44**

### Eating & Drinking
AT & T — **Page 142**

### Shopping
Virgin Megastore — **Page 176**

### Arts & Entertainment
Sunny Leigh Gallery — **Page 178**

### Clubs
i-D Magazine — **Page 196**

### Maps
AT & T — **Page 284**

**Where do you find out what's happening in London?**

http://www.timeout.co.uk

# Time Out

**Your weekly guide to the most exciting city in the world**

Section sponsored by
**AT&T**

# Maps

| | | | |
|---|---|---|---|
| Aerial Map | **276** | Santa Monica & Venice | **283** |
| Freeway Map | **278** | Street Index | **285** |
| Westside | **280** | Trips Out of Town | **288** |
| Downtown | **282** | Metro/Metrolink | **290** |

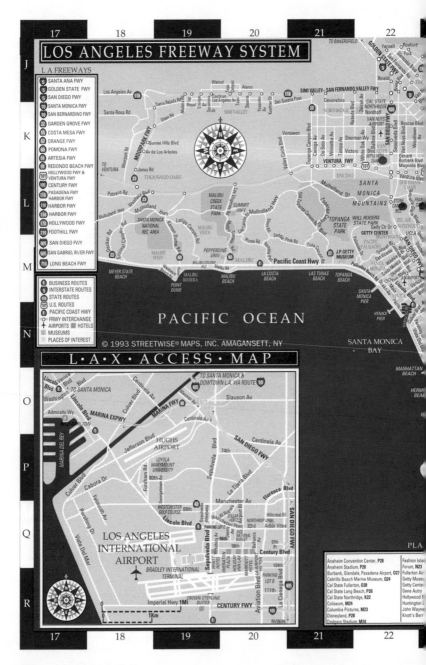

CARTOGRAPHY BY MICHAEL E BROWN

# SANTA MONICA
# VENICE

BRENTWOOD COUNTRY CLUB

**HOSPITALS**
Santa Monica Hospital, M 5
St. John's Hospital, L 5

**PARKS**
Clover, N-O 7-8
Douglas, K-L 5
Joslyn, O 5
Lincoln, M 4
Los Amigos, O 5
Marine, P 6-7
Mary Hitchcock, O 5
Memorial, M-N 5
Palisades, J-L 1
Virginia Av, M-N 6-7

**PLACES OF INTEREST**
Automobile Club, L 6
Brentwood Country Club, J 5-6
City Hall, O 4
Civic Auditorium, O 4
County Bldg, O 4
Greyhound Bus Terminal, N 4
Heritage Museum, P 5
Kinney Plz., R 6
Museum of Flying, N 8
Penmar Golf Course, O-P 6-7
Post Office, N 3
Riveria Country Club, J-K 3-4
S. Cal. Inst. of Architecture, L 7
Santa Monica Airport, O 8
Santa Monica Art Museum, P 5
Santa Monica College, N 6
Santa Monica High School, O 5
Santa Monica Place, N 4
Santa Monica Visitors Ctr., N 3
Third Street Promenade, N 3-4
Venice Pavilion, R 5

© 1993 STREETWISE®
MAPS, INC.
AMAGANSETT, NY

CARTOGRAPHY BY MICHAEL E BROWN  RV0696

SCALE

0         1/2 Mi

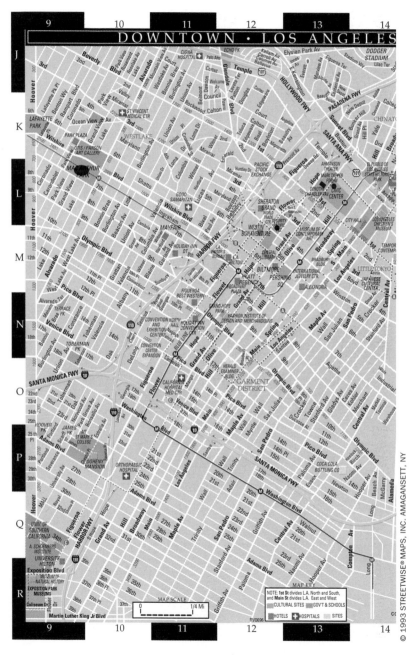

+

## Call The World On Your Card.

Calling the world is easy using your card. You can do it from any telephone in the U.S. to over 100 countri
Just dial 1 800 CALL ATT® (1 800 225-5288) and a voice will tell you exactly what to do.

# Street Index

## Westside

**Map page 280-281**

*(Includes Beverly Hills, Century City, Hancock Park, Hollywood, Midtown, Mid-Wilshire, Miracle Mile, Fairfax, Park La Brea, West Hollywood)*

## Streets

Adams Blvd, I 13-19
Aiken Ave, H 8
Airdrome, G-H 11-14
Alandele, F 14
Alcott, G 10-13
Alden Dr, D 10-12
Alfred, B-G12
Allenford Ave, F-G 1
Almayo Ave, G-H 8-9
Almont Dr, D-F 11
Alsace, H-I 14-15
Alta Dr, C-D 11
Alta Loma Rd, B 12
Alta Vista Blvd, A-E 15
Alvira, F-H 12-13
Anchor Ave, H 10
Apple, I 13-14
Arden Blvd, C-F 17
Arden Dr, C-D 10-11
Argyle Ave, A 17
Arlington Ave, G-I 18
Arnaz Dr, E-F 12
Ashby Ave, H-I 8
Ashcroft Ave, D 11-12
Ashton Ave, E-F 8
Avenue of the Stars, F-G 8-9
Avondale Ave, F-G 1
Ayres Ave, H-I 8
Bagley Ave, G-I 10-11
Balsam Ave, G 8
Bangor, I 14-15
Barbydell Dr, I 10
Baroda Dr, C-D 8
Barrows Dr, F 13-14
Barton Ave, C 18-19
Beachwood Dr, A-D 18
Beckwith Ave, F-G 1
Bedford Dr, D-G 8-10
Bedford, F-I 12
Benecia Ave, F-G 8
Benedict Canyon Dr, A-C 8
Beverly Blvd, D 11-19
Beverlycrest Dr, A 10
Beverly Dr, A-I 9-10
Beverly Glen Blvd, A-H 8
Beverly Green Dr, G 9-10
Beverly Pl, D 12
Beverlywood, I 11-12
Beverwil Dr, F-I 10
Blackburn Ave, E 12-15
Blythe Ave, H-I 8
Bolton Rd, H 10-11
Bonner Dr, D 12
Bradbury Rd, H-I 8
Bridlevale Dr, H-I 9-10
Brighton Way, E 10
Bronson Ave, A-I 17-18
Buckingham Rd, H-I 16
Burnside Ave, E-I 14-15
Burton Way, D-E 10-12
Butterfield Rd, H-I 8
Cabrillo Dr, F 13
Cadillac Ave, H-I 11-13

Cahuenga Blvd, A-D 17
Calvin Ave, G 8
Cambridge, H 19
Camden Dr, D-F 9-10
Camino Ave, A 15
Canfield Ave, G-I 11
Canon Dr, D-G 9-10
Canyon Dr, A 18
Carla Ridge, A 10
Carling Way, F 16
Carlos Ave, A 17-18
Carlton Wy, A 18-19
Carlyle Ave, G-H 1
Carmelita Ave, C-E 8-11
Carmona Ave, G-I 13-14
Carolwood Dr, C-D 8
Carolyn Way, B 8
Carsonm Dr, E-F 12
Cashio, G 10-13
Cassil Pl, A 16
Castello Ave, G 10
Castle Heights Ave, H-I 10
Cattaraugus Ave, I 10-12
Cavendish Dr, H-I 9
Century Hill, G 9
Century Park East, F-G 9
Century Park West, F-G 8
Chadbourne Ave, F-G 1
Chalmers Dr, F 12
Charleville Way, E 9-12
Charton, H-I 12
Cherokee Ave, A-D 16
Chevy Chase Dr, C 8
Cheviot Dr, I 8-9
Cimarron Ave, H-I 18
Citrus Ave, B-G 16
Civic Center Dr, D 10-11
Clark Dr, D-G 11-12
Claudina Ave, I 15-16
Claymont Dr, D 1
Clifton Way, E 10-12
Clinton, C 12-19
Cloverdale Ave, E-I 14-15
Club Dr, H-I 9-10
Club View , D-E 8
Club View Dr, E-F 8
Clyde Ave, H-I 13
Cochran Ave, E-I 14-15
Cochran Pl, H 14
Coldwater Canyon Dr, A-B 9
Cole Ave, B-C 17
Colgate Ave, E 12-14
Cologne, H-I 13-15
Comey Ave, I 12-13
Commodore Sloat Dr, F 13
Comstock Ave, D-G 8
Constellation Blvd, F 8-9
Corning, F-H 12
Cory Ave, B 11
Cosmo, A 17
Council, D 18-19
Country Club Dr, F-G 17-19
Courtney Ave, A 14
Cove Way, B-C 8
Coventry Pl, I 8
Crenshaw Blvd, F 16-18
Crescent Dr, C-G 9-11
Crescent Heights Blvd, A-H 12-14
Crest Dr, F-G 11
Cresta Dr, H 9-11
Croft Ave, B-D 13
Curson Ave, A-I 14
Cushdon Ave, H 8
Cynthia, B-C 11

Danalda Dr, I 10
Daniels Dr, F-G 10
Dannyhill Dr, I 10
Dauphin Ave, I 12-13
David Ave, H-I 11
Dayton Way, E 10-12
DeLongpre Ave, B 13-19
DelValle Dr, F 13-14
Detroit, A-F 15
Dockweiler, G 16
Doheny Ave, G11
Doheny Dr, A-G 11
Doheny Rd, B 9-11
Dorrington Ave, D 11-12
Drexel, E 12-14
Drury Ln, B 10
Dunleer Dr, I 8-9
Dunsmuir Ave, F-I 14-15
Durango, Ave, G-H 11
Durant Dr, E-F 9
Duxbury Rd, H 11
Earlmar Dr, I 9-10
Eastborne Ave, F-G 8
Edgewood Pl, G 14-17
Edinburgh Ave, B-F 13-14
Edris Dr, G 10
El Camino Dr, E-F 10
El Tovar Pl, C 11-12
ElCentro Ave, A-C 17
Elden Way, C 8
Eleanor Ave, B 17-18
Elevado Ave, C-E 8-11
Elm Dr, C-G 10-11
Elmwood Ave, D 18-19
Empyrean Way, G 9
Ensley Ave, F 8
Esther Ave, H-I 8
Euclid, I 1
Fairburn Ave, F-G 8
Fairfax Ave, A-I 13-14
Fernwood, B 18-19
Flores, B13
Foothill Dr, D-E 9-10
Formosa Ave, A-E 15
Forrester Dr, H 10
Foster Dr, F 13
Fountain Ave, B 12-19
Fox Hills Dr, F-G 8-9
Franklin Ave, A 15-19
Fremont Pl, F-G 17
Fuller Ave, A-E 15
Galaxy Way, F-G 9
Gale Dr, F 13
Gardner, A-E 15
Garth Ave, G-I 12
Genesse Ave, A-I 13-14
George Burns Rd, D 12
Georgina Ave, G-H 1
Gibson, I 11
Glen Way, C-D 9
Glenbarr Ave, H 9
Glendon Ave, E-I 8
Glenville, F-G 11
Gordon, A-B 18
Gower St, A-E 18
Grace Ave, A 17
Gramercy Dr, F-G 19
Gramercy Pl, C-I 19
Greenacre Ave, B 15
Greenway Dr, D 8
Gretna Green Way, F-G 3
Guthrie Ave, H-I 11-13
Guthrie Dr, H 11
Hacienda Pl, B12
Halm Ave, I 12
Hamel Dr, E-F 12

Hamilton Dr, E-F 12
Hammond, B-C 11
Hampton Ave, B 14-15
Hancock Ave, B-C 12
Harcourt Ave, I 15-16
Hargis, I 10-11
Harold Wy, A 18-19
Harper Ave, B-E 13
Harratt, B11-12
Hartford Way, C 8
Harvard Blvd, A-I 19
Hauser Blvd, E-I 14-15
Havenhurst Dr, B 13
Hawthorne Ave, A 15-16
Hayes Dr, F 13
Hayworth Ave, A-H 13-14
Heath Ave, F-G 9
Hi Point, F-H 13
Highland Ave, A-I 15-16
Hillcrest Dr, H 16
Hillcrest Rd, A-D 10-11
Hilldale Ave,C 11
Hillgreen Dr, G 9
Hillsboro Ave, H 11
Hobart Blvd, A-I 19
Holloway Dr, B 12
Hollywood Blvd, A 13-19
Hollywood FrWay, A-D 17-19
Holman Ave, F 8
Holmby Ave, E-G8
Holt Ave, D-I 12
Homewood, B 18-19
Horn Ave, B 12
Horner, G 10-13
Hudson Ave, A-F 16-17
Hudson Pl, D-E 17
Huntley Dr, C-D 12
Ilona Ave, G-H 8-9
Ingraham, F 18-19
Irving Blvd, C-F 18
Ivar Ave, A-B 17
June, B-E 16
Kelton Ave, H7
Keniston Ave, F-G 16
Kerwood Ave, G 8
Keswick Ave, G 8
Kilkea Dr, B-E 13
Kincardine Ave, I 10-11
Kings Rd, B-D 13
Kingsley Dr, A-F 19
Kinnard Ave, F 8
Kirkside Rd, G 10-11
La Cresta Ct, C 9
LaBrea Ave, A-I 15
LaCienaga Blvd, B-I 12-13
LaCollina Dr, B 10
Ladera Dr, C-D 8
LaJolla Ave, B-J 13
LaMirada, B 16-19
Lanewood Ave, A 15-16
LaPeer Dr, D-F 11
Larchmont Blvd, C-E 17
Larke Ellen Cir, G-H 11
Larrabee, B-C 12
Las Palmas Ave, A-E 16
LaSalle Ave, H-I 19
Lasky Dr, E-F 9
Laurel Ave, A-E 13
Laurel Way, A-C8-9
Lauriston Ave, G-H 8
Le Doux Rd, E-F 12
Leeward Ave, F 18-19
Leland Way, B 16-17
Lemon Grove Ave, C 18-19
Lexington Ave, B 14-19

Lexington Rd, C-D 8-9
Lillian Wy, B-D 17
Lindbrook Dr, E-F 8
Linda Crest Dr, A 9
Linden Dr, D-F 8-9
Lindenhurst Ave, E 13-15
Linnington Ave, G-H 8
Little Santa Monica Blvd, E 9-10
Livonia Ave, F-G 11
Loma Linda Dr, A-B 9
Loma Vista Dr, A-C 10
Lomita, H 16
Lomitas Ave, C-E 8-10
Londonderry Pl, A-B 12
Longwood Ave, F-I 15-16
Longworth Dr, F 1
Lorenzo Dr, H 9
Lorenzo Pl, H 9
Lorraine Blvd, E-F 18
Louisiana Ave, G 8
Lucerne Blvd, C-F 17
Malcolm Ave, E-I 8
Manderville Canyon Rd, C-E 1
Manhatten Pl, C-I 19
Manning Ave, E-I 8-9
Mansfield Ave, A-I 15-16
Maple Dr, C-G 10-11
Maplewood Ave, C-D 18-19
Marathon, C 18-19
Martel Ave, A-E 15
Marvin Ave, H-I 14
Maryland, E 13-14
Mascot, H 15-16
Masselin Ave, E-G 14-15
McCadden Pl, A-F 16
McCarty Dr, E-F 9
McCarthy Dr, F 13
McConnell Dr, H 10
Meadowbrook Ave, F-H 15
Melrose Pl, C 12-13
Melrose, C-D 11-19
Midvale Ave, E-I 8
Miradero Rd, A 10
Mississippi Ave, G-I 8
Missouri Ave, E-I 8
Monovale Dr, C-D 8
Monte Mar Dr, G-H 9-11
Moore Dr, F 9
Moreno Dr, F 9
Morningside Ct, A 17
Motor Ave, G-I 9-10
Motor Pl, H 10
Mountain Dr, C 10
Mullen Ave, F-G 16-17
Muirfield Rd, E-G 16-17
National Blvd, I 8
National Pl, I 8-9
Northvale Rd, I 8-9
Norton Ave, B-F 13-18
Oakhurst Ave, I 10
Oakhurst Dr, C-G 11
Oakmore Rd, H 10-11
Oakwood Ave, D 12-19
Ogden Dr, A-H 13-14
Olive Dr, B 13
Olympic Blvd, F-I 3-19
Orange Dr, A-I 15-16
Orange Grove Ave, A-F 13-14
Orange, E-F 13-14
Orlando Ave,B-G 13
Orton Ave, G 8
Overland Ave, G-I 8
Oxford Ave, B-I 19

Oxford Way, C 8
Packard, G 12-15
Palm Ave, B-C 12
Palm Dr, C-F 10-11
Palm Grove Ave, I 15-16
Pandora Ave, G 8
Park Way, E 10
Parnell Ave, G-H 8
Patricia Ave, G-I 8-10
Peck Dr, E-F 10
Pelham Ave, G-H 8
Phyllis Ave, B-C 11
Pickford, G-H 11-16
Pico Blvd, G-I 8-19
Plymouth Blvd, C-G 17-18
Poinsettia Dr, B-E 15
Poinsettia Pl, A-B 15
Point View, F-H 13
Preuss Rd, F-H 11-12
Prosser Ave, G-H 8
Putney Rd, H-I 8
Queen Anne Pl, G 17
Queensbury Dr, H-I 9
Raleigh, C 18
Rangely Ave, C 12-13
Rangely, D 11-12
Readcrest Dr, A 9-10
Redondo Blvd, F-I 14-15
Reeves Dr, E 10
Rexford Dr, C-G 9-11
Reynier Ave, I 11
Ridgeley Dr, E-I 14-15
Ridgewood Pl, B-E 18
Rimpau Blvd, E-I 16-17
Robbins Dr, F 9
Robert Ln, B 10
Robertson Blvd, E 12-15
Rochester Ave, E-F 8
Rodeo Dr, D-F 9-10
Romaine, B-C 12-19
Rosewood Ave, D 8-19
Rossbury Pl, I 9-10
Rossmore Ave, D-F 17
Roundtree Rd, H-I 8
Roxbury Dr, C-H 8-10
Rugby Dr, C 12
Russell Ave, A 19-19
San Marino, G 18-19
San Vicente Blvd, B-G 8-16
San Ysidro Dr, A-B 8
Santa Monica Blvd, B-I 8-19
Santa Monica FrWay,
I 8-19
Saturn, G-H 10-16
Sawyer, H 10-13
Schumacher Dr, F 12-13
Schuyler Rd, A-C 10
Selma Ave, A 13-18
Serrano Ave, A-F 19
Seward, A17
Shadow Hill Way, A-B 9
Shanandoah, F-I 16-12
Shelby Dr, I 10
Sherbourne Dr, D-H 12
Sherwood Dr, C 12
Sierra Alta Way, B 11
Sierra Bonita Ave, A-H 14
Sierra Dr, C-D 11
Sierra Vista Ave, B 18-19
Snowy Pl, I 9
Spaulding Ave, A-I 13-14
Spalding Dr, E-F 9
St Andrews, A-I 19
St Charles Pl, H 16-17
St Elmo, H 15-16
Stanley Ave, A-H 14
Stanley Dr, E-F 12
Stearns, Dr, F-H 13
Strathmore Dr, E 8
Summit Dr, B 8
Sunset Blvd, A-F 8-19
Sunset Hills Rd, B 11
Sunset Plaza Dr, A-B 12
Swall Dr, D-F 11
Sweetzer Ave, B-F 13
Sycamore Ave, A-I 15-16
Taft Ave, A 19

Tamarind Ave, A-B 18
Tennessee Ave, G-I 8-9
Thurman, H-I 8
Tower Rd, A-B 8
Tower Dr, F 13
Tremaine Ave, F-G 16
Trenton Dr, E 8-9
Troon Ave, H-I 8-9
Van Ness Ave, A-F 8
Venice Blvd, H-I 12-19
Veteran Ave, D-I 8
Victoria Ave, F-I 16-17
Victoria Park Dr, H 16-17
Vidor Dr, G 10
Vine, A-C 17
Vineyard Ave, H-I 16
Virgina Ave, B 18-19
Virginia Pl, F 10
Virginia Rd, H-I 16
Vista Ave, A-E 15
Vista Del Mar, A 17
Vista, F 13
Walden Dr, E 8-9
Wallace, A 10
Waring Ave, C 12-17
Warnall Ave, F 8
Warner Dr, F 13-14
Washington Blvd, F-I 12-19
Wellington Rd, H-I 16-17
West Blvd, G-I 16-17
West Knoll Dr, B-D 12
West View, I 15
Westbourne Dr, C-D 12
Westchester Pl, F-H 18
Western Ave, A-I 19
Westminster Ave, E 18
Westmoreland Blvd, F-I 19
Westmount Dr, B-D 12
Westwood Blvd, E-I 8
Wetherly Dr, A-F 11
Whitley Ave, A 17
Whittier Dr, D-E 8-9
Whitworth Dr, F-G 10-14
Wilcox Ave, A-D 17
Wilcox Pl, B 17
Wiley Ln, C 11
Willaman Dr, E-F 12
Willoughby Ave, C 12-17
Wilshire Blvd, E-I 8-19
Wilton Pl, A-F 18
Windsor Blvd, C-F 17-18
Winona Blvd, C 18
Woodland Dr, B-C 9
Wooster, F-H 12
Yucca, A 16-18

## Hospitals

Beverly Hills Med. Ctr.,
G 10
Ceders-Sinai Med. Ctr., D 12
Century City Hospital, F 9
Doctors Hospital, F 8
Kaiser Foundation, I 12
LA Doctors Hospital, I 19
Midway Hospital, F 14
Westside, F 14

## Places of interest

American Film Inst, A 19
Beverly Center, D 12
Beverly Hills City Hall, E10
Beverly Hills Shopping ,
E 9-10
Beverly Theater, E 10
Capitol Records, A 17
CBS TV, D 14
Century Plaza Towers,
F 8-9
Century Square, F 8
Cold Water Canyon Pk, B 9
Doheny Mansion,C 10
Farmers Market, E 14
George Page Museum ,
F 14
Henry Fonda Theater,
A 17-18

Hollywood Mem Pk
Cemetary, B-C 18
Hollywood Paladium, A 17
Hollywood Sign (take
Beachwood Rd north),
A 18
Hollywood Walk,
A16
LACE, B17
LA County Museum of Art,
F 14
Los Angeles Country Club,
D-F 8-9
Mann's Chinese Theatre,
A 16
Miracle Mile, F 14-15
Museum of TV and Radio,
E 10
Museum of Tolerance, G 10
Pacific Design Center, C 12
Pantages Theater, A 17
Paramount Studios, C 18
Rancho La Brea Tar Pits,
F 14
Rancho Pk. Golf Course,
G-F 8-9
Santa Monica Mountains
National Rec. Area, A-B 9
Scenic Gardens, A 16
Sunset Strip, B 11-12
20th Century Fox Studios,
G 9
Ward Plaza, F 12
Warner Hollywood Studios,
C 15
Westside Pavilion, H 8
Whittier Law School, E 16
Will Rogers Mem Pk, C-D 9
Wilshire Country Club,
D-E 16-17
Wilshire Ebell Theater,
F 17
Wilshire Theater, F 12-13
Wiltern Center &
Theater, F 19

## Downtown

### Map page 282

### Streets

Adair St, P 12
Adams Blvd, P-R 10-13
Adobe, J-K 14
Agatha, O 13
Alameda, J-Q 14
Albany, M-N 10-11
Alpine Ave, J 13
Alpine, K 13-15
Alvarado, J-N 10-11
Angelina, K 13
Arcadia, L 14
Bamboo Ln, J 14-15
Banning, M 14-15
Bartlett, K 13
Bay, P 14-15
Beacon Ave, L-M 10
Beaudry, J-M 11-13
Bellevue, J 12
Belmont, J-K 11
Benton Way, J-K 10
Bernard, J 15
Beverly Blvd, J-M 10-14
Birch, P 13-14
Bixel, K-N 11-12
Blaine, M-N 10-11
Bond, N 10
Bonnie Brea, J-N 10-11
Bonsallo Ave, Q-P 10
Boston, K-L 13-14
Boyd, M-N 13-14
Boylston, K-L 12-13
Broadway Pl, N-O 12
Broadway Pl, R 10
Broadway, J-R 10-15

Bunker Hill, K 14
Burlington, J-O 10-11
Byram, N 11
Calumet, J 12
Cambria, L-M 10
Carondelet, J-L 10
Carroll, J 12
Cecilia, N-O 13
Centenial Ave, J-K 13
Central Ave, M-R 12-14
Ceres Ave, N 13-14
Cherry, N 10
Cleveland, K 14
Clock, O 14
College, J-K 13-15
Colton, K 11-12
Columbia Ave, M 10-11
Columbia Ave, K-L 11
Colyton, N 14-15
Commercial, L 14-15
Compton Ave, Q-R 13-14
Connecticut, M 10
Coronado, J-L10
Cortez, J 11-12
Cottage Pl, M-N 11
Council, K 11-12
Court, J-K 10-13
Crandall, J-K 10
Crawford, R 11
Crocker, N-P 13-14
Crownhill, K 11
Dawson, J-K 11
Delong, N-O 10
Dewap Rd, K-L 13
Diamond, K-L12-13
Douglas, J-K 12
Ducasse Al, O-P 13
Ducommun, M 14-15
Edgeware, J-K 12
Eighteenth, N-Q 10-13
Eighth Pl, M 11
Eighth, L-P 10-15
Eleventh Pl, M 10
Eleventh, M-P 10-13
Elysian Park Ave, J 13-14
Emerald, K-L 12
Essex, P-Q 13
Estrella Av , O-P 10
Everett, J 13
Factory Pl, O 14-15
Fifteenth, O-Q 11-15
Fifth, K-N 10-15
Figueroa Ter, J 13-14
Figueroa Way, P 10
Figueroa, K-R 10-13
First, J-M 10-15
Florida, M 11
Flower,L12, O11
Fourteenth Pl, O-P11-13
Fourteenth, N- Q 10-15
Fourth Pl N 14-15
Fourth, K-N 10-15
Francisco, M 11
Fremont Ave, K-L12-13
Garey, M 15
Garland Ave, M 11
Georgia Pl, N 11
Georgia, O-N 10
Gladys Ave, N-O 13-14
Glendale Blvd, J-K 12
Grand Ave, K-R 10-14
Grand View, J10
Grattan, M 10
Green Ave, M 10
Griffith, P- R 11ꓹ13
Hartford Ave, M 11
Hartford, L 11
Hemlock, O-P 13-14
Hewitt, M-N 14-15
Hill Pl, K 14
Hill, J-R 10-15
Hooper Ave, P-R 13-14
Hope, L-Q 10-13
Huntley Dr, L 12
Industrial, O 14-15
Ingraham, L-M 10-11
Innes Ave, J 13

Jefferson Blvd, Q-R 10-11
Kellam Ave, J 12
Kensington, J-K 12-13
Kohler, O 13-14
Lake, J-M 10
Lakeshore Ter, J-K 12
Laveta Ter, J-K 12
Lilac Ter, J 14
Linden, O-P 14
Little, L 10
Loma Dr, K-L 11
Long Beach Ave, Q-R 14
Los Angeles, L-P 11-14
Lovelace Ave, O 10
Lucas Ave, K-M 11-12
ML King Jr. Blvd, R 10-12
Macy, L15
Main, K-R 10-15
Maple Ave, N-R 10-13
Margo, O 11
Market, O 14
Marview Ave, J13
Maryland, K-L 10-12
McGarry, P-Q 14
Merchant, O-P 13-14
Merrick, N 15
Mignonette, K 12-13
Mill, O 15
Miramar, K-L 10-12
Molino, N 15
Mountain View Ave,
J-K 10-11
Myrtle, P 12
Nagoya, N 11
Naomi Ave, P-R 12-14
New Depot, J-K13-14
New High, K-L 14
Newton, P-Q 13-14
Ninth Pl, O 13
Ninth, L-O 10-13
Norwood Ave, O10
Oak, N-O 10
Olive, L-P 10-13
Olvera, L 14
Olympic Blvd, M-Q 10-15
Omar Ave, M-N 14
Ord, K 14
Paloma Ave, P-R 12-13
Palmetto, N 14-15
Park Grove Ave, O-P 10
Park View, J-L 10
Patton, J-K 12
Pico Blvd, M-P 10-13
Pizarro, J 12
Produce, O 14-15
Rampart Blvd, J-L10
Ravine, J 14
Rockwood, K 11-12
Rose, M 14
Roselake, J 10
Rosemont, J 10
S. Flower, L-R 10-13
S. Pembroke, N 11
San Julian, N-O 12-13
San Pedro, M-R 11-14
Santee, N-P 11-13
Seaton, N 14
Second, J-M 10-15
Seventeenth, N-P 10-11
Seventh Pl, M 11-12
Seventh Pl, O 14-15
Seventh, K-O 10-15
Shatto, L 10-11
Sixteenth, P-Q 11-14
Sixth, K-O 10-15
Spring, K-N 12-15
St Josephs Pl, O-P 12
St Paul Ave, L-M 11
Stadium Way, J13-14
Stanford Ave, N-R 12-14
Sunbury, M 11
Sunset Blvd, J-L 12-14
Tehran, N 11
Temple, J-M 11-15
Tenth Pl, M 10
Tenth, L-P 10-13
Terminal, O 14

Third, J-M 10-15
Thirtieth, P-R 10-11
Thirty Eighth, R 10
Thirty Fifth, R 10-11
Thirty First, Q-R 10-12
Thirty Ninth, R 10-12
Thirty Second, Q-R 10- 12
Thirty Seventh, R10
Thirty Sixth, R 10-11
Thirty Third, Q-R 10-12
Toberman, N-P 10
Tolica, K 12
Towne, N-P 13-14
Traction Ave, M-N 14-15
Trenton, N 11
Trinity, P-R 10-12
Twelfth Pl, N 10
Twelfth, M-P10-13
Twenty Eighth, P-R 10-13
Twenty Fifth, O-R 10-13
Twenty First, O-R 10-14
Twenty Fourth, O-R 10-14
Twenty Ninth, P-R 10-12
Twenty Second, O-R 10-14
Twenty Seventh, P-R 10-13
Twenty Third, O-R 10-14
Union Ave, J-O 10-11
Union Dr, L 11
Union Pl, K 11
Valencia, L-N 10-11
Valley, J-K 10
Venice Blvd, N-O 10-11
Wall, M-R 10-14
Walnut, Q 13
Warehouse, O-P 14
Washington Blvd,
N- R 10-15
Welcome Ave,J-K 11
Westlake Ave, J-M 10-11
White Knoll Dr, J 13
Wholesale, O 14-15
Wilde, O 14
Wilshire Blvd, K-M 10-12
Wilson, P-Q 15
Winston, M-N 13-14
Witmer, K-M 10-12
Woodlawn Ct, R 10
Wright, N 10
Yale, K 14
Westin Bonaventure, M 12

**Places of interest**

Angelus Plaza, L13
Arco Plaza, M 12
Beaudry Center, L 12
Biltmore Hotel, M 12
Bradbury Bldg, M 13
Broadway Plaza, M 12
Broadway Trade Ctr, N 12
Bunker Hill, L 13
California Apparel
Mart, O12
Central Library, M 12
City Hall, L 14
Civic Center, L 13
County Courthouse, L 13
Criminal Courts, L 14
Dept. of Water & Power,
L 13
Dodger Stadium, J 14
Doheny Mansion, P10
Dorothy Chandler PAve,
L 13
El Pueblo De Los Angeles
State Historic Park, L 14
Fashion Institute of Design,
N 12
Federal Building, L 14
Federal Reserve, N 12
First Interstate, M 12
The Forum, L 13
Hall of Justice, L 14
Hall of Records, L 14
Herald Examiner Bldg, O 12
International Jewelry Ctr,
M 13

Japanese Cultural Ctr, M 14
LA Chamber of Commerce,
L 12
LA Childrens Museum,
L 14
LA Convention Center,
N 10-11
LA Theater Center, M-N 13
LA Trade Tech College,
P 10
LA Visitor's Bureau, M 12
Law Library, L 13
Loyola Univ Law School,
M 10
MacArthur Park, K-L 10
Mt St Mary's College, P 10
Museum of Contemporary
Art, L 13
Old Plaza, L 14
One Bunker Hill, M 12
Pacific Stock Exchange,
L 12
Parker Center, M 14
Pershing Square, M 12-13
Security Pacific Plaza,
L 12-13
Temporary Contemporary,
M 14
Term. Annex Post Office,
L 15
Times Mirror, M 13
US Courthouse, L 14
Union Bank, L 12
Union Station, L 14-15
Wells Fargo Center, M 13
World Trade Center, L 12

### Santa Monica & Venice

**Map page 283**

Streets

A. Kinney Blvd, Q-R 4-6
Adelaide Pl, K1
Admiralty Way, R 5-6
Airport Ave, N-O 5-6
Alta Ave, K-M 1-3
Amherst Ave, L-M 6
Amherst, J-L 4-6
Amoroso Ct, Q-R 5-6
Appian Way, O 2
Appleby, P 5
Appleton Way, P 5-6
Arizona Ave, K-N 3-4
Armacost Ave, J-L 5-6
Ashland Ave, O-P 3-6
Ashland Pl. N, N-O 4-5
Baltic, J 3
Barnard Way, P-Q 2-3
Barrington Ave, J-K 5-6
Barry Ave, J-K 6
Bay, N-O 2-3
Benvenue, J 3
Berkeley, J-L 3-5
Bernard Ave, P 4
Beverly Ave, O-P 3
Boccaccio Ave, Q-R 5
Breeze Ave, Q-R 3
Brentwood Ter, J-K 3-3
Bricknell, O 2
Bristol Ave, J 3-4
Broadway, K-N 3-5
Brockton Ave, J-L 5-6
Brooks Ave Q-R 3-5
Brooks Ct, Q 4
Bryn Mawr Ave, O 5
Bundy Dr, J-M 4-6
Butler Ave, J-K 6
Cabrillo Ave, R 4
California Ave, K-R 3-5
California Ct, Q-R 5
California Incline, M 3
Canal Ct, R 4
Carlyle Ave, J-L 3-3

Carmelina Ave, J-M 4-6
Cedar, N-O 3-4
Center, R 4
Centinela Ave, J-M 4-6
Chelsea Ave, K-L 3-4
Chelsea Ct, K 3
Clark Ave, R 5
Clement Ave, R 5
Cloverfield Blvd, L-N 4-5
Club House Ave, Q-R 3-4
Colby Ave, J-K 6
Colorado Ave, L-O 2-5
Commonwealth Ave, P 4
Courtland, P 5
Darlington Ave, J 4-5
Delaware Ave, M-N 3-6
Dell Ave, R 4
Dewey, O-P 3-5
Dimmick Ave, P 4
Doreen Pl, P 5
Dorothy, J 4-5
Dudley Ave, Q 3
Dudley Ct, Q 3
Electric Ave, Q-R 4-5
Elkgrove Ave, P 5
Euclid, K-O 3-4
Exposition Blvd, L-M 5-6
Federal Ave, J-K 6
Flower Ave, P 4-5
Franklin, J-L 4-5
Frederick, P 4-5
Frey Ave, R 5
Georgina Ave, J-L1-2
Glenn Ave, O-P 4
Goshen Ave, J 5-6
Grand Blvd, R 4
Grant, N-O 3-4
Granville Ave, J 5
Gretna Green Way, J 4-5
Hampton Dr, P-Q 2-4
Harbor, R 5
Harvard, K-L 3-4
Highland Ave, P 3
Hill, N-P 3-5
Hollister Ave, O-P 2-3
Horizon Ave, R 3-4
Idaho Ave, K-M 3-3
Indiana Ave, P-Q 4-5
Indiana Ct, Q 4-5
Iowa Ave, K-L 5-6
Kansas Ave, M 5
Kensington Rd, O 3
Kingsman Ave, K 1-3
Kiowa Ave, J 5
La Grange Ave, L 6
La Mesa Dr, J-K 3-2
Lake, O-P 5-6
Lincoln Blvd, L-Q 3-6
Linden Ave, Q 5
Lipton Ave, K 4
Main N-R 2-4
Maple, O 3-5
Marco Ct, Q 5
Marco Pl, P-Q 5-6
Marguerita Ave, J-M 1-3
Marine Pl. N, P 4
Marine, Q 3-5
Market, R 3-4
Marr, R 5-6
Mayfield Ave, J 5
McClellan Dr, K 4
McKinley Ave, R 5
Michigan Ave, M-O 3-5
Mildred Ave, R 4-5
Milwood Ave, Q-R 5
Milwood Ct, Q-R 5
Mississippi Ave, L 6
Missouri Ave, K-L 6
Montana Ave, J-M 3-4
Moreno Ave, J 3
Morningside Way, P 5-6
Navy Ct, Q 3
Navy Marine Ct, Q 3
Navy, O-P 4-5
Nebraska Ave, K-L 5-6
Neilson Way, O-P 2-3
Norfork Ave, Q 5

Nowita Pl, P-Q 5
Oak, N-O 4-5
Oakwood Ave, Q 5
Ocean Ave, L-R 1-5
Ocean Park Blvd, M-P 2-6
Ocean Park Pl. N, N-O 4-5
Ocean Park Pl. S, N-P 3-5
Ohio Ave, K 5
Olive Ave, R 5
Olympic Blvd, L-N 2-6
Ozone Ave, Q 3
Ozone Ct, Q 3
Ozone, P 4
Pacific Ave, R 3-4
Pacific, N-O 2-4
Palisades Ave, L-M 1-3
Palisades Beach Rd, L-O 1
Palms Blvd, P-R 5-6
Paloma Ave, Q 3
Park Ave, Q 3
Park Ct, Q 3
Pearl Pl, N 5
Pearl, M-O 3-6
Penmar Ave, P 5-6
Pennsylvania Ave, L 4-5
Pico Blvd, M-O 2-6
Pier Ave, O-P 3-6
Pine, N-O 3-4
Pisani Pl, Q 5
Preston Way, P 5-6
Princeton Ct, K 4
Princeton, J-L 3-4
Raymond Ave, P 3-4
Rennie Ave, P-Q 4
Rialto Ct, Q-R 4-5
Robson, O-P 5
Rochester Ave, K 5
Rose Ave, O-Q 3-6
Rose Ct, P-Q 3-4
Royal Ct, Q 3
Ruth Ave, O-P 3-4
Saltair Ave, J-K 5
San Juan Ave, Q-R 4-5
San Miguel Ave, Q 5
San Vicente Blvd, J-L 1-3
Santa Clara Ave, Q 4-5
Santa Monica Blvd, J-N 3-6
Santa Monica FWay,
M-N 2-6
Santa Monica Pl. N, K-L 4
Seaside Ter, O 1-2
Shell Ave, Q 5
Speedway, Q-R 3-4
Stanford, J-L 3-5
Stewart, L-M 5
Stoner Ave, J-L 5-6
Strand, O 2-3
Sunset Ave, O-Q 3-5
Sunset Ct, P-Q 3-4
Superba Ave, Q-R 5
Texas Ave, J-K 5-6
Thornton Ave, Q 3
Thornton Ct, Q 3
Urban Ave, M 5-6
Valita, P 5
Venezia Ct, Q-R 5-6
Venice Blvd, Q-R 4-6
Venice Way, R 4
Vernon Ave, P-Q 4-5
Vicente Ter, O 2
Victoria Ave, Q-R 5
Village Park W, N 5
Virginia Ave, M-N 4-6
Walgrove Ave, O-P 6
Warren Ave, P 4
Warwick Ave, M 6
Washington Ave, K-M 1-3
Washington Blvd, R 5-6
Washington Way, R 5
Wave Crest Ave, Q-R 3-4
Wellesley Ave, J-M 4-6
Wellesley Dr, O 5
Westgate Ave, J-L 5-6
Westminster Ave, Q-R 3-5
Wilshire Blvd, J-N 1-6
Wilson Pl, P 4
Windward Ave, R 3-4

Woodacres Rd, K 1
Woodlawn Ave, Q-R 5-6
Yale, J-L 3-4
Yorkshire Ave, M-N 5-6

*For hospitals, parks and
places of interest, see map.*

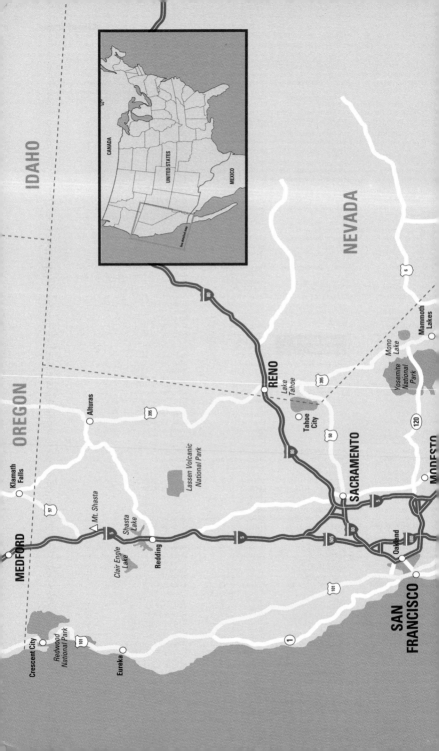

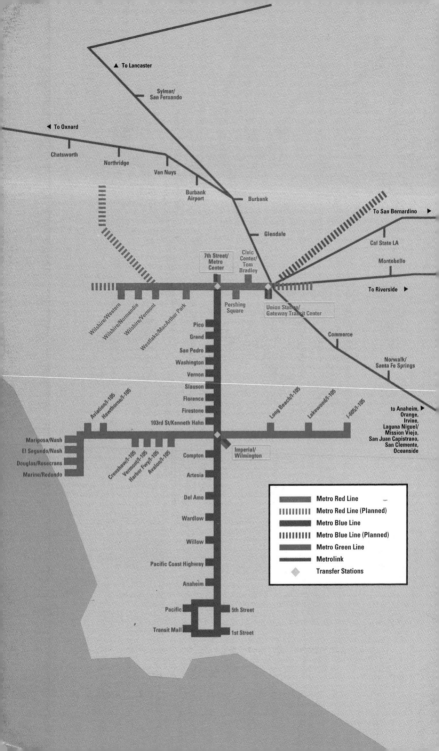

▲ To Lancaster

Sylmar/
San Fernando

◄ To Oxnard

Chatsworth

Northridge

Van Nuys

Burbank
Airport

Burbank

Glendale

To San Bernardino ►

Cal State LA

Montebello

7th Street/
Metro
Center

Civic
Center/
Tom
Bradley

To Riverside ►

Union Station/
Gateway Transit Center

Pershing
Square

Wilshire/Western

Wilshire/Normandie

Wilshire/Vermont

Westlake/MacArthur Park

Commerce

Pico

Grand

San Pedro

Washington

Vernon

Slauson

Norwalk/
Santa Fe Springs

Florence

Firestone

Aviation/I-105

Hawthorne/I-105

103rd St/Kenneth Hahn

Long Beach/I-105

Lakewood/I-105

I-605/I-105

Mariposa/Nash

El Segundo/Nash

Douglas/Rosecrans

Marine/Redondo

Crenshaw/I-105

Vermont/I-105

Harbor Fwy/I-105

Avalon/I-105

Compton

Imperial/
Wilmington

to Anaheim, ►
Orange,
Irvine,
Laguna Niguel/
Mission Viejo,
San Juan Capistrano,
San Clemente,
Oceanside

Artesia

Del Amo

Wardlow

Willow

Pacific Coast Highway

| | |
|---|---|
| | **Metro Red Line** |
| | **Metro Red Line (Planned)** |
| | **Metro Blue Line** |
| | **Metro Blue Line (Planned)** |
| | **Metro Green Line** |
| | **Metrolink** |
| ◆ | **Transfer Stations** |

Anaheim

Pacific

5th Street

Transit Mall

1st Street